THE AMERICANA ANNUAL

2003

AN ENCYCLOPEDIA
OF THE EVENTS OF 2002

YEARBOOK OF THE
ENCYCLOPEDIA AMERICANA

GROLIER

Published 2003 by Grolier Incorporated

Library of Congress Control Number: 23-10041
ISBN: 0-7172-0234-8
ISSN: 0196-0180

Printed in the United States of America.

Staff

Contributors

Contributors not listed on these pages are members of the editorial staff.

- **ANDREWS, PETER J.,** B.A., M.S.; Free-lance writer. **[Chemistry]**

- **APSELOFF, MARILYN FAIN,** B.A., M.A.; Professor of English, Kent State University, Ohio. **[Literature for children]**

- **ASKER, JAMES R.,** B.A.; Washington bureau chief, *Aviation Week & Space Technology* magazine. **[Space exploration]**

- **BARNHART, BILL,** B.A., M.S.T., M.B.A.; Financial markets columnist, *Chicago Tribune*. **[Stocks and bonds]**

- **BARRETT, NORMAN,** M.A.; Free-lance writer. **[Soccer]**

- **BAYNHAM, SIMON,** B.A., M.A., Ph.D.; Senior research associate, Centre for Defence & International Security Studies, University of Lancaster, U.K. **[Africa and African country articles]**

- **BERGER, ERIC R.,** B.A, M.A.; Science writer, *Houston Chronicle*. **[Houston]**

- **BOULDREY, BRIAN,** B.A., M.F.A.; Assistant professor of English, Northwestern University. **[Literature, American; Literature, World; Poetry; Prison; Pulitzer Prizes; San Francisco]**

- **BOYD, JOHN D.,** B.S.; Managing news editor, *Transport Topics*. **[Economics; International trade; Manufacturing]**

- **BRADSHER, HENRY S.,** A.B., B.J.; Foreign affairs analyst. **[Asia and Asian country articles]**

- **BRETT, CARLTON E.,** B.A., M.S., Ph.D.; Professor of geology, University of Cincinnati. **[Paleontology]**

- **BUERKLE, TOM,** B.A.; European editor, *Institutional Investor*. **[Europe and Western European country articles]**

- **CAMPBELL, GEOFFREY A.,** B.J.; Free-lance writer. **[U.S. government articles]**

- **CARDINALE, DIANE P.,** B.A.; Public information manager, Toy Industry Association, Incorporated. **[Toys and games]**

- **CASEY, MIKE,** B.S., M.A.; Assistant editor, *Kansas City Star*. **[Automobile]**

- **DeFRANK, THOMAS M.,** B.A., M.A.; Washington bureau chief, *New York Daily News*. **[Armed forces]**

- **DILLON, DAVID,** B.A., M.A., Ph.D.; Architecture and design editor, *The Dallas Morning News*. **[Architecture]**

- **ELLIS, GAVIN,** Editor in chief, *The New Zealand Herald & Weekend Herald*. **[New Zealand]**

- **FARR, DAVID M. L.,** D.Phil., LL.D.; Professor emeritus of history, Carleton University. **[Canada; Canada, Prime Minister of; Canadian provinces; Canadian territories]**

- **FISHER, ROBERT W.,** B.A., M.A.; Free-lance writer. **[Labor and employment]**

- **FITZGERALD, MARK,** B.A.; Editor at large, *Editor & Publisher* magazine. **[Magazine; Newspaper]**

- **FOX, THOMAS C.,** B.A., M.A.; Publisher, *The National Catholic Reporter*. **[Roman Catholic Church]**

- **FRIEDMAN, EMILY,** B.A.; Health policy and ethics analyst. **[Health care issues]**

- **GADOMSKI, FRED,** B.S., M.S.; Meteorologist, Pennsylvania State University. **[Weather]**

- **GATTY, ROBERT C.,** Executive editor and publisher, *Food Distributors* magazine. **[Food]**

- **GOLDEN, JONATHAN J.,** B.A., M.J.Ed.; Ph.D. candidate, Brandeis University. **[Judaism]**

- **GOLDNER, NANCY,** B.A.; Free-lance dance critic. **[Dance]**

- **GROGAN, TIM,** B.S., M.S. Ph.D.; Senior economics editor, *Engineering News-Record* magazine. **[Manufacturing Special Report: Hard Times for the U.S. Steel Industry]**

- **HALES, DIANNE,** B.A., M.S.; Author and free-lance writer. **[U.S. Government Special Report: One System, Two Missions]**

- **HARAKAS, STANLEY SAMUEL,** B.A., B.Th., Th.D.; Archbishop Iakovos Professor (Emeritus) of Orthodox Theology, Holy Cross Greek Orthodox School of Theology. **[Eastern Orthodox Churches]**

- **HAVERSTOCK, NATHAN A.,** A.B.; Affiliate scholar, Oberlin College. **[Latin America and Latin American country articles]**

- **HELMS, CHRISTINE,** B.A., Ph.D.; Writer and Middle East analyst. **[Middle East and Middle Eastern country articles; North African country articles]**

- **HENDERSON, HAROLD,** B.A.; Staff writer, *Chicago Reader*. **[Chicago]**

- **HIGGINS, FITZGERALD,** B.A.; Free-lance writer. **[City; Crime]**

- **HOFFMAN, ANDREW J.,** B.S., M.S., Ph.D.; Assistant professor of organizational behavior, Boston University. **[Environmental pollution]**

- **JOHANSON, DONALD C.,** B.S., M.A., Ph.D.; Director and professor, Institute of Human Origins, Arizona State University. **[Anthropology]**

- **JOHN, NANCY R.,** A.B., M.L.S.; Assistant university librarian, University of Illinois at Chicago. **[Library]**

- **JOHNSON, CHRISTINA S.,** B.A., M.S.; Free-lance science writer. **[Ocean]**

- **KATES, MICHAEL,** B.S.J.; Associate sports editor, *Chicago Tribune*. **[Sports articles]**

- **KENNEDY, BRIAN,** M.A.; Free-lance writer. **[Australia; Australia, Prime Minister of; Australian rules football]**

- **KILGORE, MARGARET,** B.A., M.B.A.; Free-lance writer, Kilgore and Associates. **[Los Angeles]**

- **KING, MIKE,** Reporter, *The* (Montreal) *Gazette*. **[Montreal]**

- **KLINTBERG, PATRICIA PEAK,** B.A.; Internal communications coordinator, Office of Communications, U.S. Department of Agriculture. **[Agriculture]**

- **KNIGHT, ROBERT,** B.A., M.M.; Free-lance writer. **[Nobel Prizes; People in the news]**

- **KORMAN, RICHARD,** Journalist and author; senior editor, *Engineering News-Record* magazine. **[Immigration** Special Report: **Passport to Reform: The INS and Homeland Security]**

- **KRONHOLZ, JUNE,** B.S.J.; Staff reporter, *The Wall Street Journal.* **[Education]**

- **LAWRENCE, ALBERT,** B.A., M.A., M.Ed.; Executive director, World Chess Hall of Fame. **[Chess]**

- **LEWIS, DAVID C.,** M.D.; Professor of medicine and community health, Brown University. **[Drug abuse]**

- **LIEBENSON, DONALD,** B.A.; Free-lance writer. **[Popular music; Television]**

- **LYE, KEITH,** B.A., F.R.G.S.; Free-lance writer and editor. **[Cricket]**

- **MARCH, ROBERT H.,** A.B., M.S., Ph.D.; Professor emeritus of physics and liberal studies, University of Wisconsin at Madison. **[Physics]**

- **MARSCHALL, LAURENCE A.,** B.S., Ph.D.; W.K.T. Sahm Professor of Physics, Gettysburg College. **[Astronomy]**

- **MARTY, MARTIN E.,** Ph.D.; Fairfax M. Cone Distinguished Service Professor Emeritus, University of Chicago. **[Protestantism]**

- **MAUGH, THOMAS H., II,** Ph.D.; Science/medical writer, *Los Angeles Times.* **[Biology]**

- **MAY, SALLY RUTH,** B.A, M.A.; Free-lance art writer. **[Art]**

- **MAYES, BARBARA A.,** M.A.; Free-lance writer and editor. **[Nobel Prizes]**

- **McWILLIAM, ROHAN,** B.A., M.A., D.Phil; Senior lecturer in history, Anglia Polytechnic University, Cambridge, U.K. **[Ireland; Northern Ireland; United Kingdom; United Kingdom, Prime Minister of]**

- **MINER, TODD J.,** B.S., M.S.; Meteorologist, Pennsylvania State University. **[Weather]**

- **MORITZ, OWEN,** B.A.; Urban-affairs editor, *New York Daily News.* **[New York City]**

- **MORRIS, BERNADINE,** B.A., M.A.; Free-lance fashion writer. **[Fashion]**

- **MULLINS, HENRY T.,** B.S., M.S., Ph.D.; Professor of geology, Syracuse University. **[Geology]**

- **NGUYEN, J. TUYET,** M.A.; United Nations correspondent, Deutsche Presse-Agentur. **[Population; United Nations]**

- **OGAN, EUGENE,** B.A., Ph.D.; Professor emeritus of anthropology, University of Minnesota. **[Pacific Islands]**

- **PAETH, GREGORY,** B.A.; Business writer, *The Cincinnati Post.* **[Radio]**

- **REINHART, A. KEVIN,** B.A., M.A., Ph.D.; Associate professor of religious studies, Dartmouth College. **[Islam]**

- **RICCIUTI, EDWARD,** B.A.; Free-lance writer. **[Conservation; Zoos]**

- **ROSE, MARK J.,** B.A., M.A., Ph.D.; Executive editor, *Archaeology* magazine. **[Archaeology]**

- **RUBENSTEIN, RICHARD E.,** B.A., M.A., J.D.; Professor of conflict resolution and public affairs, George Mason University. **[Terrorism]**

- **SALOPEK, PAUL,** B.A.; Foreign correspondent, *Chicago Tribune.* **[Newspaper** Special Report: **In Harm's Way: Reporting From the Front Lines]**

- **SARNA, JONATHAN D.,** Ph.D.; Joseph H. & Belle R. Braun Professor of American Jewish History, Brandeis University. **[Judaism]**

- **SAVAGE, IAN,** B.A., Ph.D.; Assistant professor of economics and transportation, Northwestern University. **[Aviation; Transportation]**

- **SHAPIRO, HOWARD,** B.S.; Staff writer, *The Philadelphia Inquirer.* **[Philadelphia; Washington, D.C.]**

- **SOLNICK, STEVEN L.,** B.A., M.A., Ph.D.; Associate professor of political science, Columbia University. **[Russia and other former Soviet republic articles]**

- **STEIN, DAVID LEWIS,** B.A., M.S.; Former urban affairs columnist, *The Toronto Star.* **[Toronto]**

- **STOCKER, CAROL M.,** B.A.; Reporter, *The Boston Globe.* **[Gardening]**

- **STREITFELD, DAVID,** B.A.; writer, *Los Angeles Times.* **[Collectibles** Special Report: **Mining the American Attic: Collecting and Collectibles]**

- **STUART, ELAINE,** B.A.; Free-lance public policy writer and editor. **[State government]**

- **TANNER, JAMES C.,** B.J.; Former news editor—energy, *The Wall Street Journal.* **[Energy supply]**

- **TATUM, HENRY K.,** B.A.; Associate editor, *The Dallas Morning News.* **[Dallas]**

- **THOMAS, PAULETTE,** B.A.; Free-lance writer. **[Bank]**

- **VAN, JON,** B.A., M.A.; Technology writer, *Chicago Tribune.* **[Telecommunications]**

- **von RHEIN, JOHN,** B.A.; Classical music critic, *Chicago Tribune.* **[Classical music]**

- **WILSON, DAVE,** B.A.; Producer, Cable News Network. **[Internet; Telecommunications** Special Report: **The Second Wireless Revolution]**

- **WOLCHIK, SHARON L.,** B.A., M.A., Ph.D.; Professor of political science and international affairs, George Washington University. **[Eastern European country articles]**

- **WOODS, MICHAEL,** B.S.; Science editor, *The Toledo* (Ohio) *Blade* and *Pittsburgh Post-Gazette.* **[AIDS; Computer; Drugs; Electronics; Medicine; Mental health; Public health and safety]**

- **WRIGHT, ANDREW G.,** B.A.; Managing senior editor, *Engineering News-Record* magazine. **[Building and construction]**

- **WUNTCH, PHILIP,** B.A.; Film critic, *The Dallas Morning News.* **[Motion pictures]**

- **YEZZI, DAVID,** B.F.A., M.F.A.; Free-lance theater critic. **[Theater]**

Contents

▲ Page 119

Page 410

Page 195

▲ Page 119

Update 36 to 432

The major world events of 2002 are reported in more than 250 alphabetically arranged Update articles—from "Afghanistan" and "Africa" to "Zimbabwe" and "Zoos." Included are Special Reports that provide an in-depth focus on especially noteworthy developments.

Supplement 433

New encyclopedia articles are devoted to the following topics:

Index 497

A 15-page index covers the contents of this book.

Page 410

2002 The Year's Major News Stories

From drought and forest fires in the western United States to a rise in terrorism around the world, 2002 was a year of extraordinary events. On these three pages are stories the editors picked as some of the most important of the year, along with details on where to find more information about them in this volume.
The Editors

Western wildfires

Drought conditions in the spring and summer of 2002 resulted in a series of devastating wildfires that burned out of control across huge areas of the western United States. See **Conservation,** page 139; **Weather,** page 427.

Sniper suspects arrested

Police on Oct. 24, 2002, arrested 41-year-old Army veteran John Allen Muhammad and his 17-year-old companion John Lee Malvo (above), on charges that they carried out 13 random sniper-style shootings that terrorized residents of the Washington, D.C., metropolitan area. See **Crime,** page 143; **Washington, D.C.,** page 426.

Terrorism on the rise

A series of dramatic terrorist attacks, many attributed to the al-Qa'ida terrorist network, signaled an upsurge in Islamic militancy in 2002. In Russia, armed Chechen rebels (left) held over 700 people hostage in a Moscow theater for 57 hours in October. In Indonesia, bomb blasts at two nightclubs in Bali killed more than 180 people. See **Asia,** page 61; **Australia,** page 68; **Indonesia,** page 222; **Islam,** page 229; **Israel,** page 230; **Middle East,** page 272; **Pakistan,** page 313; **Russia,** page 340; **Terrorism,** page 386; **United States, Government of the,** page 405.

Confronting Iraq

U.S. President George W. Bush (above) urges the United Nations (UN), in a speech before the General Assembly on Sept. 12, 2002, to pass a resolution to force Iraqi leader Saddam Hussein to dismantle his country's weapons of mass destruction and end the oppression of the Iraqi people. See **Armed forces,** page 56; **Iraq,** page 228; **United Nations,** page 404; **United States, Government of the,** page 405; **United States, President of the,** page 424.

Department of Homeland Security

The United States Congress in November passed legislation creating the new Cabinet-level Department of Homeland Security. The department consolidated 22 existing agencies, including the Coast Guard, Secret Service, and Immigration and Naturalization Service. See **Cabinet, U.S.,** page 95, **Congress of the United States,** page 133; **Immigration,** page 207; **Immigration: A Special Report,** page 208; **United States, Government of the,** page 405; **United States, President of the,** page 424.

Uprising in Israel

The Palestinian uprising, or Intifada, that began in September 2000 moved into its third year in 2002. A series of suicide bombings that left dozens of Israelis dead prompted repeated Israeli military incursions into Palestinian-held territory in the West Bank and Gaza Strip. See **Israel,** page 230; **Middle East,** page 272; **Terrorism,** page 386.

West Nile outbreak

The worst recorded outbreak of West Nile virus in the United States swept through the Midwest and South during the summer of 2002, resulting in more than 200 deaths and thousands of cases of the disease, which is carried by birds and spread by mosquitoes. See **Chicago,** page 110; **Houston,** page 203; **Public health and safety,** page 334.

Republicans take control of Congress

Republicans under the leadership of President George W. Bush gained control of the U.S. Senate and enlarged their hold over the U.S. House of Representatives in elections on November 5 that political experts characterized as historic. George W. Bush was the first president in nearly 70 years to see his party gain strength in both the House and the Senate in the midterm elections of his first term. See **Congress of the United States,** page 133; **Democratic Party,** page 160; **Elections,** page 174; **Republican Party,** page 337; **United States, Government of the,** page 405; **United States, President of the,** page 424.

Corporate scandals

A Federal Bureau of Investigation agent escorts Andrew Fastow (above), the former chief financial officer of Enron Corp., the failed energy trading company, into a federal courthouse in Houston in October to be indicted on 78 counts of fraud, money laundering, conspiracy, and obstruction of justice. Fastow was accused of artificially inflating Enron profits in order to skim off millions of dollars at the expense of stockholders. The Enron accounting scandal and a series of corporate bankruptcies shook the faith of investors in U.S. markets in 2002. See **Economics,** page 169; **Houston,** page 203; **Labor and employment,** page 239; **Stocks and bonds,** page 363; **Telecommunications,** page 371.

Recession in Latin America

A deep economic recession continued to plague several nations in Latin America during 2002, sparking a banking crisis in Argentina and social and political upheavals in Brazil and Paraguay. See **Argentina,** page 55; **Brazil,** page 92; **Latin America,** page 242.

Copy Cat

Executives with Texas biotech company Genetic Savings and Clone announced in February 2002 the first successful cloning of a domestic cat, a breakthrough step toward the commercial cloning of pets. See **Biology,** page 87.

2002 YEAR IN BRIEF

A month-by-month listing of the most significant world events that occurred during 2002.

Attorneys representing investors arrive at the U.S. District Court in Houston in January with evidence that Enron Corp. executives and the firm's auditor, Arthur Andersen LLP of Chicago, shredded incriminating documents after learning that the government was investigating the spectacular collapse of the energy trading company.

1 A convoy of U.S. Marines leaves Kandahar airport for neighboring Helmand Province, where they are to secure an abandoned Taliban compound. U.S. officials describe the mission as the most extensive U.S. ground operation in the war.

3 An unusual storm moving in a northeast direction from the Gulf of Mexico hits the southern United States with from 1 inch (2.5 centimeters) to 11 inches (28 centimeters) of snow in a swath from Louisiana to southeastern Virginia.

4 The government of Israel accuses Yasir Arafat, leader of the Palestinian Authority, of attempting to smuggle 50 tons (45 metric tons) of antitank missiles, mines, rockets, and other munitions into the West Bank from Iran.

5 Pakistan steps up the arrest of Islamic militants in an attempt to ease tensions with India. Both countries have troops massed along their common border and their missile systems on full alert.

6 The government of Argentina devalues the peso by nearly 30 percent in an attempt to jump-start the economy, which has been in recession for nearly four years.

8 U.S. President George W. Bush signs an education reform bill that requires public schools nationwide to raise the reading and math proficiency of all students over the next 12 years.

9 One-fifth of the population of the 22 nations that make up the Arab League, approximately 68 million people, are illiterate, announces the director general of the Arab League Educational, Cultural, and Scientific Organization.

10 Officials at Chicago-based accounting firm Arthur Andersen LLP disclose that Andersen employees had destroyed a "significant ... number" of paper and electronic documents pertaining to the failed Houston-based energy trading company Enron Corp.

13 *The Fantasticks*, the longest-running play in American theater history, closes after more than 41 years.

16 Investigators in the financial collapse of Enron Corp. disclose that the energy trader paid no U.S. income taxes in four out of five years between 1996 and 2000. During the same period, Enron claimed $382 million in IRS refunds by deducting the expense of the stock options with which Enron rewarded its executives. Enron executives sold more than $1 billion of company stock in the months before Enron filed for bankruptcy in early December 2001.

18 Hundreds of thousands of people in Congo (Kinshasa) flee their houses as a river of lava from Mount Nyiragongo flows at a depth of 6 feet (1.8 meters) through Goma, a city of 500,000 people near the Rwanda border.

19 The Republican National Committee confirms Marc Racicot as chairman of the Republican Party. Most recently, Racicot was employed as a lobbyist in Washington, D.C., for Enron Corp., the Houston-based energy trading company that filed for bankruptcy on Dec. 2, 2001.

21 Executives at Enron Corp. of Houston continued to have company documents destroyed after the U.S. government began investigations into the company's finances, announces a former executive, Maureen Castaneda. Federal authorities are already investigating the deliberate destruction of documents pertaining to Enron by executives at the energy trading company's former auditor, Arthur Andersen LLP of Chicago.

22 Discount department store chain Kmart Corporation of Troy, Michigan, files for Chapter 11 protection in what economists describe as the largest bankruptcy of a retailer in U.S. history.

22 At least 114,800 men and women from the Middle East reside in the United States illegally, announce officials with the U.S. Bureau of the Census. The U.S. Department of Justice currently seeks the whereabouts in the United States of some 6,000 Middle Eastern men for ignoring deportation orders.

24 U.S. Army Special Forces in Afghanistan attack two Taliban camps north of Kandahar, killing at least 15 Taliban soldiers and capturing 27 others. Military experts believe the raids, surprise attacks carried out shortly after midnight, are an attempt by U.S. forces to capture high-ranking Taliban leaders and to obtain computer hard drives that could be used to track down terrorist groups.

27 An 81-year-old man is killed and dozens of people are injured in Jerusalem when a bomb carried by a Palestinian woman explodes on Jaffa Street. The attack is the first suicide bombing carried out by a woman in the current Israeli-Palestinian conflict.

28 U.S. Army Special Forces and Afghan militiamen raid a hospital in Kandahar in which six al-Qa'ida fighters have been holed up since early December 2001. All six members of al-Qa'ida are killed during the 10-hour battle. Five Afghan militiamen are wounded.

29 U.S. President George W. Bush, delivering his first State of the Union address before a joint session of Congress, labels Iran, Iraq, and North Korea "an axis of evil."

30 The head of the U.S. General Accounting Office (GAO), an investigative arm of Congress, announces that the GAO is filing a lawsuit to force Vice President Richard Cheney to turn over documents detailing meetings between an energy task force chaired by Cheney and energy industry executives. The matter has gained new prominence because of investigations of Enron Corp., the energy company that in 2001 filed the largest bankruptcy in U.S. history.

31 More than 100 U.S. troops begin participating in military training exercises with Philippine soldiers in Mindanao province. The troops are the first wave of more than 600 soldiers the United States has promised to send to the Philippines to train the Philippine army in counterterrorism tactics and to provide technical assistance in the army's battle against Abu Sayyaf, a militant Islamic group on the island of Basilan.

2 A committee appointed by the Enron board of directors to investigate the company's financial collapse reports that Enron executives used a complex network of partnerships to hide financial problems and overstate profits. The report discloses that certain executives realized enormous personal profits from these partnerships at Enron's expense. The former chief financial officer, Andrew Fastow, enjoyed a $4.5-million return on a $25,000 investment.

3 Adam Vinatieri of the New England Patriots kicks a 48-yard, last-second field goal to give his team a victory in the National Football League's Super Bowl XXXVI. The Patriots beat the St. Louis Rams 20-17 in New Orleans.

4 The Bush administration submits to the U.S. Congress details of a proposed military buildup that would increase the budget of the Department of Defense by $120 billion over the next five years and boost annual spending on weapons and other military supplies from $61 billion to $99 billion.

6 The United Kingdom launches a yearlong celebration of the Golden Jubilee of Queen Elizabeth II with a 40-gun salute in London's Hyde Park and a 62-gun salute from the Tower of London.

8 The 19th Winter Olympics open in Salt Lake City, Utah, with the largest program in the history of the winter games—78 events scheduled over 16 days at 5 indoor and 5 mountain facilities. The opening ceremony, with U.S. President George W. Bush in attendance, culminates with 2,318 athletes from 77 nations parading into Rice-Eccles Stadium for the lighting of the Olympic cauldron.

10 A fire driven by winds of up to 100 miles (160 kilometers) per hour burns across 2,000 acres (810 hectares) near Fallbrook, California, some 60 miles (95 kilometers) north of San Diego. A second fire scorches 1,400 acres (565 hectares) outside Anaheim Hills about 40 miles (65 kilometers) southeast of Los Angeles.

11 Prosecutors open their case against former Yugoslav President Slobodan Milosevic before the UN International Criminal Tribunal for the former Yugoslavia in The Hague, Netherlands. Milosevic is the first former head of state to be placed on trial for crimes against humanity and genocide.

11 Federal Bureau of Investigation (FBI) officials place the United States on high alert for possible terrorist attacks against U.S. interests either at home or abroad.

12 Former Enron Chairman Kenneth L. Lay invokes his Fifth Amendment rights against self-incrimination and refuses to answer questions posed by members of the U.S. Senate Commerce Committee about the failure of the Houston-based energy trading company.

14 The United States House of Representatives passes legislation designed to curb the influence of money on U.S. politics by banning political parties from raising or spending so-called "soft money"—unlimited contributions from corporations, labor unions, and individuals. Political experts suggest that support for the campaign finance reform bill grew after the collapse of Houston-based Enron Corp. focused public attention on the political influence of many large corporations.

A domestic cat has been cloned by a group of scientists in Texas, announce executives with Genetic Savings and Clone, a company in College Station, Texas, that invested $3.7 million in the project.

15 U.S. President George W. Bush approves a plan to move radioactive waste from all of the nation's nuclear power plants to a former nuclear test site at Yucca Mountain some 90 miles (145 kilometers) northwest of Las Vegas, Nevada.

20 Israel launches rocket strikes and ground assaults against Yasir Arafat's headquarters in Gaza City, killing at least 16 people, including 3 members of the Palestinian leader's elite guard. The raids are a reprisal for a Palestinian attack on an Israeli military outpost in the West Bank on February 19.

More than 360 people are killed and hundreds of others badly injured when a fire spreads through seven crowded passenger carriages of an Egyptian train en route from Cairo, the capital, to Luxor, in upper Egypt.

21 Daniel Pearl, a U.S. reporter kidnapped by Islamic militants in Pakistan

Spectators at the 19th Winter Olympic Games in Salt Lake City, Utah, cheer on the German team at the two-man bobsled competition on February 16. Germany was the overall winner of the games with 35 medals. The United States came in second with 34 medals.

on January 23, is dead, announce executives of *The Wall Street Journal*, the newspaper for which Pearl was on assignment. Authorities in Pakistan, who showed U.S. diplomats a videotape with graphic images of Pearl's murder, arrested a number of suspects.

24 The 2002 Winter Olympics in Salt Lake City, Utah, close with Germany the big overall winner with 35 medals. The United States captures 34 medals, and Norway comes in third with 24 medals.

27 Fifty-nine people are killed in Godhra in northwestern India when an angry mob of Muslim activists attacks a train packed with more than 2,500 Hindu nationalists. After throwing rocks to force the train to stop as it left the Godhra station, the Muslims toss gasoline bombs into passenger carriages. The people aboard the train were returning home from a pilgrimage to Ayodhya, where Hindu nationalists in 1992 destroyed a 450-year-old mosque. Recent attempts to construct a Hindu temple on the site had aggravated religious tensions.

1 Israeli troops attack Palestinian refugee camps on the West Bank. At least 19 Palestinians and 2 Israelis are killed in what Israeli officials describe as the most explosive confrontations between the two groups since violence erupted in September 2000.

President George W. Bush orders U.S. Special Operations forces to Yemen to train the Yemeni military in antiterrorist operations. The anouncement comes only days after President Bush sent U.S. forces to the country of Georgia to train troops in counterinsurgency against Islamic militants in the area.

2 A lone sniper kills 10 Israelis at a checkpoint on the West Bank. Earlier, a suicide bomber blew himself apart in an ultra-orthodox neighborhood in Jerusalem, killing nine people walking home from services at the end of the Jewish Sabbath. The al-Aqsa Martyrs Brigades, a militant group with connections to Yasir Arafat's Fatah faction, claims responsibility for both attacks.

3 The people of Switzerland vote to join the United Nations (UN). Political experts suggest that the Swiss have resisted UN membership in the past because of a long history of neutrality.

4 Seven U.S. soldiers are killed when two MH-47 Chinook helicopters are hit by enemy fire during intense fighting in the Shahi Kot mountain region of eastern Afghanistan.

5 A Palestinian gunman armed with an M-16 assault rifle fires into a Tel Aviv nightclub, killing 3 Israelis and wounding at least 10 other people before being gunned down by police. The Palestinian militant group al-Aqsa Martyrs Brigades takes credit for the attack.

U.S. President George W. Bush imposes tariffs of up to 30 percent on most types of steel imported into the United States.

6 Independent counsel Robert W. Ray issues a 237-page report on the seven-year, $70-million investigation of former President Bill Clinton and U.S. Senator Hillary Rodham Clinton (D., New York). Ray does not recommend bringing criminal charges against either of the two.

7 Alan Greenspan, chairman of the Federal Reserve, the central bank of the United States, tells the Senate Banking Committee that he is encouraged by recent trends in key economic indicators and believes that the recession that began in 2001 is over.

9 A suicide bombing that kills 12 people in a Jerusalem cafe caps the most violent weekend yet in the 17-month-long Israeli-Palestinian conflict. On March 8, Israeli soldiers killed 39 people in a series of strikes in the West Bank and the Gaza Strip after five Israeli teen-agers had been gunned down by the Islamic militant group Hamas.

11 The Federal Aviation Administration reports that the number of flights at 31 hub U.S. airports declined by 12.2 percent in the five months following the terrorist attacks on the United States on Sept. 11, 2001, compared with the same period in 2000.

U.S. President George W. Bush orders an inquiry into operations at the U.S. Immigration and Naturalization Service (INS) after INS officials issued student visas to two of the dead hijackers who carried out the terrorist attacks on the United States in 2001.

13 Zimbabwe officials declare incumbent Robert Mugabe the winner in the recent presidential election, which officials from the United Kingdom and the United States condemn as rigged.

14 Accounting firm Arthur Andersen LLP of Chicago has been indicted on a charge of obstruction of justice, reveals the U.S. Department of Justice, alleging that Andersen employees systematically shredded records relating to the financial collapse of Enron Corp. of Houston.

17 Two men walk into a nondenominational Protestant church in Pakistan's capital,

Israeli tanks shell Yasir Arafat's compound in the West Bank on March 29. The attack, launched in retaliation for the suicide bombing of a hotel dining room on Passover that resulted in the deaths of 29 Israelis, destroyed much of Arafat's headquarters but left the Palestinian leader unharmed.

Islamabad, and toss grenades into the sanctuary, killing five people, including two Americans.

19 More than two-thirds of Antarctica's Larsen Ice Shelf, 3,420 square miles (8,860 square kilometers) of ice 700 feet (213 meters) thick, has disappeared since 1998, report scientists with the National Snow and Ice Data Center (NSIDC) in Boulder, Colorado. A section 50 percent larger than the state of Rhode Island fractured and disintegrated into the ocean during a 35-day period ending on March 7.

20 The U.S. Senate votes 60 to 40 to approve legislation designed to curb the influence of money on U.S. politics. The bill bans political parties from raising or spending so-called "soft money." President George W. Bush has stated that he will sign the bill.

25 The Argentine peso tumbles on international markets by 20 percent in a single day, sending thousands of people into banks to exchange pesos for U.S. dollars to protect their savings.

27 A Palestinian suicide bomber with the Islamic militant group Hamas detonates a bomb in a hotel dining room in Netanya, Israel, killing 29 people and injuring more than 100 others.

29 Israeli shelling of Yasir Arafat's Ram Al-lah headquarters gives Israeli troops access into the compound, where they battle Arafat's personal guards room by room. Although the Israeli government announced that Arafat is not to be harmed, the Palestinian leader, who is locked in a windowless office, claims he is prepared to die as a martyr.

31 Israeli Prime Minister Ariel Sharon announces that Israel is engaged in a "war against terrorism" and labels Palestinian leader Yasir Arafat "the enemy of the entire free world." Sharon's pronouncement comes after a Palestinian suicide bomber blew himself apart in a crowded restaurant in Haifa, killing 15 Israelis and wounding several other people. Five suicide bombings in five days in various locations throughout Israel left more than 40 people dead.

1 Pakistani authorities transfer custody of senior al-Qa'ida leader Abu Zubaydah to U.S. authorities in Pakistan. He was captured in Pakistan, where he appeared to be setting up a new base of operations.

2 Firefights between Israeli troops and Palestinian snipers rage around the Church of the Nativity in Bethlehem. According to Israeli officials, at least 200 armed men are holed up in the church, which many Christians believe marks the birthplace of Jesus.

4 U.S. President George W. Bush demands that Israel withdraw its troops from Palestinian territories in the West Bank and sends Secretary of State Colin Powell to the Middle East to negotiate a cease-fire.

7 The Israeli Army steps up its offensive in the West Bank as Israeli troops continue to battle Palestinian militants in Nabulus and Janin.

8 Shareholders of the failed energy trading company Enron file a lawsuit against some of the world's top financial institutions, including J. P. Morgan Chase, Citigroup, Merrill Lynch, and Bank of America. In the complaint, the shareholders allege that the executives of financial institutions realized enormous personal profits by crafting deals that funneled millions of dollars in loans to Enron, which were used to disguise that company's lack of profits.

9 Businesses and schools throughout the United Kingdom close to honor Queen Elizabeth, the Queen Mother (1900-2002), during her funeral at Westminster Abbey in London. At least 1 million people line a 23-mile (37-kilometer) route between Westminister Abbey and St. George's Chapel at Windsor Castle, where the queen mother is interred beside her husband, King George VI.

An honor guard, followed by members of the British royal family, bears the coffin of Queen Elizabeth, the queen mother, at her funeral at Westminster Abbey on April 9. The queen mother, who was 101 years old at the time of her death, was widely admired for her ability to inspire the British public, particularly during World War II.

10 Palestinian militants shoot and kill 2 monks from among the 40 priests, monks, and nuns that the militants are holding hostage inside the Church of the Nativity in Bethlehem. A third monk is seriously wounded.

12 Venezuelan President Hugo Chavez resigns under pressure from the military. Military leaders turned against Chavez after a massive demonstration ended in a massacre in the streets of Caracas, the capital. Officials estimated that as many as 150,000 people marched through Caracas on April 11, demanding the president's resignation. Nineteen people were killed when Chavez ordered National Guard troops and civilian gunmen to stop the crowd from reaching the presidential palace.

14 Hugo Chavez regains the presidency of Venezuela two days after being forced from office in a military *coup* (overthrow). The reversal in Chavez's political fortunes was driven by divisions between the leaders of Venezuela's military and rank-and-file soldiers and by the enormous support Chavez enjoys among Venezuela's poor.

U.S. golfer Tiger Woods wins the 66th Masters Tournament at the Augusta National Golf Course in Georgia, defeating Retief Goosen by three strokes for a 12-under-par 276 total.

17 Much of Italy comes to a standstill when trade unions call the country's first one-day general strike in 20 years. The strike is to protest Prime Minister Silvio Berlusconi's attempt to reform Italy's labor laws, which make it virtually impossible for Italian companies to dismiss or lay off any employee.

A U.S. District Court judge in Portland, Oregon, rejects an attempt by the U.S. Department of Justice to overturn an Oregon law that allows assisted suicide for the terminally ill. In November 2001, Attorney General John Ashcroft issued an order that physicians who dispensed controlled substances to terminally ill patients risked having their licenses revoked.

18 A U.S. fighter pilot flying an F-16 jet accidentally attacks allied forces in Afghanistan. The pilot drops a 500-pound (227-kilogram), laser-guided bomb on Canadian soldiers conducting a training mission south of Kandahar. Four Canadians are killed, and eight others are wounded.

18 Members of the U.S. Senate vote 54 to 46 to block President George W. Bush's proposal to drill for oil and natural gas in the Arctic National Wildlife Refuge in Alaska.

19 The FBI issues a warning that U.S. banks in the Northeast could be the targets of al-Qa'ida terrorist attacks.

Israeli troops pull out of Nabulus and much of Ram Allah after Israeli Prime Minister Ariel Sharon declares that the first phase of the army's offensive in the West Bank is over. Troops remain stationed around Palestinian leader Yasir Arafat's headquarters in Ram Allah.

21 French Prime Minister Lionel Jospin receives 16.2 percent of the vote in a preliminary election for the French presidency. He comes in third after the incumbent, Jacques Chirac, and an extreme right-wing candidate, Jean-Marie Le Pen. Political experts describe the results as a "political earthquake" that will likely force Jospin, the leader of French Socialists, to retire.

Fourteen people die in a string of bombings in General Santos, a largely Christian city approximately 600 miles (965 kilometers) south of the Philippine capital, Manila. An Islamic extremist group takes credit.

22 Banks in Argentina close for an indefinite period, virtually shutting down all financial systems, including the stock market in Buenos Aires, the capital. Argentine President Eduardo Duhalde ordered the bank holiday in an effort to save the nation's banks from failing.

28 Leaders of the Israeli government and the Palestinian authority agree to terms proposed by U.S. Secretary of State Colin Powell to end the Israeli siege of Palestinian leader Yasir Arafat's headquarters in Ram Allah in the West Bank.

30 President Robert Mugabe of Zimbabwe declares a national state of emergency due to food shortages, which he attributes to drought. Local authorities cite a breakdown in the country's agricultural system due to government seizure of farms owned by white citizens. Representatives of relief agencies in Zimbabwe fear widespread starvation among the nation's poor, who make up more than half of the country's population of nearly 13 million people.

1 Israeli troops withdraw from Ram Al-lah, ending the siege that kept Palestinian leader Yasir Arafat imprisoned within his headquarters compound since March 29.

3 The U.S. unemployment rate climbed from 5.7 percent in March to 6 percent in April, its highest level since August 1994, report officials with the U.S. Department of Labor.

5 French voters reelect President Jacques Chirac with 82 percent of the vote, the highest margin in the 44-year history of the French Republic. Chirac's opponent, right-wing candidate Jean-Marie Le Pen, takes 18 percent of the vote.

6 Myanmar's military government releases prodemocracy leader Aung San Suu Kyi after 19 months of house arrest with the guarantee that she is free to pursue her activities as head of Myanmar's prodemocracy opposition party.

Maverick right-wing Dutch politician Pim Fortuyn is assassinated as he leaves a radio station in Hilversum, the Netherlands. Fortuyn, a sociology professor, was campaigning for the upcoming Dutch parliamentary elections on an anti-immigrant, law-and-order platform.

Energy traders at Enron increased corporate profits by driving up the price of electricity in California during the height of the state's energy crisis in 2000 and 2001, reveals the Federal Energy Regulatory Commission.

The Bush administration formally renounces a United Nations-sponsored treaty establishing the world's first permanent court for the prosecution of war criminals and dictators.

7 State police in Nevada arrest a 21-year-old student for placing 18 pipe-bombs in mailboxes in rural areas of Illinois, Iowa, Nebraska, Colorado, and Texas. The attacks began on May 3.

8 A suicide bomber detonates a car bomb alongside a shuttle bus in front of the Sheraton Hotel in downtown Karachi, Pakistan, killing 15 people, including 11 French engineers. Authorities characterize the bombing as an al-Qa'ida attack on Pakistan's Western community.

9 At least 35 people, including 12 children, are killed when a bomb packed with nails and bolts explodes in Kaspiisk, a Caspian Sea port about 1,000 miles (1,610 kilometers) south of Moscow in the Russian republic of Dagestan. The explosion rips through a marine band and spectators lining the route of a parade commemorating the anniversary of the end of World War II.

10 The siege of Bethlehem's Church of the Nativity ends after five weeks with 123 unarmed Palestinians and 84 civilians leaving the ancient complex.

A British passenger train derails at a speed of 100 miles (160 kilometers) per hour and smashes into a commuter platform at Potters Bar, a suburb north of London. Seven people are killed in the crash, which is the fifth fatal train accident in England in six years.

11 A top planning official with the Chinese government in Beijing, the capital, warns Chinese bankers that a rapidly widening gap between rich and poor, which was virtually nonexistent in China 20 years ago, now threatens the nation's stability.

14 Former U.S. President Jimmy Carter, speaking in a live television broadcast on Cuba's state-controlled network, calls on President Fidel Castro to adopt democratic reforms. Carter also appeals to U.S. President George W. Bush to end more than 40 years of economic embargo against Cuba.

17 Temperatures in southern India hit 122 °F (50 °C). A month-long heat wave has resulted in the deaths of as many as 600 people in the state of Andhra Pradesh.

18 War Emblem wins the second leg of horseracing's Triple Crown, the Preakness Stakes, at Pimlico Race Course in Baltimore, in 1 minute, 56.35 seconds.

19 UN Secretary General Kofi Annan hands control of East Timor over to Jose Alexandre Gusmao, president of the new nation, in a ceremony in Dili, the capital, attended by thousands of East Timorese and representatives of more than 90 nations. The ceremony marks the end of nearly 500 years of foreign domination.

22 Indian Prime Minister Atal Behari Vajpayee tells Indian troops massed along the border between the Pakistani- and Indian-administered parts of Jammu and Kashmir to prepare for a "decisive battle." Nearly 1 million troops backed by tanks, warplanes, and missiles stand

U.S. President George W. Bush and Russian President Vladimir Putin announce on May 24 at the Kremlin in Moscow the completion of a landmark arms treaty in which the two leaders pledged to cut their nuclear arsenals by two-thirds over the next 10 years.

on the highest alert on both sides of the border between the two nuclear-armed countries.

24 U.S. President George W. Bush and Russian President Vladimir Putin sign a landmark nuclear arms treaty in which the governments of both countries pledge to cut their nuclear arsenals by two-thirds over the next 10 years.

26 A bridge on Interstate Highway 40 in southeast Oklahoma collapses into the Arkansas River after barges smash into concrete pylons supporting the span. At least 12 cars and trucks fall 75 feet (23 meters) into the fast-moving river, killing 14 people.

26 Voters in Colombia elect 49-year-old Alvaro Uribe, who was educated in the United States and United Kingdom, president with 53 percent of the vote. Political experts see the rare majority vote as a clear mandate for Uribe's hard-line stance against the country's leftist rebels.

28 Intelligence agents from the United States, Pakistan, and India confirm that al-Qa'ida leaders appear to have filtered across the border from Afghanistan into major Pakistani cities, where they are apparently collaborating with Islamic extremists who bitterly oppose U.S.-Pakistani cooperation in the war on terrorism.

2 At least 67 percent of all prisoners released from state penal institutions in 1994, the latest year for which data are available, were returned to prison within three years, announces the U.S. Department of Justice.

4 Enormous crowds cheer Queen Elizabeth II of the United Kingdom as a national holiday celebrating her 50 years on the throne ends with her appearance on the balcony of Buckingham Palace in London. At least 1 million people fill the streets of the capital for the end of the four-day Golden Jubilee in what observers describe as a tremendous show of loyalty and affection.

5 U.S. Attorney General John Ashcroft announces that the government intends to begin fingerprinting and photographing all foreign visitors who fit a profile of potential terrorists.

6 U.S. President George W. Bush proposes a new Cabinet department for domestic defense. The secretary of the Homeland Security Department is to oversee the domestic war on terrorism, specifically coordinating efforts to protect the country from terrorist attack.

FBI agent Coleen Rowley tells the Senate Judiciary Committee that a rigid hierarchy within the FBI discourages initiative and punishes those who challenge the system. She testifies that agents are hamstrung by a computer system that is less sophisticated than most personal computers. Rowley told FBI Director Robert Mueller in May that the plot behind the terrorist attacks in 2001 might have been uncovered if important memos had not been left to languish on agents' desks.

Israeli tanks shell Yasir Arafat's compound headquarters in Ram Allah. Two people are killed in the assault, which is launched in retaliation for the suicide car bombing on June 5 of a commuter bus that killed 17 Israelis.

7 Muslim rebels kill U.S. missionary Martin Burnham and Philippine nurse Deborah Yap as Philippine troops attack the rebel's jungle compound on the island of Mindanao. The two victims were kidnapped with 18 other people from a seafront resort in May 2001.

9 An enormous wildfire burns out of control near Glenwood Springs in west-central Colorado. The blaze burned across 2,000 acres (809 hectares) and leveled 40 structures in less than 24 hours. A second fire 50 miles (80 kilometers) southwest of Denver destroys 5,000 acres (2,023 hectares) of forest. A third fire threatens oil and gas fields in southwest Colorado.

10 India lifts its ban on Pakistani aircraft flying over Indian airspace and orders its ships home from Pakistan's coast in an effort to ease tensions between the two countries.

13 Afghanistan's loya jirga, or grand council, votes overwhelmingly to elect Hamid Karzai president of the ruling council.

14 A suicide bomber drives a car loaded with explosives into a guard post outside the U.S. Consulate in Karachi, Pakistan, killing at least 10 people and injuring more than 40 others.

15 The U.S. District Court in Houston finds the Chicago-based accounting firm Arthur Andersen LLP guilty of obstruction of justice for interfering in a federal investigation of Andersen's client, the Houston-based Enron Corp.

16 Golfer Tiger Woods wins the 102nd U.S. Open Championship by defeating Phil Mickelson by three strokes for a 3-under-par 277 total.

Residents of Show Low, Arizona, flee from the Rodeo-Chediski fire, burning out of control across two Arizona counties northwest of Phoenix in late June. The fire, the largest in Arizona's history, developed when two wildfires connected to form a single line 50 miles (80 kilometers) long.

17 Senior Enron executives awarded themselves $300 million in bonuses in the 12 months before the company filed for bankruptcy in 2001, reveal documents filed in bankruptcy court.

19 Israeli tanks and troops enter the West Bank and seize Palestinian-held territory in Nabulus and Janin. The raids are a response to a June 18 suicide bombing that killed 19 people on a Jerusalem bus.

20 The U.S. Supreme Court rules, in a 6-to-3 decision, that the execution of a mentally retarded person is cruel and unusual punishment and in violation of the Eighth Amendment.

22 Prime Minister Mahathir Mohamad of Malaysia announces that he intends to leave office in 2003. The 76-year-old Mahathir has held power for 21 years.

23 Fires have leveled at least 2.28 million acres (923,000 hectares) of forest in the United States in 2002, the National Interagency Fire Center reports. Drought-related fires currently burn out of control in Utah, New Mexico, Colorado, and Arizona.

25 WorldCom Inc. discloses that the Mississippi-based telecommunications company lost $3.8 billion in 2001, instead of posting $1.4 billion in profits as previously reported. Chief Executive Officer Bernard Ebbers resigned in April when it was disclosed that he had borrowed $409 million in company funds.

26 The State Duma, Russia's lower house of parliament, passes legislation that legalizes the sale of Russian farmland for the first time since the Bolsheviks gained control of the government in the revolution of 1917.

The Ninth U.S. Circuit Court of Appeals in San Francisco rules in a 2-to-1 decision that the recitation of the Pledge of Allegiance in public schools is unconstitutional because of the phrase "one Nation under God."

27 The U.S. Supreme Court rules that taxpayer money can be used to send children to private schools, including religious schools. In a 5-to-4 decision, the court decides that the Cleveland, Ohio, school-voucher program does not violate the constitutional clause separating church and state.

1 A Bashkirian Airlines jet with 52 Russian school children en route from Moscow to Spain collides with a cargo plane over Germany. All 69 passengers and crew members aboard the jet and the 2 crew members flying the cargo plane are killed.

2 The crew of a U.S. AC-130 gunship accidentally targets Afghan civilians approximately 100 miles (160 kilometers) north of Kandahar. Mistaking guns being shot off in celebration for anti-aircraft fire, the crew attacks a wedding party, killing up to 40 people.

5 The U.S. unemployment rate climbs to 5.9 percent in June from 5.8 percent in May, reports the Department of Labor.

6 Serena Williams of the United States takes her first Wimbledon title and her third Grand Slam tennis championship by beating her sister, Venus Williams, 7-6 (4), 6-3 at the All-England Lawn Tennis Club in Wimbledon, England.

7 About 45 forest fires burn out of control in northern Quebec. Canadian authorities estimate that 100,000 acres (40,470 hectares) of forest have burned since the fires were started by lightning on July 2.

7 AIDS will kill 68 million people in the next 20 years, more than triple the number who died in the first 20 years of the epidemic, report scientists at the 14th International AIDS Conference in Barcelona, Spain.

8 Michigan takes control of the city government of Flint, which is nearly $40 million in debt. Officials revealed earlier in 2002 that the city's debt doubled between June 2001 and June 2002.

9 Senators Tom Daschle (D., South Dakota) and John McCain (R., Arizona) call for the resignation of Securities and Exchange Commission (SEC) Chairman Harvey Pitt. McCain accuses Pitt of being slow to address corporate accounting abuses. Daschle notes that Pitt in 2001 told business leaders that accounting firms could expect a "kinder, gentler" SEC under his leadership.

A stock trader stops to catch his breath on July 22 when the Dow Jones industrial average of 30 corporations listed on the New York Stock Exchange declined below 8,000 for the first time in nearly four years. On the previous trading day, July 19, the Dow fell 390 points, the largest one-day decline of 2002. On July 12, the Dow closed the week down 7 percent, its worst weekly performance on record.

9 President George W. Bush announces the creation of a special task force to investigate questionable corporate accounting practices. The president accuses corporate America of failing to police itself and proposes increasing funding of the Securities and Exchange Commission.

10 More than 13 million children worldwide have been orphaned by AIDS since 1991, report scientists at the International AIDS Conference in Spain.

12 The Dow Jones industrial average of stock prices of 30 leading U.S. corporations listed on the New York Stock Exchange closes the week down 694.97 points, a drop of more than 7 percent and the Dow's worst weekly performance on record.

The Bush administration announces that officials expect the federal government to post a deficit of $165 billion this fiscal year, a 56-percent increase over earlier projections.

The Superior Court of Ontario, Canada, rules that Ontario's provincial government must recognize the rights of gay men and lesbian women to marry people of their own sex.

15 The value of the euro, the common currency of 12 of 15 European Union nations, edges past the U.S. dollar for the first time since the euro was introduced more than two years ago.

John Walker Lindh, the so-called American Taliban, avoids life in prison by pleading guilty to 2 counts of a 10-count indictment that he conspired with the Taliban to kill Americans.

16 Palestinian militants bomb an Israeli bus between Nabulus and Qalqilyah in the West Bank. Gunmen shoot the passengers as they attempt to flee the bus, killing seven Israeli civilians.

More than 50 people are injured in widespread clashes in Paraguay between police and demonstrators protesting the government's failure to pull the country back from an economic decline tied to recessions in Argentina and Brazil.

18 Zacarias Moussaoui, the so-called 20th hijacker, tells U.S. District Judge Leonie Brinkema that he is a member of the al-Qa'ida terrorist network and helped plan the terrorist attacks on the United States on Sept. 11, 2001.

18 More than 600 immigrants have been jailed and subjected to secret hearings since the terrorist attacks on the United States on Sept. 11, 2001, reports the U.S. Department of Justice.

19 The Dow Jones industrial average of 30 leading U.S. corporations on the New York Stock Exchange falls 390 points, the index's largest one-day drop in 2002 and the seventh biggest decline in history.

21 WorldCom Inc., a Mississippi-based telecommunications company, files for bankruptcy in Federal District Court in New York City. The bankruptcy, involving more than $100 billion in assets, including long-distance giant MCI, is the largest in U.S. history.

22 The Dow Jones industrial average of 30 leading U.S. corporations declines below 8,000 for the first time in nearly four years.

24 The Dow Jones industrial average surges up 488.95 points, the average's biggest one-day rally in 15 years.

Adelphia Communications founder John J. Rigas and two of his sons are arrested for looting the Coudersport, Pennsylvania-based cable TV company. Prosecutors allege that the Rigases borrowed as much as $66 million in company money and mired Adelphia in $18.6 billion of debt. Adelphia, with 15,000 employees, sought bankruptcy protection in June.

25 The U.S. Senate votes 99-0 and the House of Representatives votes 423-3 to approve a corporate reform bill that stiffens penalties for corporate fraud.

28 Lance Armstrong of the United States wins his fourth consecutive Tour de France bicycle race, crossing the finish line on the Champs-Elysees in Paris 7 minutes, 17 seconds before Joseba Beloki of Spain.

30 The presidents of Congo (Kinshasa) and Rwanda, meeting in South Africa, sign a treaty designed to end four years of armed conflict.

31 A powerful bomb, concealed in a bag left on a restaurant table by Islamic militants, tears apart a cafeteria in the student center at Hebrew University in Jerusalem. Seven people are killed, including five Americans.

1 Federal authorities arrest two former executives of WorldCom, Inc., the bankrupt Mississippi-based telecommunications company. Scott D. Sullivan, WorldCom's former chief financial officer, and David F. Myers, the former controller, are accused of using illegal accounting procedures to artificially inflate WorldCom earnings.

2 Four people in Louisiana have died of West Nile virus and at least 58 other residents of the state have been infected, announce health officials in Baton Rouge, the capital.

3 Floods have left at least 560 people dead in India, Nepal, and Bangladesh since the monsoon season began in June, report government officials in the three countries.

5 Israel places a total ban on Palestinian travel in the West Bank after a series of Palestinian attacks left 14 people dead in a period of less than 24 hours.

Employees at the U.S. Department of Justice have lost track of nearly 800 weapons and 400 laptop computers, many of which had national security or sensitive law-enforcement information on their hard drives, reports the department's inspector general.

The gun turret from the U.S.S. *Monitor*, an ironclad Union warship from the U.S. Civil War (1861-1865), is raised 240 feet (73 meters) from the floor of the Atlantic Ocean 16 miles (25 kilometers) off Cape Hatteras, North Carolina.

6 Louisiana's Office of Public Health confirms that a fifth resident of the state has died from the mosquito-borne West Nile virus. Officials also announce that 14 additional cases of the disease have been diagnosed in Louisiana, bringing the total to 71.

Argentina's unemployment rate hits 21.5 percent, the highest in the country's history.

8 WorldCom, the bankrupt Mississippi-based telecommunications company, announces the discovery of an additional $3.3 billion in accounting misstatements.

Ten people, including four children, plunge into a shark tank at the Aquarium of the Americas in New Orleans when a catwalk suspended above the water collapses. All are rescued without injury.

9 At least 60 percent of Zimbabwe's 2,900 white farmers ignore threats of fines or jail and defy President Robert Mugabe's order that all of the nation's white farmers must leave their land by August 9.

The George W. Bush administration issues a directive that allows physicians and hospitals to share medical records of U.S. citizens with health insurance companies, health maintenance organizations, marketing companies, and law-enforcement agencies.

11 US Airways, the sixth-largest air carrier in the United States, files for Chapter 11 bankruptcy protection.

12 Flooding in central and eastern Europe produced by torrential rains during the week of August 4 has left at least 70 people dead, estimate European officials.

15 At least 900 people have died in floods in Nepal, northern India, and Bangladesh, government officials report.

The director of the U.S. Immigration and Naturalization Service, James Ziglar, tenders his resignation to President George W. Bush.

18 The governments of Russia and Iraq announce plans to sign a new five-year, $40-billion economic cooperation agreement.

19 A Russian military transport helicopter crashes into a minefield in Chechnya, killing 116 of the 147 people aboard. Russian officials believe that the Mi-26 helicopter was downed by Chechen rebels.

20 Moscow police rescue 25 people from the rubble of a five-story apartment building that was nearly destroyed in an explosion that left eight people dead. Residents pulled from the rubble

In mid-August, floodwaters drench the court-yard of the Dresdener Zwinger, a museum complex built as a palace in Dresden, Germany, in the 1700's. Thousands of the city's residents evacuated as the Elbe River rose to a record-breaking level.

claim to have smelled gun powder be-fore the blast. Russian authorities sus-pect Chechen rebels were responsible for the explosion.

21 A former Enron executive, Michael J. Kopper, pleads guilty to money laun-dering and conspiracy to commit wire fraud in U.S. District Court in Houston and tells a federal judge that he paid huge kickbacks to Enron's chief finan-cial officer, Andrew S. Fastow.

Canadian Prime Minister Jean Chretien announces that he will not seek a fourth term and will leave office in February 2004.

25 More than 6.6 million Americans, 1 of every 32 U.S. adults, were in prison, jail, or on probation or parole in 2001, report officials with the U.S. Depart-ment of Justice. The U.S. prison popula-tion increased by 2.3 percent between 2000 and 2001.

26 The Sixth Circuit U.S. Court of Appeals in Cincinnati, Ohio, rules that the U.S. government cannot conduct deporta-tion cases in secret. The U.S. Depart-ment of Justice held hundreds of closed deportation hearings, primarily against Muslim men, in the wake of the terrorist attacks on Sept. 11, 2001.

28 Federal authorities in Detroit charge four Arab men with being members of the al-Qa'ida terrorist network and with plotting attacks in the United States, Jordan, and Turkey.

30 Major League Baseball union represent-atives and team owners reach a four-year contract agreement just hours be-fore a scheduled strike that threatened to end the 2002 baseball season.

1 Typhoon Rusa dumps nearly 36 inches (91 centimeters) of rain in South Korea, triggering massive flooding and landslides that kill more than 130 people.

3 The Dow Jones average of 30 leading stocks on the New York Stock Exchange falls 355 points. The Dow index has dropped for five consecutive months, the longest decline since 1981.

4 U.S. President George W. Bush pledges that he will seek congressional approval before launching any military campaign in Iraq and promises to present his case against Iraqi President Saddam Hussein at the United Nations.

5 President Hamid Karzai of Afghanistan survives an assassination attempt in the southern Afghan city of Kandahar.

7 British Prime Minister Tony Blair, meeting with U.S. President George W. Bush, endorses the president's drive to topple Iraqi President Saddam Hussein from power.

8 All violent crime in the United States except murder fell by 9 percent between 2000 and 2001, report officials with the U.S. Department of Justice. The 2001 decline pushes the crime rate nationwide to its lowest level since the government began tracking violent crime in 1973.

10 Senator Bob Smith loses to John Sununu in New Hampshire's Republican primary. Elizabeth Dole wins the Republican primary for the North Carolina Senate seat held by retiring Senator Jessie Helms. In Florida, attorney Bill

United States President George W. Bush addresses the United Nations (UN) General Assembly on September 12, challenging the UN to force Iraqi President Saddam Hussein to disarm or face the consequences.

McBride leads former U.S. Attorney General Janet Reno for the Democratic nomination for governor in a race marred by irregularities at the polls.

11 Communities across the United States commemorate the first anniversary of the terrorist attacks on the United States on Sept. 11, 2001.

12 U.S. President George W. Bush presents his rationale for military action against Iraq before the United Nations General Assembly in New York City.

13 Ramzi bin al-Shibh, alleged to be a high-ranking member of the al-Qa'ida terrorist network who was involved in planning the attacks on the United States in 2001, has been captured in Pakistan, announce U.S. officials.

14 Five Arab-American men are charged with operating an active al-Qa'ida terrorist cell in western New York State, according to the Federal Bureau of Investigation.

15 Federal Bureau of Investigation agents arrest a sixth man who U.S. officials believe was involved in an al-Qa'ida terrorist cell in western New York State.

17 Japan and North Korea end more than 50 years of hostility with an agreement to reestablish diplomatic relations.

Former U.S. Attorney General Janet Reno concedes defeat in her bid for the Democratic nomination for governor of Florida.

19 Federal health officials confirm that some cases of West Nile virus have been transmitted through blood transfusions.

Israeli tanks encircle Palestinian leader Yasir Arafat's compound in Ram Allah in the West Bank, demanding that he surrender various men wanted by Israeli authorities.

A *coup* (overthrow) attempt against the government of President Laurent Gbagbo of Cote d'Ivoire (Ivory Coast) leaves 19 people dead.

22 Gerhard Schroeder retains his position as chancellor of Germany in parliamentary elections.

23 The El Paso Corporation, the largest supplier of natural gas in the United States, illegally drove up the price of natural gas in California in 2000 and 2001, contributing to that state's energy crisis, rules the Federal Energy Regulatory Commission.

24 British Prime Minister Tony Blair informs the House of Commons that the Iraqi military is capable of launching warheads armed with biological or chemical weapons within 45 minutes of receiving the order from Iraqi President Saddam Hussein. According to Blair, Iraq is one to five years away from completing a nuclear weapon.

The U.S. Department of Defense dispatches 200 soldiers stationed in Germany to West Africa to protect hundreds of U.S. citizens, including 161 schoolchildren, endangered by civil unrest in Cote d'Ivoire (Ivory Coast).

25 The United States is reestablishing diplomatic relations with North Korea, announces a spokesperson for President George W. Bush's administration.

26 Some 1,200 people are killed when a ferry sinks in a violent storm in the Atlantic Ocean off the coast of Gambia in western Africa.

27 The administration of U.S. President George W. Bush proposes a United Nations (UN) resolution that calls on Iraq to give UN weapons inspectors immediate access to all suspect sites in Iraq. The United States also proposes that the UN authorize the use of military force if Iraq interferes with inspections.

The Dow Jones Industrial average of 30 major corporations traded on the New York Stock Exchange closes at 7,701.45, down 295.67 points. The average is down by 11.1 percent for the month. The decline of the market during the third quarter of 2002 was the greatest since the fourth quarter of 1987.

30 Operators of ports on the U.S. West Coast shut down operations over a contract dispute with union dockworkers. The shutdown leaves hundreds of cargo and passenger ships bottled up in 29 West Coast ports.

The foreign ministers of the European Union agree to exempt U.S. soldiers and government officials from prosecution for war crimes by the International Criminal Court in The Hague, Netherlands. U.S. President George W. Bush had demanded immunity for all U.S. government personnel on the grounds that U.S. officials could become targets of politically motivated persecution.

1 Iraqi officials, meeting in Vienna with representatives from the United Nations (UN), agree to allow UN weapons inspectors into Iraq.

2 Federal Bureau of Investigation agents arrest Andrew S. Fastow, former chief financial officer of Houston-based Enron Corp. Fastow is charged with fraud, money laundering, and conspiracy for his alleged participation in schemes to artificially inflate Enron profits.

4 A sniper armed with a high-powered rifle wounds a woman outside a strip mall in Fredericksburg, Virginia, a suburb of Washington, D.C. Police believe the same person shot and killed a man in Washington, D.C., and four other people in Montgomery County, Maryland, on October 3, and one man in Wheaton, Maryland, on October 2.

5 An Islamic militant stabs the mayor of Paris, Bertrand Delanoe, in the abdomen while the mayor entertained guests in his office at city hall.

6 An explosion aboard a French oil tanker off the southeastern coast of Yemen sets the vessel on fire and releases thousands of barrels of oil into the sea. Intelligence agents attribute the explosion to terrorists.

7 U.S. President George W. Bush declares in a nationally televised address that Iraq's biological and chemical weapons are an immediate and deadly threat to the United States as well as to U.S. allies in the Middle East and Europe.

A sniper wounds a 13-year-old boy outside his middle school in Bowie, Maryland, a suburb of Washington, D.C.

8 A United States marine is killed and another severely wounded when two Kuwaitis, later found to be connected to the al-Qa'ida terrorist network, open fire on a group of marines on the Kuwaiti island of Failaka.

9 U.S. President George W. Bush invokes the Taft-Hartley Act to halt the lockout of 10,500 dockworkers at 29 West Coast ports.

The U.S. Department of Justice alleges that the executive director of the Benevolence International Foundation in Palos Hills, Illinois, funneled money collected for humanitarian purposes to Islamic terrorist organizations.

9 A man is shot and killed while pumping gas at a station near Manassas, Virginia. Police confirm the man is the ninth victim of an area sniper.

11 The U.S. Congress authorizes President George W. Bush to use military force against Iraq.

The Washington, D.C.-area sniper kills an eighth person. The latest victim is shot while filling his car with gas at a station near Fredericksburg, Virginia.

Former U.S. President Jimmy Carter wins the Nobel Peace Prize for his "untiring effort to find peaceful solutions to international conflicts."

12 Terrorist bombs destroy two nightclubs on the Indonesian island of Bali. More than 180 people are killed, primarily Australians and Europeans.

15 U.S. Secretary of Defense Donald Rumsfeld provides military surveillance aircraft to police authorities in Washington, D.C., and its suburbs in Virginia and Maryland to help search for the sniper who has shot 11 people since October 2. The latest victim was killed in Falls Church, Virginia, on October 14.

16 The government of North Korea admitted to U.S. officials that it has conducted a secret nuclear-weapons program in defiance of a 1994 agreement, reveal U.S. government officials.

18 United Airlines, the second-largest U.S. air passenger carrier, lost $889 million in the third quarter of 2002, reports United's parent company UAL Corp., of Elk Grove Village, Illinois.

19 A man is shot and seriously wounded outside a restaurant in Ashland, Virginia, near Richmond. A letter left behind the restaurant ties the shooting to the Washington, D.C.-area sniper.

Irish voters pass by a wide margin a referendum that clears the way for the European Union (EU) to admit 10 additional nations, all in eastern Europe. The treaty had been ratified by the EU's 14 other member nations.

21 An unusually powerful electronic attack of unknown origin strikes 9 of the 13 computer servers that manage global Internet traffic. The attack disables seven servers for one hour and causes intermittent problems on two others.

At a Maryland rest stop on October 24, state police examine the car in which they found John Allen Muhammad and John Lee Malvo, suspects in a string of sniper shootings in the Washington, D.C., area. Police also discovered a .223-caliber semiautomatic assault rifle.

22 The sniper who has killed nine people and wounded three others since October 2 shoots and kills a bus driver in Silver Spring, Maryland, a Washington, D.C., suburb.

23 Some 50 Chechen guerrillas, armed with automatic rifles, storm a Moscow theater and take more than 750 people hostage. The guerrillas announce they will begin killing the hostages unless the Russian government withdraws its troops from Chechnya.

24 Police arrest John Allen Muhammad, a 41-year-old U.S. Army veteran, and John Lee Malvo, his 17-year-old companion, at a Maryland rest stop in connection with the string of sniper shootings in the Washington, D.C., area.

25 Senator Paul Wellstone (D., Minnesota), his wife, and their daughter are killed when Wellstone's campaign plane crashes in northeastern Minnesota. Three campaign aides and the plane's two pilots are also killed.

26 Russian commandos free several hundred hostages from a Moscow theater occupied by Chechen rebels since October 23. The commandos first pumped a narcotic-based gas through the ventilation system. The gas incapacitated the

rebels, who were then shot. However, more than 120 hostages also died, most from the effects of the gas.

27 Brazilian voters elect Luiz Inacio Lula da Silva, of the leftist Workers' Party, president with more than 61 percent of the vote.

The Anaheim Angels collect the team's first World Series championship with a 4-1 victory over the San Francisco Giants in Game 7 of the series.

30 Israeli Prime Minister Ariel Sharon's coalition government collapses with the resignation of Labor Party ministers. The Labor Party protests financial support that Sharon has earmarked for Israeli settlers in the West Bank and Gaza Strip.

31 Federal prosecutors indict former Enron Corp. Chief Financial Officer Andrew Fastow on 78 counts of fraud, money laundering, conspiracy, and obstruction of justice.

31

Wrecked cars crush seats inside a destroyed movie theater in Van Wert, Ohio, on November 11, one day after a severe tornado struck the town. The twister was one of dozens of tornadoes that swept across 13 states in November, killing 36 people and injuring more than 200 others.

1 Ballistics tests on the rifle used in the Washington, D.C.-area sniper killings link a shooting in Silver Spring, Maryland, on September 14 to John Allen Muhammad and John Lee Malvo. Muhammad and Malvo are accused of at least 15 other shootings that left 12 people dead in four states and the District of Columbia in September and October.

3 Voters in Turkey turn the incumbent prime minister, Bulent Ecevit, and his Democratic Left Party out of office in parliamentary elections. A one-year-old political party with Islamic roots, the Justice and Development Party, wins enough votes to form a government without a coalition partner.

4 A U.S. missile strike killed Qaed Salim Sinan al-Harethi, a senior leader of the al-Qa'ida terrorist network, and five associates in Yemen on November 3, announce officials with the Central Intelligence Agency.

5 Republicans under the leadership of President George W. Bush regain control of the U.S. Senate and enlarge their hold over the U.S. House of Representatives in midterm elections.

5 The chairman of the Securities and Exchange Commission, Harvey Pitt, resigns under intense criticism that he was too closely associated with the corporations and accounting firms that he was supposed to be regulating.

Prime Minister Ariel Sharon of Israel dissolves the Israeli parliament, the Knesset, and calls for early elections in January 2003.

6 Representative Richard A. Gephardt (D., Missouri) resigns as minority leader in the U.S. House of Representatives after Democrats lost at least five seats in midterm elections.

8 The UN Security Council unanimously endorses a resolution demanding that Iraq give UN inspectors access to all programs, plants, and materials that could be used for weapons production.

9 A crowd of some 450,000 European protesters marches through Florence, Italy, in an antiglobalization demonstration that turns into a rally against a possible U.S.-led war on Iraq.

10 Severe storms that spawn dozens of tornadoes sweep across 13 states, from Illinois and Louisiana on the west to Pennsylvania and North Carolina on the east. The storms kill 36 people.

12 Students at Tehran University and at schools in five other Iranian cities stage massive demonstrations to protest the death sentence issued to a scholar, Hashem Aghajari, for challenging the authority of Iran's hard-line clerics.

The Arab satellite television network, al Jazeera, broadcasts an audiotape in which an individual purported to be Osama bin Laden, leader of the al-Qa'ida terrorist network, praises recent terrorist strikes in Moscow and Bali. The tape could be evidence that the man credited with masterminding the terrorist attacks on the United States on Sept. 11, 2001, may still be alive.

14 Democrats in the U.S. House of Representatives choose Nancy Pelosi, who represents a district in San Francisco, as their new minority leader.

China's Communist Party announces that Hu Jintao, a 59-year-old government official little known outside the party's inner circle, is replacing Jiang Zemin as party leader.

16 Abdullah Gul, of the pro-Islamic Justice and Development Party, is chosen to be Turkey's prime minister.

18 A special spy review court grants U.S. Attorney General John Ashcroft and the Federal Bureau of Investigation broad new powers to wiretap the telephones of individuals who may be associated with foreign terrorists.

19 The U.S. Senate passes legislation, previously passed in the House, to create the Department of Homeland Security, which is to coordinate government efforts in the war on terrorism.

Congress passes legislation that makes U.S. taxpayers, rather than private insurance companies, liable for the first $90 billion in financial losses in case of future terrorist attacks.

The Liberia-registered tanker *Prestige* breaks apart and sinks off Spain's northwest coast. The tanker's cargo of fuel oil threatens coastal areas with massive contamination.

21 Abd al-Rahim al-Nashiri, a top leader of the al-Qa'ida terrorist network, has been captured and is in U.S. custody, confirm U.S. law enforcement officials.

22 The North Atlantic Treaty Organization extends invitations to seven Eastern European nations to join the military alliance and votes to create a 20,000-member rapid-response force.

23 Four days of riots leave at least 215 people dead and force hundreds of Christians to flee the Nigerian city of Kaduna. The violence between Muslims and Christians was sparked by a newspaper article written in response to Islamic criticism of the Miss World beauty pageant, which was to be staged in Nigeria in early December. The author of the article suggested that Mohammed, the founding prophet of Islam, might have regarded the pageant as an opportunity for choosing a new wife from among the contestants.

25 United Nations weapons inspectors arrive in Iraq to begin their search for weapons of mass destruction.

U.S. President George W. Bush signs the Homeland Security bill into law and nominates Tom Ridge, the former governor of Pennsylvania who has been the Bush administration's domestic security coordinator, to run the new Department of Homeland Security.

26 Women, for the first time, account for 50 percent of adults infected with HIV—more than 42 million people worldwide in 2002, reports the United Nations.

27 U.S. President George W. Bush appoints former Secretary of State Henry Kissinger to head an independent investigation into the Sept. 11, 2001, terrorist attacks.

28 A terrorist bombing of an Israeli-owned hotel in Mombassa, Kenya, kills 10 Kenyans and 3 Israelis. Minutes before the bombings, terrorists fired shoulder-launched missiles at an Israeli passenger jet taking off from the Mombassa airport. The rockets missed their target.

Israeli Prime Minister Ariel Sharon defeats Foreign Minister Benjamin Netanyahu in an election for leadership of the governing Likud Party.

1 Senator John Kerry (D., Massachusetts) announces that he is contemplating running for president of the United States in 2004.

4 The Air Transportation Stabilization Board refuses to approve a loan guarantee to United Airlines, the second largest U.S. commercial carrier. Aviation industry experts suggest that the decision will force United into bankruptcy.

5 President Hugo Chavez of Venezuela orders the armed services to protect the nation's oil industry from opposition groups attempting to drive the president from office by cutting off the country's flow of oil.

Widespread ice storms leave much of North Carolina and South Carolina under a heavy layer of ice that snaps electric lines, leaving as many as 1.2 million households without electricity or heat. Officials believe at least 20 people are dead as a result of the storms.

6 Secretary of the U.S. Treasury Paul H. O'Neill and President George W. Bush's top economic adviser, Lawrence Lindsey, resign.

7 Voters in a run-off election in Louisiana return Democrat Mary L. Landrieu to the U.S. Senate for a second term. Landrieu's victory gives the Democrats 48 Senate seats, compared with the Republicans, who hold 51 seats. The Senate also has one independent aligned with the Democrats.

8 Serbian voters fail for a second time to elect a new president. Serbia's election commission reports that 45 percent of eligible voters turned out for the election. Serbia's Constitution requires that at least 50 percent of voters must cast ballots for the results to be valid.

9 United Airlines, the world's second largest air carrier, files for bankruptcy protection. United executives disclose that the airline is currently losing as much as $22 million a day.

U.S. President George W. Bush nominates John Snow, the president and chief executive officer of the railroad giant, CSX Corp, to replace Paul O'Neill as secretary of the U.S. Treasury.

10 Two Spanish warships halt a North Korean cargo vessel in the Gulf of Aden and discover a cache of Scud missiles hidden beneath sacks of cement in the ship's hold. U.S. military experts, called in by the Spanish Navy, believe the ship was headed for a port in Yemen.

10 U.S. President George W. Bush nominates William H. Donaldson, a former investment banker and chairman of the New York Stock Exchange, as head of the Securities and Exchange Commission.

Former U.S. President Jimmy Carter accepts the Nobel Peace Prize in Oslo, Norway. In his acceptance speech, Carter notes that meeting challenges to world peace is best handled by the United Nations.

12 U.S. President George W. Bush publicly rebukes the incoming majority leader of the Senate, Trent Lott (R., Mississippi), for comments Lott made during a televised 100th birthday celebration for retiring Senator Strom Thurmond (R., South Carolina). Lott said that the United States would have fewer problems today if Thurmond, formerly an avowed segregationist, had been elected president in 1948.

13 Leaders of the European Union vote to expand the organization of 15 Western European nations with the addition of 10 Eastern European countries—Cyprus, the Czech Republic, Estonia, Hungary, Latvia, Lithuania, Malta, Poland, Slovakia, and Slovenia.

Pope John Paul II accepts the resignation of Cardinal F. Bernard F. Law of the Roman Catholic Archdiocese of Boston. Law had been under attack for the manner in which he handled priests under his supervision who had been accused of sexual abuse.

19 U.S. Secretary of State Colin Powell declares Iraq in "material breach" of a United Nations resolution demanding that Iraq must supply complete details of all its weapons programs.

19 At least 10 of the largest U.S. brokerage firms agree to pay more than $1 billion in fines to end an investigation into whether the companies had given customers misleading stock recommendations. Federal regulators and the New York State attorney general accused the companies of misinforming customers about the value of stocks in exchange for investment banking fees.

20 Senator Trent Lott announces that he is stepping down as majority leader in the

U.S. Senate for the 108th Congress, which is scheduled to begin on Jan. 6, 2003.

23 U.S. Senate Republicans, by acclamation, elect Senator Bill Frist (R., Tennessee) as their new majority leader.

U.S. Secretary of Defense Donald Rumsfeld issues a warning to North Korea that a possible U.S. war against Iraq would not deter the United States in its determination to force North Korea to halt its nuclear arms program.

25 North Korea has begun moving fresh fuel into a nuclear reactor, announces a spokesperson for the International Atomic Energy Agency. The five-megawatt reactor is one of four in Yongbyon, North Korea, that is capable of producing nuclear weapons. The agency also has evidence that North Korea has disabled UN monitoring devices at the four facilities.

27 North Korean officials announce that inspectors with the United Nations' International Atomic Energy Agency have been ordered out of North Korea. North Korean officials reveal plans to reopen a nuclear laboratory that some experts believe is capable of producing weapons-grade plutonium.

The president of Clonaid, a Bahamas-based company founded by a sect that believes that life on Earth was created by space aliens, announces the birth of the first human clone. Many scientists express skepticism of the claim.

28 A Russian counterterrorism official announces that Muslim fundamentalists were responsible for bombings that killed more than 80 people in Grozny, the Chechen capital, on December 27. The attack was one of the deadliest in Russia's three-year campaign to crush a rebellion in the breakaway republic.

30 A gunman enters a hospital run by the Southern Baptist International Mission Board in Yemen and kills three U.S. citizens, including a physician and two additional members of the hospital staff. The gunman, an Islamic extremist, tells police that he attacked the Christian outpost in order to get closer to God.

35

Ocean
Space
People in the news
Astronomy
Geology
Architecture
Biology

South Africa
Transportation
Nobel Prizes
Economics
Canada
New York City
Chemistry
Popular music
Disasters
Archaeology

2002 UPDATE

Stocks and bonds
Conservation
Australia
Classical music

The major events of 2002 are summarized in more than 250 alphabetically arranged articles, from "Afghanistan" to "Zoos." Included are Special Reports that offer in-depth looks at subjects ranging from collectibles to the new Department of Homeland Security. The Special Reports are found on the following pages.

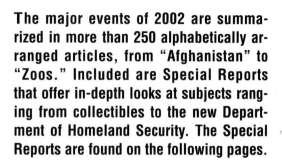

Afghanistan established a new government in 2002 and struggled to recover from decades of drought and war that left many Afghans homeless and in danger of starvation. The new government continued to work with United States and allied troops to root out terrorists operating within the country's borders.

New government. The United Nations (UN) helped establish a temporary government in Afghanistan in 2001 following the overthrow of the Taliban, an extremist Islamic group that ruled the country beginning in the mid-1990's. The Taliban allowed international terrorist organizations—including al-Qa'ida, a network headed by Saudi-born millionaire Osama bin Laden—to create training camps in Afghanistan. Following terrorist attacks against the United States on Sept. 11, 2001, the United States and allied troops joined with anti-Taliban forces within Afghanistan to drive the Taliban from power.

In June 2002, a traditional Afghan council known as a loya jirga met in Kabul, the capital, and elected Hamid Karzai, the head of the temporary government, president of Afghanistan. Karzai was to hold office until 2004, when Afghans were scheduled to democratically elect a permanent government. Karzai won 1,295 of 1,575 ballots, easily defeating his two challengers, one of whom made Afghan history as the first woman to run for president.

Muhammad Zahir Shah, the former king of Afghanistan and Karzai's strongest challenger, dropped out of the race shortly before the election and endorsed Karzai. Zahir Shah had been king until he was overthrown in 1973. He lived in exile in Italy until his return to Kabul in 2002.

Ethnic tensions. Karzai, a Pashtun ethnic leader, assembled a cabinet with a careful ethnic balance to reflect the diverse Afghan population, which consisted of about 20 ethnic groups. The cabinet included five vice presidents, including three regional warlords—Mohammad Qassim Fahim, a Tajik ethnic, who also served as the Afghan defense minister; Karim Khalili, leader of the Hazara ethnic group; and Abdul Qadir, a Pashtun who was assassinated later in 2002.

The variety of ethnic groups had long made it difficult for Afghanistan to develop into a unified, modern nation. The formation of the new, diverse government in 2002 did little to ease ethnic tensions, and some observers feared that political infighting among tribes might jeopardize the stability of the government. The government's key ministries were dominated by Tajiks, an ethnic minority group that led the fight to overthrow the Taliban. Many Pashtuns, the country's largest ethnic group, complained that they did not have enough representatives in the government.

Delegates of a *loya jirga* (traditional Afghan council) pause to pray during a meeting in June in Kabul, the capital, to establish a new Afghan government. The loya jirga, which assembled in an enormous tent, elected Hamid Karzai as president of Afghanistan.

Security issues plagued the new government in 2002. An assassin killed Abdul Rahman, the aviation minister, in February, and Qadir was shot to death in July. On September 5, Karzai narrowly escaped an assassination attempt in Kandahar. The gunman was killed by a detachment of U.S. soldiers that had replaced Afghan soldiers as Karzai's bodyguard earlier in 2002. Also on September 5, a powerful car bomb exploded in Kabul, killing some 30 people. Afghan officials said the assassination, murder attempts, and the many bombings that killed dozens of people in Kabul and other cities in 2002 were aimed at sabotaging the new government.

An international peacekeeping force policed Kabul but did not patrol outlying areas, which were plagued by crime, civil unrest, and banditry. U.S. and allied forces trained Afghan soldiers to take on security duties, but military officials said Afghan troops would not be fully trained until

2004. Karzai urged the UN to expand peacekeeping operations to enhance the central government's authority.

Hunt for terrorists. U.S.-led troops continued to battle al-Qa'ida and the Taliban forces in 2002. In March, U.S. troops launched a two-week campaign against terrorists in eastern Afghanistan. The battle forced senior leaders of the Taliban and al-Qa'ida to flee across the border into Pakistan, which harbored the world's largest concentration of al-Qa'ida operatives, according to U.S. intelligence officers. Military leaders said that U.S. troops would likely remain in Afghanistan for several years to prevent terrorists from regaining control of the country.

The U.S. military drew international criticism in July when U.S. planes attacked villages in Oruzgan province, killing at least 40 civilians and wounding nearly 100. Military officials said the airstrikes took place after U.S. planes were at-tacked from the ground. However, a UN investigation found no evidence that people on the ground had fired at the planes.

Refugees and foreign aid. Afghanistan struggled to lift itself out of destitution in 2002. The country, which was recovering from 20 years of war and a 4-year drought, did not have the resources necessary to feed the 1.7 million refugees who returned to Afghanistan following the overthrow of the Taliban. In January, several nations agreed to provide Afghanistan with $4.5 billion by 2007. However, most donor countries failed to provide the financial aid promised for 2002.

The UN warned that failure to provide food and agricultural aid would lead to massive famine in 2003. The agency also cautioned that a lack of foreign aid would undermine Karzai's government.   □ Henry S. Bradsher

See also **Asia; Newspaper: A Special Report; Pakistan; Terrorism.**

Africa

The African Union (AU), which includes almost all African nations, came into being on July 9, 2002, replacing the Organization of African Unity (OAU). Violent conflict in Congo (Brazzaville), Cote d'Ivoire (Ivory Coast), and Madagascar—together with AIDS, poverty, and a continuing political crisis in Zimbabwe—presented the newly created AU with formidable challenges. Several African nations, however, emerged in 2002 from what many observers had called seemingly irreconcilable military conflicts. In January, Sierra Leone celebrated the end of an 11-year civil war. In Angola, the death of rebel leader Jonas Savimbi in February led to a cease-fire in that country's civil war. Participants in the four-year war in Congo (Kinshasa) made progress in the second half of 2002 toward an eventual peace.

African Union. On July 9 and 10, leaders of the member nations of the new African Union gathered in Durban, South Africa, for the organization's first summit. They pledged to work to bring peace, security, and development to Africa. The AU is designed to exercise more authority than the Organization of African Unity (OAU). The OAU had provided a forum for the postcolonial nations of Africa but lacked authority to deal with such problems as genocide, war crimes, or serious human rights violations. By contrast, the new AU was structured to address such issues by allowing member nations to intervene in situations spelled out in the organization's charter.

NEPAD. The creation of the AU was closely aligned to the initiative known as the New Partnership for Africa's Development (NEPAD). Designed by South African President Thabo Mbeki and other African leaders, NEPAD offered wealthy industrial nations a compact in which African nations promised to embrace human rights and the rule of law in return for financial aid, investment, and favorable trading terms. Participants in the Group of 8 summit in Kananaskis, Alberta, Canada, in June 2002 endorsed NEPAD and pledged $6 billion in additional aid to Africa over a four-year period. The Group of 8 is an informal association of eight industrialized nations.

Africa experts lauded NEPAD's potential for rescuing the continent from the malaise of violence, corruption, and underdevelopment that had afflicted it since the 1970's. However, some analysts questioned whether African leaders were willing to embrace the requirements of the NEPAD program. They pointed, in particular, to those African nations that endorsed Zimbabwe's March 2002 presidential election, which was condemned for corruption by many human rights groups and a number of Western nations.

Poverty. Poverty in Africa's least developed countries rose rapidly in 2002, according to a report released by the United Nations Conference on Trade and Development (UNCTAD) in June. UNCTAD reported that the proportion of people in 29 African countries living on less than $2 per day increased from 82 percent in the late 1960's to 87.5 percent in the late 1990's. The proportion of people living on less than $1 per day increased from 55.8 percent to 64.9 percent during the same period. The 2002 Human Development Report, issued by the United Nations Development Program, noted that the rapid expansion of democracy in sub-Saharan Africa since 1990 had been accompanied by widening and deepening poverty, which threatened to stall the spread of democracy.

West Africa. On May 14, 2002, Ahmad Tejan Kabbah was reelected to another five-year term as president of Sierra Leone in peaceful polling. Voters gave Kabbah 70 percent of the presidential vote and his ruling Sierra Leone's People's Party (SLPP) 74 percent of contested seats in the parliament. The election had originally been scheduled to take place in early 2001, but government authorities postponed it because of widespread violence.

In January 2002, Kabbah and the leader of the rebel Revolutionary United Front (RUF)—chief protagonists in Sierra Leone's civil war—declared the conflict officially ended. Eleven years of fighting had claimed as many as 100,000 lives and left thousands of others maimed.

In Liberia, an upsurge in fighting by the Liberians United for Reconciliation and Democracy (LURD)—the rebel group opposed to the regime of President Charles Taylor—led Taylor to declare a state of emergency in February. Late in 2002, rebel leaders predicted they would capture Monrovia, the capital, within six months.

A farm couple in Zimbabwe visits the grave of their child for the last time before leaving their land in August. President Robert Mugabe, after being reelected in March in a highly controversial and violent election, notified nearly 3,000 white farmers that they had until August 9 to vacate their land.

A bloody mutiny erupted in Cote d'Ivoire's largest city, Abidjan, and a number of other towns on September 19, threatening regional stability. Officials said the uprising was an unsuccessful attempt by former military ruler General Robert Guei to overthrow President Laurent Gbagbo. Guei was killed during the operation.

The uprising triggered sporadic violence throughout the country, as rebel factions took control of towns. Ex-soldiers who had been dismissed from the regular Army for disloyalty were at the core of the rebellion, according to some experts. Some 500 people had died and thousands of others had been injured by the time loyalists and rebels agreed to a cease-fire in October. However, fighting broke out again in late November. In December, France, the former colonial ruler of Cote d'Ivoire, dispatched more than 2,500 troops to the country to back up government forces.

In late March, bloody ethnic clashes erupted between the Andani and Abudu people in northern Ghana. At least 40 people were killed, including a powerful tribal leader.

In Senegal's worst maritime disaster, more than 1,000 people drowned when a crowded Senegalese ocean ferry capsized off the Gambian coast during a storm on September 26. Officials said the vessel was designed to carry only 550 passengers.

Eastern Africa and the Horn. The United Nations (UN) Security Council voted unanimously twice during 2002—in March and September—to extend by six months the mandate of the UN mission in Ethiopia and Eritrea. The UN mission consisted of a 4,000-strong peacekeeping force patrolling a security zone between the two countries. Ethiopia and Eritrea had fought a war between 1998 and 2000 over disputed territory along their common border. At least 100,000 people died in that conflict.

An international boundary commission issued a ruling on April 13, 2002, on a definitive border between Ethiopia and Eritrea. The two countries

Country	Population	Government	Monetary unit*	Foreign trade (million U.S.$)	
				Exports[†]	Imports[†]
Algeria	32,813,000	President Abdelaziz Bouteflika; Prime Minister Ali Benflis	dinar (80.30 = $1)	19,600	9,200
Angola	13,684,000	President Jose Eduardo dos Santos	readj. kwanza (49.90 = $1)	7,800	2,500
Benin	6,422,000	President Mathieu Kerekou	CFA franc (669.55 = $1)	396	566
Botswana	1,661,000	President Festus Mogae	pula (6.23 = $1)	2,600	2,200
Burkina Faso	12,600,000	President Blaise Compaore	CFA franc (669.55 = $1)	220	610
Burundi	7,044,000	President Pierre Buyoya	franc (1,026.12 = $1)	32	110
Cameroon	15,855,000	President Paul Biya	CFA franc (669.55 = $1)	2,100	1,600
Cape Verde	447,000	President Pedro Pires; Prime Minister Jose Maria Pereira Neves	escudo (119.80 = $1)	40	250
Central African Republic	3,746,000	President Ange-Felix Patasse	CFA franc (669.55 = $1)	166	154
Chad	8,081,000	President Idriss Deby	CFA franc (669.55 = $1)	172	223
Comoros	582,000	Head of State Assoumani Azali	franc (498.83 = $1)	8	55
Congo (Brazzaville)	3,105,000	President Denis Sassou-Nguesso	CFA franc (669.55 = $1)	2,600	870
Congo (Kinshasa)	54,768,000	President Joseph Kabila	Congolese franc (365.00 = $1)	960	660
Cote d'Ivoire (Ivory Coast)	15,417,000	Head of State Laurent Gbagbo	CFA franc (669.55 = $1)	3,800	2,500
Djibouti	665,000	President Ismail Omar Guelleh; Prime Minister Mohamed Dileita Dileita	franc (164.90 = $1)	260	440
Egypt	70,818,000	President Hosni Mubarak; Prime Minister Atef Mohammed Obeid	pound (4.62 = $1)	7,300	17,000
Equatorial Guinea	475,000	President Teodoro Obiang Nguema Mbasogo; Prime Minister Candido Muatetema Rivas	CFA franc (669.55 = $1)	860	300
Eritrea	4,044,000	President Isaias Afworki	nafka (13.50 = $1)	26	560
Ethiopia	65,579,000	President Girma Wolde-Giorgis	birr (8.40 = $1)	460	1,250
Gabon	1,280,000	President El Hadj Omar Bongo; Prime Minister Jean-François Ntoutoume-Emane	CFA franc (669.55 = $1)	3,400	1,000
Gambia	1,372,000	Head of State Yahya Jammeh	dalasi (22.68 = $1)	126	203
Ghana	21,318,000	President John Agyekum Kufuor	cedi (8,154.00 = $1)	1,600	2,200
Guinea	7,794,000	President Lansana Conte	franc (1,971.00 = $1)	820	634
Guinea-Bissau	1,264,000	President Kumba Yala	CFA franc (669.55 = $1)	80	55
Kenya	31,069,000	President Mwai Kibaki	shilling (79.20 = $1)	1,700	3,000
Lesotho	2,237,000	King Letsie III; Prime Minister Pakalitha Mosisili	maloti (10.43 = $1)	175	700
Liberia	3,385,000	President Charles Taylor	dollar (1 = $1)	55	170

*Exchange rates as of Oct. 4, 2002, or latest available data.   [†]Latest available data.

Country	Population	Government	Monetary unit*	Foreign trade (million U.S.$)	
				Exports[†]	Imports[†]
Libya	5,869,000	Leader Muammar Muhammad al-Qadhafi; General People's Committee Secretary (Prime Minister) Mubarak Abdullah Al-Shamikh	dinar (1.25 = $1)	13,900	7,600
Madagascar	16,811,000	President Marc Ravalomanana	franc (6,450.00 = $1)	538	693
Malawi	11,449,000	President Bakili Muluzi	kwacha (80.03 = $1)	416	435
Mali	11,810,000	President Amadou Toumani Toure; Prime Minister Ahmed Mohamed Ag Hamani	CFA franc (669.55 = $1)	480	575
Mauritania	2,814,000	President Maaouya Ould Sid Ahmed Taya	ouguiya (272.76 = $1)	333	305
Mauritius	1,177,000	President Carl Auguste Offmann; Prime Minister Sir Anerood Jugnauth	rupee (29.70 = $1)	1,660	2,300
Morocco	29,248,000	King Mohamed VI; Prime Minister Abderrahmane Youssoufi	dirham (10.70 = $1)	7,600	12,200
Mozambique	20,367,000	President Joaquim Alberto Chissano; Prime Minister Pascoal Manuel Mocumbi	metical (23,550.00 = $1)	390	1,400
Namibia	1,768,000	President Sam Nujoma; Prime Minister Theo-Ben Gurirab	dollar (10.42 = $1)	1,400	1,600
Niger	11,395,000	President Mamadou Tandja; Prime Minister Hama Amadou	CFA franc (669.55 = $1)	385	317
Nigeria	128,886,000	President Olusegun Obasanjo	naira (126.75 = $1)	22,200	10,700
Rwanda	8,063,000	President Paul Kagame	franc (475.71 = $1)	68	246
São Tomé and Príncipe	153,000	President Fradique de Menezes	dobra (9,019.70 = $1)	3	40
Senegal	9,969,000	President Abdoulaye Wade; Prime Minister Mame Madior Boye	CFA franc (669.55 = $1)	959	1,300
Seychelles	79,000	President France Albert Rene	rupee (5.62 = $1)	111	440
Sierra Leone	5,067,000	President Ahmad Tejan Kabbah	leone (1,930.00 = $1)	65	145
Somalia	10,837,000	Interim President Abdikassim Salad Hassan; Interim Prime Minister Hassan Abshir Farah	shilling (2,620.00 = $1)	186	314
South Africa	40,952,000	President Thabo Mvuyelwa Mbeki	rand (10.57 = $1)	30,800	27,600
Sudan	30,742,000	President Umar Hasan Ahmad al-Bashir	dinar (258.70 = $1) pound (2,587.00 = $1)	1,700	1,200
Swaziland	1,064,000	King Mswati III; Prime Minister Barnabas Sibusiso Dlamini	lilangeni (10.43 = $1)	881	928
Tanzania	35,090,000	President Benjamin William Mkapa; Prime Minister Frederick Sumaye	shilling (976.00 = $1)	937	1,570
Togo	4,865,000	President Gnassingbe Eyadema	CFA franc (669.55 = $1)	336	452
Tunisia	9,845,000	President Zine El Abidine Ben Ali; Prime Minister Mohamed Ghannouchi	dinar (1.39 = $1)	6,100	8,400
Uganda	23,199,000	President Yoweri Kaguta Museveni; Prime Minister Apollo Nsibambi	shilling (1,815.00 = $1)	500	1,100
Zambia	9,549,000	President Levy Mwanawasa	kwacha (4,500.00 = $1)	928	1,050
Zimbabwe	11,896,000	President Robert Mugabe	dollar (55.45 = $1)	1,800	1,300

A river of lava from Mt. Nyira-gongo volcano flows 6-feet (1.8-meters) deep through Goma in Congo (Kinshasa) in January. The volcanic eruption destroyed at least half of the city on the country's eastern border and displaced as many as 500,000 people.

had pledged in 2000 to accept the decision of such a commission. On Aug. 23, 2002, Ethiopia and Eritrea agreed to free all prisoners of war still being held by the two countries.

The transitional government of Somalia agreed to cooperate with the United States and its allies to combat terrorism in early 2002 after reconnaissance revealed what U.S. intelligence agents suspected were al-Qa'ida terrorist training camps in Somalian territory. The transitional government had come to power in 2000 after a UN-sanctioned reconciliation conference in neighboring Djibouti. However, powerful warlords refused to support the government and continued to operate independently in 2002.

One of the warlords, Muhammad Ibrahim Egal, the leader of Somaliland, one of Somalia's three breakaway enclaves, died on May 3. Since taking power in 1993, Egal had worked to gain

international recognition for Somaliland but with little success. Nevertheless, regional experts described Somaliland as "an island of peace" in the turbulent Horn of Africa.

Tanzania suffered the worst train disaster in its history on June 24, 2002. A packed train carrying some 1,600 passengers derailed after it struck a freight train on an overnight run between Dar es Salaam, the capital, and Kigoma. At least 200 people died and as many as 800 others were injured in the disaster.

Madagascar. A series of protests and strikes in the Madagascar capital, Antananarivo, plunged the island country into crisis for much of the first six months of 2002. The trouble began when President Didier Ratsiraka refused to step down after opposition leader Marc Ravalomanana was declared the winner of a disputed December 2001 election. On May 6, 2002, the country's High Constitutional Court ruled in favor of Ravalomanana.

Ratsiraka, who had ruled Madagascar for 23 years, finally left office to retire to France on July 5, removing the threat of civil war. At least 200 people died during the six months of turmoil, and the capital and most ports were repeatedly blockaded. The violence also battered Madagascar's tourist industry, a critical revenue source.

Central Africa. Angola's brutal civil war came to an end on April 4, when the government of President Jose Eduardo dos Santos signed a cease-fire with rebel forces. The deal followed the death in battle of rebel leader Jonas Savimbi in late February, fundamentally weakening his UNITA guerrilla movement. Angola's almost continuous civil war had erupted with its independence from Portugal in 1975. The war left at least 1 million people dead, 4 million people displaced, and tens of thousands of people mutilated.

A peace pact between the Democratic Republic of Congo (DRC)—also known as Congo (Kinshasa)—and Rwanda on July 30, 2002, boosted prospects for peace in war-torn central Africa. Rwanda agreed to withdraw its troops from DRC territory in return for a pledge by Congo officials to *repatriate* (send back to their home country) Rwandan Hutu extremists who had slaughtered up to 1 million mainly Tutsi Rwandans in 1994.

The agreement was the first of several developments in 2002 that raised hopes for an end to the four-year DRC war that had drawn in six African nations and claimed at least 2.5 million lives. After the July peace agreement, DRC allies—Namibia, Angola, and Zimbabwe—agreed to withdraw from Congo, and in August, Ugandan officials moved to withdraw Uganda's rebel-allied troops from the country. In October, negotiators representing the DRC government and two Congolese rebel groups began talks in Pretoria, South Africa. They emerged in December with plans for a new power-sharing government.

The president of oil-rich Congo (Brazzaville), Denis Sassou-Nguesso, won a new, seven-year term in a March 10, 2002, election, with 89 percent of votes. According to regional experts, dissatisfaction with the election may have contributed to renewed attacks by a shadowy militia known as the "Ninjas."

Southern Africa. Zimbabwe's political crisis and economic collapse dominated events in southern Africa during 2002. In March, President Robert Mugabe won a presidential election that most international observers condemned as neither free nor fair. Evictions of white farmers from their land, displacing not only the white owners but also hundreds of thousands of black farmworkers, followed the election, which had been tainted by as many as 200 murders.

South African President Thabo Mbeki drew sharp attacks from domestic and foreign critics when he endorsed Mugabe's reelection. Economists said that instability in Zimbabwe, South Africa's chief trading partner, was damaging South Africa's own economic health in 2002.

In Johannesburg, South Africa, an estimated 65,000 delegates and 100 world leaders attended the United Nations World Summit on Sustainable Development—popularly known as "Earth Summit 2002"—between August 26 and September 4. Summit organizers defined the agenda as an attempt to find ways to improve the lives of the world's billions of poor people while protecting the environment from destructive consequences of economic growth.

The summit coincided with UN warnings that southern Africa faced its worst food crisis in a decade, with more than 14 million people threatened by starvation in six countries. Up to half of Zimbabwe's 12.5 million people faced famine in 2002, with food production down by 40 percent. Agricultural experts blamed the situation on low rainfall and President Mugabe's campaign of farm seizures, which severely disrupted agriculture in a country that was once known as the breadbasket of southern Africa.

The Botswana government, in the face of intense local and international opposition, began the forceful eviction of the remaining San people from the Central Kalahari Game Reserve in January 2002. The San are a small ethnic group who have lived as hunter-gatherers in the Kalahari region for perhaps 10,000 years. Government officials withheld water and medicines to force the San to leave their ancestral homeland for resettlement camps hundreds of miles away.

Botswana's President Festus Mogae, who had called the San "Stone Age creatures," claimed that the relocation was for their benefit. However, some international critics accused Mogae of practicing "ethnic cleansing" in order to open up the reserve for diamond mining. In April, the UN condemned Botswana for the forced relocations.

AIDS. The UN Program on HIV/AIDS in its 2002 report, released in July, predicted that 55 million Africans would die prematurely of AIDS by 2020 in the absence of suitable mass treatment. The report also revealed that 2.2 million Africans had died of AIDS in 2001 and an additional 3.5 million had become infected. The new infections increased the total of Africans living with HIV/AIDS to 28.5 million, 70 percent of the worldwide total. The report named seven southern African nations—Botswana, Lesotho, Namibia, South Africa, Swaziland, Zambia, and Zimbabwe—in which more than 20 percent of populations were infected with HIV.   □ Simon Baynham

See also **AIDS; Terrorism; United Nations;** various African country articles.

Agriculture. Drought in many parts of the world in 2002 broke a six-year record of bumper harvests. Australia, Canada, and the United States were the most affected. Nevertheless, record crops in China and South America tempered overall losses.

World crop production. According to a U.S. Department of Agriculture (USDA) report released in December, small grain production—including corn, rye, sorghum, barley, oats, and millet—totaled 861 million metric tons in 2002, nearly 3 percent less than in 2001. Drought reduced crops in the United States and Australia, while Brazilian farmers cut corn production to plant more acres in soybeans. A 9-percent increase in China's production in 2002 eased the drought's impact on total small grain supply.

The production of oilseeds—soybeans, sunflower seeds, cottonseed, rapeseed, and peanuts—nearly equalled that of the 2001 bumper crop at 322 million metric tons. Argentina's and Brazil's combined soybean harvest in 2002 of 82 million metric tons exceeded U.S. production for the first time, by 10 percent, making South America the largest soybean producer in the world. Drought reduced Australia's rapeseed crop and the U.S. peanut and cottonseed crops.

The rice harvest, at 380 million tons, was down only slightly from 2001. A smaller crop in India was offset by larger crops in the United States and Vietnam.

World wheat production totaled 569 million metric tons in 2002, about 2 percent less than in 2001. Drought cut Australia's crop by more than 50 percent, to just 11 million metric tons in 2002. Losses in Australia, Canada, and the United States were offset by bumper crops in Russia, India, and the European Union. Wheat production in Ukraine, Kazakhstan, and Russia was so prolific in 2002 that those countries exported about 19 million metric tons, compared with 5 million metric tons in 2000.

World cotton production at 87 million bales was 10 percent less than the 2001 harvest. (One bale is equal to 480 pounds of cotton.) Drought and untimely rains cut the U.S. crop, as well as those of India, China, Pakistan, Greece, Uzbekistan, Turkmenistan, Brazil, and Cote d'Ivoire.

U.S. crop production. Drought cut yields of corn, soybeans, cotton, and wheat in the United States in 2002. Corn production at 9 billion bushels was 5 percent below 2001 levels and the smallest crop since 1995.

Soybean production, at 2.69 billion bushels in 2002, declined 7 percent from 2001. In October and November 2002, the effects of drought and untimely rains in the southeastern United States slashed cotton yields. Experts forecast that total cotton production would fall to 17.4 million

bales, 12 percent below the record high produced in 2001.

Drought sapped the wheat crop in the Great Plains states, reducing it to 1.62 billion bushels, 17 percent below 2001. The rice crop was up slightly, at 6.64 million tons, largely because of farmers' use of high-yielding, disease-resistant varieties.

Genetically modified (GM) crops. Plantings of GM crops in the United States continued to increase in 2002. The number of acres planted with GM corn jumped from 26 percent in 2001 to 34 percent in 2002. GM soybean acreage increased from 68 percent to 75 percent, and GM cotton plantings increased from 69 percent to 71 percent. The European Union continued its four-year ban on imports of new GM varieties during 2002.

Organic crops and food. On October 21, U.S. Agriculture Secretary Ann M. Veneman replaced a hodge-podge of state regulations governing organic agriculture with new national standards. These standards required all but those farmers with less than $5,000 in annual sales to have a state or private agency accredited by the USDA certify their farming systems.

Under the standards, farmers could not use pesticides, chemical fertilizers, or genetically modified seeds to grow organic crops. Products that were 95 percent organically grown were allowed to display a USDA organic seal. The Organic Trade Association forecast that sales of organic foods would reach $11 billion in 2003.

The standards were expected to accelerate growth of the organic food industry, which in 2002 remained small. Only 2.3 million acres were devoted to organic crops and pasture, compared with about 325 million acres of nonorganic crops.

A new farm law. On May 13, U.S. President George W. Bush signed into law the Farm Security and Rural Investment Act of 2002. The law was to be in effect for six years, but it increased spending for farming by more than $80 billion between 2002 and 2011, bringing total spending to $170 billion over the next 10 years. The increase gave farmers an additional $5.5 billion in direct payments each year, the same amount that had been provided in 1998, 1999, 2000, and 2001 as "emergency" income aid. In addition, farmers with crop insurance received more than $4 billion in payments for weather-damaged crops in 2002.

The farm law continued the policy, established in 1996 legislation, of allowing farmers to plant the crops of their choice. A new feature—called countercyclical payments—provided additional funds to growers of corn, wheat, cotton, rice, peanuts, and soybeans when market prices fell below a legislated "target" price. In 2002, drought-driven higher market prices denied most growers income from this new program. Only cotton, rice, and peanut growers received the new payments.

The farm law also funded conservation, nutrition, research, energy, trade, and rural development programs. The largest increase, about $17 billion to be spent over 10 years, was earmarked to help farmers preserve wetlands, grasslands, and farmland and to make farm operations comply with environmental regulations aimed at curtailing water and air pollution from farms.

Exports and food aid. In 2002, exports of U.S. agricultural products reached $53.5 billion, a slight increase over 2001. Several factors prevented a greater increase, including strong competition from Brazil. The devaluation of the Brazilian currency—the real—gave the country a 40 percent price advantage in international trade over more expensive U.S. commodities. In addition, U.S. poultry exports declined after Russia banned imports for nearly six months. The ban ended in August 2002. In October, concerns about China's blocking of soybean imports from the United States were alleviated when the Chinese government extended temporary provisions regulating trade in GM commodities. China, which imports $1 billion worth of U.S. soybeans each year, had passed stricter safety regulations in early 2002 that blocked GM products.

U.S. food aid contributions of 4.7 million metric tons in 2002 were 1.3 million metric tons below 2001 levels, in part because Zimbabwe and Zambia refused to accept GM crops as aid. In August 2002, the United Nations Food and Agriculture Organization reported that 13 million people were in danger of starving in southern Africa.

Fast track. On August 6, President Bush signed the Trade Act of 2002, reinstating fast track or Trade Promotion Authority (TPA). Such legislation had been allowed to lapse in 1994. TPA allowed the administration to negotiate new trade agreements that the U.S. Congress could approve or disapprove but not revise. The law breathed new life into global talks aimed at liberalizing trade in agriculture. It also allowed the administration to pursue bilateral trade arrangements with Singapore, Australia, and Chile and a hemispherewide pact among more than 30 nations in North and South America called the Free Trade Agreement of the Americas. The agreements were to provide preferential trade treatment for goods from the participating countries.

A new Department of Homeland Security, created by law in November 2002, absorbed several border and inspection control functions previously held by the USDA, including animal disease surveillance and plant pest and disease detection.   □ Patricia Peak Klintberg

See also **Food.**

A farmer near Ulysses, Kansas, examines his drought-damaged corn in July. The drought, which affected 48 percent of the contiguous United States, resulted in a 5-percent decline in corn production in the United States in 2002, compared with 2001 levels, and the smallest corn crop since 1995.

AIDS. Officials with the U.S. Centers for Disease Control and Prevention (CDC) in Atlanta, Georgia, reported in July 2002 that the number of new cases of HIV (the virus that causes AIDS) infection in the United States had leveled off after declining since 1993. Although researchers were pleased that the numbers were not increasing, many were dismayed that the nearly 10 years of declining numbers appeared to be over.

CDC officials said that between 1998 and 2002, about 40,000 new cases of HIV infection or AIDS were reported annually. They estimated that about 1 million people in the United States were infected with HIV or had AIDS and that nearly half of those people were unaware that they were infected.

AIDS conference. The AIDS epidemic grew rapidly in the world's most densely populated countries in 2002, officials with the United Nations Aids Programme (UNAIDS) reported in July at the Fourth International AIDS Conference in Barcelona, Spain. UNAIDS officials estimated that by 2020, 68 million people will have died of AIDS. They said that most deaths would occur in Africa and Asia, where HIV infection and AIDS were spreading fastest. The researchers noted that expensive prevention and treatment programs would be required to reduce the death toll. Most countries, however, were too poor to pay for such programs. The authors of the report expressed special concern about the speed with which HIV was spreading in China, Indonesia, Russia, and Eastern Europe.

United Nations researchers also confirmed that young people were at greatest risk for infection. They found that people between 15 and 24 years of age accounted for about half of all new HIV cases. By 2002, about 20 million people had died worldwide since physicians became aware of the AIDS epidemic in 1981. In 2002, there were about 40 million people living with HIV or AIDS.

Drug treatment. The World Health Organization (WHO) in Geneva, Switzerland, in April announced a simplified method of prescribing anti-retroviral drugs to patients in developing countries. The drugs have been shown to be effective in treating AIDS in developed countries, but to be effective, they must be tailored individually to each person. These drug regimens are complex and require several physician visits.

Under the new plan, patients would receive fewer types of drugs. These drugs would be dispensed in a practical, standardized, and simplified manner that would require patients to make fewer visits to a physican. ☐ Michael Woods

Air pollution. See Environmental pollution.

Alabama. See State government.

Alaska. See State government.

Albania. Rivalry between factions in the ruling Socialist party led to the resignation of Prime Minister Ilir Meta in late January 2002 and delayed formation of a new government. The International Monetary Fund, a United Nations-affiliated organization that provides short-term credit to member nations, pressured Albania's political factions to cooperate in the formation of a new government by putting a $30-million loan on hold. In mid-February, Albania's parliament finally approved a new Socialist government led by former Prime Minister Pandeli Majko.

In June, parliament elected Alfred Moisiu to replace Rexhep Meidani as president of Albania. Political observers described Moisiu as a compromise candidate acceptable to all parties. In July, infighting among the ruling socialists led to another collapse, and the short-lived Majko government gave way to a different Socialist faction, which chose Fatos Nano as prime minister.

On September 23, the government declared a state of emergency in northern Albania, where flooding had caused extensive damage to buildings, fields, roads, and railroads and had forced thousands of people out of their houses. The government sent troops to distribute humanitarian aid and help people evacuate from flood-ravaged areas. ☐ Sharon L. Wolchik

See also **Europe.**

Algeria. Algeria's ruling National Liberation Front (FLN) won 199 of 389 parliamentary seats in May 2002 elections. The FLN's victory represented a major increase over the 62 seats the party had won in 1997. Approximately 46 percent of Algeria's registered voters turned out for the 2002 election—the lowest voter participation rate since Algerian independence in 1962.

Observers attributed the reduced turnout to several factors, including disillusionment with the government, which many Algerians believed was controlled by a small and corrupt ruling elite. Although Algeria reaped $22 billion in oil and gas revenues in 2001, more than 40 percent of Algerians earned just $2 a day. In addition, the unemployment rate stood at more than 30 percent.

A boycott and rioting by Berbers, an ethnic minority group in northern Algeria, and killings by Islamic militants also suppressed voter turnout. The militants had been waging war against the government since 1992, when the military cancelled legislative elections that Islamic conservatives were expected to win.

Berber unrest. Widespread clashes between Berbers and riot police occurred both during the May 2002 parliamentary elections and October municipal elections, in which the FLN further consolidated its power. In March, the government had tried to quell Berber dissent by announcing

Algerians survey damage from a bomb that exploded in a crowded marketplace near Algiers, the capital, on July 5, 2002, the 40th anniversary of Algeria's independence. The government blamed the attack, which killed about 50 people, on Islamic militants.

that it recognized the Berber language, Tamazight, as a national language. Berber groups, however, remained displeased because they wanted Tamazight elevated to equal status with Arabic.

Berbers also demanded that 20,000 riot police, who the Berbers accused of brutality, be withdrawn from Kabyle, the region in northern Algeria where most Berbers live. President Abdelaziz Bouteflika acknowledged police excesses but refused to withdraw the forces. However, Bouteflika granted *amnesty* (pardon) in August to dozens of Berbers who had been convicted of, or were awaiting trial for, rioting.

Islamic militants. Government security forces failed to stop attacks and killings by Islamic militants in 2002. By the end of October, more than 1,000 Algerians had been slain in the violence during the year. Since the beginning of the civil war in 1992, at least 100,000 Algerians had reportedly been killed in the conflict.

In February 2002, government forces killed Antar Zouabri, leader of the extremist Armed Islamic Group. Zouabri, renowned for brutal massacres, had been one of the government's most-wanted Islamic militants.   ☐ Christine Helms

See also **Africa; Middle East.**

Angola. See **Africa.**

Animal. See **Biology; Conservation; Zoos.**

Anthropology. The discovery of what may be the earliest-known member of the human family was reported in July 2002 by a team of anthropologists led by Michel Brunet of the University of Poitiers in France. Brunet's team dated a nearly complete skull found in Chad, a country in central Africa, to between 6 million and 7 million years ago. The scientists named the specimen *Sahelanthropus tchadensis.* They nicknamed the fossil Toumai, which means "hope of life" in the local Goran language.

Brunet said the skull has a unique combination of chimpanzee and *hominid* (humans, their ancestors, and early relatives) traits. It has a small, chimplike braincase, but it also has such features of advanced hominids as a short, relatively flat face, large brow ridges, and small canine teeth. The scientists noted that a large hole in the base of the skull—the spot where the spinal cord exited the skull—was positioned toward the front. This indicated to the scientists that *S. tchadensis* walked upright, which is a hominid characteristic.

The scientists said the location of the skull in central Africa was important for several reasons. Knowledge of early hominid evolution previously came mainly from the Rift Valley in East Africa and cave sites in South Africa. The Chad specimen provided a new region for field research. In addition, the presence of a proposed human ancestor

The discovery of two fossil skulls raised new questions about the history of the human family in 2002.

The smallest and most primitive *hominid* (humans, their ancestors, and early relatives) skull ever found outside Africa was described in July by paleoanthropologist David Lordkipanidze of the Georgia State Museum. The specimen, dated at 1.75 million years old, was discovered in the country of Georgia. It indicated to the scientists that large brains were not necessary for humans to migrate out of Africa. Scientists classified the Georgia skull as a primitive form of *Homo erectus.*

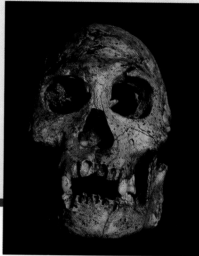

Many scientists had long believed that *H. erectus* was the first human species to migrate out of Africa, leaving between 1 million and 2 million years ago. However, the Georgia skull raised the possibility that *H. erectus* may have evolved outside Africa from an earlier species, *H. habilis,* that had already left Africa. In time, *H. erectus* or its descendants traveled to both Europe and Asia.

---

in Chad suggested that early human evolution might have included several species throughout Africa. The age of the Chad skull indicated to the scientists that the common ancestor of humans and African apes must have lived prior to 6 million or 7 million years ago. Previously, some scientists had favored a more recent date for the human-ape evolutionary split.

Not all scientists agreed that the Chad specimen was a human ancestor. Some anthropologists said it might instead be an ancestor of modern apes.

Small brains out of Africa. In July, a group of scientists led by paleoanthropologist David Lordkipanidze of the Georgian State Museum in the country of Georgia announced the discovery in the town of Dmanisi of a skull 1.75 million years old. The specimen was the smallest and most primitive hominid skull ever found outside Africa. It indicated to the scientists that humans

migrated out of Africa well before they had developed large brains.

The newly found skull was somewhat more primitive than two skulls recovered from the same area in 2000. Those specimens had been classified as *Homo erectus,* a hominid that lived from about 1.8 million to 300,000 years ago. The brain capacity of the new specimen was only 600 cubic centimeters—compared with 650 and 780 cubic centimeters for the two skulls found in 2000.

This small brain capacity, as well as other features in the face and teeth, resembled traits seen in *Homo habilis,* a small-brained hominid believed to be ancestral to *H. erectus.* The scientists classified the specimen as an early form of *H. erectus* that had not yet developed a large brain.

Anthropologists had long thought that *H. erectus* was the first human to leave Africa. The Dmanisi find, however, raised the possibility that

A skull dated to between 6 million and 7 million years ago is from the earliest known hominid, according to a July report by anthropologist Michel Brunet of the University of Poitiers in France. The specimen, named *Sahelanthropus tchadensis,* was discovered in Chad, in north-central Africa. Almost all early hominid remains had previously been found in eastern or southern Africa.

Sahelanthropus is as much as 1 million years older than the previous candidate for earliest hominid, the 6-million-year-old *Orrorin tugenensis.* Both *Sahelanthropus* and *Orrorin* lie within the possible time range—5 million to 10 million years ago—when scientists believe the ancestral lines of humans and chimpanzees split.

Genera (major groups) in the human family

Millions of years ago:

| 8 | 7 | 6 | 5 | 4 | 3 | 2 | 1 |

Sahelanthropus

Orrorin

Ardipithecus

Australopithecus

Kenyanthropus

← Possible time range when human and chimpanzee lines split →

Homo

H. habilis may have left Africa first and then evolved into *H. erectus.*

Ethiopia's *Homo erectus.* An *H. erectus* skull 1 million years old was recovered from a site known as Bouri in Ethiopia, reported a team of scientists from the United States and Ethiopia in March 2002. Three thighbones, a shinbone, and hand axes and cleavers were found with the skull.

Hominid skulls found in Africa and Europe from 1 million years ago are sometimes classified as *H. ergaster.* However, the short, bulging forehead of the Bouri specimen resembles skulls from Asia that are classified as *H. erectus.* The scientists said the new specimen suggested that *H. ergaster* and *H. erectus* were one and the same species.

The scientists concluded that by 1 million years ago *H. erectus* was a successful, widespread hominid species living throughout much of Africa, Asia, and Europe.   □ Donald C. Johanson

See also **Archaeology.**

Archaeology. In April 2002, a team of Lithuanian and French scientists completed excavating a mass grave in Vilnius, capital of Lithuania, containing the remains of as many as 2,000 soldiers. The soldiers had fought for Napoleon Bonaparte, who was the emperor of France between 1804 and 1815. The team, led by anthropologist Rimantas Jankauskas of Vilnius University, identified the skeletal remains from uniform buttons and coins found with the bones.

The scientists said the soldiers were members of the Napoleon-led forces that attacked Russia in 1812. The army was forced to retreat from Moscow during the bitterly cold winter of that year. According to historians, the bodies of tens of thousands of the soldiers were buried or burned after the men died from cold, starvation, or disease. Jankauskas's team planned to conduct genetic testing of the remains to search for evidence of diseases, including typhus.

Major *Monitor* recovery. Archaeologists raised the 120-ton (109-metric-ton) revolving gun turret of the U.S.S. *Monitor* from the floor of the Atlantic Ocean in August 2002. The *ironclad* (iron-covered ship) *Monitor* is best known for its battle with the Confederate ironclad *Virginia* on March 9, 1862, during the United States Civil War (1861-1865). The battle, which ended in a draw, demonstrated that wooden warships were obsolete. The *Monitor* sank during a storm off Cape Hatteras, North Carolina, in December 1862.

The salvage operation culminated a five-year project, directed by the Monitor National Marine Sanctuary in Newport News, Virginia, to recover and preserve pieces of the *Monitor.* The archaeologists discovered several items inside the gun turret, including uniform buttons, a pocket knife, a gold ring, a lantern, and parts of a wooden cabi-

net. The investigators also recovered the remains of two crewmembers.

Teotihuacan high society. In September 2002, an international group of scientists discovered a burial chamber containing the remains of three people within the Pyramid of the Moon at Teotihuacan, north of Mexico City. The pyramid, completed in about A.D. 250, was an important ceremonial structure at the Mexican Indian site, which was one of the largest cities in ancient North America.

Archaeologists led by Saburo Sugiyama of Aichi Prefectural University in Japan and Ruben Cabrera of the National Institute of Anthropology and History in Mexico said the skeletons were found with their legs crossed sitting on seats made of wood and fabric. Their positions differed from those of sacrificial victims that the archaeologists

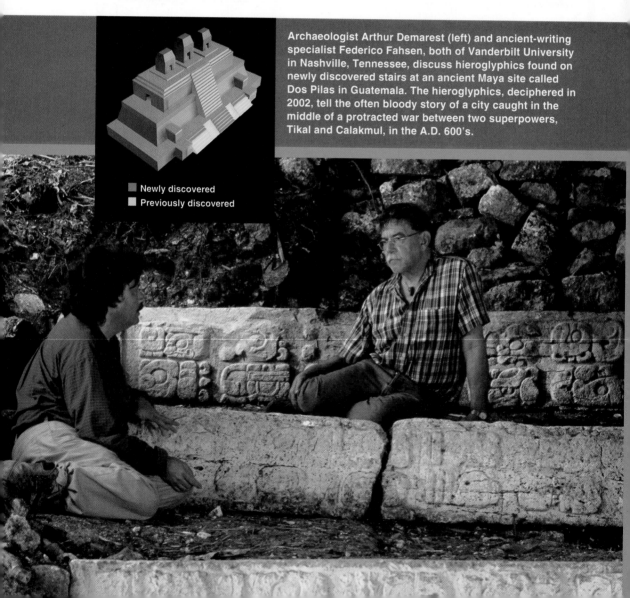

Newly discovered
Previously discovered

Archaeologist Arthur Demarest (left) and ancient-writing specialist Federico Fahsen, both of Vanderbilt University in Nashville, Tennessee, discuss hieroglyphics found on newly discovered stairs at an ancient Maya site called Dos Pilas in Guatemala. The hieroglyphics, deciphered in 2002, tell the often bloody story of a city caught in the middle of a protracted war between two superpowers, Tikal and Calakmul, in the A.D. 600's.

had discovered in the pyramid's lower chambers in 1998. Those skeletons were reclining on the floor with their hands bound. The scientists also found polished stone beads and carved obsidian figures with the newly discovered individuals. Sugiyama and Cabrera proposed that these individuals had a high status in Teotihuacan society.

Great Pyramid robot. During a live television broadcast in September 2002, Zahi Hawass, director of Egypt's Supreme Council of Antiquities, sent a small robot equipped with a camera and drill through a narrow shaft within the 4,500-year-old Great Pyramid of Khufu in Egypt. The "Pyramid Rover" robot was put into the shaft, which is about 8 inches (20 centimeters) wide, to investigate a limestone panel with two copper handles that a previous robot had discovered. The drill on the robot penetrated the limestone, revealing a small empty space behind the panel. Scientists also sent the robot up another shaft in the pyramid, where it discovered a second limestone panel.

The purpose of the shafts and panels was not clear to the investigators. However, Hawass speculated that the shafts may have been symbolic passageways for the soul of the pharaoh buried in the pyramid.

Evidence of Jesus? In October, the earliest archaeological evidence of Jesus was reported by Andre Lemaire, a specialist in ancient inscriptions, of the Sorbonne in Paris. Lemaire described an *ossuary* (limestone box containing the bones of a dead person) on which is inscribed "James, son of Joseph, brother of Jesus" in Aramaic, a language used in ancient Israel during the time of Jesus. Lemaire said the ossuary may have once contained the bones of the James who, according to many interpretations, was the brother of Jesus. James, killed by Jewish leaders in about A.D. 62, was the head of the Christian church in Jerusalem. The box was empty when it was shown to Lemaire by a private collector in Jerusalem who had purchased it on the local antiquities market.

The ossuary measures about 20 inches (51 centimeters) long, 10 inches (25 centimeters) wide, and 12 inches (30 centimeters) high. Lemaire noted that ossuaries of this type were used only in ancient Israel between about 20 B.C. and A.D. 70. In addition, he said the shapes of the letters in the inscription matched those known from other examples of Aramaic script from this period.

Not all archaeologists were convinced that the ossuary was authentic or that it had contained the remains of the brother of Jesus. Many archaeologists noted that it is usually impossible to verify the authenticity of objects obtained on the antiquities market because the location and archaeological context in which they were found are not known. □ Mark Rose

See also **Anthropology.**

Architecture. The debate over the future of the World Trade Center site in New York City intensified in 2002 with the presentation in July of six redevelopment proposals by teams of New York architects. All of the plans featured new office towers ranging from 32 to 85 stories in height—shorter than the 110-story twin towers that were destroyed by terrorist attacks on Sept. 11, 2001. Each of the plans also included a memorial park or garden, along with various combinations of retail and cultural activities. None of the plans contained housing.

Although city officials cautioned that the proposals were not final blueprints, much of the press and public denounced the ideas as monumental, impersonal, and one-dimensional. Critics argued that the developers seemed intent on merely replacing the office space lost in the terrorist attacks, instead of trying to reinvent Lower Manhattan as promised.

Following the negative reaction, the Lower Manhattan Development Corporation, the organization responsible for rebuilding the World Trade Center site, created seven new design teams. The designs, unveiled in December, represented a broader range of architectural viewpoints than the original proposals. Four of the new designs envisioned construction of what would be the world's tallest buildings, the tallest being a tower rising to 2,100 feet (640 meters). A final design was scheduled to be selected in early 2003.

Art museum. An American museum boom continued in 2002 with the December opening of the Modern Art Museum of Fort Worth in Texas. Designed by Japanese architect Tadao Ando, the museum is the second-largest institution of post-World War II (1939-1945) art in the United States. The $65-million building consists of five concrete-and-glass pavilions embracing a reflecting pool and sculpture garden. The forms and materials recalled Ando's earlier work, including the Pulitzer Foundation for the Arts in St. Louis, Missouri. At the same time, the comfortable scale and masterly construction reflected Ando's admiration for architect Louis Kahn, whose Kimbell Art Museum sits across the street.

Modernist cathedral. Los Angeles found itself in the architectural spotlight in September 2002 with the dedication of Spanish architect Rafael Moneo's Cathedral of Our Lady of the Angels. The cathedral is designed as an abstract modernist sculpture with massive concrete walls and dramatically sloping roofs. From the outside, it appears dense and impenetrable, leading some critics to compare it with a prison or power plant. Yet, others praised the interior of the building as being richly evocative. Worshipers enter from the side of the cathedral. They then

The Austrian Cultural Forum, by architect Raimund Abraham, opened in April in New York City. Some critics compared the facade of the "sliver building," only 25 feet (7.6 meters) wide, with a guillotine or landslide, with layers of metal and glass about to cascade onto 52nd Street below. The building houses offices, a library, galleries, and a theater, as well as an apartment for the director.

traverse a baptistery and nave before entering the main sanctuary, a soaring space with alabaster windows, tapestries, and lights in the form of inverted trumpets. Although Moneo simplified and abstracted most of the traditional Roman Catholic iconography, the sanctuary remains a powerful sacred space.

Gehry controversy. Renowned architect Frank Gehry's new building for the Weatherhead School of Management at Case Western Reserve University in Cleveland, Ohio, was dedicated in October. Named the Peter B. Lewis Building, after a local insurance executive who was the primary donor, the building reflects the philanthropist's hope of elevating Cleveland's architectural status and encouraging business students to think more creatively. Gehry's design includes his familiar ribbons and folds of polished metal billowing over walls and around corners. Two classroom towers supported by concrete beams and walls made of Douglas fir rise from the main lobby.

Critics noted that the school's design seems more tortured than that of Gehry's previous buildings. The donor, Peter Lewis, was among those not entirely pleased with the final results. Lewis withheld the final $9 million of his gift pending revisions.

Sponge inspiration. Simmons Hall, a dormitory at the Massachusetts Institute of Technology (MIT) in Cambridge, opened in October. Designed by New York City architect Steven Holl, it was inspired partly by an ordinary bath sponge. The massive concrete-and-metal facade is honey-combed with thousands of small square windows, like the pores in a sponge. Entrances and terraces appear to be carved out of a larger block, as if from a bar of soap.

Simmons Hall includes a theater, fitness center, computer lab, and game rooms, which were all intended to generate undergraduate camaraderie. Numerous compromises in materials and construction had to be made to get the dorm open in time for the fall semester. The final cost of the building was $68 million, or roughly $200,000 per room—an amount that produced sticker shock at MIT.

Awards. Tadao Ando received the Gold Medal for lifetime achievement from the American Institute of Architects in 2002. The jury praised the Japanese architect for creating serene, contemplative buildings that "embody the timelessness of all enduring architecture."

The 2002 Pritzker Prize, widely regarded as the most prestigious international architecture award, went to Glenn Murcutt of Australia. The architect was recognized for work—mainly houses and schools—that combined the modernism of Ludwig Mies van der Rohe and Alvar Aalto with the ruggedness of the Australian outback.

☐ David Dillon

See also **Building and construction.**

Argentina. Argentines grew increasingly angry at their leaders in 2002 for failing to lift the nation out of the worst economic crisis in its history. "Get rid of them all," expressed the popular sentiment of Argentines toward a revolving-door succession of governments that had each failed to solve the country's problems.

Duhalde's struggles. On January 1, the Argentine Congress selected Eduardo Alberto Duhalde, a senator from the Peronist Party, as the country's fifth president in just two weeks. Duhalde, who took office amid widespread rioting, promised to lead a broad-based "government of national salvation."

However, President Duhalde was repeatedly frustrated by political squabbling in Congress over his proposals to reform the economy. In April, a key member of his Cabinet, Economy Minister Jorge Remes Lenicov, resigned when Congress refused to consider his plan to forestall the collapse of the banking system by allowing banks to convert fixed-term deposits into low-interest 5- to 10-year bonds.

In June, Mario Blejer, president of Argentina's Central Bank, resigned in anger over political interference in his *autonomous* (independent) institution. Blejer's resignation delayed Argentina's ongoing negotiations with the International Monetary Fund (IMF), a United Nations-affiliated

Argentines outside a bank in Buenos Aires, the capital, protest government limits on bank withdrawals and the devaluation of the national currency in March. Demonstrations continued throughout 2002 as government policies failed to lift Argentina out of the worst economic crisis in the history of the once-prosperous nation.

organization that assists nations experiencing economic difficulties. Argentine officials sought to secure a new financial aid accord from the IMF, including a rescheduling of Argentina's debts to the agency.

Protests grow over economic woes. Four years of recession had turned into a *depression* (deep, prolonged business slump) by mid-2002, and the worsening economy led to increasingly violent protests against the government. In June, at least two protesters were shot to death and more than 90 others wounded in a clash with police in a suburb of Buenos Aires, the capital. The bloodshed occurred after the protesters, some carrying gasoline bombs, slingshots, and clubs, smashed store windows and set a bus on fire.

President Duhalde announced in July that he would step down early. He said new elections for president would be moved up six months to March 2003. The elections were later pushed back further, to April. The announcement failed to stop the anti-government demonstrations, as Argentines continued to protest restrictions on withdrawals from banks, the closing of banks and stock markets, and the government's repeated inability to pay its employees on time.

By September 2002, the peso, the Argentine monetary unit, had shrunk by more than 70 percent since the beginning of the year, and unemployment reached 25 percent. Approximately half of Argentina's population lived below the poverty line in 2002. Economists estimated that, by the end of the year, inflation would soar to 80 percent, and Argentina's *gross domestic product* (the value of all goods and services produced by the country) would contract by 18 percent.

Iranian involvement in attack. On July 22, *The New York Times* published a secret deposition given to Argentine officials by a high-level defector from Iran's intelligence agency. According to the testimony, the Iranian government organized and carried out the car bombing of a Jewish community center in Buenos Aires in 1994. The bombing killed 85 people. The Iranian informant also testified that the Iranian government paid Carlos Saul Menem, then the president of Argentina, $10 million to cover up the Iranian connection to the attack. Both Menem and the Iranian government denied the charges.

Secret U.S. files released. Previously classified files released by the United States State Department in August 2002 confirmed that U.S. officials were aware of the kidnappings, killings, and torture of leftists by the military dictatorship that ruled Argentina from 1976 to 1983.

☐ Nathan A. Haverstock

See also **Iran; Latin America.**

Arizona. See State government.

Arkansas. See State government.

Armed forces. The United States armed forces faced two fronts in 2002. Throughout the year, the administration of U.S. President George W. Bush considered taking action against Iraq following U.S. allegations that Iraqi President Saddam Hussein was stockpiling weapons of mass destruction. In Afghanistan, U.S. troops continued their search for members of the al-Qa'ida terrorist network.

Iraq tensions. In 2002, the Bush administration contended that Iraq, under the leadership of Hussein, had ignored a series of United Nations (UN) resolutions and had been mass-producing chemical, biological, and possibly nuclear weapons in violation of a treaty signed at the end of the Persian Gulf War (1991). The administration maintained that Iraq posed a growing threat to the United States, Israel, and European nations.

United States Army troops from the 101st Airborne Division arrive in Afghanistan in March 2002 during Operation Anaconda, one of the largest military operations against the Taliban and al-Qa'ida terrorist network. Several hundred members of the Taliban and al-Qa'ida network were killed in the operation after they refused to surrender.

On Sept. 12, 2002, President Bush, in a speech before the UN General Assembly, called Iraq an "outlaw regime" whose weapons programs threatened world peace. He urged the organization to insist that Iraq comply with 16 previous UN resolutions passed since the Gulf War.

In October, both the U.S. House of Representatives and the Senate passed a resolution authorizing President Bush to use military force against Iraq if he felt it was necessary to protect U.S. national security. The president signed the legislation on October 16.

Although Iraqi officials agreed in November to allow UN weapons inspectors back into the country, U.S. armed forces in the Gulf region remained on alert through the end of 2002 for possible action against Iraq.

By late November, more than 57,000 reserve and National Guard soldiers had been called to active duty to support the Persian Gulf buildup and operations in Afghanistan. By the end of 2002, the Bush administration had ordered additional Army units to Kuwait, bringing the num-

ber of U.S. armed forces in that country to more than 9,000 soldiers. U.S. forces were also increased in Qatar, where runways at existing air bases were lengthened to accommodate U.S. heavy bombers and cargo jets. About 27,000 U.S. troops were stationed in the Middle East by mid-December, including three aircraft carrier battle groups and an amphibious assault force of more than 2,200 Marines.

Afghan conflict. As the U.S. military campaign in Afghanistan entered its second year, U.S. troops sought to stabilize the war-ravaged country liberated from Taliban leaders in late 2001. The troops also continued to search for the remnants of the al-Qa'ida terrorist organization alleged to be responsible for the terrorist attacks on the Pentagon Building, the headquarters of the U.S. Department of Defense outside Washington, D.C., and the World Trade Center in New York City on Sept. 11, 2001. U.S. troops were engaged in military operations throughout 2002 to find remaining Taliban and al-Qa'ida forces that had fled into the rugged, sparsely inhabited mountainous regions of Afghanistan.

The largest operation of the war in Afghanistan, Operation Anaconda, began in March 2002. The battle was waged approximately 80 miles (128 kilometers) south of Kabul, the capital, in a 60-square-mile (156-square-kilometer) area where several hundred Taliban and al-Qa'ida fighters were attempting to regroup. The operation involved special operations forces, members of the U.S. Army's 10th Mountain Division and 101st Airborne Division, and intensive aerial bombardments from B-1 and B-52 bombers. U.S. officials reported that hundreds of al-Qa'ida and Taliban fighters were killed after they refused to surrender. Eight U.S. servicemen died in the fighting.

By December 2002, more than 7,000 U.S. soldiers were stationed in Afghanistan. Several thousand other members of the U.S. Navy and Marine Corps were stationed aboard vessels in the Arabian Sea. U.S. Army General Tommy Franks, commander of the U.S. Central Command, said in August that significant numbers of U.S. military forces would remain in Afghanistan for several years to assist in eliminating remaining enemy fighters and terrorist remnants and helping with "nation building" efforts.

By December, U.S. officials reported that more than 200 U.S. troops had been wounded and more than 40 troops had been killed in the Afghan campaign. Most were killed in aircraft accidents. Military experts estimated the cost of the operation at approximately $2 billion a year.

"Friendly fire." Four Canadian soldiers were killed and eight other soldiers were wounded on April 18 after a U.S. F-16 pilot dropped a bomb on the soldiers' position during a nighttime training exercise with U.S. forces near Kandahar in Afghanistan. The U.S. pilot reported that he had been fired upon by enemy forces and responded in self-defense.

On September 13, the Air Force charged the two Illinois National Guard pilots who had flown the mission—Major Harry Schmidt and Major William Umbach—each with four counts of involuntary manslaughter and assault. The criminal charges were the first faced by Air Force pilots in connection with a friendly fire incident. A joint U.S.-Canadian investigation concluded that Schmidt, who was flying the aircraft, ignored instructions from ground controllers to withhold fire.

Shifting operations. As Afghanistan became relatively pacified, the U.S. military began focusing efforts on other countries known to harbor large groups of terrorists. U.S. officials confirmed that special forces and Central Intelligence Agency paramilitary troops were engaged in several secret operations in Pakistan during 2002. The Department of Defense sent more than 600 special forces soldiers to the Philippines in January to help the Philippine army track down terrorists allied with al-Qa'ida.

The U.S. campaign against terrorism also moved to Yemen and Georgia, where U.S. intelligence agents believed remnants of the al-Qa'ida terrorist network were attempting to regroup after the U.S.-led invasion of Afghanistan in 2001. Defense Department officials confirmed in September 2002 that about 800 soldiers, including several hundred special forces commandos, had been stationed in Djibouti in preparation for a series of covert operations into Yemen.

Guantanamo Bay. The U.S. military established a prison for more than 500 Taliban and al-Qa'ida members at the U.S. naval base at Guantanamo Bay, Cuba, in 2001. U.S. officials categorized the detainees as enemy combatants and announced that they would be detained "indefinitely" for interrogation.

Defense Department officials said that special military commissions established by President Bush in November 2001 might ultimately prosecute some of the detainees. After several months of consultations with legal experts, the Defense

Department issued procedures for the commissions on March 21, 2002. The tribunals would consist of three to seven members, and a guilty verdict would require evidence beyond a reasonable doubt. A two-thirds vote would be required for conviction, but a death sentence would need a unanimous vote.

Arms control. President Bush and Russian President Vladimir Putin signed an arms-control treaty on May 24, 2002, in which the United States and Russia agreed to slash their respective nuclear arsenals by two-thirds. Under the terms of the agreement, the two nations will reduce their nuclear warheads to approximately 2,000 each by the end of 2012. Both the United States and Russia had approximately 6,000 warheads in 2002.

ABM treaty. The United States formally withdrew from the 1972 anti-ballistic missile (ABM) treaty on June 13, 2002. Under provisions in the treaty, either the United States or Russia could withdraw from the treaty by providing advance notice. President Bush notified Putin of his decision in December 2001. The treaty, negotiated with the former Soviet Union during the *Cold War* (an intense rivalry that developed after World War II [1939-1945] between groups of Communist and non-Communist nations), included provisions that forbid the development and testing of ballistic missile defense systems. President Bush said that developing a missile defense system was vital to preventing nuclear attacks by terrorists and rogue nations.

The withdrawal of the United States from the treaty cleared the way for the Bush administration to proceed with construction on the first interceptor missile base in the administration's strategic missile defense program. President Bush announced in December that the first interceptor missiles would be deployed by 2004.

Defense budget. In February, the Bush administration released its budget for fiscal year 2003 (Oct. 1, 2002 to Sept. 30, 2003). The Department of Defense requested $379.3 billion, a $48-billion increase over fiscal year 2002 and the largest percentage increase since the 1980's. The budget included approximately $27 billion for the war on terrorism and $10 billion as a contingency fund for future military operations. Spending on new weapons was projected at $68.7 billion.

The Defense Department also requested $7.8 billion for strategic missile defense research and development; $5.2 billion for 23 F-22 Raptor air superiority fighters; $4 billion for 12 C-17 strategic airlift jets; $3.5 billion for the Joint Strike Fighter; $3.3 billion for 44 F/A-18 Hornet jet fighters; $2.7 billion for two Burke-class Aegis guided missile destroyers; $2.5 billion for a Virginia-class nuclear attack submarine; $2 billion for 11 V-22 Osprey tilt-wing helicopters; and $1.1

billion for various unmanned aerial vehicles like those used by the U.S. armed forces in Afghanistan.

On Oct. 16, 2002, Congress approved a $355.1-billion defense appropriations bill. President Bush signed the legislation on October 23. Although Congress had approved much of what the Defense Department had requested, the bill did not include a $10-billion contingency fund the president sought for combating terrorism.

Command changes. North Atlantic Treaty Organization (NATO) officials appointed General James Jones, commandant of the Marine Corps, as NATO commander in chief in July. Jones was the first Marine officer to command NATO and U.S. military forces in Europe.

Air Force General Ralph Eberhart assumed command of the new U.S. Northern Command (NORTHCOM) in October. NORTHCOM is designed to prevent large-scale terrorist attacks within the United States and to give emergency aid to police, firefighters, and rescue workers if an attack occurs. □ Thomas M. DeFrank

See also **Afghanistan; Congress of the United States; Iraq; Russia; Terrorism; United States, Government of the; United States, President of.**

Art museum attendance rebounded somewhat in 2002, recovering from a sharp decline that many experts attributed to a drop in tourism following the terrorist attacks on the United States on Sept. 11, 2001. An informal survey published in *The New York Times* in April 2002 reported that attendance at the Metropolitan Museum of Art in New York City rose in the spring of 2002 but still remained around 20 percent lower than during the same periods of 2000 and 2001.

Attendance also rallied nationwide, as numbers of visitors nearly returned to normal at the Smithsonian Institution in Washington, D.C., the Museum of Fine Arts in Boston, and the Los Angeles County Museum of Art. Attendance at the Art Institute of Chicago rose from about 1.3 million in 2001 to about 1.7 million in 2002. Museum officials attributed the rise largely to the institute's blockbuster exhibition "Van Gogh and Gauguin: The Studio of the South."

Despite the rebound in attendance, art museums in large urban centers still faced money problems as state and local funding began to reflect the economic slowdown. Cutbacks in public financing, along with loss of revenue from visitors, forced several art museums to lay off employees and cancel or postpone exhibitions.

A 2002 exhibition by the American master Thomas Eakins (1844-1916) at the Metropolitan Museum of Art in New York City featured the well-known work *The Champion Single Sculls (Max Schmitt in a Single Scull).* "Thomas Eakins: American Realist" originated at the Philadelphia Museum of Art.

Discoveries. In July 2002, officials at the Cooper-Hewitt National Design Museum in New York City announced that a rare drawing by Italian artist Michelangelo had been discovered among the museum's collections. Scottish museum director Timothy Clifford discovered the unsigned design for a seven-branched *candelabrum* (ornamental candlestick) in a collection of sketches of Renaissance lighting fixtures. Art experts confirmed that the drawing was Michelangelo's.

Archaeologists uncovered 1,900-year-old wall paintings in the rain forests of Guatemala in March 2002. Experts said the murals, which date to about A.D. 100, may be the earliest intact murals of the Maya civilization, a culture that flourished from 250 to around 900 in southern Mexico, Guatemala, Belize, and Honduras. The newly discovered mural depicted scenes of Maya ritual and mythology.

Italian officials revealed the discovery of frescoes painted in the 1200's beneath the main cathedral of Siena, Italy, in 2002. The paintings cover nearly 2,000 square feet (190 square meters) of wall space and depict scenes from the Bible. Experts dated the frescoes to about 1270, placing them within the early Italian Renaissance period.

New museums. In January 2002, the Daum Museum of Contemporary Art opened in Sedalia, Missouri. The museum's permanent collection features works by artists Andy Warhol, Sol LeWitt, and Robert Motherwell from the collection of Sedalia millionaire Harold F. Daum.

The Pasadena (California) Museum of California Art also opened in 2002. The privately funded museum showcases the range of arts in California, including painting, sculpture, architecture, and design.

MoMA-QNS. In June, the Museum of Modern Art (MoMA) in New York City moved to MoMA-QNS, its temporary quarters in Long Island City, Queens. MoMA is scheduled to remain in the Queens location until 2005 while the museum completes the final stage of expansion on its Midtown site. The 160,000-square-foot (15,000-square-meter) MoMA-QNS facility features galleries, administrative offices, storage space, a restaurant, and a museum store in a former Swingline Stapler factory.

Egyptian treasures. The National Gallery of Art in Washington, D.C., presented in 2002 the largest group of artifacts ever loaned to North America by Egypt in the exhibition "The Quest for Immortality: Treasures of Ancient Egypt." The exhibition featured 115 objects, many never seen outside Egypt, that reflected ancient Egyptian beliefs and practices concerning the afterlife, including a full-size reconstruction of an ancient Egyptian burial chamber.

At the Met. The Metropolitan Museum of Art displayed the first extensive U.S. survey in 25 years of some of the finest European tapestries from 1420 to 1560 in "Tapestry in the Renaissance: Art and Magnificence." The show featured large tapestries woven from silk and gold thread by leading Renaissance artists. Such tapestries are rarely lent because they are extremely fragile.

Also on view at the Metropolitan during 2002 was a survey of the work of American realist painter Thomas Eakins that originated at the Philadelphia Museum of Art. The exhibit featured many of Eakins's paintings of athletes shown in periods of calm during or between competitions. Also included were shocking, realistic paintings of surgeons operating in an auditorium.

Warhol retrospective. "Andy Warhol Retrospective" at the Museum of Contemporary Art in Los Angeles in 2002 spanned the entire career of Pop artist Andy Warhol. The museum displayed around 200 works from the early 1940's through 1986, including some of Warhol's most famous series, such as his paintings of Campbell's Soup cans and Marilyn Monroe. Also on view were the artist's early drawings and his first pictures of everyday objects drawn from popular culture. The exhibit also brought together groups of Warhol's works that are rarely seen together, such as his series entitled "Most Wanted Men."

Other exhibitions. In 2002, the Kimbell Art Museum in Fort Worth, Texas, presented "Piet Mondrian: 1892-1914: The Path to Abstraction," the first exhibition ever devoted to the early career of the Dutch abstract artist. "Salvador Dali: Dream of Venus" at the Museum of Contemporary Art in North Miami, Florida, offered photographs, drawings, and films documenting a famous installation by the artist originally displayed at the 1939 New York World's Fair. In Chicago, paintings by Mexican artists Diego Rivera, Jose Clemente Orozco, and David Alfaro Siqueiros were displayed in the recently expanded Mexican Fine Arts Museum Center.

Art world deaths. J. Carter Brown, former director of the National Gallery of Art, died on June 17, 2002. Brown helped introduce art museums to the concept of blockbuster exhibitions—large, heavily attended shows that transformed museums into popular destinations. Many of these exhibitions took place in the museum's East Building, which was built during Brown's directorship.

Paul Gottlieb, former publisher, president, and editor in chief of the New York City art-publishing firm Harry N. Abrams, died on June 5. Gottlieb helped establish Abrams as a leading art publisher in the United States by producing expensive, high-quality art books that became an integral part of major museum exhibitions.   ☐ Sally Ruth May

See also **Deaths.**

Asia was a center of terrorist activity in 2002. Attacks in countries from Pakistan to Indonesia wreaked destruction and left hundreds of people dead, slowing economic progress in the region. Asian nations harbored many Islamic extremist groups, including al-Qa'ida, the terrorist network that the United States government blamed for planning the terrorist attacks on the United States on Sept. 11, 2001.

Asian governments attempted to secure the region and reassure jittery investors and tourists in 2002 by cooperating among themselves and with Western nations to crack down on extremist groups. As a result, dozens of terrorist suspects were arrested in Pakistan, Afghanistan, Indonesia, Singapore, the Philippines, and Malaysia, and authorities thwarted several planned attacks.

ASEAN action. The 10 members of the Association of Southeast Asian Nations (ASEAN)

signed a landmark agreement in August with the United States to "prevent, disrupt, and combat" global terrorism through increased sharing of information and intelligence. The antiterrorism agreement committed the countries to mutual assistance in a crackdown on the movement of terrorists, including border controls and detection of fake passports. In addition, member nations, Brunei, Cambodia, Indonesia, Laos, Malaysia, Myanmar, Philippines, Singapore, Thailand, and Vietnam, joined the United States, China, and 11 other countries in agreeing to block extremists from accessing the money they need to carry out terror attacks. The pacts dovetailed with a plan forged by ASEAN in May to develop

Hundreds of children participate in East Timor's independence celebration in late May, when the former Portuguese colony, which had been occupied by Indonesia from 1975 until 1999, became an independent nation.

Country	Population	Government	Monetary unit*	Foreign trade (million U.S.$)	
				Exports[†]	Imports[†]
Afghanistan	24,977,000	President Hamid Karzai	afghani (4,750.00 = $1)	80	150
Armenia	3,543,000	President Robert Kocharian	dram (558.14 = $1)	284	913
Australia	19,231,000	Governor General Peter Hollingworth; Prime Minister John Howard	dollar (1.84 = $1)	69,000	77,000
Azerbaijan	7,854,000	President Heydar A. Aliyev	manat (4,905.00 = $1)	1,900	1,400
Bangladesh	133,557,000	President Iajuddin Ahmed; Prime Minister Khaleda Zia	taka (57.85 = $1)	5,900	8,100
Bhutan	2,238,000	King Jigme Singye Wangchuck	ngultrum (48.36 = $1)	154	269
Brunei	340,000	Sultan Sir Hassanal Bolkiah	dollar (1.78 = $1)	2,550	1,300
Cambodia (Kampuchea)	12,269,000	King Norodom Sihanouk; Prime Minister Hun Sen	riel (3,835.00 = $1)	942	1,300
China	1,303,875,000	Communist Party General Secretary Hu Jintao; Premier Zhu Rongji	yuan (8.28 = $1)	232,000	197,000
East Timor	911,000	President Jose Alexander Gusmao Prime Minister Mari Bin Amude Alkatiri	dollar (1 = $1)	NA	NA
Georgia	4,969,000	President Eduard Shevardnadze	lari (2.06 = $1)	372	898
India	1,042,249,000	President Abdul Kalam; Prime Minister Atal Behari Vajpayee	rupee (48.36 = $1)	43,100	60,800
Indonesia	217,314,000	President Megawati Sukarnoputri; Vice President Hamzah Haz	rupiah (9,017.13 = $1)	64,700	40,400
Iran	69,049,000	Supreme Leader Ayatollah Ali Hoseini-Khamenei; President Mohammed Khatami-Ardakani	rial (1,741.25 = $1)	25,000	15,000
Japan	127,018,000	Emperor Akihito; Prime Minister Junichiro Koizumi	yen (122.71 = $1)	450,000	355,000
Kazakhstan	16,191,000	President Nursultan Nazarbayev	tenge (154.45 = $1)	8,800	6,900
Korea, North	24,585,000	Korean Workers' Party General Secretary Kim Chong-il	won (2.20 = $1)	520	960
Korea, South	47,521,000	President Lee Hoi-chang; Prime Minister Sang Chang	won (1,222.94 = $1)	172,600	160,500
Kyrgyzstan	4,784,000	President Askar Akayev	som (47.72 = $1)	482	579
Laos	5,709,000	President Khamtai Siphandon; Prime Minister Boungnang Volachit	kip (7,600.00 = $1)	323	540
Malaysia	23,002,000	Paramount Ruler Sultan Syed Sirajuddin Syed Putra Jamalullail; Prime Minister Mahathir bin Mohamad	ringgit (3.80 = $1)	97,900	82,600

regional training programs and improve coordination in law enforcement and intelligence sharing among member nations.

The rise in terrorist threats in 2002 galvanized many governments to share resources. In May, China, Russia, Kazakhstan, Kyrgyzstan, and Tajikistan agreed to pool their efforts to quash terrorism and battle violent separatists. China, Pakistan, India, the Philippines, and other Asian countries also entered into counterterrorism agreements with the United States.

Despite global efforts to crack down on extremists, terrorists continued to cause misery across Asia's broad expanse. One of the deadliest terrorist attacks on civilians took place in October, when two powerful bombs exploded on the Indonesian resort island of Bali. The blast resulted in the deaths of more than 180 people at a discotheque. Indonesian police said the bombs were planted by a radical Islamic organization based in Indonesia, Jemaah Islamiyah. Police in Singapore and Malaysia arrested more than 30 members of Jemaah Islamiyah in 2002 on charges that they had plotted, but failed, to blow up British, Australian, and U.S. embassies and other Western interests in the region.

Country	Population	Government	Monetary unit*	Foreign trade (million U.S.$)	
				Exports[†]	Imports[†]
Maldives	302,000	President Maumoon Abdul Gayoom	rufiyaa (11.77 = $1)	88	372
Mongolia	2,455,000	President Natsagiyn Bagabandi; Prime Minister Namburiin Enkhbayar	tugrik (1,117.00 = $1)	454	511
Myanmar (Burma)	46,648,000	Prime Minister, State Peace and Development Council Chairman Than Shwe	kyat (6.43 = $1)	1,300	2,500
Nepal	25,009,000	King Gyanendra Bir Bikram Shah Dev; Prime Minister Lokendra Bahadur Chand	rupee (76.77 = $1)	485	1,200
New Zealand	3,930,000	Governor General Dame Silvia Cartwright; Prime Minister Helen Clark	dollar (2.12 = $1)	14,600	14,300
Pakistan	144,135,000	President and Chief Executive Pervez Musharraf	rupee (59.14 = $1)	8,600	9,600
Papua New Guinea	5,015,000	Governor General Sir Silas Atopare; Prime Minister Sir Michael Somare	kina (3.99 = $1)	2,100	1,000
Philippines	78,850,000	President Gloria Macapagal-Arroyo	peso (52.44 = $1)	38,000	35,000
Russia	146,376,000	President Vladimir Putin	ruble (31.71 = $1)	105,100	44,200
Singapore	3,641,000	President Sellapan Rama Nathan; Prime Minister Chok Tong Goh	dollar (1.78 = $1)	137,000	127,000
Sri Lanka	19,415,000	President Chandrika Kumaratunga; Prime Minister Ranil Wickremesinghe	rupee (96.25 = $1)	5,200	6,100
Taiwan	22,735,000	President Chen Shui-bian; Vice President Lu Annette	dollar (34.87 = $1)	148,380	140,010
Tajikistan	6,347,000	President Emomali Rahmonov; National Assembly Chairman Makhmadsaid Ubaydulloyev	somoni (2.59 = $1)	761	782
Thailand	62,422,000	King Phumiphon Adunyadet; Prime Minister Thaksin Chinnawat	baht (43.38 = $1)	68,200	61,800
Turkmenistan	4,605,000	President Saparmurat Niyazov	manat (5,200.00 = $1)	2,400	1,650
Uzbekistan	25,355,000	President Islam Karimov	som (682.00 = $1)	2,900	2,600
Vietnam	79,387,000	Communist Party General Secretary Nong Duc Manh; President Tran Duc Luong; Prime Minister Phan Van Khai	dong (15,345.00 = $1)	14,300	15,200

*Exchange rates as of Oct. 4, 2002, or latest available data.
[†]Latest available data.

Terrorist threats forced the United States to shut down its embassies in Cambodia, Indonesia, Malaysia, and Vietnam on the eve of the anniversary of the Sept. 11, 2001, attacks. U.S. officials said they closed the embassies after receiving "credible and specific" terrorist threats, but reopened the embassies later in 2002.

The global war on terrorism continued in 2002 as United States and allied troops battled extremists and helped Asian governments root out terrorists. In Afghanistan, U.S.-led troops searched for members of al-Qa'ida and the Taliban, an extremist Islamic group that had ruled Afghanistan until their overthrow in 2001. Pakistan cooperated with U.S. forces in 2002 by arresting several al-Qa'ida and Taliban leaders who had fled across the Afghan border into Pakistan.

U.S. forces also participated in a six-month mission to help Philippine forces battle rebel separatist groups and terrorists. U.S. military advisers arrived in the Philippines in January to share intelligence and equipment and to train Philippine troops in counterterrorism tactics.

India and Pakistan engaged in a tense 10-month military standoff in 2002. The countries amassed nearly 1 million soldiers along their shared border as tensions escalated between the countries over terrorism and control of the state of Jammu and Kashmir—territory largely held by India but claimed by Pakistan since 1947. In October 2002, India and Pakistan agreed to end the standoff after Pakistani officials promised an end to cross-border terrorism.

Other regional disputes broke out between neighboring countries in 2002. In May, Thai and Myanmar soldiers traded fire after Myanmar launched an offensive against ethnic Shan rebels near the Thai-Myanmar border. In August, the governments of the Philippines and Indonesia protested Malaysia's expulsion of nearly 300,000 foreign workers. In September, Vietnamese forces shot at a Philippine military reconnaissance plane while it was flying over an island in the South China Sea that was occupied by Vietnam but claimed by the Philippines.

Separatist violence. Fighting between government troops and separatist rebels in Indonesia, Myanmar, China, and Sri Lanka resulted in thousands of deaths in 2002. In December, the Sri Lankan government and the rebel Liberation Tigers of Tamil Eelam agreed to end a 19-year conflict that had resulted in the deaths of some 64,000 people.

Nepal. King Gyanendra Bir Bikram Shah Dev of Nepal dismissed the government headed by Prime Minister Sher Bahadur Deuba on Oct. 4, 2002, after the king called Deuba "incompetent." The king installed an interim government headed by royalist Lokendra Bahadur Chand. The king also suspended parliamentary elections, which were scheduled for November. Most observers condemned the king's moves as unconstitutional.

Nepal had been in turmoil since Gyanendra assumed the crown in June 2001 after his brother, King Birendra, was gunned down in a royal palace massacre apparently committed by Birendra's son, the crown prince, who also died. Riots shook Kathmandu, the capital, after the killings. Soon after, fighting intensified between government forces and rebels inspired by Chinese revolutionary Mao Zedong.

The rebels began fighting in 1996 to replace Nepal's constitutional monarchy with a Communist government. By early 2002, rebels controlled several districts and were active throughout much of the country. The rebels used ruthless violence and intimidation against the people of Nepal. By 2002, approximately 7,000 people had been killed as a result of rebel violence. In May 2002, Nepalese forces launched an offensive against the rebels, killing 650 Maoists. The rebels retaliated in September by killing nearly 100 people, including 49 police officers. In November, rebels killed more than 150 people in rural Nepal. The violence damaged Nepal's economy,

which relied heavily on tourism. In 2000, more than 460,000 tourists visited Nepal. In 2002, the number fell to about 150,000. The nation also suffered from flooding and landslides, which killed more than 500 people in 2002.

Economy. The increase in terrorist activity and a worldwide economic slowdown softened economic growth in Asia in 2002. However, economists still expected most Asian economies to expand at an average rate of 5.6 percent annually from 2002 to 2006—faster than the global average of less than 4 percent.

China led Asian growth in 2002. The economy expanded by an annual rate of 7.9 percent, according to the Asian Development Bank (ADB), a United Nations (UN) affiliate based in Manila. The economies of Malaysia, Vietnam, South Korea, Thailand, and the Philippines were expected to grow by more than 4 percent in 2002, according to the ADB. Taiwan and Singapore pulled out of recession and experienced growth of more than 3.5 percent. Japan remained mired in its worst recession since World War II (1939-1945), however. The ADB warned that Japan's crippling problems of high unemployment, government debt, and unpaid bank loans might derail growth in other Asian countries.

Laotians elected a new parliament in February 2002. Only 1 of the 109 assembly deputies elected was not a member of the Lao People's Revolutionary Party, the ruling Communist party.

Floods caused by monsoon rains swept across Asia in 2002 and resulted in the deaths of thousands of people. In China, more than 1,500 people were killed as the result of floods and flood-related disasters. More than 1,000 people died in Bangladesh, India, and Nepal.

Pollution. A thick blanket of pollution over South Asia may be causing the premature deaths of 500,000 people in India each year, deadly flooding in some areas, and drought in other areas, according to a report published in August by the UN Environment Program. The pollution, knows as "the Asian brown cloud," is a mixture of ash, soot, acids, and other particles. The cloud cuts the amount of sunlight reaching the ground and the oceans by 10 to 15 percent, cooling the land and water while heating the atmosphere.

Human rights experts met in Bangkok in October for a UN-sponsored conference aimed at combating the global scourge of human trafficking, a business that generates about $7 billion annually. The U.S. State Department reported that as many as 2 million people—the vast majority of them women and children—are smuggled across international borders each year and sold into various forms of slavery.   □ Henry S. Bradsher

See also **Armed forces; Newspaper: A Special Report**; various Asian country articles.

Astronomy. Astronomers in 2002 found the strongest evidence yet that Mars has an abundance of frozen water; discovered 11 new moons of Jupiter; and found a frozen world 1 billion miles (1.6 billion kilometers) beyond Pluto. Astronomers also located a planetary system similar to our own and found evidence of a new type of black hole.

Water on Mars. In May, scientists controlling the National Aeronautics and Space Administration's (NASA) Mars Odyssey spacecraft announced the discovery of a vast amount of water ice on Mars. Instruments aboard the spacecraft, in orbit around Mars, detected large amounts of hydrogen, a main ingredient of water, beneath the surface near the planet's south pole.

The instruments indicated that the hydrogen is less than 3.3 feet (1 meter) below the planet's surface. NASA scientists estimated that if the ice were to melt, it would create a lake twice as large as Lake Michigan. Mars Odyssey was unable to determine if the same amount of ice was present near the north pole of Mars.

Quaoar. Astronomers announced in October 2002 that they had found the largest object in the solar system since the discovery of Pluto in 1930. Michael Brown and Chadwick Trujillo of the California Institute of Technology in Pasadena reported discovering an asteroidlike object nearly 800 miles (1,287 kilometers) in diameter about 1 billion miles (1.6 billion kilometers) beyond Pluto. Astronomers named the object "Quaoar" (pronounced *KWA-whar*), after a Native American creation god.

Although Quaoar is only about half the size of Pluto, it contains more mass than all other asteroids in the solar system combined. Astronomers believe Quaoar is an icy ball made up of bits of rock and frozen gases, much like a comet. The astronomers originally spotted Quaoar with an Earth-based telescope, but the object was so faint that they needed the Hubble Space Telescope to determine its size.

Jupiter moons found. Astronomers at the University of Hawaii at Manoa announced in May 2002 that they had found 11 previously undiscovered small moons in orbit around Jupiter. They found the moons using the Canada-France-Hawaii telescope on Mauna Kea in Hawaii. Although the moons are too small for surface features to be seen, astronomers believe them to be irregular-shaped rocks no more than 2 miles (3.2 kilometers) in diameter. The newly found moons orbit in the opposite direction to Jupiter's rotation. They are probably the remains of asteroids that were captured by Jupiter's gravitational field during the formation of the solar system.

Extrasolar system. In June, a team of astronomers announced that they had found a plane-

The bright area near the center of a highly detailed image of the Milky Way, taken by the Chandra X-ray Observatory and released in January, contains a super-massive black hole.

The Cone Nebula (right), in an image released by NASA in 2002, is a towering pillar of gas and dust. Its red glow is produced by energy emitted by millions of stars forming inside the nebula.

Two small galaxies (below), called the Mice because of their tails, collide about 30 million light-years from Earth. The two will eventually combine to form a single galaxy.

New images of the far reaches of the universe from the Hubble Space Telescope.

A galaxy called the Tadpole swirls before a backdrop of faraway galaxies. The long tail of dust and gas was created by the gravitational effects of another galaxy—visible as a blue spot at the upper left—interacting with the Tadpole.

2002 the discovery of a new type of black hole, which could help astronomers learn more about how black holes form. Astronomers Roeland Van Der Marel of the Space Telescope Science Institute in Baltimore and Michael Rich of the University of California at Los Angeles independently discovered evidence of medium-sized black holes located in the cores of groups of stars that are known as globular clusters.

Astronomers had previously known of only two types of black holes. The first type is about 10 times the mass of the sun. The other type, called a supermassive black hole, is millions or even billions of times more massive than the sun. Supermassive black holes are found at the centers of galaxies, such as our own Milky Way.

Van Der Marel and Rich found black holes of a mass in between the two previously discovered varieties. Van Der Marel discovered a black hole about 4,000 times more massive than the sun in the globular cluster M15 in the Milky Way. Rich's group found a black hole about 20,000 times more massive than the sun in globular cluster G1 in the neighboring Andromeda Galaxy.

While noting that the black holes were of a mass never before seen, astronomers also were very interested in the fact that the discoveries seem to imply a relationship between the mass of a black hole and the size of the galaxy or globular cluster in which it resides. Astronomers had already noted that larger galaxies have more massive black holes at their centers than do smaller galaxies. Many astronomers believe the new discovery could provide a clue to how black holes are formed.

The two main theories of how midsized and supermassive black holes form hold that they either all formed at the beginning of the universe; or grow around a "seed," or smaller black hole. Astronomers said the new findings seem to support the second theory.   ☐ Laurence A. Marschall

tary system similar to our own. The team, led by Geoffrey Marcy of the University of California at Berkeley and Paul Butler at the Carnegie Institute of Washington, D.C., said the planets orbit the star 55 Cancri, which is about 41 light-years from Earth.

Astronomers were excited about the discovery. For the first time, they had found a planet somewhat similar to Jupiter in both size and orbital distance from its star. The newly found planet, which is the second to be found around 55 Cancri, is about five times as massive as Jupiter and orbits its star every 13 years, similar to Jupiter's orbit of 12 years. The discovery was important because all other planetary systems found so far are very different from our own.

"Midsized"black holes. Astronomers announced in September

Australia

Australians were deeply shocked by a terrorist attack on the Indonesian island of Bali on Oct. 12, 2002, which killed a number of Australian citizens. Two bombs, exploding just seconds apart, destroyed a bar and nightclub at Kuta, a popular beach resort, killing more than 180 people. Australians, mainly young people in their 20's, made up nearly half the dead. Among the victims were members of several amateur Australian football teams who had flown to Bali to celebrate the end of the football season. Australian Prime Minister John Howard flew to Bali on October 17 and proclaimed October 20 a national day of mourning.

Although no group claimed responsibility for the attack, authorities suspected that Jemaah Islamiyah, an Indonesian Islamic terrorist group, was behind the bombings. Experts believed that Jemaah Islamiyah was linked to the al-Qa'ida terrorist network responsible for the attacks on the United States on Sept. 11, 2001. The Australian government offered a reward of $2 million for information leading to the arrests of the terrorists. (All figures are in Australian dollars.) In November and December 2002, Indonesian authorities arrested a number of suspects, including the alleged "mastermind" of the attack.

Drought. A severe drought worsened in Australia in 2002. In July, farmers in northern and western Victoria reported the lowest rainfalls ever recorded in those areas. In the wheat-growing regions of New South Wales and Queensland, farmers planted only half the potential winter crops. By November, virtually all of New South Wales was affected by the drought, which was the worst since 1903, according to government officials. The government offered $100 million in drought relief to Australian farmers in 2002. Economists calculated that the dry conditions would cost the Australian economy as much as $1 billion. Retailers estimated that food prices would rise by up to 20 percent as a result of the drought. The dry weather also led to many fires.

Commonwealth of Nations. Queen Elizabeth II of the United Kingdom visited Australia in 2002 in her capacity as head of the Commonwealth of Nations, a voluntary association of independent countries and other political units that meets every other year. The queen arrived in Adelaide, South Australia, in late February. She then traveled to Queensland, where she opened the Commonwealth Heads of Government Meeting (CHOGM) at Coolum.

Debate over Commonwealth member Zimbabwe, whose president, Robert Mugabe, was not present, dominated the CHOGM. A number of participants at the conference accused Mugabe of using political intimidation to silence his opponents. Some Commonwealth leaders, including Prime Minister Tony Blair of the United Kingdom, wanted the CHOGM to take immediate action against the Mugabe government. Other leaders urged a slower approach. The delegates reached a compromise, appointing Prime Minister Howard and two senior African leaders to decide on a course of action following upcoming elections in Zimbabwe. After Commonwealth observers reported adversely on the way the elections were conducted, Howard announced in mid-March that Zimbabwe would be suspended from the Commonwealth for one year.

The 2002 Commonwealth Games were held in Manchester in the United Kingdom in July. The games attracted athletes from 72 nations, who took part in 17 different events. Australian athletes dominated the games, winning a total of 206 medals. Australia's final tally included 82 gold, 62 silver, and 62 bronze medals. Australian Olympic swimming champion Ian Thorpe won six gold medals, the most ever won by a competitor in the Commonwealth Games.

Governor-general trouble. A child-abuse scandal surrounding Governor-General Peter Hollingworth that began in 2001 continued in 2002. The governor-general, a largely ceremonial position, represents Queen Elizabeth, who is Australia's head of state. Hollingworth found himself under intense criticism for the way he had handled a case of child abuse committed by a counselor at a church school during the early 1990's. During this time, Hollingworth was Anglican Archbishop of Brisbane.

Pressure mounted for Hollingworth to resign in February 2002, as Simon Crean, the leader of the Australian Labor Party (ALP), and several state Labor premiers called for the governor-general to step down. Because of Hollingworth's role as the queen's representative, his fate threatened to provoke a constitutional crisis.

Hollingworth, appearing on a national television program in February, admitted that he had made errors of judgement in the way he handled the child-abuse case. He insisted, however, that he had done nothing wrong personally, and he resisted calls for his resignation. Public calls for Hollingworth's removal were repeated in October, after the governor-general delayed visiting the surviving victims of the Bali bombings.

Other political events. In mid-2002, a leadership crisis plagued the Australian Democrats, a small but important party whose members, along with independents, held the balance of power in Australia's Senate. The crisis began in late July, when Senator Meg Lees, the former head of the Democrats, announced that she was leaving the party and would sit as an independent. Lees had been ousted from the party's leadership in 2001 by a rival senator, Natasha Stott Despoja. After Lees announced her switch, Stott Despoja demanded that Lees quit the Senate and relinquish her seat back to the Democrats. Lees refused.

In August 2002, Stott Despoja announced that she would resign as party leader because she could not accept a 10-point list of demands presented to her by Democrats at a party meeting.

The Democrats then installed Senator Brian Greig of Western Australia as their temporary leader. In October, party leaders replaced Greig with Queensland senator Andrew Bartlett after a poll of members.

Simon Crean put his leadership of the ALP on the line in 2002 with his controversial attempts to modernize the party. Crean had been elected party leader following a big ALP defeat in the elections of 2001, when the party attracted only a third of the primary vote. Crean, a former trade union official, clashed in 2002 with union leaders over his plans to reduce the power of the unions in the party. He claimed his plans would help attract more public support for the ALP. Union officials maintained that the changes advocated by

Mounted police clash with demonstrators outside the Woomera Detention Center in South Australia in late March. The demonstrators, who had previously helped refugees escape from the facility, protested the policy of holding all captured refugees in detention, sometimes for months, while the government considered their applications for asylum.

the national conferences. Under the new rules, the three senior ALP leaders were to rotate jobs every 12 months. Crean claimed this reform would ensure that a woman would become ALP president within three years.

Economic issues. Treasurer Peter Costello introduced his seventh federal budget into Parliament in May 2002. The Australian media tagged the budget "the khaki budget" because of its emphasis on meeting Australia's growing military commitments. Labor Party leaders and other political opponents of the conservative administration criticized a number of other items, especially proposed higher charges for prescription drugs and tighter controls over health and welfare spending.

Australia experienced a relatively high growth rate, about 4 percent, in 2002, when most countries were suffering from a downturn in their economies. The Reserve Bank of Australia, the nation's central bank, raised the *official interest rate*, the rate that banks charge other banks for overnight loans, from 4.25 percent in May to 4.75 percent in June. The rate remained at 4.75 percent throughout the rest of the year, despite a boom in housing prices.

Agriculture. A low Australian dollar, which hovered around U.S. 55 cents for most of 2002, helped Australia's agricultural exports. The wine industry was one of the brightest Australian economic success stories in 2002. Lower production costs gave Australia's producers a competitive advantage in the huge U.S. market. The value of wine sales to the United States in 2002 for the first time approached the value of wine sales to the United Kingdom, which had long been the mainstay of the Australian wine industry.

Not all sectors of Australian agriculture enjoyed the good fortune of the wine producers in 2002. Australian wheat farmers, who were already suffering from the worst drought in 100 years, had more bad news in July, when the government of Iraq threatened to cancel lucrative wheat purchases. The threat came in retaliation for the Australian government's support for a threatened U.S. military attack against Iraq.

The Australian sugar industry, which faced low world prices, was also thrown into crisis by the 2002 drought. In September, the federal government unveiled a $150-million rescue package that included a tax-free $50,000 payment for growers who wanted to leave the industry. The bailout was to be funded by an 18-cent increase in the price of every kilogram of sugar.

Mining. The mining sector, like agricultural exports, benefited in 2002 from the low Australian dollar. In May, Prime Minister Howard visited Beijing, China's capital, to discuss future sales of Australian natural gas. In August, the

Crean would make no difference in the party's electoral appeal.

Crean won a major victory for his plans at an ALP conference in October, when the ratio of union votes to those of ordinary party members at state conferences was reduced to 50 percent in 2002, compared with 60 percent in 2001. The ALP also endorsed the direct election of the party's president and two vice presidents by a vote of grass-roots members, rather than by delegates to

Members of the Australian House of Representatives

The House of Representatives of the 40th Parliament first met Feb. 12, 2002. As of Dec. 1, 2002, the House of Representatives consisted of the following members: 68 Liberal Party of Australia, 64 Australian Labor Party, 13 National Party of Australia, 3 independents, 1 Northern Territory Country Liberal Party, and 1 Australian Greens. This table shows each legislator and party affiliation. An asterisk (*) denotes those who served in the 39th Parliament.

Australian Capital Territory
Annette Ellis, A.L.P.*
Bob McMullan, A.L.P.*

New South Wales
Tony Abbott, L.P.*
Anthony Albanese, A.L.P.*
John Anderson, N.P.*
Peter Andren, Ind.*
Larry Anthony, N.P.*
Bruce Baird, L.P.*
Bob Baldwin, L.P.
Kerry Bartlett, L.P.*
Bronwyn Bishop, L.P.*
Laurie Brereton, A.L.P.*
Alan Cadman, L.P.*
Ross Cameron, L.P.*
Ian Causley, N.P.*
John Cobb, N.P.
Janice Crosio, A.L.P.*
Pat Farmer, L.P.
Laurie Ferguson, A.L.P.*
Joel Fitzgibbon, A.L.P.*
Joanna Gash, L.P.*
Jennie George, A.L.P.
Sharon Grierson, A.L.P.
Jill Hall, A.L.P.*
Luke Hartsuyker, N.P.
Michael Hatton, A.L.P.*
Kelly Hoare, A.L.P.*
Joe Hockey, L.P.*
John Howard, L.P.*
Kay Hull, N.P.*
Julia Irwin, A.L.P.*
Jackie Kelly, L.P.*
Peter King, L.P.
Mark Latham, A.L.P.*
Sussan Ley, L.P.
Jim Lloyd, L.P.*
Robert McClelland, A.L.P.*
Leo McLeay, A.L.P.*
Daryl Melham, A.L.P.*
Frank Mossfield, A.L.P.*
John Murphy, A.L.P.*
Gary Nairn, L.P.*
Brendan Nelson, L.P.*
Michael Organ A.G.
Tanya Plibersek, A.L.P.*
Roger Price, A.L.P.*
Philip Ruddock, L.P.*
Alby Schultz, L.P.*
Ken Ticehurst, L.P.
Mark Vaile, N.P.*
Danna Vale, L.P.*
Tony Windsor, Ind.

Northern Territory
Warren Snowdon, A.L.P.*
David Tollner, C.L.P.

Queensland
Arch Bevis, A.L.P.*
Mal Brough, L.P.*
Steven Ciobo, L.P.
Peter Dutton, L.P.
Kay Elson, L.P.*
Craig Emerson, A.L.P.*
Warren Entsch, L.P.*
Teresa Gambaro, L.P.*
Gary Hardgrave, L.P.*
Michael Johnson, L.P.
David Jull, L.P.*
Robert Katter, Ind.*
De-Anne Kelly, N.P.*
Peter Lindsay, L.P.*
Kirsten Livermore, A.L.P.*
Ian Macfarlane, L.P.*
Margaret May, L.P.*
Paul Neville, N.P.*
Bernie Ripoll, A.L.P.*
Kevin Rudd, A.L.P.*
Con Sciacca, A.L.P.*
Bruce Scott, N.P.*
Peter Slipper, L.P.*
Alexander Somlyay, L.P.*
Wayne Swan, A.L.P.*
Cameron Thompson, L.P.*
Warren Truss, N.P.*

South Australia
Neil Andrew, L.P.*
David Cox, A.L.P.*
Alexander Downer, L.P.*
Trish Draper, L.P.*
Martyn Evans, A.L.P.*
Christine Gallus, L.P.*
Christopher Pyne, L.P.*
Rodney Sawford, A.L.P.*
Patrick Secker, L.P.*
Andrew Southcott, L.P.*
Barry Wakelin, L.P.*
Trish Worth, L.P.*

Tasmania
Dick Adams, A.L.P.*
Duncan Kerr, A.L.P.*
Michelle O'Byrne, A.L.P.*
Harry Quick, A.L.P.*
Sid Sidebottom, A.L.P.*

Victoria
Kevin Andrews, L.P.*
Fran Bailey, L.P.*
Phillip Barresi, L.P.*
Bruce Billson, L.P.*
Anna Burke, A.L.P.*
Anthony Byrne, A.L.P.*
Bob Charles, L.P.*
Ann Corcoran, A.L.P.*
Peter Costello, L.P.*
Simon Crean, A.L.P.*
Michael Danby, A.L.P.*
Martin Ferguson, A.L.P.*
John Forrest, N.P.*
Petro Georgiou, L.P.*
Steve Gibbons, A.L.P.*
Julia Gillard, A.L.P.*
Alan Griffin, A.L.P.*
David Hawker, L.P.*
Greg Hunt, L.P.
Harry Jenkins, A.L.P.*
David Kemp, L.P.*
Catherine King, A.L.P.
Jenny Macklin, A.L.P.*
Stewart McArthur, L.P.*
Peter McGauran, N.P.*
Brendan O'Connor, A.L.P.
Gavan O'Connor, A.L.P.*
Sophie Panopoulos, L.P.
Chris Pearce, L.P.
Nicola Roxon, A.L.P.*
Bob Sercombe, A.L.P.*
Tony Smith, L.P.
Sharman Stone, L.P.*
Lindsay Tanner, A.L.P.*
Kelvin Thomson, A.L.P.*
Maria Vamvakinou, A.L.P.
Christian Zahra, A.L.P.*

Western Australia
Kim Beazley, A.L.P.*
Julie Bishop, L.P.*
Graham Edwards, A.L.P.*
Barry Haase, L.P.*
Sharryn Jackson, A.L.P.
Carmen Lawrence, A.L.P.*
Jann McFarlane, A.L.P.*
Judi Moylan, L.P.*
Geoffrey Prosser, L.P.*
Don Randall, L.P.
Stephen Smith, A.L.P.*
Wilson Tuckey, L.P.*
Mal Washer, L.P.*
Kim Wilkie, A.L.P.*
Daryl Williams, L.P.*

High Court of Australia upheld a law passed in Western Australia denying Aborigines any rights to minerals or oil found beneath tribal lands worked by mining companies.

Tourism. Australia's $70-billion tourism industry, which rivals the mining industry in economic importance, suffered from the worldwide downturn in tourism that followed the terrorist attacks on the United States on Sept. 11, 2001. Many large Australian hotels reported running 40 percent below capacity in 2002.

Refugees. Human rights activists in 2002 criticized the Australian government's strict policies toward people seeking *asylum* (refuge or safety in a foreign country). In January, a facility detaining refugees at Woomera in South Australia was the site of rallies, hunger strikes, and self-mutilation in protest of government policies allegedly delaying the processing of refugee applications. More than 60 of the Woomera refugees, including many children, sewed their lips—or had their lips sewn—together as part of this protest. Most of the people seeking asylum in Australia were Muslims from Iraq or Afghanistan who had been transported to Australia by "people smugglers" operating out of Indonesia.

In June, the United Nations Working Group on Arbitrary Detention claimed that Australia treated asylum seekers like criminals. The group reported that refugees were usually locked behind barbed wire in camps in remote parts of the continent or sent to Pacific Islands while their cases were decided. Immigration Minister Philip Ruddock defended the government's practices, maintaining that the policies were designed to allow for orderly decisions to be made about the number of asylum seekers accepted each year.

As 2002 progressed, political observers noted that the government's tough stance on illegal immigrants was proving successful. By September, no new illegal refugees had arrived by boat on the Australian mainland for more than a year. In addition, the detention camps had begun to empty as the cases of individual refugees and families were processed.

In September, the Department of Immigration announced that 647 of the 1,217 people detained on the Pacific islands of Nauru and Manus had qualified for asylum. Approximately half of the more than 400 detainees who were rescued by the Norwegian freighter *Tampa* when their vessel sank off the northwest coast of Australia in August 2001 were classified as refugees or resettled in New Zealand.

Insurance reform in Australia was spurred on by a court ruling in May 2002. The court required the Waverley City Council to pay $3.7 million to a man who became paralyzed after striking his head on a sandbar while diving at Sydney's Bondi Beach. The size of the award produced public outrage. An panel chaired by New South Wales Judge David Ipp subsequently recommended several changes to federal laws governing personal liability. Among other proposals, Ipp recommended a single nationwide statute limiting liability and capping damage awards; laws barring injured adults from initiating legal action if the injury happened three or more years before; and measures to encourage people who engage in risky activities to assume greater personal responsibility.

Several states introduced their own insurance reforms in 2002. New South Wales proposed laws to protect volunteers against litigation; prevent people from suing for injuries sustained while they were playing contact sports; and ban people from winning damages for injuries incurred while they were drunk or committing a crime.

Steve Fossett, a U.S. businessman and adventurer, became the first person to successfully pilot a balloon around the world by himself when he took off from Northam, in Western Australia, on June 19 and landed at Lake Yamma Yamma in Queensland on July 4. The 21,000-mile (33,900-kilometer) trip was restricted to the Southern Hemisphere.   □ Brian Kennedy

See also **Australia, Prime Minister of; Iraq; News bytes; Terrorism; Zimbabwe.**

Australia, Prime Minister of. John

Howard brokered an agreement at the Commonwealth Heads of Government Meeting (CHOGM) in Queensland in March 2002 addressing concerns about Zimbabwe. The CHOGM is a conference of the Commonwealth of Nations, an association of independent countries and other political units. The agreement stipulated that Howard chair a committee to consider any evidence of wrongdoing by Zimbabwe's President Robert Mugabe in an upcoming presidential election. Following reports of political intimidation in the election, Howard announced that he and the presidents of Commonwealth members Nigeria and South Africa had decided that Zimbabwe would be suspended from the CHOGM for one year.

In May, Prime Minister Howard attended independence celebrations in East Timor and held trade talks in China. He also discussed trade issues during a 12-day trip to Europe in July. In October, Howard flew to the site of terrorist bombings in Bali, Indonesia, that resulted in the deaths of about 180 people, including many Australians.

The prime minister publicly lent support to United States President George W. Bush in September for a possible U.S. military attack against Iraq.   □ Brian Kennedy

See also **Australia; Indonesia; Iraq; Terrorism; Zimbabwe.**

Australian rules football. The Brisbane Lions edged out the Collingwood Magpies for the Australian Football League (AFL) premiership on Sept. 28, 2002, in what fans described as one of the best grand finals in years. The young Magpies team performed well against heavily favored Brisbane but lost in front of a crowd of nearly 92,000 at the Melbourne Cricket Ground.

Collingwood led by a goal near the end of the third quarter. Brisbane's Alastair Lynch scored to give the Lions the lead, and Jason Akermanis kicked a goal to seal the win. Brisbane won 10 goals, 15 behinds, and 75 points to Collingwood's 9 goals, 12 behinds, and 66 points. Collingwood's Nathan Buckley won the Norm Smith medal for the best player on the field. Brisbane midfielder Simon Black won the 2002 Brownlow medal for the best and fairest player.

Regionals. In Queensland, the Mount Gravatt Vultures defeated the Southport Sharks 20.11 (131) to 10.10 (70). In South Australia, Sturt beat Central 13.14 (92) to 6.9 (45). In Tasmania's Southern Football League, Clarence overpowered North Hobart by 21 points in the premier league grand final, and Cygnet beat Lauderdale 9.13 (67) to 4.7 (31) in the regional grand final. In New South Wales, the Cardiff Hawks defeated the Terrigal-Avoca Panthers to take the 2002 Black Diamond Cup. □ Brian Kennedy

Austria underwent dramatic political change in 2002. The conservative People's Party of Chancellor Wolfgang Schuessel emerged as Austria's dominant political party in parliamentary elections in November after the right-wing Freedom Party split over tax policy and who was to lead the party.

The controversial Freedom Party had grown rapidly in the 1990's by challenging the status quo, under which the People's Party and the Social Democrats shared political power and jobs in state-run companies. However, the extreme views of party leader Joerg Haider, who praised Nazi Germany's employment policies and opposed immigration, made the party an outcast with the leaders of the European Union (EU). When the party formed a coalition with the People's Party after winning second place in parliamentary elections in 1999, Austria's partners in the EU refused direct contacts with the government for several months in protest.

Party rift. Tensions grew inside the Freedom Party in 2002 between Haider, who remained governor of the state of Carinthia, and party members in the national coalition government, who moderated their stance while in power. In February, Peter Westenthaler, the Freedom Party leader in parliament, and Finance Minister Karl-Heinz Grasser criticized Haider for traveling to Baghdad to meet Iraqi President Saddam Hussein. In August, the government decided to postpone planned tax cuts to cover the costs of devastating floods that caused an estimated $5 billion worth of damage. Haider led a protest inside the party that stripped his former protege, Susanne Riess-Passer, of her position as Freedom Party leader. Riess-Passer, who had become vice chancellor in the coalition government, and Grasser then resigned from the governing coalition.

Election. Schuessel seized on the Freedom Party's disarray to call for early parliamentary elections. He campaigned in favor of a continuation of the government's economic policies of gradual deregulation and privatization of state-owned companies. He also promised to support the expansion of the EU to admit 10 countries from Eastern and Southern Europe.

The People's Party won 42 percent of the vote in the November 24 election, short of a majority in parliament but up sharply from 27 percent in 1999. The opposition Social Democrats won 37 percent, up from 33 percent in 1999. The Freedom Party's share of the vote collapsed to 10 percent from 27 percent. Schuessel began negotiations to form either a minority government led by the People's Party or a coalition with one of the other parties. □ Tom Buerkle

See also **Europe**.

Automobile industry analysts reported in late 2002 that the sales of light trucks and cars in the United States remained relatively steady compared with sales in 2001 despite an economic slowdown. By the end of September 2002, sales of cars and light trucks totaled 12.9 million units, 0.08 percent ahead of the same period in 2001. However, industry analysts predicted that 2002 sales would not pass the 17.2 million light trucks and cars sold in 2001. Analysts noted that to entice more consumers into dealers' showrooms in 2002, automakers were forced to offer large rebates and zero-percent financing—that is, interest-free loans. Such incentives cut into corporate earnings.

Top sellers. Ford remained the top seller of light trucks during the 2002 model year with its F-series pickup. Sales of the F-series truck totaled more than 880,000 units. The Toyota Camry captured the car sales title for the 2002 model year. The Camry sold approximately 435,000 units.

Sales trends. Despite overall steady sales during the first nine months of 2002, officials at the three largest automobile manufacturers in the United States—General Motors Corporation (GM) of Detroit, Ford Motor Company of Dearborn, Michigan, and the U.S. division of Daimler-Chrysler AG of Germany—reported that sales and market shares declined during much of the year.

Two extremes—tiny, environmentally friendly automobiles and giant sports utility vehicles—competed for buyers in 2002.

BMW took a page from the past when it reintroduced the Mini Cooper in 2002. The vehicle is under 12 feet (3.6 meters) long and features a four-cylinder, 115-horsepower engine. The Mini Cooper, inspired by the "sub-subcompact" Mini Cooper of the 1960's, was the latest "retrostyle" offering from car manufacturers.

Takara Co. of Japan introduced the Qi in 2002. The single-seat electric vehicle travels up to 50 miles (80 kilometers) with a single charge of its battery.

Sales for the top three manufacturers totaled 8.1 million units for the first nine months of 2002, 1.2 percent lower than during the same period in 2001. Market share through September 2002 dropped to 63 percent, compared with 64.3 percent for the first nine months of 2001.

Officials at Asian automobile manufacturers reported that their sales rose through September 2002 to 4 million units, or 4.7 percent higher than the same period in 2001. Their market share increased to 31.7 percent, compared with a market share of 30.5 percent for the first nine months of 2001. European automakers increased their market share through September 2002 to 5.3 percent, compared with 5.2 percent for the first nine months of 2001.

The Big Three. GM's fortunes marginally improved in 2002. GM, the number-one automaker in the United States, reported that sales increased 1.9 percent to 3.6 million vehicles in the first nine months of 2002, compared with the same period in 2001. GM's market share in 2002 increased to 28.4 percent, compared with 28.1 percent for the same period in 2001. The improvement came, in part, because of better sales of sports utility vehicles (SUV's) such as the Chevrolet Avalanche, Suburban, and GMC Envoy.

GM reported net income of $716 million through September 2002, a sizable increase compared with the $346 million reported for the first nine months of 2001.

Despite higher earnings, GM officials faced financial problems in 2002. In October, GM announced that it had adjusted the value of its investment in the Italian auto company Fiat Auto Holdings by $1.37 billion on an after-tax basis. GM paid $2.4 billion for a 20 percent stake in the company in 2000.

GM expanded its presence in Asia in 2002, when company officials agreed in April to take over debt-ridden Daewoo Motor Co. of South Korea. The new company was named GM Daewoo Auto & Technology Co.

GM officials announced plans in late 2002 to

General Motors Corporation issued a redesigned Hummer in 2002. The new H2 model is 16 feet (4.5 meters) long and features a 6.0-liter V-8 engine and a suspension system similar to that of a full-sized truck.

The Cadillac Escalade EXT combined the features of a pickup truck and an SUV to create a "sport utility truck." The Escalade is 18 feet (5.5 meters) long and features a 345-horsepower V-8 engine and three rows of seating.

offer a number of new and remodeled cars, including the Saturn Ion, a 50th-anniversary Chevrolet Corvette, and a new Pontiac GTO. The move was made to increase company sales figures during the 2003 model year.

Officials at Ford, the second-largest U.S. automaker, announced in January 2002 that the company would close four plants in the United States and one plant in Canada. The measure was part of a plan that began in 2001 to cut 35,000 jobs to return the company to profitability. Ford reported that the closings will take place by 2005. The company also phased out production of the Ford Escort, Mercury Cougar, Mercury Villager, and Lincoln Continental.

Ford lost $5.4 billion in 2001. Through the first nine months of 2002, Ford sales fell 6.2 percent to 2.7 million units, and its market share dropped 1.6 percentage points to 21.2 percent. For the first three quarters of 2002, Ford reported a net loss of $556 million, compared with a net loss of $385 million in the same period in 2001. Compa-

ny officials planned to improve sales in the 2003 model year with the addition of the Lincoln Aviator, a midsized SUV.

DaimlerChrysler officials in 2002 continued to explore ways to make its Chrysler Group more profitable. In 2001, the Chrysler Group announced a 20 percent work force reduction by 2004. In September 2002, company officials said that its Chrysler Group would earn more in 2002 than originally expected. Chrysler's market share stood at 13.4 percent in the first nine months of 2002, unchanged from the same period in 2001. Chrysler's total sales rose to 1.72 million vehicles in the first three quarters of 2002, due in part to increased sales of its PT Cruiser and Jeep Liberty. Overall, DaimlerChrysler reported a net income of $4.5 billion through September 2002, compared with a net loss of $589 million through September 2001. In 2003, Chrysler planned to introduce a new vehicle, the Pacifica, which combined the features of an SUV and a minivan, in the hope of attracting more customers.

Asian manufacturers, including three automakers headquartered in Japan, reported increased sales and market shares in the United States through September 2002. Officials at Nissan reported that sales increased 8.5 percent to 567,245 units, while Honda's sales rose 3.1 percent to 945,767 units. Toyota officials reported that U.S. sales increased 3.7 percent to 1.3 million units.

Other Asian automakers announced plans in 2002 to enlarge their U.S. manufacturing facilities. In April, officials at Hyundai, based in Seoul, South Korea, revealed that the company planned to construct a $1-billion automotive plant in Montgomery, Alabama. Company officials said that the facility, Hyundai's first in the United States, would employ 2,000 people and produce 300,000 vehicles annually by 2005.

Nissan officials announced in June 2002 that the company would add 1 million square feet (90,000 square meters) to a 2.5 million-square-foot (225,000-square-meter) plant under construction in Canton, Mississippi. The expansion would enable the plant to produce an additional 150,000 Altima family sedans.

Honda officials said in July that the company would invest $425 million in its Lincoln, Alabama, plant to produce 150,000 additional Odyssey minivans. To increase sales in 2003, Honda introduced a redesigned Accord.   □ Mike Casey

Automobile racing.

The rift between the Indy Racing League (IRL) and Championship Auto Racing Teams (CART) widened significantly in 2002, with Honda Motor Company, Ltd., announcing in May that it was leaving CART for the IRL. Racing officials introduced a new type of race-track wall designed to make racing safer for drivers. The 2002 Indianapolis 500 proved to be one of the most hotly contested in history. Tony Stewart took NASCAR's Winston Cup series.

Honda leaves CART. In May, CART suffered a major blow when Honda Motor Company, Ltd., of Tokyo announced it was leaving to join the IRL in 2003. Honda was the latest in a long line of major car manufacturers, racing teams, and drivers to defect from CART, helping tip the advantage toward the IRL in the bitter rivalry between the two open-wheel racing organizations.

Soft walls. Race officials in 2002 experimented with walls designed to absorb energy in crashes. The "soft walls" system uses special barriers in an attempt to reduce injuries. It was first used at the Indianapolis 500 in May and kept in place for the Brickyard 500. However, the walls were increased in thickness from 16 inches (41 centimeters) to 26 inches (66 centimeters) to account for the heavier cars used in the Brickyard 500.

IRL. Sam Hornish Jr. won his second consecutive IRL title on September 15, edging Helio Cas-

Eighteen cars pile up at the Daytona 500 in Daytona Beach, Florida, on February 17 after a driver, forced into the wall, rolled into oncoming cars. No one was injured in the crash. Ward Burton went on to win the race.

troneves to win the Chevy 500 at the Texas Motor Speedway in Fort Worth. The victory was Hornish's record-breaking fifth of the season. He is the first IRL driver to win the title twice.

CART. Cristiano da Matta of Brazil clinched the CART title on October 6 with a victory at the Grand Prix Americas in Miami, Florida. Da Matta finished with 237 points, 73 ahead of Bruno Junqueira of Brazil. Da Matta won five of the season's first eight races, including a record-tying four in a row, to gain a huge early points lead.

Indianapolis 500. On May 26, Helio Castroneves took the checkered flag in one of the most disputed Indy 500's in history. On the second-to-last lap, Castroneves was nearly out of fuel when the caution flag was raised because of a crash. Castroneves crossed the finish line, but Paul Tracy and his team leader, Barry Green, protested that Tracy had passed Castroneves just before the caution flag was raised. In the IRL, drivers cannot pass each other under the caution flag. In July, race officials finally ruled against Tracy's protest, making Castroneves the first person to win back-to-back Indy 500's since Al Unser Sr. in 1971.

NASCAR. Tony Stewart won the Winston Cup Series Championship on Nov. 17, 2002. Stewart finished the season with 4,800 points to second-place finisher Mark Martin's 4,762.

In August, NASCAR officials had fined Stewart $10,000 and put him on probation for the rest of the season for punching a photographer at the Brickyard 400 on August 4. Stewart's main sponsor, Home Depot, Inc., of Atlanta, Georgia, fined him $50,000.

Formula One. Michael Schumacher of Germany won his third straight and record-tying fifth overall world driver's title with a victory on July 21 in the French Grand Prix. Schumacher won a record 11 races in 2002 and became the first driver to finish in the top three in every race.

Endurance. In the Rolex 24-hour race on February 3 in Daytona Beach, Florida, Didier Theys of Belgium, Fredy Lienhard of Switzerland, and Italians Mauro Baldi and Max Papis became the first team with the fastest preliminary times to win since 1993. They drove the 2,549 miles (4,102 kilometers) at an average speed of 106.142 miles (170.819 kilometers) per hour.

Vehicles made by Audi AG of Germany swept the 24 Hours of Le Mans on June 16, 2002. Frank Biela of Germany, Tom Kristensen of Denmark, and Italy's Emanuele Pirro became the first team to win three consecutive Le Mans titles. The second- and third-place teams also drove Audi's.

Dragsters. Cory McClenathan won the 2002 National Hot Rod Association (NHRA) top fuel division championship; John Force won the funny car division; and Kurt Johnson took the pro stock division. ☐ Michael Kates

Aviation. The aviation industry continued in 2002 to suffer the worst economic downturn in its history. According to aviation experts, there were two main causes for the downturn. People were afraid to fly after the terrorist attacks on the United States on Sept. 11, 2001, and the U.S. economy was slow to recover from recession. Airlines responded by reducing flights by nearly 10 percent and laying off thousands of employees.

Bankruptcies. United Airlines, Inc., of Elk Grove Village, Illinois, declared bankruptcy on Dec. 9, 2002, becoming the largest airline ever to seek bankruptcy protection. United, the second-largest airline in the United States, lost more than $2.5 billion in 2002. Company officials cut costs to forestall the bankruptcy by laying off thousands of employees and negotiating about $1.5 billion in wage concessions from unions.

In August, United officials applied for a $1.8-billion loan guarantee from the Air Transportation Stabilization Board. The board was established in September 2001 to provide up to $10 billion in government loan guarantees to help airlines that were struggling financially after the attacks on Sept. 11, 2001. But the board denied United's application on Dec. 4, 2002, ruling that the airline's restructuring plan was flawed.

US Airways Group, Inc., of Arlington, Virginia, the nation's sixth-largest carrier, filed for bankruptcy in August. The airline continued to operate while it reorganized. US Airways had been especially affected by the extended closure of its main airport, Ronald Reagan Washington National Airport in Washington, D.C., after the terrorist attacks in 2001. US Airways officials also pointed out that, after the attacks, many passengers took trains or cars instead of flying.

Several small airlines ceased operations in 2002. Midway Airlines Corporation of Morrisville, North Carolina, and Vanguard Airlines, Inc., of Kansas City, Missouri, ceased operations in July and National Airlines, Inc., of Las Vegas, Nevada, did so in November.

Federal loan guarantees. America West Airlines of Phoenix became the first company to be granted a loan guarantee from the Air Transportation Stabilization Board. The airline secured a $900-million guarantee in January before declaring bankruptcy. American Trans Air, Inc., of Indianapolis, Indiana, received a $148.5-million guarantee in September.

Security. The Transportation Security Administration (TSA), an agency of the U.S. Department of Transportation, hired more than 44,000 security screeners in 2002 to replace employees of private companies that had previously conducted airport security procedures. As a result, passengers faced shorter lines at security checkpoints than they had immediately after the September

A German official surveys the wreckage of a Russian jetliner that collided with a cargo plane over Uberlingen, Germany, on July 1, 2002. All 69 passengers aboard the Russian jet, including 52 children, and the two pilots of the cargo plane were killed.

11 attacks. Security screeners asked many people to remove their shoes so that they could be examined for explosives. This measure was taken after a man who later claimed to be a terrorist attempted to light explosives packed into his shoes aboard an American Airlines flight from Paris to Miami, Florida, in December 2001.

President George W. Bush established the TSA in November 2001 to make air travel safer. The agency had required security screeners to hold U.S. citizenship, but in November 2002 a federal judge ruled that this requirement was unconstitutional. In late 2002, it was unclear whether the ruling, which was made as part of a lawsuit filed by several noncitizens, would apply nationwide.

A federal law passed in 2001 also required that by Dec. 31, 2002, all checked bags must be inspected for explosives. By the end of 2002, however, the majority of airports had not yet met this requirement, and airport operators were seeking more time to implement this change.

Electronic ticketing. During 2002, most airlines announced that they would begin charging additional fees to passengers who wanted traditional paper tickets. The airlines said they were moving toward electronic ticketing in an effort to save money and speed travel. In electronic ticketing systems, details of passengers' reservations are stored electronically on the airlines' computer systems. Passengers in 2002 increasingly used computers at major airports to access these electronic records, print out boarding passes, and check their luggage. In an effort to control costs, most airlines also urged travelers to book their tickets directly through the airlines rather than using travel agents or Web sites. Airlines had previously eliminated the sales commissions that they had paid to agents, forcing agents to charge fees. Airlines also began to offer their best fares to customers purchasing tickets from the airlines' official Web sites.

Deep vein thrombosis. In 2002, relatives of several airline passengers filed lawsuits against airlines in the United States, the United Kingdom, and Australia, claiming that long-distance airplane flights had led to the deaths of their family members. The deaths were blamed on a disorder called deep vein thrombosis (DVT), which can occur as a result of cramped conditions in economy-class airline seats. The disorder, which is sometimes called "economy class syndrome," can develop when blood clots form after a person sits still for extended periods of time.

Physicians in Britain and Australia testified in 2002 that the cramped conditions on long flights contribute to an increased risk of DVT. Airline officials disputed this claim.　　□ Ian Savage

See also **United States, Government of the.**

Azerbaijan. President Heydar Aliyev joined the presidents of Georgia and Turkey in September 2002 to launch the construction of a new oil pipeline. The Baku-Tbilisi-Ceyhan pipeline was to carry Azerbaijani oil from the Caspian Sea to the Turkish Mediterranean port of Ceyhan beginning in 2005. Construction of the pipeline was budgeted at nearly $3 billion. Azerbaijani politicians hoped that the new southerly oil export route would reduce the nation's dependence on Russia.

Azerbaijani voters approved a constitutional referendum in August 2002 reforming the country's electoral system. Under the new law, the prime minister, rather than the speaker of the legislature, would replace the president should he die or step down. Because the prime minister is appointed directly by the president, the new system greatly strengthens presidential power. Opposition parties organized a boycott of the vote and claimed that the result was invalid because only 20 percent of the electorate participated. However, the country's Central Electoral Commission claimed that 88 percent of the electorate voted and that 97 percent of them supported the new measure.   □ Steven L. Solnick

See also **Asia; Georgia; Turkey.**

Bahamas. See West Indies.

Bahrain. See Middle East.

Ballet. See Dance.

Bangladesh experienced its worst flooding in four years in 2002. Summer monsoon rains in combination with runoff from rivers that flow into Bangladesh from neighboring countries washed away entire villages, forcing more than 6 million people to evacuate. Approximately 200 people drowned, and dozens of others died from dengue fever, a disease spread by mosquitoes in flooded areas. More than 2,000 people were infected with the disease.

Parliament elected Iajuddin Ahmed, a retired professor, president of Bangladesh in September 2002. He succeeded A. Q. M. Badruddoza Chowdhury, who resigned in June. The position of president is mainly ceremonial.

The United States Department of State in May included a Bangladeshi group among the organizations listed in its annual report on state-sponsored terrorism. The U.S. action followed signs of a growing Islamic fundamentalist movement in Bangladesh, a moderate Islamic country.

The World Bank and the Asian Development Bank, both affiliates of the United Nations, reported in March that Bangladesh's economy grew in the 1990's at a rate of about 5 percent annually. In addition, the percentage of Bangladeshis living in poverty fell from 59 to 50 during the 1990's.   □ Henry S. Bradsher

See also **Asia; Terrorism.**

Bank. Most banks in the United States were profitable in 2002. However, some of the nation's largest banks spent much of the year dealing with the fallout from corporate accounting scandals that shook the business world.

Corporate loans. Several of the largest U.S. banks were troubled in 2002 because of loans to large corporations that later collapsed into bankruptcy. Citigroup, Inc., of New York City, loaned $300 million to WorldCom, Inc., of Clinton, Mississippi, before the telecommunications giant disclosed massive financial fraud in June and in July became the largest U.S. coporation ever to file for bankruptcy. J.P. Morgan Chase & Co., of New York City, made huge loans to Kmart Corporation, of Troy, Michigan, before the retailer filed for protection from its creditors in January; and to Adelphia Communications Corp., of Coudersport, Pennsylvania, which filed for bankruptcy in June.

Enron. Bankers from Citigroup, J.P. Morgan, and Merrill Lynch & Co., also of New York City, faced questions in 2002 from the U.S. Congress, the Justice Department, and the Securities and Exchange Commission (SEC) about loans the banks provided to Houston-based Enron Corp. The SEC is an independent government agency that administers federal laws covering the sale of stocks and bonds. Enron, formerly the largest U.S. energy-trading concern, had filed for bankruptcy in December 2001 after disclosing massive accounting irregularities.

In July 2002, officials from Citigroup and J.P. Morgan were forced to testify before the Senate Permanent Subcommittee on Investigations. Documents disclosed at the hearings revealed that the banks took part in more than $8 billion worth of "prepay deals," in which Enron received money upfront in exchange for agreeing to deliver commodities at a later date. This scheme allowed Enron to keep the transactions off its official accounting records. The bank officials testified that they did not intend to mislead regulators with the transactions.

In August, Citigroup announced that it would no longer provide financing for companies that, like Enron, conceal debts by keeping them off their balance sheets.

Citigroup analyst resigns. One of Citigroup's most prominent analysts, Jack Grubman, who evaluated telecommunications stocks to recommend whether investors should buy them, resigned in August. Grubman had published optimistic earnings forecasts for several companies that had investment banking business with Citigroup. After a large number of the companies he recommended performed poorly, many investors complained that they had been misled by his advice. Government authorities, including Manhattan's district attorney and New York's attorney general, began in 2002 to investigate Grubman's activities.

Other Citigroup problems. In September, Citigroup agreed to pay $215 million in compensation to consumers who were victimized by "predatory lending" by Associates First Capital Corp., a Dallas-based lender that Citigroup acquired in 2000. Predatory lending involves deceptive marketing of mortgages with hidden fees, often to people with poor credit histories.

In October 2002, Citigroup disclosed that it would cut more than 1,000 employees from its corporate and investment banking departments.

The Fed. The Federal Reserve Board (the Fed), an independent government agency that oversees the U.S. banking system, held interest rates steady throughout most of 2002. However, amid signs of a continuing weak economy in November, the Fed cut the *federal funds rate,* the interest rate that banks charge each other for overnight loans, from 1.75 percent to 1.25 percent. The Fed tends to reduce interest rates during times of economic weakness to spur business borrowing. Following the rate cut, some commercial banks lowered their prime lending rate by a half point to 4.25 percent, the lowest rate since 1959.

Overall good health. Despite the weak economy and loans to failing companies, the overall condition of the U.S. banking industry appeared healthy in 2002. For the first half of the year, commercial banks posted earnings of $45.3 billion, a $6.5-billion increase over the first half of 2001. The banking industry's *total assets*—the amount of loans, leases, mortgages, and other investments—increased by $245.1 billion during the second quarter of 2002, ending June 30. This was the largest quarterly increase of industry assets on record. *Interest rate spreads,* the difference between what banks charge for loans and what they pay depositors, were also very favorable for the industry.

Bank profits were bolstered in 2002 by strong demand from consumers for loans. However, commercial loans to businesses showed weakness. The second quarter's net *charge-offs*—loans that banks remove from their books after nonpayment—were about 33 percent higher than a year earlier. Commercial and industrial loans were the largest part of these charge-offs.

Consolidation continues. The banking industry continued to consolidate, a trend that began in the early 1990's. The total number of insured U.S. banks fell to 7,966 during the first half of 2002, compared with more than 9,000 banks in 1997. One commercial bank failed during the second quarter of 2002; 66 banks were merged into other institutions; and 26 new banks began operations.

Deposit insurance bill. The U.S. Congress began considering deposit insurance changes in 2002. A government corporation called the Federal Deposit Insurance Corporation (FDIC) has insured deposits since the 1930's. If a bank fails, insured deposits are guaranteed by the U.S. government up to $100,000 per account.

In May 2002, the House of Representatives voted to raise the limit on federal deposit insurance to $130,000 per account. The legislation would also merge the deposit insurance funds of the banking industry with those of the savings and loan industry. Federal Reserve Chairman Alan Greenspan had earlier expressed his opposition to raising the insurance limit. He said the move would increase the risk that government insurance funds face without adding to the stability of the banking system. The Senate had not voted on the issue by the end of 2002.

The proposed deposit insurance change was controversial because the insurance increase made in 1980, from $40,000 to $100,000 per account, contributed to a huge taxpayer bailout of the savings and loan industry. Hundreds of savings and loans failed in the late 1980's and early 1990's, and the insurance change made the taxpayer liability larger than it would have been otherwise.

☐ Paulette Thomas

See also **Crime; Economics.**

Baseball. The Anaheim Angels capped a remarkable 2002 season by winning their first World Series title in the team's 42-year history. The Angels edged the San Francisco Giants and their star slugger Barry Bonds in a dramatic seven-game World Series that was the first ever between two wild-card teams. The teams set World Series records for most runs scored by two teams (85) and most combined home runs (21).

Strike averted. The Major League Baseball (MLB) Players' Association and baseball team owners averted a season-threatening strike on August 30, when the two groups agreed to a new four-year labor contract. The deal, which was announced just hours before the strike was to begin, avoided what many people expected to be the MLB's ninth work stoppage since 1972. The previous eight labor negotiations had all resulted in a work stoppage.

The owners, who were planning on eliminating two teams—most likely the Minnesota Twins and Montreal Expos—for economic reasons at the end of the 2002 season, agreed to delay any such move until 2006. They also raised the minimum player's salary from $200,000 to $300,000. The players agreed to an increase in the percentage of revenues shared among teams. The system is designed to level the disparity among teams, some of which make much more money than others. The players also agreed to a penalty for teams with payrolls of more than $117 million. Some team owners had long wanted such a "luxury tax," to penalize owners who paid sky-high salaries. For the first time, the players also agreed to submit to random testing for *steroids*, drugs that can enhance a player's performance.

While the strike was averted, the possibility of a work stoppage and fans doubtful about the future of baseball, caused average MLB attendance to drop by more than 6 percent in 2002. The decline in attendance, the second in a row, was the biggest since a strike in 1994 and 1995.

World Series. The Anaheim Angels beat the San Francisco Giants 4 games to 3 in a thrilling series in which the Angels came from behind in each of their wins. The Angels won Game 7 on Oct. 27, 2002. However, the most critical moment of the series came in Game 6, when the Angels, facing elimination, stormed back from a 5-0 deficit to win 6-5 and force Game 7. In Game 6, Scott Spiezio sparked the Angels' rally in the seventh inning with a three-run homer to make the score 5-3. Darin Erstad followed with a solo homer to make it 5-4. In the eighth, the Angels' Troy Glaus, who was later named the Series Most

Final standings in Major League Baseball

American League

American League champions—
Anaheim Angels (defeated Minnesota Twins, 4 games to 1)
World Series champions—
Anaheim Angels (defeated San Francisco Giants, 4 games to 3)

Eastern Division	W.	L.	Pct.	G.B.
New York Yankees	103	58	.640	—
Boston Red Sox	93	69	.574	10½
Toronto Blue Jays	78	84	.481	25½
Baltimore Orioles	67	95	.414	36½
Tampa Bay Devil Rays	55	106	.342	48
Central Division				
Minnesota Twins	94	67	.584	—
Chicago White Sox	81	81	.500	13½
Cleveland Indians	74	88	.457	20½
Kansas City Royals	62	100	.383	32½
Detroit Tigers	55	106	.342	39
Western Division				
Oakland Athletics	103	59	.636	—
Anaheim Angels*	99	63	.611	4
Seattle Mariners	93	69	.574	10
Texas Rangers	72	90	.444	31

Offensive leaders

Batting average	Manny Ramirez, Boston	.349
Runs scored	Alfonso Soriano, New York	128
Home runs	Alex Rodriguez, Texas	57
Runs batted in	Alex Rodriguez, Texas	142
Hits	Alfonso Soriano, New York	209
Stolen bases	Alfonso Soriano, New York	41
Slugging percentage	Jim Thome, Cleveland	.677

Leading pitchers

Games won	Barry Zito, Oakland	23
Earned run average (162 or more innings)—	Pedro Martinez, Boston	2.26
Strikeouts	Pedro Martinez, Boston	239
Saves	Eddie Guardado, Minnesota	45
Shut-outs	Jeff Weaver, Detroit	3
Complete games	Paul Byrd, Kansas City	7

Awards†

Most Valuable Player.........................Miguel Tejada, Oakland
Cy Young ....Barry Zito, Oakland
Rookie of the Year ....Eric Hinske, Toronto
Manager of the Year ....Mike Scioscia, Anaheim

National League

National League champions—
San Francisco Giants (defeated St. Louis Cardinals, 4 games to 1)

Eastern Division	W.	L.	Pct.	G.B.
Atlanta Braves	101	59	.631	—
Montreal Expos	83	79	.512	19
Philadelphia Phillies	80	81	.497	21½
Florida Marlins	79	83	.488	23
New York Mets	75	86	.466	26½
Central Division				
St. Louis Cardinals	97	65	.599	—
Houston Astros	84	78	.519	13
Cincinnati Reds	78	84	.481	19
Pittsburgh Pirates	72	89	.447	24½
Chicago Cubs	67	95	.414	30
Milwaukee Brewers	56	106	.346	41
Western Division				
Arizona Diamondbacks	98	64	.605	—
San Francisco Giants*	95	66	.590	2½
Los Angeles Dodgers	92	70	.568	6
Colorado Rockies	73	89	.451	25
San Diego Padres	66	96	.407	32

Offensive leaders

Batting average	Barry Bonds, San Francisco	.370
Runs scored	Sammy Sosa, Chicago	122
Home runs	Sammy Sosa, Chicago	49
Runs batted in	Lance Berkman, Houston	128
Hits	Vladimir Guerrero, Montreal	206
Stolen bases	Luis Castillo, Florida	48
Slugging percentage	Barry Bonds, San Francisco	.799

Leading pitchers

Games won	Randy Johnson, Arizona	24
Earned run average (162 or more innings)—	Randy Johnson, Arizona	2.32
Strikeouts	Randy Johnson, Arizona	334
Saves	John Smoltz, Atlanta	55
Shut-outs	A.J. Burnett, Florida	5
Complete games	Randy Johnson, Arizona	8

Awards†

Most Valuable Player ....Barry Bonds, San Francisco
Cy Young ....Randy Johnson, Arizona
Rookie of the Year ....Jason Jennings, Colorado
Manager of the Year......................Tony La Russa, St. Louis

*Qualified for wild-card play-off spot.
†Selected by the Baseball Writers Association of America.

the West Division crown and a 103-59 record, second best in baseball behind the New York Yankees, who won the AL East with a 103-58 mark. The Twins rolled to the AL Central crown by 13 ½ games with a 94-67 record. Anaheim won the wild-card spot with a 99-63 mark.

In the NL, Atlanta posted a record of 101-59 and captured the East Division by 19 games over Montreal. St. Louis easily captured the NL Central with a 97-65 mark. Arizona won the West Division with a 98-64 record. The Giants secured the wild-card with a 95-66 record.

Troy Glaus of the Anaheim Angels hits a double in the eighth inning of game 6 of the World Series, driving in what proved to be the winning runs. The victory forced Game 7, which the Angels won on October 27. Glaus was later named World Series Most Valuable Player.

Valuable Player (MVP), hit a clutch two-run double, driving in what proved to be the game-winning runs.

During the World Series, Barry Bonds, who became the first player to hit a home run in his first three World Series games, was 8 for 17 at the plate with 4 home runs and 13 walks. Bonds hit a record eight home runs during the Giants' 2002 postseason run.

Play-offs. The Angels caught fire in the play-offs, coming from behind in 8 of their 11 victories. They stunned New York 3 games to 1, then ended Minnesota's run in the American League (AL) Championship Series 4 games to 1. Minnesota had ousted Oakland 3 games to 2. In the National League (NL), San Francisco toppled Atlanta 3 games to 2, and St. Louis swept Arizona 3 games to none in the first round. San Francisco beat St. Louis 4 games to 1 in the NL Championship Series.

Regular season. In August and early September, the Oakland A's won 20 straight games, setting an AL record. The streak propelled the A's to

Bonds milestones. On August 9, Barry Bonds became only the fourth MLB player to hit 600 career homers, joining Hank Aaron (755), Babe Ruth (714), and Willie Mays (660). Bonds drew a record 68 intentional walks and a record 198 total walks. He also set a record for on-base percentage (.582) and, at 38, became the oldest player to win his first batting title.

Other highlights. Mike Cameron of the Seattle Mariners in a game against the Chicago White Sox on May 2 became only the 13th player to hit four home runs in one game. On May 23 in a game with the Milwaukee Brewers, L.A. Dodgers right fielder Shawn Green matched Cameron's feat, becoming the 14th player to hit four homers in one game. He also set a record for total bases in a game (19). But Green was not finished. He added three homers over the next two games to set a record of seven homers in three games.

Pedro Martinez and Derek Lowe of the Boston Red Sox became the first pair of Red Sox pitchers to win 20 or more games since 1949. Arizona's Curt Schilling and Randy Johnson became the first pitchers on the same team to each strike out 300 batters in a season.

College. The University of Texas at Austin won its fifth National Collegiate Athletic Association

(NCAA) title in school history and its first since 1983 with a 12-6 win over South Carolina on June 22, 2002, in Omaha, Nebraska.

Youth. On August 25, a team from Louisville, Kentucky, became the first team from the United States to win the Little League World Series since 1998. They beat a team from Sendai, Japan, 1-0.

Deaths. St. Louis Cardinals pitcher Darryl Kile, 33, was found dead in his Chicago hotel room on June 22. Medical authorities said his death was due to a heart attack that occurred because of a blocked artery. Kile was the first active player to die during the season since New York Yankees catcher Thurmon Munson in 1979.

Ted Williams, 83, whom many considered to be one of the greatest hitters in the history of baseball, died July 5, 2002, of cardiac arrest in a hospital in Inverness, Florida.

Enos Slaughter, a Hall-of-Fame outfielder best known for scoring the winning run in the 1946 World Series while with the St. Louis Cardinals, died August 12. Knuckleball pitcher Hoyt Wilhelm, who appeared in 1,070 games, died on August 23 at age 86.   □ Michael Kates

See also **Deaths: A Special Report; Sports.**

Basketball. The Los Angeles Lakers won their third straight National Basketball Association (NBA) title in 2002 by sweeping the New Jersey Nets 4 games to 0. The Lakers became only the fifth team in NBA history to win three consecutive titles. Los Angeles head coach Phil Jackson won his ninth title, tying an NBA coaching mark.

Michael Jordan, one of the NBA's all-time great players, attempted another comeback in 2001-2002. His quest ended prematurely when he injured his knee in February. The injury put Jordan, who was playing for the Washington Wizards, on the injured list for only the second time in his career. Jordan ended his season on April 3.

In college basketball, the University of Maryland (College Park) won its first National Collegiate Athletic Association (NCAA) men's title in 2002 and the University of Connecticut, which went undefeated, won the women's title.

Professional men. In the NBA play-offs, the Los Angeles Lakers defeated the New Jersey Nets 113-107 on June 12 in East Rutherford, New Jersey, rallying from a three-point deficit as late as the fourth quarter to seal the title. Lakers center Shaquille O'Neal scored 34 points in the final

National Basketball Association standings

Eastern Conference

Atlantic Division	W.	L.	Pct.	G.B.
New Jersey Nets*	52	30	.634	—
Boston Celtics*	49	33	.598	3
Orlando Magic*	44	38	.537	8
Philadelphia 76ers*	43	39	.524	9
Washington Wizards	37	45	.451	15
Miami Heat	36	46	.439	16
New York Knicks	30	52	.366	22
Central Division				
Detroit Pistons*	50	32	.610	—
Charlotte Hornets*	44	38	.537	6
Toronto Raptors*	42	40	.512	8
Indiana Pacers*	42	40	.512	8
Milwaukee Bucks	41	41	.500	9
Atlanta Hawks	33	49	.402	17
Cleveland Cavaliers	29	53	.354	21
Chicago Bulls	21	61	.256	29

Western Conference

Midwest Division	W.	L.	Pct.	G.B.
San Antonio Spurs*	58	24	.707	—
Dallas Mavericks*	57	25	.695	1
Minnesota Timberwolves*	50	32	.610	8
Utah Jazz*	44	38	.537	14
Houston Rockets	28	54	.341	30
Denver Nuggets	27	55	.329	31
Memphis Grizzlies	23	59	.280	35
Pacific Division				
Sacramento Kings*	61	21	.744	—
Los Angeles Lakers*	58	24	.707	3
Portland Trail Blazers*	49	33	.598	12
Seattle Supersonics*	45	37	.549	16
Los Angeles Clippers	39	43	.476	22
Phoenix Suns	36	46	.439	25
Golden State Warriors	21	61	.256	40

Individual leaders

Scoring	G.	F.G.	F.T.	Pts.	Avg.
Allen Iverson, Philadelphia	60	665	475	1,883	31.4
Shaquille O'Neal, L.A. Lakers	67	712	398	1,822	27.2
Paul Pierce, Boston	82	707	520	2,144	26.1
Tracy McGrady, Orlando	76	715	415	1,948	25.6
Tim Duncan, San Antonio	82	764	560	2,089	25.5
Kobe Bryant, L.A. Lakers	80	749	488	2,019	25.2
Vince Carter, Toronto	60	559	245	1,484	24.7
Dirk Nowitzki, Dallas	76	600	440	1,779	23.4
Karl Malone, Utah	80	635	509	1,788	22.4
Antoine Walker, Boston	81	666	240	1,794	22.1
Gary Payton, Seattle	81	737	267	1,815	22.1

Rebounding	G.	Off.	Def.	Tot.	Avg.
Ben Wallace, Detroit	80	318	721	1,039	13.0
Tim Duncan, San Antonio	82	268	774	1,042	12.7
Kevin Garnett, Minnesota	81	243	738	981	12.1
Danny Fortson, Golden State	77	290	609	899	11.7
Elton Brand, L.A. Clippers	80	396	529	925	11.6
D. Mutombo, Philadelphia	80	254	609	863	10.8
Jermaine O'Neal, Indiana	72	188	569	757	10.5
Dirk Nowitzki, Dallas	76	120	635	755	9.9
Shawn Marion, Phoenix	81	211	593	804	9.9
P.J. Brown, Charlotte	80	273	513	786	9.8

NBA champions—Los Angeles Lakers
(defeated New Jersey Nets, 4 games to 0)

*Made play-offs

game, giving him 145 points in the four games. This made him the all-time highest scorer in a four-game series. O'Neal also broke NBA finals records for free-throw attempts (68), free throws made (45), and shots blocked (11) in a four-game series. He averaged more than 36 points and 12 rebounds per game. O'Neal was named the Finals Most Valuable Player for the third straight year, a feat that had previously been accomplished only by Michael Jordan.

Phil Jackson's ninth NBA title tied him with legendary Boston Celtics head coach Arnold "Red" Auerbach, whom many fans considered to be one of the greatest innovators of the game. Jackson also picked up his 156th career play-off win, passing the Miami Heat's Pat Riley to become the coach with the most play-off victories.

During their play-off run, the Lakers received their strongest challenge in the Western Conference finals from the Sacramento Kings. The Kings, who had posted the best regular-season record, 61 wins and 21 losses, grabbed a 3-games-to-2 lead on Los Angeles with a 92-91 victory on May 28. The Lakers came back to win Game 6 in Los Angeles and then prevailed 112-106 in overtime on June 2 in Sacramento in Game 7. To reach the conference finals, the Lakers had defeated Portland in three games in the first round and beat the San Antonio Spurs 4 games to 1 in the conference semifinals.

The Nets reached the NBA finals by defeating the Boston Celtics 4 games to 2 in the Eastern Conference finals in a battle between two teams that had failed to make the play-offs in the 2001-2002 season. In Game 3 of the series on May 25, 2002, the Boston Celtics pulled off the biggest fourth-quarter comeback in NBA play-off history, rallying from 21 points down to win 94-90. The Celtics' victory, which gave them a 2-games-to-1 lead in the series, was the first time in NBA play-offs history that a team leading by 19 points going into the fourth quarter had ever lost.

Many observers did not think that the Nets could recover from such a devastating defeat, but the team surprised its critics, winning three consecutive games to take the best-of-seven series. To reach the conference finals, the Nets had beaten the Indiana Pacers 3 games to 2 in the first round and Charlotte 4 games to 1 in the semifinals.

The Nets and the Detroit Pistons surprised many fans with their success in the regular season. The Nets finished with a record of 52 wins and 30 losses, the best in the Eastern Conference. The Pistons, which were not expected to be a strong team, won the Central Division with a regular-season record of 50 wins and 32 losses.

In the Western Conference, the Sacramento Kings won the Pacific Division with a regular-sea-

The 2001-2002 college basketball season

College tournament champions

NCAA	(Men)	Division I:	Maryland
		Division II:	Metropolitan State (Colorado)
		Division III:	Otterbein
	(Women)	Division I:	Connecticut
		Division II:	California State Polytechnic
		Division III:	Wisconsin-Stevens Point
NAIA	(Men)	Division I:	Science and Arts (Oklahoma)
		Division II:	Evangel (Missouri)
	(Women)	Division I:	Oklahoma City
		Division II:	Hastings (Nebraska)
NIT	(Men)		Memphis

Men's college champions

Conference	School
America East	Vermont
	Boston University (tournament)
Atlantic 10	
East Division	Temple
West Division	Xavier*
Atlantic Coast	Maryland
	Duke (tournament)
Atlantic Sun	Georgia State
	Florida Atlantic (tournament)
Big 12	Kansas
	Oklahoma (tournament)
Big East	
East Division	Connecticut*
West Division	Pittsburgh
Big Sky	Montana State
	Montana (tournament)
Big South	Winthrop
Big Ten	Ohio State*–Illinois–Indiana–Wisconsin
Big West	Utah State–California (Irvine) (tie)
	California (Santa Barbara) (tournament)
Colonial	UNC Wilmington*
Conference USA	
American Division	Cincinnati*
National Division	Memphis
Horizon League	Butler
	Illinois at Chicago (tournament)
Ivy League	Pennsylvania†
Metro Atlantic	Marist–Rider (tie)
	Siena (tournament)
Mid-American	
East Division	Kent State*
West Division	Ball State
Mid-Continent	Valparaiso*
Mid-Eastern	Hampton*
Missouri Valley	Creighton*–Southern Illinois
Mountain West	Wyoming
	San Diego State (tournament)
Northeast	Central Connecticut*
Ohio Valley	Tennessee Tech
	Murray State (tournament)
Pacific 10	Oregon
	Arizona (tournament)
Patriot League	American
	Holy Cross (tournament)
Southeastern	Mississippi State (tournament)
Eastern Division	Florida–Georgia–Kentucky (tie)
Western Division	Alabama
Southern	
North Division	Davidson*–NC Greensboro–E. Tenn. St.
South Division	Charleston–Georgia (S.)–Chattanooga
Southland	McNeese State*
Southwestern	Alcorn State*
Sun Belt	
East Division	Western Kentucky*
West Division	Louisiana (Lafayette)
West Coast	Gonzaga*–Pepperdine (tie)
Western Athletic	Hawaii*

*Regular season and conference tournament champion.
†No tournament played.
Sources: National Collegiate Athletic Association (NCAA); National Association of Intercollegiate Athletics (NAIA); National Invitation Tournament (NIT); Conference Web sites.

Lonny Baxter (#35) of Maryland goes up for a rebound with Jeff Newton (#50) of Indiana during the NCAA championship game on April 1, 2002, in Atlanta, Georgia. Maryland won the game, defeating Indiana 64 to 52 for the men's national basketball crown.

son record of 61 and 21, three games ahead of the Lakers. The San Antonio Spurs won the Midwest Division with a record of 58 and 24.

Detroit captured three regular season awards, for coach of the year (Rick Carlisle), defensive player of the year (Ben Wallace), and sixth-man of the year (Corliss Williamson). San Antonio's Tim Duncan won the regular-season MVP award. He was joined on the All-NBA first team by the Lakers' O'Neal and Kobe Bryant, Orlando's Tracy McGrady, and the Nets' Jason Kidd. Pau Gasol of the Memphis Grizzlies was named rookie of the year.

Professional women. On August 31, the Los Angeles Sparks won their second straight Women's National Basketball Association title by defeating the New York Liberty 69 to 66. The Sparks swept the Liberty two games to none.

College men. On April 1, the University of Maryland Terrapins beat the Indiana University Hoosiers 64-52 in Atlanta, Georgia, to win the NCAA basketball championship. Maryland's Juan Dixon netted a game-high 18 points.

To get to the title game, Maryland, the top seed in the East bracket, beat the University of Kansas at Lawrence, the top-seed in the Midwest, by a score of 97 to 88 on March 30. Indiana, a fifth seed in the South bracket, stunned top-seeded Duke in the third round. Indiana ended the impressive run of 10th-seeded Kent State in the fourth round, 81 to 69. Indiana then beat the University of Oklahoma at Norman, the second seed in the West, 73-64, in the national semifinals. The top seed in the West, the University of Cincinnati, had already been upset by the University of California at Los Angeles (UCLA).

In November, officials at the University of Michigan at Ann Arbor punished the school's basketball program after a fan was found to have given more than $600,000 to several players in the 1990's. The team forfeited 112 regular-season and tournament games dating back to 1992, including two NCAA tournament appearances, and was banned from postseason play in 2003.

College women. The University of Connecticut (UConn) Huskies (39-0) capped their undefeated season by toppling the University of Oklahoma at Norman, 82 to 70, on March 31 in San Antonio, Texas. Connecticut's Swin Cash scored 20 points and grabbed 13 rebounds in the game and was named the Final Four most outstanding player. The Huskies became only the fourth team to go unbeaten since women's basketball came under NCAA control in 1981. Some observers claimed that UConn was the best team in the history of women's college basketball. Not only did they win every game they played, but they never trailed in the second half. UConn's 39 victories tied the NCAA record.

To reach the final game, UConn beat Tennessee, the second seed in the West, 79 to 56 in the national semifinals on March 29, 2002. Oklahoma reached the finals by beating Duke, the top seed in the East, 86 to 71.   ☐ Michael Kates
See also **Sports.**

Belarus. Plans for Belarus to reunite with Russia stumbled in 2002. Belarusian President Aleksandr Lukashenko complained in April that the integration process was proceeding too slowly. In June, he proposed an accelerated timetable for unifying the two nations' economies during a meeting with Russian President Vladimir Putin in St. Petersburg. Political analysts noted that following the meeting, Putin appeared to be withdrawing his support for some of the unification measures endorsed by former Russian President Boris Yeltsin in a 1997 charter between the two countries. In particular, Putin offered Belarus little more than the prospect of becoming a constituent province within the Russian Federation.

The Russian president forced the issue in August 2002 by proposing a timetable for integrating Belarus into Russia. Putin's proposal called for a referendum on the merger in May 2003 with an election of a unified parliament the following December. Lukashenko called the plan an "insulting" attempt to "dissolve" Belarus, making it clear that he would not support any reunification plan in which Belarus was not an equal partner. Political experts believed that Putin's unwillingness to accept Lukashenko's demands could spell the end of efforts to reunify the two nations.

☐ Steven L. Solnick
See also **Europe; Russia.**

Belgium. The Belgian economy remained sluggish for a second straight year in 2002, as the country was affected by the widespread slowdown across Europe. European Union economists forecast that Belgium's *gross domestic product* (the value of all goods and services produced in a year) would increase by only 0.7 percent in 2002, compared with a 0.8 percent increase in 2001. The unemployment rate edged up slightly in 2002, to 6.8 percent from 6.6 percent, after several years of decline.

The government pursued a policy of tax cuts designed to stimulate growth by reducing tax rates, which were among the highest in Europe. The government launched the first of a series of income-tax reductions that were supposed to cut taxes by 15 percent between 2002 and 2006. In March 2002, the government announced that it would reduce the tax rate on corporate profits to 34 percent from 40 percent, effective in 2003.

A new national airline, SN Brussels Airlines, was launched in February 2002. SN was formed using some of the aircraft, workers, and flight routes of Sabena, the old Belgian airline, which began liquidation proceedings in November 2001. Aviation industry experts attributed Sabena's demise to the bankruptcy of its controlling owner, Swissair, and the slowdown in air traffic after the terrorist attacks on the United States in 2001.

Euthanasia. A national debate about euthanasia, or mercy killing, erupted in 2002, after Belgium became the second European country (after the Netherlands) to legalize the procedure. Parliament passed a law legalizing euthanasia, which took effect in September. One week later, Mario Verstraete, a 39-year-old man with multiple sclerosis, requested and received a lethal injection. His death angered opponents of euthanasia, because Verstraete was not in the final stages of a terminal illness, and his physician did not respect the law's one-month waiting period.

Sex crimes. A court case in 2002 renewed national concerns about pedophilia. The case was the most notorious sex crime since the 1996 arrest of Marc Dutroux for the kidnapping, rape, and murder of four girls.

In September 2002, a former bar owner in the southern Belgian town of Sainte-Ode was convicted of sexually abusing his two daughters and prostituting one of them. The man and six other people, including the girls' stepmother and the family physician, were imprisoned. Also in September, a Belgian court instituted proceedings to begin Dutroux's trial in 2003.   ☐ Tom Buerkle
See also **Europe.**

Belize. See Latin America.
Benin. See Africa.
Bhutan. See Asia.

Biology. Biologists discovered a number of previously unknown animal species in 2002. Most were found in largely unexplored regions of the world, such as the Amazon jungles in South America. However, one species was found in a very surprising place—Central Park in New York City.

Researchers from the American Museum of Natural History in New York City, searching through leaf litter in Central Park, discovered a new type of centipede. The scientists reported in July that the creature, named *Nannarrup hoffmani,* may be the smallest centipede on Earth. It is about half an inch (1.3 centimeters) long—less than half the length of the previously known smallest centipede.

N. hoffmani is light yellow with short antennae and 41 pairs of legs. The scientists said it is not only a new species, but it also belongs to a brand new *family* (large group of related species) of centipedes. They added, however, that *N. hoffmani* resembles some centipedes that live in Asia. This raised the possibility that the Central Park centipede may be descended from centipedes that were brought to the United States in potting soil.

New Amazon monkeys. In June, researchers from Conservation International, a conservation organization based in Washington, D.C., an-

nounced the discovery of two new species of titi monkey in the central Amazon basin in Brazil. Primate expert Marc van Roosmalen of the National Institute for Amazon Research in Brazil identified the monkeys.

Titi monkeys are about the size of a small house cat. They live in the dense *understory* (low-level trees and plants) of South American forests in small family groups. One of the new species, named *Callicebus bernhardi,* has dark orange sideburns and orange fur on its chest and the inner sides of its arms and legs. Its back is reddish-brown, and it has a white-tipped black tail. The other species, *Callicebus stephennashi,* is mainly silver with a black forehead and red sideburns. Its chest and inner sides of limbs are also red.

The monkeys were the 37th and 38th new primate species discovered worldwide since 1990, according to Conservation International. With the 2002 discoveries, Brazil had 95 known species of primates, far more than any other country.

New Brazilian parrot. Biologists at the University of Sao Paulo in Brazil reported in May that they had identified a previously unknown species of parrot in the Brazilian state of Para. The parrot was found in the Amazon jungle near the Madeira River. The bird is about 10 inches (25 centimeters) long from head to tail. It has mostly green feathers, with an orange head and a vul-

The first kitten created through cloning snuggles against its surrogate mother, the female that gave it birth. Scientists at Texas A&M University in College Station announced in February 2002 that the kitten was genetically identical to a 2-year-old female cat from which a body cell had been taken.

turelike hooked neck. The bird was the fourth new parrot species discovered in South America since 1988.

Flying snakes explained. A small group of snakes in Southeast Asia has long puzzled biologists by their ability to "fly," or glide for long distances from trees to the ground. In August 2002, *herpetologist* (amphibian and reptile expert) John J. Socha of the University of Chicago offered an explanation.

Other animals that can glide for long distances, such as flying squirrels and lizards, do so by spreading skin flaps that act somewhat like miniature wings. Flying snakes, however, do not have skin flaps, so scientists did not understand how they accomplished their "flights." Socha studied the paradise tree snake, or *Chrysopelea paradisi*. He brought the snakes to the top of a tower 33 feet (10 meters) high and observed the reptiles as they launched themselves into the air. Socha videotaped the flights from two different angles. This allowed him to later view the snakes' motions in three dimensions.

Socha reported that the snakes flatten their bodies to twice the normal width and form a concave channel in their bellies. This makes the snakes' bodies function like an *airfoil* (a surface that helps create lift). The snakes sway their bodies from side to side while they are airborne, steering with their heads. They can even change course in midair. Most of the snakes landed about 33 feet (10 meters) from the tower, but one long-distance champion consistently traveled more than 66 feet (20 meters). These distances were much farther than would be possible if the snakes were simply falling.

Socha said the unusual behavior probably evolved to prevent injury or death from falls and to help the snakes move quickly from treetop to treetop as they chase prey or escape predators.

Super ants. A supercolony of ants that stretches more than 3,700 miles (5,950 kilometers) from Italy to Spain was described in April by biologist Laurent Keller of the University of Lausanne in Switzerland. A supercolony is a collection of colonies operating as a single colony. A similar kind of ant supercolony stretches from Mexico to Oregon, but it is only one-third as large as the one in Europe.

The European supercolony consists of billions of Argentine ants, or *Linepithema humile*, living in millions of nests. The ants were accidentally introduced into Europe during the 1920's, possibly on imported plants. Normally, Argentine ants from different nests fight each other to the death whenever they meet. Keller proposed that the Argentina ants in Europe cooperate because they are genetically similar, even though they come from different queen ants. This lack of ge-

netic variability is due to the fact that the ants are all descended from the relatively small number of ants that arrived in the 1920's.

Keller said cooperative behavior allows the ants to live in a much more dense distribution than normal. He explained that Argentine ants from different nests work together to eliminate other species of ants in the area rather than fight other ants of their own kind.

Love those hot peppers. Some tropical birds are known to regularly eat the hottest of chili peppers—peppers that bring tears to the eyes of people and send them running for water. Molecular biologists at the University of California at San Francisco explained in February how the birds tolerate such spicy foods.

The key ingredient in chili peppers is a chemical called capsaicin. This chemical produces the burning sensation in people by binding to a *receptor* (the part of a cell that attaches to and reacts with chemical compounds) on tongue cells. This receptor is called vanilloid receptor 1, or VR1. The biologists reported that birds have a slightly different version of VR1 than people. The bird receptor does not bind to capsaicin. Thus, to birds, peppers are as mild as peas.

This ability of birds to eat peppers actually benefits the pepper plants. The pepper seeds pass through the birds' digestive system and are widely dispersed in their droppings.

War on northern snakehead. In September, officials with the Maryland Department of Natural Resources (DNR) poisoned a pond in Crofton, Maryland, that had become infested with an alien fish called the northern snakehead. Northern snakeheads are a predatory fish native to China. They can grow to 3 feet (0.9 meter) in length and will eat virtually anything they can fit into their large jaws. Snakeheads also have an air sac in their digestive system that can take in oxygen from the atmosphere. The air sac makes it possible for the fish to flop from one waterhole to another, an adaptation useful when rice paddies and irrigation ditches in China dry out seasonally. Maryland officials feared that the air-breathing fish might migrate from the Crofton pond to the Little Patuxent River, which is only 75 yards (69 meters) away. Once in the river, the snakehead could have destroyed many native species.

A local man admitted to dumping a pair of the snakeheads into the pond in 2000 after purchasing them at a New York City market. By the time of the poisoning, there were at least 100 snakeheads in the pond.

After the poisoning, DNR officials reported that tests indicated the alien fish had been wiped out. The officials planned to restock the pond with native fish. □ Thomas H. Maugh II

See also **Conservation.**

Team New Zealand sails toward the finish line ahead of OneWorld Challenge of the United States on its way to winning the Road to the America's Cup regatta on Feb. 12, 2002. The race was held off the coast of New Zealand near Auckland.

Boating. Germany's *Illbruck Challenge* won the Volvo Ocean Race on June 9, 2002, beating Sweden's *Assa Abloy*. The race began on Sept. 23, 2001. It was the 29th running of the 32,700-mile (52,600-kilometer) race but the first under its new name. The race had previously been called the Whitbread.

Assa Abloy was the only close competitor to *Illbruck Challenge*. Going into the final leg, a 250-mile (402-kilometer) sprint from Goteborg, Sweden, to Kiel, Germany, *Assa Abloy* needed to take first place and *Illbruck* had to finish worse than fifth place for *Assa Abloy* to win.

The critical moment in the ninth leg came when leaders *SEB* of Sweden, Australia's *News Corporation,* and Bermuda's *Tyco* headed west of Anhalt Island in the Baltic Sea, lost the wind and were forced to drop anchor. Norway's *Djuice*, *Illbruck*, and *Assa* chose to hug the Swedish coast

and took the lead. *Djuice* won the leg, followed by *Illbruck* and *Assa Abloy*. Still, *Illbruck* maintained enough of a lead to win the overall race.

World championships. Pasquale Landolfi's *Brava Q8* captured the Division A class in the Rolex IMS Offshore World Championship on May 25, 2002. Manfredo Toninelli's *Team Revolution* won the Division B class. Spain's Iker Martinez and Xabi Fernandez took the 49er World Championship regatta on June 22 in Kaneohe Bay, Hawaii, edging out two British teams—Chris Draper and Simon Hiscocks, who took second, and Paul Brotherton and Mark Asquith, who finished third. Monica Azon, Laia Tutzo, and Sandra Azon of Spain won the women's Yngling World Championship on July 26. Simon Cooke and Peter Nicholas of New Zealand won the 470 World Championships on September 11. Robert Scheidt of Brazil secured the Laser World Masters Championship September 18, while Darren Bundock and John Forbes of Australia won the Tornado world championship on September 28.

World Sailing Games. France took the King's Cup at the World Sailing Games held June 29 through July 10 off Marseille, France. The French captured four golds, four silvers, and one bronze. Australia and Italy tied for second.

Powerboats. Dave Villwock captured the fifth Gold Cup of his career on July 14 in Detroit, piloting his Unlimited Hydroplane, *Miss Budweiser,* to victory.

Jones dies. Warren Jones, 65, who played a critical role in Australia's snapping the United States 132-year winning streak in the America's Cup, died May 17, 2002, after a stroke. Jones directed the Australia II syndicate that beat U.S. skipper Dennis Conner in Newport, Rhode Island, to win the Cup in 1983.   □ Michael Kates

Bolivia. See Latin America.

Books. See Literature, American; Literature, World; Literature for children.

Bosnia-Herzegovina. Officials of the
United Nations, the North Atlantic Treaty Organization (NATO), and other international entities urged leaders in Bosnia-Herzegovina in 2002 to strengthen multiethnic institutions. However, nationalist parties, which represent specific ethnic groups, defeated more moderate, multiethnic parties in nationwide elections in October.

Bosnian leaders found it difficult to strengthen multiethnic institutions because of the way the country is structured. The Dayton Accords, the 1995 agreement that ended the civil war between Bosnian Serbs and Muslims, created two mini-states within Bosnia—the Serb-controlled Republika Srpska and the Muslim-controlled Muslim-Croat federation. The two entities share power, but each has its own parliament and president. Bosnia also has a national government, with a national parliament and a joint presidency. Three individuals—a Muslim, a Croat, and a Serb—share this largely symbolic office.

Elections. Nationalist parties made gains at most levels of Bosnia-Herzegovina's government in elections held on Oct. 5, 2002. In the multiethnic Muslim-Croat federation, the moderate, governing Socialist Democratic Party lost ground to the chief nationalist Muslim and Croat parties. In the all-Bosnia national parliament, the three main nationalist parties—Muslim, Croat, and

Serb—also did well, winning about half the available seats. Hardline nationalists also won the three positions in Bosnia's joint presidency, replacing moderates elected in 2000.

International relations. Under pressure from NATO officials, the three presidents of Bosnia's joint presidency agreed in August 2002 to set up a standing committee for military matters to coordinate the separate Muslim-Croat and Serb armed forces in Bosnia. NATO officials said that Bosnia could not join the Partnership for Peace until it integrated its armed forces. NATO established the Partnership for Peace program in 1994 to allow nonmembers, especially formerly Communist countries of Eastern Europe, to participate in NATO military planning and exercises.

Bosnian Foreign Minister Zlatko Lagumdzija pledged in 2002 to cooperate with the United States in the U.S. war on terrorism. In April, Bosnian officials supplied U.S. law enforcement officials with information that led to the arrest in Chicago of a suspect with alleged links to the al-Qa'ida terrorist network. In July, Bosnian police in Sarajevo, the capital and largest city of Bosnia-Herzegovina, arrested two men believed to be linked to terrorist leader Osama Bin Laden.

□ Sharon L. Wolchik

See also **Europe.**

Botswana. See Africa.

Bowling. Walter Ray Williams, Jr., and Chris
Barnes were locked in a tight race for the PBA Player of the Year Award midway through the 2002-2003 Professional Bowlers Association (PBA) season. Both were at the top of the major statistical categories on the men's tour. In the Professional Women's Bowling Association (PWBA), Michelle Feldman and Leanne Barrette ended the season leading the major statistical categories.

PBA. Walter Ray Williams, Jr., of Ocala, Florida, led in earnings ($105,250) and in average (227.43) midway through the 2002-2003 PBA season. Chris Barnes of Dallas led in player point rankings, was second in earnings, and third in average, despite the fact that he did not win a single title in 2002. Williams won only one tournament in 2002, the Greater Detroit Open in November. He defeated Brian Voss of Atlanta, Georgia, in the championship match 215 to 193.

Williams nearly won the Miller High Life Open in Vernon Hills, Illinois, on November 3, only to be defeated by Danny Wiseman of Baltimore in the championship match. Wiseman nearly bowled a perfect game in the match, defeating Williams 277 to 237.

Parker Bohn III, who won PBA Player of the Year honors in 2001-2002, won his 29th and 30th career titles in 2002. On January 6, he captured the Earl Anthony Memorial Classic in Kirkland,

Washington. On March 17, Bohn won the Battle of Little Creek in Norfolk, Virginia.

PWBA. Michelle Feldman of Skaneateles, New York, and Leanne Barrette of Pleasanton, California, battled throughout the 2002 PWBA season, but Feldman ended the season leading in both earnings ($82,405) and points (11,101.875). Barrette had the best average (216.45) but finished behind Feldman with $72,960 in earnings and 11,041.563 points.

Carolyn Dorin-Ballard of North Richland Hills, Texas, also enjoyed a winning season. Dorin-Ballard, who was named PWBA Player of the Year in 2001, captured two titles in 2002. She took the Dallas Open in July and won the Burlington Open in Burlington, North Carolina, in September.

Seniors. Pete Couture of Titusville, Florida, became the only player on the PBA Senior Tour to win more than one title in 2002, when he captured the PBA Senior Jackson Open in Jackson, Michigan, in August. Couture had already won the American Bowling Congress Senior Masters in May. At the Senior Jackson Open, Couture defeated rookie Senior Tour bowler Vince Mazzanti, Jr., of Levittown, Pennsylvania, 2 games to 1 in the best-of-three final. Couture ranked second in earnings on the Senior Tour but did not finish in the top 10 in average or points. □ Michael Kates

Boxing. Two big bouts highlighted the 2002 boxing season. In June, Michael Tyson and Lennox Lewis tangled in a long-awaited heavyweight title fight. In September, Oscar de la Hoya faced his bitter superwelterweight rival Fernando Vargas.

Lewis vs. Tyson. Lennox Lewis tamed the legend of "Iron" Mike Tyson by knocking out the ex-champion in the eighth round on June 8 in Memphis, Tennessee. With the win, Lewis retained his International Boxing Federation (IBF) and World Boxing Council (WBC) heavyweight titles. Tyson won the first round but quickly faded to Lewis's barrage of right-hand blows. Lewis knocked Tyson out with a crushing right 2 minutes and 25 seconds into the eighth round.

The Tyson-Lewis fight was notable in that it almost did not happen. Tyson bit Lewis on the leg during a January press conference in Las Vegas, Nevada. After the altercation, the Nevada State Athletic Commission rejected Tyson's application for a boxing license, forcing promoters to move the fight to Memphis.

De la Hoya vs. Vargas. In the second high-profile fight, Oscar de la Hoya scored a technical knockout against his bitter rival Fernando Vargas on September 14 in Las Vegas. De la Hoya, who had not fought in 15 months, battled with a bloody nose before wearing Vargas down. He won 1 minute and 48 seconds into the 11th round. With the win, de la Hoya, with 35 career wins and 2 losses, retained his WBC super welterweight title and captured Vargas's World Boxing Association superwelterweight title.

On September 27, officials with the the Nevada Athletic Commission announced that steroids had been found in Vargas's urine in a test taken after his bout with de la Hoya. Vargas disputed the results, saying he only took nutritional supplements provided by his trainers. He requested a second test. Commission officials had warned both fighters that they would be tested after the bout.

Trinidad retires. Felix "Tito" Trinidad, who fought in three weight classes and compiled a career record of 41 wins and 1 loss, retired in July. Trinidad said he retired after learning he would likely not get a rematch with Bernard Hopkins, who had knocked out Trinidad in September 2001 to take his WBC middleweight title.

Fighter dies. Pedro Alcazar of Panama died on June 24, 2002, in Las Vegas, 36 hours after losing a World Boxing Organization junior bantamweight title fight with Fernando Montiel. Physicians who examined Alcazar after the fight noticed no major injuries, but he suffered brain swelling hours later. □ Michael Kates

World champion boxers

World Boxing Association

Division	Champion	Country	Date won
Heavyweight	John Ruiz	Puerto Rico	3/01
Light heavyweight	Bruno Girard	France	12/01
Middleweight	William Joppy	United States	11/01
Welterweight	Ricardo Mayorga	Nicaragua	3/02
Lightweight	Leonard Dorin	Canada	1/02
Featherweight	Derrick Gainer	United States	9/00
Bantamweight	Johnny Bredahl	Denmark	4/02
Flyweight	Eric Morel	Puerto Rico	8/00

World Boxing Council

Division	Champion	Country	Date won
Heavyweight	Lennox Lewis	United Kingdom	11/01
Light heavyweight	Roy Jones, Jr.	United States	7/97
Middleweight	Bernard Hopkins	United States	9/01
Welterweight	Vernon Forrest	United States	1/02
Lightweight	Floyd Mayweather	United States	4/02
Featherweight	Erik Morales	Mexico	11/02
Bantamweight	Veeraphol Sahaprom	Thailand	12/98
Flyweight	Pongsaklek Wonjongkam	Thailand	3/01

Brazil. Luiz Inacio Lula da Silva of the leftist Workers Party was sworn in for a four-year term as Brazil's president on Jan. 1, 2003. Da Silva, known as "Lula" by Brazilians, won over 61 percent of the vote—more than 52 million votes—in runoff elections in October 2002. His opponent, Jose Serra of the ruling Social Democratic Party, received about 39 percent of the final tally. The almost two-to-one electoral margin was the widest in Brazil's history.

Da Silva was born to peasant parents and had been a lathe operator. He had run unsuccessfully for president of Brazil three previous times as the candidate of the Workers Party. After his election, da Silva sought to reassure Brazilian business leaders and international investors that Brazil would live up to its financial obligations—even while striving to create 10 million new jobs. Da Silva also invited the business leaders and investors to participate in a new "social pact" aimed at reducing disparities between the country's rich and poor.

IMF loan. In August, the International Monetary Fund (IMF), a United Nations-affiliated organization that assists nations in financial difficulties, approved $30 billion in new financing for Brazil. The IMF mandated that the bulk of this assistance—$24 billion—could go to Brazil only if the incoming government was able to maintain a budget surplus of at least 3.75 percent of the national economic output. Many Brazilians condemned this IMF condition as improper meddling in Brazilian affairs that would limit the flexibility of the new administration. However, the IMF's loan approval helped dispel uncertainty among international investors, who were concerned about da Silva's intentions, including the possibility that Brazil might default on its $264-billion public debt.

Milestone for black women. In April, Benedita da Silva became the first black woman in Brazilian history to hold the post of governor. Benedita da Silva, who had been the lieutenant governor of the state of Rio de Janeiro, became governor when Anthony Garotinho resigned the office to make what proved to be an unsuccessful run for the presidency. Da Silva was born in a Rio slum and worked as a maid and street vendor before entering politics as a Worker Party official in the early 1980's. She achieved a succession of firsts for black women in Brazil—member of Rio's city council, federal deputy and senator, and finally, lieutenant governor and governor. In October 2002, she lost her bid for a gubernatorial term in her own right.

Drug gangs. Many political experts blamed Governor da Silva's defeat on an outbreak of violence in Rio de Janeiro before the election. On September 30, slum-based gangs armed with machine guns terrorized the city. The gangs, which were engaged in illegal drug trafficking, shut down stores, schools, banks, offices, and markets to protest allegedly poor conditions in prisons, where many of their fellow gang members were confined. In mid-October, gang members sprayed machine gun fire at the governor's palace, threw a hand grenade at a shopping mall, and assaulted police stations and patrol cars. Rio drug gangs were also involved in a number of prison uprisings in 2002.

Oil company deal. Officials with Brazil's state-controlled oil company, Petroleo Brasileiro (Petrobas), announced in July that the company had acquired a controlling stake in Perez Companc, the second-largest Argentine oil company.

Petrobas, which already owned 700 gasoline stations in Argentina, predicted that the $1-billion acquisition would expand its production by 12 percent.

World Cup. Brazilians celebrated a record fifth World Cup victory in August. Their national soccer team defeated Germany 2 to 0 before a capacity crowd at the International Stadium in Yokohama, Japan. Brazil's star striker Ronaldo scored both goals. ☐ Nathan A. Haverstock

See also **Argentina; Latin America; People in the news** (da Silva, Luiz Inacio Lula; Ronaldo); Soccer.

British Columbia. See Canadian provinces.

Brunei. See Asia.

Building and construction. Major progress was made in 2002 on the cleanup of the World Trade Center complex in New York City, one of the sites of the terrorist attacks against the United States on Sept. 11, 2001. Experts said that, despite the progress, it would take years to rebuild the complex and to clean up the damage done in the area surrounding the Trade Center.

Scotland's Falkirk Wheel, which opened in June 2002, raises and lowers up to four boats at a time 115 feet (35 meters) between two canals that connect Glasgow and Edinburgh. The wheel, part of a $127-million waterways renovation project, replaced a system of 11 locks through which boats previously had to travel to transfer from one canal to the other.

In all, seven buildings that had been part of the World Trade Center complex either collapsed or were demolished for safety reasons. In addition, several surrounding structures were severely damaged in the terrorist attacks. By April 2002, workers had removed more than 1.5 million tons (1.36 million metric tons) of debris from the site. This, however, was just the beginning of the cleanup effort.

Winter Garden rebuilt. The biggest and most visible repair project at the World Trade Center site was the $50-million renovation of the 45,000-square-foot (4,180-square-meter) Winter Garden, which was reopened to the public on September 17. Designed by Cesar Pelli and first opened in 1988, the glass atrium had provided a pedestrian link between the World Financial Center, the Trade Center, and mass transit systems. Immediately after the attack, engineers doubted that the 10-story steel and glass barrel vault that is the centerpiece of the structure would remain standing.

However, a team of architects, engineers, and community groups set an ambitious goal of reopening the Winter Garden by September 2002. To accomplish this, engineers devised an ingenious exterior hoist-and-trolley system to speed the repairs of the building's structural steel. Using the new hoist-and-trolley system, workers were able to replace 60,000 square feet (5,570 square meters) of glass in only four and a half months. Such a huge job would normally have taken more than two years. Many people viewed the completion of the reconstruction project at the Winter Garden as symbolic of the rebuilding of New York City itself after the terrorist attacks.

Subway stations reopened. Officials with the New York Metropolitan Transit Authority (MTA) reopened three subway stations on September 15 that had been damaged when the towers collapsed. The stations were finished more than one month ahead of schedule. With the reopenings, the MTA resumed full service of the rail system that serves about 4.8 million passengers daily. Workers continued to rebuild two commuter rail tunnels that had provided access to the World Trade Center from New Jersey before the attacks. The tunnels were to be reopened in 2003. By late 2002, New York City transit agencies were expected to unveil plans for a major transit hub in Lower Manhattan that would integrate subways, commuter rail, and ferries.

Redeveloping the Trade Center. The Lower Manhattan Redevelopment Corporation, the agency charged with implementing the final rebuilding plan for the World Trade Center, chose six teams of architects in September to develop preliminary plans. The final plan must include a memorial to those who died in the attacks, preferably located on the exact site where the World Trade Center towers stood; a panoramic view of New York City's skyline; and approximately the same amount of commercial office space as the original World Trade Center.

Desalination plant. The largest and most efficient desalination plant in North America began operating in Tampa Bay, Florida, in December 2002. Desalination plants produce drinkable water by removing the salt from seawater. The $110-million Tampa Bay Seawater Desalination plant produces 25 million gallons (95 million liters) of fresh, drinkable water daily from the waters of Tampa Bay.

Groundwater wells are the most common source of drinking water in Florida. However, population growth in the Tampa Bay area has pushed demand for water beyond the available supply of fresh water available from wells.

The desalination plant uses a process called reverse osmosis to remove salt from the water. The plant takes salt water from Tampa Bay and pumps it through a series of filters to remove sediment. The water is then forced through special membranes that catch the salt and allow only fresh water to pass through. The fresh water is either stored or added to the delivery system and the concentrated salt water that is left behind is returned to Tampa Bay.

Millennium footbridge. The Millennium pedestrian footbridge over the River Thames in London reopened in February 2002. Officials had closed the slender footbridge, which is 1,050 feet (320 meters) long, just days after its opening in June 2000. When the first crowds crossed the bridge, it began to sway noticeably. Engineers later learned that the swaying was caused by people's footsteps. Because of bridge's slight sway, people tended to fall into step, amplifying the forces of their steps. This created unanticipated stress on the bridge. To prevent the swaying, engineers installed shock-absorbing dampers that reduced stress.

Wacker Drive renovation. A large section of Wacker Drive, a major traffic artery through downtown Chicago, reopened in November 2002 after a $200-million rebuilding project that began in February 2001. About 60,000 vehicles daily use the double-decked street, which provides access to Chicago's central business district, known as the Loop. Years of heavy traffic and freeze-and-thaw seasonal cycles had left the riverside drive, built in 1926, in an advanced state of decay. Engineers used a new type of high-performance concrete to make the repairs more durable
□ Andrew Wright

See also **Architecture**.

Bulgaria. The government of Prime Minister Simeon Saxe-Coburg-Gotha pressed forward on anticorruption and privatization measures in Bulgaria in 2002. Saxe-Coburg-Gotha, who as Simeon II reigned as king of Bulgaria from 1943 to 1946, heads a political party called the National Movement for Simeon II, which swept parliamentary elections in June 2001.

The prime minister pressed for Bulgaria's admission to the European Union (EU) and the North Atlantic Treaty Organization (NATO). By late 2002, Bulgaria had completed 11 of 30 chapters (topics for negotiation) in talks with the EU, and officials of the organization expressed support for Bulgaria's goal of joining the EU by 2007. In November 2002, NATO officials formally invited Bulgaria to join the defensive military alliance.

Unemployment in Bulgaria remained high in 2002, boosted by the rapid privatization of state industries urged by the EU and endorsed by the prime minister. Official sources reported an unemployment rate of 17.6 percent in August, up 1 percent from August 2001.   □ Sharon L. Wolchik
See also **Europe.**

Burkina Faso. See Africa.

Burma. See Myanmar.

Burundi. See Africa.

Business. See Bank; Economics; Labor and employment; Manufacturing.

Cabinet, U.S. President George W. Bush, on June 6, 2002, proposed the creation of a new Cabinet department for domestic defense, the Department of Homeland Security. According to the president, the secretary would oversee the domestic war on terrorism, specifically coordinating efforts to protect the country from terrorist attack. The department was designed to incorporate the Office of Homeland Security, a government agency created in response to the terrorist attacks on the United States on Sept. 11, 2001.

The plan shifted the Bush administration's original proposals for domestic defense following the terrorist attacks. The president initially established the Office of Homeland Security and named Pennsylvania Governor Tom Ridge as the office's director.

The U.S. House of Representatives and the U.S. Senate approved legislation in November 2002 authorizing the creation of the new department. Before the final vote, Democratic leaders in the Senate unsuccessfully tried to block what they called "special interest" provisions inserted by House Republicans that aided industries that develop antiterrorism technologies.

The new Department of Homeland Security is responsible for border security and transportation, emergency preparedness, and intelligence analysis. It also coordinates and develops coun-

termeasures in defense of potential chemical, biological, and nuclear terrorist attacks. The Bush administration projected that the new department would have 170,000 employees and a budget of $37 billion. It consolidated 22 existing agencies, including the Federal Emergency Management Agency, the Immigration and Naturalization Service, and the U.S. Secret Service. The president nominated Ridge as the department's secretary.

Political experts described President Bush's new department as the most dramatic government restructuring in more than 50 years. The department's head occupies the first new Cabinet position to be created since 1988, when the Department of Veterans Affairs was established.

Paul O'Neill, the U.S. secretary of the treasury since 2001, resigned on Dec. 6, 2002. Political experts suggested that O'Neill's resignation was tied to problems with the economy, which remained slow in 2002. On December 9, President Bush nominated John W. Snow as treasury secretary. Snow was the chief executive officer of CSX Corporation, a railroad company headquartered in Richmond, Virginia.   □ Geoffrey A. Campbell
See also **Congress of the United States; Immigration; Immigration: A Special Report; United States, Government of the; United States, President of the.**

Cambodia. The party of Prime Minister Hun Sen won a landslide victory in February 2002 in Cambodia's first local elections in nearly 50 years. The Cambodian People's Party (CPP) won control of approximately 1,600 of the 1,621 commune councils. The communes are administrative clusters of villages. The elections introduced multiparty politics to commune government after years of control by CPP-appointed chiefs. A party led by Sam Rainsy, a former finance minister and a critic of the CPP, won control of more than 10 communes. The royalist party, Funcinpec, finished first in the remaining communes.

The elections were part of an agreement brokered by the United Nations (UN) under a 1992 peace accord that helped end Cambodia's civil war and establish a democratic government.

The UN decided in November 2002 to resume long-dormant efforts to establish an international tribunal to try former leaders of the Khmer Rouge (KR). The KR was a Communist regime that ruled Cambodia from 1975 to 1979 and was responsible for the deaths of more than 1.5 million people. The UN had said that Prime Minister Hun Sen, a former KR officer who had long resisted internationally supervised trials, refused to accept conditions the UN deemed critical to ensuring fair trials.   □ Henry S. Bradsher
See also **Asia.**

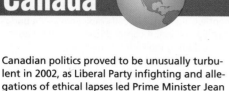

Canadian politics proved to be unusually turbulent in 2002, as Liberal Party infighting and allegations of ethical lapses led Prime Minister Jean Chretien to announce his retirement. The war on terrorism, a United States-led campaign for military action against Iraq, and lumber duties dominated Canada's foreign affairs.

Showdown in the Cabinet. Chretien on June 2, 2002, dropped political rival Paul Martin from his post as minister of finance. Chretien cited "irreconcilable differences" between the two men, which prevented them from working together comfortably.

Chretien and Martin had been political rivals since 1990, when they competed against each other for leadership of the Liberal Party. Chretien won but invited Martin to become minister of finance when the Liberal Party came to power three years later. A successful businessman, Martin became a highly regarded finance minister by eliminating a massive federal budget deficit inherited from the previous administration. Martin balanced the budget every year from 1998 to 2001. By 2002, his successful management of Canada's finances had become a hallmark of Chretien's government.

The two politicians, however, were uneasy colleagues, and by early 2002, Martin was raising funds to run for party leadership. At a tense Cabinet meeting on May 30, Chretien ordered Martin and others to stop campaigning, as their activities were undermining his ability to govern. When Martin refused to put aside his leadership ambitions, the prime minister dropped him from the Cabinet. Martin remained a member of Parliament and began actively enlisting support to challenge Chretien for Liberal Party leadership.

An embattled prime minister. Martin found fertile ground for his challenge as unhappiness with Chretien's leadership grew in 2002. Chretien's administration, and even the prime minister himself, had been rocked by allegations of ethical misconduct. In May, Chretien forced Defense Minister Arthur Eggleton to resign after it was revealed that he had granted a lucrative defense-consulting contract to a former girlfriend. Opposition parties accused Solicitor General Lawrence MacAulay of lobbying the head of the Royal Canadian Mounted Police to donate $3.5 million to a college administered by MacAulay's brother. (All amounts are in Canadian dollars.) MacAulay denied any wrongdoing but resigned from the government in October. Eggle-

ton's dismissal and other scandals led many politicians and media officials to call for Chretien's resignation.

Critics had in recent years accused him of becoming increasingly authoritarian and relying for advice on a small group within his office. Chretien in 2001 had refused to disclose when he planned to step down as Liberal Party leader, claiming that after three successive electoral victories, he had a mandate to continue in office. Dissatisfaction within the Liberal Party reflected a similar mood within the country, with polls in 2002 suggesting that the time had come for Chretien to step down.

Chretien, fearing a humiliating review of his leadership at a Liberal Party convention scheduled for February 2003, announced on Aug. 21, 2002, that he had decided to retire from politics. He declared that he would continue as party leader, however, until February 2004, giving himself 18 months to introduce legislation that would define his place in Canadian history.

Chretien's legacy agenda. Chretien revealed his agenda in the traditional Speech from the Throne at the opening of the second session of the 37th Parliament on Sept. 30, 2002. The prime minister disclosed that his government would invest significantly in strengthening public health care, attack the social problem of child poverty, and attempt to close the gap in living conditions between *First Nations* (native) people and other Canadians. Chretien proposed doubling Canada's foreign assistance to developing countries by 2010, with half the aid earmarked for Africa, an area of priority attention for Chretien. The government also pledged to cooperate with the United States in security measures in North America and would work to establish "smart" borders designed to ease vital trade flows between Canada and the United States. Chretien coupled the ambitious agenda with a promise to restrain spending in order to continue to achieve balanced budgets. The prime minister did not propose to increase support for Canada's military, which many critics considered underfunded.

Chretien vowed that efforts to protect the environment would continue and repeated his pledge that, before the end of the year, Canada would ratify the Kyoto Protocol, an international agreement to reduce the release of gases that

An honor guard in Kandahar, Afghanistan, flanks the coffin of a Canadian soldier accidentally killed by a U.S. bomb on April 18, 2002. Four Canadians died when a U.S. fighter pilot mistakenly dropped a laser-guided bomb on them during a night training exercise.

contribute to global warming. Canada's Parliament ratified the agreement in December.

Commentators pointed out that most of the items on the Chretien agenda had been put forward earlier. The throne speech also did not specify dates by which goals would be completed or the amount of money to be devoted to its various programs. Political analysts said a great deal would depend upon Paul Martin's view of the programs, as he appeared virtually certain to assume leadership of the Liberal Party in 2004. As finance minister, Martin had discouraged overspending, and it was unclear how he would finance Chretien's expensive legacy.

John Manley. Chretien made clear in 2002 that he favored John Manley, an Ottawa-area member of Parliament who had served as minister of foreign affairs and international trade since October 2000, as his successor. Chretien re-

portedly admired the firmness that Manley had shown during tense security discussions with the United States following the terrorist attacks on Sept. 11, 2001. During a major reshuffling of the Cabinet in January 2002, Chretien promoted Manley to deputy prime minister. When Paul Martin was dropped as finance minister, Manley was given that post while still retaining the title of deputy prime minister. Manley showed himself to be Chretien's closest colleague, one whom the prime minister could rely on to handle difficult assignments.

Political parties. The Liberal Party suffered a setback during by-elections in May, losing two seats in Parliament that most political experts had believed to be secure. However, the party still held a comfortable majority with 169 seats in the 301-seat House of Commons. Public opinion polls during 2002 showed the party with a 44 percent standing, almost larger than that of the combined opposition. Experts speculated that the party's support would increase in the future if Martin succeeded Chretien as prime minister.

The official opposition party, the Canadian Alliance, settled upon a new leader in March. Stockwell Day, the party's former leader, lost out to challenger Stephen Harper. Harper advocated a leaner federal government, disciplined management of expenditures, lower taxes, and more powers for provincial governments. He did not favor a special status for Quebec in the federation. Harper was elected to the House of Commons from Calgary in the May elections and was later sworn in as official leader of the opposition.

Although the Alliance held 63 seats in Parliament, its popular standing across the country languished at about 15 percent. Harper sought to broaden the base of the Alliance's support from the party's homeland in the West. The Liberal Party had benefited for years from a division between Canada's two conservative parties—the Alliance and the Progressive Conservative Party (PCP). Harper sought cooperation with the PCP in running a joint slate of candidates, but the older party rejected his overtures.

The PCP also faced a leadership contest. Joe Clark, prime minister for a short term in 1979 and 1980, had served as party leader since 1998 and was considered a veteran of Canadian politics. He had worked to strengthen his party following its disastrous electoral defeat in 1993. But the PCP held only 14 seats in Parliament and enjoyed the same popular support as the Alliance. Clark announced in August that he wished to step down and asked that a successor be chosen before the autumn of 2003.

Leadership changes were not confined to the parties of the center and the right. Canada's party of the left, the New Democratic Party (NDP), also faced the prospect of a new leader. Alexa McDonough of Nova Scotia had led the NDP since 1995. McDonough worked to broaden the party's popular support. Under her leadership, the NDP made some gains in Quebec and the Maritime Provinces, but its main support remained in the West. The party held 14 seats in the Commons, but its national popular standing stood at only 13 percent. Discouraged by these figures, McDonough announced her resignation in June 2002. Her successor was to be chosen by a convention in January 2003.

Canada's fifth party, the Bloc Quebecois (BQ), the national party of the movement for the independence of Quebec, showed little vigor in 2002. Although the movement still held power in Quebec, the results of by-elections and public opinion polls indicated that the movement was in decline. The BQ still held 37 seats in the Commons, but party experts suggested that this strength was likely to erode at the next general election. They noted that the challenge for all of the opposition parties was to define themselves and their policies as Canada moved into a post-Chretien period.

Economy. Canada's economy gathered momentum in late 2001 and moved forward robustly until mid-2002, when the pace slackened. The downturn in the U.S. economy did not strongly hurt exports to Canada's largest foreign market. Economists noted that the continued low value of the Canadian dollar in relation to the U.S. dollar helped keep exports to the United States steady.

Economic analysts said the sluggish performance of international stock markets in 2002 did not severely hurt Canada's economy because Canadians had a much smaller proportion of their wealth invested in stock than U.S. citizens. Also, the corporate accounting scandals that eroded confidence in the U.S. economy had no counterpart in the Canadian business world. Job creation was strong in early 2002. However, Canada's unemployment rate climbed to 7.5 percent by November. The consumer price index, a statistical measurement of changes in the price of goods and services bought by most people, rose 2.3 percent between September 2001 and September 2002.

The Bank of Canada projected in July that the country's *gross domestic product* (the total value of goods and services produced within a country in a given year) would rise by 3 to 4 percent by the end of 2003, the highest level of growth among the G7 industrialized nations. Further evidence of the economy's strength came in May 2002 when Canada regained the Triple A credit rating that it had lost in 1994, when the government's operating deficit reached a high of $42 billion. Under Paul Martin's management, Canada's budget had been in surplus since 1998.

Finance Minister John Manley announced in 2002 that he would not introduce a new federal budget until early 2003. In the meantime, Manley stated his intention of following his predecessor's policy of tight fiscal management in an effort to assure the international financial community that no major changes were planned for 2002. Although federal revenues were expected to be lower in 2002 than in 2001, Manley announced in October 2002 that the 2001-2002 budget surplus of $8.9 billion was higher than expected.

War on terrorism. Canada pledged support in January for the international struggle against terrorism by announcing that it would send nearly 800 soldiers to Afghanistan to work under U.S. command. The mission represented the largest overseas deployment of Canadian combat forces since the Korean War (1950-1953). The detachment arrived in Kandahar in western Afghanistan in February 2002 to guard the city's airport. Canadian troops also helped search for elusive forces loyal to Afghanistan's former Taliban government and members of the al-Qa'ida terrorist organization. A naval detachment of six ships was sent to the Arabian Sea. The naval group, together with a small contingent of transport and reconnaissance aircraft, brought an additional 1,700 personnel to the area of operations.

An unfortunate incident on April 18 marred the mission. Four Canadian soldiers were killed and eight others wounded when a U.S. Air National Guard F-16 mistakenly dropped a 500-pound (226-kilogram) laser-guided bomb on Canadian forces participating in a night training exercise. Boards of inquiry set up by both countries issued reports blaming the incident on two U.S. pilots for failing to observe rules of engagement. The report also criticized U.S. military command and communication procedures.

The declining size of Canada's defense forces made it difficult to conduct military operations in Afghanistan while maintaining large-scale peacekeeping duties in other areas. In August, Canada withdrew its ground forces from Afghanistan, though the naval and air personnel remained.

International relations. Canadian officials expressed unhappiness in 2002 with the *unilateralist* (one-sided) stance adopted by U.S. President George W. Bush in the conduct of foreign policy. Disagreement came to the fore as the United States considered military action against the regime of Saddam Hussein in Iraq. Canada had criticized Iraq since 1998 for its refusal to permit United Nations (UN) weapons inspectors to examine whether it was building weapons of mass destruction in violation of the 1991 Gulf War peace settlement. Canada advocated a vigorous UN diplomatic push for the renewed weapons inspections before resorting to military force. Canada also argued that any military strikes should be conducted on a multinational basis under UN auspices. Canadian officials also did not believe that the United States had made the case that Iraq was a direct threat to U.S. security.

Canada hosted an economic summit of the G8 leading industrial nations at a Rocky Mountain resort in Kananaskis, Alberta, on June 26 and 27, 2002. The remote site kept the meeting free from the noisy and sometimes violent demonstrations that had marred earlier summits. Prime Minister Chretien, who chaired the meeting, emphasized the pressing need for assistance to Africa, the world's poorest continent. Chretien said aid should be coupled with the requirement that African nations adopt more democratic reforms

Federal spending in Canada
Estimated budget for fiscal 2002-2003*

Department or agency	Millions of dollars†
Agriculture and agri-food	2,270
Canada customs and revenue agency	3,364
Canadian heritage	3,362
Citizenship and immigration	1,051
Environment	734
Finance	65,132
Fisheries and oceans	1,438
Foreign affairs and international trade	3,756
Governor general	18
Health	3,009
Human resources development	29,069
Indian affairs and northern development	5,158
Industry	5,044
Justice	1,196
National defence	11,846
Natural resources	1,014
Parliament	403
Privy Council	2,470
Public works and government services	2,248
Solicitor general	3,477
Transport	1,084
Treasury board	2,144
Veterans affairs	2,273
Total	**151,560**

* April 1, 2002, to March 31, 2003.
† Canadian dollars; $1 = U.S. $0.63 as of Oct. 4, 2002.

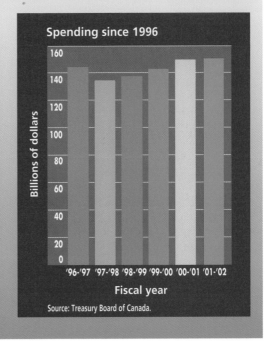

Spending since 1996

Billions of dollars

160
140
120
100
80
60
40
20
0

'96-'97 '97-'98 '98-'99 '99-'00 '00-'01 '01-'02

Fiscal year

Source: Treasury Board of Canada.

Members of the Canadian House of Commons

The House of Commons of the second session of the 37th Parliament convened on Sept. 30, 2002. As of Dec. 10, 2002, the House of Commons consisted of the following members: 169 Liberal Party, 63 Canadian Alliance, 37 Bloc Québécois, 14 New Democratic Party, 14 Progressive Conservative Party, 3 Independents, and 1 vacancy. This table shows each legislator and party affiliation. An asterisk (*) denotes those who served in the 36th Parliament.

Alberta
Diane Ablonczy, C.A.*
Rob Anders, C.A.*
Leon E. Benoit, C.A.*
Rick Casson, C.A.
David Chatters, C.A.*
Joe Clark, P.C.
Ken Epp, C.A.*
Peter Goldring, C.A.*
Deborah Grey, C.A.*
Art Hanger, C.A.*
Stephen Harper, C.A.
Grant Hill, C.A.*
Rahim Jaffer, C.A.*
Dale Johnston, C.A.*
Jason Kenney, C.A.*
David Kilgour, Lib.*
Anne McLellan, Lib.*
Rob Merrifield, C.A.
Bob Mills, C.A.*
Deepak Obhrai, C.A.*
Charlie Penson, C.A.*
James Rajotte, C.A.
Monte Solberg, C.A.*
Kevin Sorenson, C.A.
Myron Thompson, C.A.*
John Williams, C.A.*

British Columbia
Jim Abbott, C.A.*
David Anderson, Lib.*
Andy Burton, C.A.*
Chuck Cadman, C.A.*
John Cummins, C.A.*
Libby Davies, N.D.P.*
Stockwell Day, C.A.
Herb Dhaliwal, Lib.*
John Duncan, C.A.*
Reed Elley, C.A.*
Paul Forseth, C.A.*
Hedy Fry, Lib.*
Jim Gouk, C.A.*
Gurmant Grewal, C.A.*
Richard Harris, C.A.*
Jay Hill, C.A.*
Betty Hinton, C.A.
Sophia Leung, Lib.*
Gary Lunn, C.A.*
James Lunney, C.A.
Keith Martin, C.A.*
Philip Mayfield, C.A.*
Grant McNally, C.A.*
Val Meredith, C.A.*
James Moore, C.A.
Stephen Owen, Lib.
Joe Peschisolido, Lib.
John Reynolds, C.A.*
Svend Robinson, N.D.P.*
Werner Schmidt, C.A.*
Darrel Stinson, C.A.*
Chuck Strahl, C.A.*
Randy White, C.A.*
Ted White, C.A.*

Manitoba
Reg Alcock, Lib.*
Bill Blaikie, N.D.P.*
Rick Borotsik, P.C.*
Bev Desjarlais, N.D.P.*
John Harvard, Lib.*
Howard Hilstrom, C.A.*
Inky Mark, P.C.*
Pat Martin, N.D.P.*
Anita Neville, Lib.
Rey Pagtakhan, Lib.*
Brian Pallister, C.A.
Raymond Simard, Lib.
Vic Toews, C.A.
Judy Wasylycia-Leis, N.D.P.*

New Brunswick
Claudette Bradshaw, Lib.*
Jeannot Castonguay, Lib.
Yvon Godin, N.D.P.*
John Herron, P.C.*
Charles Hubbard, Lib.*
Dominic LeBlanc, Lib.
Andy Savoy, Lib.
Andy Scott, Lib.*
Greg Thompson, P.C.*
Elsie Wayne, P.C.*

Newfoundland
Rex Barnes, P.C.
Gerry Byrne, Lib.*
Norman Doyle, P.C.*
R. John Efford, Lib.
Loyola Hearn, P.C.
Bill Matthews, Lib.*
Lawrence D. O'Brien, Lib.*

Northwest Territories
Ethel Blondin-Andrew, Lib.*

Nova Scotia
Scott Brison, P.C.*
Bill Casey, P.C.*
Rodger Cuzner, Lib.
Mark Eyking, Lib.
Gerald Keddy, P.C.*
Wendy Lill, N.D.P.*
Peter MacKay, P.C.*
Alexa McDonough, N.D.P.*
Geoff Regan, Lib.
Peter Stoffer, N.D.P.*
Robert Thibault, Lib.

Nunavut
Nancy Karetak-Lindell, Lib.*

Ontario
Peter Adams, Lib.*
Sarkis Assadourian, Lib.*
Jean Augustine, Lib.*
Sue Barnes, Lib.*
Colleen Beaumier, Lib.*
Réginald Bélair, Lib.*
Mauril Bélanger, Lib.*
Eugène Bellemare, Lib.*
Carolyn Bennett, Lib.*
Maurizio Bevilacqua, Lib.*
Ray Bonin, Lib.*
Paul Bonwick, Lib.*
Don Boudria, Lib.*
Bonnie Brown, Lib.*
John Bryden, Lib.*
Sarmite Bulte, Lib.*
Charles Caccia, Lib.*
Murray Calder, Lib.*
John Cannis, Lib.*
Elinor Caplan, Lib.*
Aileen Carroll, Lib.*
Marlene Catterall, Lib.*
Brenda Chamberlain, Lib.*
David M. Collenette, Lib.*
Joe Comartin, N.D.P.
Joe Comuzzi, Lib.*
Sheila Copps, Lib.*
Roy Cullen, Lib.*
Paul DeVillers, Lib.*
Stan Dromisky, Lib.*
Art C. Eggleton, Lib.*
John Finlay, Lib.*
Joe Fontana, Lib.*
Cheryl Gallant, C.A.
Roger Gallaway, Lib.*
John Godfrey, Lib.*
Bill Graham, Lib.*
Ivan Grose, Lib.*
Albina Guarnieri, Lib.*
Mac Harb, Lib.*
Tony Ianno, Lib.*
Ovid Jackson, Lib.*
Joe Jordan, Lib.*
Jim Karygiannis, Lib.*
Stan Keyes, Lib.*
Bob Kilger, Lib.*
Gar Knutson, Lib.*
Karen Kraft Sloan, Lib.*
Walt Lastewka, Lib.*
Derek Lee, Lib.*
Judi Longfield, Lib.*
Paul H. Macklin, Lib.
Steve Mahoney, Lib.*
Gurbax Malhi, Lib.*
John Maloney, Lib.*
John Manley, Lib.*
Diane Marleau, Lib.*
Brian Masse, N.D.P.
John McCallum, Lib.
Larry McCormick, Lib.*
John McKay, Lib.*
Dan McTeague, Lib.*
Peter Milliken, Lib.*
Dennis Mills, Lib.*
Maria Minna, Lib.*
Andy Mitchell, Lib.*
Lynn Myers, Lib.*
Robert Nault, Lib.*
Pat O'Brien, Lib.*
John O'Reilly, Lib.*
Carolyn Parrish, Lib.*
Janko Peric, Lib.*
Jim Peterson, Lib.*
Beth Phinney, Lib.*
Jerry Pickard, Lib.*
Gary Pillitteri, Lib.*
David Pratt, Lib.*
Carmen Provenzano, Lib.*
Karen Redman, Lib.*
Julian Reed, Lib.*
Scott Reid, C.A.
Allan Rock, Lib.*
Benoît Serré, Lib.*
Judy Sgro, Lib.*
Alex Shepherd, Lib.*
Bob Speller, Lib.*
Brent St. Denis, Lib.*
Paul Steckle, Lib.*
Jane Stewart, Lib.*
Paul Szabo, Lib.*
Andrew Telegdi, Lib.*
Tony Tirabassi, Lib.
Alan Tonks, Lib.
Paddy Torsney, Lib.*
Rose-Marie Ur, Lib.*
Tony Valeri, Lib.*
Lyle Vanclief, Lib.*
Joseph Volpe, Lib.*
Tom Wappel, Lib.*
Susan Whelan, Lib.*
Bryon Wilfert, Lib.*
Bob Wood, Lib.*

Prince Edward Island
Wayne Easter, Lib.*
Lawrence MacAulay, Lib.*
Joe McGuire, Lib.*
Shawn Murphy, Lib.*

Quebec
Carole-Marie Allard, Lib.
Mark Assad, Lib.
Gérard Asselin, B.Q.*
André Bachand, P.C.*
Claude Bachand, B.Q.*
Eleni Bakopanos, Lib.*
Stéphane Bergeron, B.Q.*
Robert Bertrand, Lib.*
Bernard Bigras, B.Q.*
Gérard Binet, Lib.
Diane Bourgeois, B.Q.
Pierre Brien, B.Q.*
Serge Cardin, B.Q.*
Jean-Guy Carignan, Ind.
Martin Cauchon, Lib.*
Yvon Charbonneau, Lib.*
Jean Chrétien, Lib.*
Denis Coderre, Lib.•
Irwin Cotler, Lib.•
Paul Crête, B.Q.*
Madeleine Dalphond-Guiral, B.Q.*
Odina Desrochers, B.Q.*
Stéphane Dion, Lib.*
Nick Discepola, Lib.*
Claude Drouin, Lib.*
Antoine Dubé, B.Q.*
Gilles Duceppe, B.Q.*
Claude Duplain, Lib.
Georges Farrah, Lib.
Raymonde Folco, Lib.*
Ghislain Fournier, B.Q.*
Liza Frulla, Lib.

Christiane Gagnon, B.Q.*
Marcel Gagnon, B.Q.
Sebastien Gagnon, B.Q.
Roger Gaudet, B.Q.
Michel Gauthier, B.Q.*
Jocelyne Girard-Bujold, B.Q.*
Monique Guay, B.Q.*
Michel Guimond, B.Q.*
André Harvey, Lib.*.
Marlene Jennings, Lib.*
Mario Laframboise, B.Q.
Francine Lalonde, B.Q.*
Robert Lanctôt, B.Q.
Ghislain Lebel, Ind.*
Clifford Lincoln, Lib.*
Yvan Loubier, B.Q.*
Richard Marceau, B.Q.*
Serge Marcil, Lib.
Paul Martin, Lib.*
Réal Ménard, B.Q.*
Gilbert Normand, Lib.*
Massimo Pacetti, Lib.
Pierre Paquette, B.Q.
Denis Paradis, Lib.*
Bernard Patry, Lib.*
Gilles-A. Perron, B.Q.*
Pierre Pettigrew, Lib.*
Pauline Picard, B.Q.*
Louis Plamondon, B.Q.*
David Price, Lib.*
Marcel Proulx, Lib.*
Lucienne Robillard, Lib.*
Yves Rocheleau, B.Q.*
Jean-Yves Roy, B.Q.
Jacques Saada, Lib.*
Benoît Sauvageau, B.Q.*
Hélène Scherrer, Lib.
Caroline St-Hilaire, B.Q.*
Diane St-Jacques, Lib.*
Guy St-Julien, Lib.*
Yolande Thibeault, Lib.*
Suzanne Tremblay, B.Q.*
Pierrette Venne, B.Q.*

Saskatchewan
David Anderson, C.A.
Roy Bailey, C.A.*
Garry Breitkreuz, C.A.*
Brian Fitzpatrick, C.A.
Ralph E. Goodale, Lib.*
Rick Laliberte, Lib.*
Lorne Nystrom, N.D.P.*
Jim Pankiw, Ind.*
Dick Proctor, N.D.P.*
Gerry Ritz, C.A.*
Carol Skelton, C.A.
Larry Spencer, C.A.
Maurice Vellacott, C.A.*
Lynne Yelich, C.A.

Yukon Territory
Larry Bagnell, Lib.

The Ministry of Canada*

Jean Chretien—prime minister
John Manley—deputy prime minister; minister of finance; minister responsible for border issues
David Michael Collenette—minister of transport and minister responsible for five Crown Corporations
David Anderson—minister of the environment
Ralph Goodale—minister for public works and government services; minister responsible for the Canadian Wheat Board; minister responsible for the Office of Indian Residential Schools Resolution; Federal Interlocutor for Métis and Non-Status Indians
Sheila Copps—minister of Canadian heritage
Anne McLellan—minister of health
Allan Rock—minister of industry and minister responsible for infrastructure
Wayne Easter—solicitor general of Canada
Lucienne Robillard—president of the Treasury Board; minister responsible for Crown Corporations Policy
Martin Cauchon—minister of justice, attorney general of Canada
Jane Stewart—minister of human resources development
Stéphane Dion—president of the Queen's Privy Council for Canada; minister of intergovernmental affairs
Pierre Pettigrew—minister for international trade
Don Boudria—leader of the government in the House of Commons
Lyle Vanclief—minister of agriculture and agri-food
Herb Dhaliwal—minister of natural resources
Claudette Bradshaw—minister of labour; Federal Coordinator on Homelessness
Robert Daniel Nault—minister of Indian affairs and Northern development
Elinor Caplan—minister of national revenue
Denis Coderre—minister of citizenship and immigration
Sharon Carstairs—leader of the government in the Senate; minister with the Special Responsibility for Palliative Care
Robert G. Thibault—minister of fisheries and oceans
Rey Pagtakhan—minister of veterans affairs; secretary of state (science, research, and development)
Susan Whelan—minister of international cooperation
Bill Graham—minister of foreign affairs
Gerry Bryne—minister of state (Atlantic Canada Opportunities Agency)
John McCallum—minister of national defence
Ethel Blondin-Andrew—secretary of state (children and youth)
David Kilgour—secretary of state (Asia-Pacific)
Andrew Mitchell—secretary of state (rural development)
Maurizio Bevilacqua—secretary of state (international financial institutions)
Paul DeVillers—secretary of state (amateur sport); deputy leader of the government in the House of Commons
Gar Knutson—secretary of state (Central and Eastern Europe and Middle East)
Denis Paradis—secretary of state (Latin America and Africa; Francophonie)
Claude Drouin—secretary of state (Economic Development Agency of Canada)
Stephen Owen—secretary of state (Western economic diversification; Indian affairs and northern development)
Jean Augustine—secretary of state (multiculturalism/status of women)
*As of Dec. 31, 2002.

Premiers of Canadian provinces

Province	Premier
Alberta	Ralph Klein
British Columbia	Gordon Campbell
Manitoba	Gary Doer
New Brunswick	Bernard Lord
Newfoundland	Roger Grimes
Nova Scotia	John Hamm
Ontario	Ernie Eves
Prince Edward Island	Patrick George Binns
Quebec	Bernard Landry
Saskatchewan	Lorne Albert Calvert

Government leaders of territories

Northwest Territories	Stephen Kakfwi
Nunavut	Paul Okalik
Yukon Territory	Dennis Fentie

and respect human rights. Chretien secured a pledge from the G8 nations to earmark half of their foreign aid for Africa, but he received no guarantee as to how and when the funds would be provided. However, some progress was achieved in getting the countries to open their domestic markets to imports from Africa.

Lumber dispute. Softwood lumber continued to bedevil trade relations between Canada and the United States in 2002. In May, the U.S. Department of Commerce imposed a 27 percent

2002 Canadian population estimates

Province and territory populations

Alberta	3,036,134
British Columbia	3,946,189
Manitoba	1,120,726
New Brunswick	727,791
Newfoundland and Labrador	505,705
Northwest Territories	36,925
Nova Scotia	906,553
Nunavut	27,181
Ontario	11,549,356
Prince Edward Island	135,442
Quebec	7,329,921
Saskatchewan	976,698
Yukon Territory	28,284
Canada	30,326,905

City and metropolitan area populations

	Metropolitan area	City
Toronto, Ont.	4,774,965	2,501,482
Montreal, Que.	3,447,294	1,821,062
Vancouver, B.C.	2,020,658	552,394
Ottawa-Hull	1,077,498	
Ottawa, Ont.		785,436
Hull, Que.		*
Calgary, Alta.	981,447	904,219
Edmonton, Alta.	854,207	676,868
Quebec, Que.	684,966	509,612
Winnipeg, Man.	672,115	619,758
Hamilton, Ont.	670,473	494,978
London, Ont.	435,753	338,786
Kitchener, Ont.	421,066	192,956
St. Catharines-Niagara Falls	377,941	
St. Catharines, Ont.		128,824
Niagara Falls, Ont.		79,204
Halifax, N.S.	362,580	362,517
Victoria, B.C.	313,463	74,250
Windsor, Ont.	312,400	210,660
Oshawa, Ont.	302,367	140,021
Saskatoon, Sask.	227,344	197,453
Regina, Sask.	192,630	177,794
St. John's, Nfld. Lab.	172,693	98,646
Sherbrooke, Que.	154,683	75,744
Chicoutimi-Jonquière	153,873	
Chicoutimi, Que.		59,427
Jonquière, Que.		54,520
Greater Sudbury, Ont.	153,719	153,319
Abbotsford	149,722	117,667
Trois-Rivières, Que.	137,026	45,852
Saint John, N.B.	122,678	69,117
Thunder Bay, Ont.	121,986	108,125

*Hull became part of the city of Gatineau in 2002. Gatineau's projected 2002 population was 229,643.

Source: World Book estimates based on data from Statistics Canada.

duty on construction lumber imports from Canada, which total about $10 billion annually. U.S. officials argued that the Canadian practice of selling cutting rights to private operators on *Crown* (public) land for low prices represented an unfair government subsidy and that the duty was needed to protect U.S. lumber companies. In the first month after the duties went into full effect, Canadian lumber exports fell by 40 percent. Communities dependent upon the logging industry were hard hit by the trade stoppage. Economists estimated that as many as 25,000 lumber industry workers could lose their jobs if the dispute continued for two years. At the end of September, the Chretien government approved an aid package of $247 million for the affected communities.

In September, a panel of the World Trade Organization, an organization that promotes international trade, declared that the Canadian practice of selling cutting rights on Crown lands to private operators did not constitute a subsidy and that the U.S. duties, therefore, were illegal. Trade experts expected the United States to appeal the Canadian victory and the legal battle over lumber duties to continue.   □ David M. L. Farr

See also **Afghanistan; Canada, Prime Minister of; Canadian provinces; Canadian territories; Iraq; Montreal; Toronto; United States, Government of the.**

Canada, Prime Minister of.

Prime Minister Jean Chretien announced in 2002 that his long political career was drawing to a close. Chretien served in Canada's Parliament almost continuously since 1963. He worked to unite the country, control government spending, and promote social and economic justice both at home and abroad. In 2002, allegations of ethical lapses increasingly touched Chretien's government, and many Canadians called for him to step down. In August, Chretien announced that he would retire from politics by February 2004. Political experts predicted that he would use the remaining 18 months of his term to pass legislation that would define his place in Canadian history.

G8 summit. Chretien hosted a G8 summit of the leaders of eight of the world's richest nations at the Rocky Mountain resort of Kananaskis, Alberta, in June 2002. The prime minister's agenda focused on the needs of Africa, the world's poorest continent. Chretien urged the G8 leaders to increase economic assistance to Africa in return for an African commitment to democratic institutions and human rights. Chretien argued that the widening gap between the rich and poor nations had led to a deep resentment of the West in many countries.   □ David M. L. Farr

See also **Canada; Canadian provinces; Canadian territories.**

Canadian provinces. Economic conditions varied across Canada in 2002. A drought hurt agricultural production on the prairies, and British Columbia's lumber industry suffered under import duties imposed by the United States. Provincial governments continued to wrestle with relations with *First Nations* (native) people.

Alberta, with an economy that relies heavily on farming and ranching, suffered under a drought that affected 70 percent of the province during 2002. Many areas of Alberta received less than half of normal rainfall. Three days of unusually heavy rain in June caused flooding and further crop damage in southern Alberta. The provincial government stepped in to help farmers with more than $324 million in aid. (All amounts are in Canadian dollars.) The government gave half of the money to buy feed for livestock, and the rest went to farmers who had lost their crops.

Depressed public revenues led the Progressive Conservative government under Premier Ralph Klein to produce a "bad news budget" in March. The budget for fiscal year 2002-2003 imposed or raised 70 different taxes and fees in order to bring in an additional $722 million, in spite of Klein's 2001 election promise not to raise taxes. However, Alberta's taxes remained the lowest of any Canadian province in 2002, and Alberta carried the smallest per-capita government debt in the country. The provincial government planned to use a surplus of $724 million from the 2001-2002 budget to pay down the province's debt, which was about $5.2 billion in 2002. Klein's government predicted better conditions for economic growth in 2002.

British Columbia. Premier Gordon Campbell's Liberal government struggled during 2002 to manage the province's finances. The provincial budget, introduced in February, raised the retail sales tax to 7.5 percent, the same level as in heavily taxed Quebec. Facing a possible deficit of $4.4 billion, Finance Minister Gary Collins ordered all ministries except health and education to cut their expenditures by 25 percent over the next three years. The civil service was to be reduced by about the same amount over the same period.

British Columbia's lumber industry suffered under U.S. import duties in 2002. In May, the U.S. government imposed a 27-percent duty on construction lumber imports from Canada. Canada's lumber exports fell by 40 percent within a month. Economists estimated that as many as 25,000 lumber industry workers could lose their jobs if the dispute continued for two years. Logging communities in the province received their share of $247 million in federal aid approved by the federal government in September.

Relations between British Columbia's government and its more than 100,000 First Nations people deteriorated in 2002. The province's native people do not enjoy the special status accorded native people by treaty in many other parts of Canada, and progress in negotiating native rights has been limited. Campbell's government decided to make a fresh start in 2002 by asking voters for their views on a bargaining position for future negotiations. The government sent an unprecedented mail-in referendum to the province's 2.1 million registered voters.

The referendum asked voters to give their opinion on eight questions posed by the government. The questions included: Was the self-government of native people to be based on the model of municipal administration or was it to be something more? Should hunting rights on *Crown* (public) lands be open to all citizens or confined to native groups? Should existing tax concessions to native people be phased out? The referendum proved highly controversial. Opponents claimed that the questions posed were one-sided and designed to strengthen the government's position. Many native groups urged voters to protest the referendum by not returning their ballots. Only 36 percent of voters responded by the July deadline.

Among the ballots that were returned, the approval rate for the government's stand on the issues ran between 84 and 95 percent. Around 87 percent of participating voters agreed that native settlements should be given a form of government similar to municipalities, which many experts deemed the key question on the ballot. The province's native people, who desired complete self-government, had already rejected the government's stand on the issue.

Manitoba. Canada's first crop of medicinal marijuana was produced in an abandoned mine in northern Manitoba in 2002. The federal government harvested 550 pounds (250 kilograms) of the drug, which was placed in storage under police protection. However, the government backed away from distributing marijuana to ease the pain and suffering of terminally ill patients despite a 2001 law legalizing its use for medicinal purposes. Anne McLellan, Canada's new minister of health, decided that more clinical trials were necessary to assess the efficacy of the drug.

The provincial budget, introduced in April 2002, utilized a new method of financing. For the first time, the government dipped into the operating profits of a Crown utility corporation, Manitoba Hydro, for the sum of $150 million to balance the previous year's budget. Furthermore, the government announced its intention to take more profits from the company over the next two years. The budget also took $93 million from the province's Fiscal Stabilization Fund, a "rainy day" fund. This provided a modest $10-million surplus in a budget of over $7 billion.

New Brunswick. The governments of Canada and New Brunswick reached an agreement over fishing rights with the province's Micmac Indians in August 2002. The agreement followed a heated dispute that arose from a 1760 treaty that gave the Micmac the right to fish whenever and wherever they wished. A Supreme Court of Canada decision in 1999 that upheld this interpretation of the treaty led to three years of confrontation between the Burnt Church Indian band and commercial fishermen. Under the 2002 agreement, Indians and non-Indian fishermen accepted regulations and quotas governing the fishing of valuable lobster and snow crab.

New international rules imposed in 2002 diverted shipping traffic in the Bay of Fundy in order to protect the bay's threatened right whale population. The waters off the mouth of the bay provide a rich feeding ground for the right whales, which in 2002 numbered fewer than 350 in Canadian waters. Oil tankers passing through the bay have collided with right whales, disabling or killing them. The International Maritime Commission in London stepped in on July 14, declaring the area of the bay with the highest concentration of right whales off-limits to tanker traffic.

The provincial budget, released in March, revealed that an extra $104 million in federal government funds had greatly boosted New Brunswick's finances. The federal funds, along with higher tax revenues, allowed Finance Minister Peter Mesheau to balance the budget for the third consecutive year without increasing taxes.

Newfoundland and Labrador. The provincial government in June reached agreement with the International Nickel Co. (INCO), of Toronto, on a multibillion-dollar project to mine nickel at Voisey's Bay in Labrador. INCO purchased the property in 1996 but wanted to process the ore at its smelters in Ontario and Manitoba. The government insisted that the project could not proceed unless the ore was processed within the province. In 2002, INCO agreed to build an experimental processing plant in Newfoundland, which was to be in operation by 2010. The province agreed to allow INCO to begin mining at Voisey's Bay and process the ore outside Newfoundland until the new plant becomes operational.

In February 2002, a group of oil companies shelved the development of a third oil field on the Grand Banks off the eastern coast of Newfoundland. The companies dropped the Hebron-Ben Nevis project because the site's oil proved too heavy to be profitably extracted and refined. The provincial government expected a fourth site, White Rose, to begin production by 2004.

An increase in oil production from Newfoundland's two operating oil fields helped fuel economic growth in the province during 2002. The provincial government predicted in March that the *gross domestic product* (the total value of goods and services produced within the province in a given year) would grow by 3.7 percent in 2002, the highest growth rate of any Canadian province. However, Newfoundland and Labrador's unemployment rate, after hitting a 10-year low in 2001, began to climb again in 2002, reaching 16.8 percent by September.

Nova Scotia, which was hard-pressed financially, appeared to turn a corner in 2002. The provincial budget, presented in April, was balanced after 40 years of deficits. However, the surplus was a razor-thin $1.3 million in a $5.3 billion budget. Increased revenues came from higher license fees for motorists, higher cigarette taxes and liquor prices, and greater profits from provincially regulated gambling. The provincial debt stood at $11.6 billion in 2002.

Ontario. Premier Mike Harris, author of Ontario's "common sense revolution," announced his intention to step down in 2002 as head of the Progressive Conservative Party (PCP). Coming to office in 1995 and reelected five years later, Harris reduced the size of Ontario's government, cut the province's taxes, slashed welfare payments, and brought in a string of balanced budgets.

Lawyer Ernie Eves won leadership of the PCP at a convention held in March 2002, gaining 55 percent of the votes cast. Eves had shown strict fiscal management as Harris's finance minister but left the government to enter private banking in 2001. He returned to politics when Harris announced his resignation and was sworn in as Ontario's 23rd premier on April 15, 2002. Eves declared that he intended to follow the principal policies laid down by Harris, emphasizing sound management over new initiatives.

Eves's new government immediately faced problems. On April 19, a court decision halted the province's plan to sell the distribution arm of its public utility company, Ontario Hydro, to private interests. In August, Eves faced a showdown with three of the province's largest school boards. Harris's administration had ordered local school boards to maintain educational services in their districts without operating at a deficit. The school board of the Ottawa-Carleton School District, the second largest school district in the province, refused to close schools with low enrollment and cut back on special education for disadvantaged children in order to meet budget restraints. On August 16, Eves's government suspended the Ottawa-Carleton School Board and appointed a supervisor to oversee the school district's operations. Later in the month, the province took over the boards of two other large school districts, Toronto and Hamilton-Wentworth.

Protesters parade a giant puppet of British Columbia Premier Gordon Campbell through the streets of Victoria, the provincial capital, on Feb. 23, 2002. Thousands of British Columbia residents gathered in the city to protest the legislature's plans to slash government spending and services.

Ontario's budget, introduced in June, estimated that the gross domestic product would rise about 3.1 percent in 2002. However, spending increases for education, health care, and water management forced Eves's government to delay scheduled income tax cuts until 2004.

Prince Edward Island. A sluggish economy hurt Canada's smallest province in 2002. The potato blight of 2001, which resulted in a ban on exports to the United States, as well as drought conditions, led to a 39-percent decline in potato production in 2002. The decline reduced government revenues.

The provincial government presented a budget in March 2002 with a deficit of $28.8 million for fiscal year 2002-2003. This was double the deficit of 2001. Prince Edward Island also suffered from a decline in international tourism in 2002, an important element of the small island's economy.

Quebec. The powerful Parti Quebecois (PQ), the political party committed to the independence of Quebec, suffered political losses in 2002. A series of scandals affecting lobbyists close to the party, combined with the resignation of a key minister, damaged the image of Premier Bernard Landry's administration. Landry in June called by-elections to fill four vacant seats in the National Assembly (legislature) of Quebec. The PQ held on to only one of the seats, while the Liberal Party was shut out by voters altogether. The elections left the PQ with 68 seats in the 125-seat Assembly, followed by the Liberals with 51 seats. Faced with the loss of public and legislative support, Landry began downplaying any immediate prospects for Quebec's independence.

The strongly nationalistic maverick party Action Democratique du Quebec (ADQ) proved the biggest winner in the elections, gaining the three remaining seats. The ADQ first appeared in the 1994 election when its leader, Mario Dumont, won the party's first seat. In by-elections on April 15, 2002, the ADQ picked up its second seat. After the June elections, the ADQ followed the PQ and Liberal Party with five seats in the Assembly.

The PQ government's negotiations with roughly 15,000 Cree Indians from 9 communities resulted in an agreement that gave the Cree more control over natural resources in their homeland. The deal paved the way for a massive hydroelectric project on the rivers flowing into James Bay. Quebec also reached an agreement with the 9,600 Inuit living in Nunavik, the vast area of the province lying north of the 55th parallel. Quebec gave the Inuit financial benefits in return for development rights in the region. The deal was approved by referendum in May. Critics said that the deal served the PQ's separatist agenda by challenging the federal government's constitutional jurisdiction over relations with native people.

Quebec's economy quickly recovered from a slowdown that began in late 2001. In a budget update delivered in March 2002, Finance Minister Pauline Marois predicted that the province's economy would grow by 1.7 percent in 2002 and 2.9 percent in 2003. Economists also noted that despite declining job growth in Canada's other large provinces, Quebec's industries continued to create jobs at a steady rate.

Saskatchewan. Bad weather conditions plagued Canada's major wheat-growing province in 2002. A drought left bone-dry soil and poor crops that often had to be plowed under. Authorities estimated that 17 million tons (15.4 million metric tons) of wheat would be harvested in 2002, compared with 22.7 million tons (20.6 million metric tons) in 2001. The worst grasshopper infestation in 10 years and an early cold snap in August 2002 further damaged surviving crops. The province received its share of $5.2 billion in federal aid for farmers, but the provincial government claimed the help was inadequate.

Despite the poor harvest, the province balanced its budget in 2002 for the ninth consecutive year. This required cost-cutting and the elimination of four provincial departments.

◻ David M. L. Farr

See also **Canada; Canadian territories; Montreal; Toronto.**

Canadian territories.

Plans to build a pipeline to carry natural gas from the Arctic coasts of Alaska and Canada to southern markets stalled in 2002. The project was delayed by uncertainties among business backers and disputes with native groups. Indecision also slowed the process, as two plans competed to win public and industry support. One proposed route ran through Alaska and Canada's Yukon Territory. The other route followed the Mackenzie River valley in the Northwest Territories.

Northwest Territories. Diamond mining dominated the Northwest Territories' economy in 2002. Construction continued on the territory's second diamond mine at Lac de Gras, Diavik, which was scheduled to open in 2003. Diavik's owners estimated that at its peak the mine would supply 6 million carats of diamonds annually, with an average value of about U.S. $63 per carat. Tiffany and Co., the New York City jewelers, announced that it would purchase U.S. $50 million worth of Diavik diamonds annually. The company intended to cut about 25 percent of the rough stones at a new facility to be erected in Yellowknife. A third mine, owned by the De Beers Group, a giant South African diamond company, was under regulatory review by an environmental impact board through 2002. The company expected the mine to begin operation by 2006.

Yukon. Census figures released in March 2002 showed that the boom and bust cycle of the mining industry had led the territory's population to decline from about 30,800 in 1996 to around 28,700 in 2001. Not a single mine remained in operation in the territory in 2002. However, 120 placer operations, mostly small and family-owned, continued to sluice gold from riverbanks in the Klondike district.

The territorial budget, presented in April 2002 by Premier and Finance Minister Patricia Duncan, showed that the population drop hurt government revenues. Total revenues for fiscal year 2002-2003 were estimated at $529 million, of which only $73 million came from the territory's own revenue sources. (All amounts are in Canadian dollars unless otherwise noted.) The budget projected a deficit of $41.5 million. Duncan also announced that four more land claims and self-government agreements had been reached with *First Nations* (native) groups as part of a plan to transfer local authority to native bands.

Three members of the Yukon's legislature deserted the Liberal Party in April 2002 to sit as independents. They claimed that Duncan had failed to involve them in government decisions. Duncan called an election in November to regain a majority in the Assembly. The move backfired as 12 members of the conservative Yukon Party were elected to the 18-member legislature. The party's leader, Dennis Fentie, became the new premier. Fentie promised to revive the Yukon's mining industry and support the building of a gas pipeline along the Alaska Highway. The New Democratic Party won five seats. Duncan was the only Liberal elected to the legislature.

A new Yukon Act, the result of lengthy negotiations with the federal government, received assent in the Canadian Parliament in March 2002. The act gave the Yukon the same authority over its natural resources as that exercised by Canadian provinces. The governments of Canada and the Yukon planned to implement the new structure in 2003.

Nunavut, Canada's newest territory, faced difficult economic prospects in 2002. Census figures released in March showed that Nunavut's population grew about 8 percent between 1996 and 2001, a rate nearly double the national average. The region's extensive mineral resources were largely untapped in 2002, and experts predicted that traditional activities, such as hunting and fishing, could not continue to support Nunavut's rapidly growing population.

Finance Minister Kelvin Ng presented the territory's fourth budget in April. Expenditures of $760 million were offset by revenues of $745 million, of which $70 million was expected to come from the territory's own taxes and fees. The remainder came from the federal government. Taxes on tobacco products provided an important source of revenue.

Nunavut hosted the 17th Arctic Winter Games in 2002, held from March 17 to March 23. For the first time, Iqaluit, Nunavut's capital, shared the Games with a sister community in Greenland. Nearly 2,000 athletes, coaches, and cultural performers took part in the largest public event ever held in the territory. In addition to participants from the host countries, teams from Russia and Alaska also competed in the games. Events included traditional Inuit and *Dene* (Indian) pursuits, such as the painful sport of "knuckle hop," in which contestants must hop across the floor balanced only on their knuckles and toes. The games also included more common sports, such as snowboarding, basketball, hockey, and gymnastics. Cultural events featured contests in throat singing, a traditional Inuit art form.

Queen Elizabeth II of the United Kingdom, Canada's head of state, made her first visit to Nunavut on October 4. Arriving from London on a tour to celebrate her Golden Jubilee, the 50th anniversary of her reign, Queen Elizabeth stopped at Iqaluit to dedicate the territory's Legislative Assembly building. ☐ David M. L. Farr

See also **Canada.**

Cape Verde. See **Africa.**

Census. The United States Census Bureau in 2002 released statistics from the 2000 census on poverty, income, occupation, and housing in the United States and on the percentage of foreign-born people living in the United States. The Census Bureau collected the data from a detailed questionnaire distributed to approximately 19 million U.S. households.

Poverty levels. On June 4, 2002, the Census Bureau released figures that demonstrated that the economic gains of the 1990's had done little to eliminate poverty in the United States. According to the bureau, approximately 6.6 million U.S. families, 9.2 percent, officially qualified as poor in 1999. The Census Bureau described a family of four as poor if it had an annual income of less than $16,954. In 1989, 10 percent of families qualified as poor under federal guidelines.

The bureau found that the poverty rate among households headed by women with children under the age of 18 fell to 34.3 percent of all households in 1999 from 42.3 percent in 1989. The poverty rate among the elderly fell to 9.9 percent from 12.8 percent during the same period.

In September 2002, the Census Bureau released data that revealed that the poverty rate in the United States increased for most races between 2000 and 2001. White Americans experienced the largest increase, a rise of 7.4 percent, to 7.8 percent, in 2001. By comparison, poverty among African Americans rose 0.2 percent, to 22.7 percent, in 2001, according to the Census Bureau.

Income levels for men declined in 26 states between 1990 and 2000, according to 2000 census data released in June 2002. Average income for men fell by 2.3 percent in the 10 years since the 1990 census. Women's earnings rose 7 percent during the same period and increased in every state except Alaska. The bureau reported that median family income—the point at which half of the population earned less and half of the population earned more—increased by 9.5 percent between 1989 and 1999, to more than $50,000.

The Census Bureau revealed in a separate report issued on July 18, 2002, that people who earned a college or an advanced degree significantly increased their lifetime earnings. According to the report, high school graduates can expect to earn approximately $1.2 million over the course of their working lives, defined as the period ranging from ages 25 through 64. By contrast, those with a bachelor's degree can expect to earn $2.1 million. People with master's degrees can expect to earn $2.5 million, while those with doctoral degrees can expect to earn $3.4 million. People with professional degrees, for example, lawyers and physicians, can expect to earn $4.4 million.

Immigration statistics. The 2000 census also revealed that 31.1 million of the 281.4 million people counted in the last census came to the United States from other countries. The 2000 figure exceeded the number of foreign-born people counted in the 1990 census by 11.3 million people. The increase in foreign-born residents was the largest ever counted by the bureau. According to the census report, 52 percent of the new immigrants came to the United States from Latin America. The figure represented a 44-percent jump from 1990 census figures.

Adjusted count. A three-judge panel of the Ninth Circuit Court of Appeals in San Francisco ruled in October 2002 that the Census Bureau must release its statistically adjusted count for every state, county, and neighborhood in the United States. Some politicians had claimed that the 2000 census missed 3.2 million people, and as a result, many communities lost federal funding that is awarded based on population. The panel ruled that the public is legally entitled to see the bureau's adjusted figures, which show how many people were probably missed in the census. However, the Census Bureau was not required to use the adjusted figures to recalculate U.S. population totals.   □ Geoffrey A. Campbell

See also **Population.**

Chemistry. An international group of scientists reported in August 2002 that it had identified the key molecule responsible for creating the feeling of fullness after a meal. The researchers said their finding offered hope for treating *obesity* (extreme overweight). In obesity, some people fail to get the biochemical signal to stop eating when their stomachs are full.

Endocrinologists Rachel L. Batterham and Stephen R. Bloom, of the Imperial College of Science, Technology, and Medicine in London, and biochemist Michael A. Cowley, of Oregon Health and Science University in Beaverton, studied a molecule called peripheral hormone peptide YY, or PYY. Endocrinologists study *hormones,* chemical substances secreted by the body that affect the activity of cells, tissues, or organs. PYY is a hormone secreted by the intestines when a person eats a large amount of food.

The scientists said PYY travels through the bloodstream to the brain, where it has two effects. First, it blocks a chemical compound known to increase appetite. Second, it helps prompt the production of appetite-depressing compounds called melanocortins.

The researchers discovered the function of PYY in tests with human subjects. They injected the subjects with PYY two hours before the people went to eat at a buffet. These people ate about one-third less food than they did when not injected with PYY. In addition, the people reported that they had decreased appetites for about 12 hours after receiving the PYY injections.

According to the scientists, PYY or a synthetic version of it might be used to block the hunger pangs that cause some people to overeat.

Silk factories. In January, a team of scientists announced that it had, for the first time, developed a method that might be used to produce spider-web silk commercially. The team was led by molecular biologists Anthoula Lazaris and Costas N. Karatzas of Nexia Biotechnologies, Inc., near Montreal, Canada, and materials scientist Steven Arcidiacono of the United States Army Soldier Biological Chemical Command in Natick, Massachusetts.

Spider-web silk is five times stronger than steel by weight and nearly as elastic as nylon. However, it has never been produced commercially, mainly because spiders are cannibalistic and difficult to raise in captivity. The researchers got around this problem with *genetic engineering* (the manipulation of an organism's genes.)

The scientists first isolated the silk-making genes of the common garden spider, *Araneus diadematus.* They then spliced these genes into the genetic material of two kinds of animal cells— hamster kidney cells and cow mammary cells. The cells secreted two kinds of spider silk proteins.

The proteins contained a high proportion of the *amino acids* (building blocks of proteins) glycine and alanine, which are responsible for the silk's physical properties. The researchers collected copies of one of the proteins and put them in water to create a concentrated solution. Next, they squirted some of this solution into a new solution containing methanol (methyl alcohol). Exposure to the alcohol prompted the silk proteins to assemble themselves into long fibers, which the researchers pulled from the solution.

The resulting silk fibers were stronger than Kevlar, a tough commercial fiber product, and nearly as stretchy as nylon. The scientists said the fibers might be used to make artificial tendons and ligaments, fishing line, sutures for surgeries, and lightweight body armor for the military.

Chemical detection. A potential new way to isolate chemicals for drug production and medical tests was reported in July by chemists Stephen Zimmerman, Kenneth Suslick, and their colleagues at the University of Illinois at Urbana-Champaign. The chemists said they had created *synthetic* (artificial) chemical receptors. Chemical receptors are pocketlike molecules to which specific chemical substances, such as proteins or drugs can attach. In this way, chemical receptors can single out and identify chemicals in solution.

Scientists have long used natural chemical receptors, such as those on *antibodies* (proteins that react in the body with viruses and other foreign substances), to detect and isolate individual chemicals in complex mixtures in the laboratory. These kinds of studies have helped scientists design drug therapies and techniques to diagnose diseases. However, antibodies are costly and do not last long in the laboratory. The use of synthetic receptors would eliminate these problems.

The Illinois chemists first built a *dendrimer* (large, round molecule with branches) around a porphyrin. Porphyrins are large molecules found in such substances as *hemoglobin* (a pigment that transports oxygen in blood) and *chlorophyll* (a pigment that absorbs light energy in plants). The porphyrin served as a *template* (model of a shape) for the dendrimer. After the chemists removed this template, the dendrimer was left with a cavity in its middle shaped like the porphyrin. The cavity allowed the dendrimer to function like a receptor in that the porphyrin molecules shaped like the template attached themselves to it.

The scientists said their technique could be adapted to produce synthetic receptors for detecting many kinds of chemicals. These receptors, they added, might provide new ways to make chemical and biomedical materials; conduct certain medical tests; and identify chemical weapons and pollution. ☐ Peter J. Andrews

See also **Medicine.**

Chess. Ruslan Ponomariov of Ukraine became the youngest player to win the men's title of the Federation Internationale des Echecs (FIDE), the governing body of international chess, in January 2002. Ponomariov, who was 18 years old, beat Vassily Ivanchuk, also of Ukraine, 4.5 to 2.5 in Moscow. In chess, a win is worth one point, a draw is worth one-half, and a loss is worth zero. Ponomariov is the first Ukrainian to win the title.

Split title. Ponomariov was not the undisputed chess champion, however, because Vladimir Kramnik, who in 2000 defeated Garry Kasparov to become the Brain Games world chess champion—a rival organization to the FIDE—did not play in the FIDE tournament. (Einstein Group PLC., a London-based education firm, bought Brain Games in 2002 and changed the name of the Brain Games title to the Einstein World Chess Championship.) Chess officials were planning a world championship play-off involving Ponomariov, Kramnik, Kasparov, and Peter Leko of Hungary that could take place in early 2003.

Man vs. machine. Vladimir Kramnik and a computer named Deep Fritz battled to a draw in an eight-game, nontitle match held in Bahrain in October 2002. The Deep Fritz computer, manufactured by Chessbase, a computer company based in Hamburg, Germany, could evaluate 3.5 million moves per second. Kramnik reported that he was impressed with Deep Fritz's abilities.

Other tournaments. The favored Russian men's team won the gold medal at the World Chess Olympiad in November in Bled, Yugoslavia. Hungary took the men's silver medal, and Armenia won the bronze at the event, which is held every two years. In the women's division, China won the gold medal, Russia took the silver, and Poland captured the bronze.

China came from behind to defeat the United States 20.5 to 19.5 in the hard-fought Chess Summit held in Shanghai, China, in July. Teams included seven top male players, two top female players, and two top juniors from each country.

United States events. Larry Christiansen of Cambridge, Massachusetts, won the men's U.S. Chess Championship, and Jennifer Shahade of New York City won the women's title in January in Seattle. Gennadi Zaitshik of France and Evgeny Najer of Russia tied for first place at the U.S. Open Chess Championship in Cherry Hill, New Jersey, in August.

Young champions. The University of Texas at Dallas won the Final Four of college chess on April 7 at the World Chess Hall of Fame in Miami, Florida. Pieta Garrett of Mesa, Arizona, won the U.S. Cadet (under 16) championship held in Cleveland, Ohio, in July. A. J. Steigman of Parkland, Florida, won the U.S. Junior (under 21) Open held in Dallas in July. ☐ Al Lawrence

Broken scaffolding dangles from the 100-story John Hancock Center in Chicago in March 2002 after pieces plunged to the streets below, killing three people. High winds dislodged the scaffolding, which had not been properly secured.

Chicago. Mayor Richard M. Daley's plans to enlarge and improve Chicago's O'Hare International Airport ran into trouble in 2002. The project required buying up large tracts of suburban residential property for new runways. To obtain authority to condemn the suburban properties, Mayor Daley sought agreement from state and federal officials. Daley concluded an airport pact with Illinois Governor George Ryan in December 2001 but was unable to obtain federal approval in 2002. Although United States Senator Dick Durbin (D., Illinois) sponsored legislation in the Senate to authorize O'Hare expansion, U.S. Senator Peter Fitzgerald (R., Illinois) used parliamentary tactics to hold up the bill. The O'Hare project received a further blow in August when the two largest carriers based at O'Hare—United Airlines of Elk Grove Village, Illinois, and American Airlines of Ft. Worth, Texas—withdrew from an earlier agreement to contribute funding to terminal expansion plans. However, they remained committed to the runway expansion project.

West Nile outbreak. An outbreak of West Nile virus during the summer of 2002 resulted in the deaths of more than 12 Chicagoans, and almost 200 city residents were diagnosed with the disease. Migrating birds carry the virus, which is spread to humans by mosquitoes that bite both birds and people.

In June, city workers began placing insecticidal pellets in catch basins and lagoons in city parks and on other city property to kill young mosquitoes. On September 8, city trucks began spraying insecticide in city neighborhoods, the first widespread spraying program undertaken by Chicago since 1975.

Soldier Field project. On April 25, 2002, Cook County Judge John K. Madden ruled that a renovation of Soldier Field does not improperly use tax dollars to benefit the Chicago Bears of the National Football League. The judgment came in response to a suit brought by Friends of the Park and the Landmarks Preservation Council of Illinois, citizens' groups attempting to halt the $632-million renovation of Chicago's classically colonnaded stadium built on the city's lakefront in 1924. The groups appealed the verdict to the Illinois Supreme Court, which agreed in late 2002 to hear the case.

Despite the legal challenges, construction proceeded on the Soldier Field project. During the summer and fall of 2002, Chicago residents watched as the steel skeleton of a giant bowl took shape inside the existing colonnades. In September, city officials said that the project was on schedule to be completed in September 2003.

Law upheld. Chicago's revised antigang loitering ordinance, which allows police officers to disperse people from locales designated by the police superintendent as areas prone to gang-related or drug-related activity, survived its first court test in 2002. On July 30, a Cook County judge acquitted two alleged gang members of the loitering charge but did not question the law's constitutionality.

The U.S. Supreme Court struck down the original version of Chicago's antigang loitering law in 1999. In that decision, a majority of the court held that the law gave police officers too much discretion. Legal experts then rewrote the law to narrow its scope and resubmitted it to the Chicago City Council, which passed the revised legislation in 2001.

School scores. Students in the Chicago Public School system scored 3 to 4 percentage points higher on standardized tests in 2002 than in 2001, school officials reported in May 2002. The test statistics showed across-the-board improvements, with increases both at the high school and elementary level and in schools that have historically performed poorly, as well as in schools that have been strong academic performers.

☐ Harold Henderson

See also **City; Gardening; Houston; People in the news** (Chihuly, Dale); **Public health and safety.**

Children's books. See Literature for children.

Chile signed a free-trade agreement with the United States in December 2002 that eliminated tariffs on 85 percent of the goods traded by the two countries. Furthermore, the pact called for the elimination of all tariffs in Chile-U.S. trade after 12 years. Earlier in 2002, Chile had negotiated a similar agreement with the European Union, which eliminated tariffs on nearly 90 percent of Chilean trade with Europe. Chilean officials expected the free-trade accords to help reduce unemployment, which was unofficially estimated at 15 percent in 2002.

President Ricardo Lagos Escobar presented an ambitious social agenda to Chile's Congress in May. He proposed creating 150,000 new jobs, reforming the health care system, and expanding government spending on education to help the 20-percent of Chileans living in poverty.

Many Chileans criticized the government for increasing military spending in 2002. In January, the armed forces acquired 10 F-16 fighter jets at a cost of more than $600 million and two submarines for $500 million from the United States.

In July, Chile's Supreme Court ruled that former President Augusto Pinochet Ugarte was mentally unfit to stand trial for human rights violations that occurred during his dictatorship from 1973 to 1990. ☐ Nathan A. Haverstock

See also **Latin America.**

China. Vice President Hu Jintao of China assumed the role of general secretary of the ruling Chinese Communist Party in November 2002 at the 16th Party Congress, a meeting that takes place every five years. Party members appoint leaders and lay out the nation's goals at such meetings. The change in leaders in 2002 was the first orderly transition of power in China's modern history. Hu, a 59-year-old engineer who replaced Jiang Zemin as China's leader, pledged to adhere to the course of economic reform and openness to the outside world set by Jiang.

Hu took over leadership of a country experiencing dazzling economic and social change. He also faced rampant corruption, spreading unemployment, and growing demands for political change.

Hu had been a rising star in Chinese politics for some time. In the early 1990's, Deng Xiaoping, one of China's most influential leaders, gave Hu a seat on the Politburo, which establishes policy guidelines for the Communist Party. Hu first became prominent as leader of the powerful Communist Youth League. He served as head of the Communist Party in Tibet in 1989, when China imposed martial law to quell unrest in the region. In 1998, the Chinese parliament selected Hu to serve as vice president. He was the youngest person ever to hold the office.

Jiang's retirement in 2002 as general secretary ended months of speculation that he might try to remain in office long past the unofficial retirement age of 70. Although he relinquished the post to Hu, Jiang retained the titles of president and chairman of the Central Military Commission. Political observers expected Jiang to turn over the title of president to Hu in March 2003 at the annual meeting of parliament. Observers were not certain whether Jiang would resign the military post, which gave him the power to make decisions on security and foreign policy matters.

At the 2002 Party Congress, Jiang also succeeded in packing the Standing Committee of the Politburo—a powerful council that the congress expanded from seven to nine members in November—with at least six of his own loyalists, including Zeng Qinghong, his longtime aide and strategist. Jiang's continuing influence raised questions about the true extent of Hu's influence and power within the government.

Other powerful leaders retired in 2002, including Prime Minister Zhu Rongji and the head of parliament, Li Peng. Change also swept through the 22-member Politburo and the larger Central Committee. Two-thirds of the members of the Politburo retired in 2002. Half of the 356 members of the Central Committee also retired. In general, the new members were younger and better educated than their predecessors.

In July, a young capitalist in Shanghai hauls enormous bundles of plastic containers to a recycling depot, where he receives about 1 cent for every two pounds (0.9 kilograms). China's leaders announced in 2002 that the Communist Party represents capitalists as much as workers and peasants and amended the Constitution to allow private business owners to join the party.

Capitalism. Reconciling a modern market economy with traditional Communist principles became the recurring theme at the weeklong congress. The 2,114 delegates voted unanimously to amend the party's Constitution to include Jiang's theory of the "three represents"—which declares that the party represents capitalists as much as the workers and peasants who formed its base for more than 80 years. The amendment made it possible for private-business owners to become members of the Communist Party.

In a two-hour speech to the congress, Jiang said China would continue on its course of economic transformation but ruled out any sweeping changes in political freedom. He described economic development as the nation's central task and said China must persevere with the introduction of market forces. He also acknowledged the problems of corruption, inequality, and unemployment that had emerged along with China's spectacular economic growth.

Corruption. Government officials admitted in 2002 that corruption had become a threat to national stability. In March, Chinese legislators called for the introduction of tough legislation to target the country's endemic problem of official graft. In August, the Communist Party expelled Zhu Xiaohua, a banker in charge of China's foreign reserves and a protege of the prime minister, on charges of bribery. Chinese citizens told Western reporters that they believed many government officials were being protected from prosecution.

Unrest. Industrial workers from state-owned factories in northeastern China held massive demonstrations in March to protest unpaid wages and corruption. In the industrial city of Liaoyang, tens of thousands of workers attracted worldwide attention as they demonstrated outside bankrupt factories. Antigraft investigators later confirmed that officials at the factories had milked the assets of fading state companies, even as workers and retirees were denied their wages and pensions. In Daqing, the site of oil fields, a few thousand workers protested against inadequate severance pay. Approximately 25 million workers had been laid off from state-owned companies since 1998.

Human rights. The United Nations (UN) high commissioner for human rights, Mary Robinson, warned in August 2002 that China was using the global war on terrorism as an excuse to crack down on Islamic minorities and members of the banned Falun Gong, a spiritual movement that combines exercises, meditation, and breathing techniques with religious ideas from Buddhism and Taoism. Robinson said China had passed laws in recent years that increased the government's powers of arrest and detention. China's treatment of ethnic Uighur Muslims in the western province of Xinjiang was of particular concern, Robinson said. In March, Amnesty International, a London-based human rights group, accused China of stepping up harsh repression of Uighurs.

Xinjiang is a large province with 8 million Muslim Uighurs among its 17 million people. Opposition to rule by Chinese migrants had long festered in the province, particularly among separatists. In January, the Chinese government accused Uighurs of being linked to al-Qa'ida, a global terrorist organization that is allied with other Islamic extremist groups worldwide. In September, Chinese officials welcomed a UN decision to place an Uighur separatist group on a terrorist list. The move was supported by the United States, Afghanistan, and Kyrgyzstan, a former Soviet republic which borders Xinjiang.

Economy. Premier Zhu said in November that China hopes to quadruple the size of its economy by 2022. China grew at an annual rate of 7.9 percent in 2002, and direct foreign investment in China surged by 22.5 percent in the first nine months of 2002 compared with the same period of 2001.

In March 2002, Zhu warned that farmers were being left behind in China's pursuit of economic growth. He said rural incomes rose just 4.2 percent to the annual equivalent of $275 in 2001. Incomes in cities, in contrast, rose 8.5 percent to $837. In May 2002, Lu Zhiqiang, a senior economic planner, warned that the gap between rich and poor in China was rapidly widening and could threaten national stability.

Hong Kong. Tung Chee-hwa began his second five-year term as Hong Kong's chief executive in July 2002. He was elected by a committee selected by Chinese officials. Tung selected a cabinet of political appointees, replacing civil servants at the top levels of government. Political experts said it was Hong Kong's biggest shake-up since the United Kingdom turned the former colony over to China in 1997.

U.S. relations. China continued in 2002 to seek friendly ties with the United States. In February, U.S. President George W. Bush met with Jiang in China, and Jiang visited Bush's ranch in Texas in October. The governments drew closer in part because of shared interests in combating terrorism. However, the issue of whether China would force Taiwan to reunite with the mainland remained a point of contention between the Chinese and U.S. governments. Taiwan is an island state regarded by China as a province.

In July, Chinese officials rejected a U.S. Department of Defense report suggesting that China spent four times more on defense than it publicly acknowledged. At the urging of the United States, China in August imposed new regulations on exports of missile-related technology to a host of countries, including Iran, Iraq, North Korea, Yemen, Libya, and Pakistan.

AIDS. The UN reported in June that China was on the brink of an "explosive" AIDS epidemic and could have 10 million people infected with HIV, the virus that causes AIDS, by 2010. UN officials urged the Chinese government to spend more on education and prevention and complained that many Chinese officials lack commitment to fighting AIDS. UN officials noted that in 2002 between 800,000 and 1.5 million Chinese were infected with HIV.

Floods swept through central China in mid-2002. More than 1,500 people were killed as the result of floods and flood-related disasters. The government reported that 110 million people were affected by the floods and that more than 2.4 million had to be evacuated nationwide.

Space. China's official newspaper, *The China Daily,* reported in May that China planned to put an astronaut in space by 2005. Such as launch would make China only the third nation to send a human into space, after Russia and the United States. In addition, the government hoped to put an astronaut on the moon by 2010.

☐ Henry S. Bradsher

See also **Asia; Taiwan.**

City. The threat of terrorism was a far greater concern for cities in the United States in 2002 as a result of the terrorist attacks on Sept. 11, 2001. In a survey of 725 cities released in September 2002 by the National League of Cities (NLC), officials listed attacks involving biological and chemical weapons and cyberterrorism at the top of their list of concerns about terrorist threats. Cyberterrorism is the use of computer technology to sabotage information systems. The NLC is a Washington, D.C.-based organization that seeks to improve the quality of life in U.S. cities.

According to the survey, officials in larger cities (those with more than 100,000 people) were more likely to indicate concern about terrorist threats. Terrorism involving biological weapons was a concern for 82 percent of all cities and 95 percent of larger cities. Eighty-one percent of all cities and 92 percent of larger cities mentioned chemical weapons. Eighty percent of all cities and 91 percent of large cities listed cyberterrorism as a concern.

Funding terrorism preparedness. According to the NLC survey, city officials also included terrorism preparedness among their top priorities. Approximately 70 percent of all cities indicated the need for funding to pay for equipment, and 62 percent mentioned training to support local homeland security efforts. However, a weak

50 largest urban centers in the world

Rank	Urban center	Population
1.	Tokyo, Japan	26,444,000
2.	Mumbai, India	19,148,000
3.	Mexico City, Mexico	18,258,000
4.	Sao Paulo, Brazil	18,173,000
5.	New York City, U.S.	16,753,000
6.	Lagos, Nigeria	14,679,000
7.	Dhaka, Bangladesh	13,430,000
8.	Calcutta, India	13,390,000
9.	Los Angeles, U.S.	13,317,000
10.	Shanghai, China	12,975,000
11.	Buenos Aires, Argentina	12,815,000
12.	Karachi, Pakistan	12,639,000
13.	Delhi, India	12,359,000
14.	Jakarta, Indonesia	11,812,000
15.	Manila, Philippines	11,476,000
16.	Osaka, Japan	11,013,000
17.	Cairo, Egypt	10,957,000
18.	Beijing, China	10,917,000
19.	Rio de Janeiro, Brazil	10,754,000
20.	Istanbul, Turkey	9,964,000
21.	Seoul, Republic of Korea	9,888,000
22.	Paris, France	9,641,000
23.	Moscow, Russia	9,332,000
24.	Tianjin, China	9,281,000
25.	Lima, Peru	7,729,000
26.	London, U.K.	7,640,000
27.	Bangkok, Thailand	7,589,000
28.	Tehran, Iran	7,343,000
29.	Hyderabad, India	7,338,000
30.	Hong Kong, China	7,082,000
31.	Chicago, U.S.	7,005,000
32.	Madras, India	6,933,000
33.	Essen, Germany	6,550,000
34.	Taipei, Taiwan	6,542,000
35.	Bogota, Colombia	6,533,000
36.	Lahore, Pakistan	6,489,000
37.	Bangalore, India	5,862,000
38.	Chongqing, China	5,813,000
39.	Santiago, Chile	5,704,000
40.	Kinshasa, Congo	5,467,000
41.	Wuhan, China	5,458,000
42.	St. Petersburg, Russia	5,134,000
43.	Baghdad, Iraq	5,041,000
44.	Shenyang, China	4,892,000
45.	Toronto, Canada	4,759,000
46.	Ho Chi Minh City, Vietnam	4,757,000
47.	Philadelphia, U.S.	4,446,000
48.	Yangon, Myanmar	4,396,000
49.	Ahmedabad, India	4,353,000
50.	Belo Horizonte, Brazil	4,304,000

Source: 2002 estimates based on data from the United Nations.

economy left many U.S. cities less able to fund terrorism readiness programs. Approximately two-thirds of the cities responding to the survey mentioned a need for funding to pay for training and to support local homeland security efforts in the future.

Efforts to get the federal government to help U.S. cities fund terrorism preparedness received a major setback in November. A $3.5-billion initiative that would have provided resources for emergency management planning, training, exercises, and equipment for local police, fire, and medical services personnel was cut from federal legislation that created the Department of Homeland Security. NLC President Karen J. Anderson sharply criticized Congress's failure to provide this security assistance to U.S. cities.

Despite heightened fears of terrorism, city officials still cited traditional security and economic issues as being of greater concern than terrorist threats. The NLC survey indicated that 62 percent of all cities and 69 percent of larger cities cited public safety and crime prevention as their top priority. This was followed by economic conditions (cited by 55 percent of all cities and 53 percent of larger cities); and funding for infrastructure investment (44 percent of all cities and 26 percent of larger cities).

Decline in city economies. The economies of U.S. cities were in worse shape in 2002 than in the preceding year, according to a study by the NLC released in August 2002. This decline in the financial health of U.S. cities ended nearly a decade of improvement in urban economic conditions. According to the study, growth in city revenues, which had been nearly 6 percent in 2001, was expected to drop to 1.2 percent in 2002. An uncertain economic recovery in 2002 resulted in slower than expected growth in sales taxes and income taxes.

Furthermore, tourism declined throughout the United States following the terrorist attacks in 2001, reducing tax revenues from hotels and restaurants. U.S. Commerce Secretary Don Evans noted in September 2002 that travel and tourism industries in most major U.S. cities had begun to show some improvement. NYC & Company, New York City's convention and visitor's bureau, reported in September that the number of tourists visiting New York City in 2002 would equal the number of visits in 2001, when 29.5 million domestic tourists came to the city. The company noted, however, that visitors were spending less money than in previous years.

Quality of life. In 2002, cities in Australia, Austria, Canada, and Switzerland scored the highest ratings in an annual survey of the quality of life in cities throughout the world conducted by William M. Mercer Consulting Group of

50 largest cities in the United States

Rank	City	Population*
1.	New York, N.Y.	8,159,541
2.	Los Angeles, Calif.	3,739,291
3.	Chicago, Ill.	2,919,230
4.	Houston, Tex.	2,031,761
5.	Philadelphia, Pa.	1,504,527
6.	Phoenix, Ariz.	1,413,223
7.	San Diego, Calif.	1,248,485
8.	Dallas, Tex.	1,231,754
9.	San Antonio, Tex.	1,196,266
10.	Detroit, Mich.	937,054
11.	San Jose, Calif.	920,903
12.	Indianapolis, Ind.	802,573
13.	San Francisco, Calif.	788,115
14.	Jacksonville, Fla.	759,046
15.	Columbus, Ohio	729,224
16.	Austin, Tex.	711,504
17.	Memphis, Tenn.	658,579
18.	Baltimore, Md.	636,264
19.	Boston, Mass.	592,209
20.	Milwaukee, Wis.	591,019
21.	Nashville, Tenn.	583,189
22.	Charlotte, N.C.	581,141
23.	Denver, Colo.	575,460
24.	El Paso, Tex.	574,309
25.	Seattle, Wash.	573,674
26.	Washington, D.C.	565,556
27.	Las Vegas, Nev.	563,432
28.	Fort Worth, Tex.	555,750
29.	Portland, Ore.	551,577
30.	Oklahoma City, Okla.	520,198
31.	Tucson, Ariz.	506,461
32.	New Orleans, La.	482,254
33.	Cleveland, Ohio	473,250
34.	Long Beach, Calif.	468,471
35.	Albuquerque, N. Mex.	463,624
36.	Fresno, Calif.	445,540
37.	Kansas City, Mo.	442,871
38.	Virginia Beach, Va.	432,260
39.	Mesa, Ariz.	426,743
40.	Atlanta, Ga.	421,235
41.	Sacramento, Calif.	415,364
42.	Oakland, Calif.	405,338
43.	Omaha, Nebr.	402,666
44.	Tulsa, Okla.	398,571
45.	Minneapolis, Minn.	385,608
46.	Colorado Springs, Colo.	381,680
47.	Honolulu, Hawaii	372,922
48.	Miami, Fla.	363,268
49.	Wichita, Kan.	353,433
50.	Arlington, Tex.	351,329

*2002 World Book estimates based on data from the U.S. Census Bureau.

50 largest metropolitan areas in the United States

Rank	Metropolitan area*	Population†
1.	Los Angeles-Long Beach, Calif.	9,660,745
2.	New York City, N.Y.	9,482,646
3.	Chicago, Ill.	8,465,809
4.	Philadelphia, Pa.-N.J.	5,137,724
5.	Washington, D.C.-Md.-Va.-W.Va.	5,087,958
6.	Detroit, Mich.	4,478,046
7.	Atlanta, Ga.	4,438,350
8.	Houston, Tex.	4,395,993
9.	Dallas, Tex.	3,744,376
10.	Phoenix-Mesa, Ariz.	3,553,169
11.	Boston, Mass.	3,444,407
12.	Riverside-San Bernadino, Calif.	3,424,269
13.	Minneapolis-St. Paul, Minn.-Wis.	3,070,000
14.	Orange County, Calif.	2,950,257
15.	San Diego, Calif.	2,885,188
16.	Nassau-Suffolk, N.Y.	2,784,289
17.	St. Louis, Mo.-Ill.	2,627,092
18.	Baltimore, Md.	2,589,889
19.	Seattle-Bellevue-Everett, Wash.	2,506,259
20.	Tampa-St. Petersburg-Clearwater, Fla.	2,472,795
21.	Oakland, Calif.	2,464,386
22.	Pittsburgh, Pa.	2,351,624
23.	Miami, Fla.	2,327,420
24.	Cleveland-Lorain-Elyria, Ohio	2,260,786
25.	Denver, Colo.	2,237,737
26.	Newark, N.J.	2,057,867
27.	Portland, Ore.-Vancouver, Wash.	2,021,404
28.	Las Vegas, Nev.-Ariz.	1,834,572
29.	Kansas City, Mo.-Kan.	1,819,662
30.	Fort Worth-Arlington, Tex.	1,789,169
31.	Orlando, Fla.	1,759,313
32.	San Francisco, Calif.	1,758,993
33.	San Jose, Calif.	1,724,572
34.	Fort Lauderdale, Fla.	1,719,520
35.	Sacramento, Calif.	1,698,962
36.	Cincinnati, Ohio-Ky.-Ind.	1,672,511
37.	Indianapolis, Ind.	1,660,644
38.	San Antonio, Tex.	1,657,365
39.	Norfolk-Virginia Beach-Newport News, Va.	1,597,286
40.	Charlotte-Gastonia, N.C.-Rock Hill, S.C.	1,587,513
41.	Columbus, Ohio	1,585,145
42.	Milwaukee-Waukesha, Wis.	1,515,183
43.	Salt Lake City-Ogden, Ut.	1,399,803
44.	Bergen-Passaic, N.J.	1,393,565
45.	Austin-San Marcos, Tex.	1,371,834
46.	New Orleans, La.	1,348,718
47.	Greensboro-Winston-Salem-High Point, N.C.	1,300,028
48.	Nashville, Tenn.	1,293,646
49.	Raleigh-Durham-Chapel Hill, N.C.	1,282,160
50.	Middlesex-Somerset-Hunterdon, N.J.	1,204,281

*The U.S. Bureau of the Census defines a metropolitan area as a large population nucleus with adjacent communities having a high degree of economic and social integration.

†2002 World Book estimates based on data from the U.S. Census Bureau.

New York City. The Mercer group evaluated 215 cities on the basis of 39 criteria, including factors such as basic political, social, economic, and environmental conditions; the availability and quality of housing; health care; schools; public services; and recreation.

The report placed Zurich, Switzerland, first in the overall ranking. Vienna, Austria, and Vancouver, Canada, tied for second, followed by Sydney, Australia, and Geneva, Switzerland. Brazzaville, capital of the Republic of the Congo, received the lowest ranking. Among U.S. cities, Honolulu, Hawaii, ranked as the city with the best quality of life.

Calgary, Canada, was ranked the cleanest city in the world, according to the same Mercer group study. Honolulu, Hawaii, placed second, followed by Helsinki, Finland; Katsuyama, Japan; Minneapolis, Minnesota; and Ottawa, Canada.

Most expensive cities. Hong Kong, Moscow, and Tokyo were the world's three most expensive cities in which to live in 2002, according to a report published in July by the Mercer group. The Chinese cities Beijing and Shanghai ranked fourth and fifth on the list. Eleven of the world's most costly cities are located in Asia.

The Mercer group ranked 144 cities throughout the world by comparing city-by-city rents and the costs of over 200 items in each location. These included housing, food, clothing, and household goods, together with transportation and entertainment. The company assigned each city a numerical rating and compared it with New York City, which was assigned a rating of 100.

New York City placed seventh on the group's list, making it the most expensive city in the United States. London, in 10th place, was the most expensive city in the European Union. Toronto was the most expensive city in Canada, ranking 104th overall.

Political and economic turmoil in Argentina caused Buenos Aires to plummet from its 2001 ranking as the 23rd most expensive city in the world to the 133rd spot in 2002. Johannesburg, South Africa, was the least expensive city in the world. In the United States, Portland, Oregon, and Winston-Salem, North Carolina, were the least expensive cities. Both tied for 69th place.

Wealthiest U.S. cities. Rancho Santa Fe, California, was the wealthiest community in the United States, according to the U.S. Census Bureau, which reported that finding in June. Residents of Rancho Santa Fe had an average annual per capita income of $113,132 in 2000, the year of the last census. The Census Bureau reported that Atherton, California, was the second wealthiest U.S. city, with an average per capita income of $112,408. Palm Beach, Florida, placed third with an average income of $109,219.

September 11 memorials. On September 11, 2002, cities throughout the United States chose a variety of ways to mark the first anniversary of the terrorist attacks on Sept. 11, 2001. The ceremonies shared common themes of patriotism and unity. In New York City, a day of tributes included a moment of silence at 8:46 a.m., the moment when the first plane struck the World Trade Center. A tolling of bells at religious and academic institutions followed at 10:29 a.m., the moment when the second tower collapsed. Several people, including former New York City Mayor Rudolph Giuliani, read the names of all of the nearly 2,800 victims at the World Trade Center. New York Governor George Pataki read the Gettysburg Address during the ceremony.

In Los Angeles, residents gathered in spontaneous moments of remembrance and in large formal ceremonies to express solidarity. Despite a three-hour time difference between Los Angeles and New York City, many ceremonies coincided with the exact moments of the terrorist attacks. Similar ceremonies took place in Chicago. At one memorial service, Chicago Mayor Richard M. Daley urged residents to "recommit ourselves with the president and go after every terrorist in the world." ☐ Fitzgerald Higgins

See also **Chicago; Los Angeles; New York City.**

Civil rights. See **Human rights.**

Classical music. The drumbeat of financial trouble for symphony orchestras in the United States grew to a low roar in 2002, as one orchestra after another announced that it had lost money on the 2001-2002 season. The sagging national economy had a negative effect on all revenue sources, especially corporate, foundation, government, and individual donations. Symphony executives noted that orchestras suffer in weak economic times because of such high fixed costs as long-term contracts with musicians and commitments to guest artists booked years in advance.

The Chicago Symphony Orchestra, with a $60-million annual budget, announced in October that it faced operating losses of $6.1 million in 2002. The Houston Symphony Orchestra posted a deficit of $1.6 million, while the Dallas Symphony Orchestra was $850,000 in debt in 2002. These Texas ensembles suffered from a downturn in corporate giving tied to problems plaguing local energy companies, such as the bankruptcy of Houston-based Enron Corp. The Cleveland Orchestra posted a $1.3-million deficit in 2002 after being hit by a 29-percent drop in corporate contributions related to the departure of several companies from the city. Facing a deficit of more than $750,000, the Pittsburgh Symphony Orchestra announced in August that it might have to

The French emperor Napoleon enters a burning Moscow in a lavish production of Sergei Prokofiev's *War and Peace*, staged at the Metropolitan Opera in New York City in early 2002. The opera, with an American and Russian cast, included 52 soloists, 227 extras, 120 choristers, 41 dancers, and a live horse.

Grammy Award winners in 2002

Classical Album, *Berlioz: Les Troyens;* Various artists; London Symphony Orchestra; James Mallinson, producer.

Orchestral Performance, *Boulez Conducts Varese (Ameriques; Arcana; Deserts; Ionisation);* Chicago Symphony Orchestra; Pierre Boulez, conductor.

Opera Recording, *Berlioz: Les Troyens;* Various artists; London Symphony Orchestra; James Mallinson, producer.

Choral Performance, *Bach: St. Matthew Passion;* Arnold Schoenberg Chorus and Wiener Sanger-knaben; Concentus Musicus Wien; Nikolaus Harnoncourt, conductor.

Instrumental Soloists with Orchestra, *Strauss Wind Concertos (Horn Concerto; Oboe Concerto, Etc.);* Dale Clevenger, horn; Larry Combs, clarinet; Alex Klein, oboe; David McGill, bassoon; Chicago Symphony Orchestra; Daniel Barenboim, conductor.

Instrumental Soloist without Orchestra, *Britten Cello Suites (1-3);* Truls Mork, cello.

Chamber Music Performance, *Haydn: The Complete String Quartets;* The Angeles String Quartet.

Small Ensemble Performance, *After Mozart (Raskatov, Silvestrov, Schnittke, Etc.);* Gidon Kremer, violin; Kremerata Baltica.

Classical Vocal Performance, *Dreams & Fables—Gluck Italian Arias (Tremo Fra' Dubbi Miei; Di Questa Cetra in Seno, Etc.);* Cecilia Bartoli, mezzo soprano.

Classical Contemporary Composition, *Rouse: Concert De Gaudi for Guitar and Orchestra;* Christopher Rouse.

Classical Crossover Album, *Perpetual Motion (Scarlatti, Bach, Debussy, Chopin, Etc.);* Bela Fleck, banjo; Various other artists.

seek bankruptcy protection if it was unable to raise enough money to cover its expenses during the 2002-2003 season.

Orchestras fight back. Not all U.S. orchestra news was gloomy in 2002. The St. Louis Symphony Orchestra saved itself from bankruptcy by making $5.5 million in budget cuts and raising $29 million from the public with an appeal to civic pride. The comeback in St. Louis matched that of several other orchestras. Of the dozen orchestras that filed for bankruptcy or ceased operations since 1987, all but the Sacramento and San Jose symphonies in California were back in business by 2002. "Orchestras have proved surprisingly resilient," noted Jack McAuliffe, vice president of the American Symphony Orchestra League, a New York City-based organization that provides services for North American orchestras.

A number of symphony orchestras found creative ways in 2002 to fight the popular perception that their concerts were stuffy, intimidating rituals for elite audiences. Even in communities where this was not the prevailing image, orchestras explored new means of making concertgoers feel more personally connected to performances. Innovations included adding visual elements to selected programs, increasing interaction between the musicians on stage and audience members, and departing from the usual overture-concerto-symphony program format. In October, the Chicago Symphony Orchestra staged a special family-oriented Halloween program in which the musicians dressed in ghoulish costumes and makeup and performed amid spooky props and lighting. The Philadelphia Orchestra and the Atlanta Symphony Orchestra were among other ensembles that adopted new approaches, including integrating video images and theater into their performances.

Music critics noted that orchestras that experimented with performances may have succeeded in making the concert experience more appealing to a younger and broader community of listeners. However, they added that the innovations turned off some older, more experienced classical music lovers, who said they did not want or need such help to enjoy concerts.

Musical chairs. Several prominent conductors took up the baton at new podiums in September 2002. Great Britain's Sir Simon Rattle directed his first concerts as chief conductor of the Berlin Philharmonic Orchestra. The U.S. conductor Lorin Maazel made his debut as music director of the New York Philharmonic, succeeding Kurt Masur, and the Austrian conductor Franz Welser-Most took over the Cleveland Orchestra from Christoph von Dohnanyi. In October, the Royal Concertgebouw Orchestra of Amsterdam named the Latvian-born conductor Mariss

Jansons to succeed Riccardo Chailly as principal conductor.

New operas. *Galileo Galilei,* an opera by U.S. composer Philip Glass about the Italian astronomer whose findings led the Roman Catholic Church to convict him of heresy in 1633, was premiered at Chicago's Goodman Theatre in June 2002. The opera, with a libretto by stage director Mary Zimmerman, moved on to the Brooklyn Academy of Music in New York City and the Barbican Theatre in London. *Three Tales,* a video opera by U.S. composer Steve Reich and video artist Beryl Korot, had its world premiere in May at the Vienna Festival in Austria and its U.S. premiere later that month at the Spoleto Festival USA in Charleston, South Carolina. The opera explores three historic events in the 1900's concerning technology—the crash of the German zeppelin *Hindenburg* in 1937; the atom bomb tests at Bikini Atoll in the late 1940's; and the creation of the sheep Dolly in 1996 through *cloning* (the creation of genetically identical individuals).

New orchestral works. Two scores by the French composer Marc-Andre Dalbavie were premiered by leading orchestras in 2002. The Orchestre de Paris under Christoph Eschenbach gave the first performance of Dalbavie's *Color* at New York City's Carnegie Hall in January. The Cleveland Orchestra under Franz Welser-Most premiered Dalbavie's *Rocks Under the Water,* inspired by a building designed by architect Frank Gehry, in September.

On the Transmigration of Souls, by the U.S. composer John Adams, was first performed in September with Lorin Maazel leading the New York Philharmonic. The piece, scored for two choruses and orchestra and featuring computer-controlled electronic sound, marked the first anniversary of the terrorist attacks on the United States on Sept. 11, 2001.

Notable deaths. U.S. composer Ralph Shapey, who called himself a "radical traditionalist" because of the romantic impulse at the core of his dense, complex music, died in June 2002 at age 81. Gunter Wand, the German musician who was considered the last great orchestra conductor in the German tradition, died in February at age 90. In May, Yevgeny Svetlanov, one of Russia's foremost conductors and composers, died at age 73. In August, William Warfield, the U.S. bass-baritone best known for his portrayal of Porgy in George Gershwin's opera *Porgy and Bess,* died at age 82. Leo Ornstein, the Ukrainian-born U.S. composer whose experimental works were considered to be part of the Futurist movement, died in February at age 109. ☐ John von Rhein

See also **Popular music.**

Clothing. See **Fashion.**

Coal. See **Energy supply.**

Television and the Internet intensified a generation's mad scramble for forgotten treasures.

By David Streitfeld

Mining the American Attic: Collecting and Collectibles

COLLECTIBLES

SPECIAL REPORT

A 75-year-old retired man in Tucson, Arizona, had an old Navajo blanket that had been in his family for years. The blanket looked quite ordinary, so ordinary that it had been kept at the foot of the man's bed when he was a child. As an adult, he kept it folded over a chair. Then "Antiques Roadshow," a Public Broadcasting System (PBS) television series, came to town. The program, the most popular on public television, offered free appraisals of people's antiques in exchange for a chance to film the stories behind their possessions. Sometimes people discovered that a cherished heirloom was worth less than they guessed. Sometimes they were thrilled because some object they had taken for granted was worth thousands of dollars.

The man took his blanket to the show, where an expert closely examined the cloth, weave, and dyes used to create its stripes. The appraiser told the man that the blanket was a national treasure that had once been worn by a Ute Indian chief. The extremely rare textile dated from about 1850 and was in extraordinarily good condition. Its estimated value was $350,000 to $500,000.

The blanket was the most valuable article discovered in the program's first six years, but every episode featured some item of surprising value. A pair of wooden duck decoys turned out to be worth $10,000; a Native American tomahawk, $150,000. The message promoted by the show and others like it—that treasures lay undiscovered in attics everywhere—fueled the imagination of viewers who hoped that they too might realize a small fortune from some forgotten, dust-covered relic.

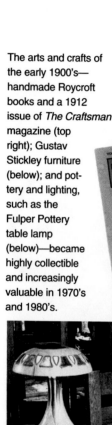

The arts and crafts of the early 1900's—handmade Roycroft books and a 1912 issue of *The Craftsman* magazine (top right); Gustav Stickley furniture (below); and pottery and lighting, such as the Fulper Pottery table lamp (below)—became highly collectible and increasingly valuable in 1970's and 1980's.

The search is on

The message was eagerly embraced by a generation that already was collecting on a scale and with intensity unlike any other generation. According to Nicholas Basbanes, the author of two books about the mania of possessions, "We have entered an age where everything is collectible"—from 1930's patent medicine bottles to doorknockers, foot-scrapers, and aged vacuum cleaners. Even Charles, the Prince of Wales, is known to collect vintage toilet seats. All the trash of earlier generations has became someone's treasure today. Studying the phenomenon, psychologists and sociologists came up with a number of explanations including an increase in disposable income, nostalgia triggered by shifts in society, the mobility of the culture, and the rise of the Internet. Most basically, it would appear to be a human impulse to acquire and cherish objects that have little or no intrinsic value.

Passion or obsession?

Collecting, originally, was called by a less elegant name—plunder. Whatever victorious armies and the kings and generals who led them liked, they claimed as their own and carried home. The museums of Europe are filled with objects looted from conquered cultures. In the United Kingdom, collecting flourished during the peak of the British Empire under Queen Victoria, from 1837 to 1901. Soldiers and sailors, adventurers and explorers, and wealthy tourists plundered treasures from around the world and carted them back home to England. In the early 1800's, Lord Elgin, the British ambassador to the Ottoman Empire, actually purchased and shipped home the ancient Greek sculptures that originally decorated the Parthenon in Athens. They remain in the British Museum in London to this day.

Individuals regarded as obsessive, even deranged, also assembled extraordinary collections. Sir Thomas Phillipps, a wealthy British book collector of the 1800's, wanted to own one copy of every book in the world. It was an impossible pursuit, but he did acquire about 50,000 books and an even more impressive 60,000 manuscripts. However, Phillipps kept his family in poverty and appeared unstable even to sympathetic friends, one of whom wrote, "the house looks more miserable and dilapidated every time I visit it, and there is not a room now that is not crowded with large boxes." Gerald Wells, a prominent British collector, described his own obsession with collecting wireless sets (an early form of radio) as "the manifestation of a psychiatric condition."

Collecting takes off in the United States

Collecting in the United States did not begin in a big way until some of its citizens began acquiring vast fortunes in the years following the Civil War (1861-1865). The newly wealthy showed off their taste by acquiring sculpture, furniture, paintings, and medieval manuscripts in enormous quantities. Industrialist Henry Clay Frick, financier J. P. Morgan, railway magnate Henry E. Huntington, and newspaper publisher William Randolph Hearst all assembled world-class collections of various items that remain

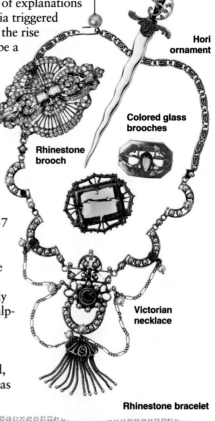

Hori ornament

Colored glass brooches

Rhinestone brooch

Victorian necklace

Rhinestone bracelet

Bakelite brooch

The author:
David Streitfeld is a writer for the *Los Angeles Times*.

on public display in the libraries and museums specifically built to house them.

William Randolph Hearst's collecting became so obsessive that it nearly broke him, and he was regarded as one of the world's richest men. Hearst had entire castles and Medieval monasteries disassembled and shipped to the United States, only to be stored away and forgotten in warehouses. His mania was so infamous that film director and actor Orson Welles caricatured it in *Citizen Kane* (1941). The film's title character, Charles Foster Kane, acquired "paintings, pictures, statues, the very stones of many another palace, a collection of everything so big it can never be catalogued or appraised."

The movie suggests that Kane's insatiable need to acquire possessions was his attempt to regain the cheerful frontier childhood lost with the acquisition of great wealth. Kane is Welles's symbol for the United States itself, and he uses the film to point how closely tied the country remained in the 1930's to its frontier period, which had only ended some 40 years before. Historians note that people on a frontier generally lack disposable incomes and are too much on the move to accumulate unnecessary belongings. They are interested in what is useful and practical and are generally unsentimental about things, which are used until worn out and then thrown away. In a frontier society, new objects, not worn-out goods, symbolize success.

A national mentality begins to change

World War II (1939-1945), more than any other event, changed the frontier mentality in the United States. The

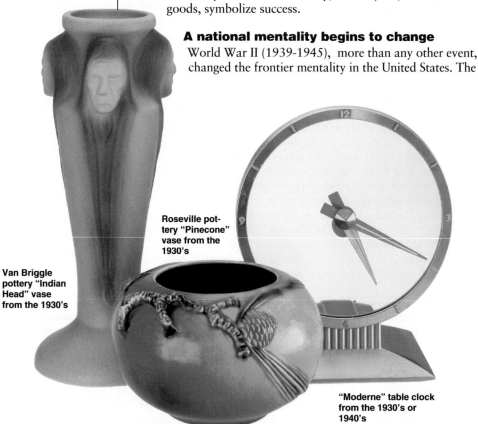

Van Briggle pottery "Indian Head" vase from the 1930's

Roseville pottery "Pinecone" vase from the 1930's

"Moderne" table clock from the 1930's or 1940's

war triggered the movement of millions of U.S. citizens, which changed their perceptions. U.S. soldiers, like their British counterparts, went off to fight a war and returned with a new appreciation of foreign cultures, even if the appreciation was symbolized only by foreign military memorabilia.

After the war, the U.S. standard of living rose dramatically. For the first time, the majority of Americans had some disposable income—and so did their children. The baby boom generation, the large group of people born in the United States from 1946 to 1964, had money to spend on baseball cards, comic books, and toys. These children often had their own bedrooms, which they filled with their own possessions, their collections. The habit stuck. As the baby boomers grew up in the 1960's and 1970's, they began collecting in a big away. Initially, they collected antiques, which the U.S. government for tax purposes defines as an object 100 or more years old that has artistic or historical value.

The baby boom generation consisted of approximately 76 million people. When that generation began acquiring in the 1960's and 1970's, the newest of antiques dated from the 1860's and 1870's, when the entire United States only had about 40 million residents. A good deal of the rather meager possessions belonging to those 40 million people had been worn out and thrown out in frontier tradition. Therefore, many people in the 1970's chased after relatively few items—a classic supply and demand situation. High demand for a low supply drives up prices, and during the 1970's, antiques became expensive. They disappeared into the private collections of a generation young enough that the items were not likely to reappear on the market anytime in the foreseeable future. So the baby boomers, not finished with collecting, turned to what became known as "collectibles." Initially, these included items of artistic value that were less than a century old, such as Tiffany lamps and arts and crafts or "mission" furniture. They also included items that were valued simply for the nostalgic appeal, such as jukeboxes and movie memorabilia.

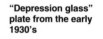

"Depression glass" plate from the early 1930's

Tin containers from the early 1900's through 1920's

COLLECTIBLES

SPECIAL REPORT

These, too, became scarce and expensive as they eventually disappeared into private collections.

Yesterday's trash becomes today's treasures

Savvy collectors next focused on recent disposable culture and on the "junk" that people had always been eager to leave behind as they climbed the economic ladder. The so-called junk included such things as Fiestaware and Depression glass. Fiestaware is the brightly colored dishes and serving pieces that graced countless kitchen tables during the worldwide economic downturn of the 1930's. Depression glass is colorful glassware that theaters and stores in the 1930's gave away to lure in customers. During the economic upswing after World War II, people threw away old dishes and glasses and other reminders of hard times. Fiestaware and Depression glass eventually went from being common to being rare enough to be desirable. High inflation in the late 1970's also fueled the collectibles market. It seemed a good idea to invest in "things" as prices continually increased and money became less valuable. Large numbers of collectors chased after a dwindling supply of pre-World War II stock, driving up prices.

This pattern next played out with items made after World War II. An item was produced in the millions, then it was relegated to the trash heap by a new model, style, or fad. Collectors in the vanguard scoured flea markets for plastic purses, vintage lunchboxes, or

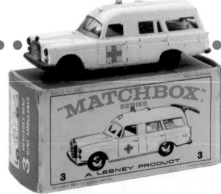

Packaging can dictate the value of a collectible. A Matchbox toy ambulance in its box from the 1960's (right) is coveted by collectors. An untouched European "Kissing Barbie" from 1978 is more valuable than an older, but "played with," Barbie (left) from the 1960's.

"Adam-12" tin lunchbox
from the 1970's

action figures of
beloved comic book
characters. Such
items could be
hard to find, and
collectors often
were subjected to
ridicule, as if no sensible person would be interested in
such trash. The eager collector, however, was driven. The objects of his or her desire still remained essentially undiscovered by
the vast herd of collectors and were, therefore, still inexpensive.
Across the country, collectors of various items formed a sort of
family, meeting at conventions and keeping in touch through
newsletters.

Packaging becomes important

During the 1960's and 1970's, the materials from which ordinary
items were made began to change. Manufacturers stopped producing toys made of wood, metal, or rubber. Toys became plastic.
The packaging of the most ordinary household items—aspirin,
patent medicines, ketchup, and syrup—changed from tin, card-
board, or glass to plastic. People slowly began to realize that their
lives were changing as well, and they began searching for the remnants of their own recent past. Suddenly glass mixing bowls and
refrigerator dishes, tin bandage boxes, and old metal electric fans
became collectibles. People even began hunting for the earliest
forms of plastic, primarily Bakelite, which was most commonly
used in utensils, jewelry, and early portable radios. They all became collectibles.

The desire to collect things continued in the 1980's, which led
to the rise of the so-called "instant collectible" in the 1990's. The
manufacturers of such instant collectibles as special edition dolls
and Christmas ornaments, or even the floppy bean-bags creations
called Beanie Babies, claimed that they were destined to gain in
value over time. In the mid-1990's, collectors willingly paid hun-

Such ordinary house-
hold items as early
electric fans (above
top) and utensils with
handles made of
Bakelite, an early
plastic (above),
gained popularity in
the collectible market
throughout the 1980's
and 1990's.

dreds of dollars for Beanie Babies that initially sold for about $5 a piece.

The instant collectible led people to think about more than just the item itself. Suddenly, the item's condition in addition to its age and desirability became a key component of the collection game. This spawned such phrases as Mint In Box (MIB). Items that were dubbed MIB were destined to remain untouched in their original packaging. Because old toys or watches were often more valuable if they remained in their original boxes, people came to believe that instant collectibles would be more valuable if they had never been opened, or even examined.

Veteran collectors voiced their doubts about both the instant collectible and MIB phenomenon, citing basic laws of supply and demand. "People who become investors in collectibles often find it doesn't work," said Terry Kovel, author with her husband, Ralph Kovel, of more than 60 guides and books about antiques and collectibles. "If everyone saves their toys in the original box, they'll be worth nothing."

The hobby turns upside down

Veteran collectors also noted that postwar collectibles, instant collectibles, and MIB phenomenon had turned traditional collecting on its head. Before, a good collector really had to work at it. Years were needed to acquire specialized knowledge. It took an expert book collector to know that Edgar Allan Poe's first book, *Tamerlane*, was published in 1827 by "A Bostonian." A man who realized what he was looking at when he found a rare copy of *Tamerlane* at a New Hampshire book barn in 1988 snapped it up for $15. He resold it at auction for $198,000.

Every longtime collector has memories of making similar if smaller scores as he or she scavenged for a long-sought

Baseball cards from the 1960's

Autographed baseballs

object for next to nothing in a flea market or junk shop. At best, collecting was a game that took vigor, skill, knowledge, and luck. There were few price guides. Information was carried in collectors' heads, where it was often jealously guarded. After all, why tip off a shop-owner about how to identify a rare object?

Collecting also took time, another way that the amateur could be distinguished from the devoted collector. A day's search might yield only one worthwhile item. And, in an era when real estate was still relatively cheap, there were endless second-hand shops. There were other possibilities as well. At library sales, where thousands of donated books would be displayed on long tables, each going for only a dollar or two, collectors would line up the night before and literally run inside once the doors opened. Seconds counted.

The Internet forever changes collecting

Then came the Internet and the introduction of the World Wide Web. The Internet turned collecting on its head. It allowed collectors to find and share information much more easily than in the past. Dealers, especially book dealers who were among the first to take to the Net, posted their catalogs online. E-mail and Web site bulletin boards allowed like-minded collectors to build closer links. The Internet turned the collecting cults populated by small groups of savvy pioneers into a mass movement.

G.I. Joe action figures from the 1960's

EBay, an auction Web site founded by a French-Iranian engineer, Pierre Omidyar, in 1995, triggered the most wide-reaching change. Ebay did what local markets for antiques and collectibles could not do—create a global market. Omidyar did not have collectibles, let alone international market forces, in mind when he started his trading post. Many of the first items offered for sale were computer-related, but there were also in those early days rare issues of comic books or posters autographed by Elizabeth Taylor and Michael Jackson. The site in 1995 was primitive, even by standards at the time, but it was appealing. Users flocked to it not only to trade, but to establish an online community, where they could chat on message boards about their collecting strategies. By early 1997, the vast majority of items on eBay were collectibles.

Like all online auctions, eBay closely followed the procedures of live auctions, except that bidders entered bids from their computers at any time of the day or night. By allowing sellers and buyers to offer a wide variety of items to a vastly expanded international audience 24 hours a day, 7 days a week, the Internet destroyed all physical boundaries in the world of collecting. No longer was a dealer limited to the number of customers who got his catalog or came into his shop. No longer was the collector lim-

Superhero comic books from the 1960's

Spider-Man, Incredible Hulk, and Green Goblin superhero action figures from the 1970's

ited to the number of shops he visited or catalogs received. But if this had obvious benefits for both buyers and sellers, it also had hidden costs.

Collectors no longer had to rely on a dealer's word about what an object was worth. They could see for themselves as it rose—or failed to rise—in price. This cut some dealers out of the market. Adam Cohen, author of *The Perfect Store*, a history of eBay, tells the story of a Pennsylvania dealer who specialized in fluters, a kind of iron that was used to put the ruffles in pillowcases. Fluters were common in Scandinavia, so the dealer would buy them there for $40 and sell them in the United States for $400. But the Scandinavians selling to the dealer soon realized they could sell their fluters directly on eBay for more than $40. The dealer, or middleman, was cut out of the market.

The global market could hurt collectors as well. The dustiest shop in the most obscure town could now be online, with all of its items priced for a global rather than a local market. Scouting the countryside for bargains became pointless to many people. In fact, many antique and curio shops and bookstores found they were doing so much business on the Internet that they closed to visitors or be-

Web sites, such as eBay (left), refocused collecting from flea markets and antique malls (far left) to the Internet. The Internet instantly shifted the trade in collectibles from a regional to a national, if not international, market, which standardized prices.

came appointment-only.

Collecting became less a matter of time or skill than of wallet. All but the most narrowly focused collectors merely had to sign on to the Internet to find dozens if not hundreds of items.

"It's like an open-air flea market operating out of the comfort of your home, 24 hours a day, seven days a week," said San Francisco comics collector and dealer Rory Root. "It's no longer an event. That takes some of the joy out of it." Yet Root, like millions, couldn't resist the pull of spending hours trolling eBay. "My weight's gone up and I need a new prescription for my glasses," he said. "It's phenomenally addictive."

The global market established on the Internet pushed some authentic baby boomer materials to astronomical prices in the late 1990's and depressed the value of others. A 1946 Dick Tracy wristwatch walkie-talkie, still in its box, fetched $10,000, and a G. I. Nurse action figure, manufactured briefly in 1967, sold for $1,200. A picture autographed by Baseball Hall of Fame member Paul Waner climbed in value to $5,000. The same market sent the value of Barbie dolls tumbling, with the auction price of a vintage 1959 doll fetching only $4,400 in 2002 after hitting a record $13,000 just a few years earlier. Barbie sellers simply outnumbered buyers. The market was saturated, and prices dropped.

The Internet also accelerated the launch of collecting fads. While the dot-com Internet companies were still crashing in the spring of 2001, collectors were already buying dot-com memorabilia—hats, keychains, bumper stickers, and mugs emblazoned with the logos of failed companies. A few months later, eBay users enjoyed a miniboom in tote bags, paperweights, and employee manuals bearing the logo of Enron Corp., the failed Houston-based energy trading company. Purchasers touted the objects as instant history, the crystallization of a moment of time. Somewhat the same phenomena occurred after terrorists attacked the United

States on Sept. 11, 2001. Sellers almost immediately began offering World Trade Center collectibles on eBay. EBay management banned all such items, but later allowed them in a special charity category.

A difference of opinion

Ebay and the Internet killed the collecting bug for some collectors. To these folks, the difficulty of the hunt was as much a part of the appeal of collecting as possessing the object. Most collectors, however, did not seem to mind that the latest technology had rendered the hunt tame. Collecting, regardless of the means, continued to satisfy some deep urge, one that philosophers and commentators have analyzed for centuries without coming to agreement.

Sigmund Freud, the Austrian physician who revolutionized human understanding of how the human mind works, called collecting "a redirection of surplus *libido* (sexual desire) onto an inanimate object." The psychoanalyst Werner Muensterberger was scarcely more sympathetic. In *Collecting: An Unruly Passion*, he wrote that collecting was linked to a memory of "deprivation or loss or vulnerability and a subsequent longing for substitution...." By their standards, there are a lot of troubled people in today's world. On the average day, eBay has approximately 8 million visitors to its Web site.

Most collectors maintain that their pursuits simply offer a little relief from the reality of the work-a-day world and some measure of control. Unlike the morning traffic, the state of the economy, or the threat of terrorism, collecting is something most individuals can control. He or she decides what to buy, how much to spend, and where to place the object. Many people find that highly satisfying in a world that appears to them to be out of control. There also may be another and deeper allure.

"After September 11, everyone was telling us that we should go out and live a normal life," noted Terry Kovel. "Collecting both gets you away from life and shows you how persistent it is. If you go to an antique show, you see a lot of things that have lasted for a long time. It's reassuring. Collectors are optimists." ■ ■ ■

Cast metal toys from the 1950's and 1960's

Colombians pay their respects to Roman Catholic priest Hilario Arango in Cali, Colombia, in June 2002. Arango, a prominent critic of leftist rebels, was murdered during a wave of attacks on Colombian leaders by the Revolutionary Armed Forces of Colombia, the country's largest rebel group.

Colombia. Alvaro Uribe Velez, a 50-year-old former state governor, was sworn in for a four-year term as the president of Colombia on Aug. 7, 2002. As Uribe was taking his oath of office, mortar fire exploded in the streets of Bogota, the capital. The attack left 21 people dead and about 60 others wounded. Authorities blamed the attack on the Revolutionary Armed Forces of Colombia (FARC), the largest leftist group engaged in a 38-year-old civil war with the government.

State of emergency. President Uribe, who had been elected in May vowing to crack down on violence, declared a state of emergency shortly after assuming office. The declaration allowed his administration to assume special powers, including imposing a 1.2-percent tax on all individuals and businesses with assets of more than $57,000. The estimated $800 million in extra revenues was to be used to create two mobile army brigades of 3,000 troops each and to hire 10,000 additional police officers. Uribe also planned to arm 20,000 "peasant soldiers," a part-time civilian force given military training to help control violence in rural areas.

Violence by FARC intensified in January after peace negotiations between the rebels and the government collapsed. In late February, FARC rebels hijacked a commercial airliner and took hostage Senator Jorge Eduardo Gechem Turbay. Then-President Andres Pastrana Arango responded to the kidnapping by ordering the armed forces to retake FARC's haven in southern Colombia, an area of 16,000 square miles (38,850 square kilometers) that the government had ceded FARC in 1998.

On Feb. 23, 2002, the rebels kidnapped Senator Ingrid Betancourt, a presidential candidate. On March 2, Senator Martha Catalina Daniels and two people accompanying her on a mission to obtain the release of rebel-held hostages were shot to death near the town of Zipacon, north of Bogota. On April 14, presidential candidate Uribe was nearly killed in a rebel bomb attack on his motorcade in Barranquilla, a town on the Caribbean coast. Rebels launched a series of attacks on lawmakers in Bogota in December, including a bombing that wounded Senator German Vargas Lleras.

Urban warfare. In October, violent urban warfare in Colombia since the 1980's broke out as soldiers and police battled leftist rebels in Medellin, the country's second-largest city. The rebels had taken control of poor neighborhoods in the city.

U.S. support. In February 2002, U.S. President George W. Bush's administration allocated $98 million for the training and equipping of special Colombian units to safeguard an oil pipeline in northern Colombia operated by Occidental Petroleum of Los Angeles. The pipeline, almost 500 miles (805 kilometers) long, had been repeatedly bombed by rebels. The Bush administration also began sharing intelligence information about rebel groups with Colombian officials. In addition, the U.S. Congress in 2002 authorized the Colombian government to use funds and equipment originally earmarked for the war against drugs to wage the war against the rebels and a right-wing paramilitary group called the United Self-Defense Forces of Colombia (AUC).

Drugs for weapons. At a federal court in Houston in November, the U.S. Justice Department charged four men with plotting to trade $25 million in cash and cocaine for assault rifles, antiaircraft missiles, and other weapons, which were to be delivered to the AUC. The charges included providing material support to a foreign terrorist organization.   □ Nathan A. Haverstock

See also **Latin America; People in the news** (Uribe Velez, Alvaro); **Terrorism.**

Colorado. See State government.
Common Market. See Europe.
Commonwealth of Independent States. See Asia; Azerbaijan; Belarus; Georgia; Kazakhstan; Russia; Ukraine.
Comoros. See Africa.

Computer. The United States Department of Labor reported in October 2002 that more than half of all U.S. workers used a computer at work. The report showed that women were more likely than men to use a computer on the job and that about 94 percent of workers with college degrees use a computer at work, compared with just 16 percent of high school dropouts.

Worldwide sales of personal computers (PC's) fell 0.6 percent in the second quarter of 2002, compared with the same period in 2001. The market research company Gartner Inc. of Stamford, Connecticut, reported in July 2002 that U.S. computer sales fell by 0.8 percent over the same period. The report blamed poor economic conditions for the decline. Hewlett-Packard Company of Palo Alto, California, led in sales, with 15.5 percent of the total market, followed by The Dell Computer Corporation of Austin, Texas, with 14.9 percent. Of the top five companies, only Dell showed strong growth in its share of the computer market, and experts predicted that the company would surpass Hewlett-Packard to become the premier manufacturer in the PC industry.

New iMacs. In January, Apple Computer, Inc., of Cupertino, California, unveiled a new version of its iMac desktop computer. The new iMac's hard drive and other components are housed in a small hemisphere-shaped base. The compact design features a 15-inch (38-centimeter) flat panel monitor connected to the base by a swiveling neck.

Apple introduced a modified version of the original iMac designed for use in schools in April. Called the eMac, it comes equipped with a larger monitor and faster processor.

Tablet PC. Officials with Microsoft Corp. of Redmond, Washington, announced the release of a new generation of tablet computers. The

Tablet PC's, which were being built to Microsoft's specifications and sold by several manufacturers, had a laptop-size screen and a detachable or pull-out keyboard. They could also lie flat on a table, like a tablet of paper. Users could type on the keyboard or write on the screen with a pencil-like device. Microsoft officials claimed that mobility was the main advantage of the Tablet PC.

The new HP. In May, Hewlett-Packard combined with Compaq Computer Corp. of Houston in the largest merger in computer industry history. The new company kept the Hewlett-Packard name and headquarters and announced that it would continue to sell products under both companies' brand names. ☐ Michael Woods

See also **Internet.**

Steve Jobs, CEO of Apple Computer, unveils the new iMac computer at the Macworld Expo in San Francisco in January 2002. The iMac's innovative design features a small base that holds the computer's hard drive and a flat screen mounted on a swiveling arm.

Congo (Kinshasa). The Democratic Republic of Congo (DRC), rebel leaders, and opposition parties signed a peace agreement in mid-December 2002 that was designed to end four years of civil war and set up a transitional government. Under the accord, DRC President Joseph Kabila was to remain interim head of state until elections could be held.

The movement toward peace began on July 30 when two of the main adversaries in the war signed an accord. Officials of Rwanda, Congo's neighbor to the east, agreed to remove all of its troops from Congo, while Kabila agreed to expel Rwandan Hutu guerrillas from Congolese soil. Rwanda, citing the need to protect its border against Hutu guerrillas, first had sent troops into eastern Congo in 1996. The Hutu had fled into the DRC after participating in a 1994 massacre of the Tutsi, Rwanda's rival ethnic group.

The complex civil war expanded into a regional conflict in 1998 when Uganda and Rwanda were drawn in on the side of rival rebel combatants in the eastern part of the country. Angola, Namibia, and Zimbabwe entered on the side of the Kinshasa-based Congolese government. The war claimed the lives of at least 2.5 million people between 1998 and 2002, according to United Nations sources.

DRC allies withdraw. Following the July 2002 peace agreement, Kabila persuaded allies Angola and Zimbabwe to withdraw from Congo. Namibia, the DRC's other ally, had pulled its troops out in 2001. Uganda's president, Yoweri Museveni, whose country had fought on the side of the rebels, agreed in August 2002 to order home Uganda's troops, and by October, only a small force of Ugandan soldiers were left.

Peace talks and agreement. Kabila's government and two of the rebel groups started peace talks in October in South Africa at the invitation of South Africa's president, Thabo Mbeki. On December 17, the government and two rebel factions—the Ugandan-backed Congolese Liberation Movement (MLC) and the Rwandan-backed Congolese Rally for Democracy (RCD)—signed the pact in which all parties shared in a transitional DRC government with Kabila serving as the country's interim leader.

Volcanic eruption. On January 17, Mount Nyiragongo, a volcano near the city of Goma in eastern Congo, erupted, killing at least 100 people and forcing the city's 500,000 inhabitants to flee from their houses. The eruption spewed rivers of molten lava that cut Goma in two and burned vast areas of the city. Lava also engulfed runways at the Goma Airport and spilled into Lake Kivu, polluting Goma's main water source.

□ Simon Baynham

See also **Africa.**

Congress of the United States.
Midterm elections held on Nov. 5, 2002, gave the Republican Party control of the U.S. Senate and left the Republicans—or GOP (for Grand Old Party)—with a greater majority in the U.S. House of Representatives. The election was the first since 1934 in which a president's party gained seats in both the House and the Senate two years into a first term. Congress during 2002 approved several measures sought by President George W. Bush. It authorized him to use the U.S. armed forces against the Iraqi regime headed by President Saddam Hussein. The Congress also approved President Bush's plan to create a new Cabinet department dedicated to homeland security. However, Congress failed to pass any of the necessary spending bills prior to the start of the new fiscal year (October 2002 to September 2003).

Major House races. There were few competitive races in the November elections for all 435 House seats. Republicans widened their majority over Democrats and retained control of the leadership of the House. Following the midterm elections, Republicans held 229 seats, and Democrats held 205. Representative Bernard Sanders of Vermont was the only independent in the House in 2002.

Major Senate races. The Republican Party scored major Senate victories in the November elections. Republicans took three seats held by Democrats, while losing only one seat, giving the GOP control of the Senate. Following the 2002 elections, Republicans held 51 seats, and Democrats held 48. James M. Jeffords of Vermont was an independent aligned with the Democrats.

In one of the most closely watched races in November, Republican Jim Talent scored an upset victory over incumbent Democratic Senator Jean Carnahan in Missouri. Carnahan had been appointed to the Senate in 2000. Also in the 2002 election, U.S. Representative Saxby Chambliss, a Republican, defeated incumbent Senator Max Cleland, a Democrat, in Georgia. Many political experts suggested that Cleland's loss was tied to his stand against adopting all of President Bush's demands in the drafting of a bill creating a new homeland security department. In Minnesota, Norm Coleman, the former mayor of St. Paul, pulled off a major victory over former Senator and Vice President Walter Mondale. Mondale ran in place of Senator Paul Wellstone, an incumbent Democrat who died in an airplane accident in October.

The Democratic Party was able to unseat just one GOP senator. Arkansas Attorney General Mark Pryor defeated incumbent Tim Hutchinson, who was seeking a second term in office.

Members of the United States House of Representatives

The House of Representatives of the first session of the 108th Congress consisted of 205 Democrats, 229 Republicans, and 1 Independent (not including representatives from American Samoa, the District of Columbia, Guam, Puerto Rico, and the Virgin Islands) when it convened on Jan. 7, 2003. This table shows congressional district, legislator, and party affiliation. Asterisk (*) denotes those who served in the 107th Congress; dagger (†) denotes "at large."

Alabama
1. Jo Bonner, R.
2. Terry Everett, R.*
3. Mike Rogers, R.
4. Robert Aderholt, R.*
5. Bud Cramer, D.*
6. Spencer Bachus, R.*
7. Artur Davis, D.

Alaska
†Donald E. Young, R.*

Arizona
1. Rick Renzi, R.
2. Trent Franks, R.
3. John Shadegg, R.*
4. Ed Pastor, D.*
5. J.D. Hayworth, R.*
6. Jeff Flake, R.*
7. Raul Grijalva. D.
8. Jim Kolbe, R.*

Arkansas
1. Marion Berry, D.*
2. Vic Snyder, D.*
3. John Boozman, R.*
4. Mike Ross, D.*

California
1. Mike Thompson, D.*
2. Wally Herger, R.*
3. Douglas Ose, R.*
4. John Doolittle, R.*
5. Robert T. Matsui, D.*
6. Lynn Woolsey, D.*
7. George E. Miller, D.*
8. Nancy Pelosi, D.*
9. Barbara Lee, D.*
10. Ellen Tauscher, D.*
11. Richard Pombo, R.*
12. Tom Lantos, D.*
13. Fortney H. (Peter) Stark, D.*
14. Anna Eshoo, D.*
15. Mike Honda, D.*
16. Zoe Lofgren, D.*
17. Sam Farr, D.*
18. Dennis Cardoza, D.
19. George Radanovich, R.*
20. Calvin Dooley, D.*
21. Devin Nunes, R.
22. Bill Thomas, R.*
23. Lois Capps, D.*
24. Elton Gallegly, R.*
25. Howard McKeon, R.*
26. David Dreier, R.*
27. Brad Sherman, D.*
28. Howard Berman, D.*
29. Adam Schiff, D.*
30. Henry Waxman, D.*
31. Xavier Becerra, D.*
32. Hilda Solis, D.*
33. Diane Watson, D.*
34. Lucille Roybal-Allard, D.*
35. Maxine Waters, D.*
36. Jane Harman, D.*
37. Juanita Millender-McDonald, D.*

38. Grace Napolitano, D.*
39. Linda Sanchez, D.
40. Ed Royce, R.*
41. Jerry Lewis, R.*
42. Gary Miller, R.*
43. Joe Baca, D.*
44. Ken Calvert, R.*
45. Mary Bono, R.*
46. Dana Rohrabacher, R.*
47. Loretta Sanchez, D.*
48. Christopher Cox, R.*.
49. Darrell Issa, R.*
50. Randy Cunningham, R.*
51. Bob Filner, D.*
52. Duncan Hunter, R.*
53. Susan Davis, D.*

Colorado
1. Diana DeGette, D.*
2. Mark Udall, D.*
3. Scott McInnis, R.*
4. Marilyn Musgrave, R.
5. Joel Hefley, R.*
6. Tom Tancredo, R.*
7. Bob Beauprez, R.

Connecticut
1. John Larson, D.*
2. Rob Simmons, R.*
3. Rosa DeLauro, D.*
4. Christopher Shays, R.*
5. Nancy L. Johnson, R.*

Delaware
†Michael Castle, R.*

Florida
1. Jeff Miller, R.*
2. Allen Boyd, D.*
3. Corrine Brown, D.*
4. Ander Crenshaw, R.*
5. Virginia Brown-Waite, R.
6. Clifford B. Stearns, R.*
7. John Mica, R.*
8. Ric Keller, R.*
9. Michael Bilirakis, R.*
10. C. W. Bill Young, R.*
11. Jim Davis, D.*
12. Adam Putnam, R.*
13. Katherine Harris, R.
14. Porter J. Goss, R.*
15. Dave Weldon, R.*
16. Mark Foley, R.*
17. Kendrick Meek, D.
18. Ileana Ros-Lehtinen. R.*
19. Robert Wexler, D.*
20. Peter Deutsch, D.*
21. Lincoln Diaz-Balart, R.*
22. E. Clay Shaw, Jr., R.*
23. Alcee Hastings, D.*
24. Tom Feeney, R.
25. Mario Diaz-Balart, R.

Georgia
1. Jack Kingston, R.*
2. Sanford Bishop, Jr., D.*

3. Jim Marshall, D.
4. Denise Majette, D.
5. John Lewis, D.*
6. Johnny Isakson, R.*
7. John Linder, R.*
8. Michael Collins, R.*
9. Charles Norwood, R.*
10. Nathan Deal, R.*
11. Phil Gingrey, R.
12. Max Burns, R.
13. David Scott, D.

Hawaii
1. Neil Abercrombie, D.*
2. Ed Case, D.*

Idaho
1. C.L. Otter, R.*
2. Mike Simpson, R.*

Illinois
1. Bobby Rush, D.*
2. Jesse L. Jackson, Jr., D.*
3. William O. Lipinski, D.*
4. Luis Gutierrez, D.*
5. Rahm Emanuel, D.
6. Henry J. Hyde, R.*
7. Danny Davis, D.*
8. Philip M. Crane, R.*
9. Janice Schakowsky, D.*
10. Mark Kirk, R.*
11. Gerald Weller, R.*
12. Jerry F. Costello, D.*
13. Judy Biggert, R.*
14. J. Dennis Hastert, R.*
15. Timothy Johnson, R.*
16. Donald Manzullo, R.*
17. Lane A. Evans, D.*
18. Ray LaHood, R.*
19. John Shimkus, R.*

Indiana
1. Peter J. Visclosky, D.*
2. Chris Chocola, R.
3. Mark Souder, R.*
4. Steve Buyer, R.*
5. Dan Burton, R.*
6. Mike Pence, R.*
7. Julia Carson, D.*
8. John Hostettler, R.*
9. Baron Hill, D.*

Iowa
1. Jim Nussle, R.*
2. Jim Leach, R.*
3. Leonard Boswell. D.*
4. Thomas Latham, R.*
5. Steve King, R.

Kansas
1. Jerry Moran, R.*
2. Jim Ryun, R.*
3. Dennis Moore, D.*
4. Todd Tiahrt, R.*

Kentucky
1. Edward Whitfield, R.*
2. Ron Lewis, R.*
3. Anne Northup, R.*
4. Kenneth Lucas, D.*
5. Harold (Hal) Rogers, R.*
6. Ernie Fletcher, R.*

Louisiana
1. David Vitter, R.*
2. William J. Jefferson, D.*
3. W. J. (Billy) Tauzin, R.*
4. Jim McCrery, R.*
5. Rodney Alexander, D.
6. Richard Hugh Baker, R.*
7. Chris John, D.*

Maine
1. Thomas Allen, D.*
2. Michael Michaud, D.

Maryland
1. Wayne T. Gilchrest, R.*
2. C.A. "Dutch" Ruppersberger, D.
3. Benjamin L. Cardin, D.*
4. Albert Wynn, D.*
5. Steny H. Hoyer, D.*
6. Roscoe Bartlett, R.*
7. Elijah Cummings, D.*
8. Chris Van Hollen. D.

Massachusetts
1. John W. Olver, D.*
2. Richard E. Neal, D.*
3. James McGovern, D.*
4. Barney Frank, D.*
5. Martin Meehan, D.*
6. John Tierney, D.*
7. Edward J. Markey, D.*
8. Michael Capuano, D.*
9. Stephen F. Lynch, D.*
10. William Delahunt, D.*

Michigan
1. Bart Stupak, D.*
2. Peter Hoekstra, R.*
3. Vernon Ehlers, R.*
4. Dave Camp, R.*
5. Dale Kildee, D.*
6. Frederick S. Upton. R.*
7. Nick Smith, R.*
8. Mike Rogers, R.*
9. Joseph Knollenberg, R.*
10. Candice Miller, R.
11. Thaddeus McCotter, R.
12. Sander M. Levin, D.*
13. Carolyn Kilpatrick. D.*
14. John Conyers, Jr., D.*
15. John Dingell, D.*

Minnesota
1. Gil Gutknecht, R.*
2. John Kline, R.
3. Jim Ramstad, R.*
4. Betty McCollum, D.*

5. Martin O. Sabo, D.*
6. Mark Kennedy, R.*
7. Collin C. Peterson, D.*
8. James L. Oberstar, D.*

Mississippi
1. Roger Wicker, R.*
2. Bennie Thompson, D.*
3. Charles Pickering, R.*
4. Gene Taylor, D.*

Missouri
1. William Clay, D.*
2. Todd Akin, R.*
3. Richard A. Gephardt, D.*
4. Ike Skelton, D.*
5. Karen McCarthy, D.*
6. Samuel Graves, R.*
7. Roy Blunt, R.*
8. Jo Ann Emerson, R.*
9. Kenny Hulshof, R.*

Montana
†Dennis Rehberg, R.*

Nebraska
1. Doug Bereuter, R.*
2. Lee Terry, R.*
3. Tom Osborne, R.*

Nevada
1. Shelley Berkley, D.*
2. Jim Gibbons, R.*
3. Joe Porter, R.

New Hampshire
1. Jeb Bradley, R.
2. Charles Bass, R.*

New Jersey
1. Robert E. Andrews, D.*
2. Frank LoBiondo, R.*
3. H. James Saxton, R.*
4. Christopher H. Smith, R.*
5. Scott Garrett, R.
6. Frank Pallone, Jr., D.*
7. Mike Ferguson, R.*
8. William Pascrell, Jr., D.*
9. Steven Rothman, D.*
10. Donald M. Payne, D.*
11. Rodney Frelinghuysen, R.*
12. Rush Holt, D.*
13. Robert Menendez, D.*

New Mexico
1. Heather Wilson, R.*
2. Steve Pearce, R.
3. Thomas Udall, D.*

New York
1. Tim Bishop, D.
2. Steve Israel, D.*
3. Peter King, R.*
4. Carolyn McCarthy, D.*
5. Gary L. Ackerman, D.*
6. Gregory Meeks, D.*
7. Joseph Crowley, D.*
8. Jerrold Nadler, D.*
9. Anthony Weiner, D.*
10. Edolphus Towns, D.*
11. Major R. Owens, D.*
12. Nydia Velazquez, D.*
13. Vito J. Fossella, R.*

14. Carolyn Maloney, D.*
15. Charles B. Rangel, D.*
16. Jose E. Serrano, D.*
17. Eliot L. Engel, D.*
18. Nita M. Lowey, D.*
19. Sue Kelly, R.*
20. John Sweeney, R.*
21. Michael R. McNulty, D.*
22. Maurice Hinchey, D.*
23. John McHugh, R.*
24. Sherwood Boehlert, R.*
25. James Walsh, R.*
26. Thomas Reynolds, R.*
27. Jack Quinn, R.*
28. Louise M. Slaughter, D.*
29. Amo Houghton, R.*

North Carolina
1. Frank Ballance, Jr., D.
2. Bob Etheridge, D.*
3. Walter Jones, Jr., R.*
4. David Price, D.*
5. Richard Burr, R.*
6. Howard Coble, R.*
7. Mike McIntyre, D.*
8. Robin Hayes, R.*
9. Sue Myrick, R.*
10. Cass Ballenger, R.*
11. Charles H. Taylor, R.*
12. Melvin Watt, D.*
13. Brad Miller, D.

North Dakota
†Earl Pomeroy, D.*

Ohio
1. Steve Chabot, R.*
2. Rob Portman, R.*
3. Michael Turner, R.
4. Michael G. Oxley, R.*
5. Paul E. Gillmor, R.*
6. Ted Strickland, D.*
7. David L. Hobson, R.*
8. John A. Boehner, R.*
9. Marcy Kaptur, D.*
10. Dennis Kucinich, D.*
11. Stephanie Tubbs-Jones, D.*
12. Pat Tiberi, R.*
13. Sherrod Brown, D.*
14. Steven LaTourette, R.*
15. Deborah Pryce, R.*
16. Ralph Regula, R.*
17. Timothy Ryan, D.
18. Bob Ney, R.*

Oklahoma
1. John Sullivan, R.*
2. Brad Carson, D.*
3. Frank Lucas, R.*
4. Tom Cole, R.
5. Ernest Jim Istook, R.*

Oregon
1. David Wu, D.*
2. Greg Walden, R.*
3. Earl Blumenauer, D.*
4. Peter A. DeFazio, D.*
5. Darlene Hooley, D.*

Pennsylvania
1. Robert Brady, D.*
2. Chaka Fattah, D.*

3. Philip English, R.*
4. Melissa Hart, R.*
5. John Peterson, R.*
6. Jim Gerlach, R.
7. W. Curtis Weldon, R.*
8. Jim Greenwood, R.*
9. Bill Shuster, R.*
10. Donald Sherwood, R.*
11. Paul E. Kanjorski, D.*
12. John P. Murtha, D.*
13. Joseph Hoeffel, D.*
14. Michael Doyle, D.*
15. Patrick Toomey, R.*
16. Joseph Pitts, R.*
17. Tim Holden, D.*
18. Tim Murphy, R.
19. Todd Platts, R.*

Rhode Island
1. Patrick Kennedy, D.*
2. James Langevin, D.*

South Carolina
1. Henry Brown, Jr., R.*
2. Joe Wilson, R.*
3. J. Gresham Barrett, R.
4. James DeMint, R.*
5. John M. Spratt, Jr., D.*
6. James Clyburn, D.*

South Dakota
†William Janklow, R.

Tennessee
1. William Jenkins, R.*
2. John J. Duncan, Jr., R.*
3. Zach Wamp, R.*
4. Lincoln Davis, D.
5. Jim Cooper, D.
6. Bart Gordon, D.*
7. Marsha Blackburn, R.
8. John S. Tanner, D.*
9. Harold E. Ford, Jr., D.*

Texas
1. Max Sandlin, D.*
2. Jim Turner, D.*
3. Sam Johnson, R.*
4. Ralph M. Hall, D.*
5. Jeb Hensarling, R.
6. Joe Barton, R.*
7. John Culberson, R.*
8. Kevin Brady, R.*
9. Nick Lampson, D.*
10. Lloyd Doggett, D.*
11. Chet Edwards, D.*
12. Kay Granger, R.*
13. Mac Thornberry, R.*
14. Ron Paul, R.*
15. Ruben Hinojosa, D.*
16. Silvestre Reyes, D.*
17. Charles W. Stenholm, D.*
18. Sheila Jackson Lee, D.*
19. Larry Combest, R.*
20. Charlie Gonzalez, D.*
21. Lamar S. Smith, R.*
22. Tom DeLay, R.*
23. Henry Bonilla, R.*
24. Martin Frost, D.*
25. Chris Bell, D.

26. Michael Burgess, R.
27. Solomon P. Ortiz, D.*
28. Ciro Rodriguez, D.*
29. Gene Green, D.*
30. Eddie Bernice Johnson, D.*
31. John Carter, R.
32. Pete Sessions, R.

Utah
1. Rob Bishop, R.
2. Jim Matheson, D.*
3. Christopher Cannon, R.*

Vermont
†Bernard Sanders, Ind.*

Virginia
1. Jo Ann Davis, R.*
2. Edward Schrock, R.*
3. Robert Scott, D.*
4. J. Randy Forbes, R.*
5. Virgil Goode, Jr., R.*
6. Robert Goodlatte, R.*
7. Eric Cantor, R.*
8. James P. Moran, Jr., D.*
9. Rick C. Boucher, D.*
10. Frank R. Wolf, R.*
11. Tom Davis, R.*

Washington
1. Jay Inslee, D.*
2. Rick Larsen, D.*
3. Brian Baird, D.*
4. Doc Hastings, R.*
5. George Nethercutt, Jr., R.*
6. Norman D. Dicks, D.*
7. Jim McDermott, D.*
8. Jennifer Dunn, R.*
9. Adam Smith, D.*

West Virginia
1. Alan B. Mollohan, D.*
2. Shelley Moore Capito, R.*
3. Nick J. Rahall II, D.*

Wisconsin
1. Paul Ryan, R.*
2. Tammy Baldwin, D.*
3. Ron Kind, D.*
4. Gerald D. Kleczka, D.*
5. James Sensenbrenner, Jr., R.*
6. Thomas E. Petri, R.*
7. David R. Obey, D.*
8. Mark Green, R.*

Wyoming
†Barbara Cubin, R.*

Nonvoting representatives

American Samoa
Eni F. H. Faleomavaega, D.*

District of Columbia
Eleanor Holmes Norton, D.*

Guam
Madeleine Bordallo, D.

Puerto Rico
Anibal Acevedo-Vila, D.*

Virgin Islands
Donna Christian-Christensen, D.*

However, Democrats also considered Senator Mary Landrieu's (D., Louisiana) reelection a major victory. Voters returned Landrieu to a second term in the Senate in a runoff election on December 7 after she failed to receive a majority of the votes in the November election. In the runoff, Landrieu defeated Republican challenger Suzanne H. Terrell, who had received considerable help from President Bush and members of the GOP.

House leadership. Republican House members elected Representative Tom DeLay of Texas as their majority leader. They also chose Representative Roy Blunt of Missouri as majority *whip* (assistant leader) and Representative Deborah Pryce of Ohio as Republican conference chair.

Representative Richard A. Gephardt (D., Missouri) resigned on November 6 as House minority leader after the poor showing by Democratic candidates in the election. House Democrats selected Representative Nancy Pelosi of California to succeed Gephardt. Pelosi was the first woman ever to be elected to lead a party in the U.S. Congress. House Democrats also elected Representative Steny Hoyer of Maryland as minority whip and Representative Robert Menendez of New Jersey as caucus chairman.

Senate leadership changed hands following the November election as Senate Republicans chose Trent Lott of Mississippi as majority leader, Mitch McConnell of Kentucky as majority whip, and Rick Santorum of Pennsylvania as secretary of the Republican Conference.

Senate Democrats chose Senator Tom Daschle of South Dakota as the Senate minority leader, Senator Harry Reid of Nevada as minority whip, and Senator Barbara A. Mikulski of Maryland as the secretary of the Democratic Conference.

Lott resigns as majority leader. On December 20, Lott announced he was stepping down as Senate majority leader for the 108th Congress, scheduled to begin on Jan. 7, 2003. Lott's resignation came two weeks after he remarked at a birthday party for Senator Strom Thurmond (R., South Carolina) that the United States "wouldn't have had all of these problems over all these years" if Thurmond had been elected president in 1948. Thurmond ran for president on a segregationist platform against Harry S. Truman. On December 23, Senate Republicans elected by acclamation Bill Frist (R., Tennessee) as their majority leader.

Homeland security. Congress undertook a major initiative designed to oversee the domestic war on terrorism. In November, both the House and the Senate approved legislation creating the Department of Homeland Security. The House passed the bill by a vote of 299 to 121. The Senate approved the measure by a vote of 90 to 9.

President Bush proposed the creation of the new Cabinet department for domestic defense in June. The new department, with a budget of $37 billion, consolidated 170,000 federal employees from 22 existing agencies.

Congressional approval came only after Senate Republicans were able to defeat an attempt by Democrats and some politically moderate Republicans to strip the legislation of provisions that allegedly favored large business interests. The measure provided protection for pharmaceutical companies against lawsuits filed because of adverse effects from their vaccines. Moderate Republicans and Democrats exacted a promise that the special interest provisions would be revisited in 2003.

Trouble with Iraq. Congress in October 2002 authorized President Bush to use the U.S. armed forces "as he determines to be necessary and appropriate" in dealing with Iraqi President Saddam Hussein. The Bush administration maintained that Hussein had stockpiled chemical and biological weapons since the end of the Persian Gulf War (1991), violating resolutions adopted by the United Nations (UN).

President Bush, in his State of the Union address to Congress on Jan. 29, 2002, warned of an "axis of evil"—Iran, Iraq, and North Korea—that threatened world security in their pursuit of weapons of mass destruction and support of terrorism. The president vowed that the United States would take military action against any regime that sponsored terrorism.

On October 10, the House of Representatives voted 296 to 133 to pass the resolution authorizing the president to use force to defend U.S. national interests. The Senate passed the legislation by a vote of 77 to 23 on October 11. President Bush signed the authorization on October 16.

Spending bills. President Bush presented his federal budget to Congress on Feb. 4, 2002. The proposed $2.13-trillion budget for fiscal year 2003 included increased spending for the military and homeland security. However, Congress failed to pass any of the required 13 spending bills in 2002 prior to the start of fiscal year 2003. By the end of 2002, only two of the spending bills had been passed. Congress approved several temporary spending measures to keep the government running without a budget. Congress was expected to pass the remaining measures when reconvening in 2003.

September 11 memorial. Approximately 300 members of the House and Senate convened in New York City on Sept. 6, 2002, as part of a ceremony commemorating the anniversary of the terrorist attacks on the United States on Sept. 11, 2001. The ceremony marked the first time that Congress had met in New York City

Members of the United States Senate

The Senate of the first session of the 108th Congress consisted of 48 Democrats, 51 Republicans, and 1 Independent when it convened on Jan. 7, 2003. The first date in each listing shows when the senator's term began. The second date in each listing shows when the senator's term expires.

State	Term
Alabama	
Richard C. Shelby, R.	1987-2005
Jeff Sessions, R.	1997-2009
Alaska	
Theodore F. Stevens, R.	1968-2009
Lisa Murkowski, R.	2003-2005
Arizona	
John McCain III, R.	1987-2005
Jon Kyl, R.	1995-2007
Arkansas	
Blanche Lambert Lincoln, D.	1999-2005
Mark Pryor, D.	2003-2009
California	
Dianne Feinstein, D.	1992-2007
Barbara Boxer, D.	1993-2005
Colorado	
Ben N. Campbell, R.	1993-2005
Wayne Allard, R.	1997-2009
Connecticut	
Christopher J. Dodd, D.	1981-2005
Joseph I. Lieberman, D.	1989-2007
Delaware	
Joseph R. Biden, Jr., D.	1973-2009
Thomas Carper, D.	2001-2007
Florida	
Bob Graham, D.	1987-2005
Bill Nelson, D.	2001-2007
Georgia	
Zell Miller, D..	2000-2005
Saxby Chambliss, R.	2003-2009
Hawaii	
Daniel K. Inouye, D.	1963-2005
Daniel K. Akaka, D.	1990-2007
Idaho	
Larry E. Craig, R.	1991-2009
Mike Crapo, R.	1999-2005
Illinois	
Richard J. Durbin, D.	1997-2009
Peter Fitzgerald, R.	1999-2005
Indiana	
Richard G. Lugar, R.	1977-2007
Evan Bayh, D.	1999-2005
Iowa	
Charles E. Grassley, R.	1981-2005
Tom Harkin, D.	1985-2009
Kansas	
Sam Brownback, R.	1996-2005
Pat Roberts, R.	1997-2009
Kentucky	
Mitch McConnell, R.	1985-2009
Jim Bunning, R.	1999-2005

State	Term
Louisiana	
John B. Breaux, D.	1987-2005
Mary L. Landrieu, D.	1997-2009
Maine	
Olympia Snowe, R.	1995-2007
Susan M. Collins, R.	1997-2009
Maryland	
Paul S. Sarbanes, D.	1977-2007
Barbara A. Mikulski, D.	1987-2005
Massachusetts	
Edward M. Kennedy, D.	1962-2007
John F. Kerry, D.	1985-2009
Michigan	
Carl Levin, D.	1979-2009
Debbie Stabenow, D.	2001-2007
Minnesota	
Mark Dayton, D.	2001-2007
Norm Coleman, R.	2003-2009
Mississippi	
Thad Cochran, R.	1978-2009
Trent Lott, R.	1989-2007
Missouri	
Christopher S. (Kit) Bond, R.	1987-2005
Jim Talent, R.	2003-2009
Montana	
Max Baucus, D.	1978-2009
Conrad Burns, R.	1989-2007
Nebraska	
Chuck Hagel, R.	1997-2009
Ben Nelson, D.	2001-2007
Nevada	
Harry M. Reid, D.	1987-2005
John Ensign, R.	2001-2007
New Hampshire	
Judd Gregg, R.	1993-2005
John E. Sununu, R.	2003-2009
New Jersey	
Jon S. Corzine, D.	2001-2007
Frank R. Lautenberg, D.	2003-2009
New Mexico	
Pete V. Domenici, R.	1973-2009
Jeff Bingaman, D.	1983-2007
New York	
Charles E. Schumer, D.	1999-2005
Hillary Rodham Clinton, D.	2001-2007
North Carolina	
John Edwards, D.	1999-2005
Elizabeth Dole, R.	2003-2009
North Dakota	
Kent Conrad, D.	1987-2007
Byron L. Dorgan, D.	1992-2005

State	Term
Ohio	
Mike DeWine, R.	1995-2007
George V. Voinovich, R.	1999-2005
Oklahoma	
Don Nickles, R.	1981-2005
James M. Inhofe, R.	1994-2009
Oregon	
Ron Wyden, D.	1996-2005
Gordon Smith, R.	1997-2009
Pennsylvania	
Arlen Specter, R.	1981-2005
Rick Santorum, R.	1995-2007
Rhode Island	
Jack Reed, D.	1997-2009
Lincoln D. Chafee, R.	1999-2007
South Carolina	
Ernest F. Hollings, D.	1966-2005
Lindsey Graham, R.	2003-2009
South Dakota	
Thomas A. Daschle, D.	1987-2005
Tim Johnson, D.	1997-2009
Tennessee	
Bill Frist, R.	1995-2007
Lamar Alexander, R.	2003-2009
Texas	
Kay Bailey Hutchison, R.	1993-2007
John Cornyn, R.	2003-2009
Utah	
Orrin G. Hatch, R.	1977-2007
Robert F. Bennett, R.	1993-2005
Vermont	
Patrick J. Leahy, D.	1975-2005
James M. Jeffords, I.	1989-2007
Virginia	
John W. Warner, R.	1979-2009
George F. Allen, R.	2001-2007
Washington	
Patty Murray, D.	1993-2005
Maria Cantwell, D.	2001-2007
West Virginia	
Robert C. Byrd, D.	1959-2007
John D. Rockefeller IV, D.	1985-2009
Wisconsin	
Herbert Kohl, D.	1989-2007
Russell D. Feingold, D.	1993-2005
Wyoming	
Craig Thomas, R.	1995-2007
Mike Enzi, R.	1997-2009

U.S. Representative Nancy Pelosi (D., California) is congratulated by her fellow representatives after being elected House minority leader on November 14. She became the first woman ever to hold a leadership position in Congress. Her predecessor, Richard Gephardt of Missouri (right), resigned after Democrats lost seats in the midterm elections.

since 1790, when the capital was moved from New York City to Philadelphia. During the tribute, Vice President Dick Cheney, the president of the Senate, paid homage to the "valor, generosity, and grace" displayed by New York residents in the weeks following the attacks.

Campaign finance reform. Congress passed legislation in 2002 designed to reform the way federal political candidates finance their election campaigns. The House voted 240 to 189 in favor of the legislation on February 14 after almost 17 hours of continuous debate. Forty-one Republicans joined all but 12 Democrats in support of the bill, which was strongly opposed by the Republican leaders of the House. The Senate approved the legislation by a vote of 60 to 40 on March 20. President Bush signed the campaign finance reform legislation into law on March 27. The restrictions went into effect on November 6, one day after the 2002 midterm elections.

The legislation targeted so-called "soft-money" contributions—unlimited contributions from corporations, labor unions, and individuals in support of a political party. It also prohibited corporations and unions from funding advertising that mentions a federal candidate within specific time periods before elections. However, the new campaign finance law doubled from $1,000 to $2,000 the amount of money that federal candidates may raise from individuals. Opponents of the legislation characterized it as an "unconstitutional infringement of free speech."

Nuclear waste repository. Congress gave final approval to a plan to establish a nuclear waste repository at the Yucca Flat Nuclear Test Site in Nevada to store up to 77,000 tons (69,300 metric tons) of high-level radioactive waste and spent nuclear fuel from nuclear reactors across the United States. Under the plan, the waste would be stored 1,000 feet (300 meters) below the peak of Yucca Mountain, which is about 90 miles (145 kilometers) northwest of Las Vegas. The facility is slated to open in 2010.

In 1982, Congress had mandated that the federal government come up with a permanent disposal site for nuclear waste, but it was not until 2001 that the U.S. Department of Energy recommended the Yucca Mountain site. The House approved the measure in May 2002. The Senate followed with a voice vote of approval in July, and President Bush signed the measure on July 23.

Trade agreement. Congress passed legislation in August that gave President Bush broad authority to negotiate trade agreements with foreign countries without congressional approval. Under the law, the president can negotiate trade pacts with other countries through 2007. Congress can approve or reject the deals but cannot alter them.

Traficant expelled. In July 2002, the House of Representatives, by a vote of 420 to 1, expelled Representative James Traficant (D., Ohio) after he was sentenced to eight years in prison. Traficant was found guilty in April of bribery, racketeering, tax evasion, and obstruction of justice. The district that Traficant had represented since 1984 was eliminated in 2002 through redistricting. Traficant lost a bid to represent a redrawn congressional district while campaigning from federal prison as an independent in the November election.

Senator Strom Thurmond retired in November 2002 after having served in the Senate since 1955. Thurmond, who turned 100 on Dec. 5, 2002, was the longest-serving senator in U.S. history. Originally elected as a Democrat, Thurmond withdrew from the party in 1964 and became a Republican. ☐ Geoffrey A. Campbell

See also **Armed forces; Cabinet, U.S.; Democratic Party; Elections; Immigration; Immigration: A Special Report; Iraq; People in the news** (Feingold, Russell; Gerberding, Julie L.; McCain, John); **Republican Party; Terrorism; United States, Government of the; United States, President of the.**

Connecticut. See **State government.**

Conservation. Extremely dry weather in the Western United States led to a catastrophic wildfire season in 2002. The U.S. National Interagency Coordination Center reported that more than 70,000 fires consumed more than 7 million acres (2.8 million hectares) of forest across the United States, more than double the annual average. From July to September, the Biscuit Fire in Oregon, the largest and most damaging fire in state history, consumed about 500,000 acres (202,000 hectares).

Healthy Forest Initiative. U.S. President George W. Bush's response to the wildfire crisis sparked its own controversy. In August, President Bush announced his Healthy Forest Initiative, which proposed that timber companies be given more access to federal lands to remove dead trees and undergrowth that some scientists said increased the risk of severe fires. Several environmental groups complained that the Bush initiative was an attempt to override environmental laws and open up national forests to uncontrolled logging.

World Summit. The habitats in which great apes—chimpanzees, bonobos, gorillas, and orangutans—live are in worse danger than had been thought, according to a study by the United Nations Environmental Program (UNEP), a Nairobi, Kenya-based agency that aims to encourage sustainable development. The authors of the study, released at the World Summit for Sustainable Development held in Johannesburg, South Africa, in August, estimated that less than 10 percent of great-ape habitat will be undisturbed by 2030. The study blamed the destruction on exploitation by such activities as mining and road-building. UNEP members called for an international effort to conserve great-ape habitats.

Delegates at the World Summit also pushed to reduce by half the estimated 1.1 billion people without access to safe drinking water by 2015. Delegates from 189 countries also agreed to restore depleted fish stocks around the world by establishing protected marine areas by 2012. The proposal called for tighter restrictions on fishing until fish populations recover. About 22,000 people attended the World Summit, including more than 100 world leaders and representatives of government agencies, environmental groups, and business interests.

Condor release. California condors returned to Mexico in August 2002 after being absent for at least 50 years. Six of the extremely rare condors—among the largest birds in North America—were bred in captivity at the Los Angeles Zoo and taken to Mexico by plane. They were released into the wild a few weeks later in the mountains of northern Mexico. California Condors nearly became extinct before scientists in the 1980's began a breeding program that had, by 2002, resulted in more than 100 condors being released into the wild in California and Arizona.

Lost and found. Scientists in 2002 discovered several animal species that were thought to be extinct. In June, a scientist from the Wildlife Conservation Society, an environmental organization based in New York City, photographed a Lowe's servaline genet, a relative of the mongoose, in Tanzania. The only previous evidence that the animal existed was a skin of one found in 1932. In May 2002, two Brazilian scientists rediscovered the golden-crowned manakin, an extremely rare bird that had not been seen since 1957. In July, *ornithologists* (scientists who study birds) in Colombia reported photographing a flock of Fuertes parrots. The birds had last been seen in 1911 and were thought to be extinct.

Two previously unknown monkey species were discovered in the Amazon rain forest in South America, Conservation International, a group based in Washington, D.C., announced in June 2002. Marc van Roosmalen of the National Institue for Amazon Research in Brazil discovered the monkeys, which are both the size of small cats. Van Roosemalen named the new species *Callicebus stephennashi* and *Callicebus bernhardi*.

Swordfish recovery. The International Commission for the Conservation of Atlantic Tunas in

A helicopter hovers over a radar installation under construction in Brazil's Amazon rain forest in 2002. The system was part of a $1.4-billion project, financed by the United States, designed to help Brazilian officials monitor and protect the rain forest from illegal logging and ranching.

Madrid, Spain, announced in October that swordfish had largely recovered from serious overfishing in the late 1990's. Swordfish, which live mainly in the North Atlantic Ocean, became a popular restaurant entree in the 1990's, leading to overfishing. Scientists credited the recovery to strict limits that had been placed on the numbers of swordfish that could be caught. They reported that the population was at 94 percent of a self-sustaining level and may make a full recovery by 2009 or earlier.

Bushmeat. The illegal hunting of African wildlife reached devastating levels in 2002, according to members of conservation groups that belong to the Bushmeat Crisis Task Force (BCTF), a Silver Spring, Maryland-based group that investigates illegal hunting. Bushmeat is the term many Africans use to mean wild creatures that are consumed by humans. Conservation officials reported in 2002 that 1.1 million tons (1 million metric tons) of wild meat is harvested from African forests each year.

BCTF members told the U.S. House of Representatives Subcommittee on Fisheries, Conservation, Wildlife, and Oceans in July that the large-scale hunting threatens both animals and people. Many Africans rely on small numbers of wild creatures for food. Commercial hunting reduces the numbers of animals these people can hunt. Witnesses at the hearing called on Congress to help make alternative food sources available to Africans. They also sought the expansion of protected forest areas in Africa.

CITES meeting. Delegates at the 12th Conference of the Convention on Trade in Endangered Species (CITES), who met in Santiago, Chile, in November, made a controversial decision to allow a one-time sale of ivory by three African countries. CITES is a treaty signed by 160 countries that regulates the commercial trade in animals and plants that are at risk of extinction. In the decision, CITES delegates voted to allow South Africa, Namibia, and Botswana to sell approximately 60 tons (54 metric tons) of elephant ivory in 2004. The ivory to be sold came mostly from elephants that died naturally. CITES had banned the sale of ivory in 1989 to prevent the poaching of elephants, whose tusks are made of ivory. Some conservation groups argued that the sale might encourage elephant poaching.

Conservationists hailed the decision by CITES delegates to restrict international sales of products from whale sharks and basking sharks. These fish—the largest fish species on Earth—are often hunted for their meat and fins, which are a popular ingredient in Asian cooking. CITES delegates also voted to restrict trade in seahorses and mahogany tree products.   □ Edward R. Ricciuti

Costa Rica. See Latin America.

Courts. Corporate scandals in 2002 led to a series of indictments in federal courts against several high-level executives. John J. Rigas, founder of Adelphia Communications, and two of his sons were arrested in July for looting the Coudersport, Pennsylvania-based cable television company. Federal prosecutors alleged that the Rigases improperly used company money to finance personal loans, buy stocks, take vacations, and purchase luxury items.

Arthur Andersen. A federal jury in Houston in June found the Chicago-based accounting firm Arthur Andersen LLP guilty of obstruction of justice for its role in covering up financial irregularities at Enron Corp. Enron is an energy trading company headquartered in Houston that declared bankruptcy in late 2001. Arthur Andersen executives allegedly ordered employees to destroy thousands of documents related to Enron's collapse after Andersen was notified that it was to be investigated by the Securities and Exchange Commission (SEC). The SEC is an independent federal agency that administers and enforces federal laws governing the purchase and sale of stocks and bonds. On Oct. 11, 2002, a judge fined Andersen $500,000 for obstruction of justice and sentenced the company to five years' probation.

Enron. In August, a former Enron executive, Michael J. Kopper, pleaded guilty to money laundering and conspiracy to commit wire fraud in U.S. District Court in Houston and told a federal judge that he paid huge kickbacks to Enron's chief financial officer, Andrew S. Fastow. The kickbacks came from funds Kopper received for managing three partnerships that Fastow set up to help Enron hide debt and increase profits. Fastow was indicted in federal court in late October on 78 counts of fraud, money laundering, conspiracy, and obstruction of justice for his alleged participation in a series of complicated schemes to artificially inflate Enron profits.

Tyco. A New York State grand jury on September 12 indicted former executives with Tyco International Ltd. on charges that they illegally funneled approximately $600 million to themselves through stock fraud, false expense reports, and unauthorized bonuses. The company, headquartered in Bermuda, manufactures and services electrical and electronic components. Former Tyco chief executive officer L. Dennis Kozlowski and former chief financial officer Mark H. Swartz were accused of using the money to pay for personal luxuries. The grand jury also indicted Tyco's former general counsel, Mark Belnick, on charges that he falsified company documents to conceal $14 million in illegal company loans to himself.

John Walker Lindh, a U.S. citizen who fought with the Taliban in Afghanistan against U.S. armed forces before being captured in 2001, pleaded guilty in July 2002 to two felony charges. Lindh pleaded guilty in U.S. District Court in Alexandria, Virginia, to a charge that he had provided service to the Taliban and to a charge of carrying explosives while serving the Taliban. On October 4, a judge sentenced Lindh to 20 years in prison.

"Shoe bomber" plea. On October 4, Richard Reid, a British citizen, pleaded guilty in U.S. District Court in Boston to eight charges in connection with a plot to detonate a bomb hidden in his shoe while on board an American Airlines flight in 2001. During his plea, Reid called himself an enemy of the United States. He was scheduled to be sentenced in 2003.

Secret deportation hearings. On Aug. 26, 2002, the U.S. Court of Appeals for the Sixth Circuit in Cincinnati, Ohio, ruled that the administration of U.S. President George W. Bush had illegally conducted hundreds of deportation hearings in secret. The U.S. Department of Justice conducted the closed hearings, mainly against Islamic men, in the wake of the terrorist attacks on the United States. The justices ruled that the administration's claim that the people involved may have links to terrorism was insufficient to warrant secrecy.

The Ten Commandments. The U.S. District Court in Montgomery, Alabama, ruled in November that a granite monument inscribed with the Ten Commandments in the lobby of the Alabama Supreme Court was unconstitutional and must be removed. Federal Judge Myron Thompson said that the monument violated the U.S. Constitution's Establishment Clause, which mandates the separation of church and state. The monument was paid for by evangelical Christians and installed in 2001.

Pledge of Allegiance. In June 2002, a three-judge panel of the U.S. Court of Appeals for the Ninth Circuit in San Francisco ruled that requiring public school children to recite the Pledge of Allegiance is an unconstitutional "endorsement of religion." The panel ruled that the words "under God," which were added by the U.S. Congress in 1954, violated the Constitution's requirement of a separation of church and state. The decision led to intense public debate on the issue and forced the Justice Department to ask the full 11-member court to reconsider the ruling.

Church bombing verdict. An Alabama jury on May 22, 2002, found former Ku Klux Klan member Bobby Frank Cherry guilty of first-degree murder for his role in a 1963 church bombing that killed four girls. Cherry maintained his innocence throughout the trial. He was sentenced to life in prison.   □ Geoffrey A. Campbell

See also **Human rights; Supreme Court of the United States; Terrorism; United States, Government of the.**

Cricket. The threat of terrorist attacks in Asia, especially in Pakistan, had serious repercussions on international cricket in 2002. In January, Pakistan rescheduled its home series against the West Indies because of anxiety over such attacks, and the series was moved to Sharjah in the United Arab Emirates. Sharjah regularly hosts one-day internationals, but it had never before hosted a test match. The test series was also the first played at a neutral venue. Pakistan beat West Indies by two test matches to one.

Test matches returned to Pakistan in May, when the home side defeated New Zealand by an innings and 324 runs in Lahore. However, officials canceled the second test scheduled to be held in Karachi because of a suicide bomb attack near the hotel where the teams were staying. The New Zealanders promptly returned home. Australia was also scheduled to visit Pakistan in October. However, both sides agreed to play one test in Colombo, Sri Lanka, and play the other two tests in the United Arab Emirates. Australia comfortably won the series 3 to 0.

Test cricket. Australia confirmed its status as the world's leading cricket nation when the team defeated rival South Africa 3 to 0 in a home test match series that ended in January. Australia also won an away series by 2 tests to 1 in South Africa in March. South Africa would have replaced Australia at the top of the championship had either series ended in a draw.

Fans attributed Australia's success to the fact that the team combined a potent offense, including the hitting of Adam Gilchrist, with an aggressive bowling attack that was spearheaded by Jason Gillespie, Glenn McGrath, and Shane Warne. In an effort to shorten long tours, Australia's captain, Steve Waugh, suggested that test matches be reduced in length from five to four days. Critics of this idea pointed out that a fifth day would probably still be required for tours held in countries where rain causes frequent interruptions to cricket matches.

Despite being defeated by Pakistan in the Lahore test in May, New Zealand had a good year, drawing a home test match series with England 1-1, with one match drawn. In the first test at Christchurch, New Zealand, Graham Thorpe of England scored the fastest double-century in English test history. In the same game, Nathan Astle of New Zealand scored an astonishing 222 from 168 balls—the fastest double-century in New Zealand test history. New Zealand then went on to beat West Indies 1-0 with one match drawn in July. The victory was New Zealand's first in a test series held in the Caribbean.

In May and June, England, which continued to improve, faced Sri Lanka in England. The fitness problems of Muttiah Muralitharan, the leading bowler for Sri Lanka, affected the team's performance, and the team went under by 2-0, with one match drawn. The test match series between England and India in July and September was drawn 1-1, with no result in the other two matches. However, the crowds enjoyed some majestic batting, especially from England's Michael Vaughan and India's Rahul Dravid and Sachin Tendulkar.

Instant replay. In a one-day international played in Sri Lanka in September, Pakistan's Shoaib Malik became the first man to be given out to a "leg before wicket" decision that was made after the third umpire had consulted television replays and transmitted the information to the umpire on the field. In 2002, third umpires commonly analyzed television replays to confirm close run outs and catches. Some cricket authorities felt that instant replay was a valuable aid to umpires. Other cricket fans felt that the use of television replays was another regrettable step towards making umpires redundant in international cricket.

One-day internationals. The ICC Champions Trophy—perhaps the most important one-day international series—was held in September in Sri Lanka. The competition included the 10 test-match-playing countries plus Kenya and the Netherlands. India and Sri Lanka shared the Trophy after rain washed out the final match.

The crowded schedule of one-day internationals included the Victorian Bitter series held in Australia between Australia, New Zealand, and South Africa. Australia failed to make the final for only the third time since the triangular one-day series began in 1979 and 1980. South Africa overwhelmed New Zealand in the final.

England and India fought to a draw in a series held in January and February 2002 in India that ended 3-3. However, in a triangular tournament with England and Sri Lanka held in England in July, India defeated England in the final. During the match, two young batsmen, Mohammad Kaif and Yuvraj Singh, led the way for India in an exciting run chase.

Cronje dies. Hansie Cronje, the former South African cricketer, was killed in a plane crash on June 1 in South Africa. Cronje was known as a match-winning all-rounder, an outstanding captain, and one of South Africa's most admired sportsmen. However, he will more likely be remembered for receiving a lifetime ban from cricket in 2000 for illegally taking money from *bookmakers* (people who make their living from taking bets) to fix cricket matches. After Cronje admitted to the charges of match-fixing, cricket officials established an anticorruption unit in an effort to prevent other players from fixing the outcome of cricket matches. ☐ Keith Lye

Crime. In October 2002, the U.S. Federal Bureau of Investigation (FBI) reported that crime in the United States had increased the previous year, reversing a 10-year trend of year-to-year declines. The FBI's Crime Index revealed that 11.8 million serious crimes had been committed in 2001, a 2.1-percent increase over the 2000 estimate and the first year-to-year increase since 1991. The Crime Index is composed of four types of violent crime—murder and non-negligent manslaughter, forcible rape, robbery, and aggravated assault—and three types of property crime—burglary, larceny and theft, and motor vehicle theft. In contrast to this increase, other FBI data recording 5- and 10-year trends indicated a long-term decline in crime levels. The crime numbers reported for 2001 showed a 10.2-percent decline, compared with 1997 data, and a 17.9-percent decline, compared with 1992 statistics.

FBI figures for the number of violent crimes in 2001 rose 0.8 percent over 2000 estimates. Robberies increased 3.7 percent; murders rose 2.5 percent; and forcible rapes increased 0.3 percent. Aggravated assault decreased 0.5 percent from 2000 data. Property crimes in 2001 were up 2.3 percent over 2000 figures. Motor vehicle thefts increased 5.7 percent; burglaries rose 2.9 percent; and larceny-thefts increased 1.5 percent.

Hate crimes. According to a November 2002 report by the FBI, 9,730 hate crime incidents were reported in 2001, a 21-percent increase from 2000. Of these, 44.9 percent resulted from racial bias; 21.6 percent were caused by bias against an ethnic group or national origin; 18.8 percent resulted from religious bias; 14.3 percent were caused by a sexual-orientation bias; and 0.4 percent resulted from bias against a disability. Reported incidents of hate crimes directed against Muslims increased from 28 in 2000 to 481 in 2001. This jump came in the wake of the attacks by an Islamic terrorist network against the United States on Sept. 11, 2001.

Prison populations. The U.S. Department of Justice announced in April 2002 that, as of late June 2001, 1,965,495 men and women were incarcerated in federal and state prisons and local jails in the United States. This amounted to 1 in every 145 U.S. residents. Between July 1, 2000, and June 30, 2001, federal, state, and local governments added 30,505 inmates, the equivalent of 587 new inmates each week. The greatest inmate increase occurred in the federal system, which grew by 7.2 percent. In the first six months of 2001, the populations of federal prisons increased by 7,372 inmates, the largest six-month increase ever recorded in the federal system.

The increase in the numbers of prisoners at the state and local level was modest by comparison. In the 12 months before June 30, 2001, the state prison population grew at a

United States Army veteran John Allen Muhammad (right) and John Lee Malvo, an illegal immigrant from Jamaica, were arrested on October 24 in connection with a series of shootings that terrorized the Washington, D.C., metropolitan area for three weeks in October. Authorities later linked the suspects to additional killings in Alabama, Louisiana, Maryland, and Washington state.

rate of 0.4 percent, the slowest rate of increase in 28 years. At the same time, the local jail population rose 1.6 percent, the slowest since the Justice Department began collecting such data in 1982.

The Beltway sniper. For three weeks in October 2002, residents of the Washington, D.C., metropolitan area were terrified by a series of seemingly random shootings. Before police arrested the sniper suspects late in the month, 10 people were known to have been killed and 3 others were seriously wounded.

The shootings began in the early evening of October 2 in Montgomery County, Maryland, where a man was shot dead while sitting in his car in the parking lot of a grocery store. This attack established the snipers' basic technique—the victim was killed by a single shot fired from a long distance. On the morning of October 3, four people were shot and killed in Montgomery County within three hours. Later that night, a 72-year-old man was shot dead while standing on a Washington, D.C., street corner.

The attacks continued on October 4, when a woman was shot and wounded in the parking lot of a shopping mall in northern Virginia. Children became a focus of concern after the next shooting, on October 7. The victim was a 13-year-old boy, who was critically wounded while being dropped off at a middle school in Prince George's County, Maryland. On October 9, the snipers killed a man at a gas station in Manassas, Virginia; and on October 11, another man was killed while pumping gas in Fredericksburg, Virginia.

The next victim, a woman who worked for the FBI, was shot and killed October 14 as she was loading her car in a store parking lot in northern Virginia. On October 19, a man was shot and wounded as he left a diner in Ashland, Virginia. The last victim was a bus driver who was shot and killed on the steps of his bus on October 22 in Montgomery County.

Although police had previously told the public that a white van or truck had been linked to the attacks, they later said they were looking for a blue Caprice automobile. On October 24, a phone call from a passing motorist led police to arrest 41-year-old U.S. Army veteran John Allen Muhammad and 17-year-old John Lee Malvo, an illegal immigrant from Jamaica, as they slept in their Caprice at a Maryland rest stop. Authorities found a .223 caliber semiautomatic rifle in the car. The trunk of the car had a gun port cut into it, and the back seat had been removed to allow the snipers access to the port from inside the car.

After the arrests, authorities linked the two suspects to additional shootings in Maryland, Alabama, Louisiana, and Washington state dating back to mid-February.   □ Fitzgerald Higgins
See also **Prison; Terrorism; Washington, D.C.**

Croatia. The moderate government of Prime Minister Ivica Racan survived the dissolution of its parliamentary coalition in mid-2002 when Racan assembled a new working coalition. In foreign affairs, Croatian leaders improved relations with some of Croatia's Balkan neighbors but displeased the international community by resisting demands made by the War Crimes Tribunal in The Hague, Netherlands.

Domestic politics. Prime Minister Racan's government fell in early July when a party in the governing coalition refused to support Racan in a critical vote in parliament. The prime minister stepped down on July 5 but was immediately appointed interim prime minister by President Stjepan Mesic. The move allowed Racan to legally reconstitute a workable coalition and, therefore, remain in power.

Economy. Racan's government proceeded in 2002 with economic reforms, particularly ongoing privatization of state-owned industries, which kept Croatia's unemployment rate high. In September, the government reported that nearly 22 percent of the country's work force was idle. Nevertheless, economic growth continued in 2002 but at a slower pace than in 2001. A report released in August 2002 by the International Monetary Fund (IMF)—a United Nations-affiliated organization that provides short-term credit to member nations—predicted that Croatia's economy would grow 3.5 percent in 2002 and 4.0 percent in 2003.

Foreign policy. Croatia took part in several initiatives in 2002 that improved relations among successor nations to Yugoslavia, which largely broke apart in the 1990's. In June 2002, Croatia's President Mesic and President Vojislav Kostunica of Yugoslavia (consisting of Serbia and Montenegro) signed an agreement to end visa requirements for travel between their two nations. In December, representatives of Slovenia, Croatia, Yugoslavia, and Bosnia-Herzegovina signed an agreement to open up the Sava River to unrestricted shipping between the four nations. However, a dispute over fishing rights between Croatia and Slovenia challenged the historically cordial relations between those two countries.

The refusal of Croatian officials to turn over Janko Bobetko, Croatia's Army chief during the 1991–1995 war with Serbia, to the War Crimes Tribunal in The Hague strained relations with the the European Union and the United Nations. In September 2002, the tribunal charged Bobetko with killing 100 ethnic Serbs in a 1993 military operation. Croatia claimed Bobetko was too ill to travel to the trial. The tribunal reissued its demand in November that Croatia surrender Bobetko for trial.   □ Sharon L. Wolchik
See also **Europe.**

Cuban President Fidel Castro (right) on May 12 welcomes Jimmy Carter to Cuba for a five-day visit, during which the former U.S. president met with Cuban dissidents and called for an end to the U.S. trade embargo.

Cuba. The Cuban government began a major overhaul of the country's agricultural sector in 2002 in response to a glut of sugar and falling prices on the world market. The government planned to replace about half of Cuba's 3.5 million acres (1.4 million hectares) of sugar cane with higher-income crops, subsistence farming, and livestock. Government officials promised that the tens of thousands of laid-off sugar industry workers would be moved into other agricultural jobs or trained in technical skills.

Carter visit. On May 12, former United States President Jimmy Carter arrived in Havana, the capital, for a five-day visit. Carter met with leading Cuban dissidents and endorsed their goals in a televised speech. In his address, Carter highlighted a little-known petition drive for a national referendum seeking the right to freely express dissent, the right to own small businesses, and *amnesty* (pardon) for political prisoners. Carter also called for the lifting of the U.S. trade embargo, which was imposed against Cuba in 1960, and the easing of travel restrictions on U.S. citizens wishing to visit Cuba.

Agribusiness exhibition. A rare exception to the trade embargo took place in September 2002 with the first U.S. agribusiness exhibition in Cuba in over 40 years. Nearly 300 U.S. agricultural companies exhibited their food products and live-stock in Havana for five days. The trade fair was held in accord with a law passed by the U.S. Congress in 2000 that allows U.S. companies to sell food to Cuba for cash. After the fair, Cuban officials announced that they expected to purchase $112 million in U.S. agricultural products.

Guantanamo prison. Twenty suspected terrorists detained by U.S. forces in Afghanistan arrived at the U.S. naval base in Guantanamo, Cuba, on Jan. 11, 2002. U.S. forces had apprehended the men while attempting to capture members of the Islamic terrorist group al-Qa'ida, which carried out the terrorist attacks on the United States on Sept. 11, 2001. By October 2002, the Guantanamo facility held more than 800 prisoners. The number of U.S. military personnel at the base increased from about 1,500 to more than 4,000 between January and October. The Castro regime, which expressed support for the U.S.-led war on terrorism, refrained from criticizing this expanded use of the base.

Spy sentenced. In October, a U.S. District Court judge in sentenced Ana Belen Montes to 25 years in prison for spying on the United States on behalf of Cuba for 16 years. Montes was fomerly a top Cuba analyst at the U.S. Defense Intelligence Agency. □ Nathan A. Haverstock

See also **Latin America; Terrorism.**

Cyprus. See **Middle East.**

Czech Republic. Parliamentary elections dominated political life in the Czech Republic in 2002. The ruling Czech Social Democratic Party emerged with enough strength in the lower house of parliament to form a new governing coalition. In August, floods damaged historic parts of Prague, the capital, and many other Czech towns and cities.

Elections. The Czech Social Democratic Party won 30.2 percent of the vote in legislative elections in June. The right-of-center Civic Democrats, with which the Social Democrats had previously participated in a parliamentary partnership, took 24.5 percent of the vote. The Czech Communist Party increased its percentage of the vote to 18.5 percent from 10 percent in 1998.

The election results allowed the Social Democratic Party to form a new governing coalition with two small centrist parties. This new Social Democrat-led coalition held a one-seat majority in the lower house of the Czech parliament. Vladimir Spidla, leader of the Social Democrats, became the prime minister, replacing Milos Zeman, who had stepped down as party leader in April 2002.

Flood disaster. The worst floods in more than 100 years swept Bohemia, the western region of the Czech Republic, in August. Unusually heavy rains in early August triggered widespread flooding throughout central Europe, sending river waters over levees and into towns and cities. Prague, the capital and largest city of the Czech Republic, was especially hard hit. The floods claimed 17 lives in the Czech Republic, and damages amounted to more than $3 billion, according to Czech officials. The European Union (EU), an organization of 15 Western European nations, pledged $500 million in immediate aid to European flood victims and promised more aid in 2003.

The Czech economy grew in 2002 but at a slower rate than in 2001. The growth in *gross domestic* product (the total value of goods and services produced in a given year) slowed to 2.5 percent in the second quarter of 2002, compared with a 3.5-percent growth rate during the same period in 2001. Officials of the Czech National Bank forecast an overall 2002 growth rate of between 2.0 and 2.7 percent. Unemployment in the Czech Republic reached 9.4 percent in August, a figure near the all-time high of nearly 10 percent in January 2000. Inflation remained low, dipping to an annual rate of 2.5 percent by mid-2002.

Foreign policy. EU officials, meeting at a summit in Copenhagen, Denmark, in December 2002, formally approved the Czech Republic's application for admission into the EU. Admission was scheduled for 2004.   □ Sharon L. Wolchik

See also **Europe.**

Dallas. City Council member Laura Miller defeated businessman Tom Dunning in a runoff election on Feb. 16, 2002, for mayor. Miller was sworn in at a city council meeting on February 20.

The runoff became necessary following the January 19 mayoral election in which no candidate received a majority of votes, though Miller took 49 percent. Miller, previously a columnist for a weekly newspaper and frequent critic of the municipal government, promised to improve basic city services and move away from the big projects that characterized the administration of her predecessor, Ron Kirk. Kirk resigned as mayor in November 2001 to run for the U.S. Senate.

Drug enforcement scandal. In January 2002, Dallas Police Chief Terrell Bolton and Dallas County District Attorney Bill Hill revealed that a significant percentage of alleged drugs seized in raids by Dallas police in 2001 were actually gypsum, a harmless substance used to make plasterboard, instead of cocaine or methamphetamine. The discovery forced prosecutors to dismiss dozens of felony drug cases.

On Jan. 26, 2002, Police Chief Bolton announced that he was turning over an internal investigation into the drug seizures to the Federal Bureau of Investigation. At least some of the bogus drug busts had been traced to two undercover narcotics officers of the Dallas Police Department and paid informants they had used.

In July, two informants pleaded guilty to planting phony drugs on people and then tipping off narcotics officers. A third informant pleaded guilty to similar charges in September. As of late 2002, no charges had been brought against members of the Dallas Police Department.

School bond. Dallas voters overwhelmingly approved a record $1.37-billion school bond issue on January 19. The bond, the largest ever approved in Texas, was to fund the construction of 20 new schools as well as major repairs to 36 existing schools in the Dallas School District. The bond was approved by more than 78 percent of voters, even though city officials had said a tax increase would be necessary if the bond issue passed.

Pay raise rejected. Dallas voters were less generous in a referendum on May 4 in which they turned down a 17-percent pay raise for police and firefighters. A coalition of police and firefighters, claiming they were underpaid compared with suburban safety officers, had collected enough signatures on petitions to put the issue to a vote. However, Dallas officials warned during the campaign that a city budget deficit, which was $50 million at that time, might balloon to more than $90 million if the pay raises were endorsed. In the balloting, more than 70 percent of voters rejected the pay raise proposal.

La Scala Ballet of Milan's La Scala Opera House performs the final scene from *Excelsior* at the Palais Garnier in Paris in January 2002. The ballet, a celebration of the triumph of civilization and progress, is based on a work originally choreographed in 1881.

Transit extensions. On July 1, the Dallas Area Rapid Transit (DART) system opened 9.3 miles (15 kilometers) of new light rail connecting Richardson, a northern suburb, to downtown Dallas. The extension added seven new rail stations to the DART network. In November, another extension brought suburban Garland, northeast of Dallas proper, into the DART network. In December, the Richardson line was extended further north to the city of Plano.

Dallas Stars for sale. Tom Hicks, owner of the Dallas Stars, announced on September 9 that he intended to sell the professional hockey team along with his half ownership in the company that operates American Airlines Center, the arena where the team plays home games. National Hockey League executives said that the Stars franchise, which won the Stanley Cup championship in 1999, was worth $300 million. Hicks said he planned to retain ownership of the Texas Rangers, Dallas's professional baseball team.

Convention center expansion. The management of the Dallas Convention Center completed a $128-million expansion in September 2002, making the center the nation's sixth largest. City officials predicted that the improved facility would draw an additional 500,000 visitors annually to Dallas. ☐ Henry Tatum

See also **City.**

Dance. The struggle for ownership of the works of choreographer Martha Graham was resolved in 2002. The dispute began when Graham died in 1991, having willed all of her ballets to Ron Protas. Protas had been Graham's personal assistant in her later years. When the Martha Graham Center for Contemporary Dance, an umbrella organization consisting of the Graham dance company and school, fired Protas as artistic director, he contested the right of the company to perform the dances. As a result, the dance company was forced to close in 2000.

On Aug. 23, 2002, a federal district court judge in New York City ruled that the Center owned the rights to 45 Graham ballets. Another 10 were judged to be in the public domain, while Protas was found to own only a single work, *Seraphic Dialogue.* Ownership of nine other works remained undetermined.

Although the judge's decision to give the Graham troupe clear control over its repertory and operations was applauded by many dance world insiders, her reasoning caused concern. The judge determined that after 1956, when Graham began to draw a salary from the center for her choreography, she became in effect an employee of the center, and her ballets were "work for hire." Her dances were not, therefore, legally hers to bequeath.

The Martha Graham Dance Company went into rehearsal in October 2002 after two years of inactivity. The company's first performances were scheduled to be held in January 2003.

The American Ballet Theater (ABT) revived several classical works in 2002. Two jewels from its list included British choreographer Frederick Ashton's *La Fille Mal Gardee (The Unchaperoned Daughter)* and *The Dream,* based on William Shakespeare's *A Midsummer Night's Dream.* ABT first presented Ashton's works during its two-month summer season at the Metropolitan Opera House (the Met) in New York City's Lincoln Center. The troupe's roster of outstanding male dancers flourished in Ashton's notoriously difficult choreography—including the parts of Oberon, king of the fairies, in *The Dream* and as innocent young farmhand Colas in *La Fille.*

Major productions such as the Ashton revivals and Russian full-length classics such as *Swan Lake* formed the bulk of ABT's repertory during its tours to Costa Mesa, California; the Kennedy Center for the Performing Arts in Washington, D.C.; and the Detroit Opera House, as well as the season at the Met.

Premieres of new work were reserved for a two-week run in October at the New York City Center. *A Tribute to George Harrison,* the late singer and guitarist with the Beatles, was the work of four choreographers—David Parsons, Natalie Weir, Stanton Welch, and Broadway star Ann Reinking. Another premiere of note featured Lar Lubovitch's choreography to the music of Richard Rodgers, in honor of the 100th anniversary of the musical theater composer's birth.

The New York City Ballet paid tribute to Rodgers by commissioning three new ballets to his music. They were performed on November 26, the opening night of the company's winter season at Lincoln Center's New York State Theater.

The focus of the troupe's activities, however, was on more classically oriented music and dance in 2002. Celebrating the 10th anniversary of the Diamond Project, a showcase for new choreography, the City Ballet presented a retrospective of Diamond Project ballets during its two-month annual spring season at the State Theater. Fifteen works from the past 10 years were revived, and seven new ballets were premiered. Among them were works by ballet master-in-chief Peter Martins and resident choreographer Christopher Wheeldon. Although no single ballet was a major artistic event, the festival as a whole highlighted the City Ballet's profile as a creative force in contemporary ballet.

Merce Cunningham, the 83-year-old U.S. choreographer whom many critics consider the strongest creative force in modern dance, began the 50th anniversary celebrations of the Merce Cunningham Dance Company with a four-day retrospective in July, as part of the Lincoln Center Festival. This brief season offered a rare look at two old dances—*Suite for Five* (1956), a surprisingly classical dance set to music by the late John Cage, Cunningham's long-time collaborator; and *How To Pass, Kick, Fall and Run* (1965), a frolicsome piece that is not set to music but to amusing anecdotes written by Cage. On this occasion, they were read by Cunningham himself and company archivist David Vaughan.

Kirov Ballet. In 2001, the Kennedy Center announced an ambitious plan to present Russia's Kirov Ballet annually for the next 10 years. In February 2002, the Kirov made the first of these visits with a repertory of *The Sleeping Beauty* and George Balanchine's *Jewels.*

However, the most interesting production, a reconstruction of *La Bayadere,* was reserved for a two-week run during the Lincoln Center Festival in July. *La Bayadere* was choreographed by Marius Petipa, who had been the head of the Imperial Theatre in St. Petersburg from 1862 to 1903. Using archival material, Sergei Vikharev, a principal dancer with the Kirov, recreated Petipa's 1900 revision of his 1877 original. Although several productions of this ballet have been performed in the West, Vikharev's version includes more mime and pageantry, elements that dominated Russian ballet until the early 1900's. Some critics thought it a mere curiosity; others loved it.

September 11. A number of dances were created in 2002 in response to the terrorist attacks on the United States on Sept. 11, 2001. However, none was so grandly conceived as Paul Taylor's *Promethean Fire.* The work premiered on June 8, 2002, at the American Dance Festival at Duke University in Durham, North Carolina. Set to pieces by Johann Sebastian Bach, the dance mirrors the architectural beauty of Bach's music with stunning physical structures created by the 16 dancers. As the piece progresses, these structures collapse. Images of despair and fury give way to a coming together. At the end, the dancers form the pyramid grouping with which *Promethean Fire* began.

Twyla Tharp created a new work in 2002 that was both a two-act ballet and a Broadway show. Tharp welded some 30 songs by Billy Joel into a story tracing the lives of five young people from their high school graduation in the 1960's, through the Vietnam War (1957-1975), to a reunion many years later. *Movin' Out,* which bowed at the Richard Rodgers Theater on Oct. 24, 2002, had no singing chorus, and not one line of dialogue was spoken. A vocalist and an onstage rock band highlighted the story and relationships between the characters as expressed by the dancers. ☐ Nancy Goldner

■ Deaths

in 2002 included those listed below, who were Americans unless otherwise indicated.

Stephen Ambrose, historian

Ambrose, Stephen E. (1936–October 13), historian whose *D-Day, June 6, 1944; Citizen Soldier;* and Dwight D. Eisenhower biographies refocused national attention on the generation that fought World War II.

Annenberg, Walter H. (1908–October 1), head of a media empire and former ambassador to the United Kingdom who gave away more than $3 billion in cash and art.

Arledge, Roone (1931–December 5), television executive and producer whose reinvention of sports and news programming is credited with changing the medium.

Barry, David Walter (1944–January 28), medical researcher who codeveloped AZT, the first effective treatment for AIDS.

Baer, Parley (1914–November 22), character actor who appeared in hundreds of television shows, most memorably as the neighbor on "The Adventures of Ozzie and Harriet" and the mayor on "The Andy Griffith Show."

Benson, Mildred Wirt (1905–May 28), journalist and author who wrote 23 Nancy Drew mysteries, including the first, *The Secret of the Old Clock* (1930), under the pen name Carolyn Keene.

Berle, Milton (Mendel Berlinger) (1908–March 27),

Bill Blass, fashion designer

vaudeville, nightclub, film, and radio comedian who became television's first star and launched a national craze for the new medium.

Berwanger, Jay (1914–June 26), football player who was the first winner of the Heisman Trophy and in 1936 was the first choice in the first National Football League draft.

Black, Joe (1924–May 17), Brooklyn Dodgers right-hander who in 1952 became the first African American

pitcher to win a World Series game.

Blackwell, Otis (1931– May 6), songwriter of some 1,000 tunes, including "Don't Be Cruel," "All Shook Up," "Return to Sender," "Great Balls of Fire," and "Fever."

Blackwood, James (1919–February 3), gospel singer who was the last surviving founding member of the Blackwood Brothers Quartet.

Blass, Bill (1922–June 12), designer whose glamorous but understated clothes kept him at the top of the fashion industry for some 30 years.

Bohlin, Nils (1920–September 21), Swedish inventor who perfected the three-point safety seat belt credited with saving the lives of 1 million drivers.

Bracken, Eddie (1915–November 14), comedian who spent more than 70 years in show business but was best known for his roles in two 1944 Preston Sturges comedies, *The Miracle of Morgan's Creek* and *Hail the Conquering Hero.*

Bradley, Ruby (1907–May 28), Army nurse who became the most decorated military woman in U.S. history.

Brown, J. Carter (1934–June 17), former director of Washington, D.C.'s National Gallery of Art whose blockbuster exhibitions and construction of the landmark East Building transformed public perception of art museums.

Brown, Claude (1937–February 2), author whose 1965 bestseller *Manchild in the Promised Land* described the violence to which children in Harlem were exposed.

Brown, Ray (1926–July 2), master jazz bassist who played with Dizzy Gillespie, Charlie Parker, and the Oscar Peterson Trio;

Milton Berle, comedian

accompanied Ella Fitzgerald; and was a charter member of the Modern Jazz Quartet.

Burton, Charles (1942–July 15), English explorer who participated in the first expedition (1979-1982) to circumnavigate the world pole to pole.

Campbell, Alec (1899–May 16), Australian World War I veteran who was the last survivor of the ill-fated 1915 Gallipoli campaign.

Cela, Camilo Jose (1916–January 17), Nobel Prize-winning Spanish novelist who wrote *The Family of Pascual Duarte* (1942).

Clooney, Rosemary (1928–June 29), singer whose

control, unique phrasing, and understated interpretations placed her in the top rank of popular musical performers.

Coburn, James (1928–November 18), tough guy actor in such films as *The Magnificent Seven* (1960) and *Our Man Flint* (1967) who won an Academy Award for *Affliction* (1997).

Cohen, Herman (1927–June 2), Hollywood "B-movie" producer who was credited with launching the teen-age horror genre with his 1957 cult classic *I Was a Teenage Werewolf*.

Conniff, Ray (1916–October 12), composer, arranger, and orchestra leader who made more than 100 recordings and 25 Top-40 "easy listening" albums.

Crosetti, Frank (1910–February 11), New York Yankees shortstop and third-base coach for 37 consecutive seasons (1932-1968), the longest run ever for a single baseball franchise.

Dancer, Faye (1925–May 22), ballplayer All-American Girls Professional Baseball League whose home runs, fly-catching, and spontaneous cartwheels earned her the title "All the Way Faye."

Davis, Jr., Benjamin O. (1912–July 4), commander of the fabled Tuskegee Airmen black fighter pilots of World War II, who was the first African American to become a U.S. Air Force general.

Deegan, Millie (1919–July 21), All-American Girls Professional Baseball League player, who from 1943 to 1952 pitched and played second base for the Rockford Peaches, the team that served as the basis for the 1992 film *A League of Their Own*.

Deutsch, Martin (1917–August 16), Austrian-born physicist who discovered positronium, an elemental form of matter.

Domingues, Adelina (1888–August 21), woman who at the age of 114 was recognized by the *Guinness Book of World Records* as the oldest living American.

Earley, Charity Adams (1918–January 13), commander of the only African American Women's Army Corps (WAC) battalion to serve overseas in World War II.

Eban, Abba (1915–November 17), Israeli statesman, whose eloquence and formidable skills as a diplomat led the United Nations in 1947 to approve the creation of Israel.

Edelson, Burton I. (1926–January 6), scientist and satellite communications expert who headed various NASA programs, including the Hubble Space Telescope and Mars Explorer missions.

Elizabeth, the Queen Mother (1900–March 30), consort of King George VI of England. As queen, Elizabeth bolstered British morale during World War II. As queen mother, she became a symbol of stability in the reign of her daughter, Queen Elizabeth II.

Entwistle, John (1944–June 27), British rock musician, who was a founding member of The Who.

Farrell, Eileen (1920–March 23), down-to-earth soprano whose repertoire ranged from opera to jazz and popular music.

Findley, Timothy (1930–June 20), prolific Canadian novelist best known for *Not Wanted on the Voyage, Headhunter,* and *The Piano Man's Daughter*.

Frankenheimer, John (1930–July 6), director who was best known for two Cold War films, *The Manchurian Candidate* (1962) and *Seven Days in May* (1964), and for made-for-television movies that garnered him four consecutive Emmys.

Fuentes, Gregorio (1897–January 13), Cuban fisherman who inspired Ernest Hemingway to write *The Old Man and the Sea* for which Hemingway received the Pulitzer Prize for fiction in 1952.

Gal, Uzi (1923–September 7), Israeli arms expert who invented the widely used 9-millimeter submachine gun dubbed the "Uzi."

Gardner, John W. (1912–February 16), educator who as secretary of Health, Education, and Welfare under President Lyndon Johnson introduced Medicare and went on to found Common Cause, an organization that encourages participation in government.

Rosemary Clooney, singer

Stephen Jay Gould, biologist

Lionel Hampton, jazz musician

Waylon Jennings, musician

dren's books who won the Newbery Medal and the National Book Award for *M.C. Higgins, the Great* (1975).

Hampton, Lionel (1908–August 31), influential jazz musician whose virtuosity and rhythmically sophisticated performances made the vibraphone an important jazz instrument.

Handler, Ruth (1916–April 27), Mattel toy company cofounder who created the Barbie doll.

Harding, Warren J. (1925?– February 27), rock climber who was one of the first persons to ascend Yosemite's "Big Walls."

Harper, John C. (1924–September 13), minister of Washington, D.C.'s "Church of the Presidents," St. John's Episcopal, who preached to eight presidents, beginning with Lyndon B. Johnson in 1963.

Harris, Richard (1930–October 25), Irish actor who portrayed King Arthur in *Camelot* (1967) and Albus Dumbledore in *Harry Potter and the Sorcerer's Stone* (2001) and *Harry Potter and the Chamber of Secrets* (2002).

Haskin, Harold Haley (1915–June 23), marine biologist who bred a strain of oysters resistant to MSX, a parasite discovered by Haskin, that nearly wiped out eastern U.S. oyster beds.

Hayes, Bob (1942–September 18), Olympic sprinter and Dallas Cowboys wide receiver called the "fastest man in the world," who remains the only athlete to win both an Olympic gold medal and a Super Bowl ring.

Heidenreich, Jerry (1950–April 18), swimmer who won four medals—two gold, one silver, and one bronze—at the 1972 Olympic Games.

Helms, Richard (1913–October 23), former CIA director whom President Richard M. Nixon fired because Helms refused to block FBI investigations into the 1973 Watergate break-in.

Hess, Orvan W. (1906–September 6), obstetrician and gynecologist who prompted the first clinical use of penicillin and was instrumental in the development of the fetal heart monitor.

Heyerdahl, Thor (1914–April 18), Norwegian anthropologist and adventurer who in 1947 sailed across the South

Gotti, John (1940–June 10), flamboyant Mafia don who allegedly headed New York City's Gambino crime family until he was convicted of murder and racketeering and sent to prison in 1992.

Gould, Stephen Jay (1941–May 20), evolutionary biologist, author, and essayist who developed the theory of punctuated equilibrium, which holds that evolutionary change comes in fits and starts rather than in a slow, steady progression.

Graves, Teresa (1949–October 10), television actress who appeared on "Rowan and Martin's Laugh-In" and starred in the television series "Get Christie Love!"

Gray, Pete (Peter Wyshner) (1915–June 30), outfielder who played with the St. Louis Browns in 1945 despite having lost his right arm in a childhood accident.

Green, Adolph (1914–October 24), playwright, performer, and lyricist who with partner Betty Comden co-wrote books and lyrics for such Broadway musicals as *On the Town* (1944) and *Bells Are Ringing* (1956) and the screenplay for *Singin' in the Rain* (1952).

Gregory, James (1911–September 16), character actor who was best known for his roles in *The Manchurian Candidate* (1962) and on the television series "Barney Miller."

Hamilton, Virginia (1936–February 19), author of chil-

Pacific aboard the balsa-log raft *Kon-Tiki*.

Howard, Harlan (1927–March 3), songwriter of more than 100 country songs, including "I Fall to Pieces," "I've Got a Tiger by the Tail," and "Heartaches by the Number."

Hunter, Kim (1922–September 11), Academy Award-winning actress who played Stella in the 1947 Broadway production and 1951 film *A Streetcar Named Desire* and Dr. Zira in *Planet of the Apes* (1968).

Inn, Frank (Elias Franklin Freeman) (1916–July 27), animal star maker who trained such dogs as Lassie and Benji.

Jam Master Jay (Jason Mizell) (1965–October 30), disc jockey and part of the rap trio Run DMC.

Jennings, Waylon (1937–February 13), singer and songwriter who recorded 60 albums and 16 hit singles, including "Mammas Don't Let Your Babies Grow Up to Be Cowboys," and "Good Hearted Woman." His brash, re-bellious attitude defined the country music "outlaw" move-ment.

Jones, Chuck (1912–February 22), Academy Award-winning ani-mator and director who created or co-created Bugs Bunny, Daffy Duck, Elmer Fudd, Porky Pig, Road Runner, and Wile E. Coyote.

Junge, Traudl (Gertraud Humps) (1920–February 10), German woman who served as Adolf Hitler's last secretary and took down the dictator's last will and testament in January 1945.

Jurado, Katy (Maria Cristina Jurado Garcia) (1924–July 5), Mexican actress who was best known in the United States for playing sultry roles in such Westerns as *High Noon* (1952) and *Broken Lance* (1954).

Kamen, Martin D. (1913–August 31), co-discoverer of the radioactive isotope carbon-14, which made radiocarbon dating possible and al-lowed biologists to decipher the chemistry of the living cell.

Karsh, Yousuf (1908–July 14), Turkish-born Canadi-an photographer—Karsh of Ottawa—who was known for insightful portraits of such notables as Winston Churchill and George Bernard Shaw.

Kelly, Thomas J. (1929–March 23), engineer who headed the team that designed and constructed the Lunar Excursion Module that landed the first humans on the moon in July 1969.

Kile, Darryl (1968–June 22), veteran St. Louis Cardi-nals pitcher who had one of the most effective curve balls in professional baseball.

Kimball, Ward (1914–July 8), Disney animator who invented Jiminy Cricket, redesigned Mickey

Mouse, and was one of the "nine old men" who cre-ated *Snow White and the Seven Dwarfs* (1937), *Pinocchio* (1940), and *Fantasia* (1940).

Kloss, Henry (1929–January 31),

Darryl Kile, pitcher

Ann Landers, advice columnist

home electronics inventor who helped develop tabletop radios, bookshelf speak-ers, Dolby tape decks, and large-screen TV.

Kneff (Neff), Hilde-gard (1925–Feb. 1), German actress who starred in Cole Porter's *Silk Stockings* (1955) and appeared in 50 films.

Koch, Kenneth (1925–July 6), leading poet of the New York School who published at least 30 vol-umes of poetry that is both lyrical and humorous.

Landers, Ann (Esther Pauline "Eppie" Lederer) (1918–June 22), advice columnist whose combina-tion of good sense backed by expert opinion was carried by more than 1,200 newspapers around the world.

Lane, Dick "Night Train" (1928–January 29), football Hall of Fame cornerback who played for the Los Angeles Rams, Chicago Cardinals, and Detroit Li-ons during the 1950's and 1960's.

Lebed, Alexander (1950–April 28), former Russian general and politician who played a key role blocking the 1991 coup that threatened post-Communist Russia's first president, Boris Yeltsin.

Lee, Peggy (Norma Deloris Egstrom) (1920–January 21), sultry-voiced singer and songwriter whose understated, melancholy delivery of such hits as "Why Don't You Do Right?" (1943), "Fever" (1958), and "Is That All There Is?" (1969) made her a jazz and pop legend.

LeNoire, Rosetta (Rosetta Burton) (1911–March 17), actress who appeared in Orson Welles's all-black *Macbeth* (1936) and *The Hot Mikado* (1939); pro-duced *Bojangles* (1976) and *Bubbling Brown Sug-ar* (1978) on Broadway; and starred in "Gimme a Break" on television.

Lindgren, Astrid (1907–January 28), Swedish author of more than 70 children's books who created the popular character Pippi Longstocking.

Littlewood, Joan (1914—September 20), British theatrical producer whose Theater Workshop was credited with revitalizing British theater in the 1950's and 1960's and formed the basis for a wide-reaching experimental theater movement.

Lomax, Alan (1915–July 19), pioneering musicologist and traditional music archivist whose discovery of songs and artists such as Woody Guthrie, Leadbelly, and Muddy Waters helped preserve the musical heritage of the United States.

Longford, Countess Elizabeth (1906–October 23), British historian who wrote acclaimed biographies of Queen Victoria and the Duke of Wellington and who was the matriarch of a family of five prominent English writers.

Lopes, Lisa "Left Eye" (1971–April 25), rap singer and songwriter who was a member of the Grammy Award-winning trio TLC.

Lord, Walter (1917–May 19), author of narrative histories who published 13 highly acclaimed best-

sellers, including *A Night to Remember* (1955) and *The Miracle of Dunkirk* (1982).

Marcus, Stanley (1905–January 22), retailer who made the Dallas-based Neiman Marcus department store synonymous with luxury and conspicuous consumption.

Margaret Rose, Princess (1930–February 9), sister of Queen Elizabeth II of the United Kingdom. Margaret was perhaps best known for her high-spirited private life.

McCluskey, Joe (1911–August 31), 1932 Olympic medalist who won 27 U.S. track and field titles, more than any other runner.

McKern, Leo (1920–July 23), Australian-born English stage and screen actor who was best known for his role as the irascible title character in the long-running British television series "Rumpole of the Bailey."

Melin, Arthur (1925–June 28), Wham-O toy company cofounder who introduced such toys as the Frisbee (1956) and the Hula-Hoop (1958).

Merli, Gino (1924?–June 11), U.S. Army private during World War II who was awarded the Medal of Honor for blocking a German advance during a firefight near Sars la Bruyere, Belgium, in 1944.

Milligan, Spike (Terence Alan Milligan) (1918–February 26), English comedian and member of The Goons comedy quartet whose word play and sense of the absurd fostered postwar England's lunatic brand of humor.

Milstein, Cesar (1927–March 24), Argentine-born molecular biologist who shared the 1984 Nobel Prize in physiology or medicine for a revolutionary technique for forcing the immune system to produce a particular kind of antibody.

Montgomery, Jack (1917–June 11), U.S. Army lieutenant in World War II who was awarded the Medal of Honor for storming three enemy positions in the Battle of Anzio in 1944.

Moore, Dudley (1935–March 27), English actor, comedian, and musician who was best known for his performances in the 1960's comic stage revue "Beyond the Fringe" and in the films *10* (1979) and *Arthur* (1981).

Morath, Inge (1923–January 30), Austrian-born photographer who was celebrated for the lyrical quality of her often whimsical images.

Nader, George (1921–February 4), "B-movie" beefcake actor who appeared in such camp classics as *Robot Monster* (1953) and *The Female Animal* (1957).

Odum, Eugene (1913–August 10), biologist who championed the concept that ecology was an integrated discipline that tied together all other scientific disciplines.

Page, LaWanda (1920–September 14), actress who portrayed Aunt Esther in the television comedy series "Sanford and Son."

Paltrow, Bruce (1943–October 3), producer and di-

Peggy Lee, singer

Margaret Rose, princess

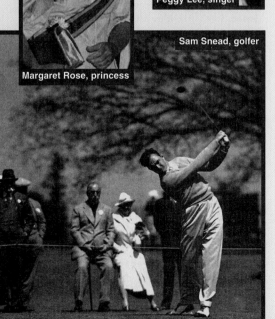

Sam Snead, golfer

rector of critically acclaimed television series, including "St. Elsewhere"; father of actress Gwyneth Paltrow.

Peet, Bill (1915–May 11), author of 35 children's books, the screenplays for *101 Dalmations* (1961) and *The Sword and the Stone* (1963) who created the title character for the film *Dumbo* (1941).

Perutz, Max (1914–February 6), Austrian molecular biologist who won the 1967 Nobel Prize in chemistry for finding the structure of the blood protein hemoglobin.

Pierce, John Robinson (1910–April 2), electrical engineer who was instrumental in creating the first communications satellite, Echo 1, and who headed the Bell Telephone Laboratory team that invented the transistor.

Porter, Darrell (1952–August 5), All-Star catcher and power hitter who played in the major leagues from 1971 to 1987 and was named the Most Valuable Player of the 1982 World Series.

Porter, Sir George (1920–August 31), British scientist who was awarded the 1967 Nobel Prize in chemistry for creating a technique to trigger and observe chemical reactions with flashes of light.

Potok, Chaim (Herman Harold Potok) (1929–July 23), rabbi and best-selling novelist who explored the relationship between Hasidic Judaism and the secular world in such books as *The Chosen* (1967) and *The Promise* (1969).

Riesman, Jr., David (1910?–May 10), sociologist who co-authored *The Lonely Crowd* (1950), one of the most influential sociological studies of the second half of the 1900's.

Riggin, Aileen (1906–October 17), diver and swimmer who at age 14 won the first Olympic gold medal for springboard diving at the 1920 games.

Riopelle, Jean-Paul (1923–March 12), Canadian artist who was celebrated for his expressionistic works that critics described as a variant of Abstract Expressionism.

Rivers, Larry (Yitzroch Loiza Grossberg) (1923–August 15), experimental artist who bridged the gap between Abstract Expressionism and Pop Art.

Robinson, Matt (1937–August 5), first actor to play Gordon on "Sesame Street" and writer of *Save the Children* (1973) and *Amazing Grace* (1974) and the TV series "Sanford and Son," "Eight Is Enough," and "The Cosby Show."

Rose, Reginald (1920–April 19), television and film playwright of social and political dramas who received Emmy Awards for "The Defenders" and "Twelve Angry Men."

Russell, Harold (1914–January 29), Canadian-born U.S. soldier who lost both hands in World War II and won an Academy Award for his portrayal of a wounded veteran in the 1947 film *The Best Years of Our Lives*.

Schreiber, Avery (1935–January 7), comedian who appeared regularly with partner Jack Burns on TV variety shows in the 1960's and later made dozens of snack-food television commercials.

Shea, Jack (1910– January 22), speed skater who won two gold medals at the 1932 Olympics; father of skier Jim Shea, Sr., who competed in the 1964 Winter Games; and grandfather of skeleton sledder Jim Shea, Jr., who won a gold medal at the 2002 Winter Games.

Shuster, Frank (1916–January 13), Canadian comedian and half of the comedy team Wayne and Shuster, who were a staple of the Canadian Broadcasting Company for more than 30 years and appeared on Ed Sullivan's television variety show a record 67 times.

Sidney, George (1916–May 5), film director who was best known for shaping such extravagant Hollywood musicals as *Ziegfeld Follies* (1946), *Show Boat* (1951), and *Kiss Me Kate* (1953).

Slaughter, Enos (1916–August 12), Hall-of-Fame baseball player who won the 1946 World Series for the St. Louis Cardinals with the famous "Mad Dash" from first base that scored the winning run against the Boston Red Sox.

Smith, Howard K. (1914–February 15), broadcast journalist and foreign correspondent who was best known for his television commentaries.

Smith, Kevin (1963-February 16), New Zealand-born actor who portrayed Ares, god of war, on the cult television program "Xena: Warrior Princess."

Snead, Sam (1912–May 23), professional golfer known for his near-perfect swing who won a record 81 PGA Tour events, including three Masters, three Professional Golfers Association championships, and one British Open.

Steiger, Rod (1925–July 9), Academy Award-winning character actor who was acclaimed for his roles in such films as *On the Waterfront* (1954), *The Pawnbroker* (1964), and *In the Heat of the Night* (1967).

Stone, W. Clement (1902–September 2), insurance tycoon who founded the Combined Insurance Corporation of America and became widely known for his multimillion-dollar campaign contributions to former President Richard M. Nixon.

Stuart, Mary (Mary Stuart Houchins) (1926–February 28), actress who played the much-married Joanne Gardner Barron Tate Vincente Tourneur throughout the 35-year run of the television soap opera "Search for Tomorrow."

Rod Steiger, actor

Thaw, John (1942–February 21), British actor who found worldwide fame portraying an irascible, music-loving police detective in the British television series "Inspector Morse."

Thomas, Dave (1932–January 8), founder of Wendy's Old Fashioned Hamburgers who became a household name when he began pitching his fast-food franchise on television in 1989.

Tobin, James (1918–March 11), Yale professor of economics who served as a top adviser in the Kennedy administration and was awarded the Nobel Prize in economics in 1981.

Todde, Antonio (1889–January 4), Italian shepherd who at 112 was listed in the *Guinness Book of World Records* as the world's oldest living man.

Trigere, Pauline (1908–February 13), French-born U.S. fashion designer who was as well known for her personal style as for timeless clothing.

Urich, Robert (1946–April 16), television actor who was best known for portraying detectives in the series "Vega$" and "Spenser: For Hire."

Vance, Cyrus R. (1917–January 12), secretary of state (1977-1980) who resigned to protest President Jimmy Carter's decision to attempt a military rescue of 52 Americans held hostage by revolutionaries in Iran.

Unitas, Johnny (1933–September 11), Baltimore Colts football star whom many sports fans considered the greatest quarterback in the history of the National Football League.

Warfield, William (1920–August 25), bass-baritone concert artist who became world famous for his portrayal of Porgy in the Gershwin opera *Porgy and Bess*.

Wasserman, Lew (1913–June 3), former head of MCA Inc., parent company of Universal Pictures, whom many considered the last of the legendary movie moguls.

Weaver, Sylvester (1908–March 15), television executive who created the "Today" and "Tonight" programs in the early 1950's; father of actress Sigourney Weaver.

Wellstone, Paul (1944–October 25), liberal U.S. Senator (D., Minnesota) who favored increased government spending on health care, welfare, and education and urged protection of the environment.

Whalen, Philip (1923–June 26), influential Beat Generation poet and major figure in the San Francisco Renaissance literary movement of the 1950's and 1960's.

White, Byron R. (1917–April 15), justice who served on the U.S. Supreme Court for 31 years (1962-1993). White, a Rhodes scholar, played professional football ("Whizzer" White) and managed the U.S. Department of Justice under Robert F. Kennedy.

Wilder, Billy (Samuel Wilder) (1906–March 27), Austrian-born filmmaker whose wit as a writer and skills as a director resulted in such classics as *Double Indemnity* (1944), *The Lost Weekend* (1945), *Sunset Boulevard* (1950), *Stalag 17* (1953), *Some Like It Hot* (1959), and *The Apartment* (1960) and earned him six Academy Awards.

Wilhelm, Hoyt (1922?–August 23), the first relief pitcher to be elected to the Baseball Hall of Fame and an early master of the knuckleball.

Wilkinson, David T. (1935–September 5), physicist who pioneered the study of microwave radiation from the big bang origin of the universe.

Williams, Ted (1918–July 5), Boston Red Sox outfielder whom many fans regarded as baseball's greatest hitter.

Worth, Irene (Harriet Abrams) (1916?–March 10), celebrated actress of the London and New York stage who was known for her classical Shakespearean and Chekovian roles and her performances in *Tiny Alice* (1965), *Sweet Bird of Youth* (1976), and *Lost in Yonkers* (1991).

Howard K. Smith, journalist

Byron R. White, U.S. Supreme Court justice

Billy Wilder, filmmaker

Sports Loses

TED WILLIAMS

By Tim Frystak

Baseball legend Ted Williams died on July 5, 2002, at age 83. Many fans and sportswriters considered Williams one of the best athletes ever to have played the game and one of the greatest hitters—if not the greatest—in baseball history.

Theodore Samuel Williams was born in San Diego on Aug. 30, 1918. He made his professional baseball debut in 1936 with the San Diego Padres of the Pacific Coast League. In 1937, the Boston Red Sox organization purchased Williams's contract. After playing for the Minneapolis Millers, a minor league team owned by Boston, he joined the Red Sox as an outfielder in 1939. He played for the Red Sox for 19 seasons until his retirement in 1960.

Williams's greatest achievement came in 1941, when he batted a historic .406 for the season. Williams was already set to go into the record books with a season average of .39955—rounded up to .400—at the start of the final game of the season, a doubleheader. Red Sox manager Joe Cronin offered to let Williams sit out the two games so that he would not risk lowering his average. Williams refused the offer and took to the field. He ended the day with six hits that boosted his average even higher. No player since has come close to a batting

(continued on page 158)

Two Legends

JOHNNY UNITAS

By Dan Blunk

Football legend Johnny Unitas, who many fans considered the greatest quarterback in the history of the National Football League (NFL), died on Sept. 11, 2002, at age 69. Unitas, who played 17 seasons with the Baltimore Colts, may be best remembered for leading the Colts to a come-from-behind overtime victory in the 1958 NFL championship game that is often referred to as the greatest NFL game ever played. Unitas also threw touchdown passes in 47 consecutive games, a record that has yet to be broken.

John Constantine Unitas was born in Pittsburgh, Pennsylvania, on May 7, 1933. He played high school football in Pittsburgh, taking over the quarterbacking duties his junior year after the starting quarterback was injured. The University of Louisville offered Unitas a football scholarship, though he was small for a quarterback, weighing only 138 pounds (63 kilograms). The NFL's Pittsburgh Steelers drafted Unitas in the ninth round in 1955, putting him on the path to a career in professional football.

(continued on page 159)

average of .400. In 1942, Williams went on to win the American League's Triple Crown by leading the league in batting average, home runs, and runs batted in. He won the Triple Crown again in 1947.

Military service twice interrupted Williams's baseball career. He missed the 1943, 1944, and 1945 seasons during World War II (1939-1945), serving as a U.S. Marine Corps pilot. Williams's reserve unit was recalled to active duty during the Korean War (1950-1953), and he missed most of the 1952 and 1953 seasons. Baseball writers have long speculated to what heights Williams might have climbed had he not lost nearly five seasons at his prime as an athlete.

Williams won the Most Valuable Player award twice and captured six American League batting titles. He took the last title in 1958 at age 40, becoming the oldest batting champion in major league history. He also led the American League in home runs four times, in runs batted in four times, and in runs scored six times. In his last at-bat in 1960, Williams hit a home run at Fenway Park—the 521st of his career. He finished his career with a lifetime average of .344. Williams was elected to the National Baseball Hall of Fame in Cooperstown, New York, in 1966. From 1969 to 1972 he managed the Washington Senators and the Texas Rangers. In the years following his playing days, Williams also worked for the Red Sox as a vice president, consultant, and hitting instructor.

An avid outdoorsman, Williams spent his time away from baseball perfecting other skills, including fishing. His dedication and concentration on his second favorite sport led to his induction in 1999 into the International Game Fish Association Hall of Fame in Dania Beach, Florida.

Williams's health began to fail in the 1990's. He suffered strokes that impaired his once-remarkable vision and was diagnosed with congestive heart failure. He had a pacemaker inserted in 2000 and underwent open-heart surgery in 2001. He died of cardiac arrest in a hospital in Inverness, Florida, not far from his home.

Williams was often quoted by the press as saying that hitting a baseball was the hardest thing to do in sports. It was an odd statement for a man who became a baseball icon for making it seem so easy. But he was a perfectionist who worked tirelessly at his craft and had no tolerance for those less dedicated than himself. He was also brash and outspoken, which coupled with the dedication, resulted in an attitude that some interpreted as arrogance. The attitude led to a turbulent relationship with Red Sox fans and the media. Some fans resented Williams's refusal to acknowledge their cheers with so much as a tip of the hat. Author John Updike, however, saw it differently. In an essay written for *The New Yorker* magazine following Williams's final game in 1960, Updike wrote: "Gods do not answer letters." ■ ■ ■

The author:
Tim Frystak is a senior editor on *The Year Book*.

However, his dream was dashed weeks later when the Steelers, who had four other quarterbacks in training camp, cut Unitas without allowing him to play in a single preseason game. Unitas took a job as a construction worker and also joined a semiprofessional football league that paid him $6 a game. Unitas generated enough attention to earn a tryout with the NFL's Baltimore Colts, who signed him in 1956.

Still, Unitas sat on the bench, waiting for his opportunity to play. That chance came in the fourth game of his first season after the Colts' starting quarterback, George Shaw, broke his leg. Unitas took over and kept the job for 17 seasons (he played his 18th and final season with the San Diego Chargers).

Unitas's main strengths were his tenacity, his coolness under pressure, and his ability to spot and exploit weaknesses in opposing defenses. He called all his own plays, a rare occurrence in contemporary football, and exhibited superior leadership. He was also admired for his modesty on the field and for his good sportsmanship.

Unitas's best-known football achievement came in the 1958 NFL championship game against the Colts' bitter rivals, the New York Giants. With only 90 seconds remaining and his team trailing by three points, a poised Unitas completed four passes to lead the Colts into range for a game-tying field goal attempt with only seconds left. The Colts made the field goal, sending the game into sudden-death overtime, the first time that had happened in a championship game. In overtime, Unitas engineered a 13-play, 80-yard touchdown drive that gave the Colts the victory and put the NFL on the map.

During Unitas's 18-year NFL career, he won championships with the Colts in 1958, 1959, and 1971. He set 22 NFL records, including records for most passes completed (2,830), most touchdown passes (290), and most 300-yard passing games (26). His 40,239 career passing yards were the most of any quarterback when he retired in 1973. While quarterbacks who benefited from rule changes eventually broke most of his records, Unitas still holds what many consider to be one of the most extraordinary records in sports. Unitas threw touchdown passes in 47 consecutive games. Only former Miami Dolphins quarterback Dan Marino came close, throwing touchdowns in 30 straight games.

Unitas played in 10 Pro Bowls, was selected to the all-NFL team five times, and was voted the NFL Player of the Year three times. He retired after the 1973 season and was voted into the NFL Hall of Fame in 1979. After his retirement, Unitas served as a television analyst and businessman.

Unitas suffered serious injuries from his playing days, including an injury to his right hand so severe that he could not use it to feed himself. He underwent triple-bypass heart surgery in 1993. On Sept. 11, 2002, Unitas suffered a fatal heart attack while exercising at a physical therapy center near Baltimore, Maryland. ∎∎∎

The author:
Dan Blunk is
a staff editor on
The Year Book.

Democratic Party. The Democratic Party was jolted by the results of the Nov. 5, 2002, midterm elections. Democrats lost control of the United States Senate and lost seats in the U.S. House of Representatives to Republicans. Political analysts suggested that most Democratic candidates could not compete with Republican candidates supported by President George W. Bush, who enjoyed enormous public popularity in 2002. The 2002 elections marked the first time since the administration of Franklin D. Roosevelt in 1934 that a president's party gained seats in both the House and Senate two years into a president's first term.

Senate races. The Democrats came out of the November 5 elections with 48 seats, compared with 50 seats prior to November 2002. They continued to control an additional seat through Senator James M. Jeffords of Vermont, an independent aligned with the Democrats.

Senator Jean Carnahan (D., Missouri) lost her seat to Republican Jim Talent in her bid for a full term in office. Carnahan had been appointed to the position in 2001. Senator Max Cleland (D., Georgia) lost to his Republican challenger, U.S. Representative Saxby Chambliss in 2002, in an election that surprised political experts. The observers later suggested that Cleland's stand against accepting all of the president's demands in the creation of a Department of Homeland Security may have cost the senator the election.

In Minnesota, former Senator and Vice President Walter Mondale, a Democrat, failed to defeat Norm Coleman, a Republican and the former mayor of St. Paul. Democratic leaders tapped Mondale after Senator Paul Wellstone was killed in an airplane accident on October 25.

Democrats scored two major victories in Senate races in 2002. In Arkansas, Attorney General Mark Pryor defeated Senator Tim Hutchinson, who was seeking his second term in office. In Lousiana, voters returned Mary L. Landrieu to the Senate for a second term in a run-off election on December 7. Political experts considered Landrieu's victory a defeat for President Bush, who had flown to Louisiana to campaign for the Republican challenger, Suzanne H. Terrell.

House races. Democrats lost ground in the House as Republicans widened their majority in November. Democrats held 205 seats in the House while Republicans increased the number of seats they held to 229. Representative Bernard Sanders of Vermont was an independent in the House.

Democratic leadership. In the wake of the November election, Representative Richard A. Gephardt (D., Missouri) resigned on November 6 as House minority leader. On November 14, House Democrats selected Representative Nancy Pelosi of California to succeed Gephardt. She de-

Senator Max Cleland (D., Georgia) greets supporters as he arrives at his campaign headquarters to concede defeat to Representative Saxby Chambliss on November 5. Cleland was one of three Democratic senators to lose their seats in the November elections, giving Republicans control of the U.S. Senate.

feated Representative Harold Ford of Tennessee for the position. Pelosi was the first woman ever to be elected to lead a party in the U.S. Congress. House Democrats had elected Pelosi *minority whip* (assistant leader) in 2001.

House Democrats on Nov. 14, 2002, elected Representative Steny Hoyer of Maryland as the new minority whip. Representative Robert Menendez of New Jersey was elected caucus chairman.

Senate Democrats chose Senator Tom Daschle of South Dakota as the Senate minority leader, Senator Harry Reid of Nevada as minority whip, and Senator Barbara A. Mikulski of Maryland as the secretary of the Democratic Conference.

Gubernatorial races. Democrats gained three governor's seats but still trailed Republicans in the total number of governorships the party held following the November election. Democrats won 14 of the 36 open governor's seats, giving the party control of 24 governorships, compared with 26 held by Republicans. Prior to the election, Democrats held 21 gubernatorial offices.

In California, Governor Gray Davis defeated Bill Simon, a Republican businessman whose campaign was criticized as having been poorly run. The party also won the governor's office in Illinois, where U.S. Representative Rod Blagojevich defeated his Republican challenger, Attorney General Jim Ryan, to became the first Democrat to hold the governorship since 1977.

State control. The November 2002 election gave Democrats control of 16 statehouses, compared with 21 legislatures controlled by Republicans. The remaining statehouses were divided. Nebraska is nonpartisan.

Fund raising. Officials with the Democratic National Committee (DNC) announced on October 15 that the DNC had received more than $62 million in contributions for the first three quarters of 2002, a party record for the period in a midterm election year. The collections surpassed the total for the same period in 1998 by more than $23 million. The $62 million total included $37 million in "soft money" contributions. Soft money refers to individual contributions to political parties.

Party agrees to fine. The DNC paid a $115,000 fine and turned over $243,000 to the Department of the Treasury after a Federal Election Committee (FEC) investigation found that the party had accepted more than $1 million in illegal foreign contributions prior to the 1996 presidential election. The settlement was disclosed in documents released by the FEC on Sept. 20, 2002.

☐ Geoffrey A. Campbell

See also **Congress of the United States; Elections; Republican Party; State government; United States, Government of the; United States, President of the.**

Denmark. The center-right government of Prime Minister Anders Fogh Rasmussen adopted a strict new law on immigration in 2002. The measure put Denmark at the forefront of a trend in Europe toward more-restrictive immigration policies.

The Danish parliament, the Folketing, passed the legislation in May. The law limited the right of asylum to groups that were entitled to protection under international conventions on asylum. It required immigrants to live in Denmark for seven years before becoming eligible for welfare benefits and required anyone seeking citizenship to pass Danish language and citizenship tests. The legislation also abolished the automatic right of refugees to bring their spouses to Denmark and raised the minimum age at which immigrants can bring a spouse into the country from 18 years to 24 years.

The legislation was the biggest initiative taken by Rasmussen's Liberal Party since it swept to power in November 2001, after campaigning on promises to crack down on immigration and crime. Nevertheless, the measure created tensions with neighboring Sweden. The Swedes, who maintain a fairly open immigration policy, criticized the Danish law as too drastic and blamed it for increasing the number of immigrants seeking asylum in Sweden. Danish officials confirmed that during the first three months of 2002, the number of people seeking asylum in Denmark fell by 38 percent, while the number increased in Sweden by 68 percent.

Economy. The Danish economy remained sluggish in 2002, as the country continued to feel the effects of the worldwide economic slump. European Union (EU) economists forecast that Denmark's *gross domestic product* (the value of all goods and services produced in a country in a year) would grow by 1.7 percent in 2002, up from 1.0 percent in 2001. The country's unemployment rate, which had fallen steadily since the mid-1990's, edged up slightly but still remained one of the lowest in the EU at 4.2 percent.

EU presidency. Denmark held the EU's rotating presidency in the second half of 2002, during which Danish leaders helped steer the EU toward enlarging its membership. At a summit meeting in Copenhagen in December, EU leaders agreed that 10 countries from Eastern and Southern Europe—Poland, Hungary, the Czech Republic, Slovakia, Slovenia, Estonia, Latvia, Lithuania, Malta, and Cyprus—had fulfilled the political and economic requirements for membership. The countries were expected to enter the EU in 2004. The expansion would be the EU's largest since the bloc was created in 1957.   ☐ Tom Buerkle

See also **Europe.**

Dinosaur. See Paleontology.

Disability. The United States Supreme Court issued several rulings related to the Americans with Disabilities Act (ADA) in 2002. The act, passed by Congress in 1990, protects disabled persons from discrimination by private employers and requires that public buildings and mass transportation systems be accessible to the disabled.

Who is disabled? In January 2002, the Supreme Court limited the definition of disability in a case involving an assembly-line worker and Toyota Motor Manufacturing, Kentucky, Inc., of Georgetown. The worker had become unable to fulfill her job requirements because of repetitive strain injury to her arms and hands. The company reassigned the woman to a position that suited her limitations but later added tasks that she claimed she could not do because of the strain injury. The worker asserted that she was entitled to protection under the ADA and should be given a job that accommodated her disability. The justices unanimously ruled that in order to qualify for protection under the ADA, a worker must be disabled in activities that are "central to daily life," not just in work-related activities.

Seniority and disability. In April, the Supreme Court ruled that, in general, employers need not accommodate a disabled worker at the expense of an employee with greater job seniority. The case involved a baggage handler who had injured his back while working at San Francisco International Airport. The man was temporarily assigned to a mailroom position. However, when two workers with greater seniority requested a transfer to that position, the handler lost the job. The worker claimed that US Airways, Inc., of Arlington, Virginia, had not made a "reasonable accommodation" for his disability by taking the job away from him.

In a 5-to-4 decision, the justices ruled that the seniority system should prevail. The author of the majority opinion wrote that seniority systems provide "important employee benefits by creating, and fulfilling, employee expectations of fair, uniform treatment." However, the court also noted that under certain circumstances, a disability may prevail over seniority. Such circumstances could include situations where an employer has made previous exceptions to the seniority system.

Threat to self. In June, the Supreme Court justices unanimously ruled that employers are not required to hire a disabled applicant if the job for which he or she is applying poses a danger to the applicant. The case, Chevron U.S.A., Inc., v. Echazabal, involved a worker with hepatitis C (a liver disease) who had applied for a job that would expose him to toxins that could affect his condition. The worker claimed that the company's refusal to hire him was the result of a paternalistic attitude by employers toward disabled people.

Mental illness as physical disability. In February, a federal district court judge in Washington, D.C., ruled for the first time that a person with a mental illness was entitled to full disability benefits under the ADA. Previous court decisions had upheld the position of employers and health insurance providers that people who are mentally ill are not entitled to the same benefits as those who are physically disabled.

In the case, an attorney with *bipolar disorder* (manic depression) was forced to quit her job because the mood swings that characterize the illness prevented her from performing day-to-day activities. The court ruled that because the woman's disorder was visible in brain scans, involved chemical imbalances, and may have a genetic basis, she qualified for benefits under the ADA.

Flagging. The College Board, which owns the Scholastic Aptitude Test (SAT), a major college admissions test, agreed in July to stop flagging the test results of disabled students. Flagging denotes some form of accommodation during the test, such as additional time. The decision was the result of a lawsuit filed in 1999 by a physically disabled student who had taken another standardized test and believed that he had been denied admission to various graduate schools because his test had been flagged.   □ Kristina Vaicikonis

See also **Supreme Court of the United States.**

Disasters. The deadliest disaster of 2002 was the capsizing of a ferry off the coast of Gambia in Western Africa in which some 1,200 people died. Disasters that resulted in 25 or more deaths include the following:

Aircraft crashes

January 28—Colombia. A Boeing 727 traveling from Quito in central Ecuador to Tulcan in the north crashes on Ecuador's border with Colombia, killing all 92 passengers and crew members aboard.

February 12—Iran. An Iran Air Tours jet, flying in dense fog, crashes into a mountain near Khorramabad, Iran, 230 miles (370 kilometers) west of Tehran, the capital. All 188 passengers and crew members aboard the Tu-154 airliner are killed.

April 15—South Korea. An Air China Boeing 767-200 crashes into a mountain as the jet attempts to land in heavy fog in the southern city of Busan. More than 120 of the 166 passengers and crew members are killed in the first fatal crash in the 47-year history of China's national carrier.

May 4—Nigeria. An EAS airliner crashes into a densely populated area of Kano, a city in north-central Nigeria, killing 72 of the 76 people aboard the BAC-1-11-500 jet and 73 people on the ground.

May 7—China. A China Northern airliner plunges into Bo Gulf in the Yellow Sea, 10 miles (16 kilometers) off the coastal city of Dalian, killing all 112 passengers and crew members aboard the MD-82 jet.

May 25—Taiwan Strait. All 225 passengers and crew members aboard a 22-year-old China Airlines jet are killed when the Boeing 747-200 breaks up off Taiwan's western coast about 180 miles (290 kilometers) from Taipei, the capital.

July 1—Uberlingen, Germany. A charter jet carrying Russian children to Spain on a vacation trip collides with a cargo plane above Lake Constance, which forms part of Germany's border with Austria and Switzerland. All 69 passengers and crew members on the jet and the 2 crew members aboard the cargo plane are killed.

July 27—Ukraine. At least 85 people are killed and 200 others injured when a Ukrainian jet fighter, swooping low during an air show at the Sk4liv airfield in the city of Lviv in western Ukraine, plows through a crowd of spectators and explodes. The jet's two pilots survive by ejecting from the plane seconds before the crash.

Earthquakes

March 3—Afghanistan. An earthquake of 7.2 magnitude shakes an area stretching from Tajikistan to India. In northern Afghanistan, at least 100 people are killed in Samangan Province, where the earthquake unleashes a landslide that buries the village of Dakhli-e-Zeu.

March 25—Afghanistan. A series of earthquakes in the Hindu Kush mountain region leaves 500 to 800 people dead and more than 20,000 others homeless. The epicenter is about 90 miles (145 kilometers) north of Kabul, the capital.

April 12—Afghanistan. At least 50 people are killed when an earthquake of 5.8 magnitude strikes the Hindu Kush mountain region in northern Afghanistan.

June 22—Iran. Nearly 100 villages are destroyed and more than 220 people are killed when an earthquake of 6.3 magnitude strikes northwestern Iran.

October 31—Italy. An earthquake of 5.9 magnitude rocks southeastern Italy. In the village of San Giuliano di Puglia, near the coast of the Adriatic Sea, 29 people are killed, including 26 children celebrating Halloween at a local school.

Explosions and fires

January 17—Congo (Kinshasa). An estimated 46 people die when Mount Nyiragongo in northeastern Congo erupts, spewing lava that partially buries the city of Goma. Four days later, an additional 50 people are killed when heat from the lava ignites gasoline and diesel fuel that residents are collecting from a burned-out gas station.

January 27—Nigeria. An estimated 700 people are killed during a series of explosions in a military munitions dump in Lagos, the capital. Most of the victims drown after being stampeded into a canal adjacent to the site as they flee the explosions.

June 16—China. A fire in an illegal Internet cafe in Beijing leaves 25 people, mostly teenagers, dead.

July 20—Peru. At least 30 people are killed in a fire in a Lima nightclub packed with as many as 1,000 young partygoers, more than double the club's capacity. The fire, which also kills several caged animals, including a lion and tiger, begins when a pyrotechnic display ignites the ceiling.

October 29—Vietnam. More than 60 people are killed and dozens of others injured when a fire sweeps through the six-story International Trade Center in the heart of Ho Chi Minh City.

December 1—Venezuela. Forty-seven people are killed and more than a dozen others are injured when a fire sweeps through a nightclub in a poor neighborhood of Caracas, the capital.

December 31—Mexico. The explosion of tons of illegally stored fireworks in Veracruz, west of Mexico City, kills at least 28 people and ignites a fire that destroys an entire city block.

Heat waves

May 21—India. Officials report that more than 760 people have died in a month-long heat wave, as temperatures rise as high as 122 °F (50 °C). Most of the deaths occurred in the southern coastal state of Andhra Pradesh. Meteorologists attribute the heat wave to an unusual low pressure system hovering over the Bay of Bengal.

Mine disasters

June 20—Northeast China. More than 100 miners die in an explosion in a coal mine in the city of Jixi in Heilongjiang Province. The state coal mine safety board closes down production in 10 other mines in the area until the cause of the explosion can be determined.

July 7—Ukraine. A malfunctioning conveyor in a coal mine in the eastern town of Ukrainsk sparks a fire that kills 35 miners.

Shipwrecks

May 3—Bangladesh. More than 200 people are killed when a ferry, carrying at least 300 passengers, sinks in the Meghna River about 40 miles (63 kilometers) southeast of Dhaka, the capital.

September 26—Gambia. Some 1,200 people are killed when a ferry sinks in a violent storm in the Atlantic Ocean off the coast of Gambia in western Africa. The ferry was crowded with almost 1,300 passengers from neighboring Senegal.

October 13—Somalia. Somali officials report that at least 70 people died from lack of food and water over a period of 17 days when the engine of their boat failed off the coast of Somalia. The victims were jobseekers from Somalia and Ethiopia traveling to Persian Gulf states.

October 22—Azerbaijan. A ferry carrying passengers and a shipment of oil from Aktau in Kazakhstan to the Azeri capital, Baku, capsizes in the Caspian Sea during a violent storm. All of the 51 passengers and crew members perish.

Storms and floods

February 19—Bolivia. At least 69 people die in La Paz, the capital, during the most destructive thunderstorm to ever strike the city. Many of those killed are street vendors caught by flash floods in underpasses.

June 29—Southeastern Russia. Russian emergency officials announce that days of heavy rain that began June 18 have caused massive flooding in the area south of Rostov-on-Don, leaving at least 90 people dead and tens of thousands of people homeless.

July 2—Micronesia. More than 35 people are killed when Typhoon Chata'an triggers landslides on the Micronesian island of Chuuk, about 600 miles (965 kilometers) southeast of Guam.

August 1—South Asia. Government officials announce that more than 500 people in Bangladesh, Nepal, and India have died in floods brought on by monsoons that began in June. An additional 5 million people in Bangladesh and 10 million people in Nepal and India are left homeless by the floods.

August 16—Europe. European officials confirm that nearly 200 people are dead as a result of flooding caused by torrential rains during the week of August 4 in central and eastern Europe. The flooding extends from France, Germany, and Austria to Romania, Bulgaria, and southern Russia. Flash floods along Russia's Black Sea coast swept away more than 50 people and stranded thousands of summer tourists. In the Czech Republic, flooding in Prague, the capital, is the most severe in more than 150 years, with 50,000 residents evacuated from the city's historic center.

September 1—China. State media officials in Beijing, the capital, announce that more than 1,200 people have died in flooding throughout China during the summer months. Most of the victims perished in flash floods and landslides.

September 1—South Korea. Typhoon Rusa dumps nearly 36 inches (1 meter) of rain in two days on the east coast of South Korea. Flooding and landslides kill more than 130 people, most of them in the resort town of Kangnung.

October 27—Europe. A violent storm out of the North Atlantic sweeps across the United Kingdom (UK) and continental Europe with winds exceeding 99 miles (160 kilometers) per hour. The storm leaves 34 people dead in the U.K., France, and Germany.

November 10—United States. Storms that spawn at least 88 tornadoes sweep across 13 states, from Illinois and Louisiana on the west to Pennsylvania and North Caronlina on the east. Thirty-six people are killed and more than 200 others are injured.

November 12—India and Bangladesh. More than 50 Indian and Bangladeshi fishermen are killed when a cyclone strikes the Bay of Bengal.

Train wrecks

February 20—Egypt. More than 360 people are killed when a passenger train enroute from Cairo, the capital, to Luxor, in the south, catches fire. Some of the victims leap from the moving train to their deaths to escape the blaze.

Part of the Russian village of Kami lies buried under a mountain of ice after a piece of the Maili Glacier weighing as much as 21 million tons (19 million metric tons) crashed down a gorge in the Caucasus Mountains in September, burying entire villages and killing as many as 150 people.

May 25—Southern Mozambique. At least 196 people are killed when railroad passenger cars packed with weekend visitors to South Africa crash into a freight train. The disconnected cars of the disabled passenger train barreled down a hill into the freight train, which was parked at a station near the town of Moambain.

June 24—Tanzania. Mechanical failure causes a passenger train to roll downhill and slam into a freight train. More than 200 passengers, traveling from Dar es Salaam, Tanzania's commercial capital, to Kigoma in the northwest, are killed.

September 9—India. A luxury train traveling from Calcutta to New Delhi, the capital, jumps its tracks near the village of Rafiganj in the eastern state of Bihar, plunging one of the cars into a nearby river. At least 120 people are killed.

Other disasters

June 9—Zimbabwe. At least 37 students from a teachers' college are killed when the bus in which they are returning from a sporting event crashes into a grain truck near Masvingo in southern Zimbabwe.

July 16—Uganda. A fuel truck with failed brakes rolls downhill and rams into a bus, killing more than 60 people some 180 miles (300 kilometers) southwest of Kampala, the Ugandan capital.

September 15—Argentina. A bus carrying 74 Roman Catholic pilgrims returning from a visit to a shrine plunges off a cliff some 600 miles (965 kilometers) northwest of Buenos Aires, the capital. At least 47 people are killed.

September 20—Russia. A wall of ice nearly 500 feet (150 meters) high breaks off a glacier in the North Caucasus Mountains, burying entire villages in the southern Russian republic of North Ossetia. As many as 150 people are killed.

November 24—India. More than 35 people traveling to a neighboring town for work are killed when a bus falls from a bridge into a dry riverbed in the Kaimur Hills of central India.

Drug abuse. The number of high school students in the United States who smoke cigarettes decreased sharply in 2001, the last year for which statistics were available. The 2001 Monitoring the Future project, an annual study sponsored by the National Institute on Drug Abuse, found that the number of students using heroin also decreased in 2001, from 1.4 percent of 10th-graders in 2000 to 0.9 percent in 2001. The number of 12th-graders using heroin fell from 1.5 percent in 2000 to 0.9 percent in 2001. The survey also found that the increase in the number of students using the stimulant drug ecstasy slowed among students in grades 8 through 10.

Tobacco use. A dramatic decline in the number of teen-agers who smoked also was confirmed in studies other than the 2001 Monitoring the Future study. The 2001 Youth Risk Behavior Surveillance System, conducted by the Centers for Disease Control and Prevention (CDC) in Atlanta, Georgia, and released in June 2002, found that 28.5 percent of high-school students had smoked a cigarette in the month before the survey, compared with 36.4 percent in 2000. The CDC study also found that the percentage of students who had ever smoked a cigarette also declined, from 70.4 percent in 1999 to 63.9 percent in 2001.

Researchers attributed the decline in teen-age smoking to prevention efforts, such as antismoking advertising campaigns, and a substantial increase in the price of cigarettes. Despite the sharp decreases in teen-age smoking, researchers pointed out that about 5.5 percent of 8th-graders and 12.2 percent of 10th-graders smoked cigarettes daily in the month before the survey.

Steroids. The number of 12th-grade students using *anabolic steroids* (drugs that make muscles grow faster and larger than they normally would) increased sharply in 2001, according to the 2001 Monitoring the Future study. The study found that 2.4 percent of 12th-graders in 2001 took steroids, compared with 1.7 percent in 2000. Steroids can greatly increase muscle mass, but they can also have serious health consequences, including hair loss, severe acne, infertility, and stunted growth. There is also some evidence that using steroids can increase the risk of stroke, heart disease, and liver cancer.

Drug testing. The U.S. Supreme Court ruled in June 2002 that public school administrators can subject students involved in extracurricular activities to mandatory drug testing. The ruling expanded upon a landmark 1995 decision that allowed random drug testing of public high school athletes. The new ruling allowed school administrators to test students even if the administrators do not have suspicions that the students are using drugs. ☐ David C. Lewis

See also **Drugs; Supreme Court.**

Drugs. The concerns of public health officials that there was an insufficient amount of smallpox vaccine in the United States to respond to a possible biological terrorist attack eased in March 2002, when researchers discovered that the existing supply of vaccine could be diluted to produce more doses. Wyeth Laboratories of Marietta, Pennsylvania, discontinued production of smallpox vaccine in 1982 after smallpox was eliminated as a naturally occurring disease. However, Wyeth kept a stockpile of 15.4 million doses in freeze-dried form.

Officials at the U.S. Department of Health and Human Services asked scientists at St. Louis University in St. Louis, Missouri, to find out if the smallpox vaccine would remain effective if diluted. The scientists concluded that each dose of the vaccine could be diluted to produce up to five doses and remain effective. The original 15.4 million doses, therefore, could be stretched to produce as many as 77 million doses. The Department of Health and Human Services announced that it had contracted with another company to make an additional 209 million doses of smallpox vaccine by the end of 2002.

Antiterrorism drugs. The U.S. Food and Drug Administration (FDA), the Rockville, Maryland, agency that administers federal laws ensuring the safety and effectiveness of drugs, in May relaxed its guidelines for permitting new drugs to be marketed. The agency's previous standards required all drugs intended for human consumption to be tested for safety and effectiveness on human volunteers. The new guidelines allow certain drugs to be approved based on evidence from animal studies alone. The new FDA guidelines were part of government-wide preparations for possible terrorist attacks.

The relaxed standards apply only to drugs and other products designed to treat people exposed to chemical, biological, or nuclear attack. An FDA official noted that testing the effectiveness of such drugs on humans was unethical, because it would involve exposing test subjects to potentially deadly or disabling toxic substances.

Drug approvals. The FDA announced in January that the agency had approved 66 new drugs in 2001. The new drugs included 24 completely new medicines with ingredients never before marketed in the United States. The FDA considered 10 of the new drugs to be urgently needed. These were approved on average six months after manufacturers submitted the drug to the agency. The FDA on average approved less urgently needed drugs 12 months after they were submitted.

Botox debut. In April 2002, the FDA approved botulinum toxin, which causes botulism food poisoning, for use as a temporary treatment for frown lines between the eyebrows. Allergan

Inc. of Irvine, California, subsequently marketed a preparation of the toxin under the name Botox Cosmetic.

The bacterium *Clostridium botulinum* produces botulinum toxin. The toxin, which can contaminate improperly prepared food, is potentially fatal when ingested because it paralyzes muscles throughout the body, including those involved in breathing. However, when the toxin is injected in small amounts into certain facial muscles, it reduces wrinkling by paralyzing the muscles, causing them to relax. The effects last about three months, after which another injection is needed to smooth the wrinkles.

"Lazy eye" drug. Eye drops containing the drug atropine can reduce the need for children with amblyopia, or "lazy eye," to wear an eye patch, reported the National Eye Institute (NEI), a government research group located in Bethesda, Maryland, in March 2002. Amblyopia is the most common cause of vision impairment in children. The disorder begins in infancy when the brain, favoring one eye more then the other, processes visual information primarily from one eye. The standard treatment involves wearing a patch or an eye bandage over the favored eye. The patch forces the brain to depend on information from the weaker eye. However, the child must wear the patch daily, which many children refuse to do.

NEI officials said new research showed that atropine eye drops, given once a day, are as effective as wearing a patch. Atropine works by temporarily blurring vision in the favored eye, forcing the brain to use the other eye.

Pfizer merger. Pfizer Inc. the world's largest drug company, announced plans in July to buy drug manufacturing giant Pharmacia Corporation for $60 billion. Pfizer, based in New York City, and Pharmacia, of Peapack, New Jersey, had cooperated in marketing the arthritis drug Celebrex since 1998. Analysts expected that the annual sales of the combined company would exceed $1 billion per year.

Drug kickbacks. Officials at the U.S. Department of Health and Human Services in September 2002 warned drug manufacturers not to offer financial incentives to physicians or other health care pro-

In April, the U.S. Food and Drug Administration approved Botox Cosmetic for use in treating facial wrinkles. Botox, a preparation made from the same toxin that causes botulism food poisoning, smooths wrinkles by paralyzing small muscles in the face.

fessionals for prescribing or recommending their products. The agency cautioned that aggressive marketing tactics commonly employed by drug manufacturers, such as offering payment, gifts, or other kickbacks, could violate federal fraud and abuse laws. □ Michael Woods

See also **Drug abuse; Health care issues; Medicine.**

East Timor became an independent nation on May 20, 2002. The country occupies the eastern side of the island of Timor, which lies in the Timor Sea, about 300 miles (480 kilometers) north of Australia.

East Timor was a Portuguese colony for centuries. In 1975, Portugal withdrew from East Timor, and Indonesia, which already possessed the western part of the island, sent military troops to take control of the eastern section. Many people in East Timor resisted Indonesian rule. During this period, as many as 200,000 East Timorese died, many from starvation and disease.

In 1999, the East Timorese voted overwhelmingly for independence. After the vote, a militia assisted by the Indonesian military launched a campaign of terror against the East Timorese. The violence left at least 1,000 people dead. In September 1999, the United Nations (UN) sent a peacekeeping force to East Timor to stop the violence. Following the UN's action, Indonesia ended its claim to the territory. The UN and East Timorese then began administering the region.

In 2001, East Timor established an 88-member Constituent Assembly (parliament). The long-time resistance leader Jose Alexandre Gusmao, commonly known as Xanana Gusmao, was elected president in April 2002.

Debris covers the floor of Bethlehem's Church of the Nativity, administered by the Orthodox Church, following a 38-day stand-off between Israeli troops and Islamic militants, who occupied the ancient shrine in April and May 2002.

Language dispute. The new government's choice of Portuguese as one of the country's official languages drew criticism from many East Timorese, who noted that only about 10 percent of the country's people spoke that language. Most East Timorese spoke either Indonesian or Tetum. Government officials said they chose Portuguese as an act of gratitude to Portugal and the Portuguese-speaking countries of Angola and Mozambique, which had supported East Timor's independence struggle.

Poverty. East Timor was one of Asia's poorest nations in 2002. At the UN's urging, donors pledged to give the fledgling country $360 million in development assistance through 2005. East Timor's economic future depended on offshore gas and oil deposits shared with Australia.

Trials. An Indonesian court sentenced the former governor of East Timor, Abilio Soares, to three years in jail in 2002 for failing to stop the violence following the vote for independence in 1999. The court acquitted six military and police officials of crimes against humanity in East Timor. The verdicts drew sharp criticism from international observers. Several countries had pressured Indonesia to hold the trials and punish the people responsible for the 1999 massacre.

☐ Henry S. Bradsher

See also **Asia; Indonesia; United Nations.**

Eastern Orthodox Churches. Ecumenical Patriarch Bartholomew I, spiritual leader of the world's Orthodox Christians, continued his support of environmental causes in 2002. In June, Bartholomew led scientists and activists on a five-day cruise of the Adriatic Sea off the east coast of Italy to draw attention to environmental problems facing the heavily polluted sea. Following the cruise, Bartholomew traveled to Oslo, Norway, to receive the Sophie prize, an annual award recognizing efforts to protect the environment. Later in June, Bartholomew and Pope John Paul II of the Roman Catholic Church signed the Joint Declaration on Articulating a Code of Environmental Ethics. The document stated that protecting the environment was a "moral and spiritual" duty for all Christians.

Russian Orthodox Church officials in February criticized the pope's decision to establish four permanent Roman Catholic dioceses in Russia. A spokesman for the church called the establishment of the new dioceses "an unfriendly act." The Russian Orthodox Church accused the Roman Catholic Church in Russia of trying to convert Orthodox Christians to Roman Catholicism, a charge that the pope denied.

In July, the Russian government announced that it would return the famous Kazan Cathedral in St. Petersburg to the Russian Orthodox Church.

The government had confiscated the cathedral during Russia's Communist period (1919-1991).

The Church of the Nativity in Bethlehem, administered by the Orthodox Church of Jerusalem, became the scene of a military stand-off in April and May between Israeli soldiers and Palestinian militants who took refuge in the shrine when the Israeli army entered the West Bank city. The siege ended 38 days later when more than 200 Palestinians surrendered.

Greek Orthodox Church Archbishop Christodoulos in April objected to plans to construct Greece's first crematorium. The church's insistence that cremation is a violation of the natural order had kept a church-administered burial service as the only legitimate means of disposing of the country's dead. Church officials also publicly opposed legislation that would legitimize artificial insemination, claiming that the measure would undermine Greek identity and beliefs.

Metropolitan Theodosius, the head of the Orthodox Church in America, retired in 2002. The Church's All-American Council, meeting in Orlando, Florida, in July, elected Metropolitan Herman as Theodosius's successor. Herman, born Joseph Swaiko, was the former archbishop of Philadelphia. □ Stanley S. Harakas

See also **Greece; Israel; Middle East; Roman Catholic Church; Russia.**

Economics. The world economy seemed poised in 2002 for a strong recovery from the 2001 recession. The recovery faltered, however, as economic growth slowed among the world's leading industrial nations.

Major stock markets declined for the third consecutive year, as investors responded to a wave of corporate accounting scandals and the largest bankruptcies in United States corporate history. Steep declines in stock values further constricted business finances and sapped the spending power of consumers who had invested heavily in stocks during the 1990's. Some analysts warned that the bear market, a market in which stock prices fall as sellers outnumber buyers, could last for a long time. Analysts said it could take years to rebuild the U.S. economy after the collapse in 2001 of the huge financial bubble that had inflated the value of stocks, particularly technology stocks, during the 1990's.

Global economic picture. Economists said a number of factors contributed to sluggish economic growth in 2002. Business leaders cited uncertainty caused by the threat of terrorist attacks and a potential U.S. war in Iraq as impediments to a solid manufacturing recovery. Demand for goods flagged in the United States and Europe even though prices and interest rates were already at their lowest levels in decades. Many ana-

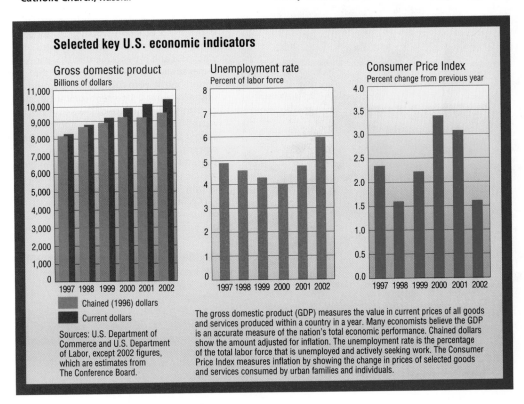

Selected key U.S. economic indicators

Chained (1996) dollars / Current dollars

Sources: U.S. Department of Commerce and U.S. Department of Labor, except 2002 figures, which are estimates from The Conference Board.

The gross domestic product (GDP) measures the value in current prices of all goods and services produced within a country in a year. Many economists believe the GDP is an accurate measure of the nation's total economic performance. Chained dollars show the amount adjusted for inflation. The unemployment rate is the percentage of the total labor force that is unemployed and actively seeking work. The Consumer Price Index measures inflation by showing the change in prices of selected goods and services consumed by urban families and individuals.

lysts blamed the sluggish economy in the United States on a phenomenon called overcapacity. They noted that during the economic boom of the late 1990's, U.S. businesses had invested heavily in expanding their production capacity. When demand levelled off in the early 2000's, companies were able to produce many more goods and services than consumers wanted, forcing them to drop prices and cut expenses by laying off staff.

Debt-strapped Latin American countries suffered several economic crises in 2002. Argentina, already in a severe contraction, defaulted on debts, including a $1-billion loan from the World Bank, a United Nations agency that provides loans to countries for development. Brazil's election of left-wing leader Luiz Inacio Lula da Silva caused international investors to worry that Latin America's largest economy might also default on loans. A short-lived *coup* (overthrow) in April and widespread labor strikes late in the year nearly halted Venezuela's already suffering economy. Other South American nations also suffered from poor economic conditions in 2002.

Emerging Asian economies were among the few countries that showed strong economic growth. China, a major force in international trade, reported a third-quarter annual growth rate of 8.1 percent and a 13.8-percent surge in industrial output. South Korea, India, and Russia also posted solid growth rates early in the year.

Oil. Early in 2002, the Organization of Petroleum Exporting Countries (OPEC), a group of oil-producing nations, tightened production quotas to boost crude oil prices. Russia, however, at times outproduced even the biggest OPEC exporters, undercutting efforts to raise prices. Still, cuts by some oil producers and the risk of war in Iraq buoyed fuel prices, putting further pressure on already sluggish industrial economies.

IMF projections. The International Monetary Fund (IMF), a United Nations–affiliated agency that provides financial assistance and economic guidance for member nations, projected in October that worldwide economic growth would improve moderately from 2.2 percent in 2001 to 2.8 percent in 2002. The IMF predicted that the U.S. economy would grow 2.2 percent in 2002 but noted gathering signs of weakness and retrenchment in U.S. consumer spending. The IMF estimated that nations in the euro currency zone would post an anemic 0.9-percent combined growth rate in the face of "extremely weak" domestic demand. The agency expected Japan's economy to contract by 0.5 percent. The IMF said Japan again appeared to be emerging from recession but forecast the nation's economy would grow by only 1.1 percent in 2003.

Collapse and scandal. The financial collapse of several large U.S. corporations produced a series of highly publicized scan-

A Federal Bureau of Investigation agent escorts former Enron Corp. chief financial officer Andrew Fastow into federal court in Houston in October to be indicted on 78 counts of fraud, money laundering, conspiracy, and obstruction of justice. Fastow was accused of artificially inflating Enron profits in order to skim off millions of dollars at the expense of stockholders.

dals in 2002 that shook investor confidence and severely weakened the U.S. economy. A panel investigating the 2001 collapse of Houston-based energy trader Enron Corp. revealed in February 2002 that Enron executives had used questionable accounting practices and a complex arrangement of partnerships to hide debt and overstate profits. The executives had realized enormous personal profits from these partnerships and sold at least $1 billion in company stock in the months before Enron collapsed. These revelations led to the indictment in March of Enron's independent auditor, Arthur Andersen LLP of Chicago, and focused public attention on corporate bookkeeping practices. In June, a federal court in Houston found Arthur Andersen guilty of obstruction of justice for destroying Enron documents.

In June, officials at WorldCom Inc. disclosed that the Mississippi-based telecommunications company had lost $3.8 billion in 2001 and 2002, instead of posting $1.4 billion in profits as previously reported. Business experts described the manipulation as the largest case of accounting deception in U.S. history. WorldCom declared bankruptcy in July.

In July, John Rigas, founder of Adelphia Communications Corp., and two of his sons were arrested for looting the Coudersport, Pennsylvania-based cable television company. They were accused of taking out $2.3 billion in bank loans guaranteed by Adelphia but never recorded on the books. Adelphia declared bankruptcy in June.

The list of bankruptcies grew to include well-known retailers, airlines, steel manufacturers, and telecommunications companies. While some business failures were tied to the poor economy, many were the result of poor management and irregular accounting practices. Critics pointed to a lack of government oversight by the Securities and Exchange Commission (SEC), an independent federal agency that enforces federal laws governing the purchase and sale of securities. SEC chairman Harvey Pitt resigned in November under intense criticism that he had been too closely associated with the corporations and accounting firms that he was supposed to have regulated.

The U.S. Congress responded to the scandals with new corporate responsibility rules, which included forcing executives to personally sign off on the accuracy of company financial statements.

Treasury Secretary Paul O'Neill and Lawrence B. Lindsey, director of the National Economic Council, resigned in December. Experts said O'Neill and Lindsey had lost public confidence by failing to effectively respond to the poor economic conditions.   ☐ John D. Boyd

See also **Cabinet, U.S.; Courts; International trade; Manufacturing; United States, Government of the.**

Ecuador. Lucio Edwin Gutierrez, of the January 21 Patriotic Movement, won the runoff election for the presidency on Nov. 24, 2002. The former colonel, whose party took its name from the date in 2000 when Gutierrez and junior army officers staged a *coup* (overthrow) attempt, defeated Alvaro Noboa, a banana tycoon, by a margin of about 54 percent to 46 percent. Gutierrez had become the surprise front-runner in the initial round of balloting in October 2002.

Gutierrez pledged to fight corruption and make Ecuador "a more honest country." Among his highest priorities was concluding an agreement with the International Monetary Fund, a United Nations-affiliated organization that provides financial assistance to nations. Such an agreement would enable Ecuador to continue making repayments on its $11.4 billion debt and tackle the problems of the estimated 60 percent of the population mired in poverty. During the final phase of his campaign, Gutierrez had sought to reassure foreign investors in visits to New York City, Washington, D.C., and Miami, Florida.

Air tragedy. On January 28, a Boeing 727 operated by Ecuador's Tame airlines crashed on the slopes of the Nevado de Cumbal volcano in southern Colombia. All 92 people on board the airliner were killed.   ☐ Nathan A. Haverstock

See also **Disasters; Latin America.**

Education. About 53.6 million students enrolled in public and private elementary and secondary schools in the United States in autumn 2002. The U.S. Department of Education estimated that 2.9 million students would graduate from high school during the 2002-2003 school year.

About 575,000 students attended nearly 2,700 charter schools operating in 36 states and the District of Columbia in fall 2002. Charter schools are taxpayer-funded schools that are not run by public school districts. The nation's experiment with public schools run by for-profit companies continued, as Edison Schools Inc. of New York City took over the operations of 20 Philadelphia schools in September. In total, Edison managed 150 public schools with about 84,000 students in 2002.

The national dropout rate, the percentage of students ages 16 to 24 who leave high school without a diploma each year, fell to a record low of 10.9 percent in 2002. However, a large gap remained between the dropout rates of white and minority students. About 28 percent of Hispanic students drop out each year, compared with 13 percent of blacks and 7 percent of whites.

The Department of Education announced that states spent an average of $6,911 a year to educate each of their students. Spending was highest in New Jersey, at $10,337 per student, and lowest in Utah, at $4,378 per student.

College and university attendance reached record highs in 2002, with about 15.6 million students estimated to have to enrolled in the fall. The Department of Education predicted that 1.3 million students would receive bachelor's degrees during the academic year.

Vouchers. The U.S. Supreme Court ruled in June that states could use taxpayer money to pay private or religious school tuition for children whose parents choose to take them out of public schools. The court ruled that these payments, called vouchers, do not violate the Constitutional separation of government and religion. The 5-to-4 ruling upheld a six-year-old voucher program in Cleveland, Ohio, and cleared the way for states that wished to create voucher programs.

The debate over vouchers moved into the state legislatures and courts. Opponents argued that vouchers drain money from public schools, making it difficult for them to improve. Voucher supporters claimed vouchers create competition between public schools and private schools that will encourage both to improve. In a sign of the battles to come, a Florida judge ruled in August that the state's voucher program violated Florida's Constitution on religious grounds.

Title IX, the education reform law that greatly expanded opportunities for women athletes, came under attack in 2002. Many colleges and universities interpret the 1972 law to mean that they should have the same proportion of men and women on their sports rosters as they do in their student bodies generally. On many campuses, women outnumbered men in 2002, meaning that more spots on sports teams and sports scholarships were allocated for women.

A group of men's wrestling coaches filed suit against Title IX in the spring, complaining that it forced colleges to cut men's teams in order to balance out their rosters. Title IX advocates blamed the cuts on men's football teams, saying that their huge rosters and budgets crowded out other men's sports, including wrestling, gymnastics, and swimming. In September, U.S. President George W. Bush appointed a commission to study the law and report its findings in January 2003.

SAT. The College Board, a nonprofit education association located in New York City, announced in June 2002 that it was redesigning its SAT I college entrance exam. The new test, to be first administered in 2005, would eliminate word analogy questions, require an understanding of more advanced math, and introduce a writing exam. The addition of the writing test would raise the perfect SAT score to 2400 points from 1600 and add 30 minutes to the test-taking time, making the SAT 3 ½ hours long. The writing exam would require students to write a brief essay in response to a written statement.

The College Board made the changes after some colleges complained that the old test measured reasoning and critical thinking skills rather than learning ability. Critics said that approach favored upper-income students who could afford to enroll in special test-preparation courses.

No Child Left Behind. State education officers ran into problems in 2002 implementing the No Child Left Behind Act of 2001. The law requires that states identify poorly performing schools and allow children in those schools to transfer to better-performing public schools in the same district. States identified more than 8,000 failing schools. However, many areas could not find enough seats in better schools for all of the students who wanted to transfer, so most of those children remained in their failing schools.

Test scores. Average math scores on the SAT I rose two points in 2002, while verbal scores fell by the same amount. The College Board attributed the rising math scores to the growing number of students taking higher-level math courses and a concerted national focus on math in the past decade. The College Board said a decline in the number of high school students enrolled in grammar and composition courses, as well as a rise in test-takers who are non-native English speakers, probably resulted in the fall in verbal scores.

The average score on the ACT, the other major college entrance exam, dropped slightly to 20.8 out of a possible 36 points. ACT Inc. of Iowa City, Iowa, said that fewer students were taking a curriculum that will enable them to do well on the exam and in college. That curriculum includes four years of English and three years each of advanced math, social studies, and natural sciences.

Paying for college. The amount of aid money available to help students attend college grew to $90 billion in 2002, with the biggest share going to students from lower-income families. However, in a continuing trend, states gave a growing share of scholarship money to students with good grades, regardless of their family incomes. More than a dozen states had begun merit scholarship programs for students who met academic goals, including minimum grade point averages and ACT or SAT scores. Colleges and universities also gave away a larger share of their own scholarship aid to students based on academic merit, athletic skill, and artistic ability, the National Association of Student Financial Aid Administrators announced in 2002.

The College Board announced in 2002 that the average yearly price of tuition, fees, and room and board was about $9,663 at a public four-year college or university and $25,052 at a private four-year institution.   □ June Kronholz

See also **State government; Supreme Court of the United States.**

Egyptian railroad officials inspect burned-out cars in which more than 360 passengers died when a portable stove sparked a fire in February. The disaster, which took place south of Cairo, the capital, was the most deadly railroad accident in Egyptian history.

Egypt. In August 2002, officials in the administration of United States President George W. Bush said that Egypt would have to improve its human rights record to qualify for additional U.S. foreign aid. The announcement was a rare rebuke for Egyptian President Hosni Mubarak, whom the U.S. government had long viewed as a key ally in the Middle East. The warning did not affect Egypt's annual U.S. grant of $2 billion.

The move by the Bush administration came after an Egyptian State Security Court resentenced Egyptian-American democracy advocate Saad Eddin Ibrahim to seven years in prison in July 2002. Ibrahim had originally been convicted and sentenced in May 2001 for tarnishing Egypt's image and accepting foreign donations for his democracy research center in Egypt. That verdict, however, had been overturned in February 2002. In December, Egypt's highest appeals court freed Ibrahim and ordered a retrial for January 2003.

Crackdown. The Egyptian government launched a major crackdown against Islamic groups that it perceived to be threats in 2002. Authorities arrested hundreds of members of the outlawed Islamic organization Muslim Brotherhood, which had long sought to establish an Islamic government in Egypt. Many members of two smaller militant Islamic groups were also arrested. In July, an Egyptian military court sentenced 16 Muslim Brotherhood members, most of whom were academics and professionals, to prison terms of up to five years for conspiring against the government. The Supreme Guide of the Muslim Brotherhood, Mustafa Mashhour, died in November.

Some experts believed that President Mubarak hoped the crackdown would deter a potential political backlash by Islamic militants against his pro-Western government. However, many Egyptians, like other people in the Arab world, grew increasingly angry about the worsening Palestinian-Israeli conflict and a possible U.S. attack on Iraq.

Train disaster. More than 360 people were killed when a fire swept through a packed passenger train south of Cairo, the capital, on February 20. The fire was sparked by a small portable stove on the train.

The Bibliotheca Alexandrina opened in the Mediterranean coastal city of Alexandria, Egypt, in October. The massive library complex, specializing in archived electronic information, is on the site where archaeologists believe the legendary library of Alexandria stood in ancient times. Egyptians hoped the Bibliotheca Alexandrina would revive cultural life and educational activities in the city. □ Christine Helms

See also **Architecture; Iraq; Israel; Middle East.**

Elections. In stunning midterm elections on Nov. 5, 2002, Republicans increased their majority in the U.S. House of Representatives and regained control of the U.S. Senate. The elections marked the first time since 1934, during the administration of President Franklin D. Roosevelt, that a president's party gained seats in both the House of Representatives and the Senate two years into the president's first term. Republicans in 2002 also won key gubernatorial races in Alabama, Florida, and Maryland. Political analysts attributed the Republican gains to President George W. Bush's popularity, which the president used to his advantage as he campaigned for Republican candidates.

Congressional elections. There were few competitive races in the November election for all 435 House seats, as Republicans increased the number of seats they held in the House to 229, compared with 205 seats held by Democrats. An independent representative held one seat in the House in 2002.

In the U.S. Senate, Republicans took three seats held by Democrats while losing only a single seat. Republican Jim Talent defeated incumbent Senator Jean Carnahan in Missouri. In Georgia, U.S. Representative Saxby Chambliss defeated Senator Max Cleland. In Minnesota, Norm Coleman defeated a last-minute entry into the race, former Senator and Vice President Walter Mondale. Mondale ran in place of incumbent Senator Paul Wellstone, who died in a plane crash in October.

Democrats managed to take one Senate seat away from the Republicans. In Arkansas, Attorney General Mark Pryor defeated Republican incumbent Senator Tim Hutchinson.

Gubernatorial races. Republicans won several gubernatorial victories in 2002 to maintain a slim margin of control over the total number of governors' offices. Of the 36 open governors' seats on the ballot, Republicans won 22 races, compared with 14 races won by Democrats. Republicans controlled 26 governorships while Democrats controlled 24 governorships after the elections.

Democrats did well in large industrial states, including Illinois, where U.S. Representative Rod Blagojevich captured the governor's office by defeating Attorney General Jim Ryan. Republicans in Illinois had held the governor's office since 1977. Other Democrats winning first gubernatorial terms included Janet Napolitano of Arizona; Kathleen Sebelius of Kansas; John Baldacci of Maine; Jennifer Granholm of Michigan; Bill Richardson of New Mexico; Brad Henry of Oklahoma; Ted Kulongoski of Oregon; Ed Rendell of Pennsylvania; Phil Bredesen of Tennessee; Jim Doyle of Wisconsin; and Dave Freudenthal of Wyoming.

Democrats retained control in California, where Governor Gray Davis won a second term by defeating Republican businessman Bill Simon. Tom Vilsack of Iowa also won reelection.

Republicans won some unexpected gubernatorial victories in the November election. For just the second time in state history, a Republican won the governor's race in Hawaii. Linda Lingle, the former mayor of Maui, defeated Lieutenant Governor Mazie Hirono, a Democrat, to replace Governor Benjamin J. Cayetano, a Democrat who retired. In Georgia, Republican Sonny Perdue defeated incumbent Democratic Governor Roy Barnes. Many political experts cited Barnes's successful effort in 2001 to remove the Confederate battle emblem from prominence on the state flag as a contributing factor in his defeat. In Alabama, incumbent Governor Donald Siegelman, a Democrat, and Bob Riley, a Republican, declared victory in the November 2002 election. Siegelman later conceded.

Other Republicans winning their first terms as governor included Frank H. Murkowski of Alaska; Robert Ehrlich, Jr., of Maryland; Mitt Romney of Massachusetts; Tim Pawlenty of Minnesota; Craig Benson of New Hampshire; Donald Carcieri of Rhode Island; Mark Sanford of South Carolina; Mike Rounds of South Dakota; and James Douglas of Vermont.

Republicans held on to power in several states. Incumbent Governor Jeb Bush, President Bush's brother, won reelection in Florida after a strong challenge by Democrat Bill McBride, a Tampa businessman. Democrats had waged a major campaign against Bush in an effort to unseat him.

Republicans also retained control of the governor's office in such large states as New York, where incumbent George Pataki won reelection by a large margin; and Texas, where incumbent Rick Perry won election to a first term. Perry had filled out the term of his predecessor, George W. Bush. Also winning reelection were Mike Huckabee of Arkansas; Bill Owens of Colorado; John G. Rowland of Connecticut; Dirk Kempthorne of Idaho; Mike Johanns of Nebraska; Kenny Guinn of Nevada; and Robert Taft of Ohio.

New limits on campaign finance went into effect on November 6. The limits targeted "soft money" contributions—individual contributions made to political parties. The campaign finance law prohibits the national political parties from raising unlimited contributions from corporations, labor unions, and other groups but doubled from $1,000 to $2,000 the amount that federal candidates may raise from individuals.

☐ Geoffrey A. Campbell

See also **Congress of the United States; Democratic Party; Los Angeles; Republican Party; State government; United States, Government of the.**

Electric power. See Energy supply.

Electronics. The Consumer Electronics Association (CEA), an industry group based in Arlington, Virginia, projected in August 2002 that retailers would sell $95.7 billion of electronics gear in 2002, compared with $93.2 billion in sales in 2001. CEA officials predicted that video-related products, including such items as DVD players, personal video recorders, satellite television systems, and digital televisions would be among the most popular.

Employment slowdown. The American Electronics Association (AEA), a high-technology trade organization with headquarters in Santa Clara, California, reported in June 2002 that the computer industry in 2001 experienced its smallest increase in jobs since 1996, when the AEA began conducting its annual employment survey. The AEA report stated that jobs in computers, software, semiconductors, Internet technology, and related high-technology fields rose by just 1 percent, or 80,000 positions, in 2001, compared with the 440,000 jobs added in 2000.

AEA officials reported that 5.6 million people were employed in the electronics industry in 2001, compared to 5.5 million in 2000. Experts blamed the slowdown in new job openings on the poor performance of the U.S. economy, which resulted in fewer investments in the electronics industry.

Better robots. Officials at Sony Corporation of Tokyo announced in May 2002 that the company would begin selling a less expensive but improved version of its Aibo electronic robot. Aibo is a small personal "entertainment" robot that uses artificial intelligence to respond to voice commands and interact with people. Sony officials claimed that the new Aibo series of robots would be equipped with superior wireless networking capabilities.

Digital television. The Federal Communications Commission (FCC) in August took a major step toward switching the United States to digital television, a technology that provides crisp images that are superior to those of nondigital transmissions. The FCC ordered that by 2004 all new televisions with screens 36 inches (91 centimeters) or larger must include tuners that can receive digital broadcasts. All new televisions will be required to have digital tuners by 2007.

Digital television, which is also called High-Definition Television (HDTV), provides extremely clear pictures and sound, but broadcasters have been slow to adopt the technology because few people have television sets capable of receiving digital signals. The FCC's August ruling was designed to encourage broadcasters to switch over to digital signals, which they are obliged to do by 2006. Consumer Electronics Association (CEA) officials complained that the decision would drive up the cost of television sets by as much as $250 per set.

Spintronics. Scientists at the University of New York at Buffalo reported in May 2002 that they had developed a new type of semiconducting material that had physical properties that were essential for use in a new generation of transistors, memory devices, and other computer components. Conventional versions of these electronic devices use electrons to turn switches known as transistors on or off. When these switches are on, they can represent a "1" and when they are off, they can represent a "0." Long strings of 1's and 0's—known as binary code—are the language of computers.

The scientists at the University of New York at Buffalo developed a type of material called gallium antimonide/manganese that will be needed in order to develop computing devices that rely on a different type of computer technology called "spintronics." Instead of using electrons to turn switches on or off, spintronic devices use the spin of electrons themselves to represent information, enabling them to process billions of pieces of information at once, greatly increasing the speed and power of computers and other electronic devices. Experts said spintronic devices would be smaller and more powerful than conventional ones.

☐ Michael Woods

El Salvador. In July 2002, El Salvador mounted a campaign aimed at doubling foreign investment in its market-oriented economy to an annual level of $500 million by 2004. The campaign focused on attracting new investment in the agribusiness, electronics, and textile sectors.

The United States Justice Department announced in July 2002 that it would allow 260,000 Salvadorans, many of them illegal immigrants, to remain in the United States until September 2003. The Salvadorans had taken refuge in the United States in 2001 following two devastating earthquakes that killed more than 1,000 people.

On July 23, 2002, a federal court in West Palm Beach, Florida, ordered two retired Salvadoran generals living in Florida to pay $54.6 million in damages to three Salvadorans tortured by units commanded by the generals during El Salvador's civil war (1979-1992). The victims sued generals Carlos Eugenio Vides Casanova and Jose Guillermo Garcia under a 1991 law that allows U.S. courts to assess damages against perpetrators of human rights abuses committed abroad.

☐ Nathan A. Haverstock

See also **Latin America.**

Employment. See Economics; Labor and employment.

Endangered species. See Biology; Conservation.

Energy supply. Global energy demand grew at a much slower pace in 2002 than in previous years. Economists said the main reason for the slower growth was the sluggishness of national economies throughout the world. Despite the slower increases in demand, fuel prices remained relatively high. Economists attributed this to worries over possible disruptions of global oil flows because of tensions in the Middle East and the threat of war between the United States and Iraq, a major Middle East oil exporter. Industry experts were also concerned that the 11 members of the Organization of the Petroleum Exporting Countries (OPEC) would tighten supplies too much, pushing up petroleum prices.

As a result of these uncertainties, crude oil prices, which began 2002 at $20 a barrel, hovered around $25 a barrel for much of the year and reached as high as $31. Energy experts said that prices were about $5 higher per barrel than normal because producers had placed a "war premium" on oil before a war had actually broken out. Prices rose to $30.10 a barrel in late December when political turmoil in Venezuela greatly reduced its oil exports. Energy experts noted that a prolonged period of such prices could threaten the global economic recovery.

Despite worries about OPEC's actions, energy supplies were ample in 2002 as oil exporters actually produced more than their self-imposed quotas. Still, consumers in the United States generally paid more for fuel than had been expected. Regular unleaded gasoline, which in January 2002 cost about $1.10 a gallon at the pump, had jumped to $1.40 by April. By October, it had risen to about $1.45 a gallon. The U.S. Department of Energy reported in October that gasoline prices nationwide were at their highest levels since September 2001.

World oil demand. The International Energy Agency (IEA), a Paris-based energy group, reported that world demand for petroleum increased in 2002 to about 76.6 million barrels a day. IEA officials said they expected global demand for oil to increase in 2003 to 77.7 million barrels a day.

The sluggishness of demand in 2002 was more pronounced in the United States, even though it still used more oil than any other nation. Officials with the Energy Information Administration (EIA), an agency within the U.S. Department of Energy, reported that the United States used about 19.6 million barrels of petroleum products a day through October 2002, compared with about 19.7 million gallons a day in 2001.

Because of lagging domestic production, the United States imported more than half of its oil in 2002, much of it from the Middle East. Energy experts expected U.S. oil imports to increase as the economy began to recover and the demand for energy rose. Officials with the EIA expected the United States to become ever more dependent on imports of both crude oil and natural gas. EIA officials reported in November that petroleum imports, including both crude oil and refined products, were expected to account for nearly 70 percent of total petroleum demand by 2025, a significant increase over 2001, when the U.S. imported 55 percent of its oil.

Fuel economy standards. U.S. President George W. Bush issued a draft of a plan in November 2002 to raise the fuel economy standards of sport utility vehicles (SUV's) by 1.5 miles (2.4 kilometers) per gallon. SUV's consume large quantities of gasoline compared with smaller vehicles. Environmental groups criticized the proposal as too small an increase in fuel efficiency standards, noting that when such standards were first implemented in 1975, light trucks were allowed to be less efficient because they were used primarily by farmers and small business owners. However, in 2002, SUV's, which are classified as light trucks, were among the most popular vehicles sold. Environmental groups, however, reported that they were pleased that people were getting a tax break for buying "hybrid" cars powered by a combination of gasoline and batteries.

Natural gas. U.S. demand for natural gas was down for much of 2002 mainly because of unseasonal warm weather in the first few weeks of the year. Natural gas use was flat for much of 2002 because of the troubled U.S. economy and a negative reaction from users to previous price increases. In the later months of 2002, cold weather caused consumption of natural gas to rise.

Energy experts predicted that, because gas was more commonly being used to generate electricity, gas consumption would grow by about 4 percent in 2003. They also said gas would account for a larger part of the U.S. energy mix in the future but questioned whether producers could meet the predicted higher demand. The EIA projected in 2002 that U.S. demand for natural gas would grow by 54 percent by 2020, to an annual rate of 35 trillion cubic feet (1 trillion cubic meters). This increase would be greater than any other fuel except petroleum.

EIA officials attributed the projected growth in natural gas use to the fact that it burns more cleanly than other sources. Natural gas can also be used as an energy source in many different applications. However, EIA officials noted that even if U.S. natural gas producers increase production, such an increase in demand would require increased imports of natural gas from Canada and elsewhere. □ James Tanner

Engineering. See Building and construction.

England. See United Kingdom.

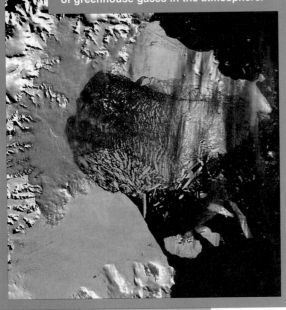

Satellite images taken in late January (above) and early March (below) show the breakup of a shelf of ice the size of Rhode Island on the eastern side of the Antarctic Peninsula. Scientists said this was the first time in thousands of years that so much ice had eroded from this part of Antarctica. They attributed the breakup to rapidly warming summer air temperatures, possibly as a result of the buildup of greenhouse gases in the atmosphere.

Environmental pollution.

An oil tanker carrying 20 million gallons (76 million liters) of heavy crude oil split in two and sank off of the northern coast of Spain on Nov. 19, 2002. Environmentalists feared that the oil escaping from the Greek-operated and Liberian-registered *Prestige* would produce one of the world's worst environmental disasters. Oil had begun seeping from the tanker after the vessel sprang a leak on November 13.

Environmental groups warned that if the entire cargo of oil from the *Prestige* poured into the ocean, the spill would be about twice as large as the amount of oil dumped when the *Exxon Valdez* hit a reef in Prince William Sound off the coast of Alaska in 1989. The *Exxon Valdez* lost nearly 11 million gallons (42 million liters) of oil, which caused severe environmental damage to the coastline of Alaska.

In late December 2002, some 8,000 people worked to clean up contaminated beaches on the Spanish Galician coast. Yet, much of the oil remained aboard the sunken halves of the *Prestige,* which lay on the ocean floor at a depth of about 11,500 feet (3,500 meters). The Spanish government announced that workers had used a French research submarine to plug five holes through which oil was leaking from the tanker. However, the workers discovered several additional cracks in the vessel. Spanish officials also said they were considering establishing a research center on water pollution, similar to a center that exists in France.

World Summit. World leaders, environmentalists, and advocates for the poor converged on Johannesburg, South Africa, in August for the United Nations (UN) World Summit on Sustainable Development. Negotiators at the meeting focused on the link between poverty and damage to the environment. At the summit, leaders of wealthy nations were asked to provide 0.7 percent of their *gross domestic product* (GDP—the value of all goods and services produced in a country over a given period) in aid to developing countries and to help reduce by half the number of people who lacked access to clean water by 2015. More than 100 presidents and prime ministers attended the summit.

Kyoto Protocol. In June 2002, the government of Japan *ratified* (approved) the 1997 Kyoto Protocol. The protocol is an international agreement to reduce the emissions of *greenhouse gases* (gases in the atmosphere, such as carbon dioxide, that trap heat and could raise temperatures). Many scientists fear that global warming is altering worldwide weather patterns and could have devastating effects on agriculture, society, and the environment in many countries.

The Kyoto Protocol, which requires participating countries to reduce emissions to below 1990 levels by 2010, goes into effect when 55 countries, accounting for at least 55 percent of industrialized emissions, ratify it. The administration of United States President George W. Bush had rejected the Kyoto treaty in 2001, citing the failure of treaty organizers to include developing countries in the protocol and expressing concern that complying with the pact might weaken the U.S. economy. Nevertheless, the Kyoto Protocol could still go into effect if ratified by the European Union, Russia, and either Canada or Poland.

Bush administration policies. In 2002, the Bush administration proposed an alternative to the Kyoto Protocol. The administration offered a plan to slow the growth of greenhouse gas emissions by nearly 18 percent by 2012. The proposed plan would reduce emissions from the 202 tons (183 metric tons) outlined in the protocol to 166 tons (151 metric tons) per every $1 million of a nation's GDP. Critics argued that this proposal would allow emissions to grow with the economy. They also complained that the program would not be mandatory.

President Bush faced mounting pressure in 2002 to deal with environmental problems related to greenhouse gas emissions. In June, the U.S. Environmental Protection Agency (EPA), a bureau within the federal government, issued a report to the UN acknowledging that the United States would be significantly affected by global warming in coming decades. In July, the attorneys general of 11 states petitioned the president for strong federal controls on greenhouse gases. Also in July, California Governor Gray Davis signed the nation's first bill to regulate greenhouse gas emissions from automobiles. The bill directed automakers to produce cars that emit less carbon dioxide by 2008. The legislation infuriated automakers, who had spent millions of dollars lobbying against the bill. Auto industry leaders claimed that the new emissions standards were a way to bypass Bush administration policy.

New air-pollution rules. The attorneys general of nine Northeastern states filed a lawsuit on Dec. 31, 2002, against the EPA, challenging new air-pollution rules that allowed utilities, refineries, and manufacturers to avoid installing expensive new antipollution equipment. The new rules, which the EPA had announced on November 22, overturned a provision of the Clean Air Act of 1970 that required companies to adopt the best available pollution controls when major sources of pollution, such as coal-fired electric plants and refineries, are upgraded or enlarged. Defending the new rules, a spokesperson for the EPA noted that the old regulations discouraged renovation and investment in new infrastructure.

Pollution-free cars. In January 2002, President Bush canceled the Partnership for a New Generation of Vehicles, an 8-year-old program in which major U.S. automakers and federal laboratories worked together to develop cars that could get 80 miles (129 kilometers) per gallon of gasoline by 2004. Both industry leaders and environmentalists considered the program, which had cost more than $1.5 billion, a failure. President Bush proposed an alternate program focused almost entirely on vehicles powered by fuel cells. Fuel cells produce electricity by combining oxygen and hydrogen without generating pollution.

National Park conflicts. Conflict continued in 2002 between protecting the environment and allowing people to use U.S. national parks for recreation. The Bush administration policy of accommodating local interests, such as various private vendors within national parks, resulted in different standards within the National Park System. In 2002, the National Park Service prohibited off-road vehicles known as swamp buggies from Big Cypress National Reserve in Florida but was unable to shut down an underground lunchroom in Carlsbad Caverns National Park in New Mexico. Scientists argued that the brightly lit lunchroom discouraged cave-dwelling bats from leaving the cave to hunt for food.

In June, Bush administration officials reversed rules that had been implemented during the administration of former President Bill Clinton banning people from driving snowmobiles in Yellowstone and Grand Teton national parks. The International Snowmobile Manufacturer's Association had challenged that ban with a lawsuit. But environmentalists countered that the noise and pollution emitted by snowmobiles posed a serious hazard to animals living within the parks. The National Park Service compromised, allowing limited recreational use of cleaner, quieter snowmobiles in supervised areas in the parks.

Toxic waste dumps. In July, the Bush administration cut funding for the cleanup of 33 toxic waste dumps in 18 states. The cuts were the latest blow to Superfund, a federal program established in 1980 to cleanup abandoned waste dumps. A special tax on chemical and oil companies, which had originally funded the program, was eliminated by Congress in 1995. To keep cleanups moving, funds were drawn from the government's general accounts. Superfund, however, fell hundreds of millions of dollars short of the amount needed to keep work on schedule.   □ Andrew Hoffman

See also **Conservation; United States, Government of the: A Special Report.**

Equatorial Guinea. See Africa.
Eritrea. See Africa.
Estonia. See Europe.
Ethiopia. See Africa.

The nations of Western Europe took two historic steps in 2002 to erase divisions between east and west that had existed since the end of World War II (1939-1945). The European Union (EU), an economic and political grouping of 15 Western European countries, agreed in December 2002 to admit 10 new members from eastern and southern Europe, including a number of countries that were once aligned with the former Soviet Union. In November, the North Atlantic Treaty Organization (NATO), a military alliance made up of the United States, Canada, and 17 European nations, invited 7 Eastern European countries to begin negotiations on joining the alliance. Both organizations expected to admit the new members in 2004.

Economic growth remained sluggish in Europe throughout 2002. Unemployment edged higher, and several EU governments violated the budget deficit rules for countries using the euro.

EU enlargement. The EU in 2002 completed membership negotiations with Poland, Hungary, the Czech Republic, Slovakia, Slovenia, Estonia, Latvia, Lithuania, Cyprus, and Malta. The agreement capped a nearly decade-long process of political and economic reform in the 10 countries. The EU determined that all 10 countries had established democratic governments that respect human rights and the rule of law. The 10 countries met a series of economic requirements that included limiting government subsidies to industry and opening their economies to foreign trade and investment.

The European Commission, the EU executive agency that led the negotiations, announced on October 9 that the 10 countries had made sufficient progress to be ready for membership by 2004. EU leaders endorsed that recommendation at a summit meeting in Brussels, Belgium, on Oct. 24 and 25, 2002. At a subsequent meeting in Copenhagen, Denmark, on December 12 and 13, EU leaders completed negotiations on the final issues, including farm subsidies and budgetary contributions. Under the agreement, the new members would become eligible for EU agricultural subsidies over a 10-year period. The EU also agreed to provide the 10 countries with $23 billion in development aid for roads, railroads, and other public works projects. The aid was crucial to most of the 10 countries, where individual incomes are less than half the average income in the 15 EU member countries.

The expansion, which must be ratified by the parliaments of all EU member nations and the 10 candidate nations, would be the largest in the history of the EU, which was founded in 1957 as the European Economic Community (EEC), a primarily economic association of six Western European countries. The 10 candidate nations would add 75 million people to the EU's existing population of 379 million and would increase the bloc's geographical area by 23 percent. The EU also agreed to accelerate negotiations with Bulgaria and Romania with the goal of achieving membership in 2007.

Relations with Turkey. The EU gave an indication in December 2002 that Turkey may eventually be considered for EU membership. The EEC first considered the possibility of Turkish membership in 1963, but the country's economic difficulties, periodic military *coups* (government overthrows), and poor human rights record prevented negotiations. The new Turkish government of Prime Minister Abdullah Gul, after taking office in November 2002, lobbied intensively to open negotiations. Turkey's bid won strong support from the U.S. government, which hoped that EU membership would strengthen democracy in Turkey and make it a model for other Islamic countries struggling to contain fundamentalism. However, many Europeans worried that admitting a predominantly Islamic and Asian country such as Turkey would stretch the EU too far and undermine its political cohesiveness.

EU convention. The task of governing an EU of 25 or more members preoccupied the group's leaders. They worried that future leaders would find it difficult to reach decisions on important economic and political issues without major changes to the bloc's governing procedures. A convention of senior EU political figures, who were appointed in 2001, met through much of 2002 to draft proposals for reform. The reforms included proposals for either a written constitution or a preamble to the EU's several hundred pages of governing treaties. The group suggested that a constitution would set out the bloc's guiding principles in clear and inspiring language, similar to the U.S. Constitution.

Other reform proposals included making decisions by a majority vote, rather than a unanimous one; strengthening links between the EU and national parliaments; and establishing a procedure for countries to withdraw from the EU. The convention was to revise its proposals during 2003, and EU governments were to agree to reforms in 2004, when the new members join the bloc.

NATO expands. The military alliance also

agreed to admit new members from Eastern Europe, a historic move that paralleled the EU's enlargement. At a summit meeting in Prague on Nov. 21 and 22, 2002, the leaders of the 19 existing NATO members agreed to start accession talks with 7 countries—Bulgaria, Romania, Slovakia, Slovenia, Estonia, Latvia, and Lithuania. The latter three, the so-called Baltic nations, were part of the Soviet Union before declaring their independence in 1990. The other four nations were former members of the Warsaw Pact, the Cold War alliance that grouped the Soviet Union and its Eastern European satellites. (The Cold War was a period of intense rivalry between Communist and non-Communist nations that lasted from 1945 to 1991.)

NATO leaders expected the accession talks to be completed in 2003 and the countries to join the alliance in 2004. The expansion would be the alliance's largest since it was founded in 1949. New members were last admitted in 1999, when NATO expanded into Poland, Hungary, and the Czech Republic.

NATO leaders also agreed to prepare the alliance for future missions, including possible operations outside of Europe. They agreed to create a NATO Response Force, which could quickly deploy land, sea, and air forces wherever needed. European members of NATO also committed to improving their military capabilities, particularly in areas such as air and sea lift, to make their forces more deployable. Years of defense cutbacks had reduced the ability of European members to fight alongside U.S. forces in areas such as Afghanistan, raising concerns about the future cohesion of the alliance.

The worst flooding in 150 years in Prague, capital of the Czech Republic, draws hundreds of people to the banks of the Vltava River in August. Torrential rains caused massive flooding throughout central Europe, killing at least 100 people and causing more than $20 billion in economic loss.

Politics shifted to the right in a number of European countries in 2002. In France, President Jacques Chirac, of the center-right Rally for the Republic, won reelection by an overwhelming margin in a May runoff against Jean-Marie Le Pen, leader of the extreme right-wing, anti-immigrant National Front. Voters in the Netherlands elected a coalition led by the center-right Christian Democratic Party and the List Pim Fortuyn, a new anti-immigrant party whose controversial leader was murdered one week before the May election. The government collapsed in October, however, because of divisions in List Pim Fortuyn. In Austria, the conservative People's Party of Chancellor Wolfgang Schuessel was reelected in November after its former coalition partner, the anti-immigrant Freedom Party, split into factions.

Bucking the trend to the right, the Social

Democratic governments of Goran Persson in Sweden and Gerhard Schroeder of Germany won reelection in September.

Economy. Europe's economy slowed sharply for a second straight year in 2002, and Germany and Italy came close to recession in the second half of the year. The region continued to feel the effects of the worldwide economic slowdown, because sharp falls in stock prices, worries about a possible war in Iraq, and high tax rates in many countries depressed consumer confidence. Unlike the United States, which cut taxes in 2001 to spur growth, many European governments with big budget deficits were unable to take strong measures to stimulate their economies.

European Commission economists estimated that economic output in the 12 EU countries that use the euro would grow by only 0.8 percent in 2002, down from 1.5 percent in 2001. Unemployment was expected to rise to 8.2 percent from 8.0 percent. The three EU countries that do not use the euro—Denmark, Sweden, and the United Kingdom—were expected to grow at a somewhat faster rate of just over 1.5 percent in 2002.

Battle over budget pact. The weak economy posed a severe test for the EU's ability to manage the euro. Under the 1997 Stability and Growth Pact, countries using the euro agreed to try to keep their budgets balanced and deficits below 3 percent of *gross domestic product* (GDP—the total value of goods and services produced in a year). EU economists wanted to avoid a situation in which a budget problem in one country could harm the currency shared by the other countries. However, as Europe's economy slowed in 2002, tax revenues fell and budget deficits increased.

In July, the new Portuguese government of Prime Minister Jose Manuel Durao Barroso announced that the country's deficit was 4.1 percent of GDP in 2001, much higher than previously reported. The government announced a package of budget cutbacks while the EU Commission, which enforces EU budgetary rules, started legal procedures that could lead to fines being imposed on Portugal.

In September 2002, the French government ignored an EU Commission recommendation to cut its deficit and introduced a budget for 2003 with a deficit projected to be 2.9 percent of GDP. The response marked the first time that an EU member country had openly flouted the bloc's budgetary rules. In October 2002, Germany announced that its deficit would exceed the 3-percent limit because of slow growth. This was a huge embarrassment for Europe's largest economy, which had once enjoyed the continent's strongest currency. Germany had insisted on the deficit rule before the euro was launched be-

Country	Population	Government	Monetary unit*	Foreign trade (million U.S.$)	
				Exports†	Imports†
Albania	3,152,000	President Alfred Moisiu; Prime Minister Fatos Nano	lek (138.30 = $1)	310	1,000
Andorra	69,000	Co-sovereigns bishop of Urgel, Spain, and the president of France; Prime Minister Marc Forne Molne	French franc & Spanish peseta	58	1,077
Austria	8,255,000	President Thomas Klestil; Chancellor Wolfgang Schuessel	euro (1.02 = $1)	63,200	65,600
Belarus	10,175,000	President Aleksandr Lukashenko	ruble (1,876.00 = $1)	7,400	8,300
Belgium	10,165,000	King Albert II; Prime Minister Guy Verhofstadt	euro (1.02 = $1)	181,400	166,000
Bosnia-Herzegovina	3,890,000	Chairman of the collective presidency Mirko Sarovic	marka (1.98 = $1)	950	2,450
Bulgaria	8,128,000	President Georgi Purvanov; Prime Minister Simeon Saxe-Coburg-Gotha	lev (1.99 = $1)	4,800	5,900
Croatia	4,460,000	President Stjepan Mesic; Prime Minister Ivica Racan	kuna (7.57 = $1)	4,300	7,800
Czech Republic	10,215,000	President Vaclav Havel; Prime Minister Vladimir Spidla	koruna (30.91 = $1)	28,300	31,400
Denmark	5,307,000	Queen Margrethe II; Prime Minister Anders Fogh Rasmussen	krone (7.58 = $1)	50,800	43,600
Estonia	1,368,000	President Arnold Ruutel; Prime Minister Siim Kallas	kroon (15.97 = $1)	3,100	4,000
Finland	5,193,000	President Tarja Halonen; Prime Minister Paavo Lipponen	euro (1.02 = $1)	44,400	32,700
France	59,411,000	President Jacques Chirac; Prime Minister Jean-Pierre Raffarin	euro (1.02 = $1)	325,000	320,000
Germany	82,286,000	President Johannes Rau; Chancellor Gerhard Schroeder	euro (1.02 = $1)	578,000	505,000
Greece	10,647,000	President Konstantinos Stephanopoulos; Prime Minister Konstantinos Simitis	euro (1.02 = $1)	15,800	33,900
Hungary	9,956,000	President Ferenc Madl; Prime Minister Peter Medgyessy	forin (247.89 = $1)	25,200	27,600
Iceland	286,000	President Olafur Grimsson; Prime Minister David Oddsson	krona (86.81 = $1)	2,000	2,200
Ireland	3,811,000	President Mary McAleese; Prime Minister Bertie Ahern	euro (1.02 = $1)	73,500	45,700
Italy	57,092,000	President Carlo Azeglio Ciampi; Prime Minister Silvio Berlusconi	euro (1.02 = $1)	241,100 (includes San Marino)	231,400
Latvia	2,305,000	President Vaira Vike-Freiberga; Prime Minister Einars Repse	lat (0.60 = $1)	2,100	3,200
Liechtenstein	34,000	Prince Hans Adam II; Prime Minister Otmar Hasler	Swiss franc	2,470	917

cause it mistrusted the ability of other EU countries to balance their budgets.

The difficulties prompted a vigorous debate about economic policy. France asked that the Stability Pact be modified. The president of the EU Commission, Romano Prodi, described the pact as "stupid" for being too inflexible. However, the European Central Bank, which sets interest rates for the euro countries, defended the budget rules as essential to maintaining confidence in the euro.

Corporate difficulties. European companies struggled with slow growth and falling stock prices in 2002. Major European stock markets fell by an average 30 percent during the year, more than those in the United States. Several major companies faced severe difficulties. Vivendi Universal, the French media group that owns the Universal movie studio and music company, fired Chairman and Chief Executive Jean-Marie Messier in July after the company lost $12 billion during the first six months of 2002, which pushed Vivendi close to bankruptcy. The new chairman, Jean-Rene

Country	Population	Government	Monetary unit*	Foreign trade (million U.S.$) Exports[†]	Imports[†]
Lithuania	3,647,000	President Valdas Adamkus;** Prime Minister Algirdas Mikolas Brazauskas	litas (3.53 = $1)	3,700	4,900
Luxembourg	438,000	Grand Duke Henri; Prime Minister Jean-Claude Juncker	euro (1.02 = $1)	7,600	10,000
Macedonia	2,048,000	President Boris Trajkovski	denar (62.66 = $1)	1,400	2,000
Malta	394,000	President Guido De Marco; Prime Minister Eddie Fenech Adami	lira (0.42 = $1)	2,000	2,600
Moldova	4,383,000	President Vladimir Voronin; Prime Minister Vasile Tarlev	leu (13.58 = $1)	500	761
Monaco	35,000	Prince Rainier III	French franc	no statistics available	
Netherlands	15,849,000	Queen Beatrix; Prime Minister Jan Peter Balkenende	euro (1.02 = $1)	210,300	201,200
Norway	4,505,000	King Harald V; Prime Minister Kjell Magne Bondevik	krone (7.48 = $1)	59,200	35,200
Poland	38,835,000	President Aleksander Kwasniewski; Prime Minister Leszek Miller	zloty (4.16 = $1)	28,400	42,700
Portugal	9,863,000	President Jorge Sampaio; Prime Minister Jose Manuel Durao Barroso	euro (1.02 = $1)	26,100	41,000
Romania	22,171,000	President Ion Iliescu; Prime Minister Adrian Nastase	leu (33,050.00 = $1)	11,200	11,900
Russia	146,376,000	President Vladimir Putin	ruble (31.71 = $1)	105,100	44,200
San Marino	28,000	2 captains regent appointed by Grand Council every 6 months	Italian lira	241,100	231,400 (includes Italy)
Slovakia	5,404,000	President Rudolf Schuster; Prime Minister Mikulas Dzurinda	koruna (42.84 = $1)	12,000	12,800
Slovenia	1,982,000	President Janez Drnovsek; Prime Minister Tone Rop	tolar (233.25 = $1)	8,900	9,900
Spain	39,567,000	King Juan Carlos I; President of the Government (Prime Minister) Jose Maria Aznar	euro (1.02 = $1)	120,500	153,900
Sweden	8,947,000	King Carl XVI Gustaf; Prime Minister Goran Persson	krona (9.27 = $1)	95,500	80,000
Switzerland	7,445,000	President Kaspar Villiger	franc (1.50 = $1)	91,300	91,600
Turkey	68,509,000	President Ahmet Necdet Sezer; Prime Minister Abdullah Gul	lira (1,666,666.67 = $1)	26,900	55,700
Ukraine	50,083,000	President Leonid Kuchma	hryvna (5.33 = $1)	14,600	15,000
United Kingdom	58,959,000	Queen Elizabeth II; Prime Minister Tony Blair	pound (0.64 = $1)	282,000	324,000
Yugoslavia	10,655,000	President Vojislav Kostunica; Prime Minister Dragisa Pesic	new dinar (61.71 = $1)	1,500	3,300

*Exchange rates as of Oct. 4, 2002, or latest available data.   [†]Latest available data.
**Lost a run-off election to Rolandas Paksas on Jan. 5, 2003; Paksas was scheduled to become president in late February 2003.

Fourtou, planned to sell $12 billion in assets to save the company.

Europe's television and telecommunications companies struggled in 2002 because of heavy debts incurred through expansion during the technology boom. Kirch Group, Germany's leading television company, filed for bankruptcy in the spring, with more than $6 billion in debts. The bankruptcy was the largest of a record number in Germany in 2002.

Deutsche Telekom AG of Germany reported a loss of $24.7 billion in the first nine months of 2002. Its chief executive, Ron Sommer, resigned and the company announced plans to cut 54,000 jobs. France Telecom removed its chief executive, Michel Bon, after reporting a first-half loss of $12.2 billion. The French government agreed in December to lend the company $9 billion to avert a bankruptcy. ☐ Tom Buerkle

See also various European country articles; **Disasters; Economics; Stocks and bonds; Turkey; Weather.**

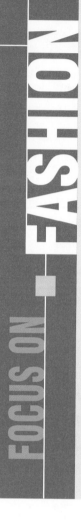

FOCUS ON FASHION

French fashion designer Yves Saint Laurent retires with a farewell show in Paris in January 2002.

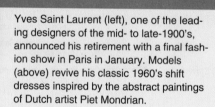

Yves Saint Laurent (left), one of the leading designers of the mid- to late-1900's, announced his retirement with a final fashion show in Paris in January. Models (above) revive his classic 1960's shift dresses inspired by the abstract paintings of Dutch artist Piet Mondrian.

Fashion in 2002 remained in its most unsettled state since the extremes of the 1960's, when hemlines moved thigh-high with the introduction of the miniskirt and then plunged to the floor with the maxiskirt. In 2002, fashion managed to avoid the extremes of the 1960's, primarily because women were not interested in bizarre colors and strangely cut garments. Unconcerned with trends, the contemporary woman primarily wanted comfort and dressed as she pleased. T-shirts, jeans, and sneakers, therefore, were considered appropriate for most occasions. Under these circumstances, fashion lost its cutting edge.

Women continued to buy clothes, of course, but unmoved by the dictates of changing fashions, they bought less. The fashion industry responded by promoting luxury clothing, which most women refused to buy. Instead, more women shopped at discount stores—Wal-Mart, Target, and Kohl's—which did relatively well in clothing sales for the year, compared with such traditional retail outlets as department stores. Women wanted to look smart but at a moderate price.

The business casual look spawned in the high-tech offices of California's Silicon Valley in the 1980's and 1990's continued to dominate men's fashion in the United States in 2002. Despite repeated announcements by clothing manufacturers that the business suit was making a comeback, many men continued to wear khaki trousers and open-neck shirts to offices.

Preadolescent girls, to the displeasure of many of their elders, copied the styles sported by pop-star entertainers, such as Jennifer Lopez and Britney Spears, and wore low-slung jeans that bared their navels. Boys and young men aped the style of rappers and hip-hoppers with baggy, low-rise jeans, a variety of fancy sneakers, and skull caps.

Model Carla Bruni reveals a contemporary Saint Laurent evening gown under a voluminous silk cape during the farewell show at the Georges Pompidou Center in Paris.

Designers. Leadership in the fashion industry changed in 2002. In the United States, Bill Blass, an industry leader for more than 50 years, died in June. He was widely known for his casual, understated, "American" style. Yves Saint Laurent, whom some critics regard as the most important *couture* (high fashion) designer of the last century, retired in January. The French designer revolutionized fashion in the 1960's with the introduction of trouser suits and tuxedos as evening wear. Oscar de la Renta left Balmain, the Paris-based fashion house, in 2002 after 10 years as designer of the couture collection. He said he would devote his attention to his ready-to-wear and accessories business based in the United States.

Miguel Adrover, Eric Bergere, Daryl Kerrigan, Olivier Theyskens, and Josephus Thimister—all young designers who had been heralded when they showed their first collections in the late 1990's—suffered major business reversals in 2002.

Industry experts blamed the failures on the overabundance of hot new designers and the difficulty of maintaining a strong creative identity season after season.

Consolidation. In 2002, small fashion companies continued to be consumed by huge conglomerates, which had the resources to adequately mass market products and streamline production costs. The Paris-based LVMH-Moet Hennessy Louis Vuitton led the trend through ownership of the products of such fashion houses and designers as Christian Dior, Marc Jacobs, Donna Karan, and Michael Kors. LVMH continued to show strong growth in 2002, despite the economic slowdown in the United States and Europe that began in 2001. Other conglomerates exerting a major influence on the fashion world in 2002 included Prada, the Italian luggage firm that expanded in the late 1990's to encompass clothing and shoe designers, and Gucci, the Italian manufacturer of luxury goods.

Fashion Walk of Fame. Contemporary designers added to the Fashion Walk of Fame on Seventh Avenue, in New York City's Garment District, in July 2002 included Stephen Burrows, Norma Kamali, Marc Jacobs, and Betsey Johnson. Perry Ellis, Mainbocher, Willi Smith, and Lilly Dache were honored *posthumously* (after their deaths).

□ Bernadine Morris

Finland continued in 2002 to suffer from the worldwide economic slowdown. The country's dependence on high-technology industries—especially mobile telephone equipment—became a liability because of the sharp decline in technology spending and a shakeout among Europe's heavily indebted telecommunications companies.

European Union economists estimated that Finland's gross domestic product, the value of all goods and services produced in a year, would grow by about 1.6 percent in 2002, up from 0.7 percent in 2001 but well below the average growth rate of 4 percent during the seven previous years. Unemployment was expected to increase to 9.3 percent from 9.1 percent in 2001.

Telecommunications. The slump in Europe's telecommunications industry hit Sonera Oy, Finland's national telephone company, in 2002. In July, Sonera wrote off 4.28 billion euros ($4.23 billion) of investments in licenses to provide so-called third-generation mobile telephone services in Germany and Italy. European telephone companies spent more than $100 billion in 2000 and 2001 for licenses to provide third-generation services, which allow users to download audio and video from the Internet on their mobile handsets. Telecommunications executives in 2002 remained unsure whether consumers would pay enough to make the services profitable. Sonera's write-off caused the company to post a loss of 2.8 billion euros ($2.7 billion) in the second quarter.

The loss proved embarrassing for the government of Prime Minister Paavo Lipponen after an anonymous book, published on the Internet in June, claimed his government had approved the company's investments. The government denied the claims, but the chancellor of justice, the government's watchdog, launched an investigation into the government's role in Sonera.

In March, Sonera announced the company was being acquired by the Swedish telecommunications company Telia AB for 7.5 billion euros ($7.3 billion). The deal was completed in November, creating the largest telephone company in Scandinavia.

Nuclear energy. The Finnish government in May approved the construction of a new nuclear power plant, the first to be built in Finland in more than 20 years. Proponents of the plant argued that it would reduce Finland's dependence on natural gas from Russia and cause less pollution. Opponents warned of the risk of an accident and the lack of any permanent storage for nuclear waste. Parliament approved the plant on May 24. Two days later, the Green Party quit Lipponen's government in protest. Lipponen's coalition retained a majority in parliament, though.

□ Tom Buerkle

See also **Europe; Sweden; Telecommunications.**

Food. On June 12, 2002, United States President George W. Bush signed the Public Health Security and Bioterrorism Preparedness and Response Act of 2002. The U.S. Congress had passed the act, the first major federal legislation to protect the nation against biological terrorism, in response to the terrorist attacks on the United States on Sept. 11, 2001. The law included provisions that gave the Food and Drug Administration (FDA) greater discretion to detain food when evidence showed that it presented a threat of serious adverse health consequences or death. The law also established record-keeping requirements for companies that manufacture, process, pack, transport, distribute, receive, hold, or import food.

Funding for bioterrorism protection was also included in the fiscal 2001-2002 Defense Appropriations Act, signed in January 2002. The act allocated $328 million in emergency funding for the U.S. Department of Agriculture (USDA), to strengthen such programs as the Food Safety and Inspection Service's monitoring and inspector training.

In February, the Food Marketing Institute (FMI), a Washington, D.C.-based industry trade association, launched a new Food Industry Information Sharing and Analysis Center in cooperation with the Federal Bureau of Investigation. The purpose of the center was to provide direct communication between law enforcement officers and the food industry to help identify and prevent terrorist threats to the U.S. food supply.

Food safety. The USDA and the Department of Health and Human Services announced in February that the government would double the number of U.S. cattle tested for bovine spongiform encephalopathy (BSE, or mad cow disease). The departments planned to complete 12,500 tests in fiscal 2002-2003, compared with 5,200 sampled in fiscal 2001-2002. BSE is a fatal brain disorder in cattle that scientists believe is related to a similar degenerative brain disease in humans called Creutzfeldt-Jakob disease. No cases of BSE have been discovered in the United States, though the disease has had a serious impact in Europe since the 1980's.

In July 2002, the Centers for Disease Control and Prevention (CDC) in Atlanta reported a number of illnesses and deaths caused by *Escherichia coli* (*E. coli,* a microorganism that is a common cause of food poisoning). The CDC traced the illnesses to fresh and frozen ground beef products made by ConAgra Beef Company of Greeley, Colorado. ConAgra recalled 19 million pounds (8.6 million kilograms) of meat nationwide. In September, FSIS announced new guidelines for the industry to help prevent *E. coli* contamination, including requirements that plants reexamine their food safety systems and establish steps to eliminate or reduce the risk of product contamination.

Bon Appetit:
The Legacy of Julia Child

On Aug. 19, 2002, the Smithsonian Institution's Museum of American History in Washington, D.C., added a unique exhibit to its collection of Americana—Julia Child's kitchen. The exhibit opened four days after Child's 90th birthday, which was celebrated with a series of events over several days.

Child, the author of numerous cookbooks, hostess of several enormously popular television cooking series, and teacher of the art of French cooking, donated the kitchen and its contents to the museum in 2001 after selling her house in Cambridge, Massachusetts, and returning to her native California. Museum officials dismantled the kitchen, which had been used as the set for Child's television shows for 45 years, catalogued some 1,200 objects—including counters, cabinets, cookbooks, and utensils—and recreated the room as an exhibit that was to be open to the public until 2004.

Child was born Julia Carolyn McWilliams in Pasadena, California, on Aug. 15, 1912. She earned a Bachelor of Arts degree from Smith College in Northhampton, Massachusetts, in 1934. During World War II (1939-1945), Child served as a clerk with the Office of Strategic Services, an intelligence agency of the United States government, where she met her future husband, Paul Child. The couple married after the war and moved to Paris, where Paul worked at the U.S. embassy.

While in France, Child attended the famed Le Cordon Bleu cooking school, where she became fascinated with French cooking. Together with two French women, she opened a cooking school of her own and wrote her first cookbook, *Mastering the Art of French Cooking,* which has sold more than 1 million copies. In 1961, the Childs returned to the United States and settled in Cambridge, where Paul Child designed the now-famous kitchen.

Child's long-running television cooking series—"The French Chef," "Julia Child & Company," "Cooking with Master Chefs," and others—greatly influenced American ideas about cooking and eating in ways that remain part of the culture today. Before Julia Child, the staples of the American diet were meat and potatoes. She popularized the idea of the kitchen as the "heartbeat of the household," even when entertaining. Most of all, her exuberant, good-humored approach to cooking helped viewers conquer their fears of exotic dishes and introduced countless Americans to such classics as French onion soup, puff pastry, and boeuf bourguignon. ■ Kristina Vaicikonis

In October, Wampler Foods Inc. of Philadelphia recalled all turkey and chicken deli products processed since May at a suburban plant. The products, which had been linked to more than 30 illnesses and 7 deaths in the Northeast, were suspected of being contaminated with *Listeria monocytogenes* bacteria. The recall involved about 27.4 million pounds (12.4 kilograms) of meat, the largest such recall in USDA history.

Organic. In mid-October, the USDA issued standards for use of the word "organic" in the marketing of food. The rules were designed to assure consumers that products carrying the organic label had been produced without pesticides, herbicides, hormones, antibiotics, irradiation, or bioengineering. Organic foods are also produced under humane conditions for animals.

Supermarkets. Wal-Mart Stores of Bentonville, Arkansas, was the top grocery retailer in the world in 2001, with $217.8 billion in sales and 4,504 stores, according to a survey published in June 2002 by the food industry trade journal *Supermarket News*. Wal-Mart led Carrefour of France, with $62.2 billion in sales and 11,338 stores, and Ahold of the Netherlands, with $59.6 billion and 9,082 stores. Kroger, of Cincinnati, Ohio, ranked number four with $50.1 billion in sales and 2,392 stores. ☐ Robert C. Gatty

See also **Agriculture.**

Football.

Football. Underdogs had their day in football in 2002. In college, the Ohio State University (Columbus) Buckeyes stunned the heavily favored University of Miami Hurricanes to win the national title with a thrilling 31-24 double-overtime victory in the Fiesta Bowl on Jan. 3, 2003, in Tempe, Arizona. In professional football, the New England Patriots scored one of the biggest upsets in National Football League (NFL) history in Super Bowl XXXVI, beating the favored St. Louis Rams 20-17 on Feb. 3, 2002, in New Orleans, Louisiana.

College. Ohio State capped an undefeated season by outlasting Miami in one of the most exciting title games in history. Miami tied the game with a field goal at the end of regulation and scored a touchdown in the first overtime. Ohio State answered with a score, sending the game into double-overtime. In the second overtime, Ohio State scored again, and their defense stopped Miami, giving the Buckeyes the victory.

In other major bowls, the University of Oklahoma (Norman) beat Washington State University (Pullman) in the Rose Bowl in Pasadena, California, and the University of Georgia (Athens) beat Florida State University (Tallahassee) in the Sugar Bowl in New Orleans, Louisiana, on Jan. 1, 2003. The University of Southern California (USC) defeated the University of Iowa (Iowa City) in the Orange Bowl in Miami, Florida, on January 2.

BCS works smoothly. With Miami and Ohio State both emerging from the regular season without a loss, there was no controversy surrounding their selection to play for the national title in the Fiesta Bowl. This marked the first time in three years that the formula used to determine the best football teams in the nation—the Bowl Championship Series (BCS)—was predictable. The BCS system takes into account polls of the media and coaches and computer programs that examine the difficulty of teams' schedules, their win-loss records, and "quality wins" against teams ranked in the top 15 of the BCS.

Bowl drama. While there was no controversy over the teams playing for the BCS title, there was drama in the selection of teams playing in other bowls. Organizers have some freedom in choosing teams that play in their bowls. Orange Bowl officials created a stir by selecting Iowa to play USC. The matchup pitted the co-champions of the Big Ten conference (Iowa) against the co-champions of the Pacific 10 conference (USC). As a result, the Rose Bowl, which usually hosts the champions of these conferences, was left with a less compelling matchup—Washington State of the Pacific 10 and Oklahoma of the Big 12.

The University of Notre Dame (South Bend) regained its reputation as a football powerhouse in 2002 after having suffered coaching turmoil and a 5-6 record in 2001. As a reward for a 10-2 record in 2002, Notre Dame was invited to play in the Gator Bowl in Jacksonville, Florida, which they lost to North Carolina State 28-6. However, Notre Dame's season could have ended on a much brighter note. Because Notre Dame finished fifth in the final 2002 BCS rankings, the team was eligible to play in the Rose, Sugar, and Orange bowls. Officials at some schools—especially USC, who had humiliated Notre Dame 44-13 during the regular season—feared that BCS officials would select Notre Dame ahead of a better team because of the large number of Notre Dame fans who could boost television ratings.

Milestones. The University of Iowa, which in 2002 clinched a share of its first Big Ten title since 1990, won 11 games for the first time in school history and went unbeaten in the conference for the first time since 1922.

The University of Nebraska (Lincoln), which lost the BCS title game to the University of Miami in January 2002, fell out of the Associated Press Top 25 on September 28 after being included on the list for 348 consecutive weeks dating back to 1981. Nebraska was dropped from the poll after losing to Iowa State (Ames). The defeat also marked the first time Nebraska had lost two consecutive regular-season games since 1976.

Heisman Trophy. USC quarterback Carson Palmer was named the winner of the 2002 Heis-

USC quarterback Carson Palmer wields the "jeweled shillelagh" trophy in celebration of his team's 44-13 defeat of the Notre Dame Fighting Irish on November 30. In December, Palmer was named the winner of the 2002 Heisman Trophy.

man Trophy on December 14. Palmer won over University of Iowa quarterback Brad Banks. Palmer received 242 first-place votes to Banks's 199.

NFL. In Super Bowl XXXVI, the Patriots jumped to a 17-3 lead over the Rams, who were favored by 14 points. The Rams, led by quarterback Kurt Warner, rallied to tie the game with just over one minute to play, but Tom Brady, the Patriots' second-year backup quarterback, marched his team to the Rams' 30-yard-line despite having no time-outs. Patriots kicker Adam Vinatieri won the game when he kicked a 48-yard field goal as time expired—the first time that the Super Bowl was decided on the final play of the game.

Play-offs. In the American Football Conference (AFC) wild-card play-offs, the Oakland Raiders beat the New York Jets 38-24 on January 12, and the Baltimore Ravens routed the Miami Dolphins 20-3 on January 13. The following weekend, New England edged Oakland 16-13 in Foxboro, Massachusetts, in a driving snowstorm. Leading by three points late in the game, Oakland appeared to have won when the team recovered a fumble by Brady with less than two minutes to play. However, referees reviewed video replays and, in a controversial decision, changed the call

The 2002 college football season

National champions

NCAA Div. I-A*	Ohio State	31	Miami	24
NCAA Div. I-AA	Western Kentucky	34	McNeese State	14
NCAA Div. II	Grand Valley State	31	Valdosta State	24
NCAA Div. III	Mt. Union	48	Trinity	7
NAIA	Carroll College	28	Georgetown	7

Bowl Championship Series games

Bowl	Result			
Fiesta*	Ohio State	31	Miami	24
Orange	USC	38	Iowa	17
Sugar	Georgia	26	Florida State	13
Rose	Oklahoma	34	Washington State	14

Other bowl games

Alamo	Wisconsin	31	Colorado	28
Capital One	Auburn	13	Penn State	9
Continental	Virginia	48	West Virginia	22
Cotton	Texas	35	Louisiana State	20
Gator	North Carolina State	28	Notre Dame	6
Hawaii	Tulane	36	Hawaii	28
Holiday	Kansas State	34	Arizona State	27
Houston	Oklahoma State	33	Southern Mississippi	23
Humanitarian	Boise State	34	Iowa State	16
Independence	Mississippi	27	Nebraska	23
Insight	Pittsburgh	38	Oregon State	13
Las Vegas	UCLA	27	New Mexico	13
Liberty	Texas Christian	17	Colorado State	3
Mobile (GMAC)	Marshall	38	Louisville	15
Motor City	Boston College	51	Toledo	25
Music City	Minnesota	29	Arkansas	14
New Orleans	North Texas	24	Cincinnati	19
Outback	Michigan	38	Florida	30
Peach	Maryland	30	Tennessee	3
San Francisco	Virginia Tech	20	Air Force	13
Seattle	Wake Forest	38	Oregon	17
Silicon Valley	Fresno State	30	Georgia Tech	21
Sun	Purdue	34	Washington	24
Tangerine	Texas Tech	55	Clemson	15

*Championship decided in the Fiesta Bowl on Jan. 3, 2003.

Conference Champions
NCAA Division I-A

Conference	School
Atlantic Coast	Florida State
Big 12	Oklahoma
Big East	Miami
Big Ten	Ohio State—Iowa (tie)
Conference USA	Texas Christian—Cincinnati (tie)
Mid-American	Marshall
Mountain West	Colorado State
Pacific 10	Southern California—Washington State (tie)
Southeastern	Georgia
Sun Belt	North Texas
Western Athletic	Boise State

NCAA Division I-AA

Conference	School
Atlantic 10	Northeastern—Maine (tie)
Big Sky	Montana—Idaho State—Montana State (tie)
Gateway	Western Illinois—Western Kentucky (tie)
Ivy League	Pennsylvania
Metro Atlantic	Duquesne
Mid-Eastern	Bethune Cookman
Northeast	Albany
Ohio Valley	Murray State—Eastern Illinois (tie)
Patriot	Fordham—Colgate (tie)
Pioneer	Dayton
Southern	Georgia Southern
Southland	McNeese State
Southwestern	Grambling State

All-America team (as chosen by the Associated Press)
Offense
Quarterback—Carson Palmer, Southern California
Running backs—Larry Johnson, Penn State; Willis McGahee, Miami
Wide receivers—Charles Rogers, Michigan State; Reggie Williams, University of Washington
Tight end—Dallas Clark, University of Iowa
Center—Brett Romberg, University of Miami
Other linemen—Shawn Andrews, Arkansas; Derrick Dockery, Texas; Jordan Gross, University of Utah; Eric Steinbach, University of Iowa
All-purpose player—Derek Abney, University of Kentucky
Place-kicker—Mike Nugent, Ohio State
Defense
Linemen—Tommie Harris, Oklahoma; Rien Long, Washington State; David Pollack, University of Georgia; Terrell Suggs, Arizona State
Linebackers—E.J. Henderson, Maryland; Teddy Lehman, Oklahoma; Matt Wilhelm, Ohio State
Backs—Mike Doss, Ohio State; Terence Newman, Kansas State; Troy Polamalu, Southern California; Shane Walton, University of Notre Dame
Punter—Mark Mariscal, University of Colorado
Player awards
Heisman Trophy (best player)—Carson Palmer, Southern California
Nagurski Trophy (best defensive player)—Terrell Suggs, Arizona State
Lombardi Award (best lineman)—Terrell Suggs, Arizona State

2002 National Football League final standings

American Conference

North Division

	W.	L.	T.	Pct.
Pittsburgh Steelers*	10	5	1	.656
Cleveland Browns*	9	7	0	.562
Baltimore Ravens	7	9	0	.438
Cincinnati Bengals	2	14	0	.125

East Division

	W.	L.	T.	Pct.
New York Jets*	9	7	0	.562
New England Patriots	9	7	0	.562
Miami Dolphins	9	7	0	.562
Buffalo Bills	8	8	0	.500

South Division

	W.	L.	T.	Pct.
Tennessee Titans*	11	5	0	.688
Indianapolis Colts*	10	6	0	.625
Jacksonville Jaguars	6	10	0	.375
Houston Texans	4	12	0	.250

West Division

	W.	L.	T.	Pct.
Oakland Raiders*	11	5	0	.688
Denver Broncos	9	7	0	.562
San Diego Chargers	8	8	0	.500
Kansas City Chiefs	8	8	0	.500

*Made play-offs

National Conference

North Division

	W.	L.	T.	Pct.
Green Bay Packers*	12	4	0	.750
Minnesota Vikings	6	10	0	.375
Chicago Bears	4	12	0	.250
Detroit Lions	3	13	0	.188

East Division

	W.	L.	T.	Pct.
Philadelphia Eagles*	12	4	0	.750
New York Giants*	10	6	0	.625
Washington Redskins	7	9	0	.438
Dallas Cowboys	5	11	0	.312

South Division

	W.	L.	T.	Pct.
Tampa Bay Buccaneers*	12	4	0	.750
Atlanta Falcons*	9	6	1	.594
New Orleans Saints	9	7	0	.562
Carolina Panthers	7	9	0	.438

West Division

	W.	L.	T.	Pct.
San Francisco 49ers*	10	6	0	.625
St. Louis Rams	7	9	0	.438
Seattle Seahawks	7	9	0	.438
Arizona Cardinals	5	11	0	.312

*Made play-offs

Team statistics

Leading offenses (yards gained)

	Yards	Per game
Oakland	6,237	389.8
Denver	6,090	380.6
Kansas City	6,000	375.0
Pittsburgh	5,952	372.0
Indianapolis	5,616	351.0

Leading defenses

	Avg. points against	Yards per game
Miami	18.8	291.0
Denver	21.5	301.6
Pittsburgh	21.6	302.2
Indianapolis	19.6	306.8
Tennessee	20.3	310.3

Team statistics

Leading offenses (yards gained)

	Yards	Per game
Minnesota	6,192	387.0
New York	5,826	364.1
Seattle	5,818	363.6
San Francisco	5,701	356.3
Philadelphia	5,604	350.3

Leading defenses

	Avg. points against	Yards per game
Tampa Bay	12.3	252.8
Carolina	18.9	290.4
Philadelphia	15.1	297.1
Washington	22.8	299.2
New York	17.4	309.3

Individual statistics

Leading scorers, touchdowns

	TD's	Rush	Rec.	Ret.	Pts.
Priest Holmes, Kansas City	24	21	3	0	144
Ricky Williams, Miami	17	16	1	0	102
Clinton Portis, Denver	17	15	2	0	102
LaDainian Tomlinson, San Diego	15	14	1	0	90

Leading kickers

	PAT made/att.	FG made/att.	Longest FG	Pts.
Adam Vinatieri, New England	36/36	27/30	57	117
Jason Elam, Denver	42/43	26/36	55	120
Sebastian Janikowski, Oakland	50/50	26/33	51	128
Mike Hollis, Buffalo	40/40	25/33	54	115

Leading quarterbacks

	Att.	Comp.	Yds.	TD's	Ints.
Rich Gannon, Oakland	618	418	4,689	26	10
Drew Bledsoe, Buffalo	610	375	4,359	24	15
Peyton Manning, Indianapolis	591	392	4,200	27	19
Tom Brady, New England	601	373	3,764	28	14
Trent Green, Kansas City	470	287	3,690	26	13

Leading receivers

	Passes caught	Rec. yards	Avg. gain	TD's
Marvin Harrison, Indianapolis	143	1,722	12.0	11
Hines Ward, Pittsburgh	112	1,329	11.9	12
Plaxico Burress, Pittsburgh	78	1,325	17.0	7
Eric Moulds, Buffalo	100	1,287	12.9	10

Leading rushers

	Rushes	Yards	Avg.	TD's
Ricky Williams, Miami	383	1,853	4.8	16
LaDainian Tomlinson, San Diego	372	1,683	4.5	14
Priest Holmes, Kansas City	313	1,615	5.2	21
Clinton Portis, Denver	273	1,508	5.5	15

Leading punters

	Punts	Yards	Avg.	Longest
Chris Hanson, Jacksonville	81	3,583	44.2	64
Tom Rouen, Pittsburgh/Denver	36	1,555	43.2	63
Brian Moorman, Buffalo	66	2,844	43.1	84
Shane Lechler, Oakland	53	2,251	42.5	70

Individual statistics

Leading scorers, touchdowns

	TD's	Rush	Rec.	Ret.	Pts.
Shaun Alexander, Seattle	18	16	2	0	108
Deuce McAllister, New Orleans	16	13	3	0	96
Terrell Owens, San Francisco	14	1	13	0	84
Tiki Barber, New York	11	11	0	0	66

Leading kickers

	PAT made/att.	FG made/att.	Longest FG	Pts.
Martin Gramatica, Tampa Bay	32/32	32/39	53	128
Jay Feely, Atlanta	42/43	32/40	52	138
John Carney, New Orleans	37/37	31/35	48	130
David Akers, Philadelphia	43/43	30/34	51	133

Leading quarterbacks

	Att.	Comp.	Yds.	TD's	Ints.
Kerry Collins, New York	545	335	4,073	19	14
Daunte Culpepper, Minnesota	549	333	3,853	18	23
Brett Favre, Green Bay	551	341	3,658	27	16
Aaron Brooks, New Orleans	528	283	3,572	27	15
Jeff Garcia, San Francisco	528	328	3,344	21	10

Leading receivers

	Passes caught	Rec. yards	Avg. gain	TD's
Randy Moss, Minnesota	106	1,347	12.7	7
Amani Toomer, New York	82	1,343	16.4	8
Joe Horn, New Orleans	88	1,312	14.9	7
Torry Holt, St. Louis	91	1,302	14.3	4

Leading rushers

	Rushes	Yards	Avg.	TD's
Deuce McAllister, New Orleans	325	1,388	4.3	13
Tiki Barber, New York	304	1,387	4.6	11
Michael Bennett, Minnesota	255	1,296	5.1	5
Ahman Green, Green Bay	286	1,240	4.3	7

Leading punters

	Punts	Yards	Avg.	Longest
Todd Sauerbrun, Carolina	104	4,735	45.5	67
Scott Player, Arizona	88	3,864	43.9	58
Sean Landeta, Philadelphia	52	2,229	42.9	63
Tom Tupa, Tampa Bay	90	3,856	42.8	71

to an incomplete pass, giving the Patriots new life. Vinatieri kicked a 45-yard field goal to send the game into overtime. New England later won when Vinatieri kicked a 23-yard field goal. The Pittsburgh Steelers eliminated Baltimore 27-10 on January 20. In the AFC title game, the Patriots defeated the host Steelers 24-17 on January 27.

In the National Football Conference (NFC) wild-card play-offs, the Philadelphia Eagles trounced Tampa Bay 31-9 on January 12 and the Green Bay Packers beat San Francisco 25-15 on January 13. In the next round, Philadelphia defeated the Chicago Bears 33-19 on January 19 and the St. Louis Rams routed Green Bay 45-17 on January 20. In the NFC title game, the Rams edged out Philadelphia 29-24 on January 27.

2002-2003 season. The NFL welcomed a new expansion team for the 2002-2003 season, the Houston Texans. To accommodate the team, the NFL shuffled its alignment, adding a fourth division to both the AFC and NFC and switching the Seattle Seahawks from the AFC to the NFC.

The San Diego Chargers, the New Orleans Saints, and the Atlanta Falcons proved to be the most surprising teams of the 2002-2003 NFL regular season. The Falcons were led by hugely talented second-year quarterback Michael Vick.

Fans were also surprised by the sudden collapse of the Rams, who began the season by losing the first five games, as quarterback Kurt Warner struggled with a hand injury. The Rams then went on a hot streak, winning five games in a row behind backup quarterback Marc Bulger. But the Rams lost two more games after Warner returned, ending the team's play-off hopes.

Payton records fall. Two records belonging to legendary Chicago Bears running back Walter Payton fell in 2002. On November 11, Oakland Raiders wide receiver Jerry Rice broke Payton's record of 21,803 career all-purpose yards. On October 27, Emmitt Smith of the Dallas Cowboys broke Payton's career *rushing* (yards running) mark of 16,726 yards. Payton, who played for the Chicago Bears from 1975 to 1987 and who was called "Sweetness" for his gracious attitude and sportsmanship, died in 1999 of liver cancer.

Unitas dies. Johnny Unitas, superstar quarterback for Baltimore who set 22 NFL passing records during a career that lasted from 1956 to 1973, died Sept. 11, 2002, at the age of 69. He was best known for keying the winning drive in overtime in the 1958 NFL championship game.

Canadian Football League. Montreal won its first Grey Cup in 25 years, defeating Edmonton 25-16 on Nov. 24, 2002. In the game, quarterback Anthony Calvillo threw a Grey Cup-record 99-yard touchdown pass to receiver Pat Woodcock.

☐ Michael Kates

See also **Deaths: A Special Report; Sports.**

France. President Jacques Chirac was reelected in 2002 after an extraordinary campaign during which an extreme right-wing National Front candidate gained more support than in any previous national election. Chirac also won a majority for his center-right party in subsequent parliamentary elections. The win gave him full political control, ending five years of so-called cohabitation between a centrist president and a Socialist government.

Political experts had expected the 2002 presidential election to be a repeat of the 1995 runoff between the country's two leading politicians, Chirac and Prime Minister Lionel Jospin, the Socialist Party leader. While Chirac succeeded in uniting the majority of center-right voters behind his candidacy with calls for tax cuts, tougher measures against crime and illegal immigration, and increased defense spending, Jospin failed to solidify the left. Several radical left-wing politicians mounted their own candidacies.

Shocking election result. In the first round of balloting on April 21, 2002, Chirac led the long list of candidates with 19.9 percent of the vote. Jean-Marie Le Pen, the National Front leader who campaigned for a halt to immigration, a crackdown on crime, and French withdrawal from the European Union (EU), came in second with 16.9 percent. Jospin trailed in third place with 16.2 percent. The result, which stunned French voters, forced a runoff between Chirac and Le Pen.

Le Pen had won a significant share of the vote in successive elections over 20 years by exploiting public concerns about immigration and crime. Mainstream parties refused to cooperate with him, however, because of his extreme views and racist rhetoric. He once dismissed the Nazi Germany death camps, where millions of Jews and other people were murdered during World War II (1939-1945), as a "detail" of history.

All major political parties, including the defeated Socialists, were united in their desire to stop Le Pen and called on their supporters to vote for Chirac in the second round of voting on May 5, 2002. Chirac was reelected with an unprecedented 82 percent of the vote, compared with 17 percent for Le Pen.

Right wins parliament. Jospin resigned as prime minister after the election and was replaced by Jean-Pierre Raffarin, a Chirac ally and regional leader from western France. Most members of the two main center-right parties, Chirac's Rally for the Republic and the Union for French Democracy, merged to create a new party, the Union for the Presidential Majority (UMP). In the two-round election in June, the UMP won a resounding majority of 355 seats in the 577-seat National Assembly, the lower house of the French parliament. The Socialists won just 140 seats.

Raffarin's government adopted a new budget in July that implemented Chirac's main economic pledges, including a 5-percent income tax rate cut and an increase in defense spending. The government also made it easier for companies to require employees to work more than 35 hours a week, a limit introduced by the Socialists over the protests of business.

Budget rift. The Raffarin government quickly clashed with the EU over its economic policies. The EU requires the 12 countries that use the euro to balance their budgets and to avoid running a deficit of more than 3 percent of gross domestic product (GDP—the total value of goods and services produced in a year). EU economists projected that the French deficit for 2002 would total just below 3 percent of GDP, and the 2003 budget called for no improvement in the deficit. Despite criticism from France's EU partners, Finance Minister Francis Mer said the government would stick with its budget priorities in 2003, the first time an EU government openly defied the rules governing the euro. The decision cast doubt on the EU's ability to coordinate economic policies in support of the currency.

Clash with United States. France provoked tensions with the administration of U.S. President George W. Bush in 2002 over issues related to terrorism and Iraq's weapons of mass destruction. For eight weeks, Chirac frustrated U.S. attempts to obtain a United Nations (UN) Security Council resolution that would automatically authorize the use of force if Iraq did not give full access to UN weapons inspectors. Chirac eventually agreed to a compromise resolution, which nevertheless freed the United States to use force if Iraq did not comply.

Economy. The French economy continued to suffer from the worldwide economic slump dur-

Demonstrators on May Day in Paris protest the candidacy of far-right presidential contender Jean-Marie Le Pen, who stunned French voters by beating Prime Minister Lionel Jospin to qualify for the runoff election. Incumbent President Jacques Chirac soundly defeated Le Pen in the May 5 runoff with an unprecedented 82 percent of the vote.

ing 2002. GDP was expected to grow by little more than 1 percent, down from 2 percent in 2001. Unemployment was expected to rise slightly in 2002, to about 8.8 percent, after declining steadily during the previous four years.

Several leading French executives were forced to resign during 2002, after their companies ran into financial difficulties. Chairman and Chief Executive Jean-Marie Messier of Vivendi Universal, one of the world's largest media companies, was dismissed in July. In March, Vivendi had reported a record loss of 13.6 billion euros ($13.3 billion) for 2001. In September 2002, shareholder pressure also forced the departure of Michel Bon, chairman and chief executive of France Telecom, the national telephone company and one of Europe's biggest mobile telephone operators. The company reported a loss of 12.2 billion euros ($12 billion) for the first half of 2002.   □ Tom Buerkle

See also **Europe; United Nations.**

Gardening. In 2002, gardeners across the United States noticed that trees were dying in unusually large numbers. Weakened by years of drought, acid rain, air pollution, and climate change, millions of trees succumbed to new insect pests and diseases.

In September, scientists reported that a fast-spreading new disease known as sudden oak death syndrome was attacking stands of redwoods in northern California. Researchers associated with the Berkeley and Davis campuses of the University of California identified the source of the disease, a microscopic fungus named *Phytophthora ramorum*. Sudden oak death syndrome kills 17 different tree and shrub species, including rhododendrons, northern red oak, and pin oak. In 2002, the disease was confined to the western United States, but botanists predicted it could easily spread.

Another potentially devastating tree pest, the emerald ash borer, claimed 100,000 native ash trees in five Michigan counties in 2002. An official of the Michigan Department of Natural Resources said in November that fully half of the ash trees in the area of infestation in southeastern Michigan had died or were dying. Experts suspected that the insect arrived in the United States 5 to 10 years earlier in packing material shipped with freight from Asia.

An exhibition of glass sculpture by master glass artist Dale Chihuly graces Chicago's Garfield Park Conservatory in 2002. The show drew nearly 500,000 visitors to a conservatory that for decades had been largely ignored by the public because of the deteriorating neighborhood in which it is located.

Several other tree pests wreaked havoc on their host species in 2002. A butternut canker of unknown origin was driving the butternut tree to the edge of extinction, experts warned. The hemlock woolly adelgid, an insect from Japan, was wiping out stands of hemlock trees in the eastern United States.

Another pest, the Asian longhorned beetle, kept cropping up in various locales in 2002. Despite aggressive eradication efforts, the beetle had spread throughout a 30-square-mile (77-square-kilometer) area of Chicago, a 120-square-mile (310-square-kilometer) area in New York City, and into several Long Island communities. In October, the beetle was found in Jersey City, New Jersey. Experts estimated that failure to control this pest, which attacks many kinds of hardwood trees, could result in $600 billion worth of damage to U.S. trees over the next 30 years.

Drought ranging from moderate to extreme affected nearly half of the lower 48 states of the United States in 2002, but conditions were worst in the Rocky Mountains and Great Plains in the West and along the middle Atlantic seaboard in the East. Garden columnists advised home gardeners to adopt principles of *xeriscaping* (dry gardening), including such strategies as using drip irrigation systems, conserving water, and planting native, drought-tolerant species. Varieties of *sedums,* drought-tolerant succulents, became the garden plant of choice for many sellers and consumers alike.

Sales. As excessive heat and drought lingered throughout the summer, nurseries and garden centers in cities as far-flung as Denver; Baltimore; and Charlotte, North Carolina, suffered sales slumps. At the same time, mass market retailers continued cutting further and further into sales of independent garden centers. According to the National Gardening Association of South Burlington, Vermont, discount garden sections at national chains and supermarkets increased their sales by 70 percent from 1997 to 2002 and were taking in 40 percent of all money spent on garden supplies in 2002. Independents that focused on specialty niches and service were most likely to survive, said industry experts.

Rare book sale. In October, the Chicago Botanic Garden announced it had purchased a major portion of the world-renowned rare book collection held by the Massachusetts Horticultural Society in Boston. The acquisition, which included about 4,200 rare books and journals, buttressed Chicago's claim of having one of the strongest natural history book collections in the world, botanical experts said.   □ Carol Stocker

See also **People in the news** (Chihuly, Dale).

Gas and gasoline. See Energy supply.
Genetic engineering. See Biology.

Geology. Two Belgian geologists reported in August 2002 that Earth's next ice age may not arrive for an extraordinarily long time. Most geologists believe that the last two *interglacials* (the warm periods between ice ages) before the current one each lasted about 10,000 years. Since the current interglacial, called the Holocene Epoch, began about 10,000 years ago, another ice age should be relatively soon. However, geologists Andre Berger and Marie-France Loutre argued that the Holocene may last 50,000 more years. They said that geologists had used outdated information for their estimates of how long interglacials last. Recent evidence indicates that previous interglacials lasted longer and were warmer than had been previously thought.

Berger and Loutre said that Earth's orbit around the sun varies over tens of thousands of years. Sometimes it is more circular and at other times more elliptical. The researchers said that Earth's orbit is now very close to circular and will remain so for thousands of years, resulting in stable temperatures. Berger and Loutre also claimed that global warming could have a more profound effect on the length of interglacials than had previously been thought. They reported that *greenhouse gases,* such as carbon dioxide, stay in the atmosphere for thousands of years and could cause long-term effects on climate. Greenhouse gases, which are generated by the burning of fossil fuels are blamed by many scientists for the gradual warming of the atmosphere.

Early life claims questioned. Two teams of geologists in 2002 cast doubt on scientific estimates of when life began on Earth, one of the most fundamental questions addressed by geologists. In March, geologists from institutions in the United Kingdom and Australia studied rocks from Australia that scientists in the late 1980's had thought contained fossilized evidence of bacteria that were 3.46 billion years old, among the oldest ever found. The British and Australian geologists who examined the rocks in 2002 said they had formed deep in the Earth, not on the floor of a shallow sea as had been proposed. They reported that the "fossils" were actually caused by chemical processes, not organisms.

In May, a second team of geologists reported that 3.8-billion-year-old *sedimentary rocks* (rocks formed in layers) from Greenland that scientists had thought contained fossilized traces of bacteria are actually not sedimentary rocks at all. Geologist Christopher Fedo of George Washington University in Washington, D.C., and geochronologist Martin Whitehouse with the Swedish Museum of Natural History in Stockholm reported that the layerlike formations were caused by temperature and pressure exerted on the rocks when they formed.

Lava spills into the Pacific Ocean from the Kilauea Volcano in Hawaii. The lava flow was named the Mother's Day flow for the day it began, May 12, 2002. While the spectacular flow attracted many tourists, scientists warned that the recent seismic activity may foreshadow a major eruption.

In 1996, geologists examining the Greenland rocks had claimed that the existence of a band of carbon in the rocks was evidence that early life-forms had once lived in the rocks. Over time, the scientists reported, the organisms decayed, leaving only the band of carbon as evidence of their existence. Fedo and Whitehouse, however, reported that the bands of carbon found in the rocks were not made by bacteria, but formed when heat and pressure deep within the Earth melted and twisted the rocks.

Volcanic hazard. A team of geologists led by Peter Cervelli of Stanford University in California reported in February 2002 that one entire side of Hawaii's Kilauea Volcano could collapse into the ocean. Such an occurrence, known as a flank collapse, would likely trigger a huge *tsunami* (wave of water) that could cause disastrous damage to coastal areas in Asia and North America. Cervelli's team estimated that such a tsunami would result in huge losses of life and property.

Cervelli and his team monitored data from satellites and sensors in 2000 and determined that a piece of Kilauea's southeast flank that was about 12 miles (20 kilometers) long, 6 miles (10 kilometers) wide, and nearly 3 miles (4.5 kilometers) thick had moved about 7 inches (18 centimeters) away from the rest of the volcano over the course of 36 hours. The scientists thought that the piece of volcano was moving along a *fault* (a weakness in the Earth's crust). This amount of movement was extraordinary because large sections of volcanos generally move only a few millimeters per year. Cervelli's team reported that the comparatively rapid movement of such a large piece of rock could be an indication that a major flank collapse could occur on Kilauea.

In a related study, Steven Ward, a geophysicist at the Institute of Geophysics and Planetary Physics at the University of California at Santa Cruz, reported in February that a flank collapse such as the kind proposed by Cervelli's team could produce a devastating tsunami. Ward used computers to determine that such a flank collapse would produce a wall of water as high as 100 feet (30 meters) by the time it struck California.

Magnetic south? Scientists in 2002 found that compass needles may start to point south sooner than expected. Compass needles point north because of the alignment of Earth's magnetic field. This alignment occasionally reverses for reasons scientists do not yet understand. In April, researchers at the Institute of Global Physics in Paris reported that they had obtained satellite data that indicated that some areas on Earth are already experiencing changing magnetic fields.   □ Henry T. Mullins

Georgia. President Eduard Shevardnadze faced mounting pressure from both inside and outside the country to resign in 2002. In June, Georgia's opposition parties turned municipal elections in Tbilisi, the capital, into a referendum on Shevardnadze's rule. Shevardnadze suffered an embarrassing setback as the propresidential Union of the Citizens of Georgia party won less than 3 percent of the vote and no seats at all on the city council. Political experts said the city's voters were responding to Shevardnadze's poor record in combating corruption, economic deterioration, and separatist movements in two provinces.

Relations with Russia also deteriorated during the summer of 2002, as Russian President Vladimir Putin threatened to invade Georgia in order to pursue terrorists allegedly hiding near the Russian border in Georgia's Pankisi Gorge. Putin claimed that rebels from Russia's breakaway region of Chechnya were receiving supplies from the Pankisi region and using the area as a base for launching terrorist operations inside Russia. In response, the Georgian army stepped up patrols in the area, and the Georgian government officially acknowledged Russia's "legitimate interests" in the region.   □ Steven L. Solnick

See also **Asia; Russia.**

Georgia. See State government.

Germany. The government of Chancellor Gerhard Schroeder won reelection in 2002, after a campaign that focused on the economy, immigration, and the possibility of war in Iraq. The Social Democratic Party's narrow victory defied a trend in other European countries, where conservative parties had replaced center-left governments.

Economic issues. Schroeder trailed his opponent, Edmund Stoiber, in opinion polls for most of 2002, because of the weakness of Germany's economy. The government forecast that growth would be stagnant at about 0.5 percent for the second straight year. Unemployment in 2002 rose to more than 9 percent of the labor force. The economic difficulties were particularly damaging for Schroeder, who had gained power in 1998 by promising to revive growth and reduce unemployment.

Stoiber, candidate for chancellor from the conservative opposition alliance Christian Democratic Union/Christian Socialist Union (CDU/CSU), was the premier of the southern state of Bavaria. The region enjoyed one of the strongest growth rates and lowest unemployment rates in Germany in recent years, and Stoiber promised to bring the same economic dynamism to the rest of the country. Neither candidate proposed the kinds of major changes in policy that economists claimed were needed to get the economy moving again.

Stoiber also campaigned on a promise to tighten German immigration laws and make it easier to deport illegal aliens, saying he did not want the country to become a multicultural society. Schroeder's government had passed a law allowing children of immigrants born in Germany to claim citizenship and establishing a quota for immigrants with skills useful in technology industries, but Germany's highest court blocked the law in December 2002.

Clash with U.S. Late in the election campaign, Schroeder promised to keep Germany out of a possible war in Iraq and criticized the policy of the United States toward Iraqi President Saddam Hussein. Schroeder's negative stance toward U.S. policy prompted the administration of U.S. President George W. Bush to suspend contacts with senior German officials for several weeks. However, Schroeder's position proved highly popular among German voters, who largely opposed a war.

Schroeder's Social Democrats won 38.5 percent of the vote in the Sept. 22, 2002, election, down from 40.9 percent in 1998. The party took 251 seats in the Bundestag, the lower house of parliament. The CDU/CSU alliance also won 38.5 percent, up from 35.1 percent in 1998, and captured 248 seats. Schroeder's coalition partner, the Greens, won 8.6 percent of the vote and 55 seats. The two parties controlled a slim majority in the Bundestag and formed a new government.

Economic policies. One of Schroeder's first moves after the election was to merge the economy and labor ministries and adopt measures designed to boost employment. The measures included reorganizing the government's labor offices and pressing the unemployed to take available jobs instead of claiming unemployment benefits.

Germany's budget difficulties threatened to slow the economy further, however. The government announced in October 2002 that the econom-

The German government welcomes U.S. President George W. Bush to Berlin in May by draping the Brandenburg Gate, undergoing restoration, with pro-U.S. coverings. The drapery, showing the White House as if it were directly behind the city's most famous landmark, was meant as a show of solidarity between German leaders and the United States.

ic slowdown was reducing tax revenues and pushing up the deficit. The government agreed on a package of spending cuts and tax increases designed to reduce the deficit by $11.6 billion. Even so, European Union economists forecast in November that Germany's deficit would grow to 3.8 percent of gross domestic product (GDP) in 2002 and 3.1 percent in 2003. (GDP is the value of all goods and services produced in a country in a year.) Both figures exceeded the limit of 3 percent for countries that use the euro. The commission began an excessive-deficit procedure against Germany in November, which could eventually lead to financial penalties.

Corporate losses. Germany's leading private television company, Kirch Group, declared bankruptcy in 2002, in what proved to be Germany's largest collapse of the year. Kirch filed for protection from creditors in the spring because of its inability to service more than $6 billion in debt. The group's owner, Leo Kirch, had become one of Germany's richest men by acquiring rights to thousands of films and major sporting events. However, his attempt to build a pay-television business in the late 1990's ran up enormous debts and failed to attract a wide customer base.

Economists estimated that a record 45,000 other German companies would declare bankruptcy in 2002, up from 34,000 in 2001. Babcock-Borsig, a major engineering firm, and the construction company Philip Holzmann AG were among the companies that failed, primarily because of the weak economy.

Germans protest President George W. Bush's Iraqi policy during his visit to Berlin in May. U.S.-German relations cooled considerably in September when Chancellor Gerhard Schroeder campaigned for reelection by denouncing Bush's hardline stance against Iraqi President Saddam Hussein.

Deutsche Telekom AG, the national phone company, reported a loss of $24.7 billion in the first nine months of 2002. Chief executive Ron Sommer, who had saddled Deutsche Telekom with massive debts through acquisitions at the peak of the technology boom, resigned in July and was replaced by Kai-Uwe Ricke, previously chief operating officer. Telekom also announced plans to cut more than 54,000 jobs—21 percent of the work force—by 2005.

Floods. Heavy rains in central Europe in August 2002 led to the worst floods in decades in parts of Germany. The hardest-hit areas were in eastern Germany, where the historic center of Dresden was inundated by the River Elbe. The floods caused an estimated $9 billion in damage. □ Tom Buerkle

See also **Disasters; Europe.**

Ghana. See **Africa.**

Golf. Eldrick "Tiger" Woods faltered midway through the 2002 professional golf season, after becoming the first golfer since Jack Nicklaus in 1972 to win the first two majors—the Masters and the U.S. Open—in a single season. With Woods not at his best, lesser-known golfers made names for themselves on the Professional Golfers' Association (PGA) tour.

On the Ladies Professional Golf Association (LPGA) tour, Karrie Webb became the first woman to win five different majors when she captured the Women's British Open (which replaced the du Maurier Classic) on Aug. 11, 2002. Webb had previously won the Nabisco Championship, the U.S. Women's Open, the LPGA Championship, and the now-defunct du Maurier Classic. On the Senior PGA circuit, a tour for pros over 50 years old, four men captured their first major championships.

PGA. At the Masters, held in April in Augusta, Georgia, Tiger Woods defeated Retief Goosen by three strokes to become the third golfer to win two Masters in a row.

Woods took control of the U.S. Open in Farmingdale, New York, by shooting a 2-under par 68 in the rain-soaked second round. He staved off Phil Mickelson on June 16 to win by three strokes.

Ernie Els of South Africa took the British Open on July 21 in Gullane, Scotland. Els's victory came after the first four-player play-off in British Open history. At the end of regulation play, Els, Thomas Levet, Stuart Appleby, and Steve Elkington were tied. Levet and Els survived the play-off and went to sudden death.

At the PGA Championship in Chaska, Minnesota, Rich Beem, a relative unknown, staved off an assault from Tiger Woods on August 18 to win the third tournament of his career and his first major. Woods birdied the final four holes, but Beem sank a critical 30-foot (9-meter) birdie putt on the 16th hole and went on to shoot 10-under par for the tournament.

LPGA. Annika Sorenstam of Sweden won the Nabisco Championship on March 31 in Rancho Mirage, California. She shot a final-round 4-under par 68 to beat countrywoman Liselotte Neumann by one stroke.

On June 9, South Korean Se Ri Pak, at age 24, became the youngest wom-

an to capture four majors, rallying from four shots down to beat Beth Daniel at the LPGA Championship in Wilmington, Delaware.

Juli Inkster edged out Sorenstam by two strokes to capture the U.S. Women's Open on July 7 in Hutchinson, Kansas. Inkster won $535,000, the largest purse in women's golf.

Karrie Webb won the Women's British Open on August 11 in Turnberry, Scotland. Webb shot

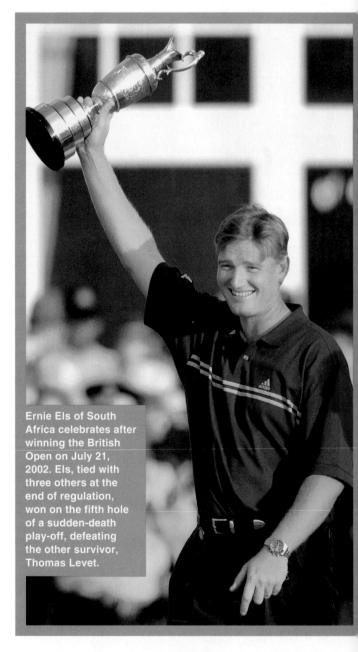

Ernie Els of South Africa celebrates after winning the British Open on July 21, 2002. Els, tied with three others at the end of regulation, won on the fifth hole of a sudden-death play-off, defeating the other survivor, Thomas Levet.

a 6-under par 66 in the final round to finish the tournament at 15 under par.

Senior PGA. Jim Thorpe won his first career major, taking the Tradition on April 28 in Superstition Mountain, Arizona. He sank a birdie putt on the first play-off hole to topple John Jacobs.

Fuzzy Zoeller won the Senior PGA Championship in Akron, Ohio, on June 9. Zoeller finished 2-under par for the tournament for his first win since joining the Senior tour earlier in 2002.

Don Pooley stunned Tom Watson on the fifth hole of their play-off to win the U.S. Senior Open June 30 in Mills, Maryland. Pooley, who had to win a play-off to even play in the tournament, became the first qualifier to ever win the event.

Stewart Ginn won the Senior Players Championship on July 14 in Dearborn, Michigan. Ginn finished 14 under par, winning by 1 stroke.

Ryder Cup. On September 30 the European team shocked the United States by winning the Ryder Cup, held in Sutton Coldfield, England. The Europeans put their best players in early matches and built up a large enough lead to win.

Snead dies. Sam Snead, 89, who won seven majors and a record 81 PGA titles, died on May 23. Snead had captured his final PGA victory in 1965 at the age of 52.   ☐ Michael Kates

See also **Deaths.**

Great Britain. See United Kingdom.

Greece. A left-wing terrorist group that staged numerous attacks against Western targets in Greece for nearly 30 years was broken up in 2002. The group was called November 17 after the date in 1973 when Greece's military government sent army tanks to crush a student protest. Until 2002, Greek authorities had never been able to uncover November 17 despite a string of attacks that had left 23 Greeks and foreign nationals dead since 1975. However, on June 29, 2002, an alleged member of the group, Savvas Xiros, was injured in a bungled bomb attack in the port city of Piraeus. Police searched his house and found a cache of weapons, including a revolver that had been used in several murders. Following evidence and tips from the public, police arrested 18 alleged members of November 17 in subsequent weeks. The group's fugitive leader, Dimitris Kourodinas, gave himself up on September 5.

Local elections. The conservative opposition party New Democracy scored significant gains in local elections in October. New Democracy won control of 45 municipalities, including Athens, the capital, and two major cities, Thessaloniki and Piraeus. The governing Panhellenic Socialist Movement (PASOK) won 30 municipalities. Voters in Athens also elected the city's first female mayor, Dora Bakoyianni, the daughter of former

Prime Minister Constantine Mitsotakis.

Economy. Greece enjoyed one of the strongest growth rates in the European Union (EU) in 2002. The low interest rates that accompanied Greece's adoption of the euro in 2001 and major investments for the Olympic Games—to be held in Greece in 2004—boosted the economy. EU economists forecast that *gross domestic product* (the value of all goods and services produced in a year) would grow by about 3.7 percent in 2002, down from 4.1 percent in 2001 but well above the EU average.

Prime Minister Costas Simitis's government approved social security reforms despite protests by public-sector workers in June 2002. The reforms raised the retirement age from 60 to 65 and were to gradually standarize pensions at 70 percent of salaries. In 2002, public-sector workers received pensions worth 80 percent of salaries. Private-sector workers got 60 percent. The changes were to avoid bankrupting the system.

The International Olympic Committee, after an inspection in April, expressed confidence for the first time that Greece would complete sports stadiums and transportation and housing facilities in time for the 2004 Olympics.

    ☐ Tom Buerkle

See also **Europe.**

Grenada. See Latin America.

Guatemala. President Alfonso Portillo Cabrera announced plans in September 2002 to cut the size of Guatemala's Army from 30,000 to 24,000 soldiers. Portillo said the military installations made vacant by these cuts would be converted into schools.

On October 3, a three-judge tribunal sentenced Colonel Juan Valencia, a former assistant director of Guatemala's presidential guard, to 30 years in prison for ordering the 1990 murder of Guatemalan anthropologist Myrna Mack. Mack had been investigating the military's alleged mistreatment of rural Guatemalans when she was stabbed to death.

In July 2002, Pope John Paul II canonized Pedro de San Jose Betancur (1619-1667), a Spanish missionary who worked in Guatemala, as Central America's first saint during a Mass in Guatemala City, the capital. Also at the Mass, Guatemalan Archbishop Rodolfo Quezada pronounced the late Guatemalan bishop Juan Jose Gerardi a martyr. Gerardi was bludgeoned to death in 1998 after blaming the military for killing vast numbers of noncombatants during Guatemala's civil war (1960-1996).   ☐ Nathan A. Haverstock

See also **Latin America; Roman Catholic Church.**

Guinea. See Africa.

Guyana. See Latin America.

Haiti. In September 2002, the Organization of American States (OAS), an association of 35 nations in North and South America, called on international financial institutions to release $500 million in aid for Haiti. The institutions had frozen the aid after international observers had judged Haitia's 2000 elections to be fraudulent. The OAS also called for the creation of an electoral council to ensure the full participation of all opposition parties in new parliamentary elections in 2003. Haitian President Jean-Bertrand Aristide said he supported the formation of such a council.

In August 2002, gunmen loyal to Amiot Metayer, a former Aristide ally who had turned against the president, crashed a tractor through the wall of a prison in northern Haiti, freeing Metayer and more than 150 other inmates.

On October 29, police near Key Biscayne, Florida, apprehended about 200 Haitians who swam to shore after their wooden freighter ran aground. Haitian-American groups condemned the U.S. government for holding the Haitians in detention and allegedly making it difficult for them to obtain *asylum* (refuge) in the United States.   □ Nathan A. Haverstock

See also **Latin America.**

Harness racing. See **Horse racing.**

Hawaii. See **State government.**

Health care issues. The United States Congress continued in 2002 to debate how to help the elderly afford expensive prescription drugs. In his State of the Union Address on January 29, U.S. President George W. Bush urged Congress to pass legislation that would make major changes in the Medicare program, including creating a drug benefit for lower-income senior citizens. Critics complained that the program would be underfunded and did not address the problem of rising prescription drug prices.

The Republican-controlled House of Representatives narrowly passed a bill in June that would help Medicare beneficiaries purchase prescription drug coverage from private insurance companies. The plan would require seniors to pay limited fees for such coverage and would provide free coverage for lower-income seniors. The federal government would pay the remaining costs.

In July, the Democrat-controlled Senate defeated the Senate version of the House proposal. The Senate also defeated a bill sponsored by Democrats that would have required the federal government to bear most of the cost of prescription drugs. Several other drug benefit proposals were also defeated.

The Bush administration announced new federal rules in October that widened the availability of cheaper, generic versions of name-brand drugs. The rules limited the length of time pharmaceutical manufacturers could keep generic versions of their products off the market. After Republicans gained control of both houses in the November 2002 elections, political experts predicted that Congress would pass some kind of a prescription drug bill in 2003.

Privacy. In August 2002, the Bush administration issued new regulations governing the privacy of personal medical records. The new rules allowed patients access to their own medical records if those records are stored electronically. However, the new rules relaxed stricter regulations imposed by former President Bill Clinton, allowing personal medical information to be used by insurers, researchers, law enforcement agencies, and others without the patient's permission. The new rules also allowed physicians to accept money from drug manufacturers to send promotional materials to patients based on information in their records. Health care providers and insurers praised the new rules. Privacy advocates condemned them.

The uninsured. In September, the U.S. Census Bureau reported that the number of U.S. citizens without health insurance had risen in 2001 to 41.2 million, an increase of 1.4 million over 2000. Census data showed that 14.6 percent of the U.S. population lacked health insurance in 2001. The Institute of Medicine, a research group located in Washington, D.C., issued a report in May 2002 estimating that 18,000 uninsured people in the United Staates die each year because they cannot obtain adquate health care.

Health care costs. In March, the federal Centers for Medicare and Medicaid Services (CMS) in Baltimore issued a report predicting that total U.S. health care spending would double by 2011, reaching $2.8 trillion per year. The report also stated that health care expenditures climbed in 2001 to 14 percent of the nation's *gross domestic product* (the value of all goods and services produced in a country in a given year). The CMS estimated an annual growth in spending of 7.3 percent until 2011, pushing annual per-person spending on health care costs in 2011 to $9,216. Experts warned that the increase would devastate government health care programs and private insurance providers.

Surgeon general. In March 2002, President Bush nominated Arizona trauma surgeon and Tucson sheriff's SWAT team member Richard Carmona as U.S. Surgeon General. He was confirmed unanimously by the Senate in July, despite some controversy surrounding his professional history and views on gun control.   □ Emily Friedman

See also **Drugs; Medicine; Public health and safety.**

Hobbies. See **Toys and games.**

National Hockey League standings

Western Conference

Central Division	W.	L.	T.	†OTL.	Pts.
Detroit Red Wings*	51	17	10	4	116
St. Louis Blues*	43	27	8	4	98
Chicago Blackhawks*	41	27	13	1	96
Nashville Predators	28	41	13	0	69
Columbus Blue Jackets	22	47	8	5	57
Northwest Division					
Colorado Avalanche*	45	28	8	1	99
Vancouver Canucks*	42	30	7	3	94
Edmonton Oilers	38	28	12	4	92
Calgary Flames	32	35	12	3	79
Minnesota Wild	26	35	12	9	73
Pacific Division					
San Jose Sharks*	44	27	8	3	99
Los Angeles Kings*	40	27	11	4	95
Phoenix Coyotes*	40	27	9	6	95
Dallas Stars	36	28	13	5	90
Anaheim Mighty Ducks	29	42	8	3	69

Eastern Conference

Northeast Division	W.	L.	T.	OTL.	Pts.
Boston Bruins*	43	24	6	9	101
Toronto Maple Leafs*	43	25	10	4	100
Ottawa Senators*	39	27	9	7	94
Montreal Canadiens*	36	31	12	3	87
Buffalo Sabres	35	35	11	1	82
Atlantic Division					
Philadelphia Flyers*	42	27	10	3	97
New York Islanders*	42	28	8	4	96
New Jersey Devils*	41	28	9	4	95
New York Rangers	36	38	4	4	80
Pittsburgh Penguins	28	41	8	5	69
Southeast Division					
Carolina Hurricanes*	35	26	16	5	91
Washington Capitals	36	33	11	2	85
Tampa Bay Lightning	27	40	11	4	69
Florida Panthers	22	44	10	6	60
Atlanta Thrashers	19	47	11	5	54

*Made play-offs   †Overtime losses

Stanley Cup champions—Detroit Red Wings
(defeated Carolina Hurricanes, 4 games to 1)

Leading scorers	Games	Goals	Assists	Pts.
Jarome Iginla, Calgary	82	52	44	96
Markus Naslund, Vancouver	81	40	50	90
Todd Bertuzzi, Vancouver	72	36	49	85
Mats Sundin, Toronto	82	41	39	80
Joe Sakic, Colorado	82	26	53	79
Jaromir Jagr, Washington	69	31	48	79

Leading goalies (26 or more games)	Games	Goals against	Avg.
Patrick Roy, Colorado	63	122	1.94
Roman Cechmanek, Philadelphia	46	89	2.05
Marty Turco, Dallas	31	53	2.09
Jose Theodore, Montreal	67	136	2.11
J. Giguere, Anaheim	53	111	2.13

Awards
Adams Award (coach of the year)—Bob Francis, Phoenix
Calder Trophy (best rookie)—Dany Heatley, Atlanta
Hart Trophy (most valuable player)—Jose Theodore, Montreal
Jennings Trophy (goalkeeper on team with fewest goals against)—Patrick Roy, Colorado
Lady Byng Trophy (sportsmanship)—Ron Francis, Carolina
Masterton Trophy (perseverance, dedication to hockey)—Saku Koivu, Montreal
Norris Trophy (best defenseman)—Nicklas Lidstrom, Detroit
Pearson Award (best player as voted by NHL players)—Jarome Iginla, Calgary
Ross Trophy (leading scorer)—Jarome Iginla, Calgary
Selke Trophy (best defensive forward)—Michael Peca, New York Islanders
Smythe Trophy (most valuable player in Stanley Cup)—Nicklas Lidstrom, Detroit
Vezina Trophy (best goalkeeper)—Jose Theodore, Montreal

Hockey. The Detroit Red Wings routed the surprisingly successful Carolina Hurricanes 4 games to 1 to take the National Hockey League's (NHL) 2001-2002 Stanley Cup. The NHL season was marred by the death of a 13-year-old fan who was struck in the head by a puck.

Season. In the Western Conference, Detroit rolled to the league's best record in the regular season, posting 51 wins and 116 points to win the Central Division. The Boston Bruins outgunned the Toronto Maple Leafs to win the Northeast by one point. In the Eastern Conference, Boston led with 43 wins. Colorado and San Jose won their divisions with 99 points. Philadelphia captured the Atlantic Division with 97 points, while Carolina won the Southeast Division with 91 points.

Play-offs. Detroit advanced to the Stanley Cup finals after a hard-fought seven-game series with Colorado for the Western Conference title. Detroit trailed 3 games to 2 but took the last two games to win the series. Detroit had defeated Vancouver 4 games to 2 in the first round and beaten St. Louis 4 games to 1 in the semifinals.

In the Eastern Conference, Carolina reached the finals by beating Toronto 4 games to 2, winning three games in overtime. Carolina had beaten New Jersey 4 games to 2 in the first round, then defeated Montreal 4 games to 2 in the semifinals. The Red Wings lost the opening game of

Detroit Red Wings defenseman Nicklas Lidstrom admires the Stanley Cup after receiving the Conn Smythe Trophy for being the most valuable player in the NHL play-offs on June 13. Detroit captured the Stanley Cup by beating the Carolina Hurricanes 4 games to 1.

the finals 3-2 in overtime but won the next four games, clinching the Cup in Detroit on June 13.

Fan death. On March 18, Brittanie Cecil of West Alexander, Ohio, became the first NHL spectator to die from being hit by a puck. Cecil was hit in the head by a deflected slapshot at a March 16 Columbus Blue Jackets home game. The puck caused her head to snap back, damaging an artery in her neck and causing internal bleeding. In June, the NHL required teams to install nets behind the goals and to raise the rinkside glass shields to a minimum of 5 feet (1.5 meters). The measures were implemented in late 2002.

Retirements. Detroit Red Wings coach Scotty Bowman retired in June after winning an NHL-record ninth Stanley Cup as head coach.

Dominik Hasek, star goaltender with Detroit, also retired after the Stanley Cup finals. Hasek won six Vezina Trophies as the league's top goaltender and several other awards.

World championships. Slovakia edged Russia 4-3 on May 11 in Goteborg, Sweden, to win the nation's first world title.

College. The University of Minnesota topped Maine 4-3 in overtime on April 6 in St. Paul, Minnesota, to win its first men's college hockey title since 1979. ☐ Michael Kates

See also **Sports.**

Honduras. See **Latin America.**

Horse racing. War Emblem, under the guidance of famed trainer Bob Baffert, became the 16th horse in racing history to win the first two races in the 2002 Triple Crown—the Kentucky Derby and the Preakness Stakes—only to lose the third, the Belmont Stakes. Also in 2002, three men were charged in the largest case of bettor fraud in racing history after allegedly rigging $3 million worth of bets on the Breeders' Cup races in October.

Three-year-olds. On May 4, War Emblem, a 21 to 1 longshot, triumphed at the Kentucky Derby in Louisville. War Emblem then won the Preakness Stakes at Pimlico Race Course in Baltimore on May 18. His quest for the Triple Crown was dashed on June 8, at Elmont, New York, when Sarava won the Belmont Stakes at 70-to-1 odds, the longest shot to ever win the race.

International. On March 23, Street Cry won the biggest purse in thoroughbred racing, $3.6 million, in a four-length victory at the Dubai World Cup in the United Arab Emirates. High Chaparral became the 15th horse to win both the English and Irish derbies. He captured the English Derby on June 8 in Epsom, England, and won the Irish Derby on June 30 at the Curragh Racecourse in Kildare, Ireland.

Bettor fraud. Three men were charged on November 12 in connection with more than $3

Major horse races of 2002		

Thoroughbred racing

Race	Winner	Value to Winner
Atto Mile (Canada)	Good Journey	$600,000
Belmont Stakes	Sarava	$600,000
Blue Grass Stakes	Harlan's Holiday	$465,000
Breeders' Cup Classic	Volponi	$2,080,000
Breeders' Cup Distaff	Azeri	$1,040,000
Breeders' Cup Filly & Mare Turf	Starine	$665,000
Breeders' Cup Juvenile	Vindication	$556,400
Breeders' Cup Juvenile Fillies	Storm Flag Flying	$520,000
Breeders' Cup Mile	Domedriver	$556,400
Breeders' Cup Sprint	Orientate	$592,800
Breeders' Cup Turf	High Chaparral	$1,258,400
Canadian International Stakes	Ballingarry	$900,000
Dubai World Cup (United Arab Emirates)	Street Cry	$3,600,000
Derby Stakes (United Kingdom)	High Chaparral	$1,244,000
Haskell Invitational Handicap	War Emblem	$600,000
Hollywood Gold Cup	Sky Jack	$450,000
Irish Derby (Ireland)	High Chaparral	$714,823
Jockey Club Gold Cup	Evening Attire	$600,000
Kentucky Derby	War Emblem	$875,000
Kentucky Oaks	Farda Amiga	$300,000
King George VI and Queen Elizabeth Diamond Stakes (United Kingdom)	Golan	$676,021
Oaklawn Handicap	Kudos	$300,000
Pacific Classic Stakes	Came Home	$600,000
Preakness Stakes	War Emblem	$650,000
Prix de l'Arc de Triomphe (France)	Marienbard	$895,772
Santa Anita Derby	Came Home	$450,000
Santa Anita Handicap	Milwaukee Brew	$600,000
Spiral Stakes	Perfect Drift	$382,160
Stephen Foster Handicap	Street Cry	$516,615
Travers Stakes	Medaglia d'Oro	$600,000

Harness racing

Race	Winner	Value to Winner
Cane Pace	Art Major	$369,188
Hambletonian	Chip Chip Hooray	$500,000
Kentucky Futurity	Like a Prayer	$202,000
Little Brown Jug	Million Dollar Cam	$309,312
Meadowlands Pace	Mach Three	$500,000
Messenger Stakes	Allamerican Ingot	$217,175
Woodrow Wilson	Allamerican Native	$325,000
Yonkers Trot	Bubba Dunn	$169,372

Sources: *The Blood Horse Magazine* and U.S. Trotting Association

million in fraudulent bets made during the Breeders' Cup races on October 26. Derrick Davis, Christopher Harn, and Glen DaSilva allegedly conspired to place off-track bets that were altered after the races to reflect the winners before being officially entered. The three allegedly pulled off the scam—the biggest in racing history—using Harn's position as a programmer with a computer company handling the bets.

Harness racing. Two horses in 2002 broke the record for fastest mile at a trot. On August 2, Victory Tilly won the Nat Ray Final at the Meadow-

War Emblem crosses the finish line to win the Preakness Stakes at Pimlico Race Course in Baltimore on May 18. War Emblem had taken the Kentucky Derby on May 4 but failed to capture the fabled Triple Crown by losing the Belmont Stakes on June 8.

lands in East Rutherford, New Jersey, in 1 minute, 50.4 seconds, breaking a 1994 record. On October 26, Allamerican Ingot won the Messenger Stakes, the final leg of the Pacing Triple Crown, at the Meadows in Meadow Lands, Pennsylvania, in 1 minute, 50.3 seconds. In the first two legs of the Pacing Triple Crown, Art Major captured the Cane Pace on September 2 and Million Dollar Cam took the Little Brown Jug on September 19. On August 3, Chip Chip Hooray held off Like a Prayer to capture the $1 million Hambletonian at the Meadowlands.

Seattle Slew dies. Seattle Slew, who had been the last living Triple Crown winner, died in his sleep on May 7 at the age of 28. His death came 25 years to the day after he had captured the Kentucky Derby en route to winning the 1977 Triple Crown. □ Michael Kates

Hospital. See Health care issues.
Housing. See Building and construction.

Houston. The revelation of massive fraud and highly questionable accounting practices at Enron Corp., formerly the world's largest energy trading company and Houston's largest corporation, cast a shadow over economic life in Houston in 2002. Enron's spectacular collapse in late 2001 set off a chain of events that hobbled the local economy. More than 5,000 Enron employees lost their jobs in December 2001. In addition, Dynegy and Reliant Energy, two other large Houston-based energy companies, laid off several thousand employees in 2002. Houston experienced a net loss of jobs during the year for the first time in a decade.

Investigations. Houston became the center of multiple federal investigations and court trials in 2002, all related to the Enron collapse. A jury in a federal district court in Houston in June found the Chicago-based accounting firm Arthur Andersen guilty of obstruction of justice for shredding Enron documents. Federal investigators also pursued possible wrongdoing on the part of Enron corporate officers. On October 31, a Houston grand jury indicted Enron's former chief financial officer, Andrew Fastow, on 78 charges, including fraud, money laundering, and conspiracy. Federal law enforcement agents also investigated Enron's former chief executive officer, Jeffrey Skilling, and its former chairman, Kenneth Lay.

Remaining Enron executives sought to reorganize the company into a smaller, profitable entity but instead watched as most of the company's assets were sold off to the highest bidder. Legal fees in the Enron case mounted to $300 million by late 2002, shattering all previous corporate records.

Football. On September 8, Houston's new football team, the Houston Texans, upset the Dallas Cowboys 19-10. The Texans' victory in their first regular season game marked only the second time that an expansion team had won its first official game. The Minnesota Vikings had won their first regular-season game in 1961. The Texans' owner, Bob McNair, won the expansion team in a 1999 bidding war with Los Angeles. The new team was quickly accepted by fans and sold out its 2002-2003 season ticket allotment.

The Texans played to a sellout crowd in the new Reliant Stadium. The $449-million stadium, which officially opened on Aug. 16, 2002, seats 69,500 people and features a fully retractable roof. Reliant Stadium dwarfs the neighboring Houston Astrodome. The Astrodome, which was once a state-of-the-art sports showplace and the home of Major League Baseball's Astros, was left without a regular tenant in 2002. The Astrodome's owners said they had no immediate plans to demolish the now-eclipsed stadium.

Basketball. The Houston Rockets basketball team acquired a new player in 2002—the towering Chinese basketball star Yao Ming. At 7 feet, 5 inches (2.27 meters), Yao Ming soon matched his immense presence on the court with a comparable presence off court. A phenomenon dubbed "Yaomania" swept Houston as the athlete's likeness appeared on billboards around the city, fans mobbed him for autographs, and Rockets games regularly sold out.

Yao's presence on the Rockets team also raised Houston's profile within Yao's home country, the People's Republic of China, where his fame was compared with that of Michael Jordan in the United States. At least 30 Rockets games were scheduled to be broadcast on Chinese television during the 2002–2003 season.

West Nile virus. Houston health officials reported more than 90 cases of West Nile virus and at least 4 deaths in 2002. Experts said that a rainy summer in the Houston area spawned a large population of mosquitoes, which spread the virus from migrating birds to people.

At least two Houston men who received donated blood were infected by the West Nile virus. Their cases helped confirm health officials' suspicions that the disease could be spread by means of blood transfusions. □ Eric Berger

See also **Basketball; City; Courts; Economics; Football; Public health and safety.**

Human rights. The United States government made combating racism and discrimination against Muslims and people of Middle Eastern descent a top priority in 2002. Government authorities reported that many Middle Easterners and Muslims in the United States had been unfairly discriminated against or threatened in the wake of the terrorist attacks on the United States on Sept. 11, 2001, which were carried out by Islamic extremists.

In July 2002, officials at the U.S. Department of Justice Civil Rights Division reported that federal authorities had investigated about 380 incidents of violence or threats against Arab Americans and other Muslims since the attacks. In August, the Justice Department reported that more than 70 cases connected to anti-Arab or anti-Muslim attacks were being prosecuted against about 80 people under state laws. Federal charges were filed against 12 people in 10 other cases.

In July, the U.S. Commission on Civil Rights, an independent government agency that works to guarantee the civil rights of minority groups, reaffirmed a commitment to protecting the rights of all U.S. citizens, regardless of religion. Commission Chairperson Mary Frances Berry said, "Maintaining a secure homeland does not justify discrimination against Arab Americans and others today, any more than World War II (1939-1945) justified the internment of innocent Japanese Americans over a half century ago."

Church bombing verdict. An Alabama jury in May 2002 convicted former Ku Klux Klan member Bobby Frank Cherry of first-degree murder for his role in a 1963 church bombing that killed four African American girls. The Ku Klux Klan is a group of white secret societies whose members oppose the advancement of blacks, Jews, and other minority groups. Cherry, who maintained his innocence during the trial, was sentenced to life in prison. Historians have described the bombing at Birmingham's 16th Street Baptist Church as a key event of the civil rights era that gave momentum to passage of various civil rights laws.

Cherry was one of four suspects in the case. One of the other suspects, Robert Chambliss, had been convicted of murder for his role in the bombing in 1977 and died in prison in 1985. A third suspect, Thomas Blanton, Jr., was convicted of murder in 2001 for his part in the bombing and was sentenced to life in prison. A fourth suspect died in 1994 without being charged.

School admissions. The U.S. Court of Appeals for the Sixth Circuit in Cincinnati, Ohio, ruled in May 2002 that colleges and graduate schools may consider race in developing admissions policies in order to ensure a "critical mass"

of black and Hispanic students. However, colleges cannot adopt strict quotas. The federal appeals court upheld admissions policies set by the University of Michigan Law School in Ann Arbor after a federal district court ruled in 2001 that the admissions policy was unconstitutional.

Civil rights commission. District Court Judge Gladys Kessler ruled in February 2002 that U.S. President George W. Bush could not appoint a new member to the U.S. Commission on Civil Rights because there were no vacancies. The Bush administration had attempted to shorten the term of Commissioner Victoria Wilson, who was appointed by former President Bill Clinton in January 2000 to replace a commissioner who had died. Kessler ruled that Wilson was entitled to serve a full six-year term and was not appointed only to serve out the two years left of the late commissioner's term.

Human rights commission. The United States regained a seat on the United Nations (UN) Commission on Human Rights in April 2002. The commission studies human rights issues and prepares recommendations and guidelines for guaranteeing such rights. In 2001, the UN Economic and Social Council, which oversees the commission, voted the United States off the panel. The move came in response to various human rights organizations that had claimed that the United States was no longer a world leader in championing human rights. The United States had been a driving force behind the creation of the commission in 1946 and had held a position on the panel until 2001.

International Criminal Court. The UN Security Council approved a resolution in July 2002 that gave U.S. peacekeeping forces temporary immunity from investigation or prosecution by the International Criminal Court (ICC). The ICC is a permanent court located in The Hague, Netherlands, for the prosecution of individuals accused of committing *genocide* (the deliberate and systematic mistreatment or extermination of a national, racial, political, religious, or cultural group), war crimes, and crimes against humanity. The court came into existence on July 1, 2002.

Passage of the resolution followed weeks of negotiations in which the administration of President Bush demanded immunity from prosecution for U.S. troops. The administration warned that the United States would withdraw peacekeeping forces from Bosnia-Herzegovina and Croatia and refuse to provide forces in the future unless U.S. troops were exempt from prosecution. The Bush administration, which argued that the court infringed on national sovereignty, refused to sign the international treaty that established the tribunal. Leaders of other nations complained that the United States, by asking for exemptions for

U.S. forces, was attempting to place itself above other nations.

New rights in Russia. Officials in Russia in July 2002 instituted a new legal code that provided broad protections for the rights of those accused of criminal activity. Under the code, people accused of a crime have the right to an attorney as soon as they are arrested, are presumed innocent until proven guilty, and are entitled to challenge the admissibility of evidence. Under Russia's previous legal system, defendants had few rights, and prosecutors had broad powers.

New human rights office. Representatives of the United Nations and Mexico signed an agreement in July to open a new UN human rights office in Mexico. UN High Commissioner for Human Rights Mary Robinson praised Mexican officials for ratifying several international rights treaties.

Milosevic trial. The trial of Slobodan Milosevic, former president of Yugoslavia, by the UN International War Crimes Tribunal in The Hague, Netherlands, began in February 2002. The tribunal had indicted Milosevic in 1999 for crimes against humanity in Kosovo, a semiautonomous province of Serbia. In 2001, the tribunal indicted him for genocide. ☐ Geoffrey A. Campbell

See also **Bosnia-Herzegovina; Courts; Mexico; United Nations; Yugoslavia.**

Hungary. The Hungarian Socialist Party defeated the center-right government of Prime Minister Victor Orban in parliamentary elections in April 2002, and a new center-left government headed by Prime Minister Peter Medgyessy came into power in May. Hungary's "status law," which grants certain privileges to Hungarians outside Hungary, continued to affect relations with neighboring Slovakia and Romania.

Elections. The Hungarian Socialists and their allies, the Alliance of Free Democrats, outpolled the ruling Young Democrats-Civic Party and their allies, the Hungarian Democratic Forum, in elections held in April. In the new parliament, the Socialists and Free Democrats held 198 seats, compared with 188 seats controlled by the conservative coalition led by the Young Democrats. The 10-seat edge in Hungary's 386-seat parliament allowed the socialist coalition to organize a new government with Medgyessy as its head.

Medgyessy's government launched a 100-day legislative program in which it raised salaries of teachers and civil service employees by 50 percent. It also authorized a one-time payment to pensioners.

Tensions with neighbors. Hungary's so-called status law, which grants ethnic Hungarians living in other nations the right to work in Hungary and to receive benefits from the Hungarian government, continued to disturb relations with Romania, Slovakia, and other neighboring countries. Officials of these nations lodged protests with Hungary's government after Hungary passed the law in June 2001. They charged that the law intruded in their internal affairs.

In September 2002, Hungary's foreign minister, Laszlo Kovacs, in talks with his Romanian counterpart, Mircea Geoana, committed the Hungarian government to amending the status law so that it would resemble the laws of other European countires. The two ministers also discussed economic, environmental, and diplomatic issues.

Economics. Growth in *gross domestic product* (the total value of goods and services produced in a given year) slowed in 2002 from rates of 5.2 percent in 2000 and 3.8 percent in 2001. Hungary's Central Statistical Bureau reported a growth rate of 2.9 percent in the first quarter of 2002 and 3.1 percent in the second quarter. The rate of unemployment, at 5.6 percent, remained virtually unchanged from a year earlier.

European Union membership. In December 2002, officials of the European Union (EU) formally approved Hungary's application for admission into the organization of 15 Western European nations. EU officials scheduled Hungary's entry into full EU membership for 2004. □ Sharon L. Wolchik

See also **Europe; Romania.**

Ice skating. A major judging scandal during the Winter Olympic Games in Salt Lake City, Utah, rocked ice skating in February 2002. The scandal centered on French judge Marie Reine Le Gougne, who admitted that French officials had pressured her to vote for the Russian pairs team of Elena Berezhnaya and Anton Sikharulidze. In return, officials said, a Russian judge would vote for the French ice dancing team.

Olympic officials began investigating when the Canadian pairs team, Jamie Sale and David Pelletier, appeared to have outperformed the Russian pair but finished in second place. Both pairs were later awarded gold medals. Le Gougne was suspended from judging for three years.

World championships. Irina Slutskaya of Russia captured her first World Figure Skating Championships title on March 23 in Nagano, Japan. Michelle Kwan of the United States took the silver medal, and Fumie Suguri of Japan won the bronze. She was the first Japanese female medalist at the world championships since 1994.

On March 21, 2002, Alexei Yagudin won his fourth gold medal in five years at the men's championships. Tim Goebel of the United States won silver, and Japan's Takeshi Honda took the bronze.

On March 20, Xue Shen and Hongbo Zhao of China captured their first world pairs title. Ta-

Jamie Sale and David Pelletier of Canada perform at the 2002 Winter Olympic Games in Salt Lake City, Utah, on February 11. After coming in second place, the team was awarded a gold medal when officials learned of vote tampering by one of the event's judges.

tiana Totmianina and Maxim Marinin of Russia won the silver, and Kyoko Ina and John Zimmerman of the United States took the bronze.

European championships. On January 20, in Lausanne, Switzerland, Maria Butyrskaya of Russia won her third European figure skating title despite struggling in the long program. Irina Slutskaya took second overall. Viktoria Volchkova of Russia was third. On January 17, Alexei Yagudin won his third men's title, ahead of fellow Russian Alexander Abt and France's Brian Joubert, who took third. Totmianina and Marinin won the pairs gold.

U.S. championships. Michelle Kwan won her sixth U.S. Figure Skating Championships title, her fifth in a row, with a dazzling performance on January 12 in Los Angeles. Sasha Cohen finished second, and Sarah Hughes, the eventual Olympic gold medalist, finished third. On January 10, Todd Eldredge captured his sixth U.S. men's title. Defending champion Timothy Goebel placed second, and Michael Weiss finished third. On January 11, 2002, Ina and Zimmerman breezed to their third straight pairs title, despite an uneven performance. ☐ Michael Kates

See also **Olympics: A Special Report; Sports.**

Iceland. See Europe.

Idaho. See State government.

Illinois. See Chicago; State government.

Immigration. The Immigration and Naturalization Service (INS) came under intense criticism in 2002 when it was learned that the INS had issued student visas to two of the highjackers who had carried out the terrorist attacks on the United States on Sept. 11, 2001. In June 2002, President George W. Bush had proposed the creation of a new Cabinet department for domestic defense. Under the proposal, the INS would become part of the new department.

In November, both the U.S. House of Representatives and the U.S. Senate approved legislation creating the new Department of Homeland Security, which consolidated 22 existing agencies and 170,000 employees. Political experts noted that it would take several months for the department to become operational.

Criticism of the INS began in March after the agency notified a flight school in Florida that the agency had approved student visas for Mohamed Atta and Marwan al-Shehhi. Government officials had already concluded that Atta and al-Shehhi had flown the two jets that demolished the twin towers of the World Trade Center in New York City. The INS blamed the error on an antiquated computer system and a heavy load of paperwork.

President Bush expressed shock at the error and ordered an investigation into the mishap. He said that the notification served as a "wake-up call for those who run the INS." In May, a report issued by the U.S. Department of Justice concluded that "widespread failure" within the INS allowed Atta and al-Shehhi to obtain student visas. In the report, Justice Department Inspector General Glenn Fine concluded that the INS failed to check immigration records, which indicated that the two men had left the United States while their applications were pending, making them ineligible for student visas had they been alive.

New database for foreign students. Attorney General John Ashcroft announced in May that U.S. colleges and universities would be required to enter student visa information on foreign students into a centralized computer system by 2003. Educators would need to notify the system—the Student and Exchange Visitor Information System—if a student left school or failed to attend classes. Government officials claimed that the new system would enable the federal government to better monitor foreign students.

National security concerns. In June 2002, Attorney General Ashcroft announced the creation of a set of rules that require some foreign visitors to the United States to be photographed and fingerprinted before entering the country. The National Security Entry-Exit Registration System focused on visitors from countries considered sponsors of terrorism, including Iran, Iraq, Libya, Sudan, and Syria. Ashcroft said that the system was designed to track nonimmigrant visa holders who might pose a national security concern. Some civil rights groups criticized the system and claimed that it amounted to racial and ethnic profiling because it focused on visitors from Middle Eastern and Arab nations.

INS Commissioner James Ziglar announced his resignation in August after one year as head of the agency. Ziglar said that he believed that the INS had made progress with security problems that existed prior to the terrorist attacks on the United States, but argued that planned improvements were often hampered by criticism of the agency.

Supreme Court ruling. The U.S. Supreme Court ruled in March 2002 that illegal immigrants working in the United States do not have the same rights as U.S. citizens if they are wrongfully discharged from their jobs. In a 5-to-4 vote, the court ruled that employers are not required to pay back wages to undocumented workers who are unjustifiably fired or demoted. The justices determined that giving back pay to people who were in the United States illegally would undermine U.S. immigration policies. ☐ Geoffrey A. Campbell

See also **Cabinet, U.S.; Congress of the United States; Immigration: A Special Report.**

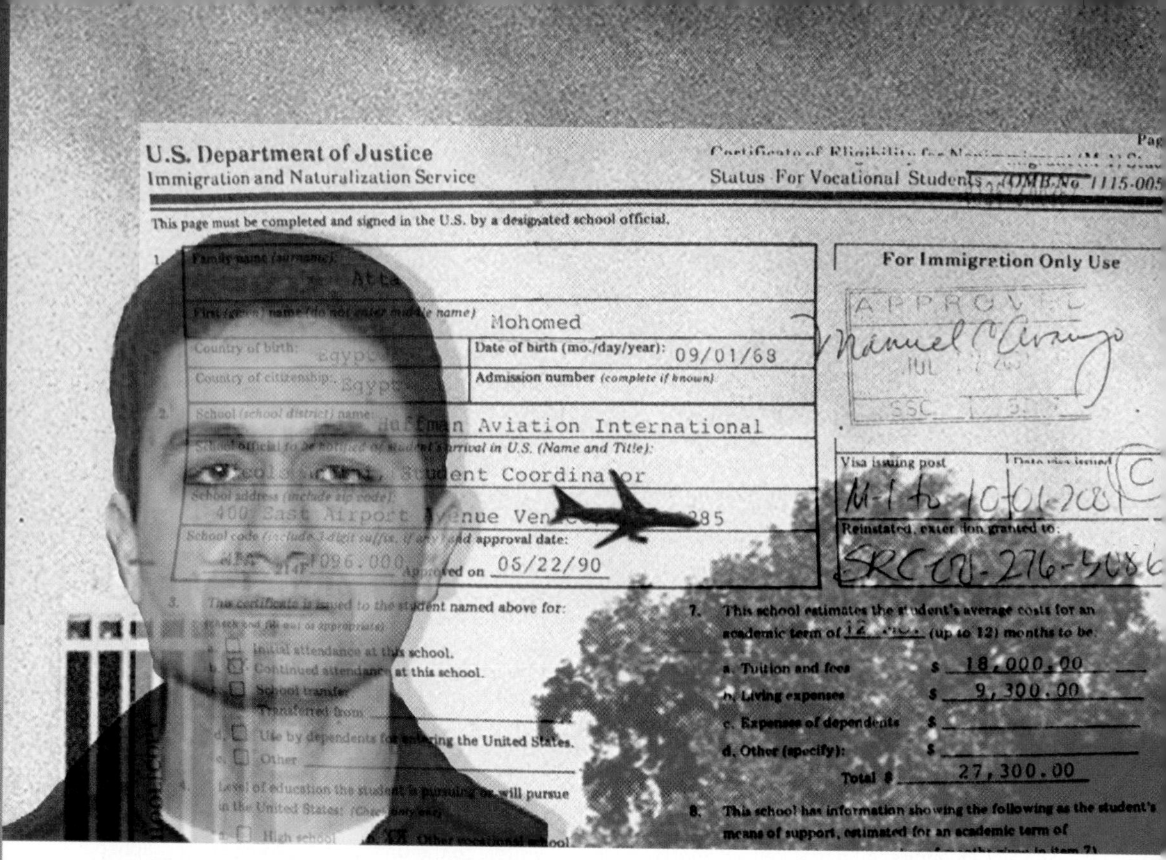

U.S. Department of Justice
Immigration and Naturalization Service

Certificate of Eligibility for N_____ (M-1) S___
Status For Vocational Students OMB No. 1115-005

Page

This page must be completed and signed in the U.S. by a designated school official.

For Immigration Only Use

Family name (surname): Atta

First (given) name (do not enter middle name): Mohomed

Country of birth: Egypt

Date of birth (mo./day/year): 09/01/68

Country of citizenship: Egypt

Admission number (complete if known):

School (school district) name: Huffman Aviation International

School official to be notified of student's arrival in U.S. (Name and Title): Student Coordinator

School address (include zip code): 400 East Airport Avenue Venice ___ 285

School code (include 3-digit suffix, if any) and approval date: MIA 214F 00096.000 Approved on 05/22/90

APPROVED
Manuel C Arango
JUL
SSC

Visa issuing post: MIA Date visa issued: 10-01-200
Reinstated, extension granted to: SRC 08-276-5086

3. This certificate is issued to the student named above for:
(check and fill out as appropriate)
a. Initial attendance at this school.
b. Continued attendance at this school.
c. School transfer. Transferred from
d. Use by dependents for entering the United States.
e. Other

4. Level of education the student is pursuing or will pursue in the United States: (Check only one)
High school   Other vocational school

7. This school estimates the student's average costs for an academic term of 12 ____ (up to 12) months to be:

a. Tuition and fees $ 18,000.00
b. Living expenses $ 9,300.00
c. Expenses of dependents $
d. Other (specify): $
Total $ 27,300.00

8. This school has information showing the following as the student's means of support, estimated for an academic term of

Passport to Reform:
The INS and Homeland Security

Terrorist attacks on the United States exposed the many problems plaguing the Immigration and Naturalization Service and sparked a national debate about the relationship between immigration services and national security.

By Richard Korman

The error could not have been more embarrassing. On March 11, 2002, Huffman Aviation International, a pilot training school in Venice, Florida, received a letter from the United States Immigration and Naturalization Service (INS). The letter informed the school that the INS had granted permission for flight training to two visitors to the United States—Mohamed Atta and Marwan Al-Shehhi. Seemingly unbeknownst to the INS was the fact that both of these men had been dead for six months. Moreover, the men were among the 19 foreign-born terrorists who had hijacked four jetliners on Sept. 11, 2001, flying two into the World Trade Center in New York City and one into the Pentagon Building outside Washington, D.C. The fourth plane crashed into a field in Pennsylvania. Some 3,000 people were killed in the attacks.

Much of the American public was outraged when the INS's mistake was disclosed. President George W. Bush ordered a complete investigation into the incident, and other angry politicians attacked the immigration agency. "We in Congress have sat back and watched the most bumbling, stumbling agency in all the land screw up case after case with no consequence to itself," said U.S. Representative Mark Foley (R., Florida).

A poll conducted soon after the attacks by the Center for Immigration Studies, a research organization based in Washington, D.C., showed that more than two-thirds of the respondents believed that border security and enforcement of immigration laws had been lax. This, the respondents felt, had made it too easy for the terrorists to enter the United States. By late 2002, INS Director James Ziglar had resigned, and the U.S. Congress had passed legislation transferring the duties of the INS and many other federal agencies into a new Cabinet department called the Department of Homeland Security. The complete implementation of the massive new department was expected to take several years.

Conflict between services and law enforcement

The advocates of the government reorganization hoped it would address a basic conflict over immigration policy that had long bedeviled the INS. On the one hand, the INS was responsible for providing many services to vast numbers of visitors and immigrants. These services included granting *green cards* (documents giving immigrants the right to permanently live, study, and work in the United States); *asylum* (refuge to an alien who has a well-founded fear of persecution in his or her home country); and U.S. citizenship. The INS's service duties also included verifying *visas* (endorsements for the right to temporarily visit, study, or work in the United States). On the other hand, INS officials were also responsible for strictly enforcing a wide range of immigration laws. These enforcement duties included inspecting all people arriving in the United States; conducting tens of thousands of criminal investigations of aliens every year; patrolling U.S. borders for illegal immigrants; and apprehending and de-

The author:
Richard Korman is a journalist and author of *The Goodyear Story: An Inventor's Obsession and the Struggle for a Rubber Monopoly.*

Immigration terms and concepts

Alien: Foreigner; person who is not a citizen of the country in which he or she lives.

Asylum: Refuge to an alien who is unable or unwilling to return to his or her country of origin because of persecution or the fear of persecution.

Deportation: Removal of an alien who has been found to violate immigration laws.

Emigrant: Person who leaves his or her country of origin to settle in another country.

Green card (or permanent visa): Document giving a person the legal right to permanently live, work, and study in the United States and to enter and leave the country freely; it also gives the bearer the right to apply for citizenship.

Illegal immigrant (or undocumented alien): Alien who enters the country in violation of immigration laws.

Immigrant: Alien admitted as a lawful permanent resident.

Legalized alien: Illegal alien who has obtained temporary resident status under laws granting *amnesty* (pardon).

Naturalization: Conferring of citizenship upon a person after birth.

Nonimmigrant: Alien who seeks temporary entry into the country for a specific purpose, such as business or pleasure.

Passport: Paper or book giving a person official permission to travel in a foreign country.

Student visa: Visa that gives a nonimmigrant alien the right to temporarily study at a school in the United States.

Temporary worker: Alien who has the right to work in the country for a temporary period.

Visa: Official signature or endorsement upon a passport showing that the bearer has been approved to temporarily visit, study, or work in the country.

porting violators of immigration law. In addition, the INS carried out its responsibilities under personnel and budgetary limits and complex rules that were frequently revised by Congress.

The first big wave

The federal government became concerned with immigration issues in the early 1890's, during an unprecedented wave of immigration to the United States. Immigration became especially intense between 1900 and 1915, when almost 14 million people arrived on U.S. shores. In an attempt to keep up with this massive flow, Congress passed a number of immigration-related laws. In 1891, the federal government took over from state boards and commissions the tasks of inspecting and either admitting or rejecting new immigrants. Congress then created a series of agencies to process immigrants and enforce immigration laws. These agencies evolved into the Bureau of Immigration, which was placed in the Department of Commerce and Labor. In 1906, Congress expanded this bureau into the Bureau of Immigration and Naturalization to better handle the growing numbers of immigrants seeking citizenship. When separate departments of commerce and labor were set up in 1913, the Bureau of Immigration and Naturalization was also divided into two agencies. Both of these agencies were assigned to the Department of Labor.

Most of the immigrants who arrived in the United States in the early 1900's were from Southern or Eastern Europe—countries such as Italy, Poland, Hungary, and Czechoslovakia. Prior to this period, the majority of immigrants to the United States had come from Western Europe. During the height of the immigration wave of the early 1900's, some people in the United States became concerned that the new immigrants were from countries and cultures that seemed very alien to most native-born

An INS agent at a U.S. airport assists visitors to the United States in understanding their passport documents. One of the main functions of the INS was to provide services to visitors and immigrants, including verifying visas and granting green cards.

citizens. As these concerns grew, a federal commission concluded that the U.S. government should impose limits on immigration. In 1917, Congress passed a law to restrict immigration. The legislation banned immigrants from South Asia, Southeast Asia, and islands in the Pacific and Indian oceans. It also established a literacy test to prove that immigrants could read and write in their native language. The test was designed to keep out immigrants who were less likely to become responsible, productive members of society.

Immigration restrictions increase

By 1918, immigration to the United States had fallen from more than 1.2 million in 1914 to about 110,000 people—the lowest level in decades. But with much of Europe in ruins after World War I (1914-1918), immigration soon began to climb again as people sought new lives in a new land. During the early 1920's, Congress responded by adopting additional limits to immigration and setting quotas for individual countries. These quotas favored Western European nations—primarily England, Sweden, Denmark, and Norway—over Italy, Poland, and other countries. The goal was to maintain the United States as a largely white, Anglo-Saxon country.

While enforcing these requirements for legal immigration, immigration authorities also had to confront a rise in illegal immigration, mainly from Mexico. In 1924, Congress created the U.S. Border Patrol to combat illegal entry. This police force was charged with pursuing, apprehending, and expelling aliens who entered the country in violation of immigration laws.

As economic conditions and joblessness worsened in the United States during the Great Depression, a worldwide business

INS Border Patrol agents arrest illegal aliens captured near the U.S. border with Mexico. Enforcing a wide range of immigration laws was an important duty of the INS.

The evolution of U.S. immigration policy

1891

An enormous wave of immigration from Europe prompts the federal government to take over enforcement of immigration laws from the states.

1903

The Bureau of Immigration moves from the Treasury Department to the Department of Commerce and Labor as concerns grow over the plight of industrial workers.

1917

The immigration bureau requires that immigrants be able to read and write in their native language in an attempt to control a massive increase in immigration.

1918

As World War I raises national security concerns, the immigration bureau requires passports for visitors and sets up internment facilities for foreign seamen who worked on captured enemy ships.

slump in the 1930's, U.S. authorities restricted immigration even more. Also during this period, the number of *ports of entry* (checkpoints where people traveling by land, sea, or air arrive in the country) grew, and this increased the demand for Border Patrol agents and inspectors. In 1933, President Franklin D. Roosevelt established a single immigration agency—the Immigration and Naturalization Service—to better handle both enforcement and service issues.

Strict immigration controls continued in the years just before and during World War II (1939-1945). In 1940, President Roosevelt, as part of a broader government reorganization, transferred the INS to the Department of Justice. The INS now came under the authority of the attorney general, the U.S. government's top law enforcement official. Roosevelt also increased the agency's staff from about 4,000 to 8,500.

After World War II, Congress passed a series of new mandates for U.S. immigration policy in response to various political concerns. Growing worries about Communists and organized crime figures living in the United States, as well as illegal Mexican immigrants, led to several programs targeting these people for deportation. Law enforcement became a much more important function of the INS. In addition, the 1952 Immigration and Nationality Act reaffirmed the national origins quotas of the 1920's, maintaining the preference for immigrants from Western Europe. The act repealed the 1917 ban on Asian immigrants and instead imposed a limit of 2,000 Asian immigrants per year.

The doors open wider

In 1965, a more tolerant approach to immigrants and a strong economy led to drastic changes in immigration policy. Congress amended the 1952 act, replacing the national origins quotas with a preference system designed to reunite immigrant families and attract skilled workers to the United States. Under the new system, legal immigration more than doubled—from about 290,000 in 1964 to 600,000 in 1978—as immigrants brought more and more relatives to join them in the United States. Illegal immigration also rose dramatically during this time.

With the liberalization of immigration policy, immigrants from Asia and Latin America began to arrive in greater numbers. By the 1970's, these immigrants outnumbered new immigrants from Europe. The size and makeup of this wave of immigration caused new worries for many people in the United States who were not used to large numbers of immigrants from these parts of the world. In 1981, a congressional commission labeled the nation's immigration system "out of control."

Amid growing public concerns over illegal immigration from Latin America, Congress in 1986 adopted the Immigration Reform and Control Act. This act granted *amnesty* (pardon) to 3 million illegal aliens, but it also, for the first time, mandated penalties for employers who hired people who were in the United States illegally. The amnesty provisions—combined with a law passed in 1990 that raised the legal immigration limit to 700,000 people per year—greatly increased the total number of permanent residents lawfully admitted into the United States. These people, who also included newcomers granted asylum, reached a record 1.8 million in 1991.

The influx of legal immigrants entering the United States in the 1990's overwhelmed the Immigration and Naturalization Service. With a limited number of personnel assigned to inspect new arrivals and keep track of

early 1920's

Congress passes restrictive immigration laws, assigning each nationality a quota, as the result of a postwar jump in immigration and concerns about immigrants bringing in Communist ideas.

1924

The U.S. Border Patrol is created within the immigration bureau following a rise in illegal immigration from Mexico.

1933

The Bureau of Immigration and the Bureau of Naturalization merge to form the Immigration and Naturalization Service (INS).

1940

The INS moves from the Department of Labor to the Department of Justice in response to renewed national security concerns related to the war in Europe and Asia.

1940's

The INS organizes and operates internment camps and detention facilities for aliens from enemy countries during World War II. Many Japanese Americans are also held in these camps.

1950's

The INS launches several deportation programs targeting illegal aliens, Communists, and organized crime figures in the United States.

1950's–1960's

Congress passes legislation that increases the number of refugees admitted into the United States as Cold War-related conflicts displace people in Hungary, Cuba, and elsewhere.

1965

Congress passes a preference system that increases the number of immigrants from Asia and Latin America, ending decades of restrictions on immigration from these areas.

1980

Congress increases the number of refugees allowed into the United States from 17,400 to 50,000 per year following political turmoil in Cuba, Haiti, and Southeast Asia.

alien visitors, the INS had to annually process hundreds of millions of legally authorized immigrants, foreign tourists, and returning U.S. citizens who arrived through more than 300 ports of entry. In late 2001, fewer than 5,000 INS inspectors staffed these ports.

Workload, record keeping, and politics

Lack of personnel also hampered the ability of the INS to track down visa violators. Officials estimated in 2001 that illegal residents in the United States—including both illegal immigrants and those people who had overstayed visas or broken other rules that apply to legal visitors—numbered between 3 million and 8 million. In 2001, there were fewer than 2,000 INS investigators around the country charged with finding these lawbreakers.

Many observers blamed various difficulties at the INS on poor record keeping and bureaucracy. According to U.S. Representative James Sensenbrenner (R., Wisconsin), the INS in October 2001 had a backlog of nearly 5 million unprocessed visas and immigration-change requests, most for green cards. Moreover, the INS was unable to account for 314,000 people who had been ordered deported.

The INS frequently turned to computer-based solutions to help it manage its workload and record keeping. Unfortunately, these attempts to solve old problems led to other problems. In 1983, the INS launched a database system called the National Automated Immigration Lookout System (NAILS). The system was designed to allow agents who inspected aliens arriving at major ports to quickly compare the arrivals with the names and physical characteristics of previous deportees or alien criminals. The NAILS system

was later upgraded and linked with other government databases, including the Interagency Border Inspection Systems (IBIS). IBIS is a database managed by the U.S. Customs Service, an agency that collects taxes on imported merchandise, that pools information from many federal and state agencies. The NAILS-IBIS linkage was supposed to enable INS agents to more efficiently check if alien applicants were classified as inadmissible or wanted by law enforcement officials. However, by mid-2002, the need to check every applicant against the IBIS database had led to greater delays and backlogging of immigration-change requests. INS district offices initially did not have a sufficient number of computers and trained personnel to carry out the required checks.

The INS also failed to implement a computer-based program that was mandated by Congress. In 1996, Congress required the INS to automate newly created records about the entries and exits of noncitizens. The system was to create a digital record for every alien arriving in the United States, later to be matched with the record of his or her departure. The INS was not able to get the program up and running. In 2000, Congress allowed the INS to use an automated system based on existing records—a less difficult assignment.

Well-intentioned congressional mandates regularly caused difficulties for the INS. In the 1996 Illegal Immigration Reform and Immigrant Responsibility Act, Congress adopted several new measures for keeping out and removing illegal aliens. This act

provided the funds for hiring 5,000 new immigration agents and 1,200 investigators to track down and deport aliens who overstayed their visas. It also mandated the building of a fence for 14 miles (23 kilometers) along the Mexican border near San Diego, California, at a cost of $12 million. However, to put these and other provisions of the act into effect, the INS was forced to change 63 sections of its regulations and rules; alter 75 immigration forms; and submit 25 new reports to Congress, 16

1986

The Immigration Reform and Control Act offers *amnesty* (pardon) to many illegal aliens in an attempt to get illegal immigration under control.

1990

Congress increases the number of legal immigrants allowed in to about 700,000 per year due to demand for low-wage workers and workers with various skills.

1996

The Illegal Immigration Reform and Immigrant Responsibility Act streamlines the deportation of illegal immigrants and makes it more difficult for them to gain asylum.

2001

On September 11, 19 aliens in the United States on non-immigrant visas hijack four jetliners and crash two of them into the World Trade Center in New York City and one into the Pentagon Building outside Washington, D.C.

2002

President Bush and Congress agree to incorporate the INS into a new Department of Homeland Security.

Source: Immigration and Naturalization Service.

Numbers revealed problems at the INS

- Fewer than 5,000 INS agents conducted more than 510 million inspections of individuals arriving legally in the United States in 2001 at more than 300 ports of entry.

- Fewer than 2,000 INS investigators were responsible for finding between 3 million and 8 million illegal residents in the United States in 2001.

- Because of a high turnover rate, the INS had 1,500 fewer Border Patrol agents and inspectors than it was authorized to hire as of mid-2002. The INS had hired 1,499 new Border Patrol agents in fiscal year 2002, but 1,459 veteran agents left at the same time, many for the Transportation Security Administration.

- Of the $6.2 billion that Congress authorized the INS to spend in fiscal year 2002, some $4 billion were appropriated for law enforcement and $1.4 billion for immigrant service programs. The rest was for support and administration.

- The increase in INS spending for law enforcement programs was nearly five times greater than the increase in spending for immigrant service programs between 1993 and 2001.

- The INS had a backlog of 5 million unprocessed applications for visa- and immigration-status changes, such as green cards, in late 2001.

- The INS reported in 2001 that it could not account for some 314,000 aliens who disappeared after receiving deportation orders.

Source: Immigration and Naturalization Service.

Limited numbers of INS agents at ports of entry cause long delays for people arriving in the United States, including immigrants seeking admission, foreign tourists, and U.S. citizens returning from abroad.

on a periodic basis. These requirements added to severe pressures on the agency's staff and budget.

New immigration policies passed by Congress, such as the 1996 act, were often the result of lobbying by various private interests. In the late 1990's, employer groups lobbied Congress to loosen some immigration restrictions as a way to obtain workers with certain skills, such as software engineers, who would work for low wages. Congress responded in 1998 by passing the American Competitiveness and Workforce Improvement Act, which raised the number of skilled temporary foreign workers allowed into the United States. In 2001, several Hispanic groups, unions, and businesses attempted unsuccessfully to persuade the government to grant amnesty to some 3 million illegal U.S. residents from Mexico.

Despite the many difficulties confronting the INS and the intense political pressures placed on the agency, experts gave the INS credit for some important accomplishments. In 2000, about 9,000 Border Patrol agents guarding the U.S. border with Mexico apprehended a record 1.6 million illegal immigrants. Experts attributed this success to the willingness of Congress to increase INS funding through the 1990's. For fiscal year 2002 (Oct. 1, 2001 to Sept. 30, 2002), Congress authorized the INS to spend $6.19 billion, about three times as much as the 1994 budget authorization of $1.57 billion. However, these appropriations emphasized law enforcement over immigrant services. In 2002, Congress appropriated some $4 billion for INS law enforcement, compared with $1.4 billion for immigrant services.

The imbalance in funding between the INS's law enforcement and service wings caused concern among some critics of the agency. They pointed out that the conflicting missions of law enforcement and immigrant services often reduced the INS's effectiveness in both areas. Many experts in 2001 and 2002 called for a major reorganization of immigration and naturalization duties within the government.

Problems exposed, solutions proposed

The terrorist attacks on the United States in September 2001 exposed serious problems within the INS. Critics initially pointed out that the agency had allowed the airplane hijackers, some of whom were known terrorists, to enter the United States. When the public learned that the INS had approved visas for flight training for two of the dead hijackers, it became obvious that something was drastically wrong with the agency. The terrorist attacks also exposed the complete inability of the INS to keep track of or locate visitors with nonimmigrant visas or determine if they were obeying the rules of their stay. The 19 hijackers, most of whom were from Saudi Arabia, were in the United States legally on nonimmigrant visas, either as students or tourists. However, some of the 19 had overstayed their visas but were never pursued by the INS.

The Bush administration took the first steps to reorganize the INS in November 2001, when Attorney General John Ashcroft announced a plan to split the INS into separate bureaus. One bureau was to be in charge of law enforcement, the other in charge of immigrant services. In addition, Congress proposed adding more agents to track down aliens, closing loopholes in student visa programs, and allocating money for new technology, such as improved information-sharing with other law enforcement agencies.

By June 2002, these and other ideas had evolved into something even more dramatic. On June 6, President Bush proposed establishing a Department of Homeland Security, involving the most extensive reorganization of the federal government since the 1940's. This new department combined 22 different federal agencies under one roof. The INS was one of the agencies moved to the new department. Others included the Customs Service, the Coast Guard, the Federal Emergency Management Agency (FEMA), and the FBI's National Domestic Preparedness Office. The three main duties of the department were to prevent terrorist attacks within the United States; reduce the country's vulnerability to terrorism; and help the nation recover from any terrorist attacks that might occur.

The Bush administration said the reorganization would help the government "manage who and what enters our homeland, and work to prevent the entry of terrorists and instruments of terrorism while simultaneously ensuring the speedy flow of legitimate traffic." In keeping with the administration's original proposal, immigration services and law enforcement are to be separated within the new department.

President George W. Bush (above) announces in June 2002 his plan to create a Department of Homeland Security, to which the functions of the INS were to be transferred. Senate Majority Leader Tom Daschle (D., South Dakota), meeting with Tom Ridge (right), director of the White House Office of Homeland Security, led Congressional opposition to certain parts of Bush's plan.

Debating the details

Although many analysts agreed with the plan to separate the enforcement and service functions of the INS, some criticized the idea of putting them both in the Department of Homeland Security. Observers noted that the INS had worked hard to develop a customer-service approach to handling green cards, citizenship, and other immigrant issues, and that this approach could be lost in the new security-conscious department. Immigration authorities feared that the department's emphasis on border security and enforcement might lead to overly aggressive actions, such as the widespread deportation of immigrants who were guilty of only minor infractions.

Many members of Congress supported the establishment of the Department of Homeland Security but favored keeping the INS service functions within the Justice Department. Furthermore, some members called for establishing a new intelligence division within the department to better analyze information on terrorist threats collected by the FBI and Central Intelligence Agency.

More funds, new rules

The integration of the INS into the new Department of Homeland Security was the most important, though not the only, step taken by the Bush administration and Congress to address the problems plaguing the INS. Congress, for example, appropriated funds that allowed the INS to hire 10,000 new Border Patrol agents, inspectors, and other personnel. However, a high turnover rate caused the INS to have 1,500 fewer Border Patrol agents and inspectors than it was authorized to hire as of mid-2002. The INS hired 1,499 new Border Patrol agents in fiscal year 2002, but 1,459 veteran agents left at the same time. Many of the departing INS agents took new airport security positions with the Department of Transportation.

In June 2002, the Justice Department introduced new rules that were intended to make it easier to track visa violators. These rules required visiting students, tourists, and workers from primarily Islamic countries to be fingerprinted, photographed, and registered with the INS. Beginning in September 2002, these visitors' fingerprints and photographs were digitized and added to a computer database that could be accessed by law-enforcement authorities. This was similar to the fingerprinting and photographing system begun for green card recipients in the late 1990's.

The Justice Department also announced in 2002 its intention to implement the Student and Exchange Visitor Information System (SEVIS) by January 2003. This Internet-based system provides the government, educational institutions, and exchange programs with an automated way to share information about foreign students. Under the system, the government requires educational institutions to record a variety of information, such as the failure of a foreign student to enroll at the required time and any disciplinary action taken against a foreign student as the result of a crime. A number of colleges and universities delayed the implementation of SEVIS, voicing concerns that the requirements violated the privacy of their students.

The INS in 2002 introduced biometric visa cards—which include digital photographs, fingerprints, and other information—to help track visitors who overstay their visas. Several of the terrorists who hijacked jets on Sept. 11, 2001, had overstayed their visas but were never pursued by the INS.

Homeland security legislation approved

Congress and the Bush administration remained locked in an impasse over the details of final Homeland Security legislation through much of 2002. The president backed legislation that gave him and future presidents the authority to freely hire, transfer, and dismiss employees of the proposed department. Democratic members of Congress, however, objected to this version of the bill because it removed civil service protections from the 177,000 federal employees who were to be transferred to the new department. Following the Republican sweep of the November 2002 congressional elections, Congress and the administration agreed on a compromise version of the legislation, which gave the president the authority over workers that he sought, while giving unions the right to challenge any proposed new rules affecting employees in the department.

Only time will tell how the Department of Homeland Security will handle future challenges in guarding the nation's borders and providing for immigrant services. Nevertheless, it was clear that the attacks on the World Trade Center and Pentagon by visa-carrying terrorists had moved the United States back to the cautious side in its long love-hate relationship with immigration.

■ ■ ■

India. Rioting between Hindus and Muslims in Gujarat, a state in western India, resulted in the deaths of at least 1,000 people in 2002. The violence was the worst between the two religious groups since 1992, when Hindus destroyed a Muslim mosque in Ayodhya, a city in the state of Uttar Pradesh. The unrest in 2002 was sparked by Hindu preparations to build a temple on the site of the former mosque. Hindus make up more than 80 percent of India's population, while Muslims make up about 12 percent. There had been relatively little violence between Indian Muslims and Hindus for the 10 years preceding the riots in 2002.

The violence erupted in February when Hindus, returning by train from a trip to Ayodhya, harassed Muslim vendors at a train station in the Gujarat village of Godhra. Muslims responded by stoning the train and setting one of its cars on fire, which resulted in the deaths of 59 Hindus. Within hours of the attack, Hindu mobs began killing Muslims throughout the state. The violence persisted for more than two months. More than 1,000 people—mostly Muslims— were killed, and 20,000 houses and businesses were damaged or destroyed. Approximately 110,000 people fled the region and traveled to other states as refugees.

Human rights groups said the Bharatiya Jana-ta Party (BJP), the Hindu nationalist group that led the national coalition government and the Gujarat legislature, was complicit in the attacks. Although BJP leaders claimed the government attempted to stop the violence, an independent police investigation concluded that BJP officials failed to halt the bloodshed and, in some cases, actually provoked the mobs.

Political backlash. The violence caused outrage among Indians, who had already turned against BJP candidates in state elections in February. Voters ousted BJP leadership in four states, including Uttar Pradesh, a BJP stronghold since the early 1990's. In city elections in March 2002, the BJP lost control of the capital, New Delhi. However, the BJP won control of the Gujarat legislature in December elections. Leaders of the Congress Party, the main opposition party, accused the BJP of exploiting religious divisions to reap Hindu votes.

The political consequences of the violence spread to the national level, shaking Prime Minister Atal Behari Vajpayee's coalition government. Vajpayee publicly condemned the attacks in Gujarat and dispatched soldiers to restore order in the state, but his government was widely criticized for not doing enough to halt the violence. Vajpayee, however, managed to maintain control of his parliamentary coalition without yielding to

Missiles line the India-Pakistan border near the Indian city of Amritsar in January when the two governments, on the brink of war, placed their armies on full alert. The countries agreed in October to pull back 1 million troops from the border after a tense 10-month military standoff.

demands to dissolve the Gujarat government.

In July, Vajpayee appeased hardline Hindu party members by elevating Lal Krishna Advani, India's home minister, to deputy prime minister. In 1992, Advani had been the leader of the Hindu mob that destroyed the Ayodhya mosque, which touched off a storm of violence, led to the BJP's rise to power, and set the stage for the deadly riots in 2002.

New president. Parliament elected Avul Pakir Jainulabdeen Adbul Kalam, a 70-year-old scientist who was widely considered the father of India's nuclear missile program, as president of India in July 2002. Political observers noted that the selection of Kalam, a Muslim, for the largely ceremonial office reflected the BJP's desire to distance itself from accusations that the party supported violence against Muslims in Gujarat.

Standoff with Pakistan. India and Pakistan engaged in a tense military standoff throughout 2002. The countries amassed approximately 1 million soldiers along their shared border as diplomats from the United States, the United Kingdom, and other countries attempted to open negotiations between the two nuclear powers.

The standoff began in December 2001, when Indian officials blamed Pakistan for an attack on India's parliament building in New Delhi. The attack escalated tensions between the countries over state-sponsored terrorism, particularly in the Himalayan state of Jammu and Kashmir—territory largely held by India but claimed by Pakistan since 1947. More than 37,000 people had died since 1989 as a result of violence in the region.

In October 2002, India and Pakistan agreed to end the standoff after President Pervez Musharraf of Pakistan promised a permanent end to state-sponsored terrorism. Observers noted, however, that the dispute over Jammu and Kashmir remained unresolved.

State assembly elections in Jammu and Kashmir, held in September and October, shook the power base of the region's ruling party, the National Conference, which had dominated the state's government for more than 50 years. The party won only 28 of 87 assembly seats and it was still the largest party in the state assembly, but it held neither the majority it needed to form a government nor sufficient allies to form a coalition. Political observers said the election might pave the way for negotiations between the new government and Kashmiri militants.

Drought. India suffered its worst drought in more than 10 years in 2002. The drought threatened the agricultural industry, which employed more than 60 percent of the population and accounted for nearly 25 percent of the nation's economic output. ☐ Henry S. Bradsher

See also **Asia; Pakistan.**

Indian, American. The largest class-action lawsuit ever filed by Native Americans continued without resolution in 2002. The suit, brought in 1996 by the Colorado-based Native American Rights Fund (a group that provides legal counsel to Native Americans) charged that the United States government had allowed more than $10 billion to be lost or stolen from American Indian trust accounts. Government agencies acknowledged the mismanagement. However, they claimed that the losses amounted to hundreds of millions of dollars, rather than billions.

American Indian trust accounts were established in 1887, when some reservations were divided up and plots of land were issued to Native Americans. The lands could not be sold. Rather, the Bureau of Indian Affairs (BIA, a division of the U.S. Department of the Interior) and other Interior Department agencies were to lease them for grazing, logging, mining, and oil drilling. Funds from the sale of natural resources on the lands were to be deposited into accounts for the individual landowners or their heirs.

By 2002, the U.S. government managed some 56 million acres (23 million hectares) of land for Native Americans. According to the Interior Department, the land is owned by about 300,000 individuals. However, Native Americans claim that 500,000 Indians—many of whose records were lost or destroyed—own the land and are entitled to payments from the trust accounts.

Lawsuit. In 1996, Elaine Cobell, a banker and member of the Blackfeet tribe, filed the class-action lawsuit with the help of the Native American Rights Fund. The suit sought to compel the Interior Department to reconcile the accounts and fix the record-keeping system.

In 1999, a U.S. District Court judge agreed that the accounts had been mismanaged. The Interior Department promised to revise its accounting procedures and correct its records by January 2001. However, problems with a new computer system and the destruction of documents pertaining to the case by Treasury Department officials hindered the process.

A court-appointed investigator determined in 2001 that the computer system on which trust information was stored was not secure. To protect the accounts, the Interior Department disconnected all of its systems that allow public access to Indian trust data through the Internet. The move halted all payments to trust fund recipients, as well as cutting off other Interior Department Web sites, such as those serving U.S. national parks. The Office of Trust Funds Management began to issue estimated payments to trust fund beneficiaries in February 2002 as an interim measure until a secure computer system could be installed.

In September 2002, a U.S. District Court judge found Interior Secretary Gale Norton guilty of contempt of court for failing to fix the error-riddled system. The Interior Department was told to pay the Indians' legal fees in the lawsuit.

Task force. Interior Secretary Norton agreed in February 2002 to the formation of a trust reform task force to improve the department's management of the trust funds. In June, the group, composed of Interior Department officials and tribal leaders, presented its report, outlining a number of improvement options. The options were to be submitted later in the year to the tribes involved in the lawsuit for their comments.

Reform begins. In July, the Interior Department's Office of Historical Trust Accounting reported that it had reconciled nearly 8,000 of the trust accounts. The reconciliation involved tracing payments due to the accounts from the late 1800's to Dec. 31, 2000. The Interior Department began to issue statements in October 2002 to trust fund owners whose accounts had been reconciled. However, the lead plaintiffs in the lawsuit expressed concern about the accuracy of the statements. The plaintiffs sought to transfer the trust accounts from the Interior Department to a neutral, court-appointed receiver who would straighten out the records. □ Kristina Vaicikonis

Indiana. See **State government.**

Indonesia. Two powerful car bombs exploded on the Indonesian resort island of Bali on Oct. 12, 2002, killing more than 180 people and wounding some 200 others at a nightclub and bar. Most of the dead and injured were tourists.

In November, police arrested Indonesian men on charges that they took part in the attack. The suspects were allegedly members of a radical Islamic organization based in Indonesia, Jemaah Islamiyah, whose leader, Abu Bakar Bashir, was arrested on separate charges two weeks after the attack. The United States and Australia called for Jemaah Islamiyah to be added to the United Nations (UN) list of terrorist organizations. The Indonesian government initially claimed Jemaah Islamiyah did not exist but eventually agreed to add the group to the UN list.

Constitutional changes. In August, the People's Consultative Assembly (parliament) attempted to ease international concerns that Indonesia, the world's most populous Islamic country, was becoming a center for Islamic militants. The assembly rejected a proposal to impose strict Islamic law on the secular country and made constitutional changes aimed at enhancing democracy in Indonesia.

The changes included the direct election of the president and the abolishment of parliamen-

tary seats reserved for the military. Under the changes, military officers were to give up the seats they held in parliament by 2004, when presidential elections were to take place. In the past, the president was chosen by a committee.

Peace plans. In December 2002, the Indonesian government and separatist rebels in Aceh, a province at the western tip of Indonesia, signed a peace accord ending a 26-year civil war. Since 1990, at least 12,000 people have been killed in the war, including nearly 2,000 people in 2002. The plan offered more autonomy for the province's 4 million people and elections for a provincial legislature.

In February, rival factions in the Moluccas Islands, formerly the Spice Islands, signed a peace plan to end violence between Christians and Muslims that had resulted in the deaths of more than 6,000 people since 2000.

Corruption. Akbar Tandjung, speaker of parliament, and Tommy Suharto, son of Indonesia's former ruler, were sentenced to prison in 2002. Tandjung was convicted of misusing $4 million in government funds, and Suharto was convicted of ordering the murder of a judge. An official of the World Bank, an affiliate of the UN, said that corruption was Indonesia's most serious economic problem.   □ Henry S. Bradsher

See also **Asia; Australia; Terrorism.**

Western tourists leave Bali's nightclub district on October 14, two days after car bombings devastated the area. More than 180 people—mostly foreign tourists—died as a result of the attack. Investigators suspected that the radical Islamic organization Jemaah Islamiyah was responsible.

International trade appeared to be making a mild recovery in the first half of 2002, as major industrial nations began to shake off the effects of the recession in 2001. However, solid growth slipped later in 2002. Emerging economies in Asia maintained somewhat stronger momentum, but key nations in Latin America suffered severe economic troubles and political upheavals that curtailed output and trade.

Global recovery. International trade in goods showed signs of growth during the first half of 2002, according to a report released in October by the World Trade Organization (WTO), a Geneva, Switzerland-based group that oversees trade agreements and arbitrates disputes among member nations. The WTO report warned, however, that the value of merchandise traded in the first half of 2002 trailed figures for the same period in 2001. Analysts at the WTO estimated that the volume of trade in goods could show a slight gain in 2002 if industrial nations maintained the levels of the first two quarters. However, demand and output slowed in the United States and key European markets in the second half of the year.

International trade in services also recovered somewhat in 2002, according to reports from the WTO and the International Monetary Fund (IMF), a United Nations-affiliated agency that provides financing and economic guidance to member nations. The IMF in October projected that the 2002 volume of world trade in both goods and services could grow by 2.1 percent after shrinking 0.1 percent in 2001.

WTO Director-General Supachai Panitchpakdi said that "the disappointing trade figures for 2001 and the first half of 2002 underscore the importance of making progress" in the Doha Development Agenda, the latest round of global negotiations to lower trade barriers. In November, U.S. officials unveiled a dramatic proposal to end all tariffs on manufactured goods worldwide by 2015. Observers said the offer was a bid to both energize the Doha talks and counter criticism of protective tariffs instituted by the United States in early 2002.

Prices. The WTO and IMF reported that prices for key commodities and goods rose slightly in 2002 as the U.S. dollar, the dominant world currency, declined in value against other major currencies. Experts said increases in oil prices were driven by concerns that a potential U.S. war against Iraq could threaten oil shipments. As industrial demand weakened later in 2002, the WTO warned that further increases in oil prices "would hurt an already fragile global recovery."

United States. The recovering U.S. economy ran up a large trade deficit during 2002 as imports eclipsed exports by a growing margin. By November, the trade deficit had reached $437.3

billion, or 4.2 percent of the entire U.S. economy.

Despite the huge trade deficit, U.S. trading partners criticized President George W. Bush for erecting several controversial trade barriers to protect U.S. industries. In March, Bush imposed import tariffs of up to 30 percent on most steel imports in an effort to protect the faltering U.S. steel industry. The government also imposed high tariffs on imports of softwood lumber from Canada. The president refused to increase the textile import quota or cut textile tariffs for Pakistan, despite that country's request for concessions in return for its cooperation in the U.S.-led war against terrorism. In December, however, Bush lifted a ban that kept Mexican trucks from carrying cargo into the United States beyond 20 miles from the U.S.-Mexican border.

In July, the U.S. Congress granted Bush so-called "fast-track" authority to negotiate trade agreements. The legislation allowed Congress to confirm or veto trade agreements negotiated by the president, but prevented it from altering the agreements' terms.

Increased security measures implemented in

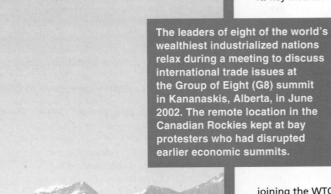

The leaders of eight of the world's wealthiest industrialized nations relax during a meeting to discuss international trade issues at the Group of Eight (G8) summit in Kananaskis, Alberta, in June 2002. The remote location in the Canadian Rockies kept at bay protesters who had disrupted earlier economic summits.

prompting calls for the European Central Bank to stimulate growth by cutting interest rates. The bank resisted until December, when it finally cut its key interest rate by half of a percentage point.

As 2002 drew to a close, several countries, including France and Germany, were running budget deficits near or over the maximum allowed without penalty by the E.U. Many member nations urged the union to relax deficit spending caps so they could stimulate their economies through deficit spending.

Asia. China, which rose to the top ranks of import/export nations shortly after joining the WTO in 2001, maintained its strength during 2002 in both economic growth and trade volume. China's trade was a key source of its economic strength, helping to spur a recovery among other nations in East Asia. Economic growth in Russia, trade liberalization measures in India, and increasing demand for computer chips from South Korea also contributed to trade recovery in Asia.

Both the WTO and IMF pressed Japan to get its weak economy on track and regain its position as an important source of growth in trade and the global economy. The IMF urged Japan to clean up the bad debt portfolios in its banking system. Economists also noted that Japan relied heavily on export sales in 2002 to help its economy in the absence of domestic demand. The country continued to suffer falling prices for domestic goods while the government still applied tariffs and duties that raised the cost of imports.

Latin America. Argentina, Venezuela, Brazil, Uruguay, and other Latin American nations underwent economic, financial, and political crises in 2002 that ravaged the region's once-strong trade. Argentina defaulted on debt payments amid a severe recession that the IMF said had cut its output by about 20 percent between 1998 and 2002. Economists considered economic strife a major reason that Venezuelans ousted President Hugo Chavez Frias for a few days in a short-lived *coup* (overthrow) in April 2002. In December, Chavez again faced growing discord as a national strike nearly halted the country's oil exports.

Hard-pressed voters in Brazil, Latin America's largest economy, elected left-wing politician Luiz Inacio Lula da Silva as president. World markets and foreign lenders nervously watched to see if the new president would lead Brazil down a confrontational path with lenders. ☐ John D. Boyd

See also **Argentina; Brazil; Economics; Japan; Manufacturing; Manufacturing: A Special Report.**

response to the terrorist attacks on the United States on Sept. 11, 2001, added costs and delays to the flow of goods into the large U.S. market throughout 2002. A 10-day lockout of dockworkers beginning on Sept. 29, 2002, shut down ports all along the West Coast, which handle a huge volume of trade with Asia.

Europe. The worldwide economic slowdown of 2000 and 2001 tested the European Union's design for a shared trading market. Major European economies including Germany, the union's largest, suffered weak economic activity in 2002,

Internet. The number of people with access to the Internet continued to grow in 2002, reaching about 450 million users worldwide. In the United States, 69 percent of adults had access to the Internet by February 2002, up from 67 percent in September 2001, according to a report by New York City-based Internet research firm Ipsos-Reid.

Digital divide. Policymakers continued to express concern in 2002 over disparities in Internet use among people of different age, gender, race, and economic background. According to a February Ipsos-Reid poll, about 73 percent of U.S. men had access to the Internet, compared with 65 percent of U.S. women. Older people were less likely to have Internet access than any other age group. About 80 percent of people ages 18 to 34 had Internet access, but only 47 percent of those age 55 and older were able to connect to the Internet. People living in higher income households were most likely to have Internet access. About 88 percent of U.S. families with an annual income of $50,000 or more had access, compared with just 48 percent of families that made $25,000 or less.

In the United States, Internet use grew faster among Hispanics than in any other ethnic group, according to a June 2002 study by Nielsen/Net-Ratings, a Milpitas, California, research group. The number of Hispanics with access to the Internet rose 13 percent from June 2001 to June 2002. However, only 7.6 million Hispanics used the Internet in June 2002, compared with 90.1 million non-Hispanic whites, who make up nearly 90 percent of U.S. Internet users. The 7.5 million African-Americans who were online made up 7.4 percent of Internet users, followed by 2.2 million Asian and Pacific Islanders, who made up 2.2 percent of users.

Spam. The use of unsolicited e-mail advertisements increased sharply in 2002. The messages, known as "spam," are the electronic equivalent of junk mail. Spam messages, sent to thousands of e-mail addresses, often use misleading subject lines to entice unwary users to open them. Spam accounted for nearly half of the traffic on some Internet servers, slowing Internet access and driving up costs for Internet service providers.

Internet users received an average of 571 pieces of spam in 2001, according to a study by Jupiter Media Metrix, a media research firm located in Darien, Connecticut. Experts at Jupiter Media Metrix predicted that the number of spam messages the average user received would top 700 in 2002 and hit 3,900 annually by 2007.

Security. An unusually powerful electronic attack in October 2002 struck 9 of the 13 root server computers that manage global Internet traffic. The attack, which consisted of data transmissions at levels 30 to 40 times greater than normal, disabled seven servers for one hour and caused intermittent problems on two others. Authorities were unable to locate the source of the attack.

Computer *crackers*, or *hackers* (people who illegally break into computer systems), launched about twice as many attacks on the Internet in 2002 as they did in 2001, according to the CERT Coordination Center, a federally funded Internet security reporting center at Carnegie Mellon University in Pittsburgh. The center reported that the number of security vulnerabilities—flaws in software that left computers open to attack—also doubled during the same period.

In February 2002, Ipsos-Reid reported that over 40 percent of Internet users were hit by a computer virus in 2001. About 40 percent of those who received a virus needed to have their computers repaired as a result of the infection. Despite the increasing danger of contracting a virus, 17 percent of Internet users reported not using widely available antivirus software.

Privacy. In November 2002, U.S. President George W. Bush signed the Cyber Security Enhancement Act of 2002 into law as part of legislation creating the U.S. Department of Homeland Security. The act protects Internet service providers from being sued by customers for sharing Internet-use information with law enforcement officials. Privacy advocates condemned the measure, which also made it easier for authorities to track the activities of Internet users who presented "an imminent threat to national security interests."

Napster, the Redwood City, California, company that popularized the practice of downloading music on the Internet, filed for bankruptcy in June. Napster had shut down after losing a legal battle with record companies in July 2001. Napster planned to reopen in partnership with Bertelsmann, a German media company, as a pay service that would provide royalties to record companies. However, Napster chief executive Konrad Hilbers announced that Napster would probably shut down permanently after a federal judge blocked the sale of Napster to Bertelsmann in September 2002.

File-swapping services similar to Napster, including KaZaA and Morpheus, quickly filled the void left by the shutdown. Music and movie companies lobbied the U.S. Congress to pass laws allowing them to take legal action against people who use file-swapping services to distribute copies of music or films. The record companies continued to develop their own music-downloading services, but limited offerings, significant restrictions, and high cost continued to drive consumers to the alternatives.   □ Dave Wilson

See also **Computers.**

Iowa. See **State government.**

Iran. The political struggle in Iran between conservatives and reformers intensified in September 2002, when moderate President Mohammad Khatami introduced two bills in the reformist-dominated parliament to weaken the power of hardline clerics. One of the bills would reduce the electoral oversight role of the Council of Guardians, a group that reviews parliamentary legislation. The council had repeatedly disqualified reformist candidates for public office. The other bill would increase the authority of Iran's president to assure that officials in other institutions and branches of government obeyed the constitution. This bill was intended to curb the power of the conservative judiciary, which had banned at least 80 reformist publications and jailed dozens of reformers since 2000. The parliament approved the outlines of both bills in November 2002, but reformers feared the Council of Guardians would later block the legislation.

Student protests. Thousands of students staged demonstrations in Tehran, the capital, and other Iranian cities in November and December to protest the death sentence given to a professor for criticizing hardline clerics. Political affairs experts suggested that the scholar, Hashem Aghajari, had been condemned as a warning to other reformers. As the protests intensified, Ayatollah Ali Khamenei, Iran's Supreme Leader, ordered an appeals court to review Aghajari's death sentence.

U.S. relations. In January, United States President George W. Bush accused Iran, along with Iraq and North Korea, of belonging to an "axis of evil" supporting terrorism and seeking weapons of mass destruction. Many Iranians viewed the accusation as hostile, bolstering support for Iran's hardliners.

U.S. concerns about Iran had increased after Israeli authorities intercepted a ship in early January carrying weapons allegedly supplied by Iran and bound for Palestinian territories. The interception occurred as U.S. officials were trying to broker a truce in the Palestinian-Israeli conflict.

In December, U.S. officials expressed concern that two new nuclear facilities in Iran could be used to develop nuclear weapons. Iran, however, claimed the facilities were for peaceful purposes.

Iraq. In August, President Khatami warned that U.S. plans to widen its war on terrorism risked unleashing new anti-U.S. violence in the Islamic world. Experts said that Khatami was apparently referring to U.S. threats to attack Iraq if Iraq failed to comply with United Nations (UN) resolutions, including fully cooperating with UN weapons inspectors. ☐ Christine Helms

See also **Afghanistan; Iraq; Israel; Middle East; Terrorism.**

An Iranian woman in Tehran mourns amid hundreds of flag-draped coffins containing the remains of Iranian prisoners of war who died in captivity during the Iran-Iraq War (1980-1988). Iran and Iraq exchanged the remains of more than 1,700 POW's in July 2002.

In December, a United Nations inspector examines dismantled equipment used in Iraq's chemical weapons program in the 1980's and 1990's. The inspectors returned to Iraq in 2002 to search for signs of chemical, biological, or nuclear weapons programs for the first time since 1998.

Iraq. Iraqi President Saddam Hussein averted the threat of imminent war by agreeing on Nov. 13, 2002, to a new United Nations (UN) resolution mandating the resumption of weapons inspections in Iraq. UN inspectors arrived in Iraq later in November to search for evidence of chemical, biological, or nuclear weapons programs. UN resolutions passed after Iraq's defeat in the 1991 Gulf War required Iraq to fully disarm. However, Iraq had refused since 1998 to cooperate with weapons inspections. The 2002 UN resolution warned Iraq of "serious consequences" if it failed to comply with disarmament requirements.

U.S. challenge. United States President George W. Bush had declared in January that Iraq was one of three nations, with Iran and North Korea, that constituted an "axis of evil" in their pursuit of weapons of mass destruction and support of terrorism. In the following months, President Bush repeatedly expressed his desire to see Iraq disarmed and called for a "regime change" in Iraq. In September, President Bush challenged the UN to join an international effort to disarm Iraq. The UN Security Council, in a unanimous vote of 15 to 0, passed the weapons-inspections resolution on November 8.

In December, Iraq provided documentation to the UN that Iraqi officials claimed proved the country no longer possessed weapons of mass de-struction. However, Hans Blix, the chief UN inspector, reported that the documentation did not contain UN-mandated evidence that Iraq had destroyed its weapons. U.S. officials declared Iraq in "material breach" of the UN resolution and warned that prospects for peace were dimming.

Referendum and pardon. In October, the Iraqi government reported that Hussein won 100 percent of the vote in a referendum on his leadership. He was the sole candidate. After the referendum, he announced that all prisoners in Iraq were granted *amnesty* (pardon) and would be freed. That same day, a crowd of relatives of prisoners broke down the gates of Iraq's main prison, Abu Ghraib, to free the inmates. Some Iraqis later demonstrated outside Iraq's Ministry of Information, claiming their relatives had disappeared without a trace while in prison.

Arab relations. Hussein sought to improve relations with other Arab and Muslim nations in 2002. At an Arab summit meeting in March, he recognized the sovereignty of Kuwait, which Iraqi forces had invaded in 1990. Hussein's statement came after other Arab leaders at the summit urged an end to UN sanctions against Iraq and expressed opposition to military action against Hussein's regime. ☐ Christine Helms

See also **Armed Forces; Congress of the United States; Middle East; United Nations.**

Ireland. The reelection of Prime Minister (Taioseach) Bertie Ahern dominated events in the Republic of Ireland in 2002. Ahern's Fianna Fail party won the most seats—81—in the Dail (the lower house of parliament) in the general election on May 17, an increase from 77 seats in the previous (1997) election. Nevertheless, Fianna Fail remained three seats short of a majority and was forced to form a new government with its former coalition partner, the Progressive Democratic Party. Political experts credited Ahern's victory to Ireland's highly successful economy, low taxes and unemployment, and increased public spending during his previous term in office.

The largest opposition party, Fine Gael, plummeted from 54 seats to 31. Fine Gael's leader, Michael Noonan, resigned the following day to be replaced later by Enda Kenny. Labour Party leader Ruairi Quinn resigned in August 2002, after his party's failure to make electoral progress. He was replaced by Pat Rabbitte in October.

Corruption. The new government came under attack almost immediately, with allegations of corruption and mismanagement. Following the election, Ahern had promised to spend millions of pounds in public funds to build Stadium Ireland, a huge sports complex on the outskirts of Dublin, the capital. The stadium was critical to a combined Irish-Scottish bid to host Euro 2008, a European soccer festival. However, a shortfall in Ireland's finances because of the worldwide economic slowdown caused the government to pull out of the project in September 2002, endangering its future. The Central Bank had forecast that the Irish economy would grow by only 4 percent in 2002, a dramatic slow-down after an average growth rate of 8.4 percent in the late 1990's.

The government was also forced to make massive spending cuts in health and education, despite having promised during the election that there would be "no cutbacks whatsoever." In addition, in September 2002, the Flood tribunal, a panel investigating illegal payments to politicians, censured Ray Burke (a former foreign minister in Ahern's government) for having received payments from building contractors in exchange for granting planning permission.

Referendum. In October, Irish voters approved a referendum on the Nice treaty, which included guidelines for admitting Eastern European countries into the European Union (EU). (The treaty needed to be ratified by all 15 EU nations in order to go into effect.) The vote was considered a triumph for Ahern, who had suffered a severe setback in 2001, when Irish voters rejected the treaty in a similar referendum despite the support of most of Ireland's political leaders.   □ Rohan McWilliam

See also **Europe; Northern Ireland.**

Islam. Muslims in 2002 experienced scrutiny and criticism primarily as fallout from the terrorist attacks on the United States on Sept. 11, 2001. These and other terrorist acts by Islamic extremists drew increasingly vehement attacks on Islam.

Several prominent U.S. evangelical leaders, such as Jerry Falwell and Jerry Vines, denounced Islam in harsh and graphic terms. In one of several attacks, Falwell referred to the prophet Muhammad, the founder of Islam, as a "terrorist" on a nationally televised appearance. Falwell's remarks elicited a public outcry, and he later apologized. Many religious and political leaders considered these attacks over-zealous and unfounded.

In the Netherlands, right-wing politician Pym Fortuyn espoused an anti-immigrant platform while campaigning on behalf of his party and attacked Muslims and Islam as a "backward culture" both in speeches and in his book *Against The Islamisation Of Our Culture.* Fortuyn, however, did not live to run in the election. He was assassinated in May by an animal rights advocate.

Moderate Muslims in Western nations tried to counter these attacks with various outreach activities. Local mosques organized seminars on Islam and made speakers available to local groups and to the press.

Increased curiosity. Observers noted an increased curiosity about Islam throughout Europe and the United States during 2002. Universities reported record numbers of students enrolling in courses in Islamic studies and Arabic language. The University of North Carolina in Chapel Hill required incoming students to read a translation of several chapters of the Quran, the sacred religious text of Islam. The assignment led to lawsuits from some political and religious organizations, which claimed that teaching about Islam violated the separation of church and state. Islamic organizations reported slight increases in rates of conversion to Islam, particularly among Hispanics in the United States.

Turkey. The pro-Islamic party in Turkey, Justice and Development, won a large plurality in elections held in November. Some observers considered the victory a challenge to secular government in Turkey. Others said it confirmed that democracy and Islam were not incompatible.

In May, Turkey's Religious Affairs Directorate broke with centuries of traditional interpretation of the Quran and urged women to participate equally with men in Islamic public religious life. The directorate, a state-controlled body that monitors Islamic communities, argued that the Quran did not prohibit women from praying with men at funerals or during menstruation, as some believers had claimed.   □ A. Kevin Reinhart

See also **Netherlands; Turkey.**

A fire triggered by an explosion rages over Bethlehem on April 6 during an Israeli military offensive in areas of the West Bank held by the Palestinian Authority. Ariel Sharon ordered the attack in response to a Passover suicide bombing in Netanya that left nearly 30 Israelis dead in a hotel dining room.

Israel. Israel's reoccupation of the West Bank in late March 2002 and the collapse of Prime Minister Ariel Sharon's coalition government in November ended any prospects for peace between Israelis and Palestinians in 2002.

Violence. Ariel Sharon, following an upsurge of Palestinian suicide bombings, adopted increasingly harsh tactics to counter spiraling Palestinian-Israeli violence. The most deadly bombing of the year occurred on March 27, when almost 30 Israelis were killed at a Passover meal in a hotel in the coastal city of Netanya.

After the Netanya attack, Sharon ordered Israeli troops to reoccupy West Bank cities that Israel had previously ceded to the control of the Palestinian Authority (PA). Israeli troops and tanks in late March attacked Palestinian leader Yasir Arafat's office compound in the West Bank city of Ram Allah. In April, Israeli forces laid siege to the Church of the Nativity in Bethlehem, where Israeli officials claimed that Palestinian extremists had taken refuge. By the end of the main part of the Israeli offensive in late April, Israel had inflicted massive damage on the PA government and economy and left much of Arafat's Ram Allah compound in ruins.

The Israeli campaign, however, failed to end Palestinian violence. Israeli troops remained in the West Bank and encamped outside the Palestinian-held Gaza Strip to retaliate against ongoing terrorist activities with quick, lethal strikes. Israel also killed leaders of the militant Palestinian groups Hamas and Islamic Jihad and destroyed the houses of families of suspected terrorists. In June, Sharon's government endorsed plans for the construction of a fence to separate the West Bank from Israel.

Economy. The cost of the military campaign in 2002 placed severe strains on Israel's economy, which was already in a serious recession. In October, the government forecast that Israel's *gross domestic product* (the total value of all goods and services produced in a given period) would decline by 0.9 percent in 2002. More than 10 percent of the workforce was unemployed, and the inflation rate reached 8 percent.

In November, the Israeli government asked the United States for approximately $4 billion in military aid and $10 billion in loan guarantees. The requests were to defray the cost of the Palestinian conflict, prepare for the possibility of a U.S.-led war against Iraq, and aid Israel's economic recovery.

Elections. In November, Prime Minister Sharon, the Likud Party leader, was forced to call early elections after members of his main coalition partner, the Labor Party, resigned from the Cabinet. Sharon was unable to form a new coalition with right-wing parties. Labor ministers, who were more moderate than Likud ministers, had protested Sharon's financial support for Jewish settlements in the West Bank at the expense of social welfare programs. Sharon, a hardliner who

An Israeli volunteer searches for human remains in July at the site of a bus bombing near a Jewish settlement in the West Bank. Palestinian gunmen set off a bomb to stop the armor-plated bus and then mowed down passengers as they tried to escape. Seven people died in the attack.

won office in 2001, found himself a target in 2002 of both moderate and right-wing groups who claimed his tactics had failed.

On November 28, Sharon fended off a challenge from Foreign Minister (and former Prime Minister) Benjamin Netanyahu in Likud Party primaries. Sharon was to face off against Labor leader Amram Mitzna in general elections in late January 2003. Mitzna, a dovish former general, had won Labor's primary in November 2002.

Al-Qa'ida attacks. On the day of the Likud primaries, suicide bombers destroyed an Israeli-owned hotel in Mombasa, Kenya, killing 10 Kenyans and 3 Israelis. Moments before, terrorists fired shoulder-launched rockets at an Israeli charter jet taking off from the Mombasa airport. The rockets missed their target. The Islamic terrorist network al-Qa'ida, which was widely considered responsible for the terrorist attacks on the United States on Sept. 11, 2001, reportedly claimed credit for the Kenyan attacks.

Abba Eban. Renowned Israeli diplomat and political leader Abba Eban died in November 2002 at age 87. ☐ Christine Helms

See also **Deaths; Iraq; Kenya; Middle East.**

Italy. The policies of Prime Minister Silvio Berlusconi faced growing opposition during 2002. Italy's three main labor unions staged the first general strike in 20 years on April 16 protesting government efforts aimed at changing labor laws so that companies could more easily fire workers. As many as 13 million workers participated in the strike, which effectively shut down the country for the day. Some 2 million people took part in street protests. The government reached a tentative agreement with two of the unions to negotiate labor reforms during the summer, but the largest union, the left-wing Confederatione Generale Italiana del Lavoro (CGIL), staged a second strike on October 18, disrupting factories and air and train travel.

The government passed judicial legislation in 2002 despite protests by opposition parties, which claimed the law was designed to personally protect Berlusconi. Berlusconi, who built a media empire that made him Italy's richest person before entering politics, was on trial in Milan on charges of having bribed judges to win the acquisition of a food company, SME, in the 1980's. The law, which was approved by parliament on Nov. 5, 2002, allows defendants to request that their trial be moved to another city if they can show credible evidence that the judge is biased. Berlusconi's lawyers said they intended to request that his trial be moved from Milan to the northern Italian city of Brescia. The change of venue was expected to delay the trial until the statute of limitations for the case expired.

Minister resigns. Berlusconi's center-right coalition suffered from infighting early in 2002 over its policy toward the European Union (EU). Berlusconi forced Renato Ruggiero, who did not belong to a coalition party but had been appointed foreign minister because of his international experience, out of office on January 5. Ruggiero had criticized other Cabinet members for attacking the EU. While Italy had traditionally been a firm supporter of the EU, several members of Berlusconi's government held that the EU interfered too much in its members' affairs. Berlusconi served as foreign minister as well as prime minister for much of 2002 before appointing Franco Frattini, a member of his Forza Italia party, to the post in November.

Andreotti trial. A murder case against former Prime Minister Giulio Andreotti took a surprising turn in November when an appeals court overturned the not-guilty verdict delivered in 1999. The court found Andreotti guilty of involvement in the 1979 murder of a journalist and sentenced him to 24 years in prison. Andreotti, who served as prime minister seven times in the 1970's and 1980's, vowed to appeal the verdict.

Economy. Italy's economy slumped to the verge of recession in 2002 as the worldwide economic slowdown hurt exports and corporate investment. EU economists forecast that the country's gross domestic product, the value of all goods and services produced in a year, would grow by 0.4 percent during 2002, down from 1.8 percent in 2001. The slowdown forced the government to make fresh budget cuts in order to reduce its deficit and the national debt, as required for countries using the euro. In September 2002, the government approved a budget for 2003 that included $20 billion of spending cuts and other measures aimed at reducing the deficit. The budget also included $7.5 billion of tax cuts, mostly for low-income people.

The weak economy caused problems for Fiat SpA, Italy's leading automaker and largest private sector employer. Weak demand for its aging car models pushed the company's auto division to post an operating loss of $1.2 billion in the first nine months of 2002. In July, Fiat sold 34 percent of its sports car subsidiary, Ferrari, to raise $770 million. In December, the company said it would lay off 2,500 workers permanently and another 5,600 workers for up to a year and reduce production sharply at its assembly plant in Sicily.

Pope John Paul II made a historic address to the Chamber of Deputies, the lower house of parliament, on November 14. His appearance before the Italian legislature was the first by a Ro-

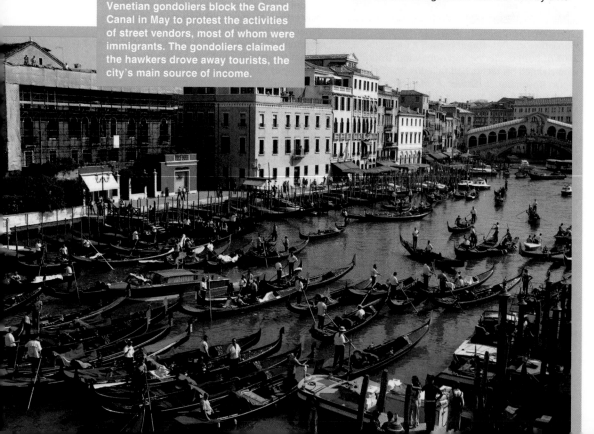

Venetian gondoliers block the Grand Canal in May to protest the activities of street vendors, most of whom were immigrants. The gondoliers claimed the hawkers drove away tourists, the city's main source of income.

man Catholic pontiff. John Paul called on EU leaders not to ignore Christian values as they expanded the union into Eastern Europe. He also cautioned against war as a response to terrorism.

Earthquake. An earthquake that struck central Italy on October 31 caused a primary school to collapse in the farming village of San Giuliano di Puglia, killing 26 children and a teacher. The tragedy prompted authorities to investigate the construction of the building.

Immigration. Authorities in 2002 continued to hunt for the crew of a ship carrying at least 283 immigrants from Asia. The ship sank off the coast of Sicily in 1996. Survivors of the wreck had claimed that the smugglers had forced hundreds of immigrants onto an old ferry and then rammed the ferry so that it sank, but their stories were disbelieved because no shipwreck was found at that time. Investigations by Italian newspapers uncovered the wrecked ferry on the sea floor in 2001. Authorities arrested the Lebanese captain of the freighter that had carried the immigrants from Asia and charged him with manslaughter, but he skipped bail. Another crew member was extradited from Malta in March 2002 to stand trial in Italy. ☐ Tom Buerkle

See also **Europe.**

Ivory Coast. See Cote d'Ivoire in **Africa.**

Jamaica. See **West Indies.**

Japan. Prime Minister Junichiro Koizumi of Japan made little progress in 2002 in reforming a political system that had left the Japanese economy mired in its worst recession, a period when the economy virtually stops growing, since World War II (1939-1945). Japan struggled in 2002 with *deflation* (decline in prices), high unemployment, and a mountain of bad loans crippling the banking system. By year's end, the Japanese economy, the second largest in the world, had sunk into its fourth recession in 10 years. The stock market had dropped to a 19-year low, and unemployment reached a postwar high of 5.5 percent. Many economists said Japan's leaders were not doing enough to solve the country's problems.

Japan's economic troubles began in the late 1980's, as Japanese manufacturers began finding it difficult to sell their products abroad. The manufacturers could not compete with low-cost goods from newly developing nations, such as China and South Korea. At the same time, the Japanese banking system began to suffer because the banks had made many loans during the late 1980's that failed when real estate prices dropped in the 1990's. Japan's problems in trade and finance resulted in a recession. In the 1990's, Japan's unemployment rate rose, average household incomes nearly stopped growing, and consumer spending declined.

In 2001, the Japanese public, desperate for change, rallied behind Koizumi, a member of the ruling Liberal Democratic Party (LDP), who promised to be a dynamic reformer. His popularity began to fall in 2002, however, as economic problems persisted and as he backed away from difficult reforms. By June, polls showed that only 37 percent of the population supported him, down from an unprecedented 85-percent approval rating the year before. Critics said Koizumi slowed his reform efforts in order to appease LDP conservatives, who opposed his plans.

Postal reform. Conservatives forced Koizumi to water down legislation in 2002 on reform of Japan's postal service, an issue he had previously claimed was a test of his government's program. The legislation allowed private companies into mail delivery and shifted control of the postal service from the government to a private corporation. Critics said Koizumi made so many concessions to guarantee passage of the legislation that real reform was unlikely.

Reform of the system was an emotional issue in Japan because postmasters played a large role in communities, particularly in remote rural areas. They delivered mail but also managed savings and life insurance accounts totaling some $3 trillion, which made the postal system the world's largest bank.

Debt woes. Public confidence in Koizumi's economic policies was shaken in May, when Moody's Investors Service, a New York City-based credit rating, research, and risk analysis firm, lowered Japan's credit rating. The move affected the rating on government bonds issued in local currency. At the new rating, bonds from Japan were considered as risky as those of Cyprus, Latvia, Poland, or Mauritius. Moody's cited government indebtedness that was rising to "levels unprecedented in the postwar era in the developed world." Because of the country's huge debt, economists urged lawmakers not to stimulate the economy with more government spending, as they had done repeatedly since 1992.

Banking crisis. In September 2002, Koizumi declared Japan's banks in a state of "emergency" and fired the economy minister, Hakuo Yanagisawa. Yanagisawa had opposed using public money to prop up banks, which were staggering under the weight of bad loans officially estimated at $423 billion. Koizumi named Heizo Takenaka, an economist, as the new economy minister.

In October, Takenaka unveiled a plan to revive the nation's ailing financial system by calling on banks to purge half of their bad loans by 2005. Bankers and their political allies opposed the plan because it would push several major banks and hundreds of debtor companies into insolvency, eliminating thousands of jobs.

In August, demonstrators decorated their faces with bar codes to protest a computerized registry of Japanese citizens. Under the system, each citizen is assigned an 11-digit number that allows online retrieval of personal information.

salaries. Political observers said the charges were made by people who wanted to punish her for questioning Koizumi's commitment to reform.

Elections. Voters turned against the LDP in three spring elections. The LDP's candidate for mayor was defeated in Yokohama, Japan's second-largest city. The LDP also lost elections for the upper house of parliament in Tanaka's home district. Observers suggested that the elections served as a referendum against Koizumi's reforms.

Korea. Japanese officials reacted in anger after North Korea admitted in October that the country had been conducting a secret nuclear weapons development program for years. The program was a violation of a pact North Korea had signed in 1994 to freeze its development of nuclear weapons.

Tanaka fired. In January, Koizumi fired Makiko Tanaka, Japan's foreign minister. Tanaka was the daughter of a former prime minister and one of Japan's most popular politicians.

Koizumi had directed Tanaka to clean up corruption in the foreign ministry and impose accountability on its bureaucrats, who had long worked without effective political oversight. Her efforts were resisted by ministry officials and key LDP members of parliament, including Muneo Suzuki, who was arrested later in 2002 on bribery charges. In an attempt to ease political tensions, Koizumi replaced Tanaka with another woman, Yoriko Kawaguchi, a former environment minister. In August, Tanaka resigned her seat in parliament over accusations that she misused public funds intended for staff

Japan vowed to withhold financial aid to North Korea until the country gave up its nuclear weapons program. It also threatened to suspend talks on normalizing relations with the isolated country, a process that had begun in September 2002 in Pyongyang, the North Korean capital. At that meeting, Japan and North Korea had ended more than 50 years of hostility with an agreement to reestablish diplomatic relations.

The summit began with North Korean leader Kim Jong Il acknowledging that North Korean agents kidnapped Japanese citizens in the 1970's and 1980's so that North Korean spies could be tutored in the Japanese language and culture. Kim also agreed to extend a moratorium on missile tests beyond 2003. In exchange, Koizumi promised North Korea billions of dollars in aid. Following the meeting, North Korea allowed five of the kidnap survivors to visit Japan. Their families, however, were not allowed to travel with them.

Japan also faced troubled relations with South Korea in 2002. In August, Japan protested South

Korea's campaign to change the name of the sea that separates the Korean peninsula from the Japanese archipelago from the Sea of Japan to the East Sea. Japan also objected to a South Korean plan to make an uninhabited islet in the sea into a national park. Japan claimed to own the islet, which it calls Takeshima.

Nuclear hopes. Japan's cabinet secretary, Yasuo Fukuda, alarmed leaders of neighboring countries in May when he suggested that Japan might consider acquiring nuclear weapons. Fukuda said that the Japanese government might rethink its self-imposed ban on nuclear weapons, which the country established in 1967.

Shrine visit. Koizumi made a surprise visit in April 2002 to a shrine that had long been at the center of a regional dispute over Japan's recognition of its wartime atrocities. The visit was Koizumi's second to the Yasukuni Shrine, which is dedicated to the 2.5 million Japanese who were killed in World War II. The visit touched off a storm of criticism from China and South Korea, which Japan occupied during the war.

Foreign aid. In 2002, Japan yielded its position to the United States as the world's top donor of foreign aid. Japan spent $9.7 billion in official development assistance in 2001, while the United States spent $10.9 billion.   □ Henry S. Bradsher
   See also **Asia; North Korea.**

Jordan. King Abdullah II remained steadfast in support of the United States in 2002. Abdullah warned, however, that a perceived U.S. bias in favor of Israel in the Palestinian-Israeli conflict and U.S. threats to attack Iraq risked the stability of both his kingdom and the entire Middle East.

Anti-U.S. violence. In October, Lawrence Foley, a senior official at the United States embassy in Amman, Jordan's capital, was shot and killed in Amman. Security forces detained dozens of Islamic militants for questioning after the slaying. In November, Jordanian authorities placed the southern city of Maan under curfew as police searched for individuals linked to the murder and people who might engage in public disorder should U.S. forces attack Iraq. In December, authorities said they arrested two men for the assassination who claimed they belonged to the Islamic terrorist network al-Qa'ida.

Palestinians. Israel's massive assault against Palestinian West Bank cities in March led to concerns that the Palestinian-Israeli conflict might spread to Jordan, where approximately 60 percent of Jordan's population, including Abdullah's wife, Queen Rania, was Palestinian. In April, Rania led a pro-Palestinian demonstration through Amman. However, the Jordanian government imposed immigration restrictions in July to try to prevent a possible Palestinian influx into Jordan.

Officials feared such an influx might occur as a result of worsening conditions in the West Bank or a mass transfer of Palestinians by Israel.

Iraq. In July, Jordan's information minister announced that Jordan would not be a "launching pad" for U.S. strikes against Iraq. Iraqi President Saddam Hussein was a longtime supporter of the Palestinian cause, and Iraq was also Jordan's largest trading partner and the major source of Jordan's oil supplies.

Water shortages. Heavy rainfall filled 40 percent of Jordan's severely depleted reservoirs in 2002. Nevertheless, the kingdom continued to suffer from declining water quality and groundwater supplies. Demand for water in Jordan greatly increased since the early 1990's because of rapid population growth, industrialization, and immigration to Jordan.

The government was engaged in several ongoing projects in 2002 to relieve the water shortages. The water ministry reduced water for irrigation by 50 percent in some areas and asked farmers to recycle water. The government also rationed water for household use, expanded and improved wastewater treatment facilities, and made repairs to an aging underground pipe network. Syria agreed in August to pump additional water to Jordan.   □ Christine Helms
   See also **Iraq; Israel; Middle East.**

Judaism. Jews around the world expressed solidarity with Israel in 2002 during a year of tense conflict between Israelis and Palestinians. *Anti-Semitism* (prejudice against Jewish people), spawned in part by the conflict, flared up in many countries.

Israel. Religion played a growing role in the Israeli-Palestinian conflict. Palestinian terrorists, in addition to attacking buses, shopping malls, and other secular (nonreligious) sites in Israel, pointedly targeted Jewish religious gatherings. On January 17, a Palestinian gunman opened fire at a *bat mitzvah* (the Jewish celebration of a girl's passage into womanhood) in Hadera, killing 6 people and injuring 25 others. A Palestinian suicide bomber killed about 30 people in an attack on March 27 at a crowded hotel dining room where Jews were celebrating the Passover meal, or *seder.* Several attacks targeted Jews gathering after the Sabbath, the weekly Jewish holy day.

The attacks led to a sharp decline in tourism to Israel and a continuation of Israel's economic downturn. In response, *diaspora* (non-Israeli) Jews organized "missions" to Israel and invited Israeli merchants to market their wares in special Israel fairs held in major diaspora communities.

United States. Concern for Israel's security and support for the war against terrorism became the major themes of Jewish life in the United States in 2002. In April, the largest Jewish rally in the United States in 10 years brought tens of thousands of Jews to Washington, D.C., to express support for Israel. Jewish fundraising for Israel also rose dramatically.

Many Jewish students sought during 2002 to counter what they saw as a growing anti-Israel bias on U.S. college campuses. Students at Harvard University in Cambridge, Massachusetts; the University of California at Berkeley; and other major universities organized protests against campaigns aimed at discouraging investment in companies doing business with Israel.

The United Jewish Communities, a Jewish organization based in New York City, released preliminary results in October from the 2000-2001 National Jewish Population Survey. The survey reported that the U.S. Jewish community was aging and declining in size. The release prompted an outcry from Jewish experts who disputed the methods used to conduct the survey. The United Jewish Communities delayed the release of further data from the survey until a panel of experts finished investigating the results.

Fears of increasing anti-Semitism rose in early 2002 following the kidnapping and murder of U.S. journalist Daniel Pearl by Islamic terrorists in Pakistan. In a taped statement preceding the murder, his captors forced him to read a confes-

sion identifying his Jewish ancestry. The statement raised fears that Pearl's kidnappers were motivated in part by Pearl's Jewish heritage.

An attack at the Los Angeles International Airport ticket counter of Israeli airline El Al on July 4 reinforced fears that international terrorists were targeting Jewish people. As a result, many synagogues and other Jewish institutions implemented unprecedented security measures during the Jewish high holidays.

Anti-Semitism increased sharply in Europe in 2002. Hundreds of incidents of vandalism and violence took place at Jewish schools and synagogues in France, particularly in April as violence escalated in the Middle East. In Russia and Ukraine, scores of people were injured in anti-Semitic attacks, and synagogues were damaged.

A television series based on "The Protocols of the Elders of Zion," which aired in Egypt in 2002, drew protests from historians, Jews, and other people around the world. Many anti-Semitic movements have drawn on the Protocols, documents dating from the 1800's that purport to reveal a Jewish plan for world domination. Nearly all historians have condemned the Protocols as a forgery, and efforts to support their claims have not turned up any credible historical evidence.

☐ Jonathan D. Sarna and Jonathan J. Golden
See also **Israel; Journalism; Middle East.**

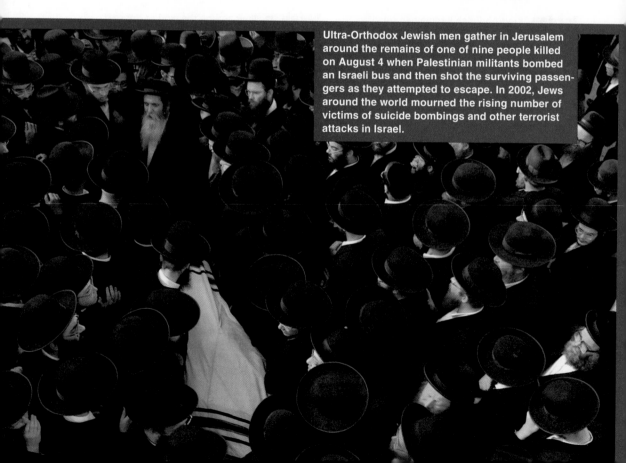

Ultra-Orthodox Jewish men gather in Jerusalem around the remains of one of nine people killed on August 4 when Palestinian militants bombed an Israeli bus and then shot the surviving passengers as they attempted to escape. In 2002, Jews around the world mourned the rising number of victims of suicide bombings and other terrorist attacks in Israel.

Kazakhstan. Prime Minister Qasymzhom-art Toqaev of Kazakhstan and his entire Cabinet resigned in January 2002 under intense pressure from a united opposition movement. President Nursultan Nazarbayev appointed his long-time ally and former deputy prime minister, Imangali Tasmagambetov, to replace Toqaev.

Western authorities and human rights groups expressed concern in 2002 over the arrests of a number of Kazakhstan's opposition leaders. In March, the police arrested former Energy, Indus-try, and Trade Minister Mukhtar Abliyazov. Abliyazov led the Democratic Choice for Kazakh-stan party (DVK), the country's main opposition movement. Authorities seized Ghalymzhan Zhaqiyanov, another DVK leader, in April after he had taken refuge in a building occupied by sever-al European embassies. Despite the objections of international human rights groups, Kazakh courts convicted both men on charges of abuse of pow-er and sentenced Abliyazov to six years in jail and Zhaqiyanov to seven. In October, police arrested journalist and human rights activist Sergei Du-vanov and subsequently charged him with rape. Duvanov protested the indictment, saying the government had trumped up the charges in or-der to discredit him.   □ Steven L. Solnick

See also **Asia**.

Kentucky. See State government.

Kenya. Terrorists, in two apparently coordi-nated attacks on Nov. 28, 2002, fired missiles at an Israeli jetliner taking off from the Mombasa airport and detonated bombs in a Mombasa ho-tel filled with Israeli tourists. The heat-seeking missiles missed their target. However, the suicide bombers' attack on the hotel left 10 Kenyans and 3 Israelis dead. Experts noted that the attacks were made on the same day that Israel was hold-ing an important primary election.

A few days after the incident, a statement claiming responsibility for the attack and at-tributed to the al-Qa'ida terrorist network was posted on an Islamic extremist Web site. U.S. in-telligence agents noted that there was evidence to validate that claim.

In elections on December 27, Mwai Kibaki of the opposition National Alliance of Kenya (NAK) was elected president with 62 percent of the vote. Kibaki had been vice president under Presi-dent Daniel arap Moi until 1988, when he be-came an opponent of Moi. Kibaki defeated Uhu-ru Kenyatta of the ruling Kenya African National Union (KANU). Kenyatta was the son of Kenya's first president, Jomo Kenyatta.

KANU had nominated Kenyatta in October 2002 as its presidential candidate. The selection was widely attributed to President Moi, who was constitutionally barred from seeking reelection

after 24 years in office. Moi described Kenyatta as a "young man who can be guided," prompting fears that Moi would hold onto power through the politically inexperienced Kenyatta. A group of KANU politicians responded to the nomination by quitting the party and forming an opposition group called "The Rainbow Coalition." The coali-tion united behind NAK candidate Kibaki.

Corruption. On January 18, Transparency In-ternational, an independent anticorruption orga-nization based in Berlin, Germany, issued a report documenting how corruption affected daily life in Kenya. The "Kenya Urban Bribery Index" was based on interviews with 1,200 Kenyans. It out-lined how corruption had permeated Kenya's po-lice, ministry of public works, and immigration office. The report's authors estimated that the widespread system of bribes for services inflated the cost of living 30 percent for average Kenyans.

Days before the report was released, Presi-dent Moi announced his appointment of a team of British anticorruption experts. Moi was re-sponding to pressure from international donors that had withheld loans and aid pending a signif-icant government response to corruption. Earlier efforts by the Kenyan government to tackle cor-ruption had yielded insignificant results, the donors claimed.   □ Simon Baynham

See also **Africa; Terrorism**.

Korea, North. Officials of North Korea shocked governments around the world in 2002 when they admitted North Korea had been con-ducting a secret nuclear weapons program for years. The program was a violation of a pact North Korea had signed in 1994 to freeze its nuclear weapons development. The announcement took place in October 2002 after a United States diplo-mat confronted North Korean officials with data that suggested a secret project was under way. The North Koreans acknowledged the nuclear pro-gram but would not comment on whether scien-tists had produced a nuclear weapon.

North Korea had long sought nuclear capabili-ty. It pursued a nuclear weapons program in the 1980's and 1990's that resulted in a confrontation with the United States in 1994. The crisis was re-solved when North Korea agreed to halt its nu-clear work, and the United States, Japan, and South Korea agreed to provide the country with oil and nuclear reactors to produce power.

U.S. reaction. After North Korea announced it had abandoned the accord in 2002, the United States pressed China to persuade North Korea to give up its weapons program. Tensions between the United States and North Korea escalated in December when North Korea reactivated nuclear facilities at Yongbyon and expelled United Na-tions inspectors monitoring its nuclear plants.

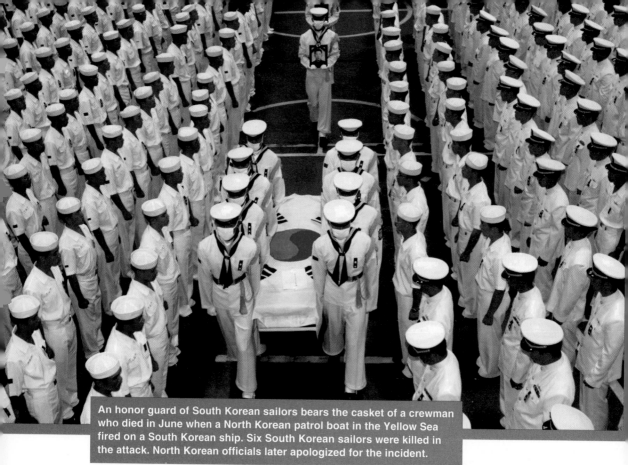

An honor guard of South Korean sailors bears the casket of a crewman who died in June when a North Korean patrol boat in the Yellow Sea fired on a South Korean ship. Six South Korean sailors were killed in the attack. North Korean officials later apologized for the incident.

Japan vowed to withhold financial aid until North Korea gave up its nuclear program. Japanese officials also threatened to suspend talks on normalizing relations with the isolated country, a process that began in September in Pyongyang, North Korea's capital. At that meeting, the countries agreed to reestablish diplomatic relations after more than 50 years of hostility.

North Korean leader Kim Jong Il revealed at the Pyongyang meeting that North Korean agents had kidnapped Japanese citizens in the 1970's and 1980's. The kidnap victims were to tutor North Korean spies in the Japanese language and culture. Also at the meeting, Kim agreed to extend a moratorium on missile tests, and Japanese Prime Minister Junichiro Koizumi promised Korea billions of dollars in aid.

Refugees. At least 100,000 North Koreans entered China illegally in 2002. The refugees, fleeing repression and starvation, sought refuge in diplomatic missions. A few dozen refugees managed to fly to South Korea from China.

Economic change. North Korea modified its rigidly Communist system in July 2002 by adopting free market reforms, such as increasing wages, eliminating food rationing coupons, and halting state subsidies for many failing industries.

□ Henry S. Bradsher

See also **Asia; Japan; South Korea.**

Korea, South. Roh Moo-hyun, the candidate of the governing Millennium Democratic Party (MDP), was elected president of South Korea on Dec. 19, 2002. Roh, who campaigned on a promise to continue South Korea's "sunshine policy" of reconciliation with North Korea, narrowly defeated his main rival, Lee Hoi-chang, leader of the conservative Grand National Party (GNP).

Roh, an attorney, overcame several political obstacles in 2002 to win the presidency. His campaign suffered a serious blow in August when the GNP won a majority of vacant seats in parliament. As a result, members of the MDP asked Roh to step down as a candidate, but he refused.

Roh's campaign gathered steam in November when Chung Mong Joon, an heir to the Hyundai business fortune, dropped out of the race and endorsed Roh. However, the day before the election, Chung withdrew his support, claiming that Roh would improve relations with North Korea at the expense of South Korea's relationship with the United States.

U.S. protest. Roh, who once called for the withdrawal of U.S. troops from South Korea, benefited from an outpouring of anti-U.S. sentiment, which was sparked by the acquittal of two U.S. soldiers in the accidental death of two schoolgirls. After his election, Roh said he would try to preserve good relations with the United States.

South Korea's relationship with North Korea was the focal point of the 2002 campaign. The issue intensified in October when North Korea admitted that for years it had been conducting a secret nuclear weapons program. Lee vowed to withhold financial aid until North Korea gave up its nuclear program. Roh promised to use gentle persuasion to get the North to renounce its nuclear ambitions.

Outgoing President Kim Dae-jung, who was not eligible to serve another term, suffered a number of political setbacks in 2002. He reshuffled his cabinet twice in an effort to win public confidence, which had waned after several of his allies were arrested for bribery. In May, he resigned from the MDP after the arrest of two of his sons on charges of influence peddling threatened to derail Roh's campaign. Kim suffered another political blow when parliament rejected two of his nominees for prime minister. In October, parliament approved Kim's third choice, Kim Suk-soo, a former Supreme Court judge.

North Korean officials issued an apology to South Korea after a North Korean patrol boat in the Yellow Sea fired on a South Korean boat in June, killing six South Korean sailors. Representatives of the two countries met for talks shortly after the incident.   □ Henry S. Bradsher

See also **Asia; North Korea.**

Kyrgyzstan. Political protests erupted in March 2002 over the trial of Azimbek Beknazarov, a member of the Kyrgyz parliament. Beknazarov, a harsh critic of Kyrgyz President Askar Akayev, was accused of misconduct in a murder trial he prosecuted in 1995. Beknazarov's supporters claimed that he was being persecuted for his opposition to Akayev and especially for his role in blocking the ratification of a border treaty with China. On March 17, 2002, police fired on a crowd of Beknazarov supporters in the village of Kerben, killing five protesters.

A government inquiry blamed the police for mishandling the situation, and in May, the prime minister and cabinet of ministers resigned after a new wave of mass protests. On May 30, the parliament approved Nikolai Tanayev as the new prime minister. Tanayev, an ethnic Russian, did not speak Kyrgyz, the country's official language, and therefore would be ineligible to run for president when Akayev's term ends in 2005.

In August 2002, Akayev convened a Constitutional Council to propose changes to the national constitution. If adopted by referendum or presidential decree, the measures would strengthen the judicial and legislative branches of the Kyrgyz government at the expense of the presidency.
          □ Steven L. Solnick

See also **Asia.**

Labor and employment. The economy of the United States emerged from recession during 2002. However, the economy's weak growth caused only a minor improvement in unemployment figures throughout the year. Most economic experts considered the recession to have been mild, particularly in comparison with the downturn of 1991 and 1992, when the overall unemployment rate hit a high of 7.8 percent. Unemployment for workers aged 16 years and older hit 6 percent in April 2002, fluctuated below that figure from May through October, then returned to 6 percent in November.

In November, the unemployment rate varied among demographic groups, according to the U.S. Department of Labor's Bureau of Labor Statistics. Jobless rates followed the usual patterns. They were lowest for all white workers (5.2 percent in November 2002) age 16 and above and highest for black workers (11 percent), with Hispanic workers in between (7.8 percent). During that same month, the jobless rate for 16- to 19-year olds was 16.8 percent.

Historically, adult white men have had the lowest unemployment rates of all ethnic-racial-gender groups. However, from June 2001 through November 2002, white women had the lowest jobless rates. In November, the unemployment rate for white women workers was 4.2 percent, compared with 5 percent for white male workers. Continuing a long-term trend, black women workers had a lower unemployment rate in November (9 percent) than black male workers (10.9 percent). The Bureau of Labor Statistics does not publish separate unemployment rates for Hispanic men and women workers.

Compensation (wages, salaries, and benefits) rose by 3.7 percent in the 12 months ending in September 2002. Wages and salaries alone increased 3.2 percent, while benefits increased 4.9 percent. The increases continued a trend of accelerating raises in both total compensation and wages and salaries that began in the early 1990's. Increases in wages and salaries had generally been above 3.5 percent since the first quarter of 2000. Increases in total compensation were 4 percent or higher during the same period. Price inflation remained low, leading to real gains in wages and benefits.

Airlines in the United States in 2002 continued to reel from financial losses totaling billions of dollars in the aftermath of the terrorist attacks on the United States on Sept. 11, 2001. Only Southwest Airlines of Dallas posted a profit for 2002. However, all of the other major airlines—American Airlines, Inc., of Fort Worth, Texas; Delta Air Lines of Atlanta, Georgia; Northwest Airlines Inc. of Saint Paul, Minnesota; United Airlines Inc. of Elk Grove Village, Illinois; and US Airways of Arlington, Virginia—suffered declines in revenue because of increased fuel costs, decreased passenger traffic after the terrorist attacks, and fierce price wars.

Early in 2002, the financially strapped airlines continued to bargain with their unions over increased wages and improved benefits. But with the specter of bankruptcy for several major airlines looming in the second half of the year, the bargaining sessions instead centered on concessions in wages and benefits.

In August, US Airways Group, Inc., the parent company of US Airways, became the first major airline to file for bankruptcy protection since the Sept. 11, 2001, attacks. The airline began a restructuring program, reaching agreements on wage and benefit concessions with its unions by September. Company officials expected to emerge from bankruptcy in 2003.

United Airlines, the second-largest U.S. carrier, agreed to wage and pension increases for its 37,500 members of the International Association of Machinists and Aerospace Workers (IAM) in March 2002. For the previous eight years, the union had frozen wages or given wage concessions in efforts to help the airline. Nevertheless, United had lost $2.1 billion in 2001. By June 2002, the company had been forced to ask for $1.5 billion in annual wage and benefit cuts over the next five years from its unions. The concessions were not enough to help the company secure a federal government-guaranteed $2 billion loan. In early December, UAL Corporation, the parent of United Airlines, filed for bankruptcy protection in Chicago, the largest airline bankruptcy in U.S. history.

Other negotiations, including those of Northwest Airlines with the Airline Pilots Association and Southwest Airlines with the Southwest Airline Pilots Association, resulted in one-year extensions of their current contracts.

Aerospace. In late April, members of the IAM voted to accept a new contract with Bethesda, Maryland-based Lockheed-Martin Corp., ending a strike that began on March 10. The three-year pact resolved the main sticking point of "outsourcing" of production by requiring the company to consult the union before it goes outside the bargaining unit for production.

In mid-September, the IAM also reached an accord with Chicago-based Boeing Co. on a three-year agreement, providing an 8-percent bonus when the union members approved the contract. The pact also provided increases of 2 percent in 2003 and 2.5 percent in 2004.

Railroads. In August 2002, members of the United Transportation Union ratified a new contract covering workers at the nation's largest rail freight companies. The pact included wage increases; the elimination of lower wages for new

Changes in the United States labor force		
	2001	**2002***
Civilian labor force . . .	141,822,000 . . .	142,412,000
Total employment	135,043,000 . . .	134,203,000
Unemployment	6,779,000	8,208,000
Unemployment rate	4.8%	5.7%
Change in real weekly earnings of production and nonsupervisory workers (nonfarm business sector)†	+0.4%	+2.1%
Change in output per employee hour (nonfarm business sector)	+1.1%	+4.8%

*All 2002 data are through the third quarter of 2002 (preliminary data).

†Real weekly earnings are adjusted for inflation by using constant 1982 dollars.

Sources: U.S. Bureau of Labor Statistics; Joint Economic Committee, U.S. Congress.

workers; no increases in health care costs for employees; and job protection whenever remote control technology is introduced.

Mail services. Members of the National Association of Letter Carriers (NALC) ratified a contract with the United States Postal Service (USPS) in May that included a wage increase of 7.1 percent over 5 years and annual cost-of-living adjustments for 238,000 workers. The wage increases were retroactive to November 2001, with increases of 1.2 percent to 1.8 percent scheduled each year through November 2005. With the acceptance of the NALC contract, all four postal unions had reached agreement with the USPS.

The International Brotherhood of Teamsters ratified a six-year contract covering 230,000 workers (including drivers and package sorters) with the United Parcel Service (UPS) in August 2002. The contract included wage increases of 22 percent over the six years. UPS also agreed to create 10,000 full-time jobs in the bargaining unit and to convert 10,000 jobs to union positions.

Communications. Members of the Communication Workers of America ratified an 18-month contract with AT&T Corp. of New York City in May. The pact provided a 6-percent wage increase and an 8-percent pension benefit increase for 27,000 technicians, operators, and customer service representatives.

Dockworkers. The International Longshore and Warehouse Union (ILWU), which represents 10,500 dockworkers on the West Coast, and the Pacific Maritime Association, the employer association, began bargaining over a new contract in July. The employers' desire to introduce new technology to help move goods through the terminals more quickly proved to be the most controversial issue. The union was concerned that such technology would result in job losses.

On September 27, the employer association locked out the union, arguing that its members were creating an artificial "slowdown" in the movement of cargo by excessive observation of safety and other contractual rules. The union responded that its members were simply exercising caution in the wake of the deaths of five longshoremen in previous months and that the movement of an unusually high volume of goods through the ports in anticipation of a strike was causing delays. Acting on the request of U.S. President George W. Bush, a federal court ordered that the docks be opened and the workers return to work on October 8. The court order marked the first time in 25 years that the 1947 Taft-Hartley Labor Relations Act has been used to end a work stoppage. The act allows the government to delay for 80 days the start of any strike that might cause a national emergency. The workers returned to the docks on Oct. 9, 2002.

Subsequently, the association and the union bargained under the auspices of a federal mediator. On November 24, the union and the Pacific Maritime Association reached agreement on a new, six-year contract. The contract allowed the association to introduce new technology but stipulated that the new jobs would be under union control. The contract, which included wage and benefit increases, was to be voted on by the union membership in January 2003.

Unions. Data released by the Bureau of Labor Statistics in January indicated that the number of U.S. workers who belonged to labor unions remained stable in 2001 at 16.3 million workers, or 13.5 percent of the work force. Almost 40 percent of government workers belonged to unions, compared with about 10 percent of private sector employees. Protective service workers, such as police officers and firefighters, had the highest proportion of workers in unions, 38 percent.

In November 2002, Edward C. Sullivan, president of the AFL-CIO's Building and Construction Trades Department, reported that the department and the Brotherhood of Carpenters were close to an agreement about the carpenters' rejoining the AFL-CIO. The carpenters' union had withdrawn from the federation in March 2001 in a dispute over organizing and spending policies. The federation board voted unaimously

in January 2002 to invite them back.

In April, the 4,000-member FEDEX Pilots Association (FPA) voted to merge the union with the 67,000-member Airline Pilots Association (ALPA). More than 90 percent of FEDEX pilots approved the move. The FEDEX pilots had withdrawn from the ALPA in 1995 to form their own union.

Federal government. In January 2002, the U.S. Department of Transportation issued eligibility requirements for federal airport passenger and baggage screeners. The U.S. Congress had placed airline security, including the screening positions, under the jurisdiction of the newly created Transportation Security Administration following the terrorist attacks on the United States on Sept. 11, 2001. One of the requirements for screeners was that applicants be U.S. citizens. The American Civil Liberties Union and the Service Employees International Union filed suit against the government, claiming that the citizenship requirement was unconstitutional. In November 2002, a federal judge put a hold on the requirement, pending a hearing.

To help the struggling U.S. steel industry, President Bush in March imposed temporary tariffs—some as high as 30 percent—on most imported steel. In August, the president signed a new Trade Promotion Authority bill allowing his administration to negotiate trade agreements with other nations. Congress could only approve or reject—not amend—the agreements. Such "fast track" authority had been allowed to expire in 1994.

International unemployment. Unemployment stood at 7 percent in October 2002 in 27 countries of the Organization for Economic Cooperation and Development (OECD). The figure represented an increase of 0.5 percent over 2001. In the OECD's "major seven" countries (the United States, Canada, Japan, France, Germany, Spain, and the United Kingdom), unemployment rose from 5.9 percent in 2001 to 6.5 percent in October 2002.

Unemployment in the euro area (Austria, Belgium, Finland, France, Germany, Greece, Italy, Ireland, Luxembourg, the Netherlands, Portugal, and Spain) was 8.4 percent in October 2002, 0.4 percent higher than in 2001. The 15 European Union nations (euro area countries plus Denmark, Sweden, and the United Kingdom) had a jobless rate of 7.7 percent in October 2002, an increase from 7.4 percent in 2001. The unemployment rate in Japan was 5.5 percent in October 2002, up from 5 percent in 2001. The rate of 6 percent in the United States in November 2002 was higher than the 4.8 percent for all of 2001. The lowest jobless rates reported by the OECD were in the Netherlands (2.8 percent) and Luxembourg (2.6 percent). ☐ Robert W. Fisher

See also **Economics; Transportation; United States, Government of the: Manufacturing: A Special Report.**

Latin America

A worsening global economic downturn severely impacted the nations of Latin America in 2002. The governments of several countries in the region, rent by partisan divisions, corruption, and mismanagement, could do little to curb ballooning deficit spending at a time of dwindling revenues. As conditions grew increasingly bleak, violence erupted in a number of countries. Many Latin Americans felt that neither the United States nor international financial institutions were doing as much as they could to help the area weather the difficult times.

Andean violence. Continuing political turmoil in Venezuela led to a bizarre *coup* (overthrow) on April 12 in which an alliance of military, business, and labor leaders ousted President Hugo Chavez Frias. Chavez returned to power just two days later with the support of some military leaders. However, neither his removal nor return quelled the increasingly frequent and violent confrontations between supporters of President Chavez and those calling for his removal, which continued throughout the year. The president's opponents complained that his leftist policies and authoritarian tactics had polarized Venezuelans along class lines.

In Colombia, President Alvaro Uribe Velez, who assumed office in August, tried to achieve a military victory in a 38-year-old civil war that had defied a peaceful resolution under his predecessor, Andres Pastrana Arango. President Uribe instituted a crackdown on leftist rebels by hiring more police, arming and training citizen "peasant soldiers," and engaging the rebels in urban warfare. The United States Congress supported Uribe's hardline approach by authorizing the use of U.S. military assistance, originally appropriated for the war on drug trafficking, for fighting the rebels and right-wing paramilitary forces.

Political feuding and corruption. In much of Latin America, governments moved at a frustratingly slow pace to address serious problems in 2002. In September, Mexican President Vicente Fox Quesada, whose election in 2000 ended 71 years of increasingly corrupt rule by the Institutional Revolutionary Party, pleaded with Mexico's Congress to stop blocking his proposals for fiscal, social, and economic reform. Many Mexicans were disappointed that Fox's administration had accomplished so little in the way of such reforms.

In 2002, corruption so plagued the Haitian government, which U.S. forces helped restore to power in 1994, that foreign donors of assistance for the nation's poor sought to bypass government channels entirely. In September, the Organization of American States, an association of 35 nations in North and South America, pledged to enlarge its role in disbursing aid from international financial institutions to ensure that the aid reached Haiti's poor.

Nicaraguan President Enrique Bolanos Geyer, shortly after taking office in January, accused his predecessor, Arnoldo Aleman Lacayo, of having stolen $100 million from the public coffers. Aleman was the chairman of the National Assembly in 2002 and the political enemy of President Bolanos, who had served in Aleman's administration as vice president. In December, the National Assembly stripped Aleman of the immunity he enjoyed as a former president, and he was placed under house arrest on the embezzlement charges.

In December, the National Congress of Paraguay voted to begin impeachment proceedings against President Luis Gonzalez Macchi, who was accused of mishandling millions of dollars in government funds. Macchi struggled with a deepening economic recession, political feuding, and antigovernment street violence throughout 2002. He claimed the violence was fomented by his own vice president, Julio Cesar Franco, and Lino Oviedo, a former Paraguayan army commander who was accused of having led several coup attempts since 1996. Franco resigned in October 2002 to run for president in April 2003 elections.

Brazilian elections. Brazilians went to the polls to elect new leaders in two rounds of voting in October 2002. The results, according to many experts, reflected a deep dissatisfaction with politics as usual, a sentiment shared by a majority of Latin Americans. Experts added that the results

Bolivian Indians line up to vote in presidential and congressional elections in late June. The top vote-getters in the presidential race were Gonzalo Sanchez de Losada, a millionaire mine owner and former president, and Evo Morales, a Bolivian Indian who promised to nationalize the country's industries. In August, the Bolivian Congress selected Sanchez de Losada in a runoff.

lathe operator and labor leader who headed the Worker's Party. Da Silva, who was commonly called "Lula," won by an almost two-to-one margin, the widest margin in the country's history. He pledged to reduce Brazil's "subservience" to foreign interests and "build a country that has more justice, brotherhood, and solidarity."

Da Silva assumed office for a four-year term on Jan. 1, 2003. He became Brazil's first president from a left-wing party and the first to have emerged from the organized labor movement. These facts were of great interest throughout Latin America, where the vast majority of people identified with da Silva's struggle to lift himself up from an impoverished childhood.

Other new leaders. The Brazilian elections were echoed in November 2002 in Ecuador, where former Army Colonel Lucio Edwin Gutierrez won a runoff election for president. Gutierrez, who vowed to fight government corruption, emerged as the front-runner in the initial round of balloting in October. He had served time under house arrest for his role in a coup attempt in 2000. After being released, Gutierrez organized an independent political party with the support of native Ecuadoran and leftist groups.

In Costa Rica, Abel Pacheco de la Espriella, of the Social Christian Unity Party, was sworn in as president in May 2002. Pacheco, a psychiatrist and former television commentator, promised to improve the lot of the 20 percent of Costa Ricans living in poverty and eliminate the country's budget deficit.

In Bolivia, Gonzalo Sanchez de Losada, of the Nationalist Revolutionary Movement, was sworn

also reflected the region's disillusionment with free-market policies and political models fashioned in the United States.

Many of Brazil's most prominent and durable politicians, including former governors, senators, deputies, and even a former president, were among the losers in the first round of balloting. One of the winners in the first round was Eneas Ferreira Carneiro, of the Party for the Rebuilding of the National Order. This 63-year-old cardiologist described Brazil as "a colony of the multinationals" and accused those in power of "pillaging this country." Political experts had previously written off Carneiro as an eccentric neofascist. However, he set an election record in his race for a seat in Congress by polling more than 1.5 million votes—more than any other congressional candidate in Brazil's history.

In the runoff round of voting, Brazilians elected as president Luiz Inacio Lula da Silva, a former in as president in August. Sanchez de Losada, a tin-mine owner, had served as Bolivia's president from 1993 to 1997. In elections in late June 2002, Sanchez de Losada had finished first in a field of 11 candidates. Evo Morales, a Bolivian Indian who pledged to nationalize Bolivian industries, finished a close second. The Bolivian Congress then selected Sanchez de Losada as president.

Voters in Peru handed President Alejandro Toledo a sharp rebuke in November elections, in which opposition candidates and independents defeated ruling-party candidates in almost all the races for 25 new regional government bodies. Experts said the results would pave the way to a long-overdue decentralization of power in Peru.

Globalization concerns. The World Bank estimated in December that *per capita* (per person) income in Latin America would fall by 2.6 percent in 2002—the region's worst performance in nearly two decades. The World Bank is an agency affiliated with the United Nations (UN) that provide loans and other assistance to countries. Statistics also revealed that the number of unemployed workers in Latin America had more than doubled during the previous decade. By late 2002, the unemployment rate for the region as a whole was over 9 percent but much higher in certain countries. Nearly 45 percent of Latin Americans lived below the poverty line in 2002.

At a UN conference on economic development in Monterrey, Mexico, in August, many Latin American leaders expressed frustration with the effects on their nations of *globalization,* the trend toward increased business, cultural, and government interaction across international borders. Cuba's President Fidel Castro received a standing ovation at the conference when he called the existing economic world order "a system of plundering and exploitation like no other in history."

The World Bank and the International Monetary Fund (IMF), another UN-affiliated agency, were singled out for the most criticism at the Monterrey meeting. Critics claimed the free-market reforms demanded by these agencies as a condition for aid had proved to be ineffective. Haiti, where the World Bank had supported 41 projects over the previous 50 years with more than $1 billion in loans, was a case in point. In addition, the IMF had provided $150 million to Haiti since the early 1980's. Despite all of this assistance, more than 80 percent of Haiti's population lived in poverty in 2002, compared with 65 percent in 1987.

Elsewhere in Latin America in 2002, people blamed much of their misery on the selling off of government-run enterprises to private foreign interests. "We privatized and we do not have less poverty, less unemployment. On the contrary, we have more poverty and unemployment," complained Juan Manuel Guillen, mayor of Arequipa, Peru. Mayor Guillen led a movement to block plans of the Peruvian government to sell two state-owned electric companies, Egasa and Egesur, to a private company based in Belgium. Guillen's campaign also highlighted how privatization has caused governments throughout Latin America to lose their ability to create jobs in tough economic times.

U.S. sends mixed signals. The administration of U.S. President George W. Bush sent mixed signals to Latin America in 2002, with U.S. actions sometimes at variance with U.S. free-trade rhetoric. In March, President Bush surprised and angered the Brazilian government by imposing tariffs of up to 30 percent on most imported steel. Brazilian officials feared the tariffs would cost Brazil, the largest Latin American supplier of steel to the United States, thousands of jobs and $1 billion in export income.

In May, President Bush signed legislation providing U.S. farmers with $248.6 billion in subsidies over a 10-year period. Large-scale U.S. producers of corn and other grain were the largest beneficiaries of the legislation. Latin America's farmers, whom the bill placed at a competitive disadvantage in trade with the United States, were among the big losers. The plight of corn producers in Mexico was especially severe in 2002, when prices were depressed by a glut of U.S. corn imported tariff-free under the North American Free Trade Agreement (NAFTA), a pact that united Mexico, the United States, and Canada in a free-trade zone.

Amazon surveillance. In July, Brazilian authorities inaugurated a U.S.-financed, $1.4-billion system of radar, sensors, and computers to monitor the Amazon rain forests. The Amazon Surveillance System (SIVAM) consisted of 900 scattered listening posts, 19 radar stations, and 8 surveillance aircraft. Data generated by these instruments was fed around the clock via satellite to three command centers in Brazil. SIVAM enabled Brazilian authorities to identify all aircraft— whether commercially or privately owned—flying through Brazilian airspace. It also enabled officials to pinpoint illegal logging operations, inhibit the smuggling of endangered plant and animal species, protect lands reserved for Indians, and detect incursions into the region by foreign guerrillas and drug traffickers.

☐ Nathan A. Haverstock

See also the various Latin American countries; **Conservation; Manufacturing: A Special Report.**

Latvia. See Europe.

Law. See Courts; Human rights; Supreme Court of the United States; United States, Government of the.

Facts in brief on Latin America

Country	Population	Government	Monetary unit*	Foreign trade (million U.S.$) Exports†	Imports†
Antigua and Barbuda	69,000	Governor General James B. Carlisle; Prime Minister Lester Bird	dollar (2.67 = $1)	38	330
Argentina	37,919,000	President Eduardo Duhalde	peso (3.72 = $1)	26,500	25,200
Bahamas	317,000	Governor General Ivy Dumont; Prime Minister Perry Christie	dollar (1.00 = $1)	377	1,730
Barbados	272,000	Governor General Sir Clifford Husbands; Prime Minister Owen Arthur	dollar (1.99 = $1)	260	800
Belize	251,000	Governor General Sir Colville Young; Prime Minister Said Wilbert Musa	dollar (1.97 = $1)	236	413
Bolivia	8,691,000	President Gonzalo Sanchez de Lozada	boliviano (7.36 = $1)	1,260	1,860
Brazil	174,222,000	President Luiz Inacio Lula da Silva	real (3.87 = $1)	55,100	55,800
Chile	15,572,000	President Ricardo Lagos Escobar	peso (550.42= $1)	18,000	17,000
Colombia	43,755,000	President Alvao Uribe Velez	peso (2,833.66 = $1)	14,500	12,400
Costa Rica	4,188,000	President Abel Pacheco de la Espriella	colon (369.76 = $1)	6,100	5,900
Cuba	11,268,000	President Fidel Castro	peso (1.00 = $1)	1,800	3,400
Dominica	71,000	President Vernon Shaw; Prime Minister Pierre Charles	dollar (2.67 = $1)	61	126
Dominican Republic	8,740,000	President Rafael Hipolito Mejia Dominguez	peso (18.00 = $1)	5,800	9,600
Ecuador	13,090,000	President Lucio Edwin Gutierrez	U.S. dollar	5,600	3,400
El Salvador	6,507,000	President Francisco Flores Perez	colon (8.75 = $1)	2,800	4,600
Grenada	95,000	Governor General Daniel Williams; Prime Minister Keith Mitchell	dollar (2.67 = $1)	62	218
Guatemala	11,980,000	President Alfonso Antonio Portillo Cabrera	quetzal (7.76 = $1)	2,900	4,400
Guyana	872,000	President Bharrat Jagdeo	dollar (179.00 = $1)	570	660
Haiti	8,136,000	President Jean-Bertrand Aristide; Prime Minister Yvon Neptune	gourde (29.00 = $1)	186	1,200
Honduras	6,812,000	President Ricardo Maduro	lempira (16.69 = $1)	2,000	2,800
Jamaica	2,628,000	Governor General Sir Howard Cooke; Prime Minister P. J. Patterson	dollar (49.00= $1)	1,700	3,000
Mexico	101,709,000	President Vicente Fox Quesada	new peso (10.18 = $1)	168,000	176,000
Nicaragua	5,350,000	President Enrique Bolanos Geyer	gold cordoba (14.48 = $1)	631	1,600
Panama	2,938,000	President Mireya Elisa Moscoso	balboa (1.00 = $1)	5,700	6,900
Paraguay	5,770,000	President Luis Gonzalez Macchi	guarani (5,950.00 = $1)	3,500	3,300
Peru	26,490,000	President Alejandro Toledo; Prime Minister Raul Diez Canseco	new sol (3.65 = $1)	7,000	7,400
Puerto Rico	3,930,000	Governor Sila Maria Calderon	U.S. dollar	38,500	27,000
St. Kitts and Nevis	38,000	Governor General Cuthbert Montraville Sebastian; Prime Minister Denzil Douglas	dollar (2.67 = $1)	53	152
St. Lucia	158,000	Governor General Perlette Louisy; Prime Minister Kenny Anthony	dollar (2.67 = $1)	68	319
St. Vincent and the Grenadines	116,000	Governor General Sir Charles James Antrobus; Prime Minister Ralph Gonsalves	dollar (2.67 = $1)	54	186
Suriname	421,000	President Runaldo Ronald Venetiaan	guilder (2,178.50 = $1)	443	525
Trinidad and Tobago	1,309,000	President Arthur Napoleon Raymond Robinson; Prime Minister Patrick Manning	dollar (6.10 = $1)	3,200	3,000
Uruguay	3,384,000	President Jorge Batlle	peso (27.32 = $1)	2,600	3,400
Venezuela	25,058,000	President Hugo Chavez Frias	bolivar (1,470.59 = $1)	32,800	14,700

*Exchange rates as of Oct. 4, 2002, or latest available data. †Latest available data.

Lebanon. In October 2002, Lebanon opened a pumping station on the Wazzani River near the Israeli border to provide drinking and irrigation water for southern Lebanese villages. The opening came despite warnings by Israeli Prime Minister Ariel Sharon that the project might provoke a war between Israel and Lebanon. The Wazzani provides more than 20 percent of the water flowing into the Sea of Galilee, a freshwater lake that is Israel's main source of water. Israeli officials were concerned that the Wazzani pumping station would reduce the water supply in the lake.

Lebanese officials countered that Israel had siphoned water from the river when Israeli troops occupied southern Lebanon between 1982 and 2000. Water experts and envoys from the European Union, France, the United States, and the United Nations sought to mediate the water dispute in 2002.

Hezbollah. In April, guerrillas belonging to the Lebanon-based Islamic group Hezbollah launched rocket and grenade attacks against Israeli military positions near Lebanon's southern border. Israeli forces retaliated with air strikes against the guerrilla hideouts. Hezbollah announced that the rocket and grenade offensive was an expression of solidarity with Palestinians in West Bank towns and refugee camps, which Israeli troops began to assault in late March. The Hezbollah guerrillas also said they hoped to "liberate" a border area called Shebaa Farms held by Israeli troops. The area was claimed by both Israel and Lebanon.

Assassinations. In January, a car bomb exploded in a suburb of the capital, Beirut, killing Elie Hobeika, a former Christian militia chief who had been allied with Israel during Lebanon's civil war (1975-1990). In May 2002, a second car bomb killed the radical Palestinian leader Jihad Jabril in Beirut. Jabril was a key leader of the Popular Front for the Liberation of Palestine–General Command (PFLP–GC). The PFLP–GC, founded by Jabril's father, Ahmed, opposed any negotiated settlement between Palestinians and Israelis. Many Lebanese alleged that Israel was behind both assassinations. The Israeli Foreign Ministry strongly denied the allegations.

Debt. Lebanese Prime Minister Rafiq Hariri secured pledges of more than $4 billion in low-interest loans at a November international aid conference in Paris to help cover the nation's debt. Lebanon's economic growth had been outstripped by high-interest loans and a crippling debt of $30 billion. The debt began to mount in the 1990's, after the civil war ended and redevelopment plans were enacted.   □ Christine Helms

See also **Israel; Middle East; Syria.**

Lesotho. See **Africa.**

Vehicles and buildings in a suburb of the Lebanese capital, Beirut, burn after a car bomb killed Elie Hobeika, a former Christian militia chief in the Lebanese civil war (1975-1990), on Jan. 24, 2002. Authorities could not identify what group was responsible for the explosion, but they noted that Hobeika's enemies included Israelis, Palestinians, and various former militia members.

Library. Libraries in the United States faced a growing shortage of librarians in 2002, and experts expected the problem to grow worse by 2010. The American Library Association (ALA), a Chicago-based organization that works to promote and improve library services and librarianship, reported in mid-2002 that there were approximately 125,000 librarians working in public, school, academic, and special libraries in the United States. By 2009, the ALA estimated that more than 30,000 of those librarians will have reached the usual retirement age of 65. The ALA reported that approximately 5,000 new librarians graduate from college annually, but the majority of graduates find employment with corporations or non-governmental organizations.

To combat the problem, the administration of President George W. Bush in February 2002 announced that the federal budget for fiscal 2003, which began Oct. 1, 2002, included $10 million to recruit and train library professionals. However, the U.S. Congress failed to pass any of the required 13 spending bills necessary for the budget prior to the beginning of fiscal year 2003.

White House conference. First Lady Laura Bush hosted a White House Conference on School Libraries in June 2002, the first national conference to focus on school libraries. The conference spotlighted research that ties academic achievement to strong school library programs. The First Lady announced that the Laura Bush Foundation for America's Libraries, which she established in 2001, had raised more than $5 million for library facilities in schools.

Internet pornography. A federal district court panel in Philadelphia ruled on May 31, 2002, that the Children's Internet Protection Act of 2001 (CIPA) violated the U.S. Constitution's guarantee of freedom of speech. CIPA required libraries to equip computers with software designed to block access to sexually explicit Web sites or other material deemed objectionable. The three-judge federal panel ruled that blocking all library patrons from gaining access to material on the Internet was unconstitutional.

The worst flooding in more than 150 years damaged special collections in Prague's Municipal Library in the Czech Republic in August 2002. A Prague Bible, published in 1488, was among the hundreds of books damaged. The library's copy of the Prague Bible is one of only 12 copies known to exist. The library froze the damaged books in order to prevent further deterioration until officials could determine the best way to repair them.

The Bibliotheca Alexandrina in Alexandria, Egypt, opened in October 2002 as a modern recreation of the ancient world's most famous library, which was founded in the 330's B.C. by Alexander the Great. The massive $200-million library complex specializes in archived electronic information.

Collection acquisition. In October 2002, the Chicago Botanic Garden in Glencoe, Illinois, paid approximately $3 million for a collection of rare botanical books and journals from the Massachusetts Horticultural Society in Boston. The collection, consisting of more than 2,000 books and 2,000 journals, included extremely rare illustrated volumes and complete series of journals. The earliest title, *The History of Plants,* a Latin translation of a Greek text written by Theophrastus, who is often called the father of botany, was published in Treviso, Italy, in 1483.

Presidential library. The Abraham Lincoln Presidential Library in Springfield, Illinois, celebrated a "ceremonial grand opening" on Nov. 18, 2002. Organizers arranged the celebration so that Illinois Governor George Ryan could preside. Ryan, a strong advocate of the presidential library's construction, would have been out of office by the time the facility officially opened to the public in 2003. The library is the first phase of the Lincoln Complex, a $115-million project that will also include a museum scheduled to be completed in 2004.

☐ Nancy R. John

See also **Egypt; Literature for children; Literature, American; Literature, World.**

Libya. Libyan leader Muammar Muhammad al-Qadhafi tried unsuccessfully to push the United Nations (UN) and United States into lifting sanctions against Libya in 2002. The UN had imposed economic and diplomatic sanctions on Libya as punishment for Libya's alleged role in the 1988 bombing of Pan Am flight 103 over Scotland. The bombing killed 270 people.

In May 2002, lawyers representing families of the victims aboard flight 103 revealed that the Libyan government had offered to pay $2.7 billion in compensation. However, the offer was never embraced by the families or U.S. officials because it was reportedly contingent on the UN and United States dropping sanctions against Libya.

Appeal denied. In March, Abdelbaset Ali Mohmed al-Megrahi, a Libyan intelligence agent, began serving a life sentence for the Pan Am bombing after a Scottish court in the Netherlands refused his appeal. Megrahi had been convicted for the attack in January 2001.

Abu Nidal role in bombing? In August 2002, relatives of the Pan Am victims called for a new inquiry into the bombing after a former aide to Abu Nidal, head of the radical Palestinian group Fatah-Revolutionary Front, said Nidal had privately claimed responsibility for the bombing to the group. Nidal had reportedly established his headquarters in Libya in 1987. The aide made his revelation following the death of Nidal in Iraq.

U.S. relations. The U.S. government in January 2002 granted U.S. oil companies permission to negotiate assets frozen by Libya in 1986. Foreign affairs experts interpreted the move as a possible thaw in U.S.-Libyan relations. However, the thaw in relations was dealt a setback in May 2002, when U.S. Undersecretary of State John Bolton delivered a speech in which he accused Libya of seeking to acquire weapons of mass destruction. Libyan officials denied the charges.

African unity. Leaders of the African Union in July rejected Qadhafi's call to create a borderless, continental African state with a single army. The African Union, made up of 53 African nations working toward greater economic and political unity, was the successor organization to the Organization of African Unity. Qadhafi had promoted his vision of African unity since announcing his disillusionment with the Arab world in the 1990's.

Arab League. In October 2002, Libya announced its intention to withdraw from the Arab League, an organization of Middle Eastern and African nations that promotes unity among members. □ Christine Helms

See also **Africa: Middle East; Terrorism.**

Liechtenstein. See Europe.

Literature, American.
First-time novelists grabbed big prizes and top sales in 2002. Several distinguished authors who published their second books failed to win the same accolades they received for their first attempts.

Notables. Alice Sebold's *The Lovely Bones* was the most successful debut novel published in 2002. Sebold's first effort, which was rewarded with both critical praise and high sales, is told from the point of view of a murdered 14-year-old girl named Susie Salmon. Salmon watches enviously from heaven as the rest of her friends and family live out their lives. Another debut novel, Jonathan Safran Foer's *Everything Is Illuminated,* is told in part from the point of view of a Ukrainian student named Alex Perchov. The story is written in broken English, full of malapropisms and other funny mistakes with words and translations.

Among the notable first collections of short stories published in 2002 was Kevin Brockmeier's *Things That Fall from the Sky.* Many of the stories in Brockmeier's collection concern objects and people that enter the lives of the characters, changing them in both pronounced and subtle ways. Prominent novelist Richard Russo also published his first book of short stories, *The Whore's Child.*

Following the success of J. K. Rowling's Harry Potter novels, several critically acclaimed U.S. writers experimented with novels for younger readers. Michael Chabon, winner of the 2001 Pulitzer Prize for his novel *The Amazing Adventures of Kavalier and Clay,* published the children's novel *Summerland* in 2002. *Summerland* tells the story of 11-year-old Ethan Feld; his father, a designer of lighter-than-air dirigibles; and a league of baseball players that recruits Ethan to help them save many worlds from an evil shapechanger named Coyote.

Second attempts. Donna Tartt, who wrote the blockbuster *The Secret History* in the early 1990's, received a less favorable response for her highly anticipated second novel, *The Little Friend.* The new novel concerns the family of Harriet Cleve, which has been all but destroyed by the murder by hanging of Harriet's 9-year-old brother, committed in a small Mississippi town when Harriet was still a baby. Critics noted that the novel had all the richness of Tartt's previous work but was less satisfying for want of a strong plot. Zadie Smith, who made a big impression on readers and critics in 2000 with *White Teeth,* also suffered a second-novel slump in 2002 with *The Autograph Man.*

More critical praise came to Jeffrey Eugenides, who followed up his 1993 novel *The Virgin Suicides* with *Middlesex* in 2002. The lines, "I was born twice: first, as a baby girl, on a remarkably smogless Detroit day in January of 1960; and then again, as a teenage boy, in an emergency room near Petoskey, Michigan, in August of 1974," open the tale of the novel's protagonist, a person with both male and female qualities.

Life after Oprah. Talk show host Oprah Winfrey in April 2002 announced that she was canceling her popular monthly television book club. Over its six-year run, Oprah's Book Club had catapulted new writers onto the best-seller list and brought wide attention and huge sales to established authors such as Toni Morrison, Maya Angelou, and Joyce Carol Oates. Winfrey, who personally selected the featured books, said it was becoming increasingly difficult to find books she felt compelled to share with her audiences. However, many observers surmised that Winfrey's enthusiasm for the club had soured following a highly publicized skirmish in 2001 with Jonathan Franzen, author of *The Corrections*, that resulted in Winfrey withdrawing the book as a club selection. Publishers and booksellers worried that the club's cancellation in 2002 would cause sales to plummet, but several newspapers and talk show hosts offered their own book club suggestions, widening readership.

Pulitzer Prizes. The 2002 Pulitzer Prize for fiction was awarded to Richard Russo for his novel *Empire Falls,* the story of rich and poor families in a crumbling Maine mill town. Also nominated as finalists in the fiction category were *The Corrections* by Jonathan Franzen and *John Henry Days* by Colson Whitehead.

Dianne McWhorter won the Pulitzer Prize for nonfiction for *Carry Me Home: Birmingham, Alabama, the Climactic Battle of the Civil Rights Revolution.* Also nominated as finalists in this category were *War in a Time of Peace: Bush, Clinton, and the Generals* by David Halberstam, and *The Noonday Demon: An Atlas of Depression* by Andrew Solomon.

National Book Awards. First-time novelist Julia Glass won the 2002 National Book Award for fiction for her novel *Three Junes.* The story, the saga of a distinguished Scottish family, spans a decade. Each of the novel's three sections takes place during the month of June in a different year and is told from the perspective of a different family member. Other nominees in the fiction category included *Big If* by Mark Costello, *You Are Not a Stranger Here* by Adam Haslett, *The Heaven of Mercury* by Brad Watson, and *Gorgeous Lies* by Martha McPhee.

The National Book Award committee also awarded a 2002 Medal for Distinguished Contribution to American Letters to writer Philip Roth. Roth won a 1960 National Book Award for his story collection *Goodbye, Columbus.* Roth's third novel, the racy coming-of-age story *Portnoy's Complaint*, received much critical praise in 1969. For 15 years, Roth served as editor of the series "Writers from the Other Europe," a group of important translations of Eastern European writers such as Milan Kundera, Danilo Kis, and Bruno Schulz. Roth won the National Book Award again in 1995 for *Sabbath's Theater.* Four of his other books had been finalists for the award over his career.

The 2002 National Book Award for nonfiction went to Robert Caro for *Master of the Senate: The Years of Lyndon Johnson*, the third in a projected four-volume biography of the former United States president. Other nominees included Devra Davis for *When Smoke Ran Like Water: Tales of Environmental Deception and the Battle Against Pollution*, Steve Olson for *Mapping Human History: Discovering the Past Through Our Genes*, and Elizabeth Gilbert for *The Last American Man.*

Other notable nonfiction. The strong tradition of personal essay writing in the United States continued to receive new life from oral readings in 2002. Radio programs such as "This American Life" continued to feature noted essayists, including David Sedaris, author of *Me Talk Pretty One Day*, and David Rakoff, author of *Fraud.* Sarah Vowell joined these writers in 2002 with her book *The Partly Cloudy Patriot,* a collection of essays in which Vowell investigates U.S. history while delving into her own personal past.

A surgeon, Atul Gawande, published *Complications: A Surgeon's Notes on an Imperfect Science,* in which he dissects and dismantles the belief that physicians are infallible and medical science is exact. Gawande's book shows how most physicians learn on the job, making mistakes and improvising solutions. The book was nominated for a Pulitzer Prize as well as a National Book Award.

Tony Horwitz in 2002 completed *Blue Latitudes,* a book that retraces the three epic voyages of British explorer Captain James Cook during the 1700's. Horwitz shows how Cook's explorations of the Pacific Ocean were the last of their kind, literally completing the map of the world. The book also deals with how the captain himself remained an enigma, even as he demystified the world.

While the boom in literary memoir writing tapered off in 2002, *Off to the Side* by novelist Jim Harrison proved a notable exception. The book recounts the author's checkered life, filled with many jobs and misadventures that led him to a successful writing career. □ Brian Bouldrey

See also **Literature for children; Literature, World; Poetry; Pulitzer prizes.**

Literature, World.
Hungarian novelist Imre Kertesz won the 2002 Nobel Prize for Literature "for writing that upholds the fragile experience of the individual against the barbaric arbitrariness of history." Kertesz, born in Budapest in 1929 and of Jewish descent, was deported in 1944 to the Nazi concentration camp at Auschwitz, in Poland, and then on to a camp at Buchenwald in Germany. Liberated in 1945, Kertesz subsequently wrote for the Budapest newspaper *Vilagossag.* The newspaper dismissed Kertesz in 1951 when he refused to submit to censorship by Hungary's Communist party. Following the dismissal, Kertesz served in Hungary's military for two years. He then translated several German works of literature into Hungarian. Kertesz translated books by fellow Nobel laureate Elias Canetti, writer Joseph Roth, and philosophers Ludwig Wittgenstein and Friedrich Nietzche—all of whom are considered important influences on Kertesz's work.

Kertesz published his first novel, *Fateless,* in 1975. He later felt that *Fateless,* which detailed life in the concentration camps, was ignored by readers and reviewers in his own country. His reflections on this national indifference inspired a second novel, *Fiasco,* published in 1988. Critics now consider *Fiasco* the second installment in a trilogy of novels completed in 1990 with *Kaddish for a Child Not Born.* All three books concern the life and times of Gyorgy Koves, a concentration camp survivor, whose *kaddish* (a Jewish prayer for the dead) is recited for the child he refuses to bring into a world that allowed the horrors of the concentration camps to exist.

"For Kertesz, Auschwitz is not an exceptional occurrence," stated the Nobel Prize committee at the announcement of the award. "It is the ultimate truth about human degradation in modern experience." Kertesz's *Fateless* and *Kaddish for a Child Not Yet Born* have been translated into English.

Post-colonial and post-empire literature, including the work of Kertesz, continued to grow and provide interesting new voices and innovative styles of writing in 2002. Writers from nations that were once part of the Soviet bloc were especially active. In an era of renewed nationalism, many writers with their own languages and cultural traditions struggled to define the identities of nations with no official borders.

Sarajevo-born author Aleksandar Hemon met the challenge of defining national identity in 2002 with the publication of his first novel, *Nowhere Man. Nowhere Man* tells the story of Jozef Pronek, a Bosnian exile first introduced to readers in Hemon's 2001 short story collection *The Question of Bruno.* In *Nowhere Man,* Pronek tries to come to terms with his Bosnian roots and feelings of alienation as he recalls his life from his adopted home in Chicago.

Whitbread Prize. *Twelve Bar Blues* by Patrick Neate won the 2002 Whitbread Novel of the Year award, a prize presented at the beginning of 2002 for the best novel published in 2001. Beginning in the 1700's in Africa and ending in the early 2000's in New York City, *Twelve Bar Blues* tells the story of the African diaspora by focusing on many pioneers of jazz music, from Fortis "Lick" Holden to Louis Armstrong. Other novels nominated for the award included *The Siege* by Helen Dunmore, *Atonement* by Ian McEwan, and *Oxygen* by Andrew Miller.

The 2002 Whitbread Prize for Best First Novel was awarded to Sid Smith for *Something Like a House.* The novel tells the story of James Stuart Fraser, a British deserter during the Korean War (1950-1953). Fraser is captured and sent to live among the Miao, a minority tribe in Communist China. Other finalists for the first novel prize included *The Oversight* by Will Eaves, *Burning Worm* by Carl Tighe, and *August* by Gerard Woodward.

Man Booker Prize. Officials with the Man Group, a British securities fund, announced in April 2002 that they had agreed to sponsor the Booker Prize for five years. The Booker Prize, the British Commonwealth's most prestigious literary award, had previously been sponsored by the food supplier Big Food Group. The prize was renamed the Man Booker Prize, and the award was raised from $30,000 to $73,000. The Booker Prize Foundation, the organization that awards the prize, announced that it was considering allowing writers in the United States to compete for the prize. However, a spokesperson for the group announced in November that the prize would continue to be restricted to writers from the United Kingdom, the nations of the British Commonwealth, and Ireland.

Canadian author Yann Martel beat several literary heavyweights to win the Man Booker Prize in 2002 with his novel *Life of Pi.* The novel's protagonist, Piscine Molitor, is an Indian immigrant to Canada. Molitor, nicknamed Pi Patel, is the son of a zookeeper who decided to move his family to North America aboard a Japanese cargo ship. When the ship sinks, Pi finds himself lost at sea, alone in a life boat for 227 days with a 450-pound (200-kilogram) Bengal Tiger.

Several other novels were shortlisted for the prize in a particularly strong year. *Family Matters* by India-born Canadian author Rohinton Mistry, tells the story of a family torn apart by love, lies, and secrets. Australian novelist Tom Winton's *Dirt Music* concerns a married woman's passionate affair with a poacher in Australia's outback. In *Unless,* Canadian writer Carol Shields relates the story of a middle-aged woman forced to reexamine her life after her daughter drops out of college. *Fingersmith,* by Welsh author Sarah Waters, tells the tale of a young girl in Victorian England sent to woo the heiress of a country estate on behalf of a mysterious benefactor. In *The Story of Lucy Gault,* perennial Irish favorite William Trevor recounts the trials of a Protestant family broken up when it is forced to flee its rural Irish home.

Prix Goncourt. France's 2002 Prix Goncourt, named for the two French brothers who were literary collaborators and given to the best novel written in French, was awarded to Pascal Quignard for *Les Ombres Errantes (Wandering Shadows).* Quignard, author of several books, is most famous in English for *Tous les Matins du Monde (All the World's Mornings),* which was also adapted into a movie. The Prix Goncourt committee described *Les Ombres Errantes* as a "work of imagination in prose" that combined elements of novel, essay, poetry, and legend.

Gabriel Garcia Marquez. Celebrated author and Nobel laureate Gabriel Garcia Marquez released the first volume of his much anticipated memoirs. *Vivir Para Contrarla (Live to Tell It)* recounts the author's youth in Colombia and his early career as a journalist. Marquez, author of the critically acclaimed *100 Years of Solitude,* is Latin America's most celebrated writer. The publication of his memoirs was met with enormous demand throughout the Hispanic world, prompting U.S. publishers to move up their scheduled release of the Spanish version of the book to late 2002 and the English version to early 2003.

Asian writers. The prolific Japanese writer Haruki Murakami continued to please Western readers with the first U.S. edition of *After the Quake*. The book is a collection of six short stories, with each story loosely linked to the others by tragic losses suffered in the 1995 earthquake in Kobe, Japan.

Another Japanese writer favored by Western readers, Banana Yoshimoto, published *Goodbye Tsugumi,* a new short novel in English in 2002. Yoshimoto, author of *Kitchen* and *Asleep,* examines the relationship between two teen-aged cousins growing up in a small Japanese town on the coast.

Chinese immigrant Ha Jin, who won the National Book Award for *Waiting,* published *The Crazed.* Set during the Tiananmen Square uprising of 1989, a prominent university professor suffers brain injury, and his favorite student and future son-in-law becomes his caretaker and begins to hear truth in the rantings of the mad professor. □ Brian Bouldrey

See also **Literature, American; Literature for children; Nobel Prizes; Poetry.**

Literature for children. Historical fiction, fantasy, and picture books were especially popular in 2002. Some of the outstanding books of 2002 included the following:

Picture books. *Angelo* by David Macaulay (Houghton Mifflin). Angelo, a master restorer of old buildings, nurses a small pigeon back to health. Later, as the old man grows weaker, the pigeon returns to him. In his last project, Angelo thanks the pigeon in a special way. Ages 5 to 8.

Knick-Knack Paddywhack! A Moving Parts Book adapted and illustrated by Paul O. Zelinsky (Dutton). Flaps to open, pull, and turn reveal comical capers to the tune of "This Old Man." All ages.

Gauchada by C. Drew Lamm, illustrated by Fabian Negrin (Knopf). Compelling paintings capture the essence of a gauchada—a selfless gift—from an Argentine cowboy to his grandmother. Ages 4 to 8.

Lapin Plays Possum: Trickster Tales from the Louisiana Bayou adapted by Sharon Arms Doucet, illustrated by Scott Cook (Farrar Straus Giroux). Three lively, humorous tales of a rabbit and the tricks he plays on Bouki, a hyena. Ages 5 to 10.

Madlenka's Dog by Peter Sis (Frances Foster Books). Madlenka, walking her imaginary dog, meets Cleopatra, a friend with an invisible horse. Ages 5 to 8.

Duck on a Bike by David Shannon (Blue Sky/Scholastic). A boy leaves his bike near Duck, who can't resist showing off to barnyard friends. Ages 4 to 8.

Frida by Jonah Winter, illustrated by Ana Juan (Scholastic). Painting helps Mexican artist Frida Kahlo, in constant pain from an accident, forget her sorrow. Ages 5 to 9.

Mud Is Cake by Pam Munoz Ryan, illustrated by David McPhail (Hyperion). A little girl shows how glorious pretending can be in this rhymed salute to imagination. Ages 2 to 5.

What's That Noise? by William Carman (Random House). A young boy hears a noise, imagines unusual causes, and investigates. Ages 4 to 8.

Zathura by Chris Van Allsburg (Houghton Mifflin). In this *Jumanji* "sequel," Walter and Danny find a board game that takes them through time and space. Ages 5 to 8.

Poetry. *The Company of Crows: A Book of Poems* by Marilyn Singer, illustrated by Linda Saport (Clarion). Twenty-three poems describe crows from various points of view, including those of other animals. All ages.

Swimming Upstream: Middle School Poems by Kristine O'Connell George, illustrated by Debbie Tilley (Clarion). Poems capture the myriad worries, minicatastrophes, and highs and lows of the first year of middle school. Ages 8 to 11.

Hey You! C'mere: A Poetry Slam by Elizabeth Swados, illustrated by Joe Cepeda (Levine/Scholastic). Rap-style poems with illustrations encourage the reader to join a group of children as they explore life on a city block. Ages 6 to 9.

Peacock and Other Poems by Valerie Worth, illustrated by Natalie Babbitt (Farrar Straus Giroux). Twenty-seven poems in free verse celebrate a variety of subjects, from ice cream and crayons to a perfect fall day. All ages.

Outside the Lines by Brad Burg, illustrated by Rebecca Gibbon (Putnam). Poems about children's games—such as skipping stones and tic-tac-toe—reveal their shapes and/or movement. Ages 4 and up.

Fiction. *Island Boyz: Short Stories* by Graham Salisbury (Wendy Lamb). Ten stories and a poem depict facets of Hawaiian life, from surfing and hurricanes to bullies and the universal experiences of boys growing up. Ages 10 and up.

Hoot by Carl Hiaasen (Knopf). New kid Roy, who is being hounded by a bully, finds a friend in Beatrice and her strange, runaway brother who tries to save endangered burrowing owls. Ages 8 to 12.

Girl in a Cage by Jane Yolen and Richard Harris (Philomel). Eleven-year old Marjorie, daughter of Robert the Bruce, king of Scotland, is captured and humiliated by the English king, Edward, in 1306. Ages 12 and up.

Wingwalker by Rosemary Wells, illustrated by Brian Selznick (Hyperion). Reuben fears for the life of his father, who is forced to walk on the wings of an airplane in a traveling circus when he loses his job during the Great Depression. Ages 9 to 12.

Secret Heart by David Almond (Delacorte). Joe Maloney, ostracized by village boys, learns from traveling circus friends why he is special and why his dreams are haunted by a tiger. Ages 10 and up.

Keeper of the Doves by Betsy Byars (Viking). Amen, the youngest of five sisters living during the late 1800's, is goaded into mischief by the twin Bellas, who believe a reclusive neighbor is responsible for the death of their dog. Ages 8 to 12.

Hush by Jacqueline Woodson (Putnam). Twelve-year-old Toswiah struggles to form a new identity after her family enters the witness protection program. Ages 12 and up.

A Company of Fools by Deborah Ellis (Fitzhenry & Whiteside). Henri, a choirboy in an abbey outside Paris in 1348, becomes friends with a new arrival who changes his life as plague engulfs Europe. Ages 12 and up.

Fantasy. *Pig Tale* by Verlyn Flieger (Hyperion). Mokie, an abandoned baby who survives despite the indifference of the village, escapes a group of boys by fleeing to the woods with her favorite pig and finds shelter, care, and danger with an unusual threesome. Ages 12 and up.

The Great Blue Yonder by Alex Shearer (Clarion). Harry, killed in a bicycle accident, cannot find peace until, as a ghost, he finds a way to help his sister, who was devastated by his terrible last words. Ages 12 and up.

The Rope Trick by Lloyd Alexander (Dutton). Lidi, a young magician, searches for Ferramondo to learn the secret of the legendary Rope Trick only to abandon her quest to save a companion. Ages 12 and up.

The Great Ghost Rescue by Eva Ibbotson, illustrated by Kevin Hawkes (Dutton). A young schoolboy helps Humphrey the Horrible, his parents, and their friends—all ghosts—when their old haunt is threatened by demolition. Ages 10 to 13.

Informational books. *This Land Was Made for You and Me: The Life and Songs of Woody Guthrie* by Elizabeth Partridge (Viking). Songwriter and folksinger Woody Guthrie's tragic childhood and troubled life is explored through excerpts from his writings, interviews with his children, and family photos. Ages 12 and up.

Ice Cream by Jules Older, illustrated by Lyn Severance (Charlesbridge). Older explores the history of ice cream, the creation of flavors, and the invention of such favorites as sundaes, banana splits, and cones. Ages 7 to 10.

Grossology and You: Really Gross Things About Your Body by Sylvia Branzei, illustrated by Jack Keely (Price Stern Sloan). Lively pictures and an informal text comically impart information on such topics as goose bumps, knuckle cracking, and warts. Ages 7 and up.

So You Want to Be an Inventor? by Judith St. George, illustrated by David Small (Philomel). The Caldecott Medal-winning team humorously tells how 50 inventors—from Benjamin Franklin to Hedy Lamar—came up with their ideas. Ages 6 to 10.

Henri Matisse: Drawing with Scissors by Keesia Johnson & Jane O'Connor, illustrated by Jessie Hartland (Grosset & Dunlap). A young student imparts her own perspective on the French artist with biographical and artistic details, examples of Matisse's art, photographs, and childlike pictures. Ages 7 to 12.

The 2002 Newbery Medal was awarded to Linda Sue Park for *A Single Shard*. The award is given by the American Library Association (ALA) for "the most distinguished contribution to children's literature" published the previous year. The ALA's Caldecott Medal for "the most distinguished American picture book" was awarded to David Wiesner for *The Three Pigs*.

☐ Marilyn Fain Apseloff

Los Angeles. A proposal to permit the sprawling San Fernando Valley and Hollywood to secede from Los Angeles and form separate governments was defeated by an almost 3-to-1 margin at the polls on Nov. 5, 2002. Separatist proponents, who had argued for a decade that the city government ignored the needs of northern Los Angeles County, were hobbled by a lack of funds. Opponents, led by Los Angeles Mayor James K. Hahn, with ample funds at their disposal, were able to run television and radio ads warning of secession's allegedly dire consequences for public safety, taxes, and utility costs.

Economy. The unemployment rate in Los Angeles County hovered around 6.9 percent for much of 2002, up a full percentage point from October 2001, according to statistics released by the California Employment Development Department in April 2002 and the Los Angeles Economic Development Corporation (LAEDC) in September. Economists predicted that unemployment would decline to 6.4 percent in 2003, due in part to hefty contracts secured by local defense-sector manufacturing companies.

A sharp decline in tourism, a result of the chilling effect of the terrorist attacks on the United States in 2001, was a major factor in the jobless rate. An October 2002 report commissioned by the U.S. Conference of Mayors revealed a loss

Clergy file through the sanctuary of Our Lady of the Angels, the new Roman Catholic cathedral in Los Angeles, during a September 2 dedication service. The $190-million cost of the 12-story cathedral in the city's downtown sparked controversy, particularly among advocates for the poor and homeless.

of $2 billion in tourist dollars and 34,000 tourism-related jobs in Los Angeles since late 2000.

Hospital crisis. While the Los Angeles City Council adopted a 2002-2003 budget to maintain existing levels of services, the Los Angeles County Board of Supervisors—the county's governing body—endorsed deep budget cuts in 2002. County supervisors ordered the closing of some clinics and considered closing several of the county's big hospitals.

Some of these facilities received a temporary reprieve on Nov. 5, 2002, when voters passed Measure B to raise property taxes solely for emergency rooms, trauma centers, and bioterrorism preparedness. Economists estimated that the tax increase would raise $168 million annually. Passage of Measure B persuaded county supervisors to postpone closing two of Los Angeles County's four full-service public hospitals. Health experts noted that closure of the hospitals would have a devastating effect on the 800,000 county residents who were without health insurance. The ultimate fate of the hospitals remained uncertain, however, as county officials negotiated with federal officials for a billion-dollar bailout.

Police Chief Bernard C. Parks announced his resignation on April 22, after being denied a second 5-year term by the police commission and the Los Angeles City Council. On October 25, William J. Bratton, former New York City police commissioner, became the 54th chief of the Los Angeles Police Department.

Ports. Beginning on September 27, a 10-day lockout kept longshore workers idle and tied up traffic in West Coast ports, including the Los Angeles-Long Beach ports. Shipping companies locked out the longshore union workers, alleging that they had engaged in an illegal work slowdown. At the center of the dispute were unproductive contract talks between shipping representatives and the longshore union. A federal court ordered that the docks be reopened on October 8. Economists said the shutdown hampered the U.S. economy and may have hurt long-term trade in West Coast ports.

The Los Angeles-Long Beach port complex handles $200 billion in cargo annually. Export/import movement through all transportation facilities in Southern California is responsible for 400,000 jobs in the region.

On April 12, Los Angeles opened the Alameda Corridor, a 20-mile (32-kilometers) high-speed rail line. The line is designed to carry containerized cargo from the Los Angeles-Long Beach ports to railheads in downtown Los Angeles for shipment throughout the country .   ☐ Margaret A. Kilgore

See also **City Labor and employment.**

Louisiana. See State government.

Luxembourg. See Europe.

Macedonia. Elections in Macedonia in 2002 produced a change of government and improved prospects for peace and stability in the former Yugoslav republic. On September 15, a moderate coalition of the Social Democratic Union (SDSM), the Liberal Democratic Party, and 10 small parties won elections that were conducted peacefully under the supervision of international monitors and 700 NATO-led peacekeepers.

Election results. The SDSM-led coalition took about 41 percent of the vote, compared with 24 percent won by the ruling coalition dominated by Prime Minister Ljubco Georgievski's Slav nationalist party, the VMRO-DPMNE. The Democratic Initiative for Integration, led by former Albanian rebel Ali Ahmeti, won about 12 percent of the vote and emerged as the strongest political representative of Macedonia's Albanian minority.

In late October, the SDSM coalition formed a multiethnic government that included Ahmeti's Albanian party. SDSM leader Branko Crvenkovski replaced Georgievski as prime minister on November 1.

Much of the international community, including NATO and the European Union, welcomed the election victory of moderate parties in Macedonia. The country stood at the brink of civil war in 2001 when Albanian guerrillas launched an armed rebellion against the government. The rebels claimed that Macedonia's majority Slavic ethnic group oppressed the Albanian ethnic minority, which accounts for nearly one-quarter of the population. In August 2001, the European Union brokered a peace pact in which the rebels agreed to lay down their arms in return for guarantees of expanded political rights for the Albanian minority.

Economy. Prime Minister Crvenkovski promised that his government would take decisive action to rebuild Macedonia's tattered economy. Months of armed conflict in 2001 had taken a heavy toll on most economic sectors, analysts said. Gross domestic product (GDP), the total value of all goods and services produced in a country in a year, fell by 4.5 percent between mid-2001 and mid-2002. Unemployment rose to more than 31 percent in 2002.

Strike. Dissatisfied workers in the state sector—including teachers, government officials, and nonmilitary workers in the defense establishment—organized a national strike in May 2002 for an increase in wages. On May 20, about 80,000 workers demonstrated in the streets of Skopje, the capital. Pressure from international donors to hold the line on the country's budget deficit limited the government's ability to respond to such demands.   ☐ Sharon L. Wolchik

See also **Europe.**

Magazine publishers in 2002 discovered the downside of tying a women's magazine to a single celebrity, after two years of fast circulation growth and widespread media exposure. Gruner & Jahr USA Publishing of New York City was forced to shut down *Rosie, The Magazine,* with its December 2002 issue when former television host Rosie O'Donnell walked away from the joint venture. *Rosie* had replaced the 125-year-old *McCall's* magazine in April 2001, and circulation quickly climbed to 4 million. The magazine weakened as O'Donnell quit her daily television show, which aired for the last time in May 2002, and clashed with Gruner & Jahr over the content and staffing of the magazine. In the first half of 2002, circulation fell to 3.5 million.

The circulation of *Martha Stewart Living* magazine, celebrating the homey lifestyle of its namesake, grew to 2.4 million in its first two years. Her company, Martha Stewart Living Omnimedia Inc. of New York City, warned in mid-2002 that its products, including the magazine, could be hurt by

widely publicized allegations that Stewart engaged in an unlawful stock transaction. The Audit Bureau of Circulations, an independent auditing firm in Schaumburg, Illinois, reported that the circulation of *Martha Stewart Living* declined 3.4 percent in the first half of 2002.

The circulation of one of the most successful celebrity magazines, *O: The Oprah Magazine,* declined 17 percent in the first half of 2002, to 2.3 million. It was the first circulation decline since Hearst Magazines of New York City launched *O* in cooperation with television host Oprah Winfrey in April 2000.

Circulation decline. Newsstand sales were down for all types of magazines in 2002. *Folio,* a magazine industry publication, reported that 60 percent of all titles lost single-copy sales in the first half of the year.

Several magazines that initially had achieved spectacular success or visibility closed in 2002. When *Talk Magazine* folded in January, its editor, Tina Brown, blamed an economy that was "the worst period in memory for general interest magazines." *Talk,* an unusual joint venture between a movie company, the Walt Disney unit Miramax, and a publisher, Hearst Magazines, was launched in September 1999.

Primedia Inc. of New York City shut down *Teen* magazine in May 2002, nine months after it bought the title from Emap USA of New York City. In August, Primedia sold *Chicago* magazine for $35 million to the Tribune Company in Chicago. *Yahoo! Internet Life,* which had grown from a 100,000-circulation monthly in 1996 to 1.1 million in 2001, fell victim to the collapse of Internet businesses and closed in July 2002.

☐ Mark Fitzgerald

Malawi. See Africa.

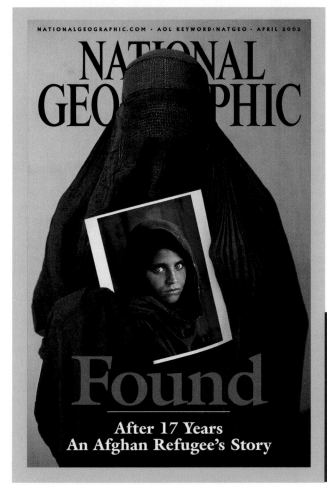

NATIONALGEOGRAPHIC.COM · AOL KEYWORD:NATGEO · APRIL 2002

NATIONAL GEOGRAPHIC

Found

After 17 Years
An Afghan Refugee's Story

The April issue of *National Geographic* magazine features an Afghan refugee holding a picture of herself first published by *National Geographic* in 1984. The photographer, Steve McCurry, returned to Afghanistan in 2002 to find the woman whose portrait had become a symbol of human suffering and one of the most recognized images ever published.

Prime Minister Mahathir bin Mohammed of Malaysia weeps as he announces in June that he will retire after more than 21 years in office. He later agreed to continue as premier until 2003.

Malaysia. Mahathir bin Mohammed stunned the Malaysian people on June 22, 2002, when he tearfully announced that he planned to retire as prime minister and chairman of the ruling National Front coalition. Shocked party leaders mobbed Mahathir after the announcement and persuaded him to stay on as premier until 2003.

In 2002, Mahathir had served as prime minister for more than 21 years and was Asia's longest-serving leader. He had overseen the transformation of his country from an impoverished nation to one of Asia's richest countries.

Mahathir said he would hand over power to Deputy Prime Minister Abdullah Ahmad Badawi in October 2003. Abdullah served Malaysia as education, defense, and foreign minister before becoming Mahathir's deputy.

Malaysia expelled nearly 300,000 foreign workers under a tough and new immigration law that went into effect Aug. 1, 2002. The law threatened the nearly 600,000 illegal workers in Malaysia with fines, prison terms, or beatings with a cane if they did not leave the country.

The crackdown on illegal workers began in January after Indonesian workers at a factory rioted during a drug raid. The riot tapped into fears that foreign workers were responsible for rising levels of crime. ☐ Henry S. Bradsher

See also **Asia.**

Manufacturing. The United States manufacturing sector experienced an up-and-down year in 2002. Early in the year, manufacturing finally pulled out of a long contraction, and the momentum continued through spring and early summer. As autumn set in, however, the manufacturing sector once again went into decline.

Analysts blamed temporary factors for some of the manufacturing drop late in 2002. A lockout of dockworkers, which shut down ports on the West Coast of the United States for 10 days beginning in September, interrupted the flow of manufactured goods to and from Asia. Tougher environmental regulations for truck engines, which went into effect in October, led to fourth-quarter layoffs in heavy truck manufacturing.

Economists noted, however, that the U.S. economy faced a broader problem. The economy had never moved onto firm ground following the recession that began in 2001. The uncertain U.S. recovery suffered a number of setbacks, so that overall demand never picked up enough to keep factories humming and shipments growing on a reliable basis.

Other key economies—including Japan's and Germany's—matched the weak performance of the U.S. economy in 2002. The world's major growth engines were running too slowly for their manufacturers to boost output significantly and keep it growing. The situation threatened to set off a new wave of weakness, and by the end of 2002, some economic analysts feared that a "double-dip" recession might be setting in.

Manufacturing trend. Manufacturers began 2002 with high hopes, as economic conditions seemed to be improving. The terrorist attacks on the United States on Sept. 11, 2001, had brought sharp disruptions to an already struggling economy. Consumers, however, began spending again early in 2002, and factories increased production.

The nation's purchasing managers reported changes in manufacturing activity through the Institute for Supply Management (ISM), a professional organization based in Tempe, Arizona. The ISM's overall index for factory activity tracks manufacturing trends, signaling a manufacturing contraction when the index falls below 50 and an expansion above that level. The index reached 49.9 in January, its highest level since August 2000 when the sector first slipped into contraction.

The index leapt to 54.7 in February 2002 and 55.6 in March, amid growing confidence that the recession might have ended. However, some analysts warned that the production surge was at least partly fueled by the need to restock inventories after a long period in which factories and retailers had been reducing stocks. The ISM index slipped to 53.9 in April but renewed its rise to 55.7 in May and 56.2 in June.

June marked the peak month for the ISM index, as some company officials began saying that the growth spurt in manufacturing had run its course. Freight carriers warned that commerce had flattened in July, which the ISM gauge confirmed with readings of 50.5 for both July and August, barely above contraction levels. The index slipped to 49.5 for September, signaling a contraction in manufacturing activity, then fell to 48.5 in October. The index rose slightly to 49.2 in November but still indicated a contraction.

Layoffs that had begun earlier, especially in the telecommunications sector, spread among other industries as consumer demand slowed and consumer confidence measures hit nine-year lows. Even automobile manufacturing, considered a bright spot in the bleak manufacturing picture, seemed in trouble. Experts warned that automobile manufacturers who were powering sales and production by offering radical incentives were borrowing from future sales.

ISM spokesman Norbert Ore noted in December that some purchasing and supply executives remained uneasy about higher air freight costs they were forced to pay because West Coast ports were still backed up. Ore said others were concerned that the ongoing risk of terrorism and the possibility of a U.S. war against Iraq would deter spending. Ore noted that new orders had

declined in November, job cuts had continued, and supply executives saw business as flat or depressed.

Orders, output, and jobs. Various government reports confirmed the manufacturing slowdown reported by purchasing managers. The reports showed the manufacturing base teetering on the line between growth and contraction, leaving the sector vulnerable to short-term problems that could offset small production gains.

The U.S. Department of Commerce reported in December that new orders for goods from U.S. factories had risen 1.5 percent in October, after falling 0.4 percent in August and 2.4 percent in September. Orders for large, expensive consumer items, such as automobiles and appliances, posted some of the largest gains. Some analysts remained concerned about the consumer sector, however, because recent sharp declines in confidence measures suggested consumers, worried about the future, might cut back on purchases.

The Labor Department announced in December that the factory sector had lost an additional 45,000 jobs during November. Job cuts had continued for 28 months, even during periods of expanding factory activity in early 2002. The overall jobless rate reached 6.0 percent in November, matching an eight-year high set in April.

The U.S. Federal Reserve (the Fed), the nation's central bank, reported in November that overall industrial production by factories, mines, and utilities declined in October for the third straight month. The drop in output included declines in the mining sector in September and reflected storm-related interruptions in production from oil and gas rigs around the Gulf of Mexico. Manufacturing output declined for all three months. Production of durable goods rose in August but fell in September and October. Production of nondurable goods fell hard in August and slipped moderately over the next two months.

As 2002 drew to a close, analysts said the contraction in the telecommunications industry had not yet run its course. Economic experts noted that the heavy truck supply market was unlikely to return to normal for months unless freight demand underwent an unexpectedly strong pickup.

Interest rate cut. The Federal Reserve Board in November cut the federal funds rate, its key interest rate, by half a percentage point to 1.25 percent in an effort to stimulate the faltering economy. Manufacturers hoped that the rate cut would bolster demand, but some feared it may have come too late for a new downturn to be avoided. □ John D. Boyd

See also **Economics; Manufacturing: A Special Report.**

Maryland. See State government.

Massachusetts. See State government.

Hard Times for the U.S. Steel Industry

By Tim Grogan

The once-mighty U.S. steel industry struggles to survive in a global economy.

Six months into the war on terrorism—launched in response to the Sept. 11, 2001, attacks on New York City and the Pentagon outside Washington, D.C.—President George W. Bush made a startling decision that angered many of the nations the United States was depending on in the fight against terror. The decision had nothing to do with ships, missiles, warplanes, or armies. It had to do with steel. On March 5, 2002, President Bush announced that he was placing stiff *tariffs* (taxes) on imports of several kinds of steel products.

He made the move to protect the U.S. steel industry, which was facing the biggest crisis in its history. Between 1997 and 2002, more than 30 U.S. steel producers had filed for bankruptcy, forcing more than 22,000 workers out of jobs. The reason, U.S. steelmakers claimed, was imported steel. They could not compete with imported steel that was so cheap it had driven steel prices in the United States to their lowest levels in 20 years. The tariffs, which were to last three years, made the price of imported steel 8 percent to 30 percent more expensive than steel produced in the United States.

The tariffs angered many U.S. allies and trading partners and drew immediate responses from the European Union, Japan, South Korea, and Russia—all of which exported large quantities of steel to the United States. The tariffs also complicated relations with developing nations, particularly large steel producers such as China. For years, the United States had pressured developing nations to open their markets, practice the principles of free trade, and bear short-term suffering for long-term economic gains. Critics were quick to question whether the United States, the world's strongest economy, had the right to ask weaker economies to lift their tariffs while providing such protection for its own steel industry.

Why did President Bush risk antagonizing allies and undermining his authority on free trade issues? And what circumstances led the once-mighty U.S. steel industry to demand such protection? The answers lie in steel's past and in its present importance to the nation's industrial and military strength.

The importance of steel

Steel is one of the most vital building blocks of a modern industrial society. Virtually all major industrial sectors from automobile manufacturers to the construction industry to food canning require steel. In 2001, U.S. steelmakers provided 99.4 million tons (90 million metric tons) of steel for use in the United States. In addition, the United States imported another 30.1 million tons (27.3 million metric tons) of steel. The largest consumers of steel produced in the United States included the construction industry, which used 17.3 million tons (15.6 million metric tons); the automobile industry, which consumed 13.8 million tons (12.5 million metric tons); and manufacturers of containers and shipping materials, which required 3.1 million tons (2.8 million metric tons) of steel, some of which was used in making the 27 billion food cans manufactured annually in the United States.

Steel also plays a major role in U.S. military operations. President Bush warned of over-dependence on foreign sources of steel in a speech he made six months before imposing the tariffs: "If you are worried about the security of the country and you become over-reliant upon foreign sources of steel, it can easily affect the capacity of our military to be well supplied." Metals designed specifically for military applications are used in virtually all armaments and military vehicles. The U.S. Army's Abrams tank requires 22 tons (20 metric tons) of steel plate. An aircraft carrier requires 50,000 tons (45,000 metric tons) of steel. Steel wire is used to make the miles of cables that connect cockpit controls to engines, landing gear, and other systems on almost all aircraft, including fighter jets.

How steel is made

To produce all this steel, the modern U.S. steel industry uses two different technologies in what are called integrated mills and minimills. Integrated mills produce about half of the steel manufactured in the United States. They are called "integrated" because they combine a number of processes that convert iron ore into finished steel. First, iron ore is dropped into a huge blast furnace, along with *coke* (a form of coal) and limestone. A blast of hot air

Major steel-producing countries	Million tons produced*
China	164.1
Japan	113.4
United States	99.3
Russia	65.0
Germany	49.4
South Korea	48.4
Ukraine	36.5
India	30.1
Brazil	29.4
Italy	29.4
France	21.3
Taiwan, China	19.0
Spain	18.2
Canada	16.9
Turkey	16.5
United Kingdom	15.1
Mexico	14.7
Belgium	11.9
South Africa	9.7
Poland	9.7

* In 2001; latest data available.
Source: International Iron and Steel Institute.

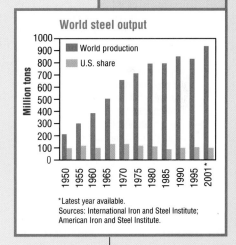

World steel output

*Latest year available.
Sources: International Iron and Steel Institute; American Iron and Steel Institute.

U.S. steelmakers produced almost half of the world's total output of steel in 1950. By 2001, the United States produced less than 10 percent of total output.

How steel is made

Integrated steel mill

An integrated steel mill performs all of the processes necessary to turn iron ore into finished steel products.

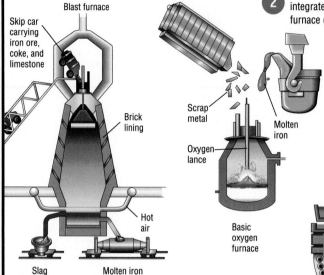

Blast furnace

Skip car carrying iron ore, coke, and limestone

Brick lining

Scrap metal

Oxygen lance

Molten iron

Hot air

Slag

Molten iron

Basic oxygen furnace

2 The molten iron is used to make steel. Most integrated mills make steel in a basic oxygen furnace (BOF). Scrap metal is dropped into the top of the BOF. Then, molten iron is poured in. Oxygen is blown into the BOF through a *lance* (pipe). The oxygen combines with carbon and silicon from the melted scrap, converting the iron to steel. Other impurities turn into slag. The BOF is tipped, and the molten steel is poured out through an opening on one side. It is tipped again, and slag is poured out from the top.

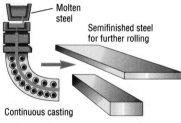

Molten steel

Semifinished steel for further rolling

Continuous casting

1 First, iron is extracted from iron ore in a blast furnace. Iron ore, *coke* (a form of coal), and limestone are dropped into the top of the furnace. Hot air is blown in at the bottom. The hot air causes the coke to burn. As it burns, oxygen in the air combines with carbon in the coke to produce carbon monoxide gas. The carbon monoxide reacts with the iron ore to form carbon dioxide gas and iron. The intense heat from the burning coke melts the iron. The molten iron is removed from the bottom of the furnace. Slag, a mixture of limestone and the leftover impurities from the process, is also removed.

3 The molten steel is mixed with small quantities of other metals to produce different *alloys* (mixtures of two or more metals) of steel. This steel is *cast* (molded) into various sizes and shapes of semifinished steel. Most integrated mills produce slabs, which are rectangular in cross section. Finally, the semifinished steel is sent to rolling mills, where it is made into finished steel products.

The author:

Tim Grogan is the Senior Economics Editor for *Engineering News-Record*.

burns the coke, which removes impurities from the iron ore and melts it. The limestone also removes impurities and combines with other waste products to form slag, which is removed from the bottom of the furnace.

The melted iron, or pig iron, is then converted into steel in a basic oxygen furnace (BOF). The BOF is loaded with a mix of about three-quarters pig iron and one-quarter scrap steel. Pig iron contains about 4 percent of the chemical element carbon. Oxygen blown into the furnace reacts with the iron to reduce its carbon content to less than 2 percent. This low carbon content is what distinguishes steel from iron.

Minimill

A minimill melts scrap metal to produce steel. Minimills in the United States use the electric arc furnace process.

Scrap metal

1 The roof of the furnace is swung aside, and scrap metal is dropped in.

Electrodes

Slag

Molten steel

Electric arc furnace

2 Electrodes are inserted into the furnace through the roof. An electric current *arcs* (jumps) between the electrodes and the scrap. The arc produces heat, which melts the scrap metal. Alloys are added to the molten metal. They change the metal to steel. At the end of the process, workers tilt the furnace to one side to release the slag and tilt it to the other side to pour out the liquid steel.

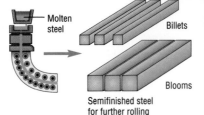

Molten steel

Billets

Blooms

Semifinished steel for further rolling

3 Minimills produce semifinished products called blooms and billets, both of which have a square cross section. As of the 2000's, they also produce thin slabs. The blooms, billets, and slabs are made into finished steel products.

Reviewed by the American Iron and Steel Institute.

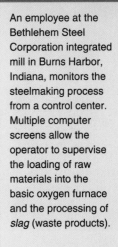

An employee at the Bethlehem Steel Corporation integrated mill in Burns Harbor, Indiana, monitors the steelmaking process from a control center. Multiple computer screens allow the operator to supervise the loading of raw materials into the basic oxygen furnace and the processing of *slag* (waste products).

Finally, the liquid steel is poured through a continuous caster, a machine that molds the steel. In a continuous caster, a large shallow vessel called a tundish holds the molten steel and releases it gradually into a water-cooled mold. The liquid steel solidifies as it travels down the mold. At the end of the caster, a torch cuts the band of red-hot steel into pieces called slabs. Slabs are either made into finished products, such as rolls of steel sheet, at the mill or sold to other mills for finishing.

Minimills are smaller than integrated mills, as their name implies. In minimills, there are no huge blast furnaces because the process begins with scrap steel rather than iron ore. Scrap steel is dropped into the top of an electric arc furnace into which carbon rods called electrodes are lowered. A powerful electric current produces intense heat that melts the metal. A continuous caster molds the liquid steel into chunks called blooms and billets—pieces that are narrower than slabs. As of the early 2000's, many minimills also began making thin slabs. The blooms, billets, and slabs are then made into finished steel products. Electric arc furnace technology is more efficient and less costly to build and maintain than the basic oxygen furnace used in an integrated mill. This makes steel produced in minimills more profitable than steel produced in integrated mills.

The history of steelmaking

Steelmaking technology has come a long way since the early 1860's, when Henry Bessemer, a British engineer, injected oxygen into molten iron to reduce the carbon content. His process allowed large quantities of steel to be made in a single day, making the mass production of high-quality, inexpensive steel possible. The new technology quickly crossed the Atlantic Ocean, and Bessemer steel was first produced commercially in the United States in 1867.

Timing played a big role in the rise of the U.S. steel industry. It coincided with the discovery in the mid-1800's of new iron-ore ranges in the region around Lake Superior. Not only was the iron ore easily accessible because it could be transported by ship on the Great Lakes, it was also of a type that was particularly suitable for the Bessemer process. The Lake Superior ore—unlike most British ores—was low in phosphorus, a chemical that makes steel brittle.

In addition, the technology to mass produce steel appeared at the same time that U.S. industries, particularly the railroad industry, began to clamor for steel. The ability of the fledgling U.S. steel industry to produce inexpensive steel rails opened the door for the golden age of railroads, as well as the further industrial development of the United States.

The U.S. steel industry began in earnest when Andrew Carnegie, a Scottish-born American, returned from a trip to Europe in 1872. During his travels, Carnegie recognized that global demand for steel would rise in the coming years. Upon his return to Pittsburgh, where he had already built a successful iron business, Carnegie constructed a new steel mill based entirely on the latest technologies. Carnegie proved to be the consummate innovator, constantly pushing to lower costs and improve quality.

As a businessman, Carnegie went about gaining control of every step in the steelmaking process. His biggest coup was acquiring the H.C. Frick Coke Company, the largest coke producer in the nation, and appointing Henry Clay Frick chairman of the Carnegie Steel Company. In 1896, Carnegie made a deal with oil tycoon John D. Rockefeller, who owned large iron ore mines in the Great Lakes region. The arrangement assured Carnegie unlimited supplies of iron ore. Carnegie also owned the ships that transported the ore, the docks where they were unloaded, and the railroad cars and rails that carried the ore to his mills.

By 1898, Carnegie and Frick had turned the Carnegie Steel Company into the largest steel producer in the nation. The legendary financier J. Pierpont Morgan owned the next three largest steel companies, and Morgan and other large producers increasingly felt threatened by the strength of Carnegie's company. In

Andrew Carnegie, a Scottish-born American, was the first major steel manufacturer in the United States. By 1898, his Carnegie Steel Company had become the largest steel producer in the nation.

1901, Morgan put together a syndicate of businesspeople with the necessary financing to buy Carnegie out for $480 million. Morgan consolidated Carnegie Steel with eight other large steel firms to form the United States Steel Corporation. In 2002, U.S. Steel of Pittsburgh, Pennsylvania, remained the largest steel producer in the United States.

"Big steel" in the United States continued to grow until U.S. production rivaled the combined steel capacity of all of Europe. By 1917, when the United States entered World War I (1914-1918), the United States produced 48 million tons (44 million metric tons) of steel and was cranking out steel-intensive armaments, such as tanks, airplanes, and battleships, that helped win the war. By the start of World War II (1939-1945), the U.S. steel industry was producing 67 million tons (61 million metric tons) a year, giving it the capacity to meet the tremendous demands of the wartime production effort. The Bethlehem Steel Corporation of Bethlehem, Pennsylvania, alone shipped enough steel during the war to build more than 1,100 ships for the U.S. Navy and the nation's civilian shipping fleet.

U.S. Steel Corporation's Gary Works in Gary, Indiana, sprawls along the Lake Michigan shoreline in 1950. The U.S. steel industry reached its zenith in the years after World War II (1939-1945), with production hitting 117 million tons (106 million metric tons) in 1955.

The beginning of the decline of U.S. steel

In the decade following World War II, the U.S. steel industry was unrivaled. In 1955, production reached 117 million tons (106 million metric tons). However, the Allied victory had sown the seeds for the eventual decline of the U.S. steel industry. World War II left European and Japanese steelmakers in ruins, which forced them to rebuild their industries. They constructed new plants with expanded capacity in waterfront locations convenient for receiving raw materials and shipping finished products. They installed the more efficient BOF and electric arc furnace technologies. U.S. producers, on the other hand, continued to rely heavily on antiquated furnaces and processes developed in the 1800's.

Another postwar trend also contributed to the U.S. steel industry's problems. A growing number of leaders of developing nations decided that a strong domestic steel industry was essential for their economic development, and their governments invested heavily in creating steel industries. Many of these nations were never able to use the steel themselves, so much of their government-subsidized steel ended up on the export market. And this steel was cheaper than U.S. steel.

Labor problems within the U.S. steel industry proved to be the final development that allowed foreign steelmakers to breach the U.S. market. In 1956, the main union for steel laborers, the United Steelworkers of America, began to represent steelworkers industrywide in collective bargaining talks. In 1959, the United Steelworkers of America staged an industrywide strike that lasted

Where steel comes from

Exporting countries	Million tons exported*
Japan	31.4
Russia	30.3
Germany	27.1
Ukraine	24.6
Belgium-Luxembourg	24.0
France	19.3
South Korea	15.3
Italy	13.0
China	11.9
Brazil	10.6
Taiwan, China	9.1
United Kingdom	8.6
Turkey	8.3
Netherlands	7.1
United States	6.8
Spain	6.8
Canada	5.6
Mexico	5.3
Austria	5.0
South Africa	4.5

* In 2000; latest data available.
Source: International Iron and Steel Institute.

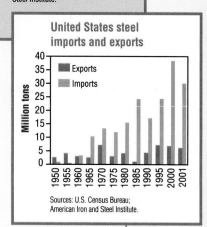

United States steel imports and exports

Million tons

■ Exports
■ Imports

1950 1955 1960 1965 1970 1975 1980 1985 1990 1995 2000 2001

Sources: U.S. Census Bureau; American Iron and Steel Institute.

a disastrous 116 days. The strike made domestic steel scarce and expensive, which forced U.S. manufacturers to turn to foreign suppliers. As a result, U.S. imports of steel products in 1959 exceeded exports for the first time since 1900. This event drew little attention at the time, because the import figure was still relatively low. However, it marked the beginning of a trend that never reversed itself.

To avoid further industrywide strikes, steelmakers conceded to an ever-increasing burden of labor costs. Labor contracts, which were renegotiated every three years, called for regular salary increases. Ever-increasing labor expenses pushed up production costs, which in turn pushed up the price of steel made in the United States. Eventually, steel companies attempted to minimize demands for higher wages by offering greater pension and retiree health care benefits—expenses that the companies could put off into the future. Although the steelmakers were expected to set aside funds for these benefits, many did not or could not.

In 1974, the U.S. economy, hurt by the oil crisis of 1973, went into a deep recession, further shaking the U.S. steel industry. Manufacturers cut back on their steel supply orders, forcing a number of steel producers into bankruptcy. The industry responded by reducing its work force by nearly 65 percent, from 512,000 employees in 1974 to 168,000 employees in 1989.

The integrated mills also dealt with the crisis by launching a much-needed modernization program. For example, by 1991, all integrated mills in the United States had adopted efficient BOF technology.

U.S. minimills were in a better position to deal with the crisis triggered by the 1974 recession than the integrated mills. The minimills were unencumbered by huge, aging physical plants and tradition-bound work practices. They generally employed nonunion workers and had fewer retirement costs. Between 1974 and 2002, U.S. minimills increased their share of the domestic market from 20 percent to nearly 50 percent.

The U.S. steel industry—both integrated mills and minimills—invested $50 billion to modernize production facilities between 1980 and 2000. During the same period, the industry continued to downsize its work force, from 168,000 employees in 1989 to 141,000 by 2001. Both moves greatly improved productivity, reducing the time needed to produce a ton of steel from 10.1 "man-hours" in 1982 to 3.4 in 2001. By 2001, the U.S. steel industry's productivity level equaled that of Germany and Japan.

Current problems for U.S. steel

However, global forces continued to work against the U.S. industry, despite its efforts to improve efficiency and lower costs. A recession in Asia in 1997 devastated the booming regional economy, which normally consumed great quantities of steel. Similar

crises in Russia and Latin America
followed Asia's economic turmoil.
With the world demand for steel dry-
ing up, the United States became the
market of last resort. Foreign producers, in an attempt to recoup some of
their losses, "dumped" steel on the
U.S. market at below-market prices.
As a result, steel imports into the
United States jumped from 29.2 million tons (26.4 million metric tons) in
1996 to 41.5 million tons (37.6 million metric tons) in 1998, a 42-per-
cent increase. Imports remained at
high levels through 2000. Although
imports fell in 2001, to 30.1 million
tons (27.3 million metric tons), prices
for U.S.-produced steel continued to drop. In 2002, prices hit a
20-year low.

Rolls of steel in a fac-
tory in Shanghai, Chi-
na, await shipment to
the West. By 2000,
China had become
one of the 10 largest
exporters of steel in
the world.

President Bush responded to the growing crisis by asking the
U.S. Department of Commerce to investigate whether foreign
steel was being dumped in the United States at below-market value or at prices lower than the producers charge in their own markets. The Commerce Department ruled that dumping had, indeed,
occurred. Next, the International Trade Commission
(ITC), an independent government agency, ruled that the
U.S. industry had been damaged by the dumping and recommended that tariffs be imposed on foreign steel. President Bush announced his decision to impose tariffs in
March 2002.

The European Union (EU) and Japan threatened to retaliate by imposing punitive duties on a variety of U.S. exports besides steel. The EU further announced that it
would impose tariffs of up to 26 percent on any steel imports exceeding 12 million tons (11 million metric tons).
EU economists feared that Latin American and Asian steel
manufacturers might divert cheap steel to Europe if they
could no longer sell it to the U.S. market.

A variety of solutions

To ease growing trade tensions, President Bush agreed to
exclude a large number of imported steel products from the
tariffs, including products difficult or impossible to obtain
from U.S. suppliers. By the end of August, fully one-quarter of all steel products exported to the United States had
been excluded from the tariffs. U.S. steel industry leaders
and representatives of labor strongly criticized the large
number of exceptions. They had wanted across-the-board
tariff protection for three years to give the industry the
time it needed to work out solutions to its problems.

Other critics also pointed out that the tariffs introduced
by the Bush administration did nothing to rid the market

Where steel goes	
Importing countries	**Million tons imported***
United States	38.4
China	22.9
Germany	22.5
France	18.8
Italy	18.4
Taiwan, China	14.3
Belgium-Luxembourg	14.2
South Korea	12.6
Spain	10.4
Canada	9.7
Hong Kong	8.9
United Kingdom	8.5
Turkey	7.9
Thailand	6.5
Netherlands	6.5
Japan	5.6
Malaysia	4.6
Mexico	4.4
Iran	4.3
Sweden	3.6

* In 2000; latest data available.

Source: International Iron and Steel
Institute.

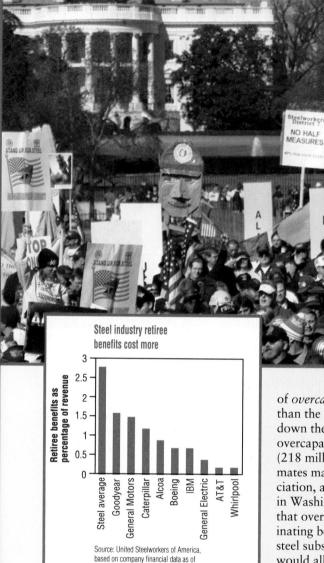

Steel industry retiree benefits cost more

Retiree benefits as percentage of revenue

3
2.5
2
1.5
1
0.5
0

Steel average · Goodyear · General Motors · Caterpillar · Alcoa · Boeing · IBM · General Electric · AT&T · Whirlpool

Source: United Steelworkers of America, based on company financial data as of Dec. 31, 2000 (latest available).

Steelworkers rally in front of the White House (top) in Washington, D.C., in February 2002 to urge President Bush to help the U.S. steel industry by setting tariffs on foreign steel imports. The U.S. steel industry's "legacy costs," the cost of benefits for retirees, are higher than those of any other U.S. industry (above), crippling profitability.

of *overcapacity* (the production of more steel than the market can absorb), which drove down the price of steel. In 2001, annual global overcapacity of steel exceeded 240 million tons (218 million metric tons), according to estimates made by the Steel Manufacturers Association, an industry trade group headquartered in Washington, D.C. Many economists argued that overproduction could only be cut by eliminating both trade barriers and government steel subsidies. Eliminating trade barriers would allow the worldwide market for steel to determine price based solely on supply and demand. Eliminating government subsidies for steel would force steel manufacturers worldwide to compete on a relatively level playing field. The elimination of both would force inefficient and unprofitable mills out of the market, cutting production. In December 2002, representatives of the major steel-producing countries met in Paris, under the auspices of the Organization for Economic Cooperation and Development (OECD), to attempt to work out such an agreement.

The steel industry proposed another solution, a major consolidation of the nation's largest integrated steelmakers that was not unlike the formation of the United States Steel Corporation in 1901. In late 2001, U.S. Steel began discussing a possible merger with the Bethlehem Steel Corporation; National Steel Corporation of Mishawaka, Indiana; Weirton Steel Corporation of Weirton, West Virginia; and Wheeling-Pittsburgh Steel Corporation of Wheeling, West Virginia. The proposed new company would produce about 30 percent of all U.S. steel.

A major hurdle stood in the way of consolidation—the burden of pension and medical benefits for retirees and their dependents.

These "legacy costs" for about 600,000 retirees and their dependents totaled about $13 billion for the entire U.S. steel industry. Any company that acquired a U.S. steel manufacturer also acquired the firm's retiree obligations, which few companies were interested in doing.

The U.S. steel industry responded to the problem of legacy costs by asking the U.S. government to absorb them. Critics argued that U.S. taxpayers—many without health insurance or retirement plans of their own—should not be expected to pay for steelworkers' benefits, which were among the most generous in the nation. The Bush administration showed little enthusiasm toward the suggestion.

Critics of the industry's consolidation proposal suggested that the weaker domestic mills simply be allowed to die through natural competition in the marketplace. They pointed out that when LTV Corporation of Cleveland, Ohio, a large integrated mill, declared bankruptcy in 2001, a large quantity of steel was taken off the market, instantly solving some of the domestic industry's problems.

However, the LTV bankruptcy also produced negative effects. Through the bankruptcy courts, LTV managed to shed its legacy costs, and many former employees found themselves facing old age without pensions or health insurance. The steelmaker did reopen in April 2002 as the International Steel Group with lowered production costs. Most of the savings came through the shedding of legacy costs and through union concessions. This allowed LTV to undercut other integrated mills on price, further weakening companies that paid pension and health care costs for retirees and provided union wages to employees.

What hope does the future hold?

By the end of 2002, both the global steel industry and the U.S. steel industry had taken tentative steps toward resolving the crisis. Industrial leaders at the OECD conference in December planned to hold an initial meeting in February 2003 to try to hammer out an agreement on cutting government subsidies to steelmakers. Nevertheless, industry analysts expected the representatives would find it difficult to agree on how much less steel should be produced and which nations should cut their production. And while many economists agreed that greater consolidation would improve the economic health of the U.S. steel industry, they also warned that mergers invariably resulted in loss of jobs and would likely threaten the pensions and health care benefits of even greater numbers of retired steelworkers.

So the U.S. steel industry, which had such a bright future at the beginning of the 20th century, faced a very uncertain one at the start of the 21st century. But one thing was clear. Both government officials and industry executives agreed that the steel industry was of vital importance to the U.S. economy and the nation's defense. It was therefore highly likely that the United States would find a way to return its once-mighty steel industry—if not to its former place as the world's greatest producer—to a position of prominence and profitability on the world economic scene. ■■■

Mauritius. In early 2002, a corruption scandal involving the state-owned airline, Air Mauritius, shook the ruling coalition of the Militant Socialist Movement/Militant Mauritian Movement (MSM/MMM), led by Prime Minister Sir Anerood Jugnauth of the MSM and Deputy Prime Minister Paul Berenger of the MMM. The scandal involved the disappearance of large sums of money from the airline's assets. The coalition survived the political fallout from the scandal, but was rocked in February by another political crisis.

Antiterrorism crisis. Sir Cassam Uteem resigned as president of Mauritius on February 15, and Vice President Angidi Chettiar, who had been promoted to the presidency, resigned on February 18. The leaders resigned rather than sign an antiterrorism bill passed by the National Assembly, the parliament of Mauritius. The legislation, which provided for cooperation with the United States in its war against terrorism, gave police and other government authorities expanded powers to bar the entry of suspected terrorists and to arrest and hold such suspects if they did enter the country.

Under the Mauritian Constitution, the presidency is largely a figurehead position. The president, who must sign a bill for it to become law, is generally expected to sign all legislation passed by parliament. President Uteem, a Muslim, said that he could not support the bill because of features that he characterized as "undemocratic." Some of the country's newspaper editors praised Uteem for his determination not to support the antiterrorism bill. Others alleged that the real reason for Uteem's departure was because his family had received free air line tickets from Air Mauritius.

Supreme Court Chief Justice Arianga Pillay became interim president according to constitutional provisions and signed the bill into law on February 19. On February 25, the National Assembly elected Karl Offmann of the MSM and Raouf Bundhun of the MMM to serve as president and vice president, respectively, until March 2003, when Jugnauth was slated to become president according to the ruling coalition's 2000 electoral pact.

Economy. In July 2002, officials of the International Monetary Fund (IMF)—a United Nations-affiliated organization that provides short-term credit to member nations—commended Mauritius for the economic reforms that its governments had pursued since the 1980's. The IMF noted Mauritius' success in achieving consistently high economic growth. Development experts praised Prime Minister Jugnauth for his role in transforming the economy of the small island nation. □ Simon Baynham

See also **Africa.**

Medicine. Surgeons in Los Angeles separated twin girls, who had been born joined at the head, in a marathon surgical operation in August 2002. The operation, which took place at Mattel Children's Hospital, lasted more than 22 hours.

The patients, Maria Teresa and Maria De Jesus, were born in Guatemala in July 2001 connected at the tops of their skulls. *Conjoined twins* (two babies born joined together) are rare, and the incidence of twins born joined at the head is less than once in every 2.5 million births.

Healing the Children, a charitable organization based in Spokane, Washington, paid for the girls and their parents to travel to Los Angeles in May 2002 for treatment. After several weeks of tests, physicians at Mattel found that the girls had separate brains and, therefore, could be separated. Following the surgery, physicians said the twins would need additional surgeries.

Hormone replacement therapy. Physicians and patients alike were shocked in July 2002 to learn that the widely accepted practice of prescribing hormones to women who have experienced menopause could actually make them sick. Two large studies indicated that the therapy, known as hormone replacement therapy (HRT), could be dangerous.

In the first case, researchers stopped a study of one type of HRT after finding that it may increase the risk of breast cancer, coronary heart disease, stroke, and blood clots in the lungs in women. The study, which was being funded by the National Institutes of Health (NIH), involved 16,608 women between the ages of 50 and 79. It had been scheduled to continue until 2005, but NIH officials halted it after finding evidence that taking hormones caused serious side effects.

HRT involves replacing hormones that women's bodies stop making after menopause. Women in the study were given Prempro, a drug that is a combination of the hormones estrogen and progestin. Other types of HRT use patches placed on the skin or pills containing only estrogen.

NIH officials recommended that women taking both estrogen and progestin talk with their physicians about continuing treatment. They said that using the medication for a short time to relieve the symptoms of menopause may be acceptable. However, scientists expressed concern about long-term use of estrogen and progestin.

In the second study, researchers with the National Cancer Institute (NCI) reported in July that women who used estrogen for more than 10 years had an 80-percent higher risk of developing cancer of the *ovaries* (reproductive organs in women) than nonestrogen users.

Mammograms. NCI officials announced in January that there would be no change in the agency's recommendations on using mammograms to screen women for breast cancer. Mammograms use X rays in an effort to detect breast cancer at an early stage.

Controversy had arisen about mammograms after a 2001 study found they were not as useful as had been thought. NCI officials cited possible flaws in the study and recommended that women 40 years old and older should have mammograms every one to two years. Women at high risk for breast cancer should consult their physicians about screening before age 40.

Knee surgery. In July 2002, scientists reported that two popular kinds of knee surgery do not relieve arthritis pain in elderly people. The operations have been performed on about 650,000 people annually in recent years at an annual cost of about $3 billion. The first surgery, lavage, involves injecting fluid into the joint to flush out material. The second surgery, called lavage plus debridement, involves using an instrument to remove sharp edges from the joint.

The study, conducted by researchers at the Houston Veterans Affairs Medical Center, involved 180 volunteers who were divided into three groups. The first group had lavage and the second group had lavage plus debridement. The third group did not have either procedure, but surgeons made cuts in their skin to make it appear that the surgery had been performed. After two years, members of all three groups experienced about the same amount of improvement in terms of reduced pain and discomfort.

Cloning ban. In January, the National Academy of Sciences (NAS), an organization in Washington, D.C., that advises the government on scientific matters, recommended that human *cloning* (producing genetically identical individuals) that would result in a baby be banned.

NAS scientists said human cloning would cause serious health risks for the mother and the baby. They cited animal studies that found that many cloned fetuses die, while other clones die shortly after birth or have severe birth defects.

Reproductive cloning involves removing the *nucleus* (central part) of an egg and replacing it with the nucleus of a cell taken from a donor, creating an *embryo* (organism in an early stage of development). If the embryo is implanted into the uterus of a woman, she will bear a baby with the exact same genetic traits as the donor.

However, the scientists said that the ban should not include therapeutic cloning, the cloning of embryos to extract *stem cells* (cells that can develop into all other kinds of cells found in the body). Stem cells could one day be used to treat disease and create organs for people who need them.   ☐ Michael Woods

See also **Health care issues; Public health and safety.**

Mental health. The United States Supreme Court on June 20, 2002, banned executions of mentally retarded criminals as "cruel and unusual punishment" that violates the Eighth Amendment to the U.S. Constitution. The court ruled in the case of convicted killer Daryl Renard Atkins, who was scheduled to be executed in Virginia. Atkins had been convicted of shooting a man during a robbery in 1996. Atkins's lawyers argued before the Supreme Court that he had an IQ (intelligence test) score of 59 and should not, therefore, be held accountable for his actions. Physicians generally consider a score of 70 to 75 or lower to be evidence of mental retardation.

In its decision, the court cited a growing national consensus against executing retarded people. By 2002, 18 of the 38 states that permit capital punishment had banned the execution of individuals who are retarded. The ruling allowed attorneys in the 20 states that permit such executions to submit appeals and ask that their clients be sentenced to life in prison instead.

Psychologists and drug prescriptions. In 2002, New Mexico became the first state in the United States to allow psychologists to prescribe antidepressants and other drugs to treat mental illness. The law went into effect July 1.

Psychologists—professionals who do not have M.D. degrees but have earned doctorates in psychology and have the right to counsel patients—had been trying to gain the right to prescribe so-called psychotropic medicines for years. However, psychiatrists—medical doctors with advanced training beyond the M.D. degree—had lobbied strongly against granting such privileges. Psychiatrists pointed out that psychotropic drugs are among the most difficult to prescribe in terms of appropriate dosage and interaction with other medications.

New Mexico passed the law in part because of a shortage of psychiatrists. Only 18 of a total 95 psychiatrists in the state serve residents who live outside of such large cities as Albuquerque and Santa Fe. The new legislation required that psychologists undergo hundreds of hours of additional training before they could be granted the right to prescribe medications. In addition, psychologists who write prescriptions must work under the supervision of a physician.

Antidepressants. A study published in July by researchers at the University of Connecticut at Storrs raised questions about the effectiveness of antidepressant drugs. Psychologist Irving Kirsch and his associates evaluated several popular antidepressant drugs, based on data submitted by the drugs' manufacturers to the U.S. Food and Drug Administration (FDA) for approval of the medications. The researchers found that the antidepressants, on average, worked better than placebos (inactive substances) but only to a very small degree. The study's authors considered that difference to be too small to be significant.

Other psychologists disagreed strongly with the study's findings. They pointed out that drug studies for FDA approval tend to choose patients who are only mildly depressed rather than those who are seriously depressed. Antidepressants tend to help people with severe depression to a much greater degree than they help those with mild depression. In addition, the dissenting psychologists pointed out, patients tend to receive smaller doses of medications during drug trials, to minimize side effects. If the patients had been given higher doses of the drugs, their responses may well have been greater.

Autism drug. Serious behavior problems in children with autism can be improved with drug treatment, a major study concluded in July. Autism is a brain disorder that appears early in childhood and affects a person's ability to communicate, form relationships with others, and respond appropriately to the environment.

Past studies had found that only one drug, haloperidol, improved behavior problems in children with autism. However, it was not widely used because of serious side effects. The new study found that risperidone—a drug successfully used to treat adult schizophrenics—helps ease serious behavior problems in children while causing fewer side effects. Children did, however, gain an average of 6 pounds (3 kilograms) while taking risperidone during the eight weeks of the study.

The new study involved 101 children between the ages of 5 and 17. It was conducted at several medical centers in the United States. Sixty-nine percent of the children treated with risperidone showed much-improved behavior, while only 12 percent of the children who received a placebo showed improvement. Lawrence Scahill of Yale University, one of the study's principal investigators, reported that risperidone produced the biggest beneficial effect of any autism drug.

Power naps. A 30-minute afternoon nap reinvigorates people mentally, reported researchers from Harvard University at Cambridge, Massachusetts, in July. Officials with the National Institute of Mental Health (NIMH), which funded the study, said people should stop feeling guilty about taking a "power nap" at work.

In one part of the study, researchers documented that volunteers' ability to perform mental tasks decreased with time. A 30-minute nap prevented further declines and a 60-minute nap boosted performance. However, naps longer than 45 to 60 minutes were not recommended because they were found to interfere with nighttime sleep.   ☐ Michael Woods

See also **Supreme Court of the United States.**

Mexico. "People want a democracy that works," declared Mexico's President Vicente Fox Quesada in his annual message to the Mexican Congress on Sept. 1, 2002. President Fox scolded the legislators for their inaction in considering proposed programs designed to help his administration address the problems of an estimated 50 million Mexicans mired in poverty.

U.S. relations. President Fox, during a state visit to the United States in early September, expressed concern about the rise in anti-immigrant sentiment in the United States following the terrorist attacks of Sept. 11, 2001. He urged President George W. Bush to keep his pledge to push for major reform of U.S. immigration policy that would benefit Mexico. Fox wanted the U.S. Congress to extend temporary legal status to some 3 million illegal Mexican workers in the United States. These workers send much of their earnings back home, where it is an important source of revenue for the Mexican economy.

Beefed-up security measures at the U.S.-Mexico border, including inspections of all Mexican vehicles entering the United States, led to a slowdown in Mexico's commerce with its northern neighbor in 2002. A recession in the United States led to high unemployment at U.S.-owned assembly plants in Mexico as companies laid off employees. Mexico was also hurt by a sharp downturn in tourism from the United States. The drop in tourism, Mexico's second-largest source of revenue after oil exports, cost the Mexican economy tens of millions of dollars in 2002.

Latin American relations. On June 28, President Fox met with the presidents of the Central American nations in the southern Mexican state of Yucatan. The leaders recommitted themselves to a regional development plan, first proposed by Fox in 2001, to use public funds and private financing for building roads, airports, railways, and energy installations throughout the area. The plan included the construction of three highways totaling 4,500 miles (7,200 kilometers) in length as part of an International Network of Mesoamerican Highways.

In July 2002, President Fox visited nations belonging to Mercosur, the South American common market. Fox signed an agreement in Brazil removing hundreds of tariffs on agricultural and industrial goods traded between Mexico and Brazil. In Argentina, he signed an accord allowing Argentina to export 50,000 cars duty-free to Mexico.

Dissident released. Mexican authorities, responding to international pressure, announced in February that General Jose Francisco Gallardo, a dissident army officer, would be released from prison. Gallardo had been imprisoned since 1993 for criticizing Mexico's human rights record.

No Pemex strike. A threatened strike at Pemex, Mexico's state-owned oil *monopoly* (a company that has exclusive control over a product), was averted in September 2002 when President Fox helped negotiate a settlement. The 90,000 unionized workers at Pemex accepted a new contract providing for a 5.5-percent increase in wages and a 1.8-percent increase in benefits. Pemex is one of the largest suppliers of foreign oil to the United States.

Hostage standoff. In August, the Fox administration canceled plans to build a $2.3-billion international airport in San Salvador Atenco, a town northeast of the capital, Mexico City. The cancellation came after violent confrontations in July between farmers in the area and police. During five days of protests against the use of their land for the airport, the farmers, armed with machetes and gasoline bombs, seized more than a dozen hostages. The hostages were released after the government freed several jailed protesters.

Mexican saint. Pope John Paul II canonized Juan Diego (1474-1548) as the first native-born saint from the Americas at a Mass in Mexico City in July 2002. Diego, whose original name was Cuauhtlatoatzin, was an Aztec who converted to Roman Catholicism in 1524 or 1525. The pope credited Diego with an important historical role in spreading Catholicism among Mexican Indians.   □ Nathan A. Haverstock

See also **Immigration: A Special Report; Latin America; Roman Catholic Church.**

Michigan. See **Detroit; State government.**

A farmer armed with a machete stands guard under a portrait of Mexican hero Emiliano Zapata in San Salvador Atenco, where local farmers seized more than a dozen hostages in July to protest government plans to build an airport on their land. The Mexican government canceled the project in August.

Middle East

The reluctance of United States President George W. Bush to intervene in the cycle of Palestinian-Israeli violence, as well as prospects of a U.S. attack against Iraq, ignited increased anti-U.S. sentiment across the Middle East in 2002. These factors also threatened regional support for the U.S.-led war against terrorism.

Palestinian-Israeli violence. In late March, Israel launched its largest ground offensive in 20 years against cities in the West Bank administered by the Palestinian Authority (PA). Israeli Prime Minister Ariel Sharon hoped the incursion would diminish the power of Palestinian militant groups that claimed responsibility for suicide bombings that killed more than 60 Israelis in the first three months of 2002. Sharon also hoped the military action would undermine Palestinian leader Yasir Arafat, whom Sharon accused of supporting terrorism. By the end of the main phase of the West Bank offensive in late April, some 170 Palestinians and 30 Israeli soldiers had been killed. In addition, Israeli forces had arrested 1,500 Palestinians.

The Israeli campaign failed to halt the suicide bombings and, in fact, prompted Palestinians to rally around Arafat. In the coming months, the number of victims on both sides mounted. Between the start of the Palestinian uprising in September 2000 and the end of November 2002, more than 1,900 Palestinians and more than 650 Israelis had been killed in the violence.

Palestinian economy. The Israeli campaign devastated the Palestinian economy. In May, the World Bank, a United Nations (UN) agency that provides loans to countries for development, estimated that the offensive had caused $361 million in damage to PA roads, buildings, cultural sites, and equipment. The World Food Program, a UN program that provides food aid to countries, launched an operation in May to help feed about 500,000 Palestinians who had lost their jobs.

U.S. involvement. Many Western and Arab leaders repeatedly warned President Bush in early 2002 that his failure to intervene in the escalating Palestinian-Israeli violence could undermine his war against terrorism. They also argued that growing perceptions in the Middle East that U.S. policies were too pro-Israeli and anti-Islamic might destabilize the entire region.

In early April, President Bush called for an immediate Israeli withdrawal from the West Bank and for an end to the construction of Israeli settlements in the Palestinian-dominated area. He also announced that U.S. Secretary of State Colin

Powell would visit the Middle East to help mediate the Palestinian-Israeli conflict. Powell's trip, however, failed to end the violence. Sharon maintained that a cease-fire must precede any peace negotiations, while Arafat said negotiations were not possible until Israeli forces withdrew from Palestinian areas.

Many experts in Middle East affairs believed that the U.S. priority to secure peace for Israel offered little incentive for Palestinians to end the violence. Experts also doubted that Arafat had control over the Palestinian militant groups Hamas and Islamic Jihad, which were responsible for many of the attacks on Israelis.

Pressure on Palestinians. President Bush delivered a speech in June that held out the prospect of a Palestinian nation and an Israeli state existing side by side in peace. The speech also recognized Israel's right to self-defense and demanded numerous reforms in the PA, including new Palestinian leadership. Many political analysts interpreted the remarks as evidence that Bush wanted Arafat either removed from office or turned into a figurehead.

Most Israelis had come to believe by mid-2002 that Arafat was no longer a credible peace partner. Prime Minister Sharon presented evidence in June that he claimed proved the PA gave financial support to the al-Aqsa Martyrs Brigades, a Palestinian group that had claimed responsibility for a suicide bombing that month. In January, Sharon had also implicated the PA in an arms smuggling operation.

Road map to peace. In October, the Bush administration, after discussions with the UN, the European Union, and Russia, presented the most complete draft yet of a "road map" to peace. The document envisioned the creation of an independent Palestinian nation by 2005. The draft also called for mutual steps by Israelis and Palestinians to put an end to the violence.

The U.S. proposals were greeted with doubts by many world leaders and experts on the Middle East. They believed that Israeli military action in PA areas, Palestinian suicide bombings, the shattered Palestinian economy, and the prospect of war with Iraq precluded any near-term peace prospects. World leaders, including many U.S. allies, were further frustrated in December 2002, when U.S. officials indicated that the United States would delay formal endorsement of the draft's concept of a Palestinian nation. Some experts believed that the Bush administration was concerned about the possible effects of the draft on Israeli elections scheduled for early 2003.

Challenges for Arafat. Yasir Arafat faced serious challenges to his leadership of the PA in 2002. Israeli tanks confined him to his headquarters in the West Bank city of Ram Allah for much of the year as they bombarded the compound in late March, June, and September, leaving it largely in ruins. In March, Israeli attacks had destroyed Arafat's headquarters in the Gaza Strip. Prime Minister Sharon considered forcing Arafat into *exile* (banishment from one's home or coun-try) but was persuaded not to do so by U.S. officials and some Israeli Cabinet ministers, who argued that exile would transform the Palestinian leader into a martyr.

In September, after the Palestinian legislature accused the PA leadership of corruption and mismanagement, Arafat accepted the resignation of

Palestinian leader Yasir Arafat stares in disbelief at the damage inflicted to his bedroom during an Israeli bombardment of his headquarters in the West Bank city of Ram Allah in June. Repeated Israeli attacks, prompted by numerous Palestinian suicide bombings against Israelis, largely destroyed the compound.

Facts in brief on Middle Eastern countries

Country	Population	Government	Monetary unit*	Foreign trade (million U.S.$) Exports[†]	Imports[†]
Bahrain	636,000	Amir Hamad bin Isa Al Khalifa; Prime Minister Khalifa bin Salman Al Khalifa	dinar (0.38 = $1)	5,800	4,200
Cyprus	798,000	President Glafcos Clerides; (Turkish Republic of Northern Cyprus: President Rauf R. Denktash)	pound (0.59 = $1)	1,051	4,002
Egypt	70,818,000	President Hosni Mubarak; Prime Minister Atef Mohammed Obeid	pound (4.62 = $1)	7,300	17,000
Iran	69,049,000	Supreme Leader Ayatollah Ali Hoseini-Khamenei; President Mohammed Khatami-Ardakani	rial (1,741.25 = $1)	25,000	15,000
Iraq	24,451,000	President Saddam Hussein	dinar (0.31 = $1)	21,800	13,800
Israel	6,425,000	President Moshe Katzav; Prime Minister Ariel Sharon	new shekel (4.85 = $1)	31,500	35,100
Jordan	6,639,000	King Abdullah II; Prime Minister Ali Abu al-Ragheb	dinar (0.71 = $1)	2,000	4,000
Kuwait	2,062,000	Amir Jabir al-Ahmad al-Jabir Al Sabah; Prime Minister & Crown Prince Saad al-Abdallah al-Salim Al Sabah	dinar (0.30 = $1)	23,200	7,600
Lebanon	3,373,000	President Emile Lahoud Prime Minister Rafiq Hariri	pound (1,513.78 = $1)	700	6,200
Oman	2,711,000	Sultan Qaboos bin Said Al Said	rial (0.38 = $1)	11,100	4,500
Qatar	617,000	Amir Hamad bin Khalifa Al Thani; Prime Minister Abdallah bin Khalifa Al Thani	riyal (3.64 = $1)	9,800	3,800
Saudi Arabia	22,910,000	King & Prime Minister Fahd bin Abd al-Aziz Al Saud	riyal (3.75 = $1)	81,200	30,100
Sudan	30,742,000	President Umar Hasan Ahmad al-Bashir	dinar (258.70 = $1) pound (2,587.00 = $1)	1,700	1,200
Syria	16,928,000	President Bashar al-Assad; Prime Minister Muhammad Mustafa Miru	pound (48.85 = $1)	4,800	3,500
Turkey	68,509,000	President Ahmet Necdet Sezer; Prime Minister Abdullah Gul	lira (1,666,606.67 = $1)	26,900	55,700
United Arab Emirates	2,522,000	President Zayid bin Sultan Al Nuhayyan; Prime Minister Maktum bin Rashid al-Maktum	dirham (3.67 = $1)	46,000	34,000
Yemen	19,391,000	President Ali Abdallah Salih; Prime Minister Abd al-Qadir Ba Jamal	rial (176.52 = $1)	4,200	2,700

*Exchange rates as of Oct. 4, 2002, or latest available data.
[†]Latest available data.

his entire Cabinet and called for elections in January 2003. (In December 2002, the elections were postponed indefinitely.) Despite these problems, Palestinian support for Arafat rose among Palestinians in reaction to Israeli attacks on PA territory and anger at U.S. pressure for changes in PA government.

Iraq war concerns. The UN Security Council unanimously passed a resolution in November 2002 that threatened Iraq with "serious consequences" if it failed to allow the resumption of UN inspections for weapons of mass destruction. Iraq had refused to cooperate with such inspections since 1998. The Bush administration had threatened to use U.S. military force to disarm Iraq if the UN failed to act. Inspections resumed in late November 2002.

The threat of U.S. military action against Iraq led to large-scale anti-U.S. demonstrations in several Arab nations during 2002. Many Muslims believed the real goal of the United States was to control access to Iraq's vast oil wealth.

Terrorist attacks. Several terrorist attacks against Israeli interests in various countries, as well as Western targets in the Middle East, occurred in 2002. In November, terrorists killed 13 people in a bombing of an Israeli-owned hotel in Kenya and fired rockets at an Israeli civilian airliner that had just taken off from a Kenyan airport. The Islamic terrorist network al-Qa'ida, which U.S. government officials believe was responsible for the attacks on the United States on Sept. 11, 2001, claimed responsibility for the Kenyan incidents. In October 2002, explosives damaged a French oil tanker off the coast of Yemen and killed one sailor. U.S. intelligence officials attributed the attack to al-Qa'ida.

Elections. Islamic parties gained ground in elections held in Turkey, Bahrain, and Morocco in 2002. Some experts believed that these parties won partly because of the perception by many Muslims that the U.S.-led war against terrorism was really a war against Islam. □ Christine Helms

See also **Terrorism**; various Middle Eastern country articles.

Mining. See **Energy supply.**

Minnesota. See **State government.**

Mississippi. See **State government.**

Missouri. See **State government.**

Mongolia. See **Asia.**

Montana. See **State government.**

Montreal. The city's most notorious criminal, the leader of Quebec's Hells Angels biker gang, was convicted in May 2002 of two counts of first-degree murder and one count of attempted murder. A Superior Court jury found Maurice (Mom) Boucher guilty for his part in ordering the killing of two prison guards and the attempted murder of a third guard in two separate 1997 incidents. Boucher, who had been acquitted of the charges in a 1998 trial, was sentenced in 2002 to serve life in prison with no eligibility for parole for at least 25 years. Fellow inmates attempted to kill Boucher in August and again in September.

The first of two Hells Angels "megatrials" began in April with 17 members of the biker gang accused of gangsterism, drug-trafficking, and conspiracy to commit murder. On July 22, Justice Jean-Guy Boilard withdrew from the trial after the Canadian Judicial Council reprimanded him for his insulting treatment of a lawyer in another case. Justice Pierre Beliveau, who presided over the Boucher case, replaced Boilard. Beliveau announced in August that the trial was being abandoned after seven months of legal proceedings in order to avoid the possibility of judicial misconduct. Critics of the decision complained that the trial had cost taxpayers millions of dollars, including $16.5 million used to build a specially fortified courthouse near the Montreal jail where the

accused were held. (All amounts are in Canadian dollars.) Awaiting the restart of the trial, one of the accused was set free due to health problems, and six others pleaded guilty. A second megatrial, in which 13 Hells Angels bikers faced 13 counts of first-degree murder, began in October.

Montreal Symphony Orchestra. Swiss-born conductor Charles Dutoit, who led the Montreal Symphony Orchestra to international prominence during his nearly 25 years as musical director, resigned in April. His resignation came in response to complaints from the Quebec Musicians Guild accusing him of tyrannical and abusive behavior on the podium. The director's resignation followed the provincial government's announcement in February that it planned to build a $281-million downtown arts complex featuring a new concert hall, which Dutoit had sought for years.

Lachine Canal reopens. The city's historic 1825 Lachine Canal, once a major commercial artery, reopened to pleasure boat traffic in May 2002 following a $100-million, five-year revitalization project. The city's environment department closely monitored the once highly polluted 8.7-mile (14-kilometer) waterway to ensure that boats did not loosen toxic sediments left behind by many years of industrial dumping.

Last Camaro. On August 27, a bright-red Camaro Z-28 became the 4,062,813th and last vehicle to roll off the assembly line at the General Motors (GM) Corp. auto plant in the Montreal suburb of Boisbriand. The event marked the final day for the factory, which opened in 1965. The closing of the plant put about 1,200 employees out of work. While the last car was sent to the GM museum in Detroit, Mark Gembinski of Michigan bought the second-to-last Camaro for $71,500 at a charity auction on Sept. 1, 2002.

Bell Centre. The Montreal-based brewery Molson Inc. surrendered its naming rights to the home arena of the Montreal Canadiens professional hockey team in February. The arena was renamed the Bell Centre after Bell Canada, a corporate sponsor of the Canadiens, agreed to a $100-million deal to obtain the naming rights for the next 20 years.

Deaths. Montreal lost a world-renowned artist when abstract painter Jean-Paul Riopelle died March 12 at age 78. The master expressionist was considered Canada's most globally celebrated painter of the past century.

Louis Laberge, lifelong trade unionist and working-class hero, died on July 18 at age 78. As president of the Quebec Federation of Labor from 1964 to 1991, Laberge was widely considered the most influential union leader in Quebec history.   □ Mike King

See also **Canada; Canadian provinces; City.**

Morocco. See **Africa.**

Motion pictures. Many critics and older movie fans regarded most films released in 2002 as little more than dreary reissues until the end-of-year holiday season, when most of the year's highly anticipated films debuted. Although global box office returns remained healthy through 2002, many people agreed that the quality of the major releases was highly erratic until December, when an unusal number of fine films pulled mature audiences into theaters.

Summer movie season. *Spider-Man* and *Star Wars: Episode II—Attack of the Clones* got the summer off to a strong box office start. *Spider-Man,* starring Tobey Maguire, swung past expectations to become a worldwide smash while receiving generally favorable reviews. The film adaptation of the comic book hero shattered box office records when it grossed $114 million in its opening weekend.

Critical reaction to *Attack of the Clones* was more reserved. Some critics and audiences generally found the film's romance between stars Natalie Portman and Hayden Christensen unconvincing. Most viewers felt that director George Lucas was more successful with the digitally enhanced battle scenes. Regardless, *Attack of the Clones* grossed $116 million in its first four days of release.

Two of the summer's most eagerly awaited films, *Road to Perdition* and *Minority Report,* received solid but less than stellar critical endorsements. Some critics and even more moviegoers felt that *Road to Perdition,* directed by Sam Mendes, was too studied and deliberate in presenting 1930's gangland vendettas. However, Paul Newman won positive reviews for his performance as a crime boss with a soft spot for his loyal henchman, played by Tom Hanks.

Steven Spielberg's *Minority Report* featured Tom Cruise as an embattled law enforcer. In the futuristic drama, murderers are arrested before they commit the crime. The film won praise for its special effects, but some critics found it emotionally cold. Audiences considered the depiction of a future world of advanced but recognizable gadgetry to be fascinating.

Robin Williams took two roles against type in 2002, portraying sinister characters in two tense thrillers, *One Hour Photo* and *Insomnia.* The intense roles caught many audiences off guard, but critics suggested that the change pointed to a possible new stage in Williams's career.

My Big Fat Greek Wedding starring Nia Vardalos proved to be one of the happiest success stories in 2002. The film was based on Vardalos's one-woman show about a Greek woman's efforts to find romance despite her traditional family's interference. *My Big Fat Greek Wedding* enjoyed an extended run in many theaters.

Another summer box office smash, *Signs,* was directed by M. Night Shyamalan, who made *The Sixth Sense* (1999). *Signs* starred Mel Gibson as a farmer who discovers mysterious crop circles made by space aliens in his field. *Signs* attracted large worldwide audiences, but some viewers and critics found the ending simplistic.

Anthony Hopkins successfully re-created his role as infamous cannibalistic serial killer Hannibal Lecter in *Red Dragon.* The film was based on the novel by Thomas Harris.

Reese Witherspoon continued her box office reign in the romantic comedy *Sweet Home Alabama.* The story of a woman who leaves her Alabama roots and reinvents herself in New York City appealed to audiences but was scorned by many critics.

Total revenue. Even though critics viewed many offerings from major film studios to be poor, fans were willing to pay to see their favorite stars. Film receipts between Memorial Day and Labor Day 2002 totaled $3.15 billion.

Battle of titans. The latest editions of two highly profitable film franchises initially launched in 2001 went head-to-head again in late 2002. *Harry Potter and the Chamber of Secrets,* based on a novel by J. K. Rowling, and *The Lord of the Rings: The Two Towers,* the latest offering based on the novels of J. R. R. Tolkien, captured the family market during the holiday season. Excitement over the motion pictures began weeks before their release, as details about both sequels became topics for discussion on numerous Web sites.

Other year-end releases that gained the attention of audiences and critics included *Chicago: The Musical,* starring Richard Gere, Renee Zellweger, and Catherine Zeta-Jones. The film, set in 1920's Chicago, was based on the Broadway musical. Also well received in 2002 were Steven Soderbergh's psychological science-fiction thriller *Solaris,* starring George Clooney, and *8 Mile,* a semiautobiographical story that explores the Detroit environment's effects on a young rapper, portrayed by Eminem.

Far From Heaven, an unsparing look at the emphasis on conformity during the 1950's, won some of the year's strongest reviews. Director Todd Haynes took his inspiration from the films of Douglas Sirk, who directed *All That Heaven Allows* (1955). In *Far From Heaven,* a suburban housewife discovers that her husband is homosexual, while also finding herself physically attracted to her African American gardener. Critics lauded the performances of Julianne Moore, Dennis Quaid, and Dennis Haysbert.

Both critical and public response to *Auto Focus,* which explored the private life of Bob Crane, the star of the 1960's television series "Hogan's Heroes," was mixed. Paul Schraeder's re-creation of the spirit of the 1960's and 1970's received overall positive reviews. Greg Kinnear also was well received as Crane, who was murdered in 1978. Even so, many people criticized the film for not delving into the psychological reasons for Crane's obsession with pornography.

Veteran actor Jack Nicholson won strong reviews in 2002 for his restrained performance as a retiree who takes inventory of his life in *About Schmidt.* Critics also lauded Kathy Bates for her role as the mother of Nicholson's future son-in-law.

Salma Hayek received critical praise for her portrayal of Mexican painter Frida Kahlo in *Frida.* Critics and audiences credited Hayek with capturing Kahlo's troubled relationship with her husband, Mexican artist Diego Rivera, as well as Kahlo's emotional and physical suffering.

Veteran actor Michael Caine received some of the finest reviews of his career for *The Quiet American,* Philip Noyce's adaptation of Graham Greene's novel. Set in Vietnam in 1952, Caine portrayed a weary *London Times* correspondent who takes a dim view of the role the United States was assuming in Southeast Asia. Caine's character in the film comes into conflict with an idealistic American played by Brendan Fraser.

The multilayered psychological drama *The Hours,* starring Nicole Kidman, Meryl Streep, and Julianne Moore as three women in three eras whose lives are affected by the works of author Virginia Woolf, was viewed by many critics as being one of the best films of the year. Critics considered Kidman's portrayal of Woolf and Streep's and Moore's portrayal of women who read Woolf's 1925 novel *Mrs. Dalloway* as outstanding.

Adaptation, written by Charlie Kaufman, was another late release that caught the attention of critics. Nicholas Cage starred as a blocked screenwriter trying to complete a screenplay he cannot write. The film was called a poignant examination of the creative process.

Two of the most heavily touted ventures released in late 2002 starred Leonardo DiCaprio. DiCaprio joined Daniel Day-Lewis and Cameron Diaz in Martin Scorsese's *Gangs of New York,* which told of urban warfare and gangland vendettas in the mid-1800's. Day-Lewis's performance as a brutal villain drew strong positive reviews from film reviewers and audiences.

DiCaprio also starred in *Catch Me If You Can,* a film by Steven Spielberg. DiCaprio portrayed real-life con artist Frank Abagnale, Jr., who successfully impersonated an airline pilot and an assistant district attorney. Tom Hanks played the federal agent assigned to track him down.

Espionage continued to be a hot movie topic in 2002. More than 10 U.S. films released during the year featured secret agents as leading or supporting characters. Two well-received offerings were based on best-sellers. *The Bourne Identity,* loosely based on Robert Ludlum's 1980 novel, and *The Sum of All Fears,* an adaptation of Tom Clancy's 1991 novel, attracted audience's attention. New chapters of such movie franchises as *Austin Powers in Goldmember; Spy Kids 2: The Island of Lost Dreams;* and the latest James Bond film, *Die Another Day,* also did well at the box office.

International fare. *Y Tu Mama Tambien,* starring Gael Garcia Bernal in the story of two teen-age boys who take a road trip with an attractive older woman, became one of the most well received films in the United States and Mexico in 2002. Audiences enjoyed accompanying the trio as they learned about life and love.

Academy Award winners in 2002

The following winners of the 2001 Academy Awards were announced in March 2002:

Best Picture, *A Beautiful Mind*
Best Actor, Denzel Washington, *Training Day*
Best Actress, Halle Berry, *Monster's Ball*
Best Supporting Actor, Jim Broadbent, *Iris*
Best Supporting Actress, Jennifer Connelly, *A Beautiful Mind*
Best Director, Ron Howard, *A Beautiful Mind*
Best Original Screenplay, Julian Fellowes, *Gosford Park*
Best Screenplay Adaptation, Akiva Goldsman, *A Beautiful Mind*
Best Animated Feature, Aron Warner, *Shrek*
Best Cinematography, Andrew Lesnie, *The Lord of the Rings: The Fellowship of the Ring*
Best Film Editing, Pietro Scalia, *Black Hawk Down*
Best Original Score, Howard Shore, *The Lord of the Rings: The Fellowship of the Ring*
Best Original Song, Randy Newman, "If I Didn't Have You" from *Monsters, Inc.*
Best Foreign-Language Film, *No Man's Land* (Bosnia and Herzegovina)
Best Art Direction, Catherine Martin and Brigitte Broch, *Moulin Rouge*
Best Costume Design, Catherine Martin and Angus Strathie, *Moulin Rouge*
Best Sound, Michael Minkler, Myron Nettinga, and Chris Munro, *Black Hawk Down*
Best Sound Editing, George Watters II and Christopher Boyes, *Pearl Harbor*
Best Makeup, Peter Owen and Richard Taylor, *The Lord of the Rings: The Fellowship of the Ring*
Best Visual Effects, *The Lord of the Rings: The Fellowship of the Ring*
Best Animated Short Film, *For the Birds*
Best Live-Action Short Film, *The Accountant*
Best Feature Documentary, *Murder on a Sunday Morning*
Best Short Subject Documentary, *Thoth*

MOTION PICTURES

Dramas with highly conflicted characters swept the Academy Awards in 2002.

The Academy Awards ceremony found a permanent home in 2002 at the Kodak Theatre on Hollywood Boulevard in Los Angeles. The theater seats up to 3,500 people and has one of the largest stages in the United States.

Best actress Halle Berry and best actor Denzel Washington display their Oscars on March 24 following the Academy Awards ceremonies. Berry became the first African American to win an Oscar for best actress.

Russell Crowe (above left) stars in *A Beautiful Mind,* which won four Academy Awards, including best picture. Ron Howard received the Academy Award for best director for the film, a factually selective biographical drama about schizophrenic mathematical genius and Nobel laureate John Forbes Nash, Jr.

Another Mexican film, *El Crimen del Padre Amaro*, broke attendance records for a film produced in Mexico. Directed by Carlos Carrera, the film also starred Bernal as a young Roman Catholic priest who impregnates a teen-age girl and encourages her abortion.

The British film *The Magdalene Sisters,* by writer and director Peter Mullan, also dealt with hypocrisy and moral flaws within the clergy. The film examined the lives of four Irish girls who are sent to live under harsh conditions in a convent.

Japanese director Hayao Miyazaki scored a major success with his animated feature *Spirited Away.* The 2001 picture, Japan's all-time box-office champion, enjoyed moderate success in the United States in 2002. The tale of a lonely 10-year-old girl who wanders into a world of wizardry was greeted with even more splendor and imagination than Miyazaki's earlier film, *Princess Mononoke* (1997).

Roberto Benigni's version of *Pinocchio*, released late in the year, proved to be the most anticipated Italian film of 2002. The new adaptation of the venerable fairy tale was Benigni's first production since *Life Is Beautiful* (1997).

The most well-received French film of 2002 was *L'Adversaire*, based on a sensational 1993 murder case in which a man who spent years posing as a physician murdered his family rather than reveal the truth that he was unemployed. The documentary *To Be and To Have,* about a school in which budget cuts force children of all ages to be taught together, was another favorite of French audiences.

Devdas, which explored an unfulfilled love between a man and woman of different social classes, proved to be India's highest grossing film of 2002. Critics called the offering an epic romance. It was the most expensive movie ever filmed in India, costing approximately $10 million to produce.   □ Philip Wuntch

See also **People in the news** (Berry, Halle; Howard, Ron; Washington, Denzel.)

Mozambique. See **Africa**.

Music. See **Classical music; Popular music.**

Myanmar. In 2002, the military rulers of Myanmar, formerly Burma, released opposition leader Aung San Suu Kyi from 19 months of house arrest. The rulers said they would allow her to pursue her political activities as leader of the National League for Democracy (NLD).

Aung San Suu Kyi, who won the Nobel Peace Prize in 1991, had been under house arrest twice. She was first arrested after the 1990 parliamentary elections in which the NLD won 82 percent of the vote. The military refused to give up power following the election, however, and

arrested NLD leaders. She was released in 1995 but was arrested again in 2000. Officials briefly negotiated with her in 2002 in an attempt to ease political tensions in Myanmar and economic pressures from abroad. However, negotiations ground to a halt late in the year, and a United Nations official who had helped win her release threatened to resign his role in protest.

In September, a court sentenced to death the son-in-law and three grandsons of former dictator Ne Win for plotting to overthrow the government. More than 80 of Ne Win's guards were sentenced to prison. Trial observers noted that the evidence was almost entirely circumstantial. Ne Win died at age 91 in December.

□ Henry S. Bradsher

See also **Asia**.

Netherlands. The Dutch people endured a tumultuous year in 2002 as the leader of one government resigned, a second government collapsed, and a controversial politician was murdered.

Bosnia scandal. Prime Minister Wim Kok, who had led the government since 1994, resigned in April 2002, after an official report blamed his government for failing to prevent the massacre of 7,000 Muslims in Bosnia. Poorly armed and trained Dutch troops were protecting the town of Srebrenica in 1995 as part of a United Nations peacekeeping mission, when the town was overrun by Bosnian Serb forces.

Assassination. The unprecedented slaying of far-right politician Pim Fortuyn stunned the Netherlands in May 2002. Fortuyn, a former sociology professor and magazine columnist, had created his own political party—List Pim Fortuyn—in February. He led the party in the national election campaign, advocating shutting the Netherlands' borders to immigrants, and labelled Islam a backward religion. List Pim Fortuyn won one-third of the vote in municipal elections in Rotterdam, the second-largest city in the Netherlands, in March. Fortuyn was shot by a gunman in an Amsterdam suburb on May 6 during the parliamentary election campaign.

Short-lived government. The Christian Democratic Party, which called for a crackdown on crime, cuts in welfare benefits, and a rolling back of the country's liberal social laws, won the largest bloc of seats in parliament in the May 15 election. Fortuyn's party won the second-largest number of seats. The Labor Party and the liberal People's Party, which had governed in coalition for the past eight years, both came in third with an equal number of seats. The Christian Democrats formed a coalition government with the List Pim Fortuyn and the People's Party.

The government took office in July under

Mourners display photographs of Pim Fortuyn, the slain leader of the right-wing, antiimmigration List Pim Fortuyn political party, in May 2002, as they prepare to enter the Laurentius and Elisabeth Cathedral in Rotterdam for the public viewing of his body. Fortuyn's murder, by an animal-rights extremist just days before a national election, shocked the Dutch people.

Prime Minister Jan Peter Balkenende, the Christian Democratic leader. With economic growth stalling and the budget in deficit after three years of surpluses, the government in September proposed $3.4 billion in spending cuts in its budget for 2003 and $4.3 billion in tax increases. However, Balkenende resigned in October in 2002, blaming continuous infighting in List Fortuyn for the coalition's inability to govern. New elections were called for January 2003.

Prince Claus, the husband of Queen Beatrix, died on Oct. 6, 2002, at the age of 76.

☐ Tom Buerkle

See also **Europe.**

Nevada. See **State government.**
New Brunswick. See **Canadian provinces.**
New Hampshire. See **State government.**
New Jersey. See **State government.**
New Mexico. See **State government.**
New York. See **State government.**

New York City. Michael R. Bloomberg, the founder of a financial and media empire, was sworn in on Jan. 1, 2002, as the 108th mayor of New York City. Bloomberg, a Republican, won the mayoral election in November 2001.

Bloomberg took over the mayor's office at a time when the city was reeling from the economic impact of terrorist attacks on the World Trade Center on Sept. 11, 2001. Following the attacks, the U.S. Congress and President George W. Bush approved appropriations totaling $21.4 billion for reconstruction of Lower Manhattan. Despite the infusion of funds, however, New York City's economy continued to erode through 2002.

The citywide unemployment rate edged up to 7.8 percent in October. As the job base shrank, the city's tax receipts fell off sharply, cutting deeply into city revenues. Mayor Bloomberg ordered a municipal hiring freeze in late October and warned that the city faced a budget deficit of as much as $6 billion in 2003.

School system. Effective control of the New York City school system of 1.1 million students passed on July 1, 2002, from the New York City Board of Education to a new department of education answering to the mayor. Legislation passed by the New York state legislature in June effected the change, which political experts described as a historic shift of power.

Two great beams of light honoring the victims of the terrorist attacks on the World Trade Center fill the night sky above New York City on March 11, six months after the collapse of the twin towers on Sept. 11, 2001. The destruction of the Trade Center made the Empire State Building (left) once again the city's tallest building.

In July, Mayor Bloomberg appointed former U.S. Assistant Attorney General Joel Klein as chancellor of the school system. Klein named Diana Lam, head of schools in Providence, Rhode Island, to serve as chief academic adviser, and Caroline Kennedy Schlossberg, daughter of President John F. Kennedy, to head an initiative to raise private funds for the schools.

Olympic nod. The U.S. Olympic Committee chose New York City over San Francisco on Nov. 2, 2002, as the U.S. nominee for host city of the 2012 Summer Olympic Games. In 2005, the International Olympic Committee will choose a finalist from an international list of cities. To enhance New York's prospects, city officials promoted an ambitious Olympic development program.

The $6-billion program called for construction of an Olympic village in Queens, a new Olympic stadium on Manhattan's West Side, and a subway extension to that site. City officials faced formidable local opposition to the proposal for the stadium, which was to be built above rail yards between 30th and 34th streets and 11th and 12th avenues. If built, the proposed 86,000-seat stadium would also serve as the new home for the New York Jets professional football team. The cost of the new stadium would be shouldered by the owners of the Jets and by taxpayers.

Penn Station development. New York-state officials struck a deal with the U.S. Postal Service on Oct. 9, 2002, to buy New York City's main post office, the James A. Farley Post Office. Plans called for transforming the huge, neoclassical building, which stands across the street from the site of the original Pennsylvania Station, into a new Penn Station. Between 1963 and 1966, officials of the Pennsylvania Railroad demolished the original station, designed by the noted architectural firm of McKim, Mead & White, leaving only an undistinguished underground facility to serve as one of New York City's main rail terminals. The October 2002 purchase paved the way for a $750-million, five-year renovation and expansion of the Farley Building—also a creation of McKim, Mead & White—to begin in 2004.

Somber anniversary. New York City marked the first anniversary of the terrorist attacks of Sept. 11, 2001, with a solemn ceremony at Ground Zero, the site where the World Trade Center towers once stood. The observance featured a reading of the approximately 2,800 names of victims who died in the World Trade Center attacks. Some 200 readers, including former New York Mayor Rudolph Giuliani, U.S. Senator Hillary Rodham Clinton (D., New York), and other civic and cultural leaders, intoned the names in succession. The reading took more than two hours.   □ Owen Moritz

See also **City.**

New Zealand. The Labour Party, headed by Prime Minister Helen Clark, increased its seats in the 120-member Parliament from 49 to 52 in a general election on July 27, 2002. The party formed a governing coalition with the centrist United Future Party headed by Peter Dunne and a smaller centrist party. Dunne's party was a big winner in the election, increasing its representation from one to eight seats.

The main opposition National Party, which had governed New Zealand for much of the time since World War II (1939–1945), suffered steep losses. Its parliamentary holding shrank from 39 to 27 seats. New Zealand's Green Party took eight seats, up from six seats in the 1999 election. Prime Minister Clark had initially negotiated with Green Party leaders to form a coalition, but the leaders refused to budge on the issue of allowing genetically modified foods to be sold in New Zealand. The prime minister said she intended to let a ban on such foods expire in October 2003.

Economy. New Zealand experienced solid economic growth in 2002, with an annual growth rate of 3.5 percent in the fiscal year ending in June. Economic analysts, who had originally predicted a 3.2-percent growth rate for the period, said that the unexpectedly strong growth was due to increases in agricultural exports, particularly the export of dairy products, which rose by 17.7 percent between June 2001 and June 2002.

Military. In January, the government announced that New Zealand planned to spend $500 million (amounts are given in New Zealand dollars) on noncombat ships for the Navy, including a multi-role vessel to carry troops and several offshore patrol craft. Parliamentary leaders of the right-of-center ACT New Zealand party accused Prime Minister Clark of turning the New Zealand Navy into a "fishing patrol." In 2001, the Labour government had drawn political fire from the right when it disbanded the combat arm of the Royal New Zealand Air Force.

In March 2002, a Web site associated with the administration of U.S. President George W. Bush inadvertently listed information that disclosed the presence in Afghanistan of New Zealand Special Air Service (SAS) troops. The New Zealand government had sent the troops to support the U.S.-led war on terrorism but did not reveal the commitment to the New Zealand public. Prime Minister Clark said the involvement was kept secret to protect the soldiers and their families.

The government of New Zealand sent the warship *HMNZS Te Kaha* to the Persian Gulf in November. The ship joined a U.S.-led task force of ships with a mission to seek out al-Qa'ida and Taliban fugitives.   □ Gavin Ellis

Newfoundland and Labrador. See **Canadian provinces.**

■ News bytes

Selected news from 2002:

Arlington National Cemetery expansion. Officials at Arlington National Cemetery in Virginia announced plans in February 2002 to add 56 acres (23 hectares) by 2014. The expansion is the cemetery's first since the 1960's.

Land for the expansion came from multiple sources. In January 2002, the National Park Service transferred 12 acres (5 hectares) of woodland behind Confederate General Robert E. Lee's resi-

An image thought to be the oldest surviving photograph sold for $398,000 in March at a Paris auction. The photograph, taken in 1825, was kept in the private collection of a French bookseller for 50 years.

dence, which is located on the cemetery grounds. Army officials at Fort Myer, Virginia, donated another 8 acres (3 hectares), adjacent to the cemetery grounds. A 36-acre (14-hectare) parcel of land came from the Navy Annex, which is owned by the U.S. Department of Defense.

Arlington officials said that the new land increases the size of the cemetery to 668 acres (270 hectares). The addition provided burial room for an additional 350,000 veterans and dignitaries. Officials estimated that the newly expanded Arlington National Cemetery will not be filled until 2060.

Sacred meteorite chip returned. In February 2002, an Oregon chiropractor paid $3,375 for a thumbnail-sized chip of the Willamette Meteorite, which is considered sacred by Oregon's Clackamas Indians. The Clackamas Indians believe the meteorite—which they called Tomanowos, or "Visitor from the Moon"—is a physical manifesta-

tion of the spiritual union between the sky, earth, and water.

The Native Americans lost control of the Willamette in 1905, when a man claimed ownership of the meteorite, which at 15 tons (13.5 metric tons) is the largest ever found in the United States, and sold it. The American Museum of Natural History in New York City eventually acquired it and allowed small pieces of the meteorite to be cut off for scientific study. The Oregon chiropractor, David Wheeler, purchased a sliver from one of those pieces. He donated it to the Confederated Tribes of the Grand Ronde, of which the Clackamas Indians are part. He said that he offered it to the Native Americans out of a "respect for the native cultures."

The first photo? The French National Library in Paris paid $398,000 at a Paris auction in March 2002 for an image believed to be the oldest surviving photograph. Joseph Nicephore Niepce, a French scientist who invented the first photographic technique, took the image of a pen-and-ink drawing of a boy leading a horse in 1825. The existence of the photograph generally was unknown until a Paris bookseller offered it at the auction. The bookseller was aware of its historic significance but chose to keep its existence secret for some 50 years.

Elvis's hair. A ball of hair reportedly clipped from the head of Elvis Presley sold for $100,105 on Nov. 15, 2002, in an Internet auction conducted by MastroNet Inc. of Oak Brook, Illinois. Homer Gilleland, who had been Presley's barber for 20 years, reportedly saved the clippings following each of the singer's haircuts and placed the dyed black strands in a plastic bag. After Presley's death in

A Japanese submarine rests on the floor of the Pacific Ocean near Pearl Harbor, Hawaii, where it was discovered in August. Historians believe the U.S. Navy sunk the vessel before the Japanese attacked Pearl Harbor on Dec. 7, 1941.

1977, Gilleland sold strands of hair in a souvenir shop in Memphis. Before Gilleland died in 1995, he gave the bag of hair to a friend who decided to put it up for auction.

Rare coin auction. In June 2002, an anonymous bidder paid a record $7.59 million for a rare 1933 Double Eagle gold coin that had never been in circulation. The coin, which features a standing Liberty figure on one side and an eagle on the other side, was sold at a live Internet auction conducted by Sotheby's, a New York City-based auction company. The price was the greatest ever paid for a coin at auction. The U.S. Mint, which owned the coin, had estimated its value at $4 million to $6 million. The U.S. government planned to use the money from the sale to help pay down the national debt.

The United States first minted Double Eagle gold coins in 1850 with a face value of $20. In 1933, President Franklin Delano Roosevelt moved the United States off the *gold standard* (the use of gold as the standard of value for the money of a country) and ordered all but two of the Double Eagle coins minted that year destroyed. However, an employee of the mint stole several of the coins. Most surfaced in the 1940's and 1950's and were confiscated by federal agents. The coin sold at the auction in 2002 also had been stolen but found its way into the col-

lection of King Faruk I of Egypt. When the king was deposed in the 1950's, the coin disappeared again. It finally resurfaced in 1995 and was confiscated by the U.S. government.

Erik Lindbergh, the grandson of aviator Charles Lindbergh, repeated his grandfather's historic solo nonstop flight from New York City to Paris in celebration of the 75th anniversary of the 1927 crossing. On May 2, 2002, Erik Lindbergh landed his plane, a single-engine Lancair Columbia 300 dubbed the *New Spirit of St. Louis,* at Le Bourget Airport outside of Paris following a 17-hour flight.

The younger Lindbergh used modern technology, including e-mail, a satellite phone, and a Global Positioning System navigation device, to assist him on his journey. Charles Lindbergh, who made the first solo nonstop flight across the At-

An anonymous bidder paid $7.59 million in June 2002 for one of the world's rarest coins, an uncirculated gold Double Eagle, which was stolen in 1933 from the U.S. Mint.

lantic Ocean flying a specially designed plane called the *Spirit of St. Louis,* used a compass and "deduced reckoning," which amounted to guessing at the wind's speed. The original flight took 33.5 hours.

Miners saved. Work crews rescued nine men who had been trapped in a coal mine in Somerset, Pennsylvania, for 77 hours in July 2002. The coal miners became trapped approximately 240 feet (73 meters) below the surface on July 24 after they dug into an adjacent vacant mine. Water from the vacant mine flooded the working mine, forcing the men to huddle together in a tiny air pocket. Rescue workers sent a steel tube to the miners and pumped warm air into the mine to try to hold down the rising water. Late in the night of July 27, crews completed a narrow rescue shaft and pulled each man to safety one at a time in a capsule that had been lowered through the shaft. All nine men had been rescued by the early morning hours on July 28.

John Phillippi, a Pennsylvania coal miner, is pulled up to safety inside a capsule after he and eight other miners spent 77 hours trapped in a flooded mine shaft in July.

Around the world. In July, Chicago businessman Steve Fossett succeeded on his sixth try to become the first person to complete a solo balloon flight around the world. Fossett's journey began on June 19 when his balloon took off from Northam, in Western Australia. He completed his trip on July 2 near Windorah, Queensland, Australia, after traveling an unofficial distance of more than 21,000 miles (33,900 kilometers). The balloon unofficially completed its circle around Earth in 13 days, 11 hours, 33 minutes. Fossett's flight also set a new unofficial record for flight duration by a solo balloonist—14 days, 19 hours, 58 minutes.

Who fired first? A Japanese submarine found on Aug. 28, 2002, in the waters near Pearl Harbor, Hawaii, may provide the first physical evidence backing U.S. military claims that it fired first against Japan in World War II (1939-1945). Researchers at the Hawaii Underseas Research Laboratory at the University of Hawaii in Honolulu discovered the submarine, which is 78 feet (24 meters) in length, in water 1,200 feet (365 meters) deep about 3 miles (5 kilometers) from Pearl Harbor. The researchers had been conducting routine test and training dives using two submersibles when they discovered the wreckage.

The find confirmed U.S. accounts that more than an hour before the Japanese actually attacked Pearl Harbor on Dec. 7, 1941, the U.S.S. *Ward,* a U.S. Navy destroyer, fired on a submarine spotted in the area.

In September 2002, U.S. State Department officials said they would handle negotiations with Japan over jurisdiction of the two-man submarine and the remains of the two crewmen believed to be onboard.

The National Civil Rights Museum in Memphis completed an $11-million expansion in September 2002. The museum was opened in 1991 at the site of the Lorraine Motel, where the Rev. Martin Luther King, Jr., was assassinated in 1968. The expansion of the museum included the former rooming house from which convicted killer James Earl Ray shot King. The rooming house was across a parking lot from the motel. The 2002 expansion offers museum visitors a view of the Lorraine Motel from the killer's perspective. The museum also placed on view a hunting rifle found inside the rooming house, personal items left in the room, and various U.S. Department of Justice documents that would have been used had the case gone to trial. Ray pleaded guilty in 1969 and died in 1998.   ■ Tim Frystak

Newspaper figures released in November 2002 by the Audit Bureau of Circulation (ABC), an industry trade group in Schaumburg, Illinois, revealed that most major newspapers in the United States essentially maintained weekday circulation in 2002. The average daily paid circulation for the 807 newspapers reporting to the ABC fell 0.3 percent to 48.5 million copies for a six-month period ending in September compared with the same period in 2001. Sunday circulation fell 0.4 percent to 53.3 million copies. Circulation increased at the largest 10 U.S. newspapers, but they struggled with declining advertising revenues, which executives blamed on decreased classified advertisement sales.

Columnist resigns. Bob Greene, a nationally syndicated columnist with the *Chicago Tribune,* resigned on Sept. 14, 2002, after admitting to "inappropriate sexual contact" in the 1990's with a high school girl in her late teens. The resignation touched off a debate among journalists because it was made in response to personal behavior rather than the violation of journalism ethics.

The Wall Street Journal published color on its front page in April 2002 for the first time since it went into circulation in 1889. *The Wall Street Journal* was the last major U.S. daily paper that did not print color on its news pages. Color in newspapers appeals to readers and many advertisers, who pay more for advertisements in color.

More changes. Two competing Chicago newspapers launched the first two U.S. daily tabloids designed specifically for young adults aged 18 to 34 on Oct. 30, 2002. Both the *Chicago Tribune's RedEye* and the *Chicago Sun-Times's Red Streak* featured short stories designed for quick reading. Newspapers in Latin America and Europe increased circulation in the late 1990's by launching similar papers for young people.

The New York Times publisher Arthur Sulzberger, Jr., announced plans in October 2002 to purchase *The Washington Post's* 50 percent partnership stake and take full control of the Paris-based *International Herald Tribune.* Sulzberger forced the *Post* into the sale by threatening to start a competing international edition and reduce his newspaper's contribution to the *International Herald Tribune.*

Daniel Pearl, a reporter for *The Wall Street Journal,* was kidnapped on Jan. 23, 2002, in Karachi, Pakistan, while researching the background of a suspected terrorist. Pakistani authorities disclosed on February 21 that they had obtained a videotape showing Pearl's murder. Officials subsequently arrested four men and charged them with the murder. In July, a Pakistan court sentenced one of the men to death. Three other men were sentenced to life in prison.

☐ Mark Fitzgerald

The New York Sun, launched on April 16, 2002, with an initial press run of approximately 60,000 copies, is New York City's first new daily paper in 17 years.

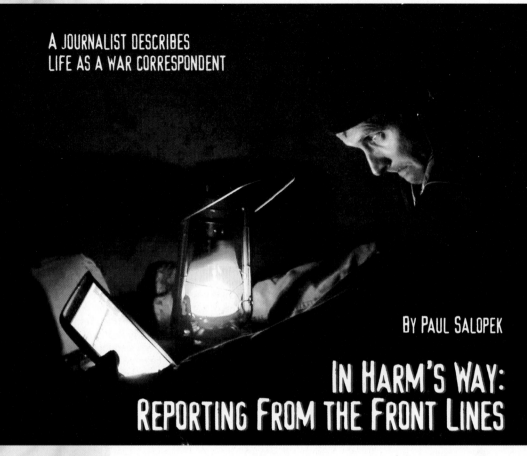

A JOURNALIST DESCRIBES
LIFE AS A WAR CORRESPONDENT

BY PAUL SALOPEK

IN HARM'S WAY:
REPORTING FROM THE FRONT LINES

The author, Paul Salopek (above), writes dispatches on his laptop computer from a cave in Afghanistan in 2001. Salopek was in Afghanistan reporting the U.S. military response to the terrorist attacks on the United States on Sept. 11, 2001.

The rocket-propelled grenade roared down from the clear sky over Afghanistan with the sound of a ripping bedsheet. The grenade, fired by a soldier of the *Taliban*, an Islamic group that once ruled Afghanistan, exploded in a walled courtyard across the street. A group of foreign journalists sought cover behind a truck of the Northern Alliance, an armed rebel group challenging the Taliban's rule. Bullets started whipping overhead. And then more rockets—one, two, three—burst nearby with ear-cracking booms. That did it. Several members of the press beat a tactical retreat. First, an Italian photographer ran. A Taliban sniper's bullet smacked into his shoulder, but he was saved by his body armor. Then, another photographer fled, a grenade exploding in his wake.

Moments later, huge explosions erupted only a few hundred yards away, causing a television technician to dive headlong into the dirt. These bigger explosions were not the work of enemy grenades, but bombs being dropped into the nearby Taliban trenches from United States B-52 bombers flying high overhead. As I lay curled up behind the truck, I felt the powerful shock waves punch my stomach and briefly wondered who would kill me first—the Taliban or my own government. I asked myself if there was any news story that was really worth risking my life.

This was in November 2001, and no doubt many journalists in Afghanistan were asking themselves the same question. Reporters were taking extraordinary risks to cover the war against global terrorism, which at that time was focused on toppling the extremist Taliban regime that controlled Afghanistan. United States officials had long believed that the Taliban was harboring terrorist groups, including al-Qa'ida ("The Base" in Arabic), the group that was believed to have carried out the suicide terrorist attacks on the United States on Sept. 11, 2001, which killed more than 3,000 people.

After the United States and its allies began conducting military operations in Afghanistan to root out members of al-Qa'ida and the Taliban, Afghanistan became an extremely dangerous place. From the start of the U.S. bombing of Taliban positions in early October, to the crumbling of Taliban forces in Kabul in mid-November, eight journalists were killed. By contrast, the number of United States military combat deaths at that point was exactly zero.

This unprecedented state of affairs—a major U.S. military operation in which reporters were dying faster than soldiers—sparked agonized soul-searching among war correspondents. What sort of chances are we now expected to take in covering our nation's wars? How can we protect ourselves in an age of murky, borderless conflicts when we can no longer count on our own soldiers to protect us in the field? And how can we continue to inform the public when the time-honored compact between the media and warring parties—we tell your story and you do not shoot us—seems to have broken down?

A dangerous occupation

Of course, the strange job of wandering unarmed into war zones for the purpose of gathering news never has been entirely without danger. During the U.S. Civil War (1861-1865), newspaper reporters considered wearing white uniforms to avoid being mistaken for soldiers and shot. And despite the unspoken agreements often made between fighters and reporters, correspondents still have been killed accidentally on the battlefield. For example, the legendary war correspondent Ernie Pyle—perhaps the most famous reporter in World War II (1939-1945)—was shot by a Japanese machine-gunner during the 1945 battle for control of the Pacific island of Okinawa. Pyle had become famous for his personal touch in reporting on the lives of U.S. soldiers on the front lines. Reporters like Pyle provide an invaluable service. They provide people with vital information about events taking place around the world. In a democracy, people depend on the media to learn what their government is doing in faraway lands.

Still, two recent trends in the nature of modern warfare have made the work of today's correspondents especially perilous. The first shift is increased restrictions on where members of the press are allowed to go in war zones. Wary of the sort of media coverage that eroded public support for the Vietnam War (1957-

The author:
Paul Salopek covers Africa for the *Chicago Tribune* and has reported on various international conflicts. He won the 1998 Pulitzer Prize for explanatory reporting.

The author crosses Afghanistan's Hindu Kush mountains on horseback to reach the front lines of the U.S. war on terrorism in late 2001. The U.S. government no longer allows correspondents to travel with U.S. military personnel, forcing reporters to find their own transportation.

Kabul

1975), officials at the U.S. Department of Defense now bar reporters from virtually all field operations. In Afghanistan, restricting reporters' movements was somewhat understandable because of the secret nature of many of the missions being carried out by highly trained Special Forces soldiers. But many editors and reporters felt the controls were excessive. For example, reporters could not even interview U.S. troops after their missions were completed.

These restrictions forced correspondents hoping to share at least part of the Afghanistan story with the U.S. public to find their own ways to the battlefields. For example, when I needed to get closer to the action, I had to pay a smuggler $250 for the honor of riding a bony horse over the snow-clogged Hindu Kush mountain range in eastern Afghanistan. Other correspondents faced rides in death-trap helicopters, terrible roads, and bandits while trying to reach the front lines unassisted. Once there, we put our safety in the hands of the Northern Alliance. Several journalists were killed in ambushes while tagging along with this tribal militia.

A new kind of enemy

The second dangerous shift involves the radically changed nature of the enemy. Gone, for the most part, are the kinds of big wars between nations that bloodied much of the 20th century. They have been replaced by small, confusing conflicts where the front lines are always shifting, if not invisible, and where the loyalties on all sides are questionable. These smoldering struggles will likely define the war on terrorism for years to come, especially as the fight goes underground and evolves into stealthy police actions. The neutrality of journalists in these chaotic situa-

tions is rarely respected. In fact, reporters are increasingly considered to be legitimate targets by both rebels and terrorists. A tragic example of this was the kidnapping and murder of *Wall Street Journal* correspondent Daniel Pearl by Muslim extremists in Pakistan in early 2002.

Given these difficult conditions, how can correspondents bring the important story of the vast, complicated, and unfolding war on terrorism to the public? First, every producer, editor, and reporter will have to set his or her own thresholds of acceptable risk. He or she will have to weigh the importance of the day's news against the need for preserving military secrecy, which all responsible journalists respect to ensure the safety of U.S. soldiers in war zones.

Lessons from African wars

A good model for the future might be the obscure, lawless wars that have been bubbling on the media back burner for years—in particular, the wars in the poorest nations of Africa. There, no army is a friend, and no one with a gun can be trusted. These blighted places have been a major part of my life for more than three years, because I cover Africa for the *Chicago Tribune*. The complete independence required to report in African war zones— a self-sufficiency that extends to carrying solar panels to power my laptop computer—is only matched by the total sense of exposure and vulnerability I sometimes feel there. In Africa, there is an absence of "good guys." This was excellent preparation for Afghanistan.

What does it take to cover wars in such bleak, remote places? It is critical to have a high tolerance for bad food (or no food), a resistance to disease, strong legs for walking or running, the gift

War correspondents hitch a ride with Northern Alliance soldiers in Afghanistan in November 2001. Some of the same reporters later died when the Taliban ambushed the vehicle. At one point, more reporters had been killed in Afghanistan than U.S. soldiers.

U.S. Marines frisk reporters in Kabul, Afghanistan, in December 2001. Such searches were performed as a security measure.

Kabul

of charming your way through roadblocks guarded by armed soldiers, and the gift of knowing when to shut up. The greatest survival skill of all is patience. War is mostly tedium. While in the Democratic Republic of Congo (Congo Kinshasa) in 2000, a colleague and I were arrested by rebels in a remote jungle town called Bumba. The local commander did not know what to do with us— and yet he was too timid to radio his superiors for orders. So we stewed in our boots for three miserable days, fending off aggressive rats at a pest-house of a hotel. To have lost our tempers would have made matters worse. Eventually, we managed to convince the commander's radio operator to broadcast our plight. A plane piloted by Russian *gunrunners* (illegal arms dealers) rescued us.

The latest tools of the trade

Modern technology helps, too. Smaller computers and portable satellite *uplinks* (devices that enable communication using satellites) have given war reporters tools that our predecessors could only dream of. During the Vietnam War, the best that

A journalist covering Afghanistan in October 2001 works on a battery-powered laptop computer (above) in a village in the remote Panjshir Valley. Another reporter in Afghanistan in 2001 (right) files a report from Kabul using a satellite telephone. Such technology enabled correspondents to remain as near the action as possible while maintaining almost instantaneous communication with editors halfway around the world.

most television crews could hope for was to get their film quickly to Japan, so that stations there could beam footage by way of satellites to the United States on the following day.

Today's technology enables reporters to broadcast live reports from any foxhole in the world. In Afghanistan, television viewers got their first glimpse of U.S. air strikes by means of a *video-phone*—a shoebox-sized device that transmits images through a small satellite telephone. These phones, which can be plugged into a car's cigarette lighter to be powered by the car's battery, have been in use for years by journalists covering the backwater wars of Africa. They are as essential for receiving information as for sending it. Using this technology, reporters, whose world is often no bigger than the trench they are sitting in, can get up-to-the-minute information from editors back home.

Human elements—and issues

Perhaps the most essential tool at the modern war reporter's disposal, however, is not mechanical, but human—the myriad of local drivers, translators, and so-called "fixers" who make war reporting possible in dangerous, remote, and politically complex environments where journalists are likely to land without even knowing friend from foe. Good fixers—who arrange travel plans and interviews—can help reporters learn the differences among Sierra Leone's competing rebel gangs or track down al-Qa'ida members. Fixers are the unsung heroes of the trade. The U.S. public gets most its war news thanks to the work and courage of these usually faceless people.

In war-fractured central Africa in late 2000, for example, I was accompanied down the Congo River in a canoe by one of these fixers, an impoverished linguist named Samuel Benda

Kabul

Daniel Pearl, a reporter for the *Wall Street Journal,* was killed in early 2002 in Pakistan after being captured by a terrorist group.

Ndomba. He not only used the sheer force of his personality to fend off predatory teenagers carrying Russian-made rifles, but he quoted the poetry of Robert Frost to boost my flagging spirits. And in June 1999 in Kosovo, a Serbian province that fought a bloody battle for independence in the late 1990's, a young woman named Delvina Hasimja left the safety of her home to translate for me in her shattered land. Not much over 5 feet (1.5 meters) tall, she was fearless at hostile Serb checkpoints.

This is without question the greatest change in the way war news will be collected and disseminated in the foreseeable future. Unlike the reporters and camera operators who palled around with the U.S. armed forces during the wars of the 20th century, the journalists of the 2000's must gather the bulk of their impressions through local civilians. This is a sad if fitting development. Journalists today must do their jobs with the help of civilians because most of the raw brutality of modern warfare is directed at *noncombatants* (the civilians in war zones who are not doing the fighting).

Journalists face other dangers in war zones, including the invisible scars caused by what they see. A study reported in April 2001 found that war correspondents suffer nearly the same amount of posttraumatic stress disorder (PTSD) as combat veterans and more than police officers. The study had been commissioned by the Freedom Forum, an Arlington, Virginia-based not-for-profit media organization dedicated to free speech. PTSD is a mental disorder that occurs as a result of witnessing or experiencing stressful, violent events, such as war. Some reporters get moody or depressed, others become short-tempered, and a few

Ernie Pyle: One of the Boys

Ernie Pyle was the most popular war correspondent of World War II (1939-1945). Pyle, who wrote in a simple style that most Americans could understand, was the only reporter of the era who focused on the daily lives of U.S. soldiers caught up in the greatest struggle in history.

Ernest Taylor Pyle was born on Aug. 3, 1900, and grew up on a farm in Indiana. He studied journalism at Indiana University in Bloomington before working for newspapers in Indiana, Washington, D.C., and New York City. In the 1930's, he landed a job as a roving reporter for the Scripps Howard Newspapers, a newspaper chain. He became known for his stories about ordinary people.

Pyle's career peaked in the 1940's with his coverage of World War II in Europe, Africa, and the Pacific islands. As a war correspondent, Pyle had unlimited access to ordinary soldiers. Many U.S. soldiers considered Pyle more a friend than a reporter. He, in turn, deeply admired the infantrymen he covered, calling them the "mud-rain-and-wind boys." Most of his dispatches focused on the sacrifices that ordinary Americans made for the war effort and how much they missed their families and friends.

Pyle received international recognition for his war reporting. In 1944, he won the Pulitzer Prize for correspondence. He was such a fixture on the front lines that he wore the same uniform as the U.S. Marines he covered. In the end, Pyle himself made the ultimate sacrifice. On April 18, 1945, Ernie Pyle was killed by a Japanese machine-gunner on the Pacific island of Ie Shima near the island of Okinawa.

Dan Blunk

succumb to what I call the "chatterbox syndrome"—manic talkativeness. In Kosovo, I once saw a colleague burst into tears in a restaurant while trying to order coffee. It was not the petty frustrations of the language barrier that had brought on the sobs; it was the burned corpses of civilians we had stumbled across that morning and had dispassionately recorded in our notebooks.

The dizzying speed of modern air travel often enhances the job's emotional whiplashes. Sixty-five years ago, fabled war reporters such as Ernest Hemingway and Martha Gellhorn could make leisurely transitions between peacetime France and the chaos of Spain raked by civil war (1936-1939), because the physical journey took at least several days. Today, that adjustment period has shrunk to mere hours. Once, after leaving the trenches of the Ethiopia-Eritrea war in Africa in 2000, I was able to jump onto a series of planes and catch the movie *American Beauty* in my home city, Johannesburg, South Africa, less than 24 hours later. I was careful not to dirty the theater seat in front of me with my war-dusted boots. Also, I have been rousted out of my bed by a phone call from an editor at night and had spears thrown at me by an angry mob in Zimbabwe the next afternoon.

Dwelling on this aspect of the job, however, is self-indulgent. After all, we volunteer for this work—unlike the brutalized soldiers and hapless civilians we cover. It is their war stories, not ours, that matter.

U.S. Army General Tommy Franks, the officer in charge of the U.S. military campaign in Afghanistan, briefs reporters in March 2002. Press conferences have become one of the only ways reporters get official information about the progress of U.S. military action since relations between the press and the military soured during the Vietnam War.

Experiences of war

Many of these peoples' stories are unforgettable. There was, for example, the one-eyed rebel commander who was sweating under a thorny tree in Sudan in northeastern Africa in April 2002. He was pleading for help from the United States to resolve his nation's seemingly endless civil war, which began in 1983. It was sad irony that the commander's men—and thousands of civilians—were dying atop a savanna that hides untold riches in the form of an almost untapped ocean of oil. (The U.S. government has, in fact, sent a mediator to Sudan to try to negotiate a peace settlement.)

There was the tough Hazara tribesman in Afghanistan digging with his bare hands through a mass grave stuffed with the bones of villagers who had been slaughtered by the Taliban. His face stiffened when he found a green pen—clearly the belonging of a beloved family member. His capacity for forgiveness—or revenge—will largely determine whether U.S. soldiers will be required to keep the peace in Afghanistan for untold years to come.

And then there are the latest and most improbable war victims of all—the millions of Americans sitting in front of their televisions, apprehensively watching dispatches from a world that seems suddenly more hostile. Hundreds of correspondents from all kinds of media outlets—print, television, and radio—are toiling to keep producing accurate and balanced stories from war-torn regions throughout the world. Unfortunately, the media still have work to do in another vital area—trust. In November 2001, a nationwide poll revealed that the U.S. Department of Defense, though it is now restricting the flow of war news as never before, enjoyed an 80-percent public approval rating. By contrast, the media earned an abysmal 43-percent approval rating. Until members of the public feel they can trust the press—and until they demand better access to U.S. troops on the battlefield—all of us may have to wait years for a U.S. soldier with a literary bent to write his or her memoirs before we can fully understand how our government is guarding our security in these critical times.

Still, I keep my assignment bag packed and ready. I cover a lot of things, not just war. But I appreciate the importance of war reporting as a window on history, as a cautionary tale, and one of the few news events in the world that cuts to the marrow of our common humanity.

Once, in Kosovo, I met a disheveled old refugee couple clearing debris from their ruined home. Serb troops had occupied the place. The soldiers had kicked apart the furniture that the old man had built, scrawled hate graffiti on the walls, and relieved themselves on the living room rug. I asked the old woman how she felt to be home again. "I am very happy," she said, starting to cry. The old man did not say anything. He just took my hand and placed it over his thumping heart.   ■■■

A grieving mother in Lagos, Nigeria, carries her dead child who drowned in a canal on January 27 attempting to escape exploding artillery shells and machine gun bullets. The flying shrapnel and bullets were caused by a massive explosion at a nearby armory. More than 1,000 people, primarily children, were killed as a result of the accident.

Nicaragua. On Jan. 10, 2002, Enrique Bolanos Geyer, the vice president in the previous government, was sworn in for a four-year term as president of Nicaragua. After becoming president, Bolanos alleged that the man he succeeded, former President Arnoldo Aleman Lacayo, had embezzled $100 million in public funds while in office. In September, the National Assembly, at the behest of President Bolanos, removed Aleman from his post as chairman of the legislative body. Also in September, a judge issued arrest warrants for several of Aleman's family members and former associates in connection with the embezzlement scheme.

In November, a special prosecutor charged President Bolanos and 23 other members of the Liberal Constitutionalist Party with electoral fraud and conspiring to steal $4.1 million in government funds to finance his 2001 campaign. Amid charges and counter-charges, a congressional committee recommended in November that the National Assembly strip both Bolanos and Aleman of the legal immunity that they enjoyed as a president and former president. In December, legislators stripped Aleman of his immunity, and he was placed under house arrest.

☐ Nathan A. Haverstock

See also **Latin America**.
Niger. See Africa.

Nigeria. More than 1,000 people died on the night of Jan. 27, 2002, when explosions ripped through a huge armory in Lagos, Nigeria's largest city. The explosion showered a crowded district with exploding artillery shells and machine gun ammunition. Most of the victims were children who fled their houses in terror and drowned in a marshy network of canals. Many people were injured by flying shrapnel. Exploding shells landed up to 15 miles (24 kilometers) away, closing Lagos's main airport.

Nigerian military leaders immediately launched an investigation into the causes of the explosion. Critics pointed out that the armory should not have been located in the center of a crowded urban area and accused the government and the army of criminal negligence.

Death sentences imposed by Nigerian courts under the Islamic law code called *Sharia* triggered an international outcry in 2002. In August, a court confirmed a sentence of death by stoning against a divorced woman for having a child out of wedlock. Human rights groups called on Nigeria's government to end *Sharia*, which 12 primarily Islamic northern states had adopted in the 1990's. President Olusegun Obasanjo warned that Nigeria risked world condemnation if public stonings were carried out. Political analysts speculated that the president was reluctant to take action that might offend Islamic leaders before the 2003 elections, in which Obasanjo planned to stand for reelection.

Deadly riots. Controversy over the Miss World pageant erupted into riots in the northern city of Kaduna in November 2002. The pageant was scheduled to be staged in Abuja, the capital, on December 7. However, Islamic youths, objecting to the pageant's "scandalous" presentation of women, protested. After a newspaper editor observed that Muhammad, the prophet whose life and teachings form the basis of the Islamic religion, might have responded to the pageant by marrying one of the contestants, the protesters went on a rampage, killing at least 215 people and destroying several churches and other buildings. Miss World pageant organizers hastily moved the event to London.

Unfavorable judgment. On October 10, the World Court in The Hague, Netherlands, ruled that Cameroon is the rightful owner of the Bakassi Peninsula on Africa's West Coast. The World Court, officially called the International Court of Justice, is a United Nations-affiliated organization that judges international disputes. Nigerian and Cameroon forces had clashed repeatedly over the oil-rich peninsula, which Nigeria has long claimed.   □ Simon Baynham

See also **Africa**.

Nobel Prizes in literature, peace, the sciences, and economics were awarded in October 2002 by the Norwegian Storting (parliament) in Oslo and by the Royal Swedish Academy of Sciences, the Karolinska Institute, and the Swedish Academy of Literature in Stockholm. Each prize was worth about $1 million.

The 2002 Nobel Prize for literature was awarded to Hungarian writer Imre Kertesz, whose works had been strongly influenced by his imprisonment as a teen-ager in a Nazi death camp during World War II (1939-1945). Kertesz, who was little known outside Europe, explores how people attempt to maintain their individuality in the face of unrelenting social and political pressure to conform. His first and best-known book, *Fateless* (1975), tells the story of a Jewish teen-ager who conforms to the brutality of life in a concentration camp and survives. *Fateless* was the first in a trilogy of semiautobiographical books that include *Fiasco* (1988) and *Kaddish for a Child Not Born* (1990).

The 2002 Nobel Peace Prize was awarded to former United States President Jimmy Carter for "decades of untiring effort to find peaceful solutions to international conflicts, to advance democracy and human rights, and to promote economic and social development." The Nobel Committee noted that Carter's role in mediating a 1979 peace treaty between Egypt and Israel alone merited the prize. In 1982, after leaving the presidency, Carter and his wife, Rosalynn, founded the Carter Center of Emory University in Atlanta, Georgia, to promote democracy and human rights and help alleviate human suffering.

The 2002 Nobel Prize for physiology or medicine went to British-born Sydney Brenner of the Salk Institute for Biological Studies in San Diego; H. Robert Horvitz of the Massachusetts Institute of Technology in Cambridge; and John E. Sulston of the Wellcome Trust Sanger Institute in Cambridge, England. The researchers discovered how genes regulate the development and death of cells, the building blocks of living things. The scientists' findings revealed how specific genes regulate a process called programmed cell death, in which sick, diseased, or even healthy cells destroy themselves to make room for new cells.

The Nobel Committee credited Brenner with laying the foundation for the discoveries by identifying *Caenorhabditis elegans*, a tiny, transparent worm, as a model for studying cell development. Sulston used *C. elegans* to demonstrate that certain cells die as a normal part of the development process. Horvitz discovered key genes responsible for controlling cell death in *C. elegans* and found corresponding human genes.

The 2002 Nobel Prize for economics was shared by Israeli-born Daniel Kahneman of Princeton University in Princeton, New Jersey, and Vernon L. Smith of George Mason University in Fairfax, Virginia. The two winners pioneered new forms of economic research that incorporate psychological findings and controlled laboratory experiments.

Kahneman, a psychologist, and his longtime collaborator, the late Amos Tversky, challenged the widely accepted economic belief that people generally rely on such rational factors as available information and self-interest when making economic decisions. Kahneman and Tversky demonstrated that people rely, instead, on a variety of strategies, including some that may be contradictory. A pioneer in experimental economics, Smith developed techniques and standards for studying economic decision-making in laboratory settings.

The 2002 Nobel Prize for chemistry went to John B. Fenn of Virginia Commonwealth University in Richmond; Koichi Tanaka of Shimadzu Corporation in Kyoto, Japan; Kurt Wuthrich of the Swiss Federal Institute of Technology in Zurich, Switzerland; and the Scripps Research Institute in La Jolla, California. The three scientists developed methods for identifying and analyzing the structures of proteins and other large biological molecules. The Nobel Committee said their work had increased understanding of the chemical processes occurring in cells and "revolutionized" the development of new drugs. Working independently, Fenn and Tanaka improved both the speed and capabilities of mass spectroscopy, a technique for identifying the chemical composition of a solution. Wuthrich developed a method of using an imaging technique called nuclear magnetic resonance spectroscopy to create three-dimensional maps of protein molecules.

The 2002 Nobel Prize for physics went to Raymond Davis, Jr., of the University of Pennsylvania in Philadelphia; Masatoshi Koshiba of the University of Tokyo in Japan; and Italian-born Riccardo Giacconi of Associated Universities, Inc., in Washington, D.C. Davis and Koshiba, working with different underground devices, detected *neutrinos,* subatomic particles formed in fusion reactions. Their findings proved that the sun derives its energy from fusion reactions.

Giacconi was honored for numerous achievements involving cosmic X rays. He became the first scientist to detect X rays outside the solar system and to prove that galaxies, quasars, and other celestial objects emit X rays. He also supervised the construction of the first X-ray telescope and spearheaded the launch of the first artificial satellites capable of detecting cosmic X rays.

See also **Literature, World**.

☐ Barbara A. Mayes

Northern Ireland. The peace process between Roman Catholics and Protestants in Northern Ireland came close to collapse in 2002. Hostility, known as the "Troubles" between the Catholic minority—or nationalists—who favored the reunification of Northern Ireland with the Republic of Ireland, and the Protestant majority—or unionists—who favored remaining in the United Kingdom (UK), had continued to flare since 1969.

An agreement on Good Friday 1998 had produced a cease-fire and created the Northern Ireland Assembly, ending a long period of direct rule by the UK. The new Assembly, led by First Minister David Trimble of the Protestant Ulster Unionist Party, included for the first time representatives of Sinn Fein, the political wing of the Irish Republican Army (IRA), a paramilitary organization. In 2001, a breakthrough in the peace process seemed to occur when the IRA began to abandon its weapons. However, continued violence and suspicions between nationalists and unionists contributed to the suspension of the Assembly and the reintroduction of direct rule by Britain in October 2002.

Riots. In early January, renewed hostility was directed toward children attending a Catholic primary school in a Protestant area of Belfast, the capital, leading to a riot in which both civilians and police officers were wounded. On January 12, a Protestant paramilitary group, the Ulster Defence Association, shot and killed a Catholic postal worker. Further riots occurred throughout the spring and summer in Belfast, especially during the "Marching Season," when the Orange Order (a militant Protestant group) paraded through a Catholic area to commemorate a Protestant victory over Catholics in 1690.

IRA. In April 2002, the IRA announced that it would give up a second cache of arms following its earlier decommissioning of weapons in October 2001. The British and Irish prime ministers, as well as David Trimble, welcomed the move. Other Unionists were more cautious, suggesting the move was a publicity stunt. On July 16, 2002, the IRA issued an unprecedented apology for the civilian deaths that had occurred since the Troubles began. The occasion was the upcoming anniversary of "Bloody Friday," July 21, 1972, on which IRA bombs in Belfast killed nine people.

Distrust between unionists and republicans worsened in March 2002, when documents relating to counterterrorist activities were stolen from Castlereagh Police Station in Belfast. Six men with links to the IRA were later arrested. In April, the police announced they had discovered a list of possible assassination targets in the home of an IRA member. The list included former British prime ministers Margaret Thatcher and John Major. The British Northern Ireland Secretary, John Reid, insisted the list did not prove the IRA intended further action.

The International Relations Committee of the United States House of Representatives subsequently issued a report claiming that the IRA was training revolutionary guerrillas in Colombia. Sinn Fein President Gerry Adams refused to appear before the committee. Unionists claimed that this series of events proved the IRA had not really renounced violence.

The Northern Ireland Assembly collapsed in October, after police claimed they had found evidence of an IRA spy ring in the Northern Ireland Office, part of the UK government. John Reid was forced to suspend the Northern Ireland Assembly, as unionists had lost confidence in it. Direct UK rule was reintroduced on October 14. Later that month, Paul Murphy replaced Reid as Northern Ireland secretary.

British Prime Minister Tony Blair urged the IRA to disband, but the organization, claiming it had been blamed unfairly, broke off contact with the commission monitoring its disarming. Nevertheless, Sinn Fein government minister Martin McGuiness stated publicly that his war with Britain was over. ☐ Rohan McWilliam

See also **Ireland; United Kingdom**.

Northwest Territories. See Canadian Territories.

Norway. The government of Prime Minister Kjell Magne Bondevik carried out a program of tax cuts in 2002. In September, the government announced tax cuts of $1.5 billion in the budget for 2003, with reductions in income tax, payroll taxes, and property taxes. Bondevik hoped the reductions would drive economic growth.

The economy picked up moderately in 2002, as strong growth in Norway's offshore oil industry offset weakness in other business sectors. Government economists estimated that the country's gross domestic product, the value of all goods and services produced in a year, would grow by 1.7 percent in 2002, up from 1.2 percent in 2001.

Merger failure. A proposal to create a dominant Norwegian financial services company by merging Den Norske Bank (DNB) and the insurance firm Storebrand ASA fell apart in 2002. The two companies announced an agreement on May 29 in which DNB was to acquire Storebrand, then abandoned the plan one month later. Storebrand objected to DNB's attempt to negotiate a lower takeover price. A proposed merger between Storebrand and Finland's Sampo Insurance PLC collapsed in 2001.

Smoking ban. The Norwegian government proposed the most restrictive smoking legislation in Europe in 2002. The bill, introduced in parliament in November, would ban smoking in all indoor public places by 2004, including bars and restaurants. Norwegians who smoke would be allowed to do so only at home or outdoors. The bill was drafted in response to pressure from restaurant workers' unions concerned about the effects of secondhand smoke.

Sri Lanka. Norwegian negotiators brokered a cease-fire in 2002 between the Sri Lankan government and the separatist Liberation Tigers of Tamil Eelam in a civil war that had begun in 1983. The cease-fire was announced on Feb. 23, 2002. Norway then led an international team to monitor the cease-fire and conducted negotiations aimed at a lasting peace agreement.

The killer whale Keiko, star of the movie *Free Willy* (1993) made his home in a Norwegian fjord in September 2002. Keiko had been captured off Iceland in 1975 and spent the next two decades in captivity before fans of the movie campaigned for his release. He was returned to Iceland in 1998, prepared for release into the wild, and then set free in July 2002. Six weeks later, he entered Skaalvik fjord, 250 miles (402 kilometers) northwest of Oslo, where he attracted thousands of sightseers. ☐ Tom Buerkle

See also **Europe; Sri Lanka.**

Nova Scotia. See Canadian provinces.
Nuclear energy. See Energy supply.
Nutrition. See Food.

Ocean. The Arctic Ocean holds much more water than scientists had thought, announced Martin Jakobsson of the Center for Coastal Ocean Mapping at the University of New Hampshire in May 2002. Jakobsson's conclusion was based on a detailed map that showed that the Arctic Ocean, on average, is about 3,940 feet (1,200 meters) deep, nearly 330 feet (100 meters) deeper than previously thought. The ocean's volume is about 90,000 cubic miles (375,000 cubic kilometers) larger than scientists had previously calculated.

The Arctic Ocean is covered by thick ice for much of the year, making it difficult for scientists to accurately survey it. The map Jakobsson analyzed—a project known as the International Bathymetric Chart of the Arctic Ocean—was created in 2000 through the use of declassified submarine data from the United States and British navies and from ice-breaking ships and satellites. The map is the most comprehensive ever made of the Arctic Ocean basin.

Jakobsson reported that more than half of the floor of the Arctic Ocean is actually part of the continental shelf, a much higher percentage than the floors of other oceans. This makes the Arctic Ocean coastline more sensitive to sea-level changes that may be caused by global warming.

Otter mystery solved. In June 2002, wildlife veterinarian Melissa Miller of the University of California at Davis offered an explanation for the mysterious decline in sea otters in California. The population of southern sea otters in California has declined 10 percent since 1995. She reported that a parasite often found in cat *feces* (solid waste) was killing the otters.

Miller examined dead otters and found that about 62 percent of them were infected with *Toxoplasma gondii.* The microscopic parasite causes brain infection in otters and can also create serious health problems in unborn human babies. Cats are the only animals known to carry the parasite.

Miller discovered that otters found near river mouths or other areas of freshwater runoff were three times more likely to be infected than other otters. This suggested that the runoff carried the parasite's eggs from cat waste on land to the ocean. Miller theorized that the otters are infected by eating mussels and other shellfish, in which the *T. gondii* eggs may accumulate.

Controversial sonar system. In November 2002, the U.S. Navy agreed to scale back the use of a controversial sonar system that environmentalists and some scientists said could harm whales and other marine life.

The system, called the Surveillance Towed Array Sensor System (SURTASS), emits very powerful low-frequency soundwaves to detect enemy submarines that are invisible to traditional sonar. Scientists believe the low-frequency blasts interfere with whale communication and navigation and can, in some cases, cause fatal brain damage. A similar sonar system was linked to the deaths of six beaked whales that became stranded in the Bahamas in March 2000.

Controversy over SURTASS erupted in July 2002 when the National Oceanic and Atmospheric Administration (NOAA), a government agency that monitors the environment, granted the Navy permission to deploy the system. Several environmental groups sued the Navy in August to prevent them from implementing the system.

Hungry sharks? Overfishing may be depleting fish stocks in the Atlantic Ocean that sharks depend on for food, causing sharks to hunt closer to the shores of the East Coast of the United States, endangering swimmers. This conclusion was reported by oceanographers at Louisiana State University in August 2002.

Richard Condrey and Kevin Barry found that blacktip sharks caught off the coast of Louisiana feed mainly on menhaden, a type of fish caught in large numbers for chicken feed. They also found that this source of food was in danger of depletion because only about 3 percent of adult menhaden in the Atlantic Ocean have a chance to reproduce before being caught.

☐ Christina S. Johnson

Ohio. See State government.
Oklahoma. See State government.
Old age. See Social Security.

Rescuers try to save pilot whales trapped in shallow waters off Eastham, Massachusetts, on July 30. At least 56 of the whales died. The whales had originally become stranded on July 29 and rescuers had freed them, but the whales beached themselves again the next day.

WINTER GAMES

THE 2002 OLYMPICS

By Dan Blunk

The 19th Winter Olympic Games opened on Feb. 9, 2002, in Salt Lake City, Utah, amid unprecedented concerns over the security of athletes and spectators. The tight security measures, costing more than $300 million and involving a huge police presence and metal detectors outside venues, were implemented in light of the terrorist attacks against the United States that occurred on Sept. 11, 2001. Despite fears of new attacks, none occurred during the Games. For 17 days, athletes from 78 countries competed on the world stage, a sign of peace in defiance of terrorism throughout the world. However, the Games were marred by one of the biggest scandals in the history of Olympic figure skating and the news that several athletes had taken performance-enhancing drugs.

German athletes dominated the Games, taking 35 medals, 12 of them gold. A greatly improved U.S. team netted 34 medals, including 10 golds, up from only 13 medals in the 1998 Winter Games. Speed skaters broke eight world records in 2002, the most in any single Olympics. Croatian skier Janica Kostelic became the first skier to win four medals in one Olympics.

The 19th Winter Olympic Games in Salt Lake City, Utah, were a sign of peace in defiance of terrorism.

**Kjetil Andre Aamodt of Norway
Men's Combined Alpine Skiing**

The reintroduction of the thrilling sport of skeleton provided one of the biggest stories of the 2002 Games. In skeleton, which is similar to the luge, athletes lie on their stomachs on a steel sled and slide down the same type of icy course used in the luge and bobsled events. However, skeleton athletes face forward, shooting down the course at more than 70 miles (113 kilometers) per hour. Skeleton was introduced as an official sport in the 1928 Winter Olympics. It appeared again in the 1948 Games but was later banned because officials deemed it too dangerous.

The 2002 Winter Games were marred by one of the biggest judging scandals in Olympics history. The scandal involved the pairs figure skating competition on February 11, in which the gold was awarded to Russians Anton Sikharulidze and Elena Berezhnaya, after a performance with several major flaws. The Canadian pairs figure skaters, Jamie Sale and David Pelletier, had skated nearly flawlessly but were only awarded the silver medal. When the judges' 5-4 decision in favor of the Russian team was displayed, the largely North American crowd loudly booed. Olympic officials later accused a French judge of vote-trading. The judge, Marie Reine Le Gougne, eventually admitted to giving high marks to the Russian pair in return for a Russian judge giving high marks to the French pair in ice-dancing, a separate event.

After a six-day investigation, Olympic officials made the unprecedented move to award gold medals to both pairs of skaters. Le Gougne was later suspended from judging for three years.

ALPINE SKIING

Women's Combined
GOLD	Janica Kostelic	Croatia
SILVER	Renate Goetschl	Austria
BRONZE	Martina Ertl	Germany

Women's Downhill
GOLD	Carole Montillet	France
SILVER	Isolde Kostner	Italy
BRONZE	Renate Goetschl	Austria

Women's Giant Slalom
GOLD	Janica Kostelic	Croatia
SILVER	Anja Paerson	Sweden
BRONZE	Sonja Nef	Switzerland

Women's Slalom
GOLD	Janica Kostelic	Croatia
SILVER	Laure Pequegnot	France
BRONZE	Anja Paerson	Sweden

Women's Super-G
GOLD	Daniela Ceccarelli	Italy
SILVER	Janica Kostelic	Croatia
BRONZE	Karen Putzer	Italy

Men's Combined
GOLD	Kjetil Andre Aamodt	Norway
SILVER	Bode Miller	United States
BRONZE	Benjamin Raich	Austria

Men's Downhill
GOLD	Fritz Strobl	Austria
SILVER	Lasse Kjus	Norway
BRONZE	Stephan Eberharter	Austria

Men's Giant Slalom
GOLD	Stephen Eberharter	Austria
SILVER	Bode Miller	United States
BRONZE	Lasse Kjus	Norway

Men's Slalom
GOLD	Jean-Pierre Vidal	France
SILVER	Sebastien Amiez	France
BRONZE	Benjamin Raich	Austria

Men's Super-G
GOLD	Kjetil Andre Aamodt	Norway
SILVER	Stephan Eberharter	Austria
BRONZE	Andreas Schifferer	Austria

On the final day of the Games, Olympic officials dismissed three cross-country skiers for failing drug tests. Two of the athletes, Larissa Lazutina of Russia and Johann Muehlegg of Spain, were stripped of one gold medal each but were allowed to keep medals they had won before the test. Olympic officials said all three skiers had tested positive for performance-enhancing drugs. British skier Alain Baxter also tested positive and he was stripped of his bronze medal in the men's slalom, the first ever won by a British skier.

The author: Dan Blunk is a staff editor on *The Year Book*.

BIATHLON

Men's 10-K Sprint
GOLD	Ole Einar Bjoerndalen	Norway
SILVER	Sven Fischer	Germany
BRONZE	Wolfgang Perner	Austria

Men's 12.5-K Pursuit
GOLD	Ole Einar Bjoerndalen	Norway
SILVER	Raphael Poiree	France
Bronze	Ricco Gross	Germany

Men's 20-K Individual
GOLD	Ole Einar Bjoerndalen	Norway
SILVER	Frank Luck	Germany
BRONZE	Victor Maigourov	Russia

Men's 4 x 7.5-K Relay
GOLD	Frode Andreson Ole Einar Bjoerndalen Egil Gjelland Halvard Hanevold	Norway
SILVER	Sven Fischer Frank Luck Peter Sendel Ricco Gross	Germany
BRONZE	Vincent Defrasne Gilles Marguet Raphael Poiree Julien Robert	France

Women's 10-K Pursuit
GOLD	Olga Pyleva	Russia
SILVER	Kati Wilhelm	Germany
BRONZE	Irina Nikoultchina	Bulgaria

Women's 15-K Individual
GOLD	Andrea Henkel	Germany
SILVER	Liv Grete Poiree	Norway
BRONZE	Magdalena Forsberg	Sweden

Women's 4 x 7.5-K Relay
GOLD	Katrin Apel Andrea Henkel Uschi Disl Kati Wilhelm	Germany
SILVER	Gunn Margrit Andreassen Liv Grete Poiree Ann Elen Skjelbreid Linda Tjoerhom	Norway
BRONZE	Olga Pyleva Galina Koukleva Svetlana Ishmouratova Albina Akhatova	Russia

Women's 7.5-K Sprint
GOLD	Kati Wilhelm	Germany
SILVER	Uschi Disl	Germany
BRONZE	Magdalena Forsberg	Sweden

Ole Einar Bjoerndalen of Norway
Men's Biathlon

Vonetta Flowers and Jill Bakken of the United States Women's Bobsled

BOBSLED

Four-Man

GOLD	Andre Lange Carsten Embach Kevin Kuske Enrico Kuehn	Germany
SILVER	Todd Hays Bill Schuffenhauer Garrett Hines Randy Jones	United States
BRONZE	Mike Kohn Doug Sharp Brian Shimer Dan Steele	United States

Two-Man

GOLD	Christoph Langen Markus Zimmermann	Germany
SILVER	Steve Anderhub Christian Reich	Switzerland
BRONZE	Martin Annen Beat Hefti	Switzerland

Women's

GOLD	Jill Bakken Vonetta Flowers	United States
SILVER	Sandra Prokoff Ulrike Holzner	Germany
BRONZE	Susi-Lisa Erdmann Nicole Herschmann	Germany

CROSS-COUNTRY SKIING

Men's 10-K Free Pursuit

GOLD	Johann Muehlegg	Spain
SILVER	Thomas Alsgaard	Norway
SILVER	Frode Estil	Norway

Men's 15-K Classical

GOLD	Andrus Veerpalu	Estonia (EST)
SILVER	Frode Estil	Norway
BRONZE	Jaak Mae	Estonia

Men's 30-K Free Mass Start

GOLD	Johann Muehlegg	Spain
SILVER	Christian Hoffmann	Austria
BRONZE	Mikhail Botvinov	Austria

Men's 4 x 10-K Relay

GOLD	Thomas Alsgaard Kristen Skjeldal Frode Estil Anders Aukland	Norway
SILVER	Giorgio di Centa Fabio Maj Pietro Pillar Cottrer Cristian Zorzi	Italy
BRONZE	Tobias Angerer Jens Filbrich Andreas Schluetter Rene Sommerfeldt	Germany

Men's 50-K Classical

GOLD	Mikhail Ivanov	Russia
SILVER	Andrus Veerpalu	Estonia
BRONZE	Odd-Bjoern Hjelmeset	Norway

Men's Sprint

GOLD	Tor Arne Hetland	Norway
SILVER	Peter Schlickenrieder	Germany
BRONZE	Cristian Zorzi	Italy

Women's 10-K Classical

GOLD	Bente Skari	Norway
SILVER	Olga Danilova	Russia
BRONZE	Julija Tchepalova	Russia

Women's 15-K Free Mass Start

GOLD	Stefania Belmondo	Italy
SILVER	Larissa Lazutina	Russia
BRONZE	Katerina Neumannova	Czech Republic

Women's 30-K Classical

GOLD	Gabriella Paruzzi	Italy
SILVER	Stefania Belmondo	Italy
BRONZE	Bente Skari	Norway

CURLING

	Men's		Women's	
GOLD	Norway	GOLD	Britain	
SILVER	Canada	SILVER	Switzerland	
BRONZE	Switzerland	BRONZE	Canada	

FIGURE SKATING

Ice Dancing

GOLD	Marina Anissina Gwendal Peizerat	France
SILVER	Irina Lobacheva Ilia Averbuch	Russia
BRONZE	Barbara Fusar Poli Maurizio Margaglio	Italy

Women's Figure Skating

GOLD	Sarah Hughes	United States
SILVER	Irina Slutskaya	Russia
BRONZE	Michelle Kwan	United States

Men's Figure Skating

GOLD	Alexei Yagudin	Russia
SILVER	Evgeni Plushenko	Russia
BRONZE	Timothy Goebel	United States

Pairs Figure Skating

GOLD	David Pelletier/ Jamie Sale	Canada
GOLD	Elena Berezhnaya/ Anton Sikharulidze	Russia
BRONZE	Zhao Hongbo/ Shen Xue	China

Women's 4 x 5-K Relay

GOLD	Viola Bauer Manuela Henkel Evi Sachenbacher Claudia Kuenzel	Germany
SILVER	Bente Skari Hilde G. Pedersen Marit Bjoerngen Anita Moen	Norway
BRONZE	Brigitte Albrecht Loretan Andrea Huber Natascia Leonardi Cortesi Laurence Rochat	Switzerland

Women's 5-K Free Pursuit

GOLD	Olga Danilova	Russia
SILVER	Larissa Lazutina	Russia
BRONZE	Beckie Scott	Canada

Women's Sprint

GOLD	Julija Tchepalova	Russia
SILVER	Evi Sachenbacher	Germany
BRONZE	Anita Moen	Norway

Sarah Hughes of the United States Women's Figure Skating

FREESTYLE SKIING

Men's Aerials

GOLD	Ales Valenta	Czech Republic
SILVER	Joe Pack	United States
BRONZE	Alexei Grichin	Belarus

Men's Moguls

GOLD	Janne Lahtela	Finland
SILVER	Travis Mayer	United States
BRONZE	Richard Gay	France

Women's Aerials

GOLD	Alisa Camplin	Australia
SILVER	Veronica Brenner	Canada
BRONZE	Deidra Dionne	Canada

Women's Moguls

GOLD	Kari Traa	Norway
SILVER	Shannon Bahrke	United States
BRONZE	Tae Satoya	Japan

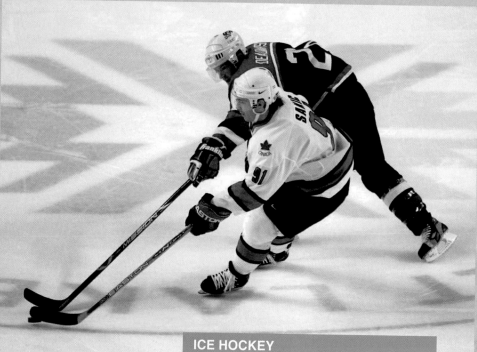

**Joe Sakic of Canada and
Adam Deadmarsh of the United States
Men's Ice Hockey**

ICE HOCKEY

Men's		Women's	
GOLD	Canada	GOLD	Canada
SILVER	United States	SILVER	United States
BRONZE	Russia	BRONZE	Sweden

LUGE

Doubles

GOLD	Patric-Fritz Leitner Alexander Resch	Germany
SILVER	Brian Martin Mark Grimmette	United States
BRONZE	Chris Thorpe Clay Ives	United States

Men's Singles

GOLD	Amin Zoeggler	Italy
SILVER	Georg Hackl	Germany
BRONZE	Markus Prock	Austria

Women's Singles

GOLD	Sylke Otto	Germany
SILVER	Barbara Niedernhuber	Germany
BRONZE	Silke Kraushaar	Germany

NORDIC COMBINED

Individual 15-K

GOLD	Samppa Lajunen	Finland
SILVER	Jaakko Tallus	Finland
BRONZE	Felix Gottwald	Austria

Sprint 7.5-K

GOLD	Samppa Lajunen	Finland
SILVER	Ronny Ackermann	Germany
BRONZE	Felix Gottwald	Austria

Team 4 x 5-K Relay

GOLD	Samppa Lajunen Hannu Manninen Jari Mantila Jaakko Tallus	Finland
SILVER	Marcel Hoehlig Bjoem Kircheisen Georg Hettich Ronny Ackermann	Germany
BRONZE	Christoph Bieler Michael Gruber Felix Gottwald Mario Stecher	Austria

SHORT TRACK SPEED SKATING

Women's 1,000-Meter
GOLD	A. Yang Yang	China
SILVER	Gi-Hyun Ko	Korea
BRONZE	S. Yang Yang	China

Women's 1,500-Meter
GOLD	Gi-Hyun Ko	Korea
SILVER	Eun-Kyung Choi	Korea
BRONZE	Evgenia Radanova	Bulgaria

Women's 3,000-Meter Relay
GOLD	Min-Kyung Choi Min-Jin Joo Hye-Won Park Eun-Kyung Choi	Korea	*4:12.793
SILVER	A. Yang Yang S. Yang Yang Wang Chunlu Sun Dandan	China	
BRONZE	Isabelle Charest Marie-Eve Drolet Amelie Goulet-Nadon Alanna Kraus Tania Vicent	Canada	

Women's 500-Meter
GOLD	A. Yang Yang	China
SILVER	Evgenia Radanova	Bulgaria
BRONZE	Wang Chunlu	China

Men's 1,000-Meter
GOLD	Steven Bradbury	Australia
SILVER	Apolo Anton Ohno	United States
BRONZE	Mathieu Turcotte	Canada

Men's 1,500-Meter
GOLD	Apolo Anton Ohno	United States
SILVER	Li Jiajun	China
BRONZE	Marc Gagnon	Canada

Men's 500-Meter
GOLD	Marc Gagnon	Canada	*41.802
SILVER	Jonathan Guilmette	Canada	
BRONZE	Rusty Smith	United States	

Men's 5,000-Meter Relay
GOLD	Eric Bedard Marc Gagnon Jonathan Guilmette Francois-Louis Tremblay Mathieu Turcotte	Canada
SILVER	Michele Antonioli Maurizio Carnino Fabio Carta Nicola Franceschina Nicola Rodigari	Italy
BRONZE	Li Jiajun An Yulong Li Ye Feng Kai Guo Wei	China

* World Record

A. Yang Yang of China
Women's Short Track Speed Skating

Jim Shea of the United States
Skeleton

SKELETON

Men's
GOLD	Jim Shea	United States
SILVER	Martin Rettl	Austria
BRONZE	Gregor Staehli	Switzerland

Women's
GOLD	Tristan Gale	United States
SILVER	Lea Ann Parsley	United States
BRONZE	Alex Coomber	Britain

SKI JUMPING

Individual K120
GOLD	Simon Ammann	Switzerland
SILVER	Adam Malysz	Poland
BRONZE	Matti Hautamaeki	Finland

Individual K90
GOLD	Simon Ammann	Switzerland
SILVER	Sven Hannawald	Germany
BRONZE	Adam Malysz	Poland

Team K120
GOLD	Michael Uhrmann	Germany
	Stephan Hocke	
	Sven Hannawald	
	Martin Schmitt	
SILVER	Janne Ahonen	Finland
	Matti Hautamaeki	
	Risto Jussilainen	
	Veli-Matti Lindstroem	
BRONZE	Damjan Fras	Slovenia
	Robert Kranjec	
	Primoz Peterka	
	Peter Zonta	

SNOWBOARD

Men's Halfpipe
GOLD	Ross Powers	United States
SILVER	Danny Kass	United States
BRONZE	Jarret Thomas	United States

Men's Parallel Giant Slalom
GOLD	Philipp Schoch	Switzerland
SILVER	Richard Richardsson	Sweden
BRONZE	Chris Klug	United States

Women's Halfpipe
GOLD	Kelly Clark	United States
SILVER	Doriane Vidal	France
BRONZE	Fabienne Reuteler	Switzerland

Women's Parallel Giant Slalom
GOLD	Isabelle Blanc	France
SILVER	Karine Ruby	France
BRONZE	Lidia Trettel	Italy

SPEED SKATING

Women's 1,000-Meter
GOLD	Chris Witty	United States	*1:13.83
SILVER	Sabine Voelker	Germany	
BRONZE	Jennifer Rodriguez	United States	

Women's 1,500-Meter
GOLD	Anni Friesinger	Germany	*1:54.02
SILVER	Sabine Voelker	Germany	
BRONZE	Jennifer Rodriguez	United States	

Women's 3,000-Meter
GOLD	Claudia Pechstein	Germany	*3:57.70
SILVER	Renate Groenewold	Netherlands	
BRONZE	Cindy Klassen	Canada	

Women's 500-Meter
GOLD	Catriona Lemay Doan	Canada	
SILVER	Monique Garbrecht-Enfeldt	Germany	
BRONZE	Sabine Voelker	Germany	

Women's 5,000-Meter
GOLD	Claudia Pechstein	Germany	*6:46.91
SILVER	Gretha Smit	Netherlands	
BRONZE	Clara Hughes	Canada	

Men's 1,000-Meter
GOLD	Gerard van Velde	Netherlands	*1:07.18
SILVER	Jan Bos	Netherlands	
BRONZE	Joey Cheek	United States	

Men's 10,000-Meter
GOLD	Jochem Uytdehaage	Netherlands	*12:58.92
SILVER	Gianni Romme	Netherlands	
BRONZE	Lasse Saetre	Norway	

Men's 1,500-Meter
GOLD	Derek Parra	United States	*1:43.95
SILVER	Jochem Uytdehaage	Netherlands	
BRONZE	Adne Sondral	Norway	

Men's 500-Meter
GOLD	Casey Fitzrandolph	United States	
SILVER	Hiroyasu Shimizu	Japan	
BRONZE	Kip Carpenter	United States	

Men's 5,000-Meter
GOLD	Jochem Uytdehaage	Netherlands	*6:14.66
SILVER	Derek Parra	United States	
BRONZE	Jens Boden	Germany	

* World Record

**Claudia Pechstein
of Germany
Women's Speed
Skating**

Pacific Islands. Parliamentary elections dominated events in the Pacific Islands in 2002. Voters went to the polls in Papua New Guinea, Vanuatu, Tonga, and Niue.

Papua New Guinea. Elections for a new parliament in the largest Pacific Island nation began in May and extended for seven weeks. Election officials took more than a month to collect all of the ballots, because of Papua New Guinea's rural and rugged terrain.

The National Alliance Party (NAP) won the most seats in the election, taking 19 in the 109-seat parliament. The NAP formed a coalition with several other parties and established a new government. NAP leader Sir Michael Somare, who had been Papua New Guinea's first prime minis-

ter when the country won independence from Australia in 1975, was elected prime minister for the third time.

The election was marred by violence in several provinces. More than 30 people were killed in tribal-related election fighting. At least 250 ballot boxes were stolen or destroyed. In the wake of the chaos, Electoral Commissioner Reuben Kainolo was charged with corruption.

Vanuatu. A record number of 261 candidates ran for the 52 seats in the Vanuatu parliament in May 2002. Prime Minister Edward Natapei's Vanua'aku Party won 14 seats. Deputy Prime Minister (and former prime minister) Serge Vohor's Union of Moderate Parties won an equal number. Natapei remained in office by forming a coalition

Facts in brief on Pacific Island countries

Country	Population	Government	Monetary unit*	Foreign trade (million U.S.$)	
				Exports†	Imports†
Australia	19,231,000	Governor General Peter Hollingworth; Prime Minister John Howard	dollar (1.84 = $1)	69,000	77,000
Fiji	840,000	President Josefa Iloilo; Prime Minister Laisenia Qarase	dollar (2.14 = $1)	537	653
Kiribati	85,000	President Teburoro Tito	Australian dollar	6	44
Marshall Islands	68,000	President Kessai Note	U.S. dollar	28	58
Micronesia, Federated States of	124,000	President Leo A. Falcam	U.S. dollar	73	168
Nauru	12,000	President Rene Harris	Australian dollar	25	21
New Zealand	3,930,000	Governor General Dame Silvia Cartwright; Prime Minister Helen Clark	dollar (2.12 = $1)	14,600	14,300
Palau	20,000	President Tommy Remengesau, Jr.	U.S. dollar	14	126
Papua New Guinea	5,015,000	Governor General Sir Silas Atopare; Prime Minister Sir Michael Somare	kina (3.99 = $1)	2,100	1,000
Samoa	187,000	Head of State Malietoa Tanumafili II; Prime Minister Tuila'epa Sailele Malielegaoi	tala (3.34 = $1)	17	90
Solomon Islands	470,000	Governor General Sir John Lapli; Prime Minister Sir Allan Kemakeza	dollar (7.22 = $1)	165	152
Tonga	100,000	King Taufa'ahau Tupou IV; Prime Minister Lavaka ata Ulukalala	pa'anga (2.23 = $1)	8	69
Tuvalu	13,000	Governor General Sir Tomasi Puapua; Prime Minister Saufatu Sopoanga	Australian dollar	1	4
Vanuatu	199,000	President Father John Bani; Prime Minister Edward Natapei	vatu (137.38 = $1)	25	77

*Exchange rates as of Oct. 4, 2002, or latest available data.
†Latest available data.

with a number of independent members of parliament.

Tonga, an absolute monarchy led by 84-year-old hereditary King Taufa'ahau Tupou IV, held parliamentary elections in March 2002. The one-chamber parliament consists of 30 members. Nine members are elected by the common people; 9 are elected by a group of 33 nobles; and the remaining 12 positions are filled by Cabinet members appointed by the king.

In the March elections, a record seven of the nine members elected by common vote belonged to the Human Rights and Democracy Movement (HRDM). The group, although it is not a formal political party, favors political reform to move the country toward a more democratic form of government. HRDM leaders were encouraged by the increase in seats, claiming it reflected the growing desire of the people for democracy.

Niue. All 20 members of parliament in Niue, a a self-governing dependency of New Zealand with fewer than 2,000 people, were reelected in April 2002. Young Vivian was chosen premier by a parliamentary vote of 14-6. Vivian replaced Sani Lakatani, whose term as prime minister was clouded by concerns that Niue was being used as a tax haven by companies involved in money laundering and tax evasion.

Fiji. In August, Fiji hosted the 33rd annual meeting of the South Pacific Forum, a group that promotes cooperation among the independent Pacific Island nations, Australia, and New Zealand. The 16 heads of government discussed such issues as development, trade, and regional security. The forum was marked by controversy as Australia announced its intention to nominate the group's secretary general when the term of the current secretary general, Noel Levi of Papua New Guinea, expires in 2003. The position has traditionally been filled by a Pacific Islander.

The Fifth Micronesian Games were held in Pohnpei, Federated States of Micronesia, in July 2002. Participants included the Republics of Palau and the Marshall Islands, the Commonwealth of the Northern Mariana Islands, Guam, Kiribati, and Nauru. Palau athletes captured the most medals, a total of 70. In addition to the usual sports, a unique event—the "Micronesian All Around"—was introduced, featuring such activities as coconut husking and spearthrowing.

Solomon Islands. A peace agreement between residents of Guadalcanal and the Malaita Islands expired in October 2002 without the militias of either group agreeing to disarm. Tensions between the groups have flared since World War II (1939-1945) when many people from Malaita moved to Guadalcanal. ☐ Eugene Ogan

See also **Australia; New Zealand.**

Painting. See Art.

Pakistan. President Pervez Musharraf of Pakistan held a controversial referendum in April 2002 that extended his presidential term by five years. Political observers said that Musharraf, who had lost much public support after he sided with the United States in 2001 against the radical Islamic Taliban regime in Afghanistan, had hoped the referendum would legitimize his leadership. Instead, the balloting, which was marred by massive fraud, weakened his popularity.

Nearly 98 percent of the ballots cast in the referendum supported extending Musharraf's term, according to the Pakistani election commission. However, a human rights group reported widespread ballot-box stuffing and other abuses. Critics also accused the election commission of grossly overestimating voter turnout. The commission claimed a 70-percent turnout, while independent poll watchers said that no more than 10 percent of voters took part in the referendum.

Constitutional overhaul. In August, Musharraf enacted sweeping constitutional changes that cemented his hold on power. The changes gave him the authority to dissolve parliament and to appoint the country's military chiefs and Supreme Court justices. He established a National Security Council—which included the president and chiefs of the armed forces—to oversee the prime minister, the cabinet, and parliament. The amendment formalized a role for the armed forces in governing the country.

Political observers said that the changes were designed to undermine parliamentary elections that Musharraf had scheduled for October. When Musharraf seized power in a military *coup* (overthrow) in 1999, he suspended parliament, but he promised to hold parliamentary elections and restore a civilian government by October 2002.

Parliamentary elections in October dealt a sharp blow to Musharraf and handed unprecedented power to hardline Islamic parties. The pro-government Pakistan Muslim League-Quaid-e-Azam won 103 of the 342 seats, the most in the election, but far fewer than needed to form a majority. An alliance of Islamic parties won 57 seats, the strongest showing ever for hardline religious parties. Political observers said the Islamic victory was a backlash against Musharraf's support of the war against the Taliban. The Pakistan People's Party (PPP), the party of former prime minister Benazir Bhutto, won 78 seats. Musharraf's ban on Bhutto leading her party hindered the PPP's chances. Bhutto, who had been convicted twice of corruption and was living in self-imposed exile, faced jail time on corruption charges if she returned to Pakistan.

Musharraf also banned former Prime Minister Nawaz Sharif, head of the Pakistan Muslim League, from participating in the election. Sharif, who had been ousted in the 1999 overthrow, was living in exile in Saudi Arabia in 2002.

In November, Musharraf swore in Zafarullah Khan Jamali, a member of the Pakistan Muslim League-Quaid-e-Azam, as prime minister.

Islamic extremists. Musharraf faced mounting criticism from Western nations about his inability to control Islamic extremists. Muslim militants killed more than 15 foreigners in 2002, including *Wall Street Journal* reporter Daniel Pearl. In addition, evidence suggested that members of the Taliban and al-Qa'ida, a global terrorist organization, were operating in Pakistan along the Afghanistan border.

End of standoff. India and Pakistan began pulling hundreds of thousands of troops back from their common border in November after the largest and longest peacetime standoff in their history. The standoff began in 2001 after India blamed Pakistan for a suicide attack on India's Parliament and demanded that Musharraf shut down Islamic groups supporting militants in Jammu and Kashmir, which is claimed by both countries. Both countries mobilized for war and moved troops to the border. In 2002, U.S. officials stepped in to help defuse the standoff and pressured Musharraf to crack down on militant groups supporting the insurgency in Kashmir.   ☐ Henry S. Bradsher

See also **Afghanistan; Asia; India; Terrorism**.

Paleontology. The dominance of dinosaurs may have begun when a large asteroid or comet collided with Earth, according to a May 2002 report. A group of scientists led by geologist Paul Olsen of Lamont-Doherty Earth Observatory in Palisades, New York, described fossil and chemical evidence linking the increased abundance of dinosaurs 200 million years ago with the same kind of cosmic crash previously blamed for their extinction.

In the 1990's, a variety of geological evidence convinced many scientists that the extinction of dinosaurs 65 million years ago was caused by an asteroid or comet striking into Mexico's Yucatan Peninsula. The collision and resulting fires would have generated vast amounts of smoke and dust that blocked sunlight for months. The lack of light and warmth would have killed many plants and animals, including dinosaurs. Evidence for an impact at this time includes a large crater in the Yucatan Peninsula and elevated levels of the chemical element iridium in geological sediment dated to 65 million years ago. Iridium is rare on Earth but common on asteroids and comets.

Olsen's team examined sediment and fossil footprints from the late Triassic Period (248 million to 213 million years ago) to the early Jurassic Period (213 million to 145 million years ago) at more than 70 sites in eastern North America. A change in the diversity and types of tracks approximately 200 mil-

Pakistani police in Karachi examine a bus destroyed in a suicide bombing in May. The attack, which authorities attributed to the al-Qa'ida terrorist network, killed 14 people, including 11 French engineers.

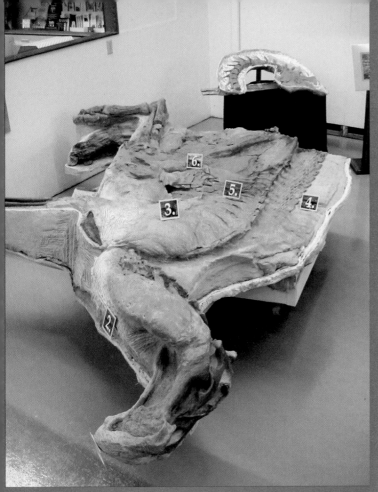

An unusually well-preserved fossil of the duckbilled dinosaur *Brachylophosaurus canadensis*, on display in October 2002, is one of the few known dinosaur fossils to have impressions of soft tissue. The 77-million-year-old fossil shows traces of muscles and tendons, skin scales the size of dimes, a long frill running along the back, and remains of plant material in the stomach. Paleontologists led by Nate L. Murphy of Phillips County Museum in Montana excavated the specimen dubbed "Leonardo," which is about 22 feet (6.7 meters) in length, near Malta, Montana, in 2001.

lion years ago revealed the change from Triassic reptiles to Jurassic dinosaurs. But an increase in the concentration of iridium in the 200-million-year-old sediment provided the most telling evidence of dramatic global change.

Olsen proposed that an asteroid or comet impact 200 million years ago wiped out many early reptile groups. This event may have cleared habitat for dinosaurs to take over, suggested Olsen.

Ancient bird tracks? Fossils of animal footprints approximately 213 million years old were described in June 2002 by paleontologists from the Universidad Nacional de La Pampa and the Museo Paleontologico, both in Argentina. The scientists said the impressions may have been left by birds. The prints are about 60 million years older than the oldest well-accepted fossil bird, *Archaeopteryx*, which lived 150 million years ago.

The scientists discovered more than 50 footprints in red siltstone in northwestern Argentina. The researchers dated the siltstone formation to the late Triassic Period. The prints average 1.1 inches (2.7 centimeters) long by 1.4 inches (3.5 centimeters) wide. The tracks resemble those made by birds in several ways, according to the scientists. For example, the prints are wider than they are long, with three long digits in front and one short digit in back.

The scientists said the tracks may represent the earliest known evidence of birds. However, they acknowledged that the impressions could have also been left by birdlike dinosaurs.

Mammal evolution. In April 2002, a team of paleontologists from China and the United States described a previously unknown fossil mammal from deposits in northeastern China. The scientists said the creature, which they named *Eomaia* ("dawn mother") *scansoria,* lived about 125 million years ago. They said it appeared to be the earliest known example of a *placental* mammal, an animal that is nourished inside its mother's womb before birth. Most mammals today are placental mammals.

The team, led by paleontologist Qiang Ji of the Chinese Academy of Geological Sciences, said the fossil is of a complete skeleton about 6.3 inches (16 centimeters) long. The fossil includes impressions of thick fur. Long fingers and toes in the skeleton indicated to the paleontologists that the animal lived in trees. Many other features of the fossil's skeleton and teeth are similar to those known from various placental mammals.

The researchers said the specimen extended the fossil record of placental mammals back 10 million to 20 million years. The discovery suggested to the team that the common ancestor of placental mammals and *marsupial* (pouched) mammals was a tree-dwelling animal that lived sometime before 125 million years ago.

Colorado rain forest. The arid plains of eastern Colorado were part of a lush rain forest 64 million years ago, according to a June 2002 report by paleobotanists Kirk Johnson and Beth Ellis of the Denver Museum of Nature and Science. The researchers found fossil leaves from almost 100 kinds of flowering plants, *coniferous* (cone-bearing) plants, and ferns southeast of Denver. The presence of pointed "drip tips" and other features on the leaves suggested that the plants were adapted to a humid rain forest environment—similar to the current ecosystem along the edges of the Amazon Basin in South America.

The leaves represented the earliest evidence of the reappearance of rain forests following the Cretaceous-Tertiary extinctions 65 million years ago, when dinosaurs and most rain forest plants were killed off. In most parts of the world, rain forest ecosystems were so severely affected by the event that similar ecosystems did not begin to redevelop until 55 million years ago. Johnson and Ellis concluded that the Colorado rain forest developed in an area with unusually high rainfall at the foothills of the newly formed Rocky Mountains. The unique local conditions in this area, they explained,probably allowed rain forests to redevelop earlier than in other areas.　　　　　□ Carlton E. Brett

Panama. The Panama Canal Authority, the *autonomous* (independent) agency that operates the Panama Canal, increased tolls for shippers by 8 percent on Oct. 1, 2002. The authority announced that it would impose a second increase of 4.5 percent in July 2003. The toll hikes were aimed at making the canal sufficiently profitable to launch a modernization program, which was to include the construction of a third set of locks to accommodate jumbo container cargo ships.

The failure of Panama's National Assembly to pass proposed tax, fiscal, and social security reforms in a timely manner forced the government to increase deficit spending in 2002.

China and Taiwan, political rivals that both manage port facilities on the Panama Canal, competed for economic and diplomatic influence in Panama in 2002. In May, Hutchison Whampoa, Ltd., a Hong Kong-based Chinese corporation, announced that it would invest $200 million to improve one of its ports on the canal. Taiwan invested a total of about $450 million in Panama between 1997 and 2002.　　□ Nathan A. Haverstock

See also **China; Latin America; Taiwan.**

Papua New Guinea. See **Asia; Pacific Islands.**

Paraguay. See **Latin America.**

Pennsylvania. See **Philadelphia; State government.**

■ People in the news

in 2002 included those listed below, who were all from the United States unless otherwise indicated.

Anaya, Rudolfo Alfonso (1937-),
noted novelist and author of children's literature, received the Medal of Arts from U.S. President George W. Bush in an awards ceremony in Washington, D.C., on April 22, 2002. The medal honors individuals who have made outstanding contributions to the arts in the United States. Anaya, who has been called "the dean of Chicano literature," received the medal for his "contributions to American literature that brought recognition to the traditions of the Chicano people."

Rudolfo Alfonso Anaya was born on Oct. 30, 1937, in Pastura, New Mexico. He attended the University of New Mexico at Albuquerque, where he earned a Bachelor of Arts degree in 1963 and Master of Arts degrees in English (1968) and guidance and counseling (1972). Anaya taught in the public school system in Albuquerque, New Mexico, in the 1960's. In 1974, he joined the English faculty at the University of New Mexico.

Critics widely praised Anaya's first novel, *Bless Me, Ultima* (1972), a coming-of-age story based on Mexican American culture and folklore. The book has become a standard text in high schools and colleges throughout the United States. Anaya also received critical acclaim for short stories, poetry, and four cultural mysteries titled "The Albuquerque Quartet." His most popular children's stories include *Farolitos of Christmas* (1995), a Mexican American Christmas story; and *Maya's Children: The Story of La Llorone* (1997), which is based on a popular Latin American folk legend.

See also **Literature, American.**

Berry, Halle (1968-),
received the Academy Award for best actress on March 24, 2002, for her performance in the 2001 film *Monster's Ball*. She was the first African American woman to win an Academy Award for a lead acting role.

Halle Berry was born on Aug. 14, 1968, in Cleveland, Ohio, and grew up in Bedford, Ohio. In 1984, she won the Miss Teen All-America Pageant title, representing Ohio. Two years later she competed in the Miss USA and Miss World contests, placing in runner-up positions. Berry then pursued a modeling career in New York City and Chicago.

In 1989, Halle Berry landed a role in a short-lived ABC television comedy series, "Living Dolls." Her debut in a serious dramatic film role came in 1991, when director Spike Lee cast her in *Jungle Fever*. Other major film roles followed, notably a romantic lead in the political satire *Bulworth* (1998) and the title role in the HBO biography, "Introducing Dorothy Dandridge" in 1999. Berry won an Emmy award in 2000 for her portrayal of Dandridge in the film.

See also **Motion pictures.**

Bloomberg, Michael Rubens

(1942-), became mayor of New York City on Jan. 1, 2002. Bloomberg, a former Democrat who had never before held public office, ran as a Republican in the city's November 2001 mayoral election. Late in the campaign, Bloomberg won the endorsement of Mayor Rudolph Giuliani, who had received high approval ratings in the wake of the terrorist attacks on New York City on Sept. 11, 2001. According to political analysts, the Giuliani endorsement—plus ample campaign funding—helped Bloomberg achieve a narrow election victory over the Democrat candidate, Mark Green. Experts estimated that Bloomberg spent more than $60 million of his own money on the campaign.

Michael R. Bloomberg was born in Boston on Feb. 14, 1942. He earned an engineering degree in 1964 at Johns Hopkins University in Baltimore and a Master of Business Administration degree in 1966 from Harvard University in Cambridge, Massachusetts. After graduation, Bloomberg took a position with Salomon Brothers, an investment company in New York City. He left the firm in 1981.

In the 1980's and 1990's, Bloomberg built a financial services and communications empire. In 1982, he launched Bloomberg LP, a computerized financial information system staffed by hundreds of researchers. The Bloomberg terminal and financial service attracted thousands of subscribers. Bloomberg later expanded into media ventures including a news wire service, publishing, radio, and television.

See also **New York City.**

Bono, *BAH-noh,* (1960-), lead performer in the Irish rock group U2 and humanitarian, accompanied United States Secretary of the Treasury Paul O'Neill on a tour of several African nations in late May 2002. Bono made the tour to focus international attention on the plight of nations in sub-Saharan Africa. Faltering economies and escalating rates of HIV infection (the virus that causes AIDS) have devastated a number of countries in the region. Bono and Secretary O'Neill called for more aid to the region and investment in Africa.

Bono was born Paul Hewson in Dublin, Ireland, on May 10, 1960. In 1976, he cofounded Feedback, a band that eventually became U2, which *Rolling Stone* magazine dubbed "the band of the '80s." The group scored Grammy wins in major categories in 2001 and 2002.

Bono participated in the 1985 Live Aid concert for famine relief in Africa and the 1986 Conspiracy of Hope tour to raise money for Amnesty International, an independent, London-based human-rights organization. In 2000, he lobbied then-President Bill Clinton and members of the U.S. Congress on behalf of the Jubilee 2000 Campaign, an international initiative to secure debt relief for developing countries. Political experts credited Bono's efforts, when Congress in October 2000 passed a nearly $500,000 debt relief bill.

See also **Africa.**

Chihuly, Dale Patrick (1941-), master glass sculptor, became known to a large audience in 2002 through a highly successful exhibition in Chicago, "Chihuly in the Park: A Garden of Glass." The exhibition, which featured 30 original Chihuly glass sculptures nestled among plants in the city's Garfield Park Conservatory,

Dale Patrick Chihuly, sculptor

drew 500,000 visitors between May and November.

Dale Chihuly was born on Sept. 20, 1941, in Tacoma, Washington. In 1965, he earned a Bachelor of Arts degree at the University of Washington–Seattle. He earned a Master of Science degree in sculpture at the University of Wisconsin–Madison in 1967 and a Master of Fine Arts degree in ceramics from the Rhode Island School of Design in Providence in 1968. Also in 1968, Chihuly won a Fulbright fellowship enabling him to study with master glassblowers in Murano, Italy, a traditional center of European glassmaking art.

Chihuly cofounded in 1971 the Pilchuck Glass School near Seattle, which has become a world center of glassmaking. Chihuly lost his left eye in a 1976 car accident, robbing him of the depth perception required to blow glass. He subsequently developed a team of glassblowers at the Pilchuck School to execute designs under his guidance. Some observers have likened Chihuly's glassmaking technique to that of a maestro conducting an orchestra. Art historians have called Chihuly the most significant glass artist since Louis Comfort Tiffany (1848–1933).

See also **Chicago; Gardening.**

da Silva, Luiz Inacio Lula (1945-),

candidate of Brazil's Workers Party, won election as president of Brazil by a landslide in a runoff election with Social Democratic candidate Jose Serra on Oct. 27, 2002. Da Silva—known to Brazilians as "Lula"—received 61 percent of the vote.

Political experts attributed the leftist politician's election triumph to widespread dissatisfaction among Brazilians over the nation's troubled economy. The value of the *real*, Brazil's currency, fell 40 percent against the U.S. dollar in 2002. Unemployment approached 10 percent, and economists estimated that as many as 30 percent of Brazil's 175 million people were living in poverty.

Luiz Inacio Lula da Silva was born on Oct. 27, 1945, to a peasant family in Pernambuco state in northeastern Brazil. The family eventually moved to Sao Paulo to find work. Da Silva dropped out of school after fifth grade to work in a factory. He later attended technical school, where he received training to become a lathe operator.

In the 1970's, da Silva rose to top leadership positions in ABC/CUT, the Brazilian metalworkers' union. As the union's president, he led a series of successful and highly publicized strikes in the late 1970's. Brazil was then under military rule, and in 1980, da Silva was arrested and convicted of violating the government's national security law. The verdict was overturned on appeal, however. In 1981, da Silva and other labor leaders began organizing the Workers Party, which first competed in elections in 1982. Da Silva ran as the party's

candidate for president in 1989, 1994, and 1998, but he was defeated in each of those elections.

See also **Brazil; Latin America.**

Feingold, Russell Dana (1953-),

United States Senator (D., Wisconsin), cosponsored with Senator John McCain (R., Arizona) campaign finance reform legislation passed by Congress in March 2002. The bill banned so-called "soft money" donations to election campaigns. Previous campaign finance laws restricted the

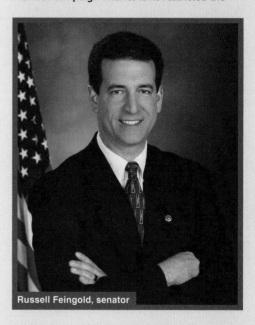

Russell Feingold, senator

amount of money donors could contribute to a single candidate but did not limit soft money donations—large contributions made to political parties by corporations, labor unions, and individuals. Political experts characterized the McCain-Feingold bill as the most sweeping reform in federal campaign financing since 1974, when Congress passed a series of campaign finance reform laws in response to the Watergate scandal.

Russell Dana Feingold was born in Janesville, Wisconsin, on March 2, 1953. He earned a bachelor's degree from the University of Wisconsin–Madison in 1975 and subsequently studied as a Rhodes Scholar at Oxford University in the United Kingdom. After earning a law degree from Harvard Law School in Cambridge, Massachusetts, Feingold returned to Wisconsin and entered private law practice. He served in the Wisconsin state Senate from 1983 to 1993. In 1992, he was elected to the U.S. Senate, and in 1998, he was reelected in a campaign in which he set and publicized his own spending limits. Feingold has served on the Senate Foreign Relations Committee, the Senate Budget Committee, and the Senate Judiciary Committee.

See also **Congress of the United States.**

Gerberding, Julie Louise (1955-),

was appointed director of the Centers for Disease Control and Prevention (CDC) by U.S. President George W. Bush in July 2002. The CDC, a federal agency based in Atlanta, Georgia, works to protect public health by administering national programs for the prevention and control of disease and disability.

Gerberding came to the attention of CDC officials and members of Congress during the anthrax attacks on various media personalities and politicians in October 2001. She was cited for her effectiveness as a CDC spokesperson and liaison with government officials.

Julie Louise Gerberding was born in Estelline, South Dakota, in 1955. Gerberding earned a Bachelor of Arts degree in chemistry and biology and a medical degree at Case Western Reserve University in Cleveland, Ohio. She served as an intern and resident at the University of California at San Francisco (UCSF).

Julie Gerberding, director of the Centers for Disease Control and Prevention

In San Francisco in the early 1980's, Gerberding became involved in the early medical response to the AIDS epidemic and helped establish the first specialized AIDS ward at San Francisco General Hospital. She also developed widely used methods to treat health care workers accidentally exposed to HIV, the virus that causes AIDS. In 1990, Gerberding received a master's degree in public health from UCSF. Gerberding joined the CDC in 1998.

See also **Public health and safety.**

Gregory, Wilton D. (1947-), bishop of

the Belleville, Illinois, Roman Catholic diocese, led the Conference of Catholic Bishops in its response to the sex abuse scandal that plagued the Roman Catholic Church in the United States in 2002. The scandal centered around a series of revelations about Catholic priests accused of sexually abusing children and young adults. The scandal widened

after the media revealed that some church leaders had concealed allegations of abuse from the public. Church leaders later confirmed that officials of some dioceses had spent millions of dollars on secret financial settlements to alleged victims of sexual abuse.

In May, Bishop Gregory was one of 10 U.S. church leaders invited to Rome by Pope John Paul II to discuss the growing scandal. After presiding over the U.S. bishops' June convention in Dallas, Gregory appointed a 13-member panel, headed by Oklahoma Governor Frank Keating, to oversee implementation of new church policy on priests and the sexual abuse of parishioners.

Wilton D. Gregory was born in Chicago on Dec. 7, 1947. He converted to Catholicism at age 11. Gregory attended St. Mary of the Lake Seminary in Mundelein, Illinois, and earned a doctorate in church liturgy from the Pontifical Liturgical Institute in Rome.

Gregory served as *auxiliary* (assistant) bishop in the archdiocese of Chicago and was appointed bishop of the Belleville, Illinois, diocese in 1994. In November 2001, Bishop Gregory was elected president of the U.S. Conference of Catholic Bishops, becoming the first African American to lead the body.

See also **Roman Catholic Church.**

Howard, Ron (1954-), received the

Academy Award for best director for *A Beautiful Mind* on March 24, 2002. The Academy also

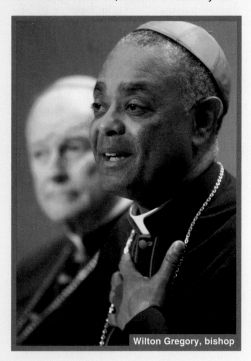

Wilton Gregory, bishop

Ron Howard, director

honored *A Beautiful Mind* with the award for best picture.

Ron Howard initially became known as a child actor in the role of Opie Taylor on the television series "The Andy Griffith Show" (1960–1968). Howard learned to write at the age of six in order to sign autographs. During the show's long run, he absorbed filmmaking fundamentals from crew members. As a child actor, Howard also performed in feature films, including *The Music Man* (1962) and *The Courtship of Eddie's Father* (1963).

Howard graduated into teen-age roles in the 1973 hit movie *American Graffiti*, which evoked teen culture of the early 1960's. Howard's portrayal of clean-cut high school graduate Steve Bolander led to the television role of Richie Cunningham on the series "Happy Days." Howard appeared in the series from 1974 to 1980.

In 1977, Howard made his debut as director of a feature film with *Grand Theft Auto*. He subsequently directed a number of critically acclaimed and financially successful films, including *Splash* (1984), *Cocoon* (1985), and *Apollo 13* (1995), which received nine Academy Award nominations.

Ron Howard was born in Duncan, Oklahoma, on March 1, 1954, into an acting family. The family eventually resettled in southern California, to be near the center of the television and film in-

dustry. Howard attended the University of Southern California at Los Angeles but did not complete a degree.

See also **Motion pictures.**

Karzai, Hamid (1957-), was elected president of Afghanistan's transitional government in June 2002, after serving as interim leader of a ruling council since December 2001. Karzai's government came to power in Afghanistan in the wake of a United States-led military campaign against the Taliban, an Islamic fundamentalist movement that had ruled the country since 1996. The Taliban sheltered Osama bin Laden and his al-Qa'ida terrorist network in defiance of U.S. demands that the regime surrender bin Laden to U.S. authorities following the terrorist attacks on the United States on Sept. 11, 2001.

In December 2001, regional Afghan leaders met in Bonn, Germany, to work out an agreement for an interim government. They named Karzai as leader and called for the convening of a *loya jirga,* or grand council of tribal and regional Afghan leaders. The *loya jirga* met in June 2002 and elected Karzai president of a transitional government to rule until at least 2004.

Hamid Karzai was on born Dec. 24, 1957, into a powerful Pashtun family in Kandahar, Afghanistan. Pashtuns are the largest ethnic group in Afghanistan. Karzai attended high school in Kabul, the capital, and then attended the University of Simla in India.

Karzai left Afghanistan for Pakistan in 1979, after the Soviet invasion of Afghanistan. He returned in 1992 to serve in a new post-Soviet government. In the early 1990's, he briefly supported the Taliban but ultimately broke with the group and went back into exile. Karzai returned to Afghanistan after the United States launched its war on terrorism and sent troops into Afghanistan in October 2001.

See also **Afghanistan.**

McCain, John Sidney, III (1936-), United States Senator (R., Arizona), cosponsored with Wisconsin Senator Russell Feingold (D., Wisconsin) campaign finance reform legislation that the U.S. Congress approved in March 2002. The bill banned "soft money" donations in federal election campaigns—that is, large contributions made to political parties by corporations, labor unions, and individuals. It attempted to close loopholes in previous campaign finance laws, which had placed limits on individual contributions while failing to stop soft money donations. Political experts characterized the McCain-Feingold bill as the most sweeping reform in the method of financing federal elections since 1974, when Congress enacted campaign finance reform

John McCain, senator

legislation in response to the Watergate scandal.

John Sidney McCain III was born on Aug., 29, 1936, in the Panama Canal Zone, where his father, a career officer, was serving in the U.S. Navy. In 1958, McCain received a bachelor's degree from the United States Naval Academy in Annapolis, Maryland, and entered the Navy.

John McCain served as a fighter pilot during the Vietnam War (1957–1975). His jet was shot down during a combat mission over North Vietnam in 1967. The North Vietnamese captured and held McCain as a prisoner of war in Hanoi, the North Vietnamese capital, until March 1973. Upon his release, McCain received the Silver Star, the Bronze Star, and the Distinguished Flying Cross for heroism and bravery.

McCain retired from the Navy in 1981 in preparation for entering politics in Arizona. He was elected to the U.S. House of Representatives in 1982. McCain was elected to the U.S. Senate in 1986 and was reelected in 1992 and 1998.

Senator McCain campaigned for the Republican nomination for president of the United States in 2000. Although he won several primaries, he withdrew from the race after George W. Bush, then the governor of Texas, amassed an overwhelming lead in the contest for convention delegates.

See also **Congress of the United States.**

Osbourne, Ozzy (John Michael) (1948-), rock music star and lead singer with the popular 1970's band Black Sabbath, gained new fame in 2002 as the real-life head of the Osbourne family on the MTV "reality" television series, "The Osbournes." The show won an Emmy its first season for outstanding nonfiction reality program. Osbourne's wife, Sharon, accepted the award on September 14.

"The Osbournes" featured the unscripted daily life of the family, which included father Ozzy, mom Sharon, and two teen-agers, Kelly and Jack. MTV launched a second season of the show in autumn 2002.

Ozzy Osbourne was born John Michael Osbourne in Birmingham, England, on Dec. 3, 1948. As a youth, Osbourne was convicted of a burglary charge and spent several months in prison. In 1969, he joined the band that became Black Sabbath. By the time Osbourne left Black Sabbath in 1978 to launch a career as a solo performer, he had gained a reputation for outrageous public behavior and controversy. In the mid-1980's, he and his record company were sued by a family claiming that their son was persuaded to commit suicide by the lyrics of the Ozzy Osbourne song "Suicide Solution." A California court eventually dismissed the case.

See also **Television.**

Ozzy Osbourne, musician

Ronaldo (1976-) led Brazil's national soccer team to a 2–0 victory over Germany in the final game of the World Cup championship on June 30, 2002, in Yokohama, Japan. Scoring both of Brazil's goals, the celebrity athlete racked up a World Cup total of 12 goals, tying the record of legendary Brazilian soccer star Pele. The victory restored Brazil to world soccer championship status after its 1998 upset loss to France, when lead player Ronaldo had been seriously hampered by knee problems.

Ronaldo Luiz Nazario da Lima was born in a suburb of Rio de Janeiro on Sept. 22, 1976. He played street ball as a child and quit school after seventh grade to play for a Rio de Janeiro soccer club. A team in Belo Horizonte, Brazil, recruited Ronaldo to play professionally in 1992. Ronaldo joined Brazil's 1994 World Cup championship team, though the 17-year-old was sidelined in the finals.

In the mid-1990's, Ronaldo signed with a succession of European soccer teams. The youthful athlete's prowess and charisma prompted "Ronaldomania" among European fans, who dubbed him "the Phenomenon." In 1997, the Nike Corporation of Beaverton, Oregon, signed the athlete to a 10-year contract to promote Nike products.

See also **Soccer; Sports.**

Stewart, Martha

(1941-), home-and-lifestyle expert and media personality, came under investigation in mid-2002 by the United States Department of Justice. The investigation concerned Stewart's sale in late 2001 of more than 3,000 shares of stock in the biotechnology company ImClone Systems. The day after the sale, officials at New York City-based ImClone Incorporated announced that the company's cancer drug Erbitux

Martha Stewart, lifestyle expert

had failed to win approval by the Food and Drug Administration. Without such approval, Erbitux could not be marketed in the United States. The announcement sent the value of ImClone's stock plummeting.

Investigators suspected Stewart of having acted on inside information from ImClone's former chief executive, Sam Waksal. Such action, known as insider trading, violates federal laws. Martha Stewart contended that the trade was "entirely lawful" and was the result of a standing order to sell her shares at a prearranged price. Under increasing media and government pressure, however, Stewart resigned her seat on the board of the New York Stock Exchange on Oct. 3, 2002.

Stewart was born Martha Kostyra in Nutley, New Jersey, on Aug. 3, 1941. She attended Barnard College in New York City, doing part-time modeling to pay tuition. In 1961, she married law student Andrew Stewart. The couple had one daughter, Alexis, in 1965 and divorced in 1990.

Martha Stewart worked as a securities trader on Wall Street in New York City until 1973. In 1976, she started a small catering business that became a multimillion-dollar enterprise and made Stewart a celebrity. In 1999, she launched Martha Stewart Living Omnimedia, a corporate umbrella for such ventures as books, radio shows, *Martha Stewart Living* magazine, and a television series of the same name. According to financial analysts, sale of stock in the company made Martha Stewart a billionaire.

See also **Economics; Stocks and Bonds.**

Uribe Velez, Alvaro

(1952-), was sworn in as president of Colombia amid rebel bombardment of the capital, Bogota, on Aug. 7, 2002. The powerful rebel group Revolutionary Armed Forces of Colombia (FARC) launched a nationwide campaign of violence to coincide with Uribe's inauguration. Four months earlier, FARC agents attempted to assassinate Uribe, then a presidential candidate, in a motorcade attack that left 3 people dead and 13 others injured. Uribe's own father was murdered by FARC agents in a 1983 kidnapping attempt.

Uribe won a landslide vote in the Colombian presidential election on May 26, 2002. He had campaigned on the slogan "Firm Hand, Big Heart," promising to beef up Colombia's military forces in their ongoing civil war with left-wing rebel groups, such as FARC, and right-wing paramilitary groups. Political experts regarded the "hard-line" approach advocated by Uribe as a significant break with the policy of his predecessor, Andres Pastrana, who tried to negotiate with the rebels.

Alvaro Uribe Velez was born on July 4, 1952, in Medellin, Colombia. He earned a bachelor's degree and a law degree in Colombia and later studied at Oxford University in Oxford, England, and at Harvard University in Cambridge, Massachusetts. Uribe served as mayor of Medellín in the early 1980's and subsequently was elected to the Colombian senate. Between 1995 and 1997, he served as governor of Antioquia province in northwestern Colombia, earning a reputation for fiscal conservatism and toughness on crime.

See also **Colombia.**

Alvaro Uribe Velez, president of Colombia

Washington, Denzel (1954-), won the

Academy Award for best actor on March 24, 2002, for his portrayal of a corrupt policeman in the 2001 film *Training Day.* Washington was only the second African American actor to receive the best-actor award. The first, Sidney Poitier, won for *Lilies of the Field* in 1963.

Denzel Washington was born on Dec. 28, 1954, in Mount Vernon, New York. He attended Fordham University in New York City, where he began acting. After graduating in 1977, Washington made his television debut in "Wilma," a made-for-television movie about African American Olympic athlete Wilma Rudolph.

In 1978, Washington studied acting at the American Conservatory Theatre in San Francisco. He returned to New York City in 1979 to pursue roles in the theater. In 1981, he won an Obie Award for his performance in *A Soldier's Play.* The actor also made his feature film debut in 1981, in *Carbon Copy.*

In 1982, Washington landed a major television role in the dramatic series "St. Elsewhere." He appeared in the series until 1988. During the same period, the actor won critical recognition for his

performances in the films *Cry Freedom* (1987) and *Glory* (1988). He was nominated for an Academy Award for best supporting actor for both roles. He won for *Glory* in 1989.

In the 1990's and 2000's, Denzel Washington continued to perform in major films, including *Mississippi Masala* (1991) and *Philadelphia* (1993). He won Academy Award nominations for leading acting roles in *Malcolm X* (1992) and *The Hurricane* (1999).

See also **Motion pictures.**

Williams, Hank, III, (1972-), released

his second solo country album, *Lovesick, Broke & Driftin',* in 2002. Recorded for Nashville-based Curb Records in late January, the album garnered rave reviews, with some critics noting a raw, steel-guitar-dominated, honky-tonk sound that recalled 1950's classic country music.

Williams is the grandson of country music pioneer Hank Williams, who died in 1953, and the son of country music performer Hank Williams, Jr. Like the two older Williamses, Hank Williams III earned the reputation of a rebel fighting the country music establishment to perform his own, deeply personal style of music. Reviewers compared the mournful, twangy voice of the younger Williams with that of his legendary grandfather.

Williams was born Shelton Hank Williams on Dec. 12, 1972, in Nashville. His parents divorced in 1977, and he was raised by his mother in Atlanta, Georgia. When he was 10 years old, he began playing drums on stage with his father's band. While in his teens, Williams played in a variety of punk rock bands. He switched to country

Hank Williams III, singer

music in the early 1990's. Hank Williams III released his first solo album, *Risin' Outlaw,* in 1999.

See also **Popular music.**

Williams, Rowan Douglas (1950-),

assumed office as the 104th archbishop of Canterbury in December 2002. The archbishop is the leader of the Church of England and Anglican churches worldwide. A native of Wales, Williams is the first archbishop of Canterbury to be appointed from outside of England since the 1500's.

The selection of Williams, confirmed by Queen Elizabeth II and made by Prime Minister Tony Blair from a list compiled by clergy and laity, stirred controversy among traditionalists. The new archbishop refused to deny priestly ordination to homosexuals and supported the ordination of women bishops as well as a more liberal stance on divorce. He angered some politicians by criticizing the United States-led war on terrorism, condemning in advance any attack on Iraq not sanctioned by the United Nations.

Rowan Douglas Williams was born on June 14, 1950, in Swansea, Wales. He studied at Cambridge and Oxford and later taught at both universities. Ordained in 1978, Williams became bishop of Monmouth in 1992 and archbishop of Wales in 2000. He has written a number of books, including *Writings in the Dust,* his reflections on the terrorist attacks on New York City on Sept. 11, 2001. Williams witnessed the attacks firsthand during a visit to the city.

See also **Protestantism; United Kingdom.**

■ Robert N. Knight

Peru. A powerful bomb planted in a car exploded across the street from the United States embassy in Lima, Peru's capital, on March 20, 2002. The blast killed 9 Peruvians and wounded 30 other people. Authorities blamed the attack on Shining Path, a leftist terrorist organization that had been trying to overthrow Peru's government since the early 1980's. The attack occurred three days before U.S. President George W. Bush was due to arrive in Peru for meetings with the heads of several Andean nations.

Bush's visit. President Bush, who arrived on March 23, 2002, was the first sitting U.S. president to visit Peru. He met in Lima with the presidents of Bolivia, Colombia, and Ecuador, as well as Peru, and pledged U.S. assistance to help their nations fight violence, terrorism, and drug trafficking. He also announced that the Peace Corps, a U.S. government program in which volunteers help people overseas improve their living conditions, would return to Peru after an absence of nearly 30 years.

Arequipa protests. In June, demonstrators staged sustained and angry protests in Arequipa, Peru's second largest city, against the government's proposed privatization of two state-owned electric companies, Egasa and Egesur. The protesters included city officials, trade unions, neighborhood organizations, and students united in their opposition to the sale of the companies to a private firm based in Belgium.

Peruvian President Alejandro Toledo responded to the Arequipa protests by declaring a state of emergency and sending 1,700 troops and police into the city to restore order. He also suspended indefinitely the proposed sale of the electric companies and revamped his Cabinet to make it more responsive to popular demands.

Finance minister resigns. Pedro Pablo Kuczynski, Peru's finance minister and one of the main architect's of Peru's free-market reforms, resigned in July. His loss was a blow to the government because he had played a key role in negotiations with international financial institutions, which had helped Peru revive its economy.

Toledo admits paternity. In a televised address in October, President Toledo acknowledged that he was the father of a 14-year-old girl whose mother had filed a paternity suit against him in 1992. Toledo had previously denied the charge, claiming it was politically motivated. Following his admission, polls indicated a modest boost in his approval ratings, which had lingered below 20 percent for several months.

Fujimori and Montesinos. Peruvian officials in 2002 repeatedly asked the government of Japan to *extradite* (turn over) former Peruvian President Alberto K. Fujimori. Japan, however, refused to honor these requests. Peruvian authorities wanted Fujimori, who had fled to Japan in 2000, to stand trial on charges of murder, bribery, and corruption during his presidency (1990-2000).

In July 2002, a Peruvian court sentenced Vladimiro L. Montesinos, who headed the National Intelligence Service in the Fujimori government, to nine years and four months in prison on the first of 70 pending criminal charges. Montesinos had been caught on videotape in 2000 bribing political, business, and military leaders to support Fujimori's administration.

Berenson sentence upheld. Peru's Supreme Court in February 2002 upheld the 20-year sentence of Lori Berenson, a New York City woman who was jailed in 1996 for conspiring with Peruvian rebels. Berenson had been convicted of working with a leftist antigovernment group in a foiled plot to seize control of Peru's Congress in 1995.

Death of Belaunde Terry. In early June 2002, Peruvians mourned the death of Fernando Belaunde Terry, 89, who had served as president from 1963 to 1968 and again from 1980 to 1985. Belaunde had appealed to Peruvians to "reconquer Peru" by fully exploiting its vast economic potential.   ☐ Nathan A. Haverstock

See also **Latin America; Terrorism.**

Petroleum and gas. See Energy supply.

Philadelphia. Public schools in Philadelphia opened on Sept. 5, 2002, under new leadership that placed one out of six schools under private managers. The move toward private management was one aspect of a state-mandated campaign to improve overall student performance in the Philadelphia school system.

The Pennsylvania state government had taken over the debt-ridden and poorly performing Philadelphia school system at the end of 2001, after Pennsylvania Governor Mark Schweiker and Philadelphia Mayor John F. Street agreed that a new school reform commission would run the school district. The five-member commission, consisting of three appointees of the governor and two of the mayor, was sworn in on Jan. 18, 2002.

In early 2002, the commission cut 325 administrative jobs and designated 45 low-performing schools to be operated under private management. The commission hired Edison Schools, Inc., of New York City, a for-profit operator of schools, to run 20 schools. Six other firms contracted to run the remainder of the troubled schools.

New school chief. The school commission named Paul G. Vallas, former head of schools in Chicago, as chief executive officer of the Philadelphia public school system in July. In August, Vallas announced a $1-billion capital improvement program that called for construction of nine new high schools. He announced a number of other measures—mandatory summer school and after-school programs for failing students; a strict discipline code; and plans for additional magnet schools, alternative schools that stress a particular field of study and draw students from throughout the school district.

Crackdown on illegal drivers. On July 1, Philadelphia started a program called "Live Stop" to crack down on illegal automobile drivers. The program allowed police officers to impound cars of drivers stopped for traffic violations whenever a driver lacked a valid driver's license or proper vehicle registration with the Pennsylvania Department of Motor Vehicles. By mid-September, police had impounded 9,000 vehicles under the program.

The city's Parking Authority spent millions of dollars to tow and store the vehicles, which were sold at auction if drivers failed to pay fines or obtain current licenses and registrations within 70 days. Officials of the Philadelphia Traffic Court projected that the court would collect $4 million in fines and costs in 2002 from drivers of impounded cars and said these revenues would help offset the city's towing costs.

Philadelphia continued in 2002 its campaign, begun in 2000, to remove abandoned cars from city streets. By September 2002, towing companies had disposed of more than 150,000 vehicles.

Convention center disagreement. Mayor Street failed to obtain approval of a new contract from the six unions working in the Pennsylvania Convention Center, the city's venue for large shows and conventions. Five of the unions approved the pact in August 2002, but the carpenter's union refused to sign.

Convention center exhibitors objected to work rules that created expenses beyond those encountered at many other U.S. convention centers. As bookings slowed, convention center management had lobbied for a new union contract that would reduce exhibitors' costs.

Under the new contract proposal, exhibitors would have been able to set up and dismantle more of their own displays, without using union labor. However, the contract reduced opportunities for union carpenters to earn overtime pay. Ed Coryell, Sr., business manager of the carpenters' union, said he refused to sign the contract because he was protecting union jobs.

The controversy stalled plans for a $464-million expansion of the convention center. The project could not proceed without state funding, and Pennsylvania legislators refused to allocate funds until Philadelphia officials settled with the unions.   ☐ Howard S. Shapiro

See also **City; Education.**

Philippines. The government of the Philippines struggled to control Islamic separatist groups and terrorist organizations that killed or kidnapped several people in 2002. The United States helped the Philippines battle rebel factions by sending troops to the region to train Filipino forces in counterterrorism.

Islamic rebel groups had been fighting for independence in the Philippines since the 1970's. In 1996, the government signed a peace agreement with the largest group, the Moro National Liberation Front. The agreement created a region of self-rule for Muslims in the southern Philippines. Despite the agreement, fighting continued between the government and other Muslim rebels, including members of Abu Sayyaf, a group responsible for much of the rebel violence in 2002. The group, which raised money for its cause by kidnapping foreigners and Christians for ransom, was linked to al-Qa'ida, an international terrorist network of Muslim extremists.

Hostilities between the Philippine government and Abu Sayyaf escalated in 2001 after the rebels kidnapped and killed several people—including a U.S. citizen—in retaliation for the government's attempts to crack down on terrorist activities. Philippine President Gloria Macapagal-

Arroyo created the National Anticrime Commission in response to Abu Sayyaf and other terror groups. However, the commission had little success in tracking down rebels and terrorists, many of whom hid in mountainous jungle regions.

U.S. involvement. In January 2002, United States military advisers arrived in the Philippines to share intelligence and equipment and to train Philippine troops in counterinsurgency tactics. U.S. troops were not directly involved in fighting the rebels, however. Nearly 4,000 U.S. advisers participated in the six-month mission, which concluded at the end of July. About 100 advisers remained in the Philippines after the mission ended to coordinate the sharing of intelligence and a long-term security assistance and counterterrorism program.

Some individuals and groups were highly critical of the U.S. mission. They claimed a U.S. military presence compromised the autonomy of the Philippines, which gained independence from the United States in 1946. The last U.S. forces withdrew from military bases on the islands in the 1990's. Vice President Teofisto Guingona resigned as foreign minister in June 2002 to protest U.S. involvement. Arroyo defended the United States, saying that U.S. troops had helped break the cycle of terrorism and crime in the Philippines.

U.S. hostages. In April, the United States offered $5 million for information leading to the arrest or capture of Abu Sabaya, a top leader of

A Philippine Navy vessel carries the coffin of Ediborah Yap, a Filipino nurse who was killed in June when Philippine troops tried to rescue her and other hostages held by Abu Sayyaf, an Islamic separatist group. A missionary from the United States was also killed during the rescue attempt.

Abu Sayyaf, and four other rebel leaders who had kidnapped several Americans, including missionaries Martin and Gracia Burnham. On June 7, Philippine troops attacked an Abu Sayyaf unit that held the hostages captive in the jungles of Mindanao Province. The troops rescued all the hostages except for Martin Burnham and a Filipino nurse, Ediborah Yap, who were killed in the fighting. Two weeks later, Sabaya was killed in a clash with Philippine troops.

Other violence. Authorities held Abu Sayyaf responsible for other violent acts in 2002. In August, rebels kidnapped six Christians on the southern island of Jolo, killing two of the captives. In October, police said members of Abu Sayyaf detonated a bomb outside a karaoke bar frequented by U.S. and Philippine troops, killing a U.S. Green Beret and two Filipinos. In October, police arrested several members of Abu Sayyaf as suspects in a deadly series of department store bombings in the southern Philippine city of Zamboanga. The bombings killed seven people and injured 152 others.

Macapagal-Arroyo vowed in her state of the nation address to the Philippine Congress in July to wage a war against crime, corruption, and poverty. She said smugglers would be treated as economic saboteurs, criminal syndicates as threats to national security, and drug lords as enemies of the state. She stressed that a decrease in crime would help win back foreign investors, who were reluctant to open businesses in the Philippines because they were targets of kidnappers. In addition, she urged the Congress to pass an antiterrorism bill. Macapagal-Arroyo announced on December 30 that she would not run in the 2004 presidential election.

Joseph Estrada, the former president who was forced from office in 2001, remained in prison in 2002 on charges he accepted $76 million in bribes and kickbacks. In February, Estrada admitted in a television interview that he had signed bank documents with a false name but insisted that he was innocent of all other charges. Following the interview, he dismissed his attorney, an action that interrupted his trial, which began in 2001.

The Philippine economy expanded by about 4.5 percent in 2002. An increase in semiconductor and computer exports and demand for domestically produced vehicles propelled growth. Economic problems loomed, however. The agricultural industry braced itself for another period of Pacific Ocean warming, a phenomenon that usually causes drought in the Philippines. To prepare, the government approved a new irrigation system, which greatly added to the country's swelling budget deficit. ☐ Henry S. Bradsher

See also **Asia; Terrorism.**

Physics. A puzzle that had stumped physicists since the 1950's was finally solved in July 2002 by a large team of physicists from Canada, the United States, and the United Kingdom. Physicists did not know why they had been detecting fewer tiny subatomic particles called neutrinos being emitted by the sun than had been predicted by theory. Physicists working at the Sudbury Neutrino Observatory (SNO) near Sudbury, Canada, learned that the type of neutrinos being emitted in vast quantities by the sun are changing into different kinds of neutrinos before they reach detectors on Earth.

Neutrinos are subatomic particles that have no electrical charge and almost no mass. There are three types: electron-neutrinos, muon-neutrinos, and tau-neutrinos. They very rarely interact with matter because atoms that make up matter are nearly transparent to neutrinos. In the 1950's, physicists theorized that staggering numbers of electron-neutrinos are produced in the sun and released. However, devices built to detect neutrinos found fewer than half the electron-neutrinos being emitted by the sun than had been predicted by theory.

In 1999, physicists began taking measurements with the SNO, a huge neutrino detector located at the bottom of a nickel mine to avoid false detections. The SNO detector could differentiate between the different types of neutrinos it was detecting. Other detectors could not do this. When the SNO detected higher numbers of muon- and tau-neutrinos than had been expected, physicists determined that electron-neutrinos from the sun are, indeed, changing into other types of neutrinos before reaching Earth. The discovery confirmed physicists' understanding of how the sun produces energy.

Fraud. The field of physics was badly shaken in 2002 by two cases of scientific fraud in which scientists were accused of falsifying data. Scientific fraud is rare but extremely serious, because scientists can waste years trying to confirm discoveries that were never actually made.

In September, an independent panel of physicists reported their findings that Jan Henrik Schon, a physicist at Lucent Technologies Inc. of Murray Hill, New Jersey, had falsified data in several major research papers dating back to 1998. The physicists began their inquiry into Schon's research in May 2002.

Schon had published what had been thought by many physicists to be groundbreaking papers on advanced technologies. Before the evidence of fraud was found, Schon's work was considered so brilliant that many physicists believed that he might one day receive a Nobel Prize.

Physicists were particularly excited about Schon's purported results showing that it was possible to make *transistors* (switchlike devices) out of single molecules that worked in the same way as the silicon transistors in modern computers. Many scientists believed that Schon's work could lead to computer chips as small as a grain of sand with the computing power of hundreds of silicon-based desktop computers. However, investigators could find no proof that Schon had actually even performed the experiments that showed that molecular transistors were possible.

Physicists at Lawrence Berkeley National Laboratory in Berkeley, California, reported in July that they had found evidence that a physicist had falsified data in the alleged discovery in 1999 of element 118. Elements are chemicals in their simplest form. Some elements do not occur naturally, but must be made in laboratories. These elements, called "heavy elements" because of the large number of subatomic particles in their *nuclei* (the central parts of atoms) can provide information about how subatomic particles *decay* (break apart). Element 118 was reported to be the heaviest element ever made.

Physicists at Lawrence Berkeley had already withdrawn the discovery of element 118 in July 2001 because physicists at other labs could not reproduce the original result. This triggered the internal investigation that revealed that a Berkeley physicist had falsified results. □ Robert H. March

Poetry. Ruth Stone won the 2002 National Book Award for poetry for her collection *In the Next Galaxy*. Stone's poems often recollect her childhood in Virginia and depict landscape in the United States. Stone, who was 86 years old when she received the award, also offers meditations on age and a lifetime of experience. In the title poem, Stone writes, "Things will be different. / No one will lose their sight, / their hearing, their gallbladder. / It will be all Catskills with brand / new wrap-around verandas. / The idea of Hitler will not / have vibrated yet." Stone's trademark lyrical lines balance thoughts, emotions, and memories. Other nominees for the 2002 National Book Award for poetry include Harryette Mullen's *Sleeping with the Dictionary,* Sharon Olds's *The Unswept Room,* Alberto Rios's *The Smallest Muscle in the Human Bod*y, and Ellen Bryant Voigt's *Shadow of Heaven*.

Pulitzer Prize. Carl Dennis won the Pulitzer Prize for poetry in 2002 for his book *Practical Gods.* Dennis's free-verse poetry is full of musings about lost opportunity and woeful experience. However, the poet often finds hope and even wry humor in the midst of despair. For example, in "Department Store" he suggests that a peaceful father-and-son exchange envied by the childless speaker is actually "only a truce / In a lifelong saga of border warfare." *The Seven Ages* by

Louise Gluck and *The Beforelife* by Franz Wright were also nominated as Pulitzer Prize finalists.

National Poetry Slam. The 2002 National Poetry Slam was held in Minneapolis, Minnesota, in August. A poetry slam is a cross between a poetry reading and a sporting event. Individual competitors and four-person teams combine poetic form, rhyme, and rhythm with fast-paced, intense performances. Audiences loudly cheer or jeer slam competitors. Slam poetry often celebrates the working class and the common person and deals with themes of political injustice, unrequited love, and everyday life. The best slam poems mix wild feeling with well-tempered form.

Sekou the Misfit, of Los Angeles, was the individual winner of the 2002 National Poetry Slam. His lyrical examinations of his place in the world are expressed with heavy rhythms and rhymes: "I speak to the silence, I sing in the dark. / I represent the last working swing in the park." Second place went to Corbet Dean, a slam poet from Mesa, Arizona, known for his accounts of life as a policeman. In "Believe," Dean asks a man he has arrested: "When you're overcome by the fumes / of this dying town / convulsing in soot, / gasping on the ground, / for consolation, / locked down / after 10 pm, / confined / in your cold / quiet cage / of desperation / tell me, what do you believe in?" Two teams—Detroit-Hamtramck and New York City-Urbana—shared first place in the teams competition.

Frank Bidart, winner of the 2001 Wallace Stevens Award, published a much-anticipated collection of poems, *Music Like Dirt,* in March 2002. Critics praised Bidart's poetry for its dramatic use of space. His poems often incorporate quoted material with free-verse lines, many of which are indented or stand alone surrounded by blank space. The subject of *Music Like Dirt* is creativity and the desire to make things. In the poem "For the Twentieth Century," Bidart writes, "you and I and Mozart / must thank the Twentieth Century, for / it made you pattern, form / whose infinite / repeatability within matter / defies matter / — Malibran, Henry Irving. The young / Joachim. They are lost, a mountain of / newspaper clippings, become words / not their own words. The art of the performer."

Poetry Magazine. Ruth Lilly, an heir of the Eli Lilly pharmaceutical fortune, announced in November 2002 that she was donating $100 million to Chicago-based *Poetry Magazine*. The highly prestigious literary journal had operated, often with little money and staff, since 1912. Lilly had submitted several poems to the magazine in the 1970's, but they were rejected. The 2002 gift placed *Poetry Magazine* among the world's richest publications. □ Brian Bouldrey

See also **Pulitzer Prizes.**

Poland. The coalition government of Prime Minister Leszek Miller confronted severe economic stagnation in 2002. The Polish financial ministry projected that Poland's gross domestic product, the value of all goods and services produced in a country in a given year, would increase by just 1.2 percent, after growing at a similar rate in 2001. Unemployment hovered around 18 percent during the first nine months of 2002, according to Poland's National Statistics Office.

Self-Defense, the radical farmers' union headed by Andrzej Lepper, launched a series of protests in mid-2002, including storming the agriculture ministry building in Warsaw, the capital, in May, and blocking roads with tractors in August. Union members demanded that the government step up state-subsidized purchases of farm products. The demands pitted the union against the government's policy of privatization of the farm economy.

Officials of the European Union (EU), meeting at a summit in Copenhagen, Denmark, in December 2002, formally approved Poland's application for admission into the organization of Western European nations. Officials scheduled Poland's entry into full EU membership for 2004.

☐ Sharon L. Wolchik

See also **Europe.**

Pollution. See Environmental pollution.

Popular music. Sales of compact discs fell 7 percent in the first six months of 2002, compared with sales from the same period in 2001, the Recording Industry Association of America (RIAA) reported in August 2002. The RIAA is a Washington, D.C.-based organization that represents the recording industry's intellectual property rights. According to the RIAA, compact disc retail sales fell from 397 million units to 369 million units. Overall sales of all recorded music, including compact discs, cassettes, vinyl albums, and music videos, fell from 442 million units in the first six months of 2001 to 398 million during the same period in 2002, a 10-percent decline. Industry experts attributed the declines to a weak economy, the illegal downloading of shared music files from the Internet, and CD *burning* (copying).

Top-selling albums. *The Eminem Show,* the third album released by white rap artist Eminem, became 2002's best-selling album, according to SoundScan, a Hartsdale, New York, company that serves as a central clearinghouse for music industry data. *The Eminem Show* sold 1.3 million copies in its first week of release in May and featured the popular single "Without Me." Eminem, whose real name is Marshall Mathers III, also had chart-topping success in November with *8 Mile,* the soundtrack to his critically acclaimed feature film debut.

Grammy Award winners in 2002

Record of the Year, "Walk On," U2

Album of the Year, "O Brother, Where Art Thou?" soundtrack, Various Artists

Song of the Year, "Fallin'," Alicia Keys

New Artist, Alicia Keys

Pop Vocal Performance, Female, "I'm Like a Bird," Nelly Furtado

Pop Vocal Performance, Male, "Don't Let Me Be Lonely Tonight," James Taylor

Pop Performance by a Duo or Group, "Stuck in a Moment You Can't Get Out Of," U2

Traditional Pop Vocal Album, "Songs I Heard," Harry Connick, Jr.

Pop Instrumental Performance, "No Substitutions— Live in Osaka," Larry Carlton and Steve Lukather

Rock Vocal Performance, Female, "Get Right With God," Lucinda Williams

Rock Vocal Performance, Male, "Dig In," Lenny Kravitz

Rock Performance by a Duo or Group with Vocal, "Elevation," U2

Hard Rock Performance, "Crawling," Linkin Park

Metal Performance, "Schism," Tool

Rock Instrumental Performance, "Dirty Mind," Jeff Beck

Rock Song, "Drops of Jupiter," Charlie Colin, Rob Hotchkiss, Pat Monahan, Jimmy Stafford, and Scott Underwood

Alternative Music Album, "Parachutes," Coldplay

Rhythm-and-Blues Vocal Performance, Female, "Fallin'," Alicia Keys

Rhythm-and-Blues Vocal Performance, Male, "U Remind Me," Usher

Rhythm-and-Blues Performance by a Duo or Group with Vocal, "Survivor," Destiny's Child

Rhythm-and-Blues Song, "Fallin'," Alicia Keys

Rhythm-and-Blues Album, "Songs in A Minor," Alicia Keys

Rap Solo Performance, "Get Ur Freak On," Missy "Misdemeanor" Elliot

Rap Performance by a Duo or Group, "Ms. Jackson," Outkast

Rap Album, "Stankonia," Outkast

New Age Album, "A Day Without Rain," Enya

Contemporary Jazz Album, "M2," Marcus Miller

Jazz Vocal Album, "The Calling," Dianne Reeves

Jazz Instrumental, Solo, "Chan's Song," Michael Brecker

Jazz Instrumental Album, Individual or Group, "This Is What I Do," Sonny Rollins

Large Jazz Ensemble Album, "Homage To Count Basie," Bob Mintzer Big Band

Latin Jazz Album, "Nocturne," Charlie Haden

Country Album, "Timeless—Hank Williams Tribute," Various Artists

Country Song, "The Lucky One," Robert Lee Castleman

Country Vocal Performance, Female, "Shine," Dolly Parton

Country Vocal Performance, Male, "O Death," Ralph Stanley

Country Performance by a Duo or Group with Vocal, "The Lucky One," Alison Krauss and Union Station

Country Vocal Collaboration, "I Am a Man of Constant Sorrow," Dan Tyminski, Harvey Allen, and Pat Enright

Country Instrumental Performance, "Foggy Mountain Breakdown," Earl Scruggs, Glen Duncan, Randy Scruggs, Steve Martin, Vince Gill, Marty Stuart, Gary Scruggs, Albert Lee, Paul Shaffer, Jerry Douglas, and Leon Russell

Bluegrass Album, "New Favorite," Alison Krauss and Union Station

The King
of Rock 'n' Roll Lives On

Enormous video images of Elvis Presley form a backdrop for a memorial concert in Memphis, Tennessee, on Aug. 16, 2002, the 25th anniversary of Presley's death.

Legions of fans around the world remembered Elvis Presley on Aug. 16, 2002, the 25th anniversary of the entertainer's death. But to many of his fans, the "King of Rock 'n' Roll" was still very much alive. Presley had a number-one single and top-selling album on the charts in 2002; his music provided the soundtrack for a new movie; and a variety of books, magazines, television shows, videos, and other products exploring his legend hit the market. Elvis seemed to be more popular than ever!

Memphis, Tennessee, where Presley lived, was the focal point of the anniversary commemorations. On the night of August 15, an estimated 35,000 people filed past Presley's gravesite at Graceland, his estate, in the pouring rain. The presidents of 500 international Elvis fan clubs led the candlelight vigil, which continued past daybreak. On August 16, more than 14,000 fans filled the Pyramid Arena in Memphis for a concert featuring many of the backup singers and musicians who had performed with Presley. Images on a giant video screen of Presley singing accompanied the live music.

Presley's lasting impact on popular culture was apparent throughout 2002. Elvis topped the singles charts in the United Kingdom (UK) and a number of other countries with a remixed, dance-club version of "A Little Less Conversation," a song that he originally sang in a 1968 movie. The hit was Presley's 18th number-one single in the UK, breaking a tie he had held with the Beatles for most chart toppers. A new compilation of Elvis's number-one songs on CD became the top-selling album in the United States upon its release in September 2002. Several of Presley's songs were featured in the 2002 animated Disney movie *Lilo & Stitch,* which exposed a new generation to music Presley had first performed for their parents or their grandparents. Presley's influence even extended into bedrooms. In 2002, Vaughan-Bassett Furniture Co., of Galax, Virginia, introduced two lines of Elvis-inspired bedroom sets—one with a "Hollywood" theme, the other with a "Graceland" theme.

Several universities, including the University of Memphis, acknowledged the 25th anniversary of Presley's death with symposiums in which scholars attempted to explain the unparalleled popularity of the "King." But Elvis's fans instinctively understood the phenomenon. In the words of one fan who attended the Memphis candlelight vigil, "Elvis is the best. He was the first and the last. There's no more to say." ■ Alfred J. Smuskiewicz

Rap artist Nelly proved to be one of the year's breakout stars following the release of *Nellyville* in June. The album, which sold more than 700,000 copies in its first week, contained the hit single "Hot in Herre," which was among the most-played songs on radio and achieved crossover success on both rap music radio stations and standard popular music formats.

Changing images. Former teen-age sensations underwent radical image changes in 2002, as they tried to make the transition from so-called "bubble gum music" to a more mature image. Some critics theorized that the changes were made as the artists searched for a more adult fan base.

Christina Aguilera released the album *Stripped* in October. A provocative music video for "Dirrty," one of the songs on the album, featured the scantily clad singer dancing suggestively with various partners. In November, Justin Timberlake of 'N SYNC released his first solo album, *Justified.* On the album, Timberlake experimented with an edgier and hipper sound than 'N SYNC fans were familiar with. Nick Carter, a member of the Backstreet Boys, released his first solo album in October. Unlike Timberlake, Carter's album, *Now or Never,* echoed the boy band's pop sound.

A female presence. Several young female singer-songwriters burst onto the music scene during 2002. Unlike many of the popular teen-pop acts of the past few years, the new artists performed songs with lyrics to which more teenagers felt they could relate.

Rhythm and blues singer Ashanti released her self-titled first album in April to positive reviews and eager audiences. Fans and critics were both drawn to her angelic voice and soothing vocals. *Ashanti* sold more than 500,000 copies its first week, a record for a female artist's debut.

Young fans looking for lyrics with more realism also turned to singer and songwriter Avril Lavigne. Lavigne's first album, *Let Go,* which was released in June, sold more than 2 million copies by the end of 2002. It contained the number-one hit, "Complicated."

Fans also applauded Michelle Branch's album *The Spirit Room* and Vanessa Carlton's album *Be Not Nobody.* Both albums offered songs with more earnest lyrics than had been offered by most other female singers in recent years. Both debut efforts sold millions of copies by the end of 2002.

Bruce Springsteen and the E Street Band released *The Rising* in July. The album was the full band's first completely new album since the 1984 release *Born in the U.S.A.* and was one of 2002's most critically acclaimed. Springsteen, a

New Jersey native whose songs often include social commentary, addressed the terrorist attacks on the United States on Sept. 11, 2001, in several songs, including "Lonesome Day," "Empty Sky," and "You're Missing."

An American idol. Kelly Clarkson, a former cocktail waitress from Texas, won a recording contract in 2002 on the Fox television show "American Idol: The Search For a Superstar." Clarkson's first single, "A Moment Like This," rocketed to the number-one spot on the *Billboard* magazine sales record chart after its release in September.

Jazz. Critics and audiences were impressed in February by *Come Away With Me,* the debut album by jazz vocalist and pianist Norah Jones. The album contained the single "Don't Know Why," which crossed musical boundaries to appeal to fans of jazz, soul, blues, and folk music. In October, vocalist Diana Krall continued her chart dominance with her first concert album, *Live in Paris.* Vocalist Patricia Barber, who had developed a cult following of fans, found a wider audience with her August release *Verse.* *Verse* was Barber's first release on a major record label and her first collection of original songs.

Box sets celebrated the careers of several jazz legends in 2002, including *The Herbie Hancock Box,* a four compact disc set; *The Genius of the Electric Guitar,* devoted to Charlie Christian, considered a forefather of the electric guitar; and *Legacy,* a compilation of saxophonist John Coltrane's recordings.

Country music. In January, Alan Jackson released *Drive.* The album became the best-selling country album of 2002 and was the number-one album on both the country and the pop charts, thanks to the crossover hit "Where Were You (When the World Stopped Turning)." Jackson wrote and released the ballad in 2001 in response to the terrorist attacks on September 11. In July 2002, Toby Keith released his most successful album, *Unleashed,* which contained his own song about the terrorist attacks, "Courtesy of the Red, White & Blue (The Angry American)."

Capitalizing on the success of the soundtrack from the motion picture *O Brother, Where Art Thou?* (2000), bluegrass and more traditional country music continued to flourish in 2002. A heavy bluegrass influence could be found on such releases as *Home* by the Dixie Chicks, *This Side* by Nickel Creek, and Dolly Parton's *Halos & Horns,* which also contained a gospel-flavored rendition of the Led Zeppelin rock classic "Stairway to Heaven."

"The Ketchup Song," a single released by Las Ketchup, a Spanish sister group consisting of

Lola, Pilar, and Lucia Munoz, became a novelty dance craze in 2002. The song, which blends Latin-pop, rumba, reggae, and hip hop, was an international sensation before it was released in September in the United States.

Grateful Dead reunion. The surviving members of the Grateful Dead, one of the most popular and longest-lasting bands in rock music history, reunited as the Other Ones and played two concerts at the Alpine Valley Music Theatre in East Troy, Wisconsin, in August. The concert marked the first time that the group's surviving members performed together since the death of founding member Jerry Garcia in 1995. Tens of thousands of devoted fans known as Deadheads welcomed the reunion.

Waylon Jennings, whom many fans considered to have defined the country music "outlaw" movement of the 1970's, died on Feb. 13, 2002. The 64-year-old Jennings released 60 albums and had 16 number-one hit singles, including "Mammas Don't Let Your Babies Grow Up to Be Cowboys" and "Good Hearted Woman," during his career. He also sang the theme song and did the narration on the CBS television series "The Dukes of Hazzard." □ Donald Liebenson

See also **Deaths; Motion pictures; People in the news** (Bono; Osbourne, Ozzy; Williams, Hank III).

Population. A United Nations (UN) Population Division study published in March 2002 reversed a previous estimate that the world population would reach 10 billion people by 2100. The revised population estimate for 2100 was between 8 billion and 9 billion. Officials said that dramatic declines in fertility rates in large, developing nations resulted in the revised estimate. According to the UN report, improved health care for children, greater acceptance of family-planning programs worldwide, marriages later in life, an increase in the number of divorces, and the increased education of women were among the factors that led to reduced fertility rates.

Fertility rates. The UN study revealed that fertility rates had declined globally, from an average of 3.4 children per woman in 1990 to 2.8 children in 2000. The rate declined in more developed countries, from an average of 1.8 children per woman in 1990 to 1.6 children in 2000. In less developed countries, it declined during the same period from 3.8 children to 3.1 children. *Demographers* (population experts) predicted that if the decline continued into the mid-2000's, fertility rates in many developing countries would fall below replacement level, which in 2002 averaged about 2.1 children per woman. Replacement level is the number of births needed to replace the existing population.

Fertility rates declined in 23 European countries, Cuba, China, Japan, and South Korea to an average of 1.5 children per woman between 1995 and 2000. In India and Bangladesh, fertility rates declined from 5.7 children per woman in the 1970's to 3.3 children by the late 1990's. A rate of less than 3 children per woman was reported in 26 developing countries, including Brazil, Colombia, Indonesia, Iran, Mexico, South Africa, Turkey, and Vietnam.

HIV/AIDS. Transmission of HIV, the virus that causes AIDS, remained high in some developing countries due to ignorance about the cause and effects of the disease, reported the Joint United Nations Programme on HIV/AIDS (UNAIDS) in June 2002. The report, "HIV/AIDS Awareness and Behavior," covered 39 countries in Africa, Asia, Latin America, and the Caribbean. It was based on surveys conducted in the mid-to-late 1990's of about 5,000 households in each country.

In more than half of the countries surveyed, 90 percent of men and women reported that they were aware of the epidemic. Overall, women were less aware of the risks of HIV and AIDS than were men. Residents in urban areas were more aware of the risks than those in rural areas, a fact the report attributed to the greater role of education in urban areas. □ J. Tuyet Nguyen

See also **AIDS; Census; City.**

Portugal. Voters in 2002 threw out the ruling Socialist Party and elected a center-right coalition led by the Social Democratic Party, as the country suffered its worst economic performance in more than 10 years. The Socialists had been in power for seven years.

The election was held 18 months early, after Prime Minister Antonio Guterres resigned in December 2001, following the defeat of his Socialist Party in local elections. The opposition Social Democrats, led by Jose Manuel Durao Barroso, campaigned on claims that the Socialists had mismanaged public services and allowed the budget deficit to rise sharply. The Social Democrats promised to slash government spending, cut taxes, and privatize some services.

The party won 105 seats in the 230-seat parliament in the election on March 17, 2002, an increase from 81 seats in the previous election in 1999. The Socialists took 96 seats, a decline from 115 seats in 1999. The Social Democrats formed a coalition with the conservative Popular Party, which won 14 seats. The new government took office on April 6, 2002, with Durao Barroso as prime minister.

Economy. Portugal's economic problems worsened in 2002. European Union economists forecast that the economy would grow by 0.7 percent, down from 1.75 percent in 2001. In

March 2002, European soccer authorities threatened to withdraw the 2004 soccer championships from Portugal, after local governments cast doubt on their ability to provide more than $4 billion for new stadiums and other facilities.

An investigation of government finances, ordered by Barroso, reported in July 2002 that Portugal's budget deficit for 2001 was 4.1 percent of *gross domestic product (GDP)*, well above the 3 percent limit set for countries that use the euro. (GDP is the total value of goods and services produced in a country in a year.) Portugal was the first of the 12 countries using the euro to incur an excessive deficit since the currency was introduced in 1999. The European Commission (EC), the agency that enforces rules for euro members, ordered Portugal to reduce its deficit by March 2003. In May 2002, the government announced that it would postpone promised tax cuts, freeze government spending, and increase some taxes. In November, the EC formally warned Portugal to cut its deficit to less than 3 percent by an even earlier deadline—the end of 2002—or face economic sanctions. □ Tom Buerkle

See also **Europe**.

President of the United States.
See **United States, President of the.**

Prince Edward Island. See Canadian
provinces.

Prison. The United States Department of
Justice reported in July 2002 that there were 1.4 million people in federal and state prisons in 2001, an increase of 1.1 percent from 2000. Despite the increase, growth in the adult prison population slowed considerably in 2001 from the average increase of 3.6 percent recorded during the mid-1990's. The prison population rose during 2001 at the lowest rate since 1972, according to the Justice Department report. Government officials credited increased efforts to control overall crime and the trafficking of illegal drugs and weapons.

The overall U.S. prison population in 2001, including local jails, military facilities, and juvenile facilities, totaled 2.1 million people. Women comprised approximately 7 percent of the total population of U.S. federal prisons.

The Justice Department reported in August 2002 that there were approximately 6.6 million men and women in prison, on probation, or on parole in 2001. That figure equaled 3.1 percent of the U.S. adult population and was a slight increase from the 6.4 million people who comprised the adult U.S. correctional population in 2000.

Statistics released in July 2002 revealed that African American males outnumbered white and Hispanic males serving more than one year in prison by a ratio that far exceeded their ratio in the general population. According to a report issued by the Justice Department's Bureau of Justice Statistics (BJS), the 585,800 African American male inmates in federal and state prisons in December 2001 made up about 46 percent of the total prison population. The 449,200 white male inmates accounted for about 36 percent of the prison population. The 199,700 Hispanic male inmates comprised 15 percent.

The BJS reported that in 2001 there were 3,535 African American males sentenced to prison for every 100,000 African American males in the general population of the United States. By comparison, 1,177 Hispanic males were sentenced per every 100,000 Hispanic males in the total population, and 462 white males were sentenced for every 100,000 white males.

Death row inmates. Prison officials executed 55 inmates between January and mid-October 2002. More than 20 of those executions were performed in Texas.

A total of 3,718 inmates, including 52 women and 83 *juveniles* (persons under the age of 18), awaited execution on death row in the United States in July 2002. All of the juvenile offenders were male and had been sentenced for murder. □ Brian Bouldrey

See also **Crime**.

Prizes. See Nobel Prizes; Pulitzer Prizes.

Protestantism. Queen Elizabeth II of the
United Kingdom named Rowan Williams, the archbishop of Wales, the 104th archbishop of Canterbury in July 2002. While the archbishop holds little direct power beyond the United Kingdom, he is the symbolic spiritual leader of the Anglican Communion, which has 70 million members worldwide and includes both the Church of England and the Episcopal Church in the United States.

Williams was widely recognized by scholars as a distinguished theologian, the only person ever to hold a chair of divinity at both Cambridge and Oxford universities in England. Church leaders regarded Williams as traditional on church doctrine and moderately liberal on social issues. Williams succeeded Archbishop George Carey, who devoted his 11-year term to reconciling disagreements between various factions in the Anglican Communion.

The Presbyterian Church (U.S.A.) took steps at its General Assembly in Columbus, Ohio, in June 2002 to help ease a bitter and longstanding debate between different factions of its membership. The debate between conservatives and liberals centered on whether faith in Jesus Christ was the only route to salvation or whether members of non-Christian faiths could also be saved. The assembly overwhelmingly approved a statement that included the phrase "Jesus is the only Savior and Lord," which pleased conservatives. The statement also noted that God's grace was beyond human definition, meaning that church doctrine did not preclude anyone from being saved.

LCMS. Controversy surrounding a memorial service for the victims of the Sept. 11, 2001, terrorist attacks on the United States divided the leadership of the Lutheran Church-Missouri Synod (LCMS) in 2002. David Benke, the church's Atlantic district president, prayed at a highly visible interfaith gathering at Yankee Stadium in New York City following the attacks.

Several LCMS clerics, including Wallace Schultz, the synodical vice president, accused Benke of violating the synod's laws that forbid members of the church to share in public prayer with ministers of other faiths. Benke announced in 2002 that he would fight to clear himself. Synod President Gerald Kieschnick, whom Benke had consulted in advance, supported Benke's decision to participate in the ceremony. Reaction against Wallace Schultz was so strong that Schultz was suspended as the main preacher on the popular radio program "The Lutheran Hour."

Publications. Evangelical interest groups battled in 2002 over a new translation of the Bible. Zondervan, a publishing company in Grand Rapids, Michigan, and the International Bible Society of Colorado Springs, Colorado, produced a new translation called *Today's New International Version.* The publishers claimed the new translation was "gender-accurate." The translators had replaced gender-specific language, such as "he" and "brother," in places where they believed the original authors of the Bible intended to refer to both men and women.

Critics of the new translation called it a "stealth Bible," saying that it eliminated gender-specific language for the purpose of political correctness, rather than accuracy. While many scholars came to the support of *Today's New International Version,* conservative Christians, including leaders of the Southern Baptist Convention, whose constituency is a huge market for Bibles, attacked the book.

In April 2002, the trade magazine *Publishers Weekly* announced that *Desecration,* the ninth novel in the "Left Behind" series by Tim LaHaye and Jerry B. Jenkins, topped the journal's annual best seller list for 2001. The "Left Behind" series deals with some evangelical views of the apocalypse in a fiction format. The books have consistently topped both religious and secular bestseller lists. In April 2002, the authors signed a $45-million contract for a new four-book series.

□ Martin E. Marty

Psychology. See **Mental health.**

Public health and safety. United States President George W. Bush in December 2002 ordered about 500,000 U.S. military personnel to be vaccinated against smallpox. He also announced that smallpox vaccination would be offered on a voluntary basis to millions of civilian health care and emergency workers, who would be on the front lines treating patients if a bioterrorist attack using the virus should occur. Routine smallpox vaccinations ended in 1972 because public health officials believed that smallpox was no longer a health threat. However, after the terrorist and anthrax attacks on the United States in 2001, officials considered resuming vaccination to protect the public against the possible use of smallpox as a terrorist weapon.

The president did not recommend mass vaccination against smallpox for the general public. In June 2002, a panel of experts at the U.S. Centers for Disease Control and Prevention (CDC) in Atlanta, Georgia, had advised against vaccinating the entire U.S. population against the disease. The CDC noted that some people, especially those with compromised immune systems, such as AIDS patients and transplant organ recipients, might actually contract smallpox from the vaccine. The CDC said that smallpox symptoms, which include a pimplelike skin rash, would quickly alert physicians to an outbreak, allowing public health officials to vaccinate populations in affected areas rapidly. Smallpox vaccine is effective even if given several days after exposure to the virus.

West Nile virus. The worst recorded outbreak of West Nile virus in the United States swept through the Midwest and South in the summer of 2002. By November, the CDC had confirmed nearly 3,500 human cases of West Nile virus and more than 200 deaths in the United States. Illinois, Michigan, Ohio, Louisiana, and Indiana led the nation in reported cases. The disease first appeared in the United States in 1999, when it caused several deaths in the New York City area.

Migrating birds carry West Nile virus, which is spread to humans when mosquitoes bite birds and then people. The infection rate drops off sharply with the onset of cold weather that kills mosquitoes. Most people exposed to the virus experience mild flu-like symptoms or no symptoms at all, according to CDC officials. In about 1 in 150 cases, however, infected people develop a life-threatening brain inflammation.

Health care. Spending on health care in the United States in 2000 rose 6.9 percent over the 1999 figure, the HHS reported in January 2002. On average, each U.S. citizen spent $4,637 on health care in 2000, up from $4,377 in 1999. Prescription drugs constituted the largest cost in-

A worker in Louisiana sprays chemicals on stacked timber in August to control the spread of the mosquito-borne West Nile virus. Communities adopted spraying programs to combat the huge outbreak, which killed some 200 people in the United States during the summer of 2002.

crease, 17.3 percent between 1999 and 2000, according to the HHS.

The Institute of Medicine, a Washington, D.C.-based division of the National Academy of Sciences, issued a report in November 2002 that criticized the public health care system of the United States as too fragmented and underfunded to respond effectively to threats posed by emerging infections and bioterrorism. The report's authors called for reforms to make health insurance available to the 41.2 million U.S. citizens without such coverage.

Teen births. The HHS announced in a June 2002 report that births to teen-age mothers in the United States had fallen to a record low in 2001. The rate dropped from 48.5 births per 1,000 girls aged 15 to 19 in 2000 to 45.9 births in 2001, a 5-percent decline. Rates among girls aged 15 to 17 dropped 8 percent. The teen birth rate had declined 26 percent since 1991.

Traffic accidents. Fatalities in U.S. traffic accidents declined in 2001, the U.S. Department of Transportation's National Highway Traffic Safety Administration (NHTSA) reported in May 2002. The NHTSA estimated that 41,730 people died in traffic accidents in 2001 compared with 41,821 people in 2000.   □ Michael Woods

See also **Chicago; Health care issues; Houston; Medicine.**

Puerto Rico. On July 25, 2002, 15,000 Puerto Ricans joined Governor Sila M. Calderon in San Juan, the island's capital, to commemorate the 50th anniversary of Puerto Rico's unique status as a self-governing commonwealth of the United States. The occasion, however, highlighted divisions among Puerto Ricans over whether the island should remain a commonwealth or work toward statehood or independence.

Governor Calderon, though a member of the procommonwealth Popular Democratic Party, expressed unhappiness with the failure of the commonwealth system to promote economic progress. In 2002, unemployment in Puerto Rico stood at approximately 13 percent; 48 percent of the population lived below the federal poverty level; and *per capita* (per person) income was approximately $8,000.

Four thousand Puerto Ricans favoring independence staged a counterdemonstration on July 25 in the southwestern city of Guanica. Speakers argued for an end to what they called Puerto Rico's "colonial status."

In September, Senator Kenneth McClintock of the New Progressive Party, which favors statehood, countered independence arguments by noting in a newspaper interview that statehood would provide Puerto Rico with increased federal financing for health and welfare programs.

Calderon's initiatives. In August, Governor Calderon announced a $1-billion program to improve living conditions in Puerto Rico's poorest communities. The development program was the first of its kind totally financed from Puerto Rican resources. Calderon hoped to bring adequate water and electrical services to almost 700 poor communities, build or rehabilitate 20,000 houses, and improve roads. The plan included a $15-million job-training program and funds for improving health and education services.

Calderon also announced a drive in 2002 to register all eligible voters of Puerto Rican descent living on the U.S. mainland. She hoped this would make the island's needs better known to U.S. legislators.

Corruption indictments. In January, federal prosecutors indicted 17 Puerto Rican officials who served in the administration of the previous governor, Pedro Rossello. The officials were charged with stealing, extorting, or laundering $4.3 million. The indictments were part of an ongoing federal investigation of corruption among Puerto Rican officials and businessmen, most of whom were associated with the New Progressive Party. By late 2002, several of the indicted officials had pleaded guilty. ☐ Nathan A. Haverstock

See also **Latin America; United States, Government of the.**

Pulitzer Prizes in journalism, letters, drama, and music were awarded on April 8, 2002, by Columbia University in New York City on the recommendation of the Pulitzer Prize Board.

Journalism. Many of the awards honored journalists covering the terrorist attacks on the United States on Sept. 11, 2001, and the aftermath. *The New York Times* won a record seven Pulitzer Prizes, including the public service award, for its special section, "A Nation Challenged," published regularly after September 11; the explanatory reporting prize for profiles of the global terrorism network; the breaking-news photography award for its coverage of the terrorist attacks on New York City and their aftermath; and the prize for feature photography for photographs of people enduring protracted conflict in Afghanistan and Pakistan.

Barry Bearak of *The New York Times* won the international reporting prize for his coverage of daily life in war-torn Afghanistan; *Times* reporter Thomas Friedman won the prize for commentary for coverage of the worldwide impact of terrorism; and Gretchen Morgenson of *The New York Times* won the beat reporting award for her Wall Street financial and economics coverage.

The Wall Street Journal staff won the breaking-news prize for its coverage of the terrorist attacks. Sari Horwitz, Scott Higham, and Sarah Cohen of *The Washington Post* won the prize for investiga-

tive reporting for a series on the neglect and death of 229 children in protective care in Washington, D.C. *The Washington Post* staff also won the national reporting prize for coverage of the U.S.-led war on terrorism.

The prize for feature writing went to Barry Siegel of *The Los Angeles Times* for his story about a man tried for negligence in the death of his son. Alex Raksin and Bob Sipchen, also of *The Los Angeles Times*, won the prize for editorial writing for a series on mentally ill people living on the streets. *Newsday* (Long Island, New York) writer Justin Davidson was awarded the prize for his reviews of classical music. Clay Bennett of *The Christian Science Monitor* won the award for editorial cartooning.

Letters, drama, and music. Richard Russo won the fiction prize for his novel *Empire Falls*. The drama prize went to Suzan-Lori Parks for her play *Topdog/Underdog*. Louis Menand won the history prize for his book *The Metaphysical Club: A Story of Ideas in America*. *John Adams* by David McCullough received the prize for biography. Carl Dennis won the prize for poetry for his collection *Practical Gods*. The general nonfiction prize was given to Diane McWhorter for *Carry Me Home: Birmingham, Alabama, the Climactic Battle of the Civil Rights Revolution*. The music prize was given to composer Henry Brant for *Ice Field*. ☐ Brian Bouldrey

Quebec. See **Canadian Provinces.**

Radio. Members of the United States Congress and the Federal Communications Commission (FCC), the agency charged with regulating communication through radio, wire, and cable, revisited the issue of deregulation in the radio industry in 2002. The Telecommunications Act of 1996 greatly loosened restrictions on the number of radio stations that a single company could own. Since then, radio conglomerates have swelled in size, causing growing concern among consumer advocates that a few large companies owning many radio stations could reduce competition. Media companies, meanwhile, claimed that the restrictions should be further loosened.

United States Senator Russell Feingold (D., Wisconsin) expressed concern in 2002 that large companies might be using their size to suppress competing stations. In June, Feingold introduced legislation that called for stations found to be engaged in such practices to lose their FCC licenses.

Feingold pointed out that various large radio conglomerates also own promotion companies. The conglomerates have been known to force record companies to hire such promotion companies when promoting a concert or other event. Feingold cited the largest radio conglomerate, Clear Channel Communications, Inc., of San Antonio, Texas, which owns more than 1,200 radio stations in the United States. Clear Channel also owns the world's largest concert promotions firm, SFX Productions. Feingold said that it was possible that companies like Clear Channel could use their exclusive arrangements with promotion companies like SFX to force record companies to pay fees in order to reach people listening to Clear Channel-owned stations. It is illegal for radio stations to charge fees to play music.

Ownership rules. While Feingold indicated that the FCC needed to tighten radio ownership regulations, the FCC in September began the most comprehensive review in the agency's history to determine whether radio station ownership restrictions should be further loosened. Among other rules, the FCC explored the validity of a current rule that no one company can own more than eight stations in any single market. The review was partially prompted by the fact that the FCC lost several court cases in 2002. The cases were filed by media companies challenging that the rules were outdated. FCC officials said they would complete their review in early 2003.

Satellite radio. The market for satellite radio, which uses satellites in orbit around Earth to transmit digital radio signals across the entire United States, heated up in 2002, with the entry of the second satellite radio company, Sirius Satellite Radio, Inc., of New York City. Sirius launched its service in July, eight months after its competitor, XM Satellite Radio Inc. of Washington, D.C., began broadcasting nationally. Both satellite radio companies offered 100 stations in various formats, including several musical categories, news, and comedy. Because the companies' satellites were about 22,300 miles (35,900 kilometers) above the Earth, people living thousands of miles away from each other could listen to the same programming.

By July, XM officials claimed to have signed up about 137,000 subscribers who paid $9.99 a month. Sirius executives said that they had about 6,500 listeners by the end of August. Sirius charged $12.95 a month, but 60 of its channels were commercial-free. In order to listen to either system, subscribers had to buy special receivers that cost about $400.

Despite the excitement generated by satellite radio, both companies faced financial problems in 2002 as they scrambled to sign up enough subscribers to make back their huge investments in equipment and programming. As a result, shares of Sirius, which in January 2002 sold at more than $10 each, were trading at less than $1 in late November. Shares of XM, which in January were valued at more than $16, had fallen to below $4 by late November.   □ Greg Paeth

Railroad. See Transportation.

Religion. See Eastern Orthodox; Islam; Judaism; Protestantism; Roman Catholic Church.

Republican Party. The Republican Party enjoyed enormous success at midterm elections on Nov. 5, 2002. The GOP (for Grand Old Party) gained control of the United States Senate and expanded its control in the U.S. House of Representatives. Republicans also maintained an edge in state governor's races. President George W. Bush barnstormed the nation for Republican candidates in 2002, and most political analysts attributed the GOP's strong election showing to the president's prestige and personal popularity. The elections in 2002 were the first since 1934 in which a president's party gained seats in both the House and Senate two years into a first term.

Senate races. The GOP regained control of the Senate from the Democratic Party, which had held a majority of Senate seats since 2001. After the 2002 elections, the Republicans held 51 seats and Democrats controlled 48 seats, plus the seat of Senator James M. Jeffords of Vermont, an independent aligned with the Democrats.

Republicans managed a major victory in Missouri where Jim Talent defeated incumbent Democrat Jean Carnahan. In Minnesota, Norm Coleman, the former Republican mayor of St. Paul, defeated a late challenge by former Senator and Vice President Walter Mondale, a Democrat.

Representative Saxby Chambliss, a Republican, scored an upset victory in Georgia over Senator Max Cleland. Political experts said that Cleland's loss was tied to his stand against adopting all of President Bush's demands in the drafting of a bill creating the Department of Homeland Security.

Voters in North Carolina selected Republican Elizabeth Dole, the wife of former Senator Bob Dole (R., Kansas), over Democratic challenger Erskine Bowles, the former chief of staff in the administration of President Bill Clinton. Dole filled the seat held by Senator Jesse Helms (R., North Carolina), who retired after 30 years in the Senate.

House races. Republicans increased the number of seats they held in the House to 229 following the midterm election, compared with 205 seats held by Democrats. Representative Bernard Sanders of Vermont was the only independent in the House.

Republican leadership. In November, Republican House members elected Representative Tom DeLay of Texas as their majority leader, Representative Roy Blunt of Missouri as majority *whip* (assistant leader), and Representative Deborah Pryce of Ohio as Republican conference chair.

Senate Republicans chose Trent Lott of Mississippi as majority leader, Mitch McConnell of Kentucky as majority whip, and Rick Santorum of Pennsylvania as secretary of the Republican Conference.

On December 20, Lott stepped down as the Senate's majority leader for the 108th Congress,

Florida Governor Jeb Bush greets supporters at the end of his reelection campaign in November. Bush handily defeated his Democratic challenger in an election that embarrassed Democratic leaders, who had vowed to defeat President George W. Bush's brother in his bid for reelection.

scheduled to begin on Jan. 7, 2003. Lott's resignation came two weeks after he commented at a party for Senator Strom Thurmond (R., South Carolina) that the nation would have been better off if Thurmond had been elected president in 1948. Thurmond had run for president on a segregationist platform.

Governors. Republicans won 22 of the 36 gubernatorial races contested in November. Before the elections, Republicans held 27 governorships, while Democrats held 21. Independents held two governor's offices. After the election, Republicans controlled 26 offices, while Democrats increased the number of governors in their camp to 24.

Florida Governor Jeb Bush, President Bush's brother, handily defeated Tampa businessman Bill McBride. Jeb Bush's reelection was a blow to the Democratic Party, which had pledged to take the office from Bush because of the pivotal role Florida had played in the 2000 presidential election.

The GOP won a surprising victory in Hawaii, where a Republican was elected governor for only the second time in state history. Linda Lingle won 51 percent of the vote, defeating Lieutenant Governor Mazie Hirono.

In another surprising victory, Republican Robert Ehrlich defeated Democratic Lieutenant Governor Kathleen Kennedy Townsend for the governorship of Maryland, an overwhelmingly

Democratic state. Ehrlich became the first GOP governor of Maryland since 1966.

U.S. Representative Bob Riley (R., Alabama) defeated Alabama Governor Don Siegelman in the closest gubernatorial race of 2002. Both candidates declared victory, and Siegelman asked for a recount after the vote total revealed he had lost by about 3,000 votes out of more than 1.3 million ballots cast. Siegelman later conceded.

State control. The November election gave Republicans control of 21 statehouses, compared with the 16 legislatures held by the Democrats. The remaining statehouses were divided between the two parties. Nebraska is nonpartisan.

Fund raising. Officials with the Republican National Committee (RNC) announced in October that the RNC had received more than $103 million in contributions for the first three quarters of 2002. The total included $32 million in "soft money" contributions—individual contributions to political parties that are not subject to the same restrictions placed on contributions to candidates. In November, a campaign finance law took effect that bars political parties from raising and spending soft money. □ Geoffrey A. Campbell

See also **Congress of the United States; Democratic Party; Elections; State government; United States, Government of the; United States, President of the.**

Roman Catholic Church.

Scandals involving allegations of sexual abuse of children by priests and the coverup of such abuse by church leaders rocked the Roman Catholic Church in the United States in 2002. An ailing pope denied rumors that he would retire and continued in 2002 to visit countries around the world.

Protecting children. Pope John Paul II called all U.S. cardinals to the Vatican in Rome in April to discuss establishing stricter policies to protect children and young people from sexual abuse by Catholic clergy. Following the meeting, the U.S. Conference of Catholic Bishops met in Dallas to draft a new document called the Charter for the Protection of Children and Young People. The authors of the charter wrote that any member of the clergy credibly accused of abusing minors would immediately be removed from the ministry. The bishops pledged to turn over to law enforcement officials the names of all clergy against whom credible charges of abuse had been made.

The bishops adopted the charter in response to widespread allegations that some priests had sexually abused children and young people. U.S. newspapers and other media outlets alleged that U.S. cardinals, archbishops, and bishops had been slow to respond to charges that the priests had acted improperly. Allegations surfaced that some church leaders had failed to punish or remove priests who had been repeatedly accused of sexual abuse dating as far back as the 1970's. Various church officials also confirmed that some archdioceses had paid out millions of dollars in settlements in exchange for the silence of children and adults claiming to be the victims of abuse.

The Vatican rejected the Charter for the Protection of Children and Young People in October 2002, saying that its aggressive, zero-tolerance approach unfairly denied accused priests of their right to defend themselves. In November, the Conference of Catholic Bishops approved a compromise policy requiring accused priests to be tried by a church tribunal before being removed from the ministry. In December, the Vatican accepted the resignation of Boston Cardinal Bernard Law, a high-ranking church official accused of sheltering wayward priests.

Ailing pontiff. The failing health of Pope John Paul II in 2002 led many people to speculate that he would retire. The pope, who turned 82 in May, suffered from Parkinson disease, a nervous system disorder that caused his left hand to tremble and his face to appear rigid and unresponsive. Problems with his hip and arthritis in his right knee often made walking difficult. However, Pope John Paul II strongly denied rumors that he intended to resign, announcing that he would leave it to Christ "to decide when and how He

Pope John Paul II addresses U.S. cardinals summoned to the Vatican in April 2002 to discuss a series of allegations that some Roman Catholic priests in the United States sexually abused children and that bishops did little to protect young people.

wants to relieve me of this service."

Although the pope's infirmities forced him to cancel or shorten some public appearances, he continued to travel, visiting Azerbaijan and Bulgaria in May. A trip to North America in July included stops in Canada, Guatemala, and Mexico. The pope concluded his summer travels with a visit to his native Poland in August.

Conference for peace. In January 2002, the pope hosted 150 representatives from a dozen different religions at a conference in Assisi, Italy. The religious leaders prayed for peace, denounced violence in the name of religion, and petitioned world leaders to respect human rights.

The Rosary. The pope in October announced changes to the Rosary, a traditional series of Catholic prayers that includes meditations on 15 momentous occasions, or "mysteries," in the life of Jesus Christ. The pope added five new mysteries, called the "mysteries of light," that deal with the miracles of Christ's public ministry. The new mysteries include Christ's baptism; the wedding feast at Cana at which He transformed water into wine; His proclamation of the Kingdom of God; His Transfiguration, when God commanded the apostles to listen to Him; and His celebration of the Last Supper or Eucharist.   □ Thomas C. Fox

See also **Eastern Orthodox Churches; Mexico; Toronto; People in the news** (Gregory, Wilton).

Romania. The Romanian government, led by Prime Minister Adrian Nastase, focused in 2002 on meeting economic requirements for eventual membership in the European Union. However, the government's economic restructuring caused hardships in some sectors of Romania's economy, prompting a series of protests.

In June, 10,000 union workers converged on Bucharest, the capital, in a mass demonstration to protest the government's economic policies. In August, thousands of defense workers, protesting planned job and salary cuts, demonstrated in towns and cities across the country.

Romania's gross domestic product (the total value of goods and services produced in a given year) increased by 4.4 percent in the first half of 2002. In November, Neven Mates, an official of the International Monetary Fund, a United Nations-affiliated organization that provides short-term credit to member nations, praised Romania's leaders for fostering an improved business climate and fighting inflation.

Romania became one of seven countries to receive an invitation in November to join the North Atlantic Treaty Organization (NATO). NATO officials extended the invitation at a summit meeting in Prague, Czech Republic.   □ Sharon L. Wolchik

See also **Europe.**

Rowing. See **Sports.**

Russia enjoyed relative calm and prosperity early in 2002. The economy grew, and President Vladimir Putin announced that Russia's war in the breakaway region of Chechnya was all but over. However, as the year drew to a close, analysts warned that the economy was not as stable as it seemed, and a spectacular hostage crisis in Moscow refocused the nation's and the world's attention on the war in Chechnya.

Economy. Russia's economy enjoyed its third consecutive year of growth, buoyed by high oil prices on international markets and strong domestic demand for consumer goods. Economists announced that the country's economy on average had grown by more than 6 percent each year from 2000 to 2002.

Despite such healthy growth, several prominent analysts began to warn in 2002 that economic reforms had stalled and that the Russian economy was too dependent on the export of natural resources. This dependency left the economy highly vulnerable to fluctuations in the price of oil, natural gas, gold, diamonds, and precious metals on international markets. Economists also noted that the country had made little progress toward reforming its banking system and shrinking the number of people employed by the government. President Putin warned in October that the economy was "stuck in a condition of sustainable stagnation" and worried that political and economic risks continued to discourage investors.

Chechnya. Russia's war in the breakaway region of Chechnya, which the government resumed in 1999, continued to claim lives in 2002. Putin declared in his state of the nation address in April that the military phase of the operation was complete, and Chechnya was under Russian control. However, violence continued through the year as Russian troops engaged in "mopping up" operations intended to round up remaining militants in Chechen villages. These activities consisted of the mass detention of Chechen civilians and led to a range of reports of brutality and human rights violations by the Russian military. Negotiations aimed at a peaceful resolution of the conflict made little progress, and both sides grew increasingly desperate.

On August 19, Chechen guerrillas shot down a Russian military transport helicopter taking off from a heavily fortified military base at Khankala in Chechnya. The helicopter crashed into a minefield, triggering explosions and making rescue efforts almost impossible. About 120 people died in the disaster, including many civilians and families of soldiers who had boarded the overcrowded helicopter in violation of military regulations. The crash ranked as the single deadliest incident since the conflict in Chechnya began.

Smoke generated by nearby peat and forest fires obscures Moscow's skyline in July 2002. An intense heat wave and a shortage of rain stoked Moscow's worst summer wildfire season since 1972, leaving the city shrouded in thick smog for several days.

In the summer of 2002, President Putin accused Georgian President Eduard Shevardnadze of doing nothing to stop Chechen rebels from hiding out in Georgia's Pankisi Gorge, near the Russian border. Putin claimed that the rebels used the gorge to smuggle weapons into Chechnya and launch attacks on Russian territory. He issued thinly veiled threats that the Russian army was prepared to invade Georgia to conduct operations in Pankisi directly, but he dropped the threat after Georgia stepped up military patrols in the region. Many observers in Russia speculated that arms traffic over the Georgian border was a minor source of supply for Chechen guerrillas. They accused corrupt Russian Army officers of selling arms directly to Chechen fighters.

Terrorism. On October 23, more than 40 heavily armed terrorists took an entire Moscow theater hostage, demanding that the Russian government withdraw immediately from Chechnya. The theater held around 800 spectators who were watching a performance of the popular Russian musical *Nord-Ost*. Some members of the audience escaped in the initial confusion, and several groups of children were subsequently released. However, the terrorists held more than 750 hostages for over 56 hours. The hostage-takers wired the theater with 250 pounds (113 kilograms) of explosives and threatened to blow up the building if police or soldiers attacked them.

Just before dawn on October 26, Russian security forces piped a sedative gas into the theater's ventilation system and then stormed the building. The gas left nearly all of the terrorists and hostages unconscious, and special forces troops were able to subdue the hostage-takers quickly.

The operation turned from triumph into scandal as details of the raid were revealed. Russian troops executed all of the terrorists they found, most of whom were still unconscious from the effects of the gas. They removed unconscious hostages from the building but were unprepared to provide medical assistance. Many were taken to hospitals where physicians were provided no information about the type of gas used in the rescue. Russian officials refused to offer any details about the gas, even as hundreds of hostages lay unconscious. More than 120 hostages died, nearly all from the effects of the gas used in the rescue operation. Officials later revealed that the gas used was a derivative of Fentanyl, an anes-

thetic commonly administered during surgery. Fentanyl is not inherently lethal but in large doses can cause heart and respiratory failure.

In a televised address, President Putin emotionally apologized for having been unable to save all of the hostages. Public frustration grew, however, as it became clear that most of the deaths were the result of the rescue and not the siege itself. Putin agreed to appoint a national commission to investigate the security breakdown that led to the crisis, as well as the conduct of the rescue operation. However, he also considered new guidelines restricting press coverage in crisis situations. Several observers voiced fears that the rules were intended to shield the military from criticism in future operations.

In the wake of the theater siege, the Russian government could no longer maintain its assertion that the conflict in Chechnya was nearly over. However, Putin rejected any suggestion

Armed Chechen terrorists keep watch at a Moscow theater during a hostage crisis in October 2002. At least 40 Chechen separatists took over the crowded theater during an October 23 performance of a popular musical. They held more than 750 people hostage for over 56 hours.

that he bargain for peace with Aslan Maskhadov, the elected Chechen leader whom Putin blamed for the theater siege. Instead, Putin proposed to continue reintegrating Chechnya by holding a referendum for a new constitution and elections for a new government for the region in 2003.

Putin also vowed to expand the war against Chechen separatists across international borders. On Oct. 30, 2002, police in Copenhagen, Denmark, arrested Akhmed Zakayev, Maskhadov's foreign envoy, at Russia's request. Authorities accused Zakayev of involvement in the hostage crisis and other incidents in the Chechen conflict. Danish officials released Zakayev in December, however, after finding there was not enough evidence to warrant extraditing him to Russia.

On December 27, Muslim fundamentalists launched one of the deadliest attacks of the past three years in Grozny, the Chechen capital. Suicide bombers drove two trucks laden with explosives into the four-story headquarters of the Russian-backed Chechen government, triggering explosions that killed more than 80 people.

International relations. On May 24, United States President George W. Bush signed a new arms control agreement with Putin during a visit to Moscow. The agreement called for the reduction of each country's stockpile of armed nuclear warheads from more than 6,000 to about 2,000 by 2012. Critics complained that the treaty contained few mechanisms for verifying disarmament and that warheads removed from missiles could be quickly redeployed.

Putin also signed an agreement with NATO in May 2002, establishing the NATO-Russia Council. The agreement promised cooperation between NATO and Russia on security matters in Europe. It marked a historic step toward Russia's acceptance in the world community, as NATO had been originally created to counter threats from Russia and other republics of the Soviet Union.

In November, Russia and the European Union (EU) struck a deal at a summit in Brussels, Belgium, to permit Russians in Kaliningrad to pass through Lithuania on their way to Russia. Kaliningrad, a Russian province that lies between Lithuania and Poland and does not border Russia, had become a source of growing tension with the EU. Putin complained that the planned EU expansion to Poland and Lithuania would require Russian citizens in Kaliningrad to obtain an EU visa to travel to the rest of Russia.

Comments Putin made during a press interview following the conference marred the Kaliningrad announcement. Normally noted for his reserve in public, Putin lashed out, warning that Islamic radicals wanted to wrest Chechnya from Russia as part of a plan to kill citizens of the United States and its allies. He followed the warning with graphic and violent threats addressed at journalists critical of Russian military actions. International affairs experts suggested that the tirade showed that the continuing conflict in Chechnya was eroding Putin's patience.

Political developments. Campaigning began in 2002 with parliamentary elections scheduled for December 2003 and presidential elections for March 2004. President Putin remained extremely popular in 2002, and few credible challengers appeared on the horizon. Attention, therefore, focused on local politics, with several important regions holding gubernatorial elections. In Krasnoyarsk, center of Russia's aluminum industry, Putin intervened to ratify the election victory of relative newcomer Alexandr Khloponin after his opponents sought to nullify the results. In the industrial center of Nizhnii Novgorod, Vadim Bulavinov was elected mayor with the support of federal authorities.

Freedom of the press. In January, Russian authorities continued a campaign against independent media companies by revoking the license of independent station TV-6 and taking it off the air. TV-6 had become a haven for journalists expelled from NTV when that station was taken over by the state-run Gazprom conglomerate. In March, a consortium of politicians and journalists reacquired the license, and the rebranded station resumed broadcasting as TV-S.

Midair collision. On July 1, a Bashkirian Airlines charter plane collided in midair with a cargo airplane over the border between Switzerland and Germany. The Bashkirian Airlines flight carried school groups from the Russian republic of Bashkortostan headed for a vacation in Spain. Seventy-one people, including 52 children, died in the crash. An investigation blamed the collision on mistakes by Swiss air traffic controllers.

Olympics. At the Winter Olympics in Salt Lake City, Utah, in February, Russian ice skaters Elena Bereznaya and Anton Sikharulidze won the gold medals in the pairs figure skating competition. However, officials also awarded gold medals to the Canadian figure skating team after a judge claimed she had been pressured to vote for the Russian team, enraging Russian skating fans. The Russian Skating Federation later protested that several of its skaters were judged unfairly, and the Russian team nearly boycotted the closing ceremonies. In July, alleged Russian crime boss Alimzhan Tokhtak-hounov was arrested in Italy and charged with attempting to manipulate the skating competition in favor of Russian teams.   ☐ Steven L. Solnick

See also **Belarus; Disasters; Europe; Georgia; Ice skating; Olympics: A Special Report; Terrorism; United States, Government of the.**

Sailing. See Boating.

Saudi Arabia. Deep divisions marred the once close relationship between Saudi Arabia and the United States in 2002. Saudi authorities feared that popular unrest might be sparked by a growing Arab perception that the U.S.-led war against terrorism was actually a war against Islam. Saudi Arabia is the guardian of the two most sacred cities in Islam—Mecca and Medina.

Terrorism. In November, Saudi Crown Prince Abdullah criticized Western portrayals of Saudis as terrorists and Islam as a religion of extremism. His remarks followed a series of events that had embittered Saudis. The *Washington Post* reported in August that a secret U.S. Department of Defense briefing paper had described Saudi Arabia as "the kernel of evil" that supports Islamic terrorism. Also in August, hundreds of relatives of the victims of the terrorist attacks on the United States on Sept. 11, 2001, filed a civil suit seeking massive financial damages from members of the Saudi royal family and Saudi charities. The suit accused the Saudis of helping to finance al-Qa'ida, the Islamic terrorist organization that U.S. officials suspected of organizing the attacks.

Iraq. The Saudi government refused to confirm in 2002 whether it would allow U.S. forces to use Saudi airspace and bases to launch attacks against Iraq. United States officials had threatened such attacks to force Iraq to comply with United Nations (UN) resolutions requiring Iraq to give up weapons of mass destruction. Many Saudis feared that U.S. military action would incite more Arab extremism as long as the Palestinian-Israeli conflict remained unresolved.

In March, Crown Prince Abdullah embraced a senior Iraqi official at an Arab summit in Lebanon. International affairs experts interpreted this gesture as a demonstration of Arab solidarity in the face of U.S. threats. In October, Saudi Arabia opened a border crossing with Iraq to facilitate trade. The crossing had been closed since the 1991 Gulf War. In November 2002, Saudi officials cautioned the United States that continued tough rhetoric could destroy the last chance for a peaceful resolution of the Iraq problem.

Palestinians. Crown Prince Abdullah received the backing of Arab leaders during the March summit for a peace overture to Israel. He proposed that Arab states normalize relations with Israel provided that Israel withdraw from occupied Arab territories, accept a Palestinian nation with East Jerusalem as its capital, and allow the return of Palestinian refugees to Israel. In April, a Saudi telethon raised $100 million in emergency aid for Palestinian families.

☐ Christine Helms

See also **Iraq; Israel; Middle East.**

School. See Education.

Senegal. See Africa.

Sierra Leone. President Ahmed Tejan Kabbah won reelection to a second five-year term in peaceful elections in Sierra Leone in May 2002. His reelection came one year after a cease-fire pact enacted on May 15, 2001, between Kabbah's government and Sierra Leone's main rebel group, the Revolutionary United Front (RUF).

Sierra Leone's civil war began in 1991. More than 100,000 people died and tens of thousands of others were mutilated in the 10-year conflict. Intervention by United Nations (UN) and British forces eventually tipped the scale, forcing the warring parties to agree to a cease-fire and a disarmament process. In a ceremony on Jan. 18, 2002, President Kabbah and RUF leader Issa Sesay declared the war officially over.

Elections. On May 14, about 80 percent of Sierra Leoneans who were eligible to vote went to the polls in the first nationwide election since 1996. International observers characterized the polling as generally free and fair.

Voters gave Kabbah 70 percent of the presidential ballots and his ruling Sierra Leone People's Party (SLPP) 83 of 112 contested parliamentary seats. Ernest Koroma's All People's Congress came in second, with 22 percent of the presidential vote and 27 seats. The Peace and Liberation Party, headed by Johnny Paul Koroma, who had once led a military *coup* (takeover) against Kabbah, won 3 percent of the presidential vote and two seats. However, Koroma's party attracted about 70 percent of the Army vote. The RUF, which in early 2000 was in control of most of the country, won no seats in parliament.

International role. The UN peacekeeping mission in Sierra Leone, comprising a force of 17,500 troops, continued to enforce peace in the country in 2002. According to UN officials, peacekeeping forces had demobilized about 47,000 government and rebel soldiers by May 2002. However, military experts speculated that illegal arms stockpiles remained in scattered locations in Sierra Leone. In September, the UN Security Council voted to reduce UN troop strength in Sierra Leone to 4,500 soldiers by June 2003. The British defense ministry began withdrawing British troops from Sierra Leone in mid-2002 but left a small force to train the Sierra Leone Army.

Fragile peace. The International Crisis Group, an independent think-tank based in Brussels, Belgium, warned in a report released in July that peace in Sierra Leone was tentative. The authors of the report said that President Kabbah and the ruling SLPP would have to give the opposition a meaningful role in the government and secure the loyalty of Army rank-and-file to build a stable society.

☐ Simon Baynham

See also **Africa; United Nations.**

Stephan Eberharter of Austria speeds down the course at Altenmarkt-Zauchensee, Austria, on his way to winning the World Cup downhill crown on March 6. Eberharter had a tremendous season in 2002, winning the World Cup overall, downhill, and Super-G titles.

Singapore. Four 7-year-old Muslim girls were expelled from school in Singapore in February 2002 for wearing traditional Islamic head scarves to class. The girls' parents said that the children wore the scarves, which violated a government ban on religious symbols at schools, as an act of civil disobedience.

The expulsion touched off a storm of protest among Muslim Malays, who make up 14 percent of the predominately ethnic Chinese population. Muslims charged the government with religious discrimination. The leader of the opposition Democratic Party, Chee Soon Juan, defended the girls in a speech at Speakers' Corner. The corner is the only place in Singapore where public speeches are legal without a permit, but discussions of race or religion are banned throughout Singapore, including Speakers' Corner. A court found Chee guilty of violating the ban.

The World Bank and the Asian Development Bank, affiliates of the United Nations, reported in September that Singapore's economy grew by a rate of more than 3.5 percent in 2002. The country's thriving petrochemical and pharmaceutical export business led growth, which helped offset losses suffered in 2001, when the country's economy experienced its worst decline since 1965. □ Henry S. Bradsher

See also **Asia.**

Skiing. Austrian skiers dominated in 2002 despite having lost their top male skier, Hermann Maier, to injury. Austria's top female skier, Renate Goetschl, also had her season cut short because of injuries sustained in a fall in March.

Stephan Eberharter of Austria finished the season with 1,702 points, the second-highest overall point total in history, behind only Hermann Maier's 2000 points in the 2000 season. Eberharter won the overall, downhill, and Super-G World Cup titles in 2002. France's Frederic Covili clinched the giant slalom title in March.

The men's slalom title came down to the season's final race at Flachau, Austria, in March. Ivica Kostelic took the slalom crown, becoming the first Croatian to win a World Cup men's title. Kostelic did not win easily, however. Bode Miller of the United States, who was trying to become the first American since Phil Mahre in 1982 to win the slalom, made a furious rush for the title. Miller, who was in eighth place after the first run, accidentally wore downhill boots instead of the stiffer slalom boots on his second run. Despite this, Miller blistered the field, winning the second run by more than 1 second. But it was not enough, and Miller finished in second place.

In women's Alpine skiing, Michaela Dorfmeister of Austria took the overall title on March 6, 2002, with her victory in the downhill at Altenmarkt-Zauchensee, Austria. Goetschl finished in second place in the overall standings, and Sonja Nef of Switzerland, the giant slalom champion, finished third. Other winners included Germany's Hilde Gerg in the Super-G, Laure Pequegnut of France in the slalom, and Italy's Isolde Kostner, who defended her downhill title.

Injuries. Hermann Maier missed the 2002 season after breaking his right leg in several places in a motorcycle accident in August 2001. Maier had won the overall, downhill, Super-G, and giant slalom in 2001. Goetschl broke her left leg, tore tendons, and injured her elbow in a crash on March 2, 2002, during a downhill run in Lenzerheide, Switzerland. Goetschl, the 2000 overall champion, underwent surgery the day of the crash. She was out for the rest of the season.

Nordic skiing. Ronny Ackermann of Germany won the Nordic combined World Cup title on March 16, 2002, in Oslo, Norway. Ackermann finished the competition with 2,110 points.

Drug scandal. The International Ski Federation in June banned Larissa Lazutina and Olga Danilova of Russia and Johann Muehlegg of Spain for two years for failing drug tests during the 2002 Winter Olympic Games. Lazutina and Muehlegg were each stripped of one gold medal they had won at the Olympics. ☐ Michael Kates

See also **Olympics: A Special Report.**

Slovakia.

Victories by center-right parties in Slovakia's September 2002 elections enabled Prime Minister Mikulas Dzurinda to again form a governing coalition. The new government, which consisted of four allied parties, amassed a 78-seat bloc in the 150-seat parliament, giving it a 3-seat governing majority. The nationalist Movement for a Democratic Slovakia, led by former Prime Minister Vladimir Meciar, and the Communist Party of Slovakia made up the opposition. The Communists in 2002 had deputies in the parliament for the first time since 1989.

Officials of the European Union (EU) and the North Atlantic Treaty Organization (NATO) hailed the election victory of Dzurinda's centrist coalition. Before the election, European and United States officials had warned that a victory by nationalist Meciar could derail Slovakia's progress toward membership in the EU and NATO.

Dzurinda's government pledged to enact reforms necessary to attract foreign investment. It also began rebuilding villages and towns damaged by severe flooding in August 2002.

In November, officials of NATO invited Slovakia to join the military alliance. In December, EU officials formally approved Slovakia's application for admission and scheduled the nation's entry into the EU for 2004. ☐ Sharon L. Wolchik

See also **Europe.**

Soccer. Brazil defeated Germany 2 to 0 on June 30, 2002, in Yokohama, Japan, to win its fifth Federation Internationale de Football Association (FIFA) World Cup title. In Major League Soccer (MLS), the Los Angeles Galaxy finally won the MLS Cup, having been defeated in three of the previous six finals. Spanish club Real Madrid won a record-extending ninth European Cup in May. The United States women's team beat Canada in the final of the Confederation of North, Central America, and Caribbean Association Football (CONCACAF) Championship in November, with both countries clinching slots in the 2003 Women's World Cup to be held in China.

International soccer. Brazil, fresh off of its World Cup triumph, toppled France from the top of the FIFA World Rankings in July 2002 and remained atop the World Rankings into December, ahead of France and Spain. The United States, which reached its highest ranking ever—eighth—in September, ahead of England and Italy, dropped to ninth by December.

Cameroon successfully defended its African Nations Cup title, defeating Senegal 3 to 2 on penalties after a 0 to 0 draw in Bamako, Mali, on February 10. Nigeria defeated Mali 1 to 0 to take third place. Sixteen countries had qualified to take part in the African Nations Cup tournament, which began January 19.

The U.S. men's team won the 2002 CONCACAF Gold Cup, defeating Costa Rica 2 to 0 in the final at the Rose Bowl in Pasadena, California, on February 2. U.S. midfielder Josh Wolff and defender Jeff Agoos provided the scoring. On its way to its first Gold Cup title since 1991, the U.S. team defeated World Cup co-host, South Korea.

Twelve countries took part in the 2002 tournament. The teams were divided into four groups of three in order to determine the eight teams that would advance to the quarterfinals. The U.S. team survived its group with single-goal wins over South Korea and Cuba. The three teams in Group D—Canada, Haiti, and Ecuador—had identical records and had to draw lots to determine who would advance, with Ecuador losing out. Canada took third place, defeating South Korea 2 to 1 on February 2. Mexico, which was criticized for bringing only a reserve squad to the tournament, won both their group matches before losing to South Korea 4 to 2 on penalties in the quarterfinals.

Canada advanced to the semifinals by defeating Martinique 6 to 5 on penalties after a 1 to 1 draw. The United States swept past El Salvador 4 to 0 thanks largely to a first-half *hat-trick* (three goals in a game) from Brian McBride. In the semifinals, the U.S. team edged Canada 4-2 on penalties after a 0-0 draw, and Costa Rica beat South Korea 3-1.

New Zealand slipped past Australia 1 to 0 to win the Oceania Nations Cup in Auckland, New Zealand, on July 14. New Zealand won the title thanks to a late goal by defender Ryan Nelsen. Australia and New Zealand were overpowering in the first round, with Australia outscoring its opponents 21 to 0 and New Zealand outscoring theirs 19 to 2. Despite its high-powered offense, Australia needed a late equalizer and a golden goal to beat Tahiti to advance to the final match. New Zealand defeated Vanuatu 3 to 0 to reach the final.

Turkey, which took third place in the 2002 World Cup, was invited to fill the last slot in the schedule for the 2003 Confederations Cup to be held in France in June 2003. Turkey joined world champion Brazil and the champions of the other six confederations—France (Europe), Colombia (South America), the United States (CONCACAF), Cameroon (Africa), Japan (Asia), and New Zealand (Oceania).

The United States defeated Ecuador 1 to 0 on Nov. 15, 2002, at Charleston, South Carolina, to advance to the 2003 World Youth (Under-20) Championship. Two days later, Canada defeated the United States 3 to 2 to also win the opportunity to participate in the tournament, which was scheduled to be held in March 2003 in the United Arab Emirates. Panama and Mexico were the two other CONCACAF countries to qualify.

International club competition. Real Madrid (Spain) defeated Bayer Leverkusen (Germany) 2 to 1 in the final of the European Cup at Hampden Park, Glasgow, Scotland, on May 15, 2002. France international captain Zinedine Zidane scored the winning goal in the 44th minute with a spectacular left-foot volley from the edge of the penalty area. In addition to Zidane's brilliant play, substitute goalkeeper Iker Casillas made a significant contribution, entering the game in the 66th minute and making three extraordinary saves in stoppage time.

Olimpia (Paraguay) won the 2002 Copa Libertadores (South American club championship) on July 31, defeating Sao Caetano 4 to 2 on penalties in Sao Paulo. Olimpia had lost the first leg of the final 1 to 0 at Asuncion, Paraguay, but came back to win the overall title.

Real Madrid defeated Olimpia 2 to 0 on December 3 in Yokohama, Japan, in the match for the 2002 World Club Cup. The match is held annually between the club champions of Europe and South America. Real Madrid's World Cup hero Ronaldo and substitute player Guti each scored a goal.

Major League Soccer (MLS). The Los Angeles Galaxy won the 2002 Major League Soccer championships, defeating the New England Revolution 1 to 0 in the final of the MLS Cup at Gillette Stadium in Foxboro, Massachusetts, on October 20. Los Angeles striker Carlos Ruiz scored the winner with eight minutes left in the second period of sudden-death overtime.

The goal capped a terrific season for Ruiz, who signed with the Galaxy in February after being discovered while playing in a Guatemalan municipal league. He scored a league-leading 24 goals during the regular season and an additional 7 goals in the play-offs, setting a new play-off record. Ruiz was named most valuable player (MVP) of both the tournament final and the regular season. The final drew a crowd of 61,316 fans, the largest in MLS Cup history.

Women's soccer. The United States won the CONCACAF Women's Gold Cup, defeating Canada 2 to 1 on a golden goal by Mia Hamm on Nov. 9, 2002, in the Rose Bowl. Striker Tiffeny Milbrett scored after 27 minutes to give the United States the lead, but Canada's Charmaine Hooper scored an equalizer two minutes into stoppage time at the end of the first half. Hamm scored her golden goal four minutes into overtime.

Eight teams from North and Central America and the Caribbean took part in the tournament. The teams were divided into two groups of four, with the first- and second-place countries in each group advancing to the semifinals. The U.S. team won all three first-round matches to win their group, including a 9 to 0 drubbing of Panama in which Milbrett scored five goals to tie the U.S. women's team record for an international match. Milbrett went on to be named MVP of the tournament and to share the Golden Boot for most goals (7) with Canada's Hooper and Christine Sinclair. Canada also went undefeated in the first round, including an 11 to 1 beating of Haiti. In the semifinals, the United States cruised past Costa Rica 7 to 0, while Canada scraped by with a 2 to 0 victory over Mexico with the help of two own-goals. By reaching the final, both the United States and Canada automatically qualified for the 2003 Women's World Cup in China.

The United States won the inaugural FIFA Under-19 Women's World Championship, beating Canada 1 to 0 in the final in Edmonton, Canada, on Sept. 1, 2002. The U.S. team won on a sudden-death golden goal by team captain Lindsay Tarpley in the 19th minute of overtime.

Player awards. Ronaldo, who played for Real Madrid and led Brazil to its World Cup title in 2002, was named FIFA men's World Player of the Year on December 17. The award was determined by a poll of 148 national coaches. Mia Hamm, a striker on the U.S. national team, was named the 2002 woman's World Player of the Year. It was the second year in a row that Hamm received the award.　　　　□ Norman Barrett

Brazil restored its reputation as a soccer power, winning its fifth World Cup title in 2002.

Two soccer powerhouses, Brazil and Germany, battled to the final in the 17th Federation Internationale de Football Association (FIFA) World Cup in 2002. Brazil overpowered Germany 2 to 0 in the final on June 30 in Yokohama, Japan, to win its record-breaking fifth World Cup. Turkey defeated South Korea 3 to 2 on June 29 in Daegu, Korea, to take third place.

The 2002 World Cup featured 32 of the best soccer teams in the world. The teams were whittled down from a large opening field with a series of qualifying tournaments taking place over the previous two years.

The 17th FIFA World Cup was the first ever to be held in Asia and the first to be hosted by two countries—South Korea and Japan. The teams of both host countries, encouraged by large and noisy crowds attending the matches, were more successful than most fans had expected. While the teams of two World Cup favorites, France, the defending champions, and Argentina, lost out far earlier in the tournament than expected.

U.S. team surprises. The United States surprised many soccer fans, battling past heavily favored Portugal 3 to 2 on June 5. The U.S. team then drew a match with South Korea and, despite losing a game to Poland, qualified for the knockout stage. The U.S. team made it all the way to the quarterfinals, the best performance of a U.S. team in a World Cup tournament since the United States took fourth place in 1930. The U.S. team's performance in 2002 was all the more impressive considering that the team had finished in last place at the 1998 World Cup tournament in France.

2002 WORLD CUP (FIRST ROUND)

W Win **L** Loss **T** Tie **PTS** Points **GF** Goals (For) **GA** Goals (Against)
x Advanced to second round

Group A	W	L	T	PTS	GF	GA
x Denmark	2	0	1	7	5	2
x Senegal	1	0	2	5	5	4
Uruguay	0	1	2	2	4	5
France	0	2	1	1	0	3
Group B						
x Spain	3	0	0	9	9	4
x Paraguay	1	1	1	4	6	6
South Africa	1	1	1	4	5	5
Slovenia	0	3	0	0	2	7
Group C						
x Brazil	3	0	0	9	11	3
x Turkey	1	1	1	4	5	3
Costa Rica	1	1	1	4	5	6
China	0	3	0	0	0	9
Group D						
x South Korea	2	0	1	7	4	1
x United States	1	1	1	4	5	6
Portugal	1	2	0	3	6	4
Poland	1	2	0	3	3	7
Group E						
x Germany	2	0	1	7	11	1
x Ireland	1	0	2	5	5	2
Cameroon	1	1	1	4	2	3
Saudi Arabia	0	3	0	0	0	12
Group F						
x Sweden	1	0	2	5	4	3
x England	1	0	2	5	2	1
Argentina	1	1	1	4	2	2
Nigeria	0	2	1	1	1	3
Group G						
x Mexico	2	0	1	7	4	2
x Italy	1	1	1	4	4	3
Croatia	1	2	0	3	2	3
Ecuador	1	2	0	3	2	4
Group H						
x Japan	2	0	1	7	5	2
x Belgium	1	0	2	5	6	5
Russia	1	2	0	3	4	4
Tunisia	0	2	1	1	1	5

The poor performance of France, the defending World Cup champion, provided one of the biggest surprises of the 2002 tournament. France opened the tournament with a stunning 1 to 0 loss to Senegal in Seoul, South Korea, on May 31 and never recovered. France finished last in its group without scoring a single goal.

Germany opened at full speed, thrashing Saudi Arabia 8 to 0 on June 1, by far the biggest win of the tournament. Argentina, which has two World Cup titles under its belt, was eliminated after drawing a match 1 to 1 with Sweden on June 12. Italy, which has won three previous World Cup titles, managed to squeeze into the knockout round after Croatia's shocking loss to Ecuador. Brazil and Spain were the only two teams in the field to win all three first-stage matches.

In the last 16, South Korea eliminated Italy with a late equalizer and a sudden-death golden-goal winner. Senegal knocked Sweden from contention with a golden-goal winner, and Spain edged Ireland 3 to 2 on penalties. The U.S. team reached the last eight for the first time since 1930, downing Mexico 2 to 0 with goals by Brian McBride and Landon Donovan in a performance that was a tribute to coach Bruce Arena's

Ronaldo, Brazil's star striker, scores the first goal in Brazil's victory over Germany in the World Cup final on June 30, 2002. Ronaldo was named the World Cup most valuable player.

tactics and organization. Although the United States lost to Germany 1 to 0 in the quarterfinals, the U.S. team confirmed that it was closing the gap with the world's top teams.

In other quarterfinal action, Brazil beat England 2 to 1, despite playing the last half hour with only 10 men. Turkey surprised many fans, reaching the semifinals for the first time and taking third place. South Korea became the first Asian team to make the semifinals, having defeated Spain 5 to 3 on penalties in the quarterfinals.

Some fans were not pleased with the lack of drama in the final match between Brazil and Germany on June 30 in Yokohama. Brazilian star Ronaldo made up for his disappointing 1998 World Cup performance and notched both of Brazil's goals. Ronaldo scored eight goals in the tournament, earning him the Golden Boot as the 2002 top scorer. Ronaldo also collected his 12th career World Cup goal, matching the mark of the legendary Brazilian player Pele.

■ Norman Barrett

SECOND ROUND

England	3
Denmark	0
Belgium	0
Brazil	2
Senegal	1 (2)
Sweden	1 (1)
Turkey	1
Japan	0
Germany	1
Paraguay	0
United States	2
Mexico	0
Spain	1 (1) (3)
Ireland	1 (1) (2)
Italy	1 (1)
S.Korea	1 (2)

QUARTERFINALS

Brazil	2
England	1
Turkey	0 (1)
Senegal	0 (0)
Germany	1
United States	0
S. Korea	0 (0) (5)
Spain	0 (0) (3)

SEMIFINALS

Brazil	1
Turkey	0
Germany	1
S. Korea	0

FINAL

Brazil	2
Germany	0

THIRD PLACE

Turkey	3
S. Korea	2

Soccer fans in Sao Paulo, Brazil, celebrate Brazil's victory in the 2002 World Cup on June 30. The victory gave Brazil its fifth World Cup title, more than any other country.

U.S. striker Landon Donovan (left) hugs U.S. goalkeeper Brad Friedel as they celebrate the U.S. team's advance to the quarterfinals after defeating Mexico.

Social Security. Social Security Administration (SSA) Commissioner Jo Anne Barnhart announced in October 2002 that Social Security benefits would increase by 1.4 percent beginning in January 2003 for more than 50 million recipients. The increase covers the 46 million people receiving Social Security benefits and 7 million recipients of Supplemental Security Income, which guarantees an annual income to needy people who are 65 years or older, blind, or disabled. The 2003 cost-of-living increase is less than the 2.6 increase received in 2002.

SSA officials announced in February the launch of a program to help people with disabilities get into the work force. The voluntary program offers people receiving disability benefits through Social Security free vocational rehabilitation, job training, and other support. Only about 1 percent of people receiving disability benefits return to work in a given year.

Approximately 2.4 million people in 13 states were invited to participate in the first phase of the program, which began in February. Another 21 states were scheduled to participate in a second phase of the program by the end of 2002. The remaining states were scheduled to implement the program in 2003.

☐ Geoffrey A. Campbell
See also **United States, Government of the.**

South Africa. Thabo Mbeki's leadership as president of South Africa continued to generate controversy in 2002. In his annual address at the opening of parliament on February 8, President Mbeki committed his ruling African National Congress (ANC) to fighting poverty but refrained from addressing the issue of providing AIDS drugs to pregnant women infected with HIV, the virus that causes AIDS. Mbeki's government had actively opposed such a policy, drawing protests from international and domestic AIDS activists and health advocacy groups. South African courts weighed in decisively on the issue in 2002.

In neighboring Zimbabwe, Robert Mugabe won reelection as president in March in polling widely regarded as rigged. Despite mounting international protest against the regime in Zimbabwe, President Mbeki continued to support Mugabe in 2002.

AIDS ruling. South Africa's most powerful judicial body, the Constitutional Court, ruled in April that Mbeki's government must obey a December 2001 court ruling regarding AIDS policy. The court had ruled that the South African government must offer a key anti-HIV medication, Nevirapine, to HIV-positive pregnant women at state hospitals and clinics. Nevirapine helps prevent mother-to-baby transmission of HIV in up to 50 percent of women receiving the drug. Mbeki's

government had repeatedly refused to allow Nevirapine to be dispensed in public health facilities, claiming it was too expensive, toxic, and difficult to administer.

According to statistics reported in July 2002 by the United Nations (UN) Program on HIV/AIDS, 70,000 babies were born HIV-positive in South Africa every year, and about 20 percent of South Africa's total population was HIV-infected.

Life expectancy. A report released in April by NGM-Levy, a financial services company based in Johannesburg, South Africa, predicted that the AIDS epidemic would drastically reduce the life expectancy of South Africans. NGM-Levy predicted that the life expectancy of women in South Africa would fall from 54 years in 1999 to 37 years in 2010. The report said that male life expectancy would decline to 38 years by 2010, down from about 52 years in 1999.

Regional relations. President Mbeki's policy of "quiet diplomacy" toward neighboring Zimbabwe came under sharp attack from domestic and international critics following the reelection of Zimbabwean President Robert Mugabe in March 2002. Mbeki—nearly alone among world leaders—endorsed the election results, despite evidence of violent intimidation and ballot-rigging on the part of Mugabe's ruling party, the Zimbabwe African National Union-Patriotic Front. Many political and business leaders in South Africa, along with the editorial boards of many of the country's newspapers, warned that Mbeki's stance on Mugabe would damage South Africa's political and economic credibility in the international arena.

Some economic analysts said that threats to democracy and economic stability in Zimbabwe were harming South Africa's economy and pointed to the decline of the *rand,* South Africa's currency, and the weak investment climate throughout southern Africa as evidence. Zimbabwe is South Africa's chief regional trading partner.

Winnie Madikizela-Mandela, ex-wife of former President Nelson Mandela, pleaded not guilty to 85 charges of fraud and theft in a Pretoria court on July 9, 2002. If convicted, she faced up to 15 years in prison.

Winnie Mandela became known to many black South Africans as the "mother of the nation" during the long battle against *apartheid,* the system of racial separation that was brutally enforced in the country before 1994. She had received a jail sentence for kidnapping and assault following the 1989 killing by her bodyguard of 14-year-old activist Stompie Moeketsi Seipei, but the sentence was suspended on appeal. Winnie Madikizela-Mandela held a seat in South Africa's national assembly in 2002 and still commanded significant support among South Africa's poorest citizens, political experts said.

White extremists. Three senior Army officers were among 23 white South Africans charged with treason and similar offenses between August and October for their part in an alleged plot to stage a military *coup* (government takeover) and restore white minority rule. When a series of bomb blasts tore through the black township of Soweto on October 30, killing one woman, a white supremacist group claimed responsibility. The explosions, together with the earlier arrests, heightened fears that right-wing groups might be conspiring to overthrow the country's black-majority government.

Sports. Disgraced former South African cricket player Hansie Cronje died at age 32 in an airplane crash in South Africa on June 1. A board of inquiry had banned Cronje from professional cricket in 2002 after the athlete admitted accepting money to help *fix* (unfairly influence the outcome of) cricket matches. Cronje, who had led the South African team in its return to the international arena in the 1990's when South Africa's apartheid-era isolation ended, remained highly popular with the public. His funeral was broadcast on South African television.   □ Simon Baynham

See also **Africa; AIDS; Cricket; Zimbabwe.**

Space exploration. The International
Space Station continued to be the focus of human space flight in 2002. Four of the five space shuttle missions were flown to the space station, to continue construction of the orbital outpost and to support research activities.

"Open-heart surgery." The first shuttle mission of 2002, however, was not to the station but to the Hubble Space Telescope, the fourth such flight to the observatory since it was launched in 1990. Seven astronauts flew on the shuttle Columbia on March 1, 2002, to undertake an 11-day repair mission. Alternating pairs of astronauts conducted a series of spacewalks to add new arrays of solar-power cells to generate electricity for the observatory. The astronauts also installed a new camera and an advanced refrigeration unit to allow another, infrared, camera to continue working. Their most delicate task, however, was replacing a power-control unit. Because the repair required shutting down the Hubble, it was likened by the telescope's controllers to open-heart surgery, during which the heart is shut down then jump-started.

Destination station. On April 8, the Atlantis lifted off with a crew of seven and a critical piece of hardware for the station. The component, called the S-Zero truss, had been designed to form a high-tech backbone for the space station.

The first piece of the truss was packed with equipment, including utility lines, computers, and rails upon which a mobile transporter, which would carry the station's 58-foot- (18-meter-) long Canadian-built robot arm, would move. The shuttle crew used the shuttle's manipulator arm to place the truss atop the Destiny module. Later in the mission, spacewalking astronauts installed the mobile transporter on the truss.

The Endeavour lifted off on June 5 with seven astronauts and an Italian-built supply module, called Leonardo, loaded with supplies and the mobile base for the Canadian robot arm's transporter. Astronauts installed the base, which allowed it to move along the space station's truss work. On the three spacewalks of the mission, the astronauts also replaced a joint in the robot arm. Three of the Endeavour's astronauts—two Russians and an American—became the station's Expedition 5 crew, replacing the Expedition 4 crew of one Russian and two Americans. The two Americans—Dan Bursch and Carl Walz—returned on the Endeavour after 196 days in space, a U.S. space endurance record. Endeavour astronaut Franklin Chang-Diaz tied Atlantis crew member Jerry L. Ross's seven-mission record.

On October 7, the Atlantis took off on an 11-day mission. The six astronauts on board installed another large section of the truss on the station.

The Endeavour lifted off on November 23 for the 113th shuttle flight, the 16th flight to the station. Endeavour carried another section of the truss and the station's Expedition 6 crew, two U.S. astronauts and a Russian cosmonaut. The truss section was installed during three spacewalks. It contained an enhanced communications system for voice and data and another mobile work platform, which was designed to help space station astronauts move along the truss. One of the astronauts aboard Endeavour, John B. Herrington of the Chickasaw tribe, was the first Native American to fly in space.

Signs of age. The National Aeronautics and Space Administration's (NASA) fleet of four shuttle orbiters, first launched in the 1980's, began showing their age in 2002. In June, technicians discovered tiny cracks in the metal liners inside pipes that carry hydrogen fuel from the shuttles' external tanks to their main engines. NASA grounded the shuttle fleet until engineers determined how to repair the cracks.

Cracks were also found in bearings on the huge mobile crawlers that move shuttles from the building where the orbiter, booster rockets, and fuel tank are assembled to their launch pads. The crawlers have been in use for more than 35 years.

China's manned spacecraft. China in 2002 took another step closer toward becoming the

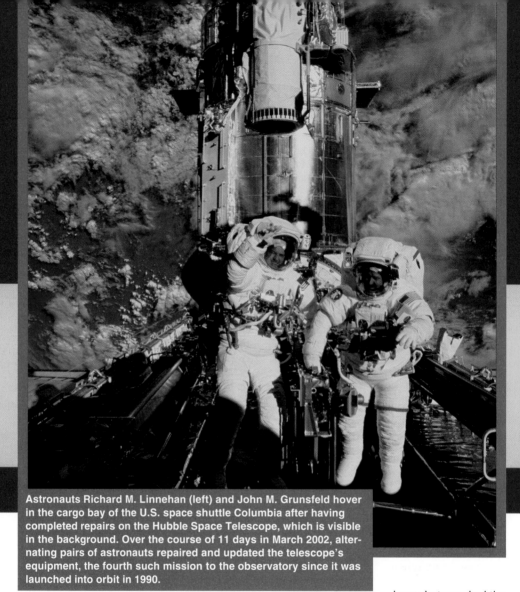

Astronauts Richard M. Linnehan (left) and John M. Grunsfeld hover in the cargo bay of the U.S. space shuttle Columbia after having completed repairs on the Hubble Space Telescope, which is visible in the background. Over the course of 11 days in March 2002, alternating pairs of astronauts repaired and updated the telescope's equipment, the fourth such mission to the observatory since it was launched into orbit in 1990.

third nation capable of launching humans into space. On March 25 and December 30, it conducted the third and fourth launches of its Shenzhou spacecraft without a crew. The Shenzhou closely resembles the three-person Russian Soyuz spacecraft but appears somewhat larger.

Space tourism. On April 25, Mark Shuttleworth, a South African Internet tycoon, became the second "tourist" to fly into space. Like U.S. entrepreneur Dennis Tito, who flew in April 2001, Shuttleworth bought a seat on one of Russia's Soyuz spacecraft, reportedly for more than $10 million. The flight delivered the Soyuz to the space station, where it would replace another Soyuz. The vehicles are kept at the station for emergency escapes. Because only two cosmonauts are needed to fly a Soyuz, the Russian space program can sell the third seat.

Lost in space. A U.S. spacecraft that was to

have photographed the *nuclei* (centers) of two comets was lost in August 2002. Its controllers believe the Contour (for Comet Nucleus Tour) exploded during the firing of a built-in, solid-fuel rocket motor that was to propel it out of Earth's orbit. Contour was launched July 3 from Cape Canaveral, Florida.

Environmental satellites. The European Space Agency on February 28 launched a satellite called Envisat from Kourou in French Guiana to study Earth's land, atmosphere, oceans, and icecaps on a five-year mission. Weighing 8.2 tons (7.4 metric tons), Envisat is the largest and heaviest satellite ever built in Europe.

With the flight of its Aqua spacecraft on April 18, NASA began a mission, costing nearly $1 billion, to study the world's oceans. Like Envisat, Aqua was launched into an orbit that takes it nearly over Earth's poles, allowing the satellite to photograph the entire surface of the planet.

Astronauts Rex J. Walheim (left) and Steven L. Smith work on a mobile transporter system just above the Destiny laboratory of the International Space Station in April 2002. The transporter will allow the station's robotic arm to move along a *truss* (the station's external framework) during future assembly and repair missions. During the same mission, astronaut Jerry L. Ross (above), tethered to the station's robot arm, installs a part that will give astronauts easy acces to the truss from the airlock, a module through which astronauts on future missions will leave and enter the station during spacewalks.

Gravity map. On March 17, a European/Russian Rockot launch vehicle blasted off from the Plesetsk Cosmodrome in Russia with a pair of satellites designed to map tiny variations in the Earth's gravity field. Although such differences had been measured before, the Gravity Recovery And Climate Experiment (Grace) was to detect differences in the gravity field over time. The differences could point to changes, such as declines in underground water supplies or oil fields.

Fire two. Two large U.S. launch vehicles flew for the first time in 2002. Both were developed by the U.S. Air Force and private industry to update the technology on U.S. single-use, or "expendable," rockets and their launch pads at Cape Canaveral, Florida. The first, Atlas V, built by Lockheed Martin Corporation, used Russian engines, and flew on August 21. It carried the Hot Bird 6 satellite into orbit for Paris-based Eutelsat. On November 20, the first Boeing-built Delta IV lifted off from Cape Canaveral. It carried another large telecommunications satellite, called W5, also for Eutelsat. ☐ James R. Asker

See also **Astronomy.**

Spain. Tensions between the government of Spain and Basque separatist groups intensified during 2002. The terrorist group ETA, whose initials stand for Basque Homeland and Freedom in the Basque language, stepped up its terror campaign for an independent Basque homeland in northern Spain and southwestern France. The violence has claimed more than 800 lives since it began in the late 1960's.

The government of Spain began a crackdown on ETA in June 2002, after parliament passed the Political Parties Law. The law allows Spain's supreme court to outlaw political parties that support terrorist attitudes. After a terrorist bomb in the resort town of Santa Pola killed a 6-year-old girl in June, a judge ordered the suspension of Batasuna, a political party linked to ETA. Police closed down the party's headquarters. In August, the parliament requested the country's supreme court to outlaw the party permanently.

Spain's economy declined dramatically in 2002 as part of the worldwide slowdown. European Union (EU) economists forecast that Spain's *gross domestic product* (the country's total output of goods and services) would grow by 1.9 percent in 2002, down from 2.7 percent in 2001. Many big Spanish companies suffered as a result of a severe recession in Argentina and other parts of Latin America, where Spanish interests had invested heavily during the 1990's.

EU policies. Spain helped forge a significant European agreement in the first half of 2002, when it held the EU's rotating presidency. At a summit meeting in Seville in June, EU leaders passed a common asylum and immigration policy. The leaders agreed that countries should take back their own nationals who have illegally immigrated to other European nations.

Territories. A dispute over an islet in the Straits of Gibraltar harmed relations between Spain and Morocco in 2002. Moroccan troops landed on the unpopulated islet in July, prompting Spanish troops to evict them at gunpoint.

Tension also flared on the issue of sovereignty over Gibraltar, a British territory located on a peninsula off Spain's southern coast. Spain ceded Gibraltar to Great Britain in 1713 but in recent years has sought its return or a possible joint rule of the area. The 30,000 inhabitants of Gibraltar expressed overwhelming disapproval of both possibilities in a referendum in November 2002.

An oil spill 150 miles (245 kilometers) off the northwest coast of Spain in November turned into a major ecological disaster as the thick fuel oil fouled the coastline, endangered wildlife, and threatened the $330-million seafood industry. The spill occurred after a tanker, the *Prestige,* broke into two pieces and sank in bad weather. □ Tom Buerkle

See also **Environmental pollution; Europe.**

People in Gibraltar wave the flags of the colony and the United Kingdom (U.K.) in March 2002 to protest the possibility that the U.K. might share sovereignty over the colony with Spain. Spain ceded Gibraltar to Great Britain in 1713. In recent years, however, Spain has sought its return or a possible joint rule.

Sports. Fans in 2002 witnessed dominating individual performances. Lance Armstrong of the United States continued to dominate cycling, winning the Tour de France in July to become the first American to win that race four consecutive times. Ed Moses of the United States broke five short-course swimming world records in eight days in January. Eldrick "Tiger" Woods dominated the sport of golf in the first half of the Professional Golfers' Association (PGA) season. Martin Strel of Slovenia in September became the first person to swim the entire length of the Mississippi River.

Venus and Serena Williams dominated women's tennis to an unprecedented degree. The sisters battled each other in the finals of three of the four Grand Slam tournaments. In June, they became the first siblings ever to hold the top two positions in the world tennis rankings.

In professional team sports, the Los Angeles Lakers won their third straight National Basketball Association (NBA) title; the Detroit Red Wings rolled to the Stanley Cup in the National Hockey League (NHL); and the Anaheim Angels won Major League Baseball's (MLB) World Series. In professional football, the New England Patriots scored one of the biggest upsets in National Football League (NFL) history, upending the defending champion St. Louis Rams in Super Bowl XXXVI in February.

Tour de France. On July 28, Lance Armstrong crossed the finish line in Paris to win his fourth consecutive Tour de France. Armstrong easily beat his closest foe in the 20-stage, 2,036-mile (3,277-kilometer) bicycle race, defeating Joseba Beloki of Spain by 7 minutes, 17 seconds.

The route of the race had been changed from previous years so that the riders faced the mountain stages later in the race. The change was made in the hope that it would make the event more competitive. However, Armstrong, as he had in his previous Tour victories, made his move in the mountains, winning stage 11, the first mountain stage, on July 18 to take a 1-minute, 12-second lead. Armstrong never looked back, finishing the race in 82 hours, 5 minutes, and 12 seconds. Armstrong averaged 24.8 miles (40 kilometers) per hour during the race.

In August, French police ended their nearly two-year investigation of the United States Postal Service cycling team, of which Armstrong is the leader. The investigation centered on allegations that Armstrong's team had used performance-enhancing drugs during the 2000 Tour de France. Authorities dropped the investigation after finding no evidence of banned substances in samples of blood and urine that had been taken from U.S. Postal Service team members during that race.

Moses dominates. Ed Moses of the United States broke five short-course world records in eight days in 2002. Moses began by breaking the 200-meter breaststroke mark in 2 minutes, 4.37 seconds. On January 22, he broke the world records in the 50-meter and 200-meter breaststroke. The following day, Moses broke the 100-meter breaststroke mark. Then, on January 26 in Berlin, Moses broke his 200-meter breaststroke record for the third time, finishing in 2 minutes, 3.17 seconds.

Tiger roars. Tiger Woods blew away the competition in the first half of the 2002 PGA season. Woods won the Masters in April and took the U.S. Open in June. With his victory at the U.S. Open, Woods became the first golfer since Jack Nicklaus in 1972 to win the first two majors in a single season. However, Woods was not able to maintain this torrid pace. He failed to win the other two majors in 2002, the British Open and the PGA Championship. He made a furious charge at the PGA Championship, making birdies on his last four holes, but lost by one stroke.

River swimmer. Martin Strel of Slovenia on Sept. 9, 2002, became the first person to swim the entire length of the Mississippi River, completing the 2,340-mile (3,766-kilometer) odyssey in 68 days. Strel began his journey on July 4 at Lake Itasca, Minnesota. He set a goal of swimming an average of 11 hours a day. On his longest single day of swimming, Strel covered 50 miles (80 kilometers). When he reached the Gulf of Mexico, Strel had bettered his own world record for the longest swim. In 2000, he swam the entire length of Europe's 1,777-mile- (2,860-kilometer-) long Danube River.

Vote-trading scandal. The figure-skating scandal that erupted in February 2002 at the Winter Olympics in Salt Lake City, Utah, exploded again in midsummer. In July, Italian police, with assistance from U.S. law enforcement officials, arrested Alimzhan Tokhtakhounov, a Russian living in Italy. Tokhtakhounov, who reportedly had ties to organized crime in Russia, was alleged to have orchestrated the Olympic vote-swapping scheme. The controversy involved the pairs skating competition at the Winter Olympics, in which Elena Berezhnaya and Anton Sikharulidze of Russia were judged the winners despite a flawed performance. The judges had voted 5-4 in favor of the Russians over the Canadian pair, Jamie Sale and David Pelletier, who had performed a nearly perfect routine. The decision came under scrutiny when French figure-skating judge Marie Reine Le Gougne told Olympic officials that she had been pressured to vote for the Russian team. Olympic officials later awarded gold medals to both pairs.

Tokhtakhounov allegedly contacted several Olympic judges in an effort to get the judges to trade votes so that the French team would win the ice-dancing competition. U.S. prosecutors al-

Lance Armstrong of the United States Postal Service team flashes four fingers, signifying his fourth Tour de France victory at the end of the prestigious bicycle race in Paris on July 28. Armstrong was the first American to win the Tour de France four times in a row.

leged that Tokhtakhounov attempted to fix the competition to win favor from French officials, from whom he was trying to secure a visa.

Mount Everest record. Fifty-four mountain climbers and their guides reached the summit of Mount Everest, the world's highest peak, on May 16, 2002, the most climbers to ever reach the summit on a single day. Mount Everest is located on the border between Nepal and Tibet. The climbers had to scale up a narrow path to the summit one person at a time.

Awards. The International Amateur Athletic Association awarded swimmer Ian Thorpe of Australia the American-International Athlete Trophy in March. The award was formerly known as the Jesse Owens International Trophy. Thorpe, an

Olympic and world champion, captured a record six gold medals at the 2001 world championships.

In April 2002, figure skater Michelle Kwan received the 2001 James E. Sullivan Award, which is presented to the best amateur athlete in the United States. Kwan is just the second figure skater to win the award, joining Dick Button, who received the award in 1949.

NBA crime. Former NBA player Jayson Williams, who retired in 2000 after suffering leg injuries, was charged with manslaughter and tampering with evidence in connection with the shooting death of limousine driver Costas Christofi on Feb. 14, 2002. According to police reports, Christofi drove some of Williams's friends to the basketball player's New Jersey estate. Christofi was invited inside and later died of a single gunshot to the chest. Police said Williams apparently fired the shot accidentally while handling a rifle. Williams and some of his friends then allegedly tampered with evidence to make it appear that Christofi had committed suicide. The trial was set to begin in 2003.

Webber indicted. Chris Webber, a member of the NBA's Sacramento Kings, was indicted on Sept. 9, 2002, for lying to a federal grand jury. The grand jury was investigating Ed Martin, a supporter of the basketball program at the University of Michigan at Ann Arbor. Officials charged Webber, who attended Michigan from 1988 to 1993, with obstruction of justice and making a false declaration before a grand jury. The indictment, which also named Webber's father and aunt, accused the three of lying to the grand jury and conspiring to conceal money and gifts that Martin allegedly gave Webber. In May 2002, Martin had pleaded guilty to conspiracy to launder money. Several of Webber's former Michigan teammates admitted receiving gifts from Martin. If convicted, Webber faced up to 10 years in prison and a $500,000 fine.

Hockey fan dies. On March 18, Brittanie Cecil, 13, became the first spectator to be killed by a puck at an NHL game. The puck struck Cecil in the head during a Columbus (Ohio) Blue Jackets home game on March 16. She died two days later. In June, the NHL Board of Governors ruled that all teams had to install safety netting behind the goals and raise the height of the glass shields around the rinks.

Other notable deaths. Several sports legends died in 2002, including baseball's Ted Williams, 83, the last Major Leaguer to hit .400 in a season; football's Johnny Unitas, 69, who threw touchdown passes in a record 47 consecutive NFL games; and golf's Sam Snead, 89, who won a record 81 PGA titles.

Among the winners in 2002 were—

Gymnastics. Tasha Schwikert of Las Vegas, Nevada, won her second straight U.S. Championships title on August 10 in Cleveland, Ohio.

Rodeo. Trevor Brazile of Anson, Texas, won the All-Around World Champion Cowboy title in the National Finals Rodeo on December 15.

Sled-dog racing. Martin Buser of Big Lake, Alaska, won the Iditarod Trail Sled Dog Race on March 12 in record time, finishing the 1,100-mile (1,770-kilometer) trip across Alaska from Anchorage to Nome in 8 days, 22 hours, 46 minutes, and 2 seconds.

Shooting. Russians took 51 medals, 21 of them gold, in July at the World Shooting Championships in Lahti, Finland.

Soap box derby. Evan Griffin of Winter Park,

Florida, won the Masters world championship race held in Akron, Ohio, on July 27.

Speed skating. Dong-Sung Kim of South Korea swept all of the men's events, and Yang Yang A. of China won the women's overall title for the sixth straight year at the World Short Track Championships, held in Montreal, Canada, in April. Yang Yang won the 500-meter, 1,000-meter, and 1,500-meter races.

Triathlon. Ivan Rana of Spain won the men's title at the World Championships in Cancun, Mexico, in November. Leanda Cave of the United Kingdom won the women's title.

Weightlifting. Hossein Reza Zadeh of Iran won the men's gold medal in the 231-pound- (105-kilogram-) plus total weight class at the World Weightlifting Championships in Warsaw, Poland, on November 24. Agata Wrobel of Poland won the women's gold medal in the 165-pound- (75-kilogram-) plus total weight class.

Wrestling. Dremiel Byers of the United States won the 264 ½-pound (120-kilogram) title at the Greco-Roman World Championships in Moscow on September 22. Two-time Olympic champion Armen Nazarian of Bulgaria won the 132-pound (60-kilogram) title; Varteres Samurgashev of Russia won at 163 pounds (74 kilograms); and Mehmet Ozal of Turkey won at 211 ¾ pounds (96-kilograms). Jimmy Samuelsson of Sweden won at 145 ½ pounds (66 kilograms); Geidar Mamedaliyev of Russia won at 121 pounds (55 kilograms); and Sweden's Ara Abrahamian won at 185 pounds (84 kilograms).

At the Freestyle World Championships in Tehran, Iran, in September, the following wrestlers won gold medals: Roberto Montero, Cuba (121 ¼ pounds [55 kilograms]); Harun Dogan, Turkey (132 ¼ pounds [60 kilograms]); Elbrus Tedeev, Ukraine (145 ½ pounds [66 kilograms]); Mehdi Hadjizadeh, Iran (163 pounds [74 kilograms]); Adam Saitiev, Russia (185 pounds [84 kilograms]); Eldar Kurtanidze, Georgia (211 ¾ pounds [96 kilograms]); and David Moussoulbes, Russia (264 ½ pounds [120 kilograms]). The United States wrestling team did not compete in Iran, citing fears of possible terrorist attacks.

Other champions

Archery. At the World Field Archery Championships in September, David Cousins of the United States won the men's compound; Catherine Pellen of France won the women's compound; Michele Frangilli of Italy won the men's recurve; Martin Ottosson of Sweden won the men's barebow; Reingold Linhart of Austria won the women's barebow. In team competition, Sweden won both the men's and women's titles.

Badminton. Thomas Cup champion: Indonesia. Uber Cup champion: China.

Canoe-kayak. Women's kayak: Rebecca Giddens, United States; men's canoe single, Michal Martikann, Slovakia; men's kayak, Fabien Le-fevre, France.

Curling. Men's world champion: Canada. Women's world champion: Scotland.

Equestrian. World Cup Equestrian Final individual show jumping champion: Otto Becker, Germany; dressage champion: Ulla Salzgeber, Germany.

Fencing. Men's world champions: Simone Vanni, Italy (foil); Pavel Kolobkov, Russia (epee); and Stanislaw Pozdniakov, Russia (sabre). Women's world champions: Svetlana Bojko, Russia (foil); Hee Hyun, South Korea (epee); Xue Tan, China (sabre).

Field hockey. Champions Trophy gold medal: women, China; men, the Netherlands.

Lacrosse. Men's NCAA champion: Syracuse University. Women's NCAA champion: Princeton University.

Modern pentathlon. Men's world team relay champion: Germany. Men's individual world champion: Michal Sedlecky, Czech Republic. Women's world team relay champion: Czech Republic. Women's individual world champion: Bea Simoka, Hungary.   □ Michael Kates

See also **Baseball; Basketball; Deaths: A Special Report; Football; Golf; Hockey; Ice skating; Olympics: A Special Report; Swimming; Tennis.**

Sri Lanka.

Sri Lanka. The Sri Lankan government and the rebel Liberation Tigers of Tamil Eelam (LTTE) began peace talks in September 2002 aimed at ending a 19-year conflict that had resulted in the deaths of some 64,000 people and devastated the country's economy. In December, Sri Lanka and LTTE representatives agreed to develop a government that would give the Tamils regional *autonomy* (self-government) and end the civil war. The talks were preceded in February by a Norwegian-brokered cease-fire.

The LTTE had been fighting since 1983 for a separate nation for 3.2 million ethnic Tamil Hindus in northeast Sri Lanka. LTTE guerrillas battled government troops controlled by the majority Sinhalese, who are Buddhists. The LTTE also attacked moderate Tamils and Muslims.

Terrorist experts estimated that the LTTE had staged more suicide bombings than all other terrorist organizations in the world combined, and the LTTE had long been listed as a terrorist group by the United States, the United Kingdom, and other countries. One of its suicide bombers killed a Sri Lankan president in 1993. India blamed the LTTE for the murder of a former prime minister in 1991.

International revulsion with terrorism after the attacks on the United States on Sept. 11, 2001, put increased political and financial pressure on the LTTE to negotiate a peace settlement. Following the attacks, several countries froze funds linked to the LTTE and other terrorist groups. This action crippled the group, which received most of its funding from foreign Tamils.

Foreign investors pressured the Sri Lankan government to enter peace talks as well. In March 2002, Sir Lanka's finance minister said the country was in a "state of economic paralysis." Officials agreed Sri Lanka would not attract foreign investment as long as the conflict continued.

Parliamentary elections in 2001 helped move the groups closer to negotiations. Ranil Wickremesinghe became prime minister in December 2001 after his United National Party vowed to renew peace talks with the LTTE, which had broken down under the previous government. In 2002, he became the first prime minister in 20 years to visit Jaffna, the center of Tamil culture.

The first round of peace talks, which took place in Thailand, focused on resettling the 1 million people displaced by the conflict. In December, LTTE and government officials met in Norway and agreed to a governing and peace plan designed to end ethnic bloodshed. The plan allowed the Tamil-dominated regions in the north and east to govern themselves.

□ Henry S. Bradsher

See also **Asia.**

State government.

State government. Republicans broadened their lead over Democrats in state government in the mid-term elections on Nov. 5, 2002. Republicans defeated Democrats in several key gubernatorial races and expanded their control in various state legislatures. Governors and legislators from both parties were forced to cope with sharp declines in their state budgets in 2002.

Election results. Republicans walked away from the November elections holding 26 governorships, compared with the Democrats, who controlled 24 governor's mansions. Republicans, for the first time since 1954, outnumbered Democrats among the more than 7,300 state legislators in the United States. The GOP (for Grand Old Party) gained control of both legislative chambers in 21 states, compared with the Democrats who finished the election in control of the legislatures in 17 states. The remaining statehouses were split between the two primary parties. Nebraska's *unicameral* (single chamber) legislature was nonpartisan.

Governor's races. The Republicans won a total of 22 gubernatorial races in November, and several popular Republican governors retained their offices. In Florida, voters reelected Governor Jeb Bush, the brother of U.S. President George W. Bush and the son of former President George H. W. Bush, to a second term. Jeb Bush

Selected statistics on state governments

State	Resident population*	Governor†	Legislature† House (D)	(R)	Senate (D)	(R)	State tax revenue‡	Tax revenue per capita‡	Public school expenditure per pupil§
Alabama	4,464,356	Bob Riley (R)	64	41	25	10	$ 16,857,000,000	$ 3,790	$ 5,300
Alaska	634,892	Frank Murkowski (R)	13	27	#8	11	8,584,000,000	13,690	9,410
Arizona	5,307,331	Jane Dee Hull (R)	21	39	13	17	16,781,000,000	3,270	4,880
Arkansas	2,692,090	Mike Huckabee (R)	70	30	27	8	10,789,000,000	4,040	5,570
California	34,501,130	Joseph Graham (Gray) Davis (D)	48	32	26	14	172,481,000,000	5,090	6,550
Colorado	4,417,714	Bill F. Owens (R)	28	37	17	18	17,060,000,000	3,970	6,440
Connecticut	3,425,074	John G. Rowland (R)	94	57	21	15	18,007,000,000	5,290	10,260
Delaware	796,165	Ruth Ann Minner (D)	12	29	13	8	5,162,000,000	6,580	9,390
Florida	16,396,515	Jeb Bush (R)	39	81	14	26	51,621,000,000	3,230	6,080
Georgia	8,383,915	Sonny Perdue (R)	**106	73	27	29	29,630,000,000	3,620	7,370
Hawaii	1,224,398	Linda Lingle (R)	36	15	20	5	6,940,000,000	5,730	6,660
Idaho	1,321,006	Dirk Kempthorne (R)	16	54	7	28	5,576,000,000	4,310	5,670
Illinois	12,482,301	Rod Blagojevich (D)	66	52	32	27	48,524,000,000	3,910	8,290
Indiana	6,114,745	Frank L. O'Bannon (D)	51	49	18	32	20,456,000,000	3,360	7,570
Iowa	2,923,179	Tom Vilsack (D)	46	54	21	29	11,340,000,000	3,880	6,360
Kansas	2,694,641	Kathleen Sebelius (D)	45	80	10	30	10,394,000,000	3,870	6,570
Kentucky	4,065,556	Paul E. Patton (D)	65	35	17	21	19,451,000,000	4,810	6,850
Louisiana	4,465,430	Murphy J. (Mike) Foster (R)	71	34	26	13	18,788,000,000	4,200	5,960
Maine	1,286,670	John Baldacci (D)	††80	67	18	17	6,294,000,000	4,940	7,910
Maryland	5,375,156	Robert Erlich (R)	98	43	33	14	21,366,000,000	4,030	7,470
Massachusetts	6,379,304	Mitt Romney (R)	**136	23	34	6	32,011,000,000	5,040	9,210
Michigan	9,990,817	Jennifer Granholm (D)	47	63	16	22	49,512,000,000	4,980	7,460
Minnesota	4,972,294	Tim Pawlenty (R)	52	82	‡‡35	31	26,889,000,000	5,470	7,940
Mississippi	2,858,029	Ronnie Musgrove (D)	§§86	33	33	18	12,181,000,000	4,280	5,270
Missouri	5,629,707	Bob Holden (D)	73	90	14	20	20,309,000,000	3,630	6,200
Montana	904,433	Judy Martz (R)	47	53	21	29	4,204,000,000	4,660	6,350
Nebraska	1,713,235	Mike Johanns (R)	unicameral (49 nonpartisan)				6,185,000,000	3,610	6,400
Nevada	2,106,074	Kenny Guinn (R)	23	19	9	12	7,285,000,000	3,650	5,600
New Hampshire	1,259,181	Craig Benson (R)	119	281	6	18	4,993,000,000	4,040	7,030
New Jersey	8,484,431	James E. McGreevey (D)	44	36	20	20	42,341,000,000	5,030	10,160
New Mexico	1,829,146	Bill Richardson (D)	42	28	24	17	10,570,000,000	5,810	6,280
New York	19,011,378	George E. Pataki (R)	103	47	25	37	111,397,000,000	5,870	10,480
North Carolina	8,186,268	Mike Easley (D)	59	61	28	22	34,361,000,000	4,270	6,170
North Dakota	634,448	John Hoeven (R)	28	66	16	31	3,295,000,000	5,130	4,430
Ohio	11,373,541	Robert Taft (R)	37	62	11	22	55,274,000,000	4,870	6,960
Oklahoma	3,460,097	Brad Henry (D)	53	48	28	20	13,116,000,000	3,800	6,330
Oregon	3,472,867	Ted Kulongoski (D)	25	35	15	15	21,321,000,000	6,230	7,560
Pennsylvania	12,287,150	Ed Rendell (D)	94	109	21	29	54,517,000,000	4,440	7,870
Rhode Island	1,058,920	Don Carcieri (R)	**63	11	32	6	5,589,000,000	5,330	8,920
South Carolina	4,063,011	Mark Sanford (R)	51	73	21	25	15,966,000,000	3,980	6,350
South Dakota	756,600	Mike Rounds (R)	21	49	9	25	2,901,000,000	3,840	5,760
Tennessee	5,740,021	Phil Bredesen (D)	54	45	18	15	18,970,000,000	3,330	5,620
Texas	21,325,018	Rick Perry (R)	62	88	12	19	72,323,000,000	3,470	6,600
Utah	2,269,789	Michael O. Leavitt (R)	19	56	7	22	10,227,000,000	4,580	4,480
Vermont	613,090	James Douglas (R)	##70	73	19	11	3,292,000,000	5,410	8,700
Virginia	7,187,734	Mark Warner (D)	***33	65	17	23	29,409,000,000	4,150	6,380
Washington	5,987,973	Gary Locke (D)	52	46	24	25	30,616,000,000	5,190	6,720
West Virginia	1,801,916	Bob Wise (D)	68	32	24	10	8,591,000,000	4,750	7,820
Wisconsin	5,401,906	Jim Doyle (D)	41	58	15	18	32,119,000,000	5,990	8,150
Wyoming	494,423	Dave Freudenthal (D)	15	45	10	20	5,740,000,000	11,620	7,650

*July 1, 2001 estimates. Source: U.S. Census Bureau.
†As of December 2002. Source: National Governors' Association; National Conference of State Legislatures; state government officials
‡2000 figures.

§2000-2001 estimates for elementary and secondary students in fall enrollment Source: National Education Association.
#One Republican moderate.
**One independent.

††One Green independent, three independents.
‡‡One independent
§§Three independents.
##Three independents, four progressives.
***Two independents.

United States Representative Rod Blagojevich greets supporters after he won the race for Illinois governor in November. Blagojevich became the first Democrat since 1976 to capture the governor's office in Illinois.

had faced a strong challenge from Democrat Bill McBride, a Tampa businessman, after the Democratic Party waged an expensive and well-publicized campaign to unseat the governor. Republicans also retained control of the governor's office in New York, where Governor George Pataki won reelection by a large margin. In Texas, Governor Rick Perry won election to his first full term. Perry had completed the final two years of the term of his predecessor, George W. Bush. Other Republican incumbents who won reelection in 2002 included Mike Huckabee of Arkansas; Bill Owens of Colorado; John G. Rowland of Connecticut; Dirk Kempthorne of Idaho; Mike Johanns of Nebraska; Kenny Guinn of Nevada; and Robert Taft of Ohio.

Republicans also managed two highly unexpected gubernatorial victories in November. In Hawaii, Linda Lingle, the former mayor of Maui, defeated Lieutenant Governor Mazie Hirono, a Democrat, to replace the Democratic incumbent, Governor Benjamin J. Cayetano. Lingle's election marked only the second time in Hawaii's history that a Republican won the governor's race.

In Georgia, Republican Sonny Perdue defeated incumbent Governor Roy Barnes, a Democrat. Various political experts suggested that Barnes's successful effort in 2001 to remove the Confederate battle emblem from prominence on the Geor-

gia state flag contributed to his election defeat.

Other Republican candidates who won first terms as governor in 2002 included Bob Riley of Alabama; Frank H. Murkowski of Alaska; Robert Ehrlich, Jr., of Maryland; Mitt Romney of Massachusetts; Tim Pawlenty of Minnesota; Craig Benson of New Hampshire; Donald Carcieri of Rhode Island; Mark Sanford of South Carolina; Mike Rounds of South Dakota; and James Douglas of Vermont.

The Democrats claimed 14 gubernatorial victories in 2002. However, only two Democratic incumbents were reelected—Gray Davis of California and Tom Vilsack of Iowa. Democrats picked up governorships in two Midwestern states—Illinois and Michigan. In Illinois, U.S. Representative Rod Blagojevich defeated Attorney General Jim Ryan. Republicans had held the governor's office in Illinois since 1977. However, the incumbent, Governor George Ryan, facing allegations of corruption, did not seek reelection in 2002. The scandal, which touched several members of the Illinois Republican Party, contributed to the defeat of several Republicans running for statewide offices.

In Michigan, Jennifer Granholm, the state's attorney general, defeated Republican Lieutenant Governor Dick Posthumus. Republicans had held the governor's office in Michigan since

1990. The incumbent, Governor John Engler, was barred from running for reelection in 2002 due to term limits.

Other Democrats winning first gubernatorial terms included Janet Napolitano of Arizona; Kathleen Sebelius of Kansas; John Baldacci of Maine; Bill Richardson of New Mexico; Brad Henry of Oklahoma; Ted Kulongoski of Oregon; Ed Rendell of Pennsylvania; Phil Bredesen of Tennessee; Jim Doyle of Wisconsin; and Dave Freudenthal of Wyoming.

The country's only two independent governors were not on the ballot in 2002. Governor Angus S. King, Jr., of Maine was prohibited by term limits from running for reelection. The highly colorful Governor Jesse Ventura of Minnesota did not seek reelection.

Ballot measures. More than 200 ballot measures in the November election in 40 states focused on such topics as education, drugs, and animal rights. Most education-related measures received voter approval. In Florida, voters authorized a measure to reduce class sizes for public elementary schools and mandate preschool programs. Voters in California endorsed a measure that extended after-school tutorial and athletic programs to all public schools.

Measures to ease drug laws failed in several states. Arizona voters rejected a proposal to approve the use of marijuana as a medical treatment for some illnesses. Voters in Nevada blocked a measure to legalize the use of small amounts of marijuana for adults over the age of 21. Ohio residents voted against a plan that would have sentenced some people convicted of a drug offense to a treatment center in lieu of a prison sentence.

Animal rights advocates won victories in two states. The voters of Oklahoma banned cockfighting. Florida voters amended the state Constitution to prohibit pork producers from placing pregnant hogs in crates or other enclosures.

State revenues underwent their sharpest decline in fiscal year 2002, which ended on June 30, since the 1980's. Fiscal 2002 state budget gaps totaled nearly $40 billion, according to a survey published in July by the National Conference of State Legislatures (NCSL).

State legislatures were forced to use a variety of measures, often in combination with other plans, to deal with their fiscal shortfalls. The NCSL reported that 29 states cut budgets in an effort to eliminate deficits, 19 states used reserve funds, and 20 states allocated money from various state funds to bolster their general funds.

At least 16 states raised taxes, and another 10 states hiked user fees, mostly involving motor vehicles and drivers licenses. The state legislatures of Indiana, New Jersey, and Pennsylvania raised taxes by more than $1 billion each. Eighteen states increased cigarette and tobacco taxes by a total of $2.9 billion. Overall, states increased taxes by $6.7 billion in 2002, marking the first net tax increase since 1994.

Budget shortfalls forced some states to curb school testing programs in 2002. Oregon officials canceled some writing, math, and science tests to save approximately $4.5 million. Officials in Missouri saved $7 million by reducing the number of state-sponsored examinations administered to schoolchildren.

Homeland security. State legislatures filed more than 1,200 pieces of legislation to combat terrorism in 2002 in response to the terrorist attacks on the United States in 2001. Legislatures increased security at public buildings; passed or increased penalties for terrorist attacks; addressed potential threats to nuclear plants and electric grids; tightened requirements for obtaining state drivers' licenses; and passed legislation aimed at dealing with bioterrorism and cyberterrorism attacks. Cyberterrorism is the use of computer technology to sabotage information systems. All 50 states established offices of homeland security by the end of 2002. □ Elaine Stuart

See also **Democratic Party; Elections; Republican Party; Supreme Court of the United States; United States, Government of the.**

Stocks and bonds. Investors in 2002 suffered a third straight yearly decline in the major stock indexes, as a sluggish United States economy and concern over a war with Iraq depressed business and investment optimism. The decline marked the first period since 1939 through 1941, during the *Great Depression* (a worldwide business slump), that the Dow Jones Industrial Average and the Standard & Poor's 500 (S&P 500) index declined for three consecutive years. The Dow is a composite of the stock prices of 30 major companies traded on the New York Stock Exchange. The S&P 500 is a set of U.S. statistics that are used to measure the level of stock market prices.

A wave of corporate scandals involving formerly prominent companies, such as Enron Corp., the Houston-based energy trading company, and WorldCom, Inc., the Clinton, Mississippi-based telecommunications company, further eroded confidence in businesses and the stock market. Investors withdrew billions of dollars from mutual funds, companies that pool funds from many investors and use them to buy stocks. Many people also switched their investments to savings bonds or low-interest bank savings accounts.

The Dow Jones industrial Average was down 11 percent to 8,896.09 by the end of November. The S&P 500 was down 18 percent in 2002. The Nasdaq Composite Index, which consists of more

than 3,000 stocks traded electronically on the system operated by the Nasdaq Stock Market, fell 24 percent during that same period. The Russell 2000 index of small-company stocks tracked by the Frank Russell Company slumped 18 percent.

The stock market had rallied early in 2002, sending the Dow above 10,600 in March. The move led many financial experts to claim that the rebound reflected evidence that the recession of 2001 had been mild and that the damaging effects of the terrorist attacks on the United States on Sept. 11, 2001, had not lingered. By mid-2002, the stock market again began to decline. After a brief rally, the Dow sank to 7,197.49 on October 10, its lowest point in five years.

Financial analysts claimed that the declining stock market in 2002 meant that whatever economic recovery was underway had not increased the number of available jobs. Economists also said that consumer spending, which had remained strong throughout 2002, would begin to suffer in 2003 without job growth.

Bonds rally. A lack of confidence in the stock market translated into popularity during 2002 for fixed-income debt securities, especially U.S. Treasury bonds issued by the federal government. The yield on 10-year U.S. Treasury bonds, which reflects changes in

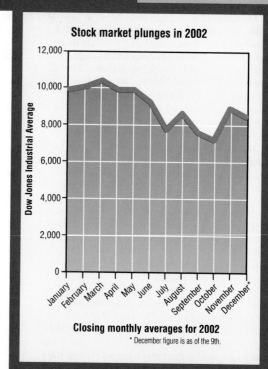

Stock market plunges in 2002

Dow Jones Industrial Average

Closing monthly averages for 2002
* December figure is as of the 9th.

On July 22, 2002, the Dow Jones Industrial average dropped below 8,000 for the first time since 1998. On Oct. 10, 2002, the Dow plunged to 7,197.49, its lowest point in since 1997.

price to accommodate current market rates, fell from 5.02 percent at the end of 2001 to 3.54 percent in October 2002. When bond yields fall, prices of older bonds with higher yields increase.

To stimulate economic growth, the Federal Reserve System (the Fed)—the central bank of the United States—cut short-term interest rates in November to 1.25 percent. The decrease left interest rates at their lowest levels since the 1960's. However, investors remained skeptical through the end of 2002. A minor stock market rally that began in early October had stalled as the year ended.

Through November, the value of mutual funds invested in bonds and other fixed-income securities had increased approximately 4 percent, compared with a 20-percent decline for the average U.S. stock fund.

Winners and losers. The stock market slump in 2002 affected nearly all sectors of the U.S. economy. Gold-mining companies were among the few sectors of the stock market to post gains. Shares of Newmont Mining Corporation based in Denver, Colorado, increased 19 percent through November.

Some companies bounced off multiyear lows amid business turnarounds. The stock of Gap Inc., a San Francisco-based apparel company, advanced 14 percent through November after having slumped badly in 2001. Several consumer product companies selling basic items also fared well in 2002. Brewery Anheuser-Busch Companies of St. Louis, Missouri, reported that its stock rose nearly 9 percent in the first 11 months of the year.

Stocks in the telecommunications sector, which continued to suffer from the over-building that took place in the 1990's and from flat demand for mobile phones, were among the biggest losers of 2002. The stock value of Lucent Technologies in Murray Hill, New Jersey, sank 65 percent, to $1.77 per share, at the end of November 2002.

International stock markets reflected the economic uncertainty in the United States. An index of 30 leading stocks at the London Stock Exchange fell 30 percent through November. Stock indices in France and Germany were also off about 30 percent through November. The Tokyo Stock Exchange fell 15 percent during the same period.

Some investors did better by investing in emerging economies. Leading stocks in Mexico fell 5 percent and stocks in Thailand gained 20 percent.

Settlement. A group of large U.S. brokerage firms agreed in late December 2002 to a series of internal reforms on how stock-research practices are conducted. The firms agreed to pay more than $1 billion in fines in order to end a joint New York State and federal investigation into whether the firms had given customers misleading stock recommendations in exchange for lucrative investment banking fees. □ Bill Barnhart

See also **Economics.**

Sudan. President Umar al-Bashir's government and the rebel group Sudan People's Liberation Army (SPLA) signed a temporary peace agreement sponsored by the United States in July 2002. Some 2 million Sudanese had been killed during a 19-year civil war between government forces in the Arab- and Muslim-dominated north and rebels in the south. Most Sudanese in the south practice Christianity or traditional African belief systems.

The peace agreement, called the Machakos Protocol after the Kenyan town in which it was signed, provided for a six-year period of limited self-rule for the south and "trust building" measures between the north and south. The protocol also promised that Sudanese in the south would not be subject to Islamic law.

Additional negotiations to establish a formal cease-fire and resolve differences in interpretations of the protocol broke down in early September after rebel forces captured the southern town of Torit from government troops. In early October, the government announced that it had recaptured Torit. In mid-October, government officials and rebels agreed to resume peace negotiations and suspend fighting. Negotiations broke down in November over unresolved issues of wealth and power sharing. However, the two sides agreed to extend the truce and continue peace talks in 2003.

U.S. peace act. U.S. President George W. Bush signed the Sudan Peace Act in October 2002. The act provided for $300 million in aid over the next three years for poor areas outside government control in the south. The act also gave the U.S. president the power to authorize economic or trade sanctions against the Sudanese government should the president determine that Sudanese officials were "not engaged in good faith negotiations" with the rebels.

Efforts to end isolation. President Bashir in August canceled a number of government restrictions on political rallies. Experts viewed the move as an attempt to end Sudan's international isolation and dilute the influence of northern *Islamists* (Islamic hardliners). However, Sudan remained under U.S. trade sanctions, which were imposed in 1997 for Sudan's alleged support of terrorism and human rights abuses.

Islamist jailed. President Bashir ordered Islamist leader Hassan al-Turabi to be transferred from house arrest to jail in September 2002. Turabi had been charged with "acts of sabotage" in February 2001 after he signed a peace agreement, not approved by the government, with the SPLA. In 1989, Turabi, the head of the Popular National Congress Party, had been credited with helping Bashir assume power. □ Christine Helms

See also **Middle East.**

Supreme Court of the United States.

In 2002, the U.S. Supreme Court issued rulings on topics including school vouchers, mandatory drug testing for students, the death penalty, civil rights protections, and online pornography.

School vouchers. The court ruled on June 27 that the federal government can provide public money to pay for school vouchers, even if parents use the money to send children to religious schools. In the 5-to-4 decision, the court ruled that a tuition voucher program in Cleveland, Ohio, does not constitute the establishment of a state religion or violate the principle of separation of church and state. The ruling reversed a decision made in 2000 by the U.S. Court of Appeals for the Sixth District in Cincinnati, Ohio, that the voucher program violated the Constitution's prohibition against the establishment of religion.

The Cleveland school system started the voucher program to provide families with educational options because the Cleveland public schools were not meeting state standards. Through the voucher program, parents with children in kindergarten through eighth grade could receive up to $2,250 to help pay private-school tuition. However, most of the private schools that accepted voucher students were church-affiliated. Critics argued that the program amounted to government sponsorship of religion and filed a lawsuit to stop it.

Random drug testing. The court in a June 27, 2002, ruling upheld the use of random drug testing on public school students. Voting 5 to 4 in a case originating in Oklahoma, the court expanded a 1995 ruling that concluded random drug testing of student athletes was not an unreasonable search prohibited by the U.S. Constitution. The court ruled that a school district does not need evidence of a drug problem to require testing of students who want to participate in clubs, band, or other school-sponsored extracurricular activities.

Death penalty decision. On June 20, 2002, the court voted 6 to 3 that the Constitution's ban on cruel and unusual punishment prevents states from executing convicted killers who are mentally retarded. The court ruled that a national consensus had developed against executing the mentally retarded, citing the fact that of the 38 states with capital punishment in 2002, 18 had already barred the execution of mentally retarded killers. In 1989, the court had ruled that states had the right to execute mentally retarded inmates. At the time, only two states banned such executions. The court determined in 2002 that in the 13 years since that decision, "evolving standards of decency" made the practice no longer acceptable.

Death sentences overturned. In a 7-to-2 vote on June 24 the court overturned death sentences against convicted murderers in several states. The court ruled that juries and not judges must decide whether the facts of a case warrant the death penalty. A sentence imposed by a judge violates a defendant's right to a trial by jury, the court ruled. In each case, a jury determined a person's guilt or innocence while judges decided whether there were factors that warranted the death penalty.

Legal experts said that the decision affected the way death sentences are imposed in Alabama, Arizona, Colorado, Delaware, Florida, Idaho, Indiana, Montana, and Nebraska. As many as 800 people in the United States could have their death sentences commuted to life imprisonment as a result of the decision.

Disability issues. The court issued several decisions during the 2002 term to better define the scope of the Americans with Disabilities Act (ADA). The law, passed by Congress in 1990, prevents employers from discriminating against workers or job applicants because of a disability.

On Jan. 8, 2002, the court unanimously ruled that for a person to qualify as disabled he or she must be restricted in performing activities that are "central to daily life," not just those that are important in the workplace. The ruling came in response to the case of a woman who developed a repetitive strain injury in her job as an assembly line worker. The court ruled that an assessment of whether she was disabled had to take into account the fact that she still could perform nonwork functions, such as personal hygiene, cooking, gardening, and some housework.

On April 29, the court ruled in a 5-to-4 decision that an employer does not have to change a valid seniority system to accommodate a disabled worker at the expense of another employee with greater job seniority. The case involved an airline baggage handler who injured his back while on the job. The man was temporarily assigned to a mailroom position while he recovered but lost that job when two workers with greater seniority requested a transfer to that position. The court ruled that the typical seniority system provides important benefits in the workplace by creating fair treatment of all employees.

Ethics ruling. In a decision handed down on June 27, the court voted 5 to 4 that a Minnesota law prohibiting candidates in judicial elections from taking stands on disputed legal or political issues was a violation of the Constitution's guarantee of freedom of speech.

Free speech made easier. The court ruled on June 17 that communities cannot require advocates of religious or political causes to get a permit before going door-to-door to spread their message. The 8-to-1 decision was a victory for the

Jehovah's Witnesses, a Christian religious group that canvasses neighborhoods in search of converts. The group had sued officials in Stratton, Ohio, who passed the permit law in an attempt to limit door-to-door solicitation in the town.

Census decision. The court ruled 5 to 4 on June 20 that a technique used by the U.S. Census Bureau to gather population data was not unconstitutional. Officials in Utah maintained that its population was undercounted in the 2000 Census when the Census Bureau used "imputation," which allowed census workers to use data from a nearby household when they were unable to reach anyone at a neighboring residence. Data gathered by the Census Bureau resulted in a shift in the total population of Utah and the loss of a seat in the U.S. House of Representatives.

Public housing agencies do not violate federal law if they evict tenants who have a family member or guest who uses drugs, even if the tenant is unaware of the activity, the court ruled on March 26, 2002. The court voted 8 to 0 that the Anti-Drug Abuse Act of 1988 does not require eviction but also does not prevent public housing authorities from following "zero tolerance" drug policies.

Internet pornography. On April 16, 2002, the court ruled that a law aimed at banning sexually explicit material online was too broad. By a 6-to-3 vote, the justices overturned the Child Pornography Prevention Act. The law, passed by the U.S. Congress in 1996, prohibited the creation of computer-generated images of child pornography. Federal law makes it illegal to make or possess child pornography that pictures children engaged in sexual conduct. However, the court said that *virtual* (computer-generated) materials cannot be banned because children are not used in making such material.

White dies. Former Supreme Court Justice Byron R. White died on April 15, 2002, at age 84. He had been one of the longest serving justices when he retired in 1993.

White, who was born in Fort Collins, Colorado, graduated from the University of Colorado at Boulder in 1938 and from Yale Law School in 1946. While attending college, he played in the National Football League for the Pittsburgh Pirates and the Detroit Lions.

President John F. Kennedy appointed White to the Supreme Court in 1962. Judicial experts noted that while White was appointed by a Democratic president, he did not vote predictably with any single faction of the court.

☐ Geoffrey A. Campbell

See also **Courts; Disability; Education.**

Surgery. See Medicine.

Suriname. See Latin America.

Swaziland. See Africa.

Sweden. The Social Democratic government of Prime Minister Goran Persson won reelection in September 2002. Debates over welfare spending, taxes, and immigration dominated the election campaign.

The Social Democrats, which had governed Sweden since 1994, claimed credit for the strong economic growth that Sweden had enjoyed since the late 1990's. They vowed to maintain Sweden's generous welfare benefits and government spending on health and education. The opposition Moderate Party called for significant reductions in spending to finance tax cuts. The Social Democrats captured 144 seats in the 349-seat parliament, a gain of 13 seats from the previous election in 1998. The Moderates' share of the vote dropped to 55 seats, from 82 seats in 1998. Sweden's 2002 election results bucked a trend in many other European countries toward center-right governments.

The election result also revealed strong support for the Liberal Party. In the campaign, the Liberals adopted some of the tough immigration stances that had proved successful for right-wing parties in neighboring Denmark and Norway in 2001. The party called for immigrants to be sent home if they were unable to find work within three months and to take Swedish language lessons before gaining citizenship. The Liberals won 48 seats in parliament, up from 17 seats in the previous election.

Persson formed a government in 2002 by reviving a coalition with two smaller parties, the Left and the Greens, which had supported the Social Democrats in the previous parliament. In an October 1 speech, Persson promised to maintain spending on education, health, and care of the elderly. He also vowed to increase the percentage of working-age adults with jobs and discourage Swedes from taking sick leave and early retirement. The number of working Swedes claiming disability rose sharply in the early 2000's, causing welfare spending on health care benefits to soar.

The Swedish economy continued to suffer from the global economic slowdown in 2002, especially from the worldwide weakness in technology and telecommunications sectors on which Sweden is heavily dependent. European Union economists forecast that gross domestic product, the total output of goods and services produced in a year, would grow by about 1.6 percent in 2002, up slightly from 1.2 percent in 2001.

Telia AB, Sweden's main telephone company, agreed in March 2002 to aquire the Finnish telephone company Sonera Oy for 7.3 billion euros ($7.1 billion). The acquisition, which was completed in November, created the largest telephone company in Scandinavia. ☐ Tom Buerkle

See also **Europe.**

Swimming. Ian Thorpe of Australia captured five gold medals at the Pan Pacific swimming championships in Yokohama, Japan, in August 2002. Despite Thorpe's performance, the United States dominated the competition, winning 21 gold medals to Australia's 11. U.S. swimmers took five gold medals on the last day of the meet, including breaking the world record in the men's 400-meter medley relay with a time of 3 minutes, 33.48 seconds.

World records. Several records fell at the European championships in Berlin in July and August. Anna-Karin Kammerling of Sweden set a new women's 50-meter butterfly record of 25.57 seconds. The German women's relay team set a new 400-meter freestyle relay record of 3 minutes, 36 seconds. Franziska van Almsick of Germany broke the 200-meter freestyle record with a time of 1 minute, 56.64 seconds. Oleg Lisogor of Ukraine broke the men's 50-meter breaststroke record in 27.18 seconds. Otylia Jedrejczak of Poland set a new women's 200-meter butterfly record of 2 minutes, 5.78 seconds.

At the U.S. National Championships in Fort Lauderdale, Florida, in August, Natalie Coughlin became the first woman to break the 1-minute mark in the 100-meter backstroke. Coughlin finished in a world-record time of 59.58 seconds.

Short-course records. On April 6 at the short-course world swimming championships in Moscow, Emma Igelstrom of Sweden set her third mark in three days, swimming the 100-meter breaststroke in 1 minute, 5.38 seconds. She had already broken the 50-meter breaststroke record and swam on the record-setting women's 400-meter medley relay team.

Geoff Huegill of Australia, Oleg Lisogor of Ukraine, and Martina Moravcova of Slovakia all set world records on January 26 in Berlin. Huegill broke his own record in the 50-meter butterfly, which he had set four days earlier. Lisogor broke Ed Moses's mark in the 50-meter breaststroke by 0.08 second. Moravcova won the 100-meter butterfly in a record 56.55 seconds. Yana Klochkova of Ukraine broke the world record in the 400-meter individual medley with a time of 4 minutes, 27.83 seconds on January 19 in Paris.

Moses leaves wake. Ed Moses of the United States broke five short-course world records in a single month in 2002. On January 18, Moses broke the 200-meter breaststroke mark with a time of 2 minutes, 4.37 seconds. On January 22, he broke two world records in Stockholm, Sweden—in the 50-meter and 200-meter breaststroke. On January 23, he broke the 100-meter breaststroke mark. On January 26 in Berlin, Moses again broke his 200-meter breaststroke record, finishing in 2 minutes, 3.17 seconds.

☐ Michael Kates

Switzerland became the 190th member of the United Nations (UN) on Sept. 10, 2002, after voters approved a reversal of the country's tradition of neutrality. The decision capped a gradual opening to the outside world, during which Switzerland deepened trade and political relations with the European Union and agreed to participate in UN peacekeeping missions.

The government campaigned in favor of UN membership, arguing that it would help the country to defend its interests in international forums. Supporters also claimed that it was hypocritical to remain outside the UN while benefitting from the presence of many UN agencies. Geneva has more UN employees than any city except New York and is home to the UN commissioners for human rights and refugees. Critics contended that Switzerland would do better to preserve its neutrality. Swiss voters approved membership in a referendum on March 3, with 54 percent voting in favor.

Economy. The Swiss economy continued to decline in 2002 as part of the worldwide slowdown. Economists predicted that the *gross domestic product* (the value of all goods and services produced in a year) would grow by only 0.7 percent, down from 1.3 percent in 2001.

Corporate woes. Several major Swiss companies ran into financial difficulties in 2002. The chief executives of Credit Suisse Group, the country's second-largest bank; Zurich Financial Services; and Swiss Life, a Zurich-based insurance company, were forced to resign after the companies reported large losses.

Scandal plagued Asea Brown Boveri (ABB), a large, Zurich-based engineering company, in early 2002. Shareholders discovered that former chief executives Percy Barnevik and Goeran Lindahl had been paid 233 million Swiss francs ($172 million) in retirement bonuses, while ABB reported a loss of 691 million Swiss francs ($468 million) for 2001. The men agreed in March 2002 to return about half of their bonuses.

Swiss corporate raider Martin Ebner saw his financial empire collapse in 2002 because of the sharp decline in stock markets. Ebner had forced changes at many Swiss companies during the 1990's by buying large stakes and demanding action to raise share prices. He reached an agreement with his creditors in August 2002 to divest himself of several investments.

A new airline, Swiss International Air Lines, began flights in March. The carrier operated a scaled-down service inherited from Swissair, which went bankrupt in October 2001. The Swiss government and major Swiss companies contributed more than $2 billion to get the new carrier flying.

☐ Tom Buerkle

See also **Europe.**

The dome from the top of a mosque is all that remains of a village in northern Syria buried in mud left by floodwaters in June. The flood was unleashed when the six-year-old Zeyzoun Dam burst, killing more than 20 people, leaving about 30,000 others homeless, and destroying livestock and crops.

Syria. Syrian President Bashar al-Assad's intervention in April 2002 halted attacks by Lebanon's Hezbollah, an Islamic political and guerrilla group, against Israeli troops near Shebaa Farms, an area claimed by both Lebanon and Israel. Experts on Middle East relations feared the attacks, which began after Israeli troops entered Palestinian cities in the West Bank in late March, would trigger a wider regional conflict.

U.S. relations. President Assad, whose troops control Lebanon, reportedly hoped that his intervention might contribute to a thaw in relations between Syria and the United States. Earlier in April, the administration of U.S. President George W. Bush had acknowledged that Syria was cooperating in the U.S.-led war against terrorism by sharing information about Islamic extremists.

The U.S. Congress began in April to consider the Syrian Accountability Act despite President Bush's acknowledgment of Syrian cooperation. The proposed law mandated that the U.S. president impose economic and diplomatic sanctions against Syria unless the Syrian government ended support for groups the United States labeled as "terrorist organizations"; withdrew Syrian troops from Lebanon; and ceased acquisition of weapons of mass destruction. In May, U.S. Undersecretary of State John Bolton accused Syria of possessing weapons of mass destruction.

In June, President Bush called upon Syria to end relations with groups the United States alleged to be terrorist organizations, including Lebanon's Hezbollah and the anti-Israel Palestinian groups Hamas and Islamic Jihad. Syrian officials rejected the demand, maintaining that the groups were legitimate political organizations resisting Israeli occupation of Arab land.

President Assad warned U.S. Deputy Secretary of State William Burns during a meeting in October that the Arab and Islamic worlds were growing more alienated from the United States. Assad attributed this to a perceived U.S. bias against Arabs in the Palestinian-Israeli conflict and a threatened U.S. military attack against Iraq.

Iraq. Syria, as a rotating member of the United Nations (UN) Security Council in 2002, voted in November to support a U.S.-proposed resolution demanding that Iraq fully cooperate with UN inspectors searching for evidence of weapons of mass destruction or face "serious consequences." Syria's foreign minister explained that Syria backed the resolution in the hopes that it would reduce the likelihood of a U.S. attack on Iraq.

Dam burst. On June 4, the six-year-old Zeyzoun Dam in northern Syria collapsed, flooding several villages in the region and killing more than 20 people.   □ Christine Helms

See also **Iraq; Israel; Libya; Middle East.**

Taiwan. Tensions between Taiwan and China intensified in 2002 after Chen Shui-bian, Taiwan's president, said that Taiwan and China existed as two separate nations. In August, Chen backed passage of a law allowing a referendum on whether Taiwan should declare its independence from China. China threatened military action if Chen continued to push for independence.

Taiwan, an island state, separated from China politically in 1949, when Communists conquered mainland China. The Communist takeover forced China's Nationalist government to flee to Taiwan. China, however, continued to regard Taiwan as a province.

A Taiwanese independence movement did not gather strength until the 1990's, when political reforms ended martial law and increased democracy. In 1999, China threatened to attack Taiwan after then-President Lee Teng-hui suggested that Taiwan and China were separate countries. Several nations were angered by China's threats. The United States, which maintained diplomatic relations with China and not Taiwan, warned that it would retaliate if China invaded Taiwan. When Chen, leader of the Democratic Progressive Party, was elected president in 2000, Chinese officials warned that any move toward independence would provoke war. Chen waited until 2002 to call for independence.

Chinese officials responded by pressuring various countries to cut ties with Taiwan. Nauru, a Pacific island nation that was 1 of only 28 countries to recognize Taiwan as a separate nation, broke diplomatic links with Taiwan and recognized the communist government in Beijing, China's capital, as the sole government of all China, including Taiwan.

Politics. In January, Chen promoted his chief of staff, Yu Shyi-kun, to prime minister. Yu replaced Chang Chun-hsiung, who held the post for more than a year as Taiwan's economy slipped into recession. In an effort to help the ailing economy, Yu named Lee Yung-san, chairman of the International Commercial Bank of China, as finance minister, and Christine Tsung, a former president of Taiwan's largest airline, as economics minister.

In March, Tsung, the first woman to head the economics ministry, was forced to resign after facing charges that she was unqualified for the position. Yu appointed Vice Economics Minister Lin Yi-fu, a veteran economist, to replace Tsung.

Elections. In December, the Democratic Progressive Party suffered a crushing defeat in a mayoral election in Taipei, the capital, but the ruling party declared victory in a crucial race in the second-largest city, Kaohsiung.

☐ Henry S. Bradsher

See also **Asia; China.**

Tajikistan in 2002 celebrated the anniversary of the end in 1997 of its civil war. While the country had managed to maintain peace for five years, the economy remained weak and prospects for economic development were limited in 2002.

The United States and other countries rewarded Tajikistan with a much-needed boost in foreign aid in 2002, after Tajikistan opened its territory to troops involved in the U.S.-led coalition fighting in Afghanistan. In addition, some of the food convoys directed to the region's Afghan refugees were diverted to help feed the Tajik population, which faced widespread famine after several years of drought. While Tajikistan's economy grew by more than 30 percent between 1999 and 2002, foreign investment in the country remained miniscule.

The government continued its crackdown on Islamic groups in 2002. In July, President Emomali Rahmonov warned members of his party that the opposition Islamic Renaissance Party (IRP) of Tajikistan was engaging in "ideological work of an extremist persuasion that may lead to a schism in society." In August, the government took the unusual step of banning 10 Muslim clerics with ties to the IRP from preaching sermons.

☐ Steven L. Solnick

See also **Afghanistan; Asia.**

Tanzania. See Africa.

Taxation. The Internal Revenue Service (IRS) announced in 2002 plans to focus IRS auditing activities as part of an attempt to increase public compliance with tax laws. IRS officials reported in September that several groups would be targeted for greater scrutiny, including high-income individuals who do not file federal income taxes and individuals who do not report all of their taxable income. IRS officials said the agency was placing a top priority on pursuing promoters "of abusive schemes, shelters, and trusts" and planned to identify people who used these means to evade taxes.

Random audits. IRS officials announced in June that the agency would revive a previously controversial practice of randomly auditing individual tax returns. In 2002, the agency planned to conduct approximately 50,000 random audits of 2001 tax returns. Officials said that taxpayers would be selected for the audits from various income groups and types of returns. Although the IRS only scheduled random audits for 2002, officials said that they intended to revive the process every few years.

The IRS ended random audits in 1988. The agency had tried to resume the policy in the mid-1990's but canceled its plans after members of the United States Congress criticized the aggressive tactics agents used in conducting such audits.

Clean-burning fuel deduction. The IRS in September 2002 certified two hybrid vehicles as eligible for a clean-burning fuel tax deduction. Hybrid vehicles are designed to combine gasoline-powered engines with battery-powered electric motors to create more fuel-efficient cars. Purchasers of the Honda Insight for model years 2000, 2001, and 2002 or the Honda Civic Hybrid for model year 2003 were eligible for a one-time deduction of $2,000 for the year the vehicle was first used.

Taxpayer rights bill defeated. The U.S. House of Representatives failed in April 2002 to approve the Taxpayer Protection and IRS Accountability Act of 2002. The proposed legislation, defeated by a vote of 219-to-205, would have provided greater protections for taxpayers when dealing with the IRS. The measure would also have given the IRS greater flexibility in dealing with people who attempt to avoid paying taxes. The legislation proposed to increase the penalty the IRS could impose against taxpayers filing fraudulent returns. Critics of the legislation argued that a section would have eased some campaign finance reporting requirement for political groups with tax-exempt status.

☐ Geoffrey A. Campbell

See also **Economics; United States, Government of the.**

Telecommunications.

The telecommunications industry lurched from economic misfortune to scandal in 2002 after revelations of questionable accounting and charges of fraud against several executives. In July, Clinton, Mississippi-based WorldCom, Inc., plagued by an accounting scandal, became the largest United States company to declare bankruptcy.

Bankruptcies. WorldCom, already suffering from the economic downturn that continued to bloody the telecom sector in 2002, declared bankruptcy in July, weeks after company officials revealed that they had wrongfully accounted for nearly $4 billion, making it appear the company had made profits when it actually suffered losses. Auditors also discovered that the company had made improper loans to executives, including about $400 million to former Chief Executive Officer Bernie Ebbers, who resigned in April. WorldCom's bankruptcy, the largest in U.S. history, further soured investors on the telecom industry.

Bermuda-based Global Crossing Ltd., which in the late 1990's built a worldwide fiber-optic network, declared bankruptcy in January 2002. Federal investigators in February began looking into allegations that Global Crossing executives had engaged in a practice known as "capacity swapping" with other carriers. In these transactions, Global Crossing allegedly bought fiber-optic capacity from another large telecom, then sold that capacity back to the same company and recorded the sale as revenue. Investigators said this practice made it appear that Global Crossing's revenues were greater than they actually were.

As a result of the accounting scandals and mismanagement uncovered in 2002, federal authorities made several high-profile arrests of telecom executives. John Rigas, the founder of Coudersport, Pennsylvania-based Adelphia Communications Corp., was arrested in July along with several other Adelphia executives. They were charged with conspiracy and fraud for failing to disclose billions in dollars of personal loans they had received from the company.

In August, authorities arrested two former WorldCom executives, Scott Sullivan and David Myers. The two men were charged with securities fraud and lying to investigators. If convicted, they faced up to 65 years in prison.

Overcapacity. The telecommunications industry continued to suffer in 2002 from a severe glut in capacity, which resulted in lower prices for telecom services. In the 1990's, the enthusiasm of investors about the future of Internet companies led many telecoms to spend billions expanding computer and telephone networks in anticipation of growing demand. With the failure of many Internet companies in the late 1990's, the industry was left with excess capacity, falling prices, and evaporating profits.

As the stock prices of telecoms plummeted, investors began to hunt for bargains amid the wreckage. In July 2002, a group of investors led by Warren Buffet invested $500 million in Level 3 Communications, Inc., a fiber-optic carrier based in Broomfield, Colorado. Some industry experts speculated that the telecom shakeout could lead to a healthier outlook for the industry.

Broadband. The steady increase in the number of consumers choosing fast broadband Internet connections provided a bright spot for the telecom industry in 2002. Dataquest, Inc., a data services firm in Harrisburg, Pennsylvania, released a survey in November revealing that nearly 30 percent of online households had broadband connections. Such connections required the high-speed data transfer made possible by the telecom industry's high-capacity networks.

A wireless technology called Wi-Fi, for "wireless fidelity," proved to be one of the most popular telecom products in 2002. Wi-Fi provided relatively low-cost broadband connections. Many colleges and businesses installed Wi-Fi systems to enable people to receive high-speed Internet access through laptop computers. ☐ Jon Van

See also **Bank; Economics; Internet; Telecommunications: A Special Report.**

The Second Wireless Revolution

A technology that is more than 100 years old is keeping people in touch in new ways.

By Dave Wilson

A harried traveler races for the airport, desperate to make it to his flight on time. While in the car, he uses the on-board computer system connected to the Internet to check for traffic patterns, quickly changing highways to avoid slow-downs. He makes it to the airport on time but discovers that his flight has been canceled. He grabs his cell phone, which also has a built-in Web browser, and quickly gets a reservation on a different airline, pays for the ticket, and e-mails the original carrier to request a refund for the canceled flight. With plenty of time to spare, the traveler takes a seat at an airport cafe equipped with a high-speed wireless Internet connection. Pulling out his laptop, he checks his e-mail, stock quotes, and sports scores while sipping on a coffee and waiting for his flight to begin boarding. On the plane, he puts on a set of wireless headphones that allows him to listen to music from his portable stereo without having to take it out of the overhead luggage compartment.

Just a few years ago, smooth, reliable, and powerful wireless connections between people and machines were in the realm of science fiction. Today, staying in constant wireless contact is a reality for many people. While microchips, portable computers, and the Internet play a big role in the story of the harried traveler, the key element is not some cutting-edge modern-day wonder. It is the same technology behind the lowly radio, which transformed the world near the turn of the last century by giving human beings a way to communicate without the use of wires.

Wireless communication—using radio waves to send information without wires—began in the early 1900's with the development of the wireless telegraph. Through the early and mid-1900's, the evolution of new wireless technologies dramatically changed the way people communicated, allowing ships to remain in contact with land bases and other ships; messages to be transmitted around the globe; police to be dispatched to stop crime; and radio broadcasters to reach audiences numbering in the millions. In the early 1980's, the development of affordable cellular telephone service launched a revolution in wireless communication. Cellular telephones allowed people to stay in constant contact and led to wireless access to the Internet. In the future, wireless technology will increasingly allow devices to communicate, connecting people and machines in vast, invisible networks.

Sending signals through the air

Wireless communication relies on radio waves, invisible patterns of electric and magnetic force that travel through the air. A device called a transmitter converts sound or information into radio waves and broadcasts them into the air. A receiver converts those signals back into sound or information. Many wireless devices, such as cell phones, are transceivers that both transmit and receive radio signals. Like waves on the ocean, radio waves move in crests and troughs. The number of crests that pass a certain spot in a set amount of time is known as the wave's frequency. Most radio transmitters generate radio waves of a certain frequency. In order to receive the signal, the receiver must be tuned to the same frequency. If more than one radio device is transmitting on the same frequency in a certain area, the two signals create interference, distorting the messages they carry.

Scientists began experimenting with radio waves in the mid-1800's. However, the application of radio waves to wireless communication began with the work of a young Italian inventor named Guglielmo Marconi. Working at his family's villa near Bologna, Italy, in the mid-1890's, Marconi developed a way of transmitting telegraph signals through the air on radio waves. His system was called wireless telegraphy.

About 60 years earlier, the telegraph, a device that used electric current to transmit messages over wires, had changed the world by allowing information to move at the speed of light (186,282 miles [299,792 kilometers] per second). Messages were sent in Morse code, a series of dots and dashes transmitted by a telegraph machine as long and short bursts of electric current. At the receiving end, a telegraph operator heard the Morse code messages as a series of clicks in his earphones.

However, the telegraph was limited by its dependence on wires. Telegraph lines were difficult and expensive to construct, and they needed frequent maintenance. They were also unsuitable for mobile communications, such as ship-to-shore. Marconi was sure that wireless telegraphy would solve these problems.

Marconi became obsessed with transmitting messages over greater distances, and in 1898, he successfully sent and received a message over a distance of 18 miles (29 kilometers). Several European navies subsequently awarded Marconi contracts to outfit ships with wireless telegraphy sets. These sets allowed ships at sea to communicate with each other and with bases on land.

Many skeptics, however, said Marconi's radio could never transmit over long distances. They believed that radio waves, which travel in straight lines, could not pass beyond the horizon. Marconi set out to prove them wrong by sending and receiving a radio transmission across the Atlantic Ocean. On Dec. 12, 1901, the 27-year-old Marconi sat in an empty room in an old hospital on the edge of a cliff in St. Johns, Newfoundland, Canada. He held his receiver's single earphone tightly against his head. As the wind howled outside, he strained to hear a signal his assistant was transmitting from a lab more than 1,700 miles (2,700 kilometers) away in Poldhu, Cornwall, on the southwest tip of England. At 12:30 p.m., Marconi heard distinct signals through the roaring static—three short bursts—Morse code for the letter "S," repeated over and over. Afraid he might be imagining the sounds, Marconi handed the earpiece to an assistant, who confirmed that he heard the message. Marconi's message had traversed the Atlantic Ocean, forever changing human communication. Although Marconi did not know it, his experiment had succeeded because certain kinds of radio waves bounce off a layer of Earth's atmosphere called the ionosphere. These waves, called sky waves, can bounce back and forth between the ionosphere and Earth's surface, traveling well beyond the horizon.

Use of wireless spreads

Wireless telegraphy spread rapidly after the success of Marconi's transatlantic experiment. Governments were the first to invest, using wireless sets to coordinate military maneuvers, manage shipping routes, and dispatch diplomatic messages.

Radio remained largely off-limits to most people because they did not know Morse code. However, a few enthusiastic amateurs, called hams, cobbled together wireless telegraphy rigs and spent hours listening to and transcribing messages in Morse code. By November 1905, the Electro Importing Co. of New York City advertised complete wireless telegraphy kits in the Scientific American magazine for the relatively low price of $8.50.

All wireless communications were conducted in Morse code until Christmas Eve, 1906, when a handful of shipboard wireless operators faintly heard through their headphones the sounds of a violin playing "O Holy Night." They had accidentally tuned into

The author:
Dave Wilson is a producer at Cable News Network (CNN) in Atlanta and former technology columnist for the *Los Angeles Times*.

an experimental broadcast by Canadian engineer Reginald A. Fessenden. During the experiment, he also read from the Bible and gave a short speech wishing listeners a merry Christmas. Most historians consider Fessenden's broadcast to be the first voice and the first music transmitted over radio. Gradually, music and voice broadcasting caught on. In 1910, radio pioneer Lee de Forest offered radio broadcasts of performances at the Metropolitan Opera House in New York City. In 1916, Frank Conrad, an engineer with the Westinghouse Electric Company of Pittsburgh, Pennsylvania, began playing records for his friends over a radio broadcast. Westinghouse executives heard about Conrad's experiments and seized on the idea of broadcast radio—transmitting radio waves containing understandable sounds, rather than just Morse code, to thousands of home radio receivers. The company correctly calculated that it could make a fortune manufacturing and selling radios to consumer audiences.

In 1920, Westinghouse established a radio station in Pittsburgh with the call letters KDKA and initiated regular broadcasting. The station remained a curiosity until it broadcast the results of that year's presidential election long before newspapers could report who had won. With that event, radio demonstrated its power to inform a large group of people very quickly about events in faraway places. Consumers began snapping up radios as fast as they could be manufactured, and broadcast radio stations began popping up all over the United States. To keep the new radio stations from interfering with one another, the U.S. government began licensing each radio station to transmit on its own unique frequency over a certain area.

How radio works

Most wireless technologies send sound or data on radio waves that travel through the atmosphere. A device called a transmitter broadcasts those waves into the air. Devices called receivers pick up the radio waves and convert them back into sound or data.

Ground waves

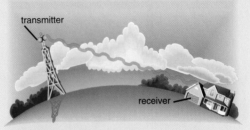

Some radio transmitters generate ground waves and sky waves. Ground waves follow the curve of the Earth, extending a short distance beyond the horizon.

Sky waves

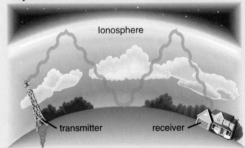

Sky waves bounce off a layer of the atmosphere called the ionosphere. These waves can travel beyond the horizon by bouncing back and forth from the surface of the Earth to the ionosphere.

Line of sight waves

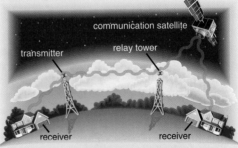

Other transmitters generate line of sight waves, which must travel in a straight line from the transmitter to the receiver. In order to pass beyond the horizon, these waves must be relayed by a relay tower or communications satellite.

How a cellular telephone works

Cellular telephones, or cell phones, use radio waves and conventional phone lines to transmit calls from a user to a receiver. A cellular telephone system uses a network of radio antennas called base stations. Each base station handles telephone calls in an area around it called a cell.

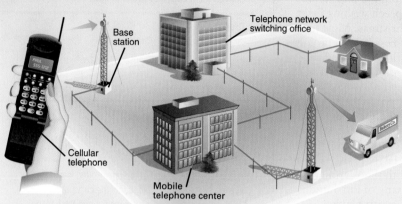

Base station

Telephone network switching office

Cellular telephone

Mobile telephone center

Transmitting a call

When a user places a call from a cell phone, radio waves carry the call from the phone to the nearest base station. The base station sends the call over wire lines to a mobile telephone center. The center routes the call to either the telephone network switching office to be sent to a regular telephone or to another base station to be transferred wirelessly to another cellular phone.

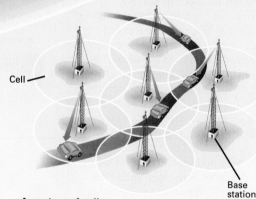

Cell

Base station

A system of cells

Each base station handles all telephone calls in an area around it called a cell. As a caller travels from one cell into another, a computerized switching system transfers the call to a new base station without interrupting the conversation.

The History of Wireless

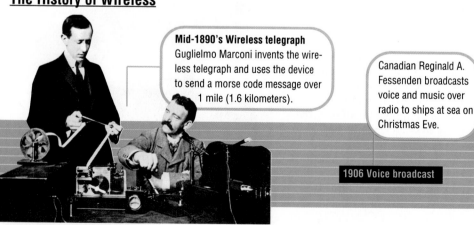

Mid-1890's Wireless telegraph
Guglielmo Marconi invents the wireless telegraph and uses the device to send a morse code message over 1 mile (1.6 kilometers).

Canadian Reginald A. Fessenden broadcasts voice and music over radio to ships at sea on Christmas Eve.

1906 Voice broadcast

Beyond broadcast radio

The next big step in wireless technology was the development of two-way radio transmission. Two-way radios like those used on ships could be made small enough to be mounted in an automobile. However, early mobile transceivers were still quite bulky and expensive, limiting their use to large companies and government services. By the 1930's, taxi companies and police and fire departments in most big cities used mobile two-way radios to dispatch cars and trucks. The United States Army began working on backpack-sized radio transceivers in the 1930's. Walkie-talkies, as they came to be called, were widely used by soldiers in the field during World War II (1939-1945).

Broadcast radio's importance as a means of mass communication began to decline with the invention of television and its rise in popularity in the 1950's. Radio technology, however, was more important than ever. Microwaves, a type of radio waves, began carrying the pictures and sounds of broadcast television. With the launching of the first communications satellites in the 1960's, radio signals could be transmitted farther and more clearly than ever before. Signals from a radio transmitter could be bounced by satellites to any location on Earth.

Advances such as satellite broadcasting benefited large companies and governments that could afford to launch such expensive equipment, but there was still a demand for cheap, reliable two-way wireless communication between individuals. Early efforts to satisfy this desire resulted in the development of the first mobile telephones. The American Telephone and Telegraph Company (AT&T) of New York City began selling mobile phone service to consumers in the 1950's.

Early mobile phone equipment was quite heavy, so it could only be used in cars, and service was only available in large cities. Each city's system operated using a single radio tower or base station that transmitted and received on a limited number of frequencies. Because two different calls could not operate on the same frequency, each city's system could only

1930's Two-way radio
Police and the military begin using two-way radios or walkie-talkies.

1920 Broadcast radio
Radio station KDKA in Pittsburgh begins regular broadcasting.

handle a few calls at a time. The limited supply of frequencies made the service very expensive.

A new wireless revolution

The modern wireless revolution began in 1983, when U.S. phone companies began offering a new option called cellular phone service. The new systems used several base stations in each city. Each station covered a smaller area, called a cell, and adjacent cells operated on different frequencies to avoid interfering with each other. Cells that were not next to each other could operate on the same frequencies without causing interference. This allowed the system to reuse the limited frequencies available, greatly expanding the number of calls that could be handled at the same time. The cellular system also used a switching system that could "hand off" a phone call as the mobile phone passed from one cell into the next, switching the call to a new frequency and a new base station without interrupting the conversation.

Cellular phone systems' ability to handle a greater number of calls brought the price of mobile telephone service within the reach of many more people. As more base stations popped up, the system's capacity grew even greater, and the price of cellular service dropped even further. By 2000, nearly 40 percent of the U.S. population, more than 100 million people, owned a cellular telephone or "cell" phone. Cell phone use skyrocketed not just in the United States but around the world. A 2001 study by the Gartner Group, a research and advisory firm located in Stamford, Connecticut, projected that 30 million people in India would own cell phones by 2005, up from about 3 million in 2000. In 2002, the International Telecommunications Union, a Geneva, Switzerland-based organization that assists governments and private companies in coordinating global telecommunication networks, predicted that wireless phones would outnumber fixed-line phones around the world by 2003. Cellular phones became popular because they allowed people to stay in contact

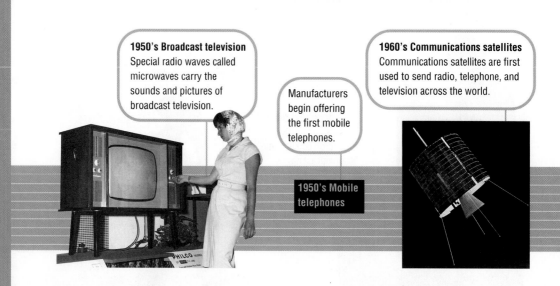

1950's Broadcast television
Special radio waves called microwaves carry the sounds and pictures of broadcast television.

Manufacturers begin offering the first mobile telephones.

1950's Mobile telephones

1960's Communications satellites
Communications satellites are first used to send radio, telephone, and television across the world.

while on the move. In developing nations that lacked widespread wire phone service, cellular service often proved cheaper because it bypassed the expense and difficulty of installing wire phone lines. In short, cellular phone systems succeeded for many of the same reasons that wireless telegraphy did after 1905.

Cellular phone systems were not without limitations. They required a network of cellular base stations. To address this issue, a number of wireless phone systems using satellites instead of land-based cell stations were proposed. In 1998, Motorola Inc. of Schaumburg, Illinois, launched Iridium service, the first global wireless telephone service that operated through a network of satellites orbiting the Earth. However, the service soon filed for bankruptcy, and as of the early 2000's, the higher cost of satellite telephone service limited its use to government agencies and private businesses that frequently operated outside the range of land-based cellular phone systems. And as the 21st century began, 80 percent of the Earth was not in range of a cell signal.

Connecting machines without wires

Until the late 1990's, most engineers and companies focused on creating wireless devices that would allow people to communicate with people. The focus eventually shifted toward creating devices that allowed people to communicate with machines and machines to communicate with other machines. Technology companies developed radio chips, tiny two-way radio transceivers that could be installed in any electronic device. The chips allowed cell phones, computers, and other devices to "talk" to each other without the need for wires.

One large group of companies—Ericsson of Stockholm, Sweden; Microsoft Corporation of Redmond, Washington; Nokia of Espoo, Finland; and IBM corporation of Armonk, New York—teamed up to develop a new type of radio chip, which was dubbed Bluetooth. The Bluetooth chip installed in a cell phone, laptop computer, or digital camera allows the device to communicate with other Bluetooth-enabled devices over a distance of about 30 feet (9 meters). Bluetooth's designers hoped that installing

Early 2000's Wireless networking
Emerging systems such as Bluetooth and Wi-Fi allow electronic devices to communicate without wires.

Cellular telephones become the first widely available mobile phones.

1983's Cellular telephones

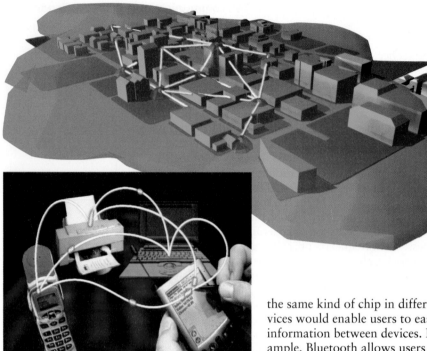

A computer model of downtown Atlanta (top) demonstrates a wireless "cloud," an invisible area of wireless Internet access created by a network of Wi-Fi transmitters. Devices with an installed Bluetooth chip (above) can communicate with one another without wires.

the same kind of chip in different devices would enable users to easily move information between devices. For example, Bluetooth allows users to download a telephone listing from a Nokia cell phone to a Microsoft database on an IBM computer—wirelessly. Bluetooth devices can also be set up to send and receive information constantly. A user could, for example, configure a cell phone to automatically connect with his or her office computer whenever the two came within range. The computer could then get updated telephone listings from the cell phone automatically as soon as the user came into the office.

Wi-Fi: The Internet goes on the air

Bluetooth is not the only wireless technology that allows machines to communicate. Another standard for wireless network connection is called IEEE 802.11b, commonly referred to as "Wi-Fi." Wi-Fi uses radio waves to create wireless links between electronic devices and the Internet over a distance of about 300 feet (90 meters). Some companies use Wi-Fi to allow their employees to carry their laptop computers around their offices without losing their connection to the company's computer network. Wi-Fi transmitters are also used to create "hot spots," public areas where computer users with Wi-Fi cards can access the Internet through a wireless connection. By the early 2000's, Wi-Fi hot spots had popped up in airport lounges, cafes, even public parks. Wi-Fi devices have also surged in popularity in the home, where families can use them to connect multiple computers in different rooms of the house to the Internet, printers, and each other without the need for hundreds of yards of tangled cords.

Wi-Fi chips transfer information faster and farther than Bluetooth chips do. In fact, some technology analysts believe that Wi-Fi will wipe out the Bluetooth market. Bluetooth, however, uses less power. Its developers also believe that Bluetooth chips, which are smaller and less complex than Wi-Fi cards, will eventually be cheaper to manufacture. Bluetooth proponents believe it is well-suited for wireless connections between devices with a limited power supply that do not demand high-speed data transfer, such as the connection between a cell phone and a wireless earpiece. Many investors believe that the two technologies will coexist. They suggest that Bluetooth's low power consumption will make it suitable for voice technologies, and Wi-Fi's high speed transmissions will make it an attractive option for connecting devices that need to transfer large amounts of information very quickly.

The next generation

Meanwhile, the cellular phone industry was at work developing new technology to compete with Bluetooth and Wi-Fi. Cellular phone providers began offering Internet access through cell phones in the late 1990's. However, the cellular phone systems in place at the time could not transfer data fast enough to satisfy the needs of most customers. In the early 2000's, engineers were designing new cellular systems that would allow people to transmit data and access the Internet at high speeds anywhere a cell phone could be used. These high-speed cellular networks, called Third Generation cellular or 3G, involved technical improvements to existing cellular phone systems that would allow them to transmit more information over the limited range of radio frequencies available. Proponents of 3G cellular networks believe the technical improvements will eventually allow users to send and receive voice, e-mail, text, and photos at speeds comparable with high-speed Internet connections that use wires.

Yet another new technology may change the way that radio signals carry information. In the 1970's, several inventors began developing a wireless technology that has variously been called baseband, carrier-free, or impulse. Today, it is generally referred to as ultrawideband wireless or UWB. Unlike other wireless technologies, which transmit information in a constant radio signal on a certain frequency, UWB systems transmit tiny radio pulses across a broad range of frequencies. UWB proponents believe that such signals will be able to transmit information more quickly than conventional radio waves. In a way, UWB brings radio full circle. Its pulses of information are similar to the dots and dashes transmitted by Marconi's wireless telegraphs.

When Marconi transmitted the first message across the Atlantic Ocean, he believed that his invention could satisfy people's appetite for information. He could scarcely have imagined how that appetite would grow or how improvements in wireless technology would allow the movement of huge volumes of information necessary to satisfy that hunger. ■ ■ ■

Video mobile phones, such as the concept model from Motorola (above), could become widespread with the launch of the proposed Third Generation or 3G cellular networks. Such networks are being designed to send sound, video, and text at much higher speeds than traditional cellular telephone systems.

Emmy Award winners in 2002

Comedy

Best Series: "Friends"

Lead Actress: Jennifer Aniston, "Friends"

Lead Actor: Ray Romano, "Everybody Loves Raymond"

Supporting Actress: Doris Roberts, "Everybody Loves Raymond"

Supporting Actor: Brad Garrett, "Everybody Loves Raymond"

Drama

Best Series: "The West Wing"

Lead Actress: Allison Janney, "The West Wing"

Lead Actor: Michael Chiklis, "The Shield"

Supporting Actress: Stockard Channing, "The West Wing"

Supporting Actor: John Spencer, "The West Wing"

Other awards

Miniseries: *Band of Brothers*

Variety, Music, or Comedy Series: "Late Show with David Letterman"

Made for Television Movie: *The Gathering Storm*

Lead Actress in a Miniseries or Movie: Laura Linney, *Wild Iris*

Lead Actor in a Miniseries or Movie: Albert Finney, *The Gathering Storm*

Supporting Actress in a Miniseries or Movie: Stockard Channing, *The Matthew Shepard Story*

Supporting Actor in a Miniseries or Movie: Michael Moriarty, *James Dean*

Television. The big success stories in 2002 were the durability of reality television and the reemergence during the fall television season of family-oriented series. Millions of television viewers followed the unconventional lives of a heavy-metal rock star and his family and picked the first "American Idol." One year after the terrorist attacks on the United States, many households continued to find comfort from the outside world as they embraced more traditional situation comedies (sitcoms).

Reality television took a bizarre turn in 2002 as two programs about the private lives of celebrities became ratings successes. "The Osbournes," which debuted in March, became a pop culture phenomenon and the highest-rated series ever to air on the cable television channel MTV. Cameras followed heavy metal-rocker Ozzy Osbourne, his wife and manager Sharon, and their teen-age children Kelly and Jack, as they moved into a new house in Beverly Hills, California, consulted psychics about their pets, and pitched food over the fence of a next door neighbor who played music too loudly. The Osbournes emerged as a close-knit family, even if their dialogue had to be censored for its profanity.

In July, E! Entertainment Television offered audiences an even more outrageous reality series. "The Anna Nicole Show" featured plus-sized model and actress Anna Nicole Smith. Critics loathed the series, which often seemed to poke fun at its own star, but audiences seemed to find Smith's antics amusing.

"American Idol: The Search for a Superstar" emerged as the television hit of the summer. Contestants competed for a record contract on this interactive talent contest, which aired on Fox. The show featured three judges from the entertainment industry who traveled the United States listening to thousands of potential contestants. The judges narrowed the field down to 30 performers. Viewers voting by phone narrowed the field down to 10 hopefuls. The final 10 performed each week, with viewers ejecting one contestant at the end of every show. In a highly rated live broadcast in September, Kelly Clarkson, a cocktail waitress from Texas, was named the winner. The final vote generated more than 15 million telephone calls.

"The Bachelor" was a ratings winner for ABC in March. In this reality series, 25 women competed for the affections of the show's designated bachelor. When the series returned in the fall, many episodes scored higher ratings than its competition, NBC's Emmy-winning series "The West Wing."

Extreme television continued to attract audiences in 2002. Viewers were drawn to series such as NBC's controversial game show "Fear Factor," in which contestants participated in such stunts as being covered with tarantulas.

Stockard Channing stars as the first lady and Martin Sheen as the president of the United States in "The West Wing," which won the Emmy Award for outstanding drama series in 2002. Channing also won an Emmy for best supporting actress.

The ABC series "The Chair," which debuted in January, proved to be one of the most bizarre programs of the season. Hosted by former tennis champion John McEnroe, contestants were attached to a heart monitor as McEnroe asked a series of questions. At various points during the game, contestants were bombarded with "environmental stimulants" such as fireworks or shocking visuals. The contestants lost money if their heart rate increased. ABC canceled the show after two months.

"The Chamber," a similar series on Fox, placed contestants in a booth to answer questions while contending with distractions such as wind, water, and temperature extremes. A critical outcry over subjecting people to what appeared to be torture for the entertainment of television viewers led Fox to cancel the series in January after one week.

"Who Wants To Be a Millionaire," the ABC quiz show that many critics had credited with revitalizing the game show format on network television following its premiere in 1999, became the victim of its own success, and subsequent overexposure, in 2002. ABC canceled the series in May.

Reunions. Networks produced several nostalgic prime time retrospectives of favorite TV series

HBO's "Six Feet Under" captured a record-breaking 23 Emmy Award nominations in 2002. However, the quirky, dark comedy, about a troubled family that operates a funeral home, garnered only one Emmy, for best director for a drama series.

in 2002. In May, NBC celebrated its 75th anniversary with a three-hour special. ABC countered with a 50th anniversary retrospective of "American Bandstand." CBS offered specials devoted to "The Mary Tyler Moore Show" and "The Honeymooners." Fox paid tribute to "M*A*S*H." NBC reunited cast members of "The Cosby Show" and "L.A. Law," while ABC reunited the cast of "Laverne and Shirley." Some TV critics claimed that the networks had flooded the market with reunion shows, though most audiences enjoyed the opportunity to return to the programs of their youth.

Thursday night, long dominated by NBC, turned into one of the season's most competitive prime-time battlegrounds in 2002. The NBC sitcom "Friends," which featured a popular storyline involving the pregnancy of one of its characters, beat both "Survivor: Africa" and "Survivor: Marquesas," two CBS reality series. In a surprising turn of events, the CBS drama "CSI: Crime Scene Investigation" beat NBC's long-running series "E.R." "CSI" emerged as one of television's most-watched series in the 2001-2002 regular season.

The fall season. Viewers embraced family-friendly series, while riskier and more daring series struggled to attract an audience. ABC enjoyed high ratings with its Tuesday night line-up

Top-rated U.S. television series

The following were among the most-watched television series for the 2001-2002 regular season, which ran from Sept. 24, 2001, to May 22, 2002.

1. "Friends" (NBC)
2. "CSI" (CBS)
3. "E.R." (NBC)
4. "Everybody Loves Raymond" (CBS)
5. "Law and Order" (NBC)
6. "Friends" (8:30 p.m. rerun) (NBC)
7. (tie) "Survivor: Africa" (CBS)
   "Survivor: Marquesas" (CBS)
9. "NFL Monday Night Football" (ABC)
10. "West Wing" (NBC)
11. "Will & Grace" (NBC)
12. "Leap of Faith" (NBC)
13. "Becker" (CBS)
14. "Law and Order: SVU" (NBC)
15. "60 Minutes" (CBS)
16. (tie) "Frasier" (NBC)
    "JAG" (CBS)
18. (tie) "Inside Schwartz" (NBC)
    "Judging Amy" (CBS)
20. "NFL Monday Showcase (ABC)

Source: Nielsen Media Research.

of comedies. Each series featured a popular comedic actor. Former "Three's Company" star John Ritter returned to series television in "8 Simple Rules for Dating My Teenage Daughter." Ritter portrayed a newspaper columnist coping with his growing children. "According to Jim" starred Jim Belushi as a blue-collar family man. "Life with Bonnie," one of the most acclaimed new fall series, starred Bonnie Hunt as a Chicago talk show host balancing a career and family. The WB series "Everwood" also proved to be a ratings success. "Everwood" starred Treat Williams as a widower physician who relocated his estranged family to a mountain town.

Phil McGraw, who dispensed folksy, no-nonsense advice as a weekly guest on "The Oprah Winfrey Show," became the host of his own syndicated talk show in October. "Dr. Phil" earned the highest ratings for a new talk show since "The Rosie O'Donnell Show" debuted in 1996.

Pay cable television stations continued their bid to lure viewers from the major networks in 2002. Fans eagerly awaited the return of "The Sopranos" to HBO in September for its fourth season after a 16-month hiatus. The season premiere was the highest-rated episode of any cable television series. It was also the first time an original cable series was watched by more viewers than any of the broadcast networks. Fans also tuned in to another HBO original series, "Six Feet Under," about a dysfunctional family that runs a funeral parlor. The highly original and unusual series garnered 23 Emmy nominations in 2002, more than any other series, but it received only one award.

Failing grades. Edgier shows did not, by and large, fare well with TV audiences in 2002. "Push, Nevada," a series cocreated by actor Ben Affleck for ABC, was canceled after only a few episodes. The series, which promised viewers clues to a real-life $1-million mystery, ended before all of the clues could be broadcast. However, the network agreed to broadcast the final clue on October 28 during ABC's "Monday Night Football."

"Watching Ellie," another NBC series, starred Julia Louis-Dreyfus as a nightclub singer. The show played in real time with an on-screen clock counting down the minutes. Audience numbers dwindled as the series unfolded. Fox canceled "girls club," a series by David Kelly, the Emmy Award-winning producer of "The Practice" and "Ally McBeal," after two episodes.

Other early ratings casualties during the fall season included the CBS sitcom "Bram & Alice," starring Alfred Molina as a scoundrel novelist who is reunited with his long-lost daughter, and the ABC drama "That Was Then," in which the main character travels back in time to relive his youth. □ Donald Liebenson

See also **People in the news** (Osbourne, Ozzy).

Tennis. Sisters Serena and Venus Williams of the United States dominated tennis in 2002, meeting in the finals of the French Open, Wimbledon, and the U.S. Open. Serena, the younger sister, prevailed in all three meetings.

Serena Williams, who missed the first major tournament of 2002—the Australian Open—because of an ankle injury, became the first woman to win three majors in one year since Martina Hingis of Switzerland in 1997. Serena and Venus had met in one Grand Slam final prior to 2002.

Pete Sampras of the United States made a comeback at the 2002 U.S. Open in September. Sampras snapped a 33-tournament losing streak to win a record 14th Grand Slam title.

Australian Open. On January 27 in Melbourne, Australia, Thomas Johansson became the first Swede since Stefan Edberg in 1992 to win a Grand Slam title. Johansson upset Russian power-server Marat Safin 3-6, 6-4, 6-4, 7-6 (4).

Jennifer Capriati of the United States captured the Australian Open women's championship for a second straight year on Jan. 26, 2002, toppling Martina Hingis 4-6, 7-6 (7), 6-2. With her victory, Capriati continued a comeback that she had begun at the 2001 Australian Open.

Mark Knowles of the Bahamas and Daniel Nestor of Canada won the men's doubles title; Hingis and Anna Kournikova of Russia won their second Australian Open women's doubles title in four years; and Daniela Hantuchova of Slovakia and Kevin Ullyett of Zimbabwe captured the mixed doubles championship.

Pete Sampras of the United States displays his trophy for winning the U.S. Open on Sept. 8, 2002, while his rival, Andre Agassi, looks on. With the victory, his record-breaking 14th Grand Slam title, Sampras broke a 33-tournament losing streak.

French Open. Albert Costa of Spain won his first career Grand Slam title, besting countryman Juan Carlos Ferrero 6-1, 6-0, 4-6, 6-3 on June 9, 2002, in Paris. Costa took the first two sets easily. After dropping the third set, he broke Ferrero's serve twice, including in the match's final game.

In the women's final on June 8, Serena Williams edged Venus Williams 7-5, 6-3 in a match that many fans considered sloppy. The two combined for 101 unforced errors, 14 double faults, and 13 breaks of serve. Before the match, officials announced that Venus had vaulted to number one in the women's rankings and that Serena had risen to number two, marking the first time in history that siblings held the top two spots in the rankings.

Russian Yevgeny Kafelnikov and Paul Haarhuis of the Netherlands won the men's doubles title; Spain's Virginia Ruano Pascual and Paola Suarez won their second women's doubles title in a row; and the brother-sister pair of Cara and Wayne Black of Zimbabwe won the mixed doubles crown.

Wimbledon. Lleyton Hewitt of Australia routed upstart David Nalbandian of Argentina 6-1, 6-3, 6-2 on July 7 to take the men's singles Wimbledon title. Nalbandian, who was playing at Wimbledon for the first time, won the fewest games by a finalist since 1984, when Jimmy Connors lost to John McEnroe 6-1, 6-1, 6-2.

Serena Williams seized the top ranking from her sister Venus and denied Venus's quest for a third straight Wimbledon title, capturing the women's crown 7-6 (4), 6-3, on July 6, 2002. A day after the women's final, the Williams sisters teamed to capture the women's doubles crown. Jonas Bjorkman of Sweden and Todd Woodbridge of Australia won the men's doubles title, and India's Mahesh Bhupathi and Russian Elena Likhovtseva won the mixed doubles title.

U.S. Open. Pete Sampras quieted critics who had written him off as a serious contender when he beat his rival Andre Agassi to win the U.S. Open on September 8. Sampras beat Agassi 6-3, 6-4, 5-7, 6-4 to become, at age 31, the oldest U.S. Open men's champion since Australian Ken Rosewall won in 1970 at age 35. Sampras had not won a tournament since Wimbledon in 2000. Before the tournament, Sampras was seeded 17th, his lowest seed ever at a U.S. Open.

Serena Williams won the U.S. Open women's title on Sept. 7, 2002. She defeated her sister Venus, the defending champion, 6-4, 6-3.

Paola Suarez and Virginia Puano Pascual won the women's doubles title; Bhupathi and Max Mirnyi of Belarus won the men's doubles title; and Lisa Raymond and Mike Bryan won the mixed doubles title.   □ Michael Kates

See also **Sports.**

Terrorism. In November 2002, United States President George W. Bush signed legislation transferring 22 federal agencies and about 170,000 federal employees into a new Cabinet department called the Department of Homeland Security. The department's mission is to guard U.S. borders and protect transportation facilities, energy plants, and other vulnerable targets against terrorist attacks. The government reorganization was prompted by the terrorist attacks against the United States on Sept. 11, 2001.

Fighting al-Qa'ida. The U.S.-led war against terrorism continued in 2002 to focus on the threat posed by al-Qa'ida, the extremist Islamic network that the U.S. government holds responsible for the September 11 attacks. By late November 2002, more than 3,000 suspected members of al-Qa'ida had been arrested worldwide. Among the most high-level people captured in 2002 were Abu Zubaydah, one of the top lieutenants in the organization; Abd al-Rahim al-Nashiri, described as al-Qa'ida's chief of Persian Gulf operations; and Ramzi bin al-Shibh, who had allegedly helped plan the September 11 attacks.

United States military guards escort a detainee to interrogation at the U.S. naval base at Guantanamo Bay in Cuba in February. The first of hundreds of suspected al-Qa'ida terrorists captured by U.S. forces in Afghanistan arrived in January at the detention facility set up at Guantanamo.

In November 2002, a *drone* (pilotless) Predator aircraft operated by the U.S. Central Intelligence Agency fired a Hellfire missile at a vehicle in Yemen. The strike killed six suspected al-Qa'ida members, including Qaed Salim Sinan al-Harethi, who U.S. officials believed played a major role in the bombing of the U.S.S. *Cole* in Yemen in 2000.

Attacks by al-Qa'ida. On Oct. 6, 2002, an explosives-laden boat rammed a French oil tanker off the coast of Yemen, damaging the vessel and killing one sailor. U.S. intelligence officials attributed the attack to al-Qa'ida.

Two bombs exploded on October 12 in a nightclub district on the Indonesian island of Bali,

More than 120 hostages also died in the rescue attempt, most from the effects of the gas.

South Asia. Militant violence spread in India, Pakistan, and Kashmir, an area claimed by both India and Pakistan, in 2002. In February, Hindu militants attacked a mosque in Rawalpindi, Pakistan, killing at least 11 worshipers. The next day, a Muslim mob in the Indian province of Gujarat set fire to a train filled with Hindu activists, killing 59 of the passengers and triggering anti-Muslim riots that left hundreds of Muslims dead. In September, Muslim gunmen attacked a Hindu temple in Gujarat, killing more than 30 people.

In June, a suicide bomb explosion outside the U.S. consulate in Karachi, Pakistan, killed more than 10 people. Authorities attributed the attack to the Islamic militant group al-Qanoon. Several lethal attacks by militants against Christian facilities in Pakistan also occurred in 2002.

In May, an attack in Kashmir by separatist militants against an Indian army base and a bus killed more than 30 people. Most of the victims were the wives and children of soldiers.

☐ Richard E. Rubenstein

See also **Australia; Immigration: A Special Report; India; Middle East; Russia; United States, Government of the.**

Texas. See **Dallas; Houston; State government.**

Thailand.
Thai Rak Thai, the party of Prime Minister Thaksin Chinnawat, expanded its governing coalition in 2002 and gained control of a record number of seats in parliament. The party, which controlled 368 out of 500 seats in the house of representatives, also held the largest number of seats in the senate. Thaksin, a billionaire, was swept into power in 2001 after leading his party to victory in parliamentary elections. The elections, however, were plagued by fraud.

Thaksin ordered pollsters to stop surveying public attitudes about his administration after polls showed that his popularity had declined sharply in 2002. Government officials also ordered television networks—most of which were owned by either the government or Thaksin—to stop attacking Thaksin's administration.

King Phumiphon Adunyadet, the widely revered monarch of Thailand, issued a statement in his annual birthday speech that was highly critical of Thaksin's government and its economic policy. The king said that Thailand "is in a state of disaster instead of prosperity." He also chided the government for its attempts to censor criticism.

Government economists estimated that Thailand's economy grew at a rate of approximately 4.5 percent in 2002. ☐ Henry S. Bradsher

See also **Asia.**

killing more than 180 people. After the bombings, Indonesian authorities arrested several members of Jemaah Islamiyah, a group that the government believed was linked to al-Qa'ida.

On November 28, explosives blew up an Israeli-owned hotel outside Mombasa, Kenya, killing three Israelis and 10 Kenyans. The attack was preceded by a failed attempt to shoot down an Israeli-chartered airliner with shoulder-fired ground-to-air missiles. Al-Qa'ida later claimed credit for both attacks.

Russia. Islamic separatists from Chechnya seized more than 750 hostages in a theater in Moscow, the capital, in October, demanding that Russia end its war against the separatists in the breakaway republic. A three-day standoff between the hostage-takers and the authorities ended when Russian security forces piped a sedative gas into the theater to disable the militants, who were then shot dead while unconscious.

Theater. Healthy ticket sales and critical acclaim for a number of ambitious Broadway shows marked 2002 as a year of rejuvenation for New York City's theater community, though no Broadway production rivaled the success of 2001's smash hit *The Producers*. Despite a dramatic drop in attendance following the terrorist attacks on the United States on Sept. 11, 2001, an upturn in attendance in early 2002 and excitement about such new shows as *Hairspray, Metamorphosis, Thoroughly Modern Milly,* and *Movin' Out* helped several theaters meet or exceed their attendance forecasts.

Changes in patterns of theater attendance, however, hurt many New York City productions. Rather than purchasing tickets for a desired performance far in advance, a significant number of theater patrons bought tickets at the last minute and at discounted prices. The decline in advance sales contributed to the closing of a number of shows, including the highly praised *Topdog/Underdog* at the Ambassador Theater. The play, which starred actor Jeffrey Wright and rapper Mos Def as brothers, won the 2002 Pulitzer Prize for its author, Suzan-Lori Parks.

The Graduate, based on the 1967 movie of the same title, continued to draw crowds, although it did not receive any Tony Awards. The show easily recouped its $1.8 million cost and, despite the trend against advance sales, sold a record $5 million in tickets before opening.

A split at the Tonys. The American Theatre Wing's 2002 Tony Awards reflected the lack of a single stand-out production. Awards given to new musicals were split between the critically undistinguished but highly popular *Thoroughly Modern Millie,* which took the award for best musical, and the quirky but much-lauded *Urinetown: The Musical,* which won best direction, book, and score of a musical. *Thoroughly Modern Millie,* based on a 1967 movie about a small town girl's move to 1920's New York City, took a total of six awards. These included best choreography, orchestration, and costume design, as well as the award for a leading actress in a musical, which went to Sutton Foster for her portrayal of Millie.

The Tony Award for best play went to Edward Albee's *The Goat or Who Is Sylvia?,* which is about an architect who conducts an extramarital affair with a member of another species. The show's original stars—Bill Pullman and Mercedes Ruehl—were replaced late in the year by actor and clown Bill Irwin, as the architect, and Academy Award-winning actress Sally Field, as his wife.

The Williamstown Theatre Festival received the 2002 Regional Theater Tony Award, making it the first summer theater to gain that honor. The festival, located in the Berkshire region of western Massachusetts, runs from mid-June to late August each year and features distinguished productions of both classic and new plays. Productions at Williamstown in 2002 included Eric Bogosian's *Red Angel,* a graphic exploration of the relationship between a male university professor and a female student, directed by Neil Pepe of the Atlantic Theater Company in New York City.

Pop musicals. Several productions in 2002 set plays to the songs of popular musicians following the pattern of the smash hit *Mamma Mia!,* which was based on the music of the pop band ABBA. In *We Will Rock You,* a science-fiction rock-musical at London's Dominion Theatre, rebels fight against the antimusic conglomerate Globalsoft. The show, which was panned by reviewers, featured the music of the British rock group Queen.

At New York City's Richard Rodgers Theater, a dance-theater piece titled *Movin' Out* featured the songs of rock performer Billy Joel and was staged by choreographer Twyla Tharp. Singer Michael Cavanaugh provided vocal renditions of Joel's songs and performed on a platform above a company of dancers. The production starred John Selya as Eddie and Elizabeth Parkinson as Brenda, the king and queen of the prom described in Joel's ballad "Scenes from an Italian Restaurant."

New shows. New shows near the end of 2002 included a much-anticipated revival of *Man of La Mancha* at the National Theatre in Washington, D.C. The play, based on the Miguel Cervantes novel *Don Quixote,* starred Brian Stokes Mitchell in the title role. The production moved to Broadway in December. *Far Away,* a new play by British playwright Caryl Churchill that premiered in London in 2000, opened to strong reviews in the United States in 2002 at the New York Theater Workshop in New York City. The show, with a cast led by actress Francis McDormand of the movie *Fargo,* runs less than an hour and relates a chilling story of wartime horror in which even animals and the elements have taken sides.

Director Baz Luhrmann, whose films include *Moulin Rouge* and *Strictly Ballroom,* brought his opulent production of Puccini's *La Boheme* to the Broadway Theater in New York City in December 2002. Set in Paris during the 1950's and sung in Italian with English subtitles, the production received rave reviews for its elaborate stage sets and colorful costuming, flourishes typical of Luhrmann's flamboyant style.

Writer Martin McDonagh, acclaimed author of the *Leenane* trilogy, enjoyed a critical success with *The Lieutenant of Inishmore,* a satirical play about terrorism in Northern Ireland. The play, featuring McDonagh's characteristically dark humor, tells the story of a violent, gun-wielding youth who seeks to make his country safe for cats. The production originated at the Royal Shakespeare Company in London and later moved to the West End.

Tom Stoppard in London. The most talked-

Edna Turnblad, played by Harvey Fierstein, sings to daughter Tracy, played by Marissa Winokur, in *Hairspray,* the 2002 hit Broadway musical. The play, based on John Waters's 1988 cult film, tells the story of a teen-ager who becomes a celebrity after appearing on a local TV dance show.

about event on the London stage in 2002 was *The Coast of Utopia,* a play in three sequential but self-contained installments by Tom Stoppard. Trevor Nunn directed the play's premiere at the Royal National Theater in London. The play's "Voyage," "Shipwreck," and "Salvage" sections take more than nine hours to perform and explore the intellectual underpinnings of the Russian Revolution. Marked by Stoppard's signature brand of philosophical and intellectual dialogue, the story follows a group of friends from their privileged youths in Russia to their subsequent exile in Western Europe. The play features heady conversations between such historical figures as activist Alexander Herzen and novelist Ivan Turgenev. An ensemble of 12 actors assuming some 70 roles supports the main cast.

Sondheim in Washington. A summer-long celebration of the work of Stephen Sondheim, the foremost musical theater composer in the United States, took place at the prestigious John F. Kennedy Center for the Performing Arts in Washington, D.C. The productions of Sondheim's plays, six in all, included *Sweeny Todd, Company,* and *Sunday in the Park with George.* The shows

Tony Award winners in 2002

Best Play, *The Goat or Who Is Sylvia?,* by Edward Albee
Best Musical, *Thoroughly Modern Millie*
Best Play Revival, *Private Lives*
Best Musical Revival, *Into the Woods*
Leading Actor in a Play, Alan Bates, *Fortune's Fool*
Leading Actress in a Play, Lindsay Duncan, *Private Lives*
Leading Actor in a Musical, John Lithgow, *Sweet Smell of Success*
Leading Actress in a Musical, Sutton Foster, *Thoroughly Modern Millie*
Featured Actor in a Play, Frank Langella, *Fortune's Fool*
Featured Actress in a Play, Katie Finneran, *Noises Off*
Featured Actor in a Musical, Shuler Hensley, *Oklahoma!*
Featured Actress in a Musical, Harriet Harris, *Thoroughly Modern Millie*
Direction of a Play, Mary Zimmerman, *Metamorphoses*
Direction of a Musical, John Rando, *Urinetown: The Musical*
Book of a Musical, Greg Kotis, *Urinetown: The Musical*
Original Musical Score, Mark Hollman and Greg Kotis, *Urinetown: The Musical*
Orchestration, Doug Besterman and Ralph Burns, *Thoroughly Modern Millie*
Scenic Design, Tim Hatley, *Private Lives*
Costume Design, Martin Pakledinaz, *Thoroughly Modern Millie*
Lighting Design, Brian MacDevitt, *Into the Woods*
Choreography, Rob Ashford, *Thoroughly Modern Millie*
Regional Theater, Williamstown Theatre Festival in Massachusetts
Special Theatrical Event, *Elaine Stritch at Liberty*
Lifetime Achievement, Julie Harris, actress, and Robert Whitehead, producer

featured some of theater's brightest stars, such as Brian Stokes Mitchell, Lynn Redgrave, Melissa Errico, and Christine Baranski. Michael Kaiser, president of the Kennedy Center, envisioned the highly successful productions as part of his plan to make the Kennedy Center a first-rate theater in its own right and not merely a venue for traveling shows.

New director at the Long Wharf. Gordon Edelstein assumed leadership of the Long Wharf Theatre in New Haven, Connecticut. The Long Wharf's previous director, Doug Hughes, who had gained attention with a production of *Wit* and had eliminated the theater's deficit of more than $500,000, left following a disagreement with the board of directors in 2001.

Edelstein pledged in 2002 to attract a younger audience for the theater and to build its diminished subscriber base back up to the high that it enjoyed in the late 1980's under longtime director Arvin Brown. Edelstein also planned to oversee the theater's move to a new building when its current lease runs out in 2007. Edelstein announced in 2002 that the first season of plays under his direction would include the rarely performed *Mourning Becomes Electra* by Eugene O'Neill, as well as plays by Ruben Santiago-Hudson and Donald Margulies.   □ David Yezzi

Togo. See Africa.

Toronto. Ontario Premier Ernie Eves and Canadian Prime Minister Jean Chretien announced in May 2002 that the federal and provincial governments were joining forces to revive Toronto's cultural institutions. The Art Gallery of Ontario, the Royal Ontario Museum, and a proposed new opera house received a total of $223 million in government funds. (All amounts are in Canadian dollars.)

Roy Thomson Hall, the city's premier concert hall, also received funds to help finance renovations and improvements completed in September to the hall's acoustics. On October 12, audiences packed the hall for a gala concert to honor Queen Elizabeth II. The queen spent two days in Toronto during a visit to Canada to celebrate her Golden Jubilee, the 50th anniversary of her reign.

City workers strike. In June, Toronto's 6,800 outdoor workers, mostly laborers who collect garbage and maintain parks, went on strike. The city's 18,000 indoor workers, the clerical staff of city offices, followed suit in July. The most visible effect of the strikes was the pile-up of garbage. Landfills on the city's outskirts remained open, but few people could reach them. As summer temperatures rose, the city turned parks into emergency garbage dumps to get rotting garbage off the streets. On July 11, the provincial government ordered an end to the strike.

World Youth Day. City workers worked overtime to clean up Toronto in time to welcome Pope John Paul II, who arrived on July 25 to attend World Youth Day celebrations. World Youth Day is a week-long gathering of Roman Catholic youth held every two or three years in a different city. The event drew hundreds of thousands of participants from more than 170 countries to Toronto. A crowd estimated at 800,000 braved pouring rain to attend an open-air Mass celebrated by the pope.

School board showdown. Ontario's provincial government took over Toronto's schools in August following a budget showdown between the province and the Toronto District School Board. The board, responsible for 300,000 pupils in 560 schools, said it needed an additional $90 million to meet operating expenses and threatened to go into debt if the province did not provide more funding. The province appointed administrators to take over the schools and make all crucial decisions, though school board members continued to hold office. Paul Christie, a popular former city councilor, was appointed administrator of Toronto's schools. In November, Christie announced that he had cut $90 million from the education budget without closing schools. He did, however, cut administrative staff, which angered parents' groups and teachers' unions.

Tent City. On September 25, Toronto police evicted a group of squatters from a patch of land near the city's waterfront. Homeless people had taken up residence for three years in what became known as "Tent City." The presence of the encampment just a few blocks east of the heart of Toronto's downtown area drew unwelcome attention to the city's housing problems. City leaders regarded an article on Tent City in *The New York Times* as a sign of Toronto's bitter descent from its reputation in the 1970's as "the city that works." Reports of drug dealing and health hazards finally prompted the owners of the land to call in the police to remove the squatters.

Official plan. In November 2002, Toronto's City Council approved the city's new official plan. The plan allowed for an additional 1 million people to join Toronto's current population of some 2.5 million over a period of 30 years. The plan called for apartment and office building construction along main suburban roads that in 2002 were occupied mostly by strip malls. The plan aroused fears that tall buildings on main roads would destabilize side-street neighborhoods made up of single family houses. However, the council approved the plan because it would enable the city to make better use of public transportation and help fight urban sprawl in areas that border Toronto.   □ David Lewis Stein

See also **Canada; Canadian provinces; City.**

Toys and games. The toy industry in the United States struggled in 2002 to recover from weak sales in 2001, the result of a recession and the after-effect of the terrorist attacks on the United States. However, the lingering fear of further terrorism, the specter of U.S. involvement in a war with Iraq, a volatile stock market, and widespread job lay-offs undermined consumer confidence in 2002, and industry sales rose less than 3 percent over 2001.

Industry observers also predicted that a 10-day lockout at 29 shipping docks on the West Coast of the United States in September and October would severely impact toy industry sales during the holiday season. About 85 percent of toys sold in the United States are manufactured elsewhere, and those made in Asia are sent via container ships that enter the United States at ports on the West Coast. However, as early as the spring of 2002, some toy manufacturers and retailers

had anticipated labor problems at the docks and had moved up shipping dates, rerouted their toy shipments to other ports of entry, or sent their products by air, resulting in fewer shortages of toys at retail stores.

Yu-Gi-Oh! My! In 2002, another character drawn from Japanese animation captured the fancy of youngsters in the United States— Yu-Gi-Oh! (king of games). Based on a comic book first produced in Japan and introduced to U.S. television audiences in 2001 via a cartoon series, Yu-Gi is a shy high-school boy who changes into a hero and commands a legion of battling monsters. The TV series spawned a number of items, aimed at boys ages 8 to 14, including trading cards, computer and video games, action figures, and puzzles. The trading card games, distributed in the United States by the Upper Deck Company, LLC of Carlsbad, California, were the most popular of the licensed items. Each player begins the game with 8,000 points and tries to reduce the other players' points to zero by acquiring their cards. The cards depict monsters and other creatures that have various powers and points.

"Lo hicimos! (We did it!)" sings Dora the Explorer, the Latina heroine of a popular cartoon series for preschoolers. During her TV adventures, Dora solves problems, figures out puzzles, and plays games, while incorporating basic Spanish words and phrases. Bilingual Dora toys, games, and accessories were big sellers in 2002, especially the We Did It! Dancing Dora from Fisher-Price Brands of East Aurora, New York. The interactive stuffed doll sings and dances to her "We

Teens show off Heelys, sneakers with a removable wheel in the heel. The shoes allow wearers to go from a walk to a roll simply by shifting their weight to their heels. More than 1.25 million pairs of the highly popular sneakers, introduced in late 2000, had been sold worldwide by the end of 2002.

Did It!" theme song and says English and Spanish phrases.

Two guys named Bob. One of the guys is a yellow sponge that lives in a pineapple under the sea, in a place known as Bikini Bottom. The other is a builder whose crew includes a talking backhoe, dump truck, steamroller, crane, and cement mixer. For kids ages 2 and up, SpongeBob SquarePants, from Mattel, Incorp., of El Segundo, California, and Bob the Builder, from Hasbro, Incorporated of Pawtucket, Rhode Island, were the must-have toys of 2002.

Based on top-rated television series, the two Bobs captured the imaginations of preschoolers. The pants-wearing sponge and his friends, including Squidward Tentacles, Patrick Star, a fish, and Mr. Krabs, learn lessons about self-esteem and accepting others. Bob the Builder, his business partner Wendy, Scoop the backhoe, Lofty the crane, and other talking building machines practice problem-solving through teamwork.

A funky chicken and hair apparent. Two of the toy industry's biggest hits in 2002 were updated classics manufactured by Mattel. Barbie as Rapunzel featured the fashion doll as the fairy-tale heroine. Her ponytail unfolds and, with a hair extension, grows to over a foot in length. The Chicken Dance Elmo interactive plush toy has the Sesame Street favorite in a chicken suit, singing and dancing to the Chicken Dance, a wedding-band favorite. □ Diane P. Cardinale

See also **Labor and employment; Transportation.**

Track and field. Tim Montgomery of the United States broke the world record in the 100-meter dash on Sept. 14, 2002, in Paris, becoming the world's fastest human. Montgomery's time of 9.78 seconds was 0.01 second better than the time of the previous record-holder, Maurice Greene of the United States.

British sprinter Dwain Chambers had a successful season, beating the usually dominant Greene five times. In June, Chambers won the European championships, running the 100 in 10.02 seconds. Greene blamed minor injuries for his 2002 slump, but observers attributed his lack-luster performances to poor conditioning.

Golden League. On September 6, three-time Olympic champion Marion Jones of the United States finished her sweep in the seven-event Golden League series by winning the women's 100-meter dash at a meet in Berlin, Germany. Jones had a time of 11.01 seconds. Jones's performances earned her a share of 110 pounds (50 kilograms) of gold bars worth about $500,000.

In addition to Jones, three other athletes took shares of the Golden League prize. Hicham el Guerrouj of Morocco became the first athlete to win a share of the jackpot four times when he won the 1,500-meter run in 3 minutes, 30 seconds. Felix Sanchez of the Dominican Republic ran the 400-meter hurdles in 48.05 seconds, and Ana Guevara of Mexico took the women's 400-meter dash in 49.91 seconds.

World track and field records established in 2002

Event	Holder	Country	Where set	Date	Record
Women indoor					
Pole vault	Svetlana Feofanova	Russia	Vienna, Austria	March 3	15' 7" (4.75 m)
800 meters	Jolanda Ceplak	Slovenia	Vienna, Austria	March 3	1:55.82
3,000 meters	Berhane Adere	Ethiopia	Stuttgart, Germany	March 2	8:29.15
Men outdoor					
100 meters	Tim Montgomery	U.S.	Paris	September 14	9.78
3,000-meter steeplechase	Brahim Boulami	Morocco	Zurich, Switzerland	August 16	7:53.17*
Marathon	Khalid Khannouchi	U.S.	London	April 14	2:05.38**
Women outdoor					
3,000-meter steeplechase	Alesya Turova	Belarus	Gdansk, Poland	July 27	9:16.51
5,000-meter walk	Gillian O'Sullivan	Ireland	Dublin, Ireland	July 13	20:02.60
25,000 meters	Tegla Loroupe	Kenya	Mengerskirchen, Germany	September 21	1:27:05.9
Marathon	Paula Radcliffe	U.K.	Chicago	October 13	2:17.18**

m = meters
* = not yet ratified.
** = not recognized as a world record, but world-best performance.
Source: International Association of Athletics Federations (IAAF).

Outdoor records. Khalid Khannouchi, a U.S. citizen born in Morocco, broke his own world mark in the men's marathon in thrilling fashion at the London Marathon on April 14. Khannouchi pulled past two runners near the end to win in 2 hours, 5 minutes, and 38 seconds.

Alesya Turova of Belarus broke the world record in the women's 3,000-meter steeplechase on July 27 in Gdansk, Poland. Russia's Svetlana Feofanova broke the women's indoor pole vaulting world record in February and went on to beat her own record four more times. On March 3 in Vienna, Austria, Feofanova set the world record at 15 feet, 7 inches (4.75 meters).

Sammy Kipketer of Kenya broke his own world record in the men's 10-kilometer run, finishing in 27 minutes, 10 seconds on March 31 in New Orleans, Louisiana. On August 16, Brahim Boulami of Morocco broke his own record in the 3,000-meter steeplechase in Zurich, Switzerland, with a time of 7 minutes, 53.17 seconds.

Indoor records. Mark Bett of Kenya broke the world record for the 10,000 meters on February 10 in Ghent, Belgium. He finished in 27 minutes, 50.29 seconds. U.S. runner Regina Jacobs broke the indoor world record for the 3-mile run on February 23 in New York City, finishing in 14 minutes, 44.11 seconds. Slovenia's Jolanda Ceplak broke the indoor world record in the 800 meters on March 3 in Vienna, Austria, with a time of 1 minute, 55.82 seconds.

Drug testing. The International Association of Athletics Federations (IAAF), the official governing body for track and field, announced on March 14 that it would conduct year-round out-of-competition testing for erythropoetin, or EPO. Because the drug increases the production of red blood cells, which carry oxygen to muscles, it can increase athletes' endurance.

The IAAF announced on August 29 that Brahim Boulami, the world-record holder in the 3,000-meter steeplechase, tested positive for EPO in a test taken the day before he broke his own world record. Boulami asserted his innocence, and results on a second part of his sample were pending in late 2002.

The IAAF said in August that Mohammed Mourhit of Belgium had tested positive for EPO in May. Mourhit, who held the European records in the 3000-, 5000-, and 10,000-meter steeplechase events, was banned for three years.

College tragedy. On February 23, Kevin Dare, a sophomore at Pennsylvania State University at University Park, died at the Big Ten men's indoor championships in Minneapolis, Minnesota. Dare died from injuries he sustained after falling and hitting his head during a pole-vault attempt. ☐ Michael Kates

Transit. See Transportation.

Transportation. The Transportation Security Administration (TSA), an agency of the United States Department of Transportation that was created in late 2001, assumed official responsibility for airport security in the United States in February 2002. U.S. President George W. Bush had signed legislation in November 2001 requiring federal employees to replace private-company passenger and baggage screeners at 424 commercial airports in the United States. (Five airports were to continue using private screeners.) The move came after 19 terrorists hijacked four commercial jets on Sept. 11, 2001. The terrorists crashed two of the planes into the World Trade Center in New York City and one into the Pentagon Building outside Washington, D.C. Another plane crashed in Pennsylvania. About 3,000 people were killed in the attacks.

The TSA announced in November 2002 that it had met its November 19 deadline to hire and train more than 30,000 new passenger screeners. Unlike previous screeners, the federal employees were required to be U.S. citizens. In addition, they had to speak English and pass drug tests and criminal background checks.

The TSA was also required to inspect all checked bags at airports for explosives. To do so, the legislation passed in 2001 required the agency to hire 22,000 baggage screeners and install more than 1,000 massive detection machines by the end of 2002. In November 2002, Congress passed legislation that allowed some airports to seek an extension of this deadline.

TSA head resigns. John W. Magaw, the head of the TSA, resigned in July after only six months on the job. Admiral James M. Loy, retired commandant of the U.S. Coast Guard, replaced Magaw as undersecretary of transportation for security. The Coast Guard, a unit of the Department of Transportation, is responsible for marine safety and other duties. Magaw had come under intense criticism from the airline industry for not consulting industry officials on proposed solutions to security problems.

Amtrak's woes. Amtrak, the semipublic corporation that provides intercity passenger rail transportation in the United States, narrowly avoided having to cease operations in June. The Federal Railroad Administration, a division of the Department of Transportation, agreed to provide a $100-million loan guarantee to cover a budget shortfall.

Amtrak's financial condition, which had been perilous since its creation in 1970, deteriorated markedly during the late 1990's. In May 2002, David L. Gunn, a railroad- and transit-industry veteran who was widely credited with rescuing the New York City Transit Authority in the late 1980's, was named Amtrak's president. Never-

Container ships lie anchored off the California coast at the ports of Los Angeles and Long Beach in October during a 10-day labor lockout that closed 29 West Coast ports and cost the U.S. economy more than $10 billion. Dock owners imposed the lockout during a labor dispute.

theless, speculation continued that Amtrak might be broken up and large parts of it closed down.

Amtrak's woes were compounded by two serious accidents in 2002. On April 18, four people were killed and more than 150 others were injured when the Amtrak Auto Train, carrying passengers from Florida to Virginia, derailed because of misaligned track near Crescent City, Florida. The accident was Amtrak's deadliest since 1999. On July 29, 2002, about 100 passengers were injured when the Capital Limited, traveling from Chicago to Washington, D.C., derailed shortly before reaching its destination. Investigators also blamed this derailment on misaligned track.

In August, Amtrak officials announced that Amtrak's high-speed Acela Express trains, which provide service between Boston, New York City, and Washington, D.C., had cracks in locomotive equipment and a number of other serious mechanical problems. Amtrak suspended most of its Acela service for about a month while it repaired the problems.

Rail privatization setback. In June, Railtrack, the private firm that owned passenger track and signaling in the United Kingdom, re-turned to public ownership. Network Rail, Inc., a not-for-profit company backed by the British government, purchased Railtrack.

Since being privatized in 1995, the passenger rail system in Great Britain had experienced many problems, including a highly publicized fatal crash in 2000, delays, and financial struggles. These incidents disappointed proponents of privatization, who had hoped privatizing state-owned passenger railroad companies would lead to reduced costs and improved service.

L.A. rail link opens. In April 2002, the Alameda Corridor opened in southern California. The corridor, a rail link 20 miles (32 kilometers) long, connected the major seaports of Los Angeles and Long Beach with nearby rail yards. The corridor is used primarily to move the growing number of containers that arrive from Asia by ship.

Barge collision. On May 26, 14 people were killed when the Interstate 40 bridge near Webbers Falls, Oklahoma, collapsed after a towboat pushed two barges into the bridge's supports. A 500-foot (152-meter) section of the bridge was destroyed, causing at least 12 vehicles to plummet into the Arkansas River. The National Transportation Safety Board, a federal agency that works to ensure the safety of all types of transportation, determined that the towboat's captain had less than 10 hours of sleep in the two days prior to the accident. ☐ Ian Savage

See also **Automobile; Aviation; Terrorism.**

Trinidad and Tobago. See Latin America.

Tunisia. See Middle East.

Turkey. The pro-Islamic Justice and Development Party (AKP) trounced entrenched political parties in general elections in early November 2002, allowing the AKP to form Turkey's first single-party government in 15 years. The AKP, headed by former Istanbul mayor Recep Tayyip Erdogan, won 363 of the parliament's 550 seats. Leaders of previously banned Islamic parties had founded the AKP in 2001, though they portrayed their new party as centrist and *secular* (nonreligious) in 2002. The secular center-left Republican People's Party claimed 178 seats in parliament.

New prime minister. Despite the AKP victory, Erdogan was ineligible to become prime minister—or even hold a seat in parliament—because of a 1998 criminal conviction for reciting a poem that "incited religious hatred." In mid-November 2002, President Ahmet Necdet Sezer appointed AKP deputy leader Abdullah Gul to the premiership. However, in late December, the parlliament voted to allow Erdogan to run for parliament in a special election in February 2003, which would clear the way for him to become prime minister.

Iraq. General Hilmi Ozkok, chief of Turkey's armed forces, urged the United States in November 2002 to avoid war with Iraq. Turkish officials feared that a threatened U.S. military attack on Iraq, Turkey's neighbor to the south, would damage Turkey's already depressed economy and unleash the aspirations for independence of Kurds, an ethnic minority in southeastern Turkey. The U.S. government viewed military bases in Turkey as critical in a military action against Iraq.

European Union. In December, the European Union (EU) announced it would begin membership meetings with Turkey in December 2004. Turkish officials had hoped for an earlier timetable. In October 2002, the EU had excluded Turkey from a list of countries eligible to join the economic association in 2004. The EU remained concerned about Turkey's record on democracy and human rights despite the passage of some reforms by the Turkish parliament in 2002.

Cyprus. Turkish-Cypriot leader Rauf Denktash rejected a United Nations-sponsored deal to reunite the island of Cyprus in December. Cyprus was divided into Turkish and Greek enclaves in 1974. The rejection led to the prospect that only the Greek-led portion of Cyprus would be granted EU membership. The EU had hoped to offer membership to a united Cyprus.

Afghanistan. Turkey took command of the 19-nation peacekeeping force in Afghanistan in June 2002. Turkey had the largest contingent—1,400 troops—in the Afghan capital, Kabul, as part of the 5,000-troop force. ☐ Christine Helms

See also **Afghanistan; Europe; Iraq; Middle East.**

Turkmenistan. See Asia.

Uganda. In March 2002, Uganda's government launched a major offensive, code-named "Operation Iron Fist," against the Lord's Resistance Army (LRA), a Ugandan rebel group hiding out in neighboring Sudan. The LRA, led by self-proclaimed prophet Joseph Kony, claimed as its objective the imposition of Christian rule in Uganda but in fact carried out a campaign of terror against civilians, especially children. Human rights experts estimated that in 16 years of armed rebellion, LRA soldiers had kidnapped and enslaved at least 10,000 children.

With the approval of the Sudanese government, Ugandan forces carried out military operations on both sides of Uganda's northern border with Sudan. By mid-2002, the Ugandan army had some 25,000 troops in the area of rebel activity, 10,000 of them based in southern Sudan, against some 3,000 to 5,000 LRA fighters.

By late 2002, the government offensive, despite overwhelming superiority of numbers, had not achieved its objective of ending the LRA rebellion. Analysts said the military campaign in Sudan had merely driven LRA troops back into northern Uganda, where they terrorized the local population. In October, an official with the Gulu Support the Children Organization, a charity operating a children's camp in northern Uganda, said that the LRA was abducting as many as 10 children per day, an all-time high.

Political retrenchment. In June 2002, President Yoweri Museveni signed a bill into law that tightened restrictions on political activity. The new law dashed hopes of opposition politicians and international human rights activists that a genuine multiparty political system might evolve in Uganda. Museveni's National Resistance Movement, which seized power in Uganda in 1986, imposed a "no-party" system in 1995 that restricted independent political activity. Kizza Besigye, a Ugandan Army officer, mounted the only serious challenge to Museveni's rule in 2001 when he ran against Museveni in a presidential election.

The Ugandan parliament had passed the new law, the Political Organizations and Parties Act, in May. It restricted all political activities to Kampala, the capital, and specified what types of meetings were legal. It also specified criminal penalties for violations.

Regional relations. President Museveni and Joseph Kabila, president of Congo (Kinshasa), signed a pact in September 2002 committing the leaders to reestablish full diplomatic ties. The two countries had severed relations in 1998 when Uganda sent troops into Congo (Kinshasa) to support a rebel faction. In August 2002, Uganda pledged to withdraw its forces.

☐ Simon Baynham

See also **Africa; Congo (Kinshasa).**

A Russian-built Sukhoi-27 jet fighter slams into the ground during an air show in Lviv, Ukraine, on July 27, 2002. At least 85 people were killed and 200 others injured when the plane crashed into a crowd of spectators after clipping the ground with its wing during a dangerous maneuver.

Ukraine. Our Ukraine, the electoral bloc led by former Prime Minister Viktor Yushchenko, took more votes than any other party in March 2002 elections for seats in Ukraine's *Verkhovna Rada* (parliament). Our Ukraine won 23.6 percent of the nationwide party-list vote, compared with 20 percent for the Communist Party and 11.8 percent for United Ukraine, the party of President Leonid Kuchma.

Despite its poor showing, United Ukraine managed to assemble a coalition of smaller parties to gain control of the Rada. On May 28, United Ukraine leader Volodymyr Lytvyn, who had previously headed President Kuchma's administration, was elected speaker of the Rada.

Kuchmagate tapes. President Kuchma continued to struggle during 2002 with the revelations contained in the "Kuchmagate" tapes—hundreds of hours of conversations secretly recorded by a presidential bodyguard and published in the national and international press. Kuchma was dogged by persistent allegations that taped remarks revealed he had ordered the murder of opposition journalist Heorhy Gongadze in 2000. In September and October 2002, tens of thousands of Ukrainians demonstrated in Kiev, the capital, and other major cities, demanding Kuchma's resignation.

In October, the Kuchmagate scandal spilled over into foreign relations as newly released recordings suggested that Kuchma authorized the sale of a sophisticated radar system to Iraq in July 2000. The system would allow Iraq to detect and shoot down U.S. fighter jets patrolling Iraqi air space. The sale, which Ukraine denied, violated United Nations sanctions established after the 1991 Persian Gulf War. As a result of the revelation, NATO withdrew its invitation to Ukraine to a November 2002 summit. Despite the withdrawal, Kuchma attended the summit, where he was greeted coldly by many world leaders.

In November 2002, Kuchma fired Prime Minister Anatoly Kinakh and nominated close political ally Viktor Yanukovich to be his successor. Political experts said Kuchma was trying to consolidate his power in the face of mounting criticism over actions revealed in the Kuchmagate tapes.

Air show disaster. On July 27, a jet fighter at an air show in Lviv crashed into a crowd of spectators while attempting a dangerous maneuver. At least 85 people were killed, and 200 others were injured. The pilots managed to eject, however, and were charged with criminal negligence for their role in one of the worst air-show disasters in history.   □ Steven L. Solnick

See also **Disaster; Europe.**

United Arab Emirates. See Middle East.

Britons expressed increased sympathy and support for the royal family in 2002, following the death of Queen Elizabeth, the Queen Mother, and during the celebration of the 50-year reign of Queen Elizabeth II. However, new scandals concerning the royal household surfaced near the end of the year. Meanwhile, Prime Minister Tony Blair's Labour government, shaken by a series of high profile Cabinet resignations, still managed to win support for increasing spending on public services.

Budget. Chancellor of the Exchequer (finance minister) Gordon Brown presented a budget to the House of Commons on April 17 that included substantial spending increases for public services. In previous years, the Labour government had been criticized by its own supporters for its failure to spend more money on such services as health and education. Discontent over the poor state of such services surfaced in the general election of 2001.

Brown's budget focused particularly on the National Health Service (NHS), which provides publicly funded medical care for all citizens. Brown provided 40 billion pounds ($64 billion) of additional money to the NHS over the next five years. Public spending overall increased by 4 billion pounds ($6 billion) in fiscal 2002-2003 to a total of 390 billion pounds ($619 billion). Spending was to increase to 471 billion pounds ($747 billion) in fiscal 2005-2006. Brown proposed increasing national insurance, a flat rate tax paid by both employers and employees, to fund the additional spending. Opposition leader Iain Duncan Smith of the Conservative Party accused Brown of, in effect, increasing income taxes, which Labour had promised not to do. Opinion polls, however, indicated that the budget was well received by the public.

Brown, in his review of spending in July 2002, announced a further increase of 14.7 billion pounds ($23.3 billion) for education (an increase of 6 percent), as well as more spending on the police, defense, and transportation. The additional funds were linked to demands for reform and greater efficiency in the delivery of public services. The government wagered that increased spending would provide Labour with a platform for the next election, expected to take place in 2005 or 2006.

Economic growth in the United Kingdom was modest in 2002. Economists forecast that the country's *gross domestic product* (the value of all goods and services produced in one year) would rise by 1.6 percent, down from 1.9 percent in 2001. The slow growth was attributed to the general slowdown in the global economy. The lack of growth led to speculation that the government may not be able to afford its proposed spending plans.

Cabinet. The Labour government in 2002 underwent a number of Cabinet reshuffles, sparked by the resignations of key ministers. The secretary of state for transport, local government, and the regions, Stephen Byers, announced his resignation on May 28, after months of allegations that he had lied about a number of matters involving his department. Byers, a close political ally of Tony Blair, was the first Cabinet minister to resign since the 2001 election.

The controversy surrounding Byers began in late 2001. Byers's political advisor, Jo Moore, sent out a departmental e-mail on September 11 (the day of the terrorist attacks on the United States). She suggested that the events of the day provided a good opportunity for the government to release unpopular news, as attention would be focused on the United States. After the e-mail was made public, Moore was forced to apologize, but the incident reinforced the Labour government's reputation for "spinning" the news (reporting events in a way that would enhance the government's image).

Moore became involved in a similar incident following the death of Princess Margaret, the sister of Queen Elizabeth II, in February 2002. Moore's suggestion to "bury" bad news about the British railway system on the day of the princess's funeral was leaked to the press by Martin Sixsmith, the ministry's communications director. Both Moore and Sixsmith were forced to resign. Byers subsequently came under further pressure when he announced Sixsmith's resignation before the secretary had actually resigned, leading the Conservatives to claim that he had lied about the circumstances of Sixsmith's departure.

In the Cabinet reshuffle that followed Byers's resignation, his ministry was broken up. Alastair Darling became transport secretary, while other responsibilities in the department were taken over by John Prescott, the deputy prime minister. As part of the reshuffle, Paul Boateng became chief secretary to the treasury, the first black person to join the Cabinet.

On Oct. 23, 2002, Education Secretary Estelle Morris resigned in the wake of a number of controversies. The most serious involved the results of the 2002 *A-Levels* (exams taken by high school students in the United Kingdom that are used as the basis for university admissions). Within hours of the publication of the test results in August, complaints began that students' scores had been deliberately downgraded to keep pass rates down, and counter criticism that the exams had become too easy. Mor-

Pageantry heralded Queen Elizabeth II's Golden Jubilee celebration, a commemoration of her 50 years on the British throne.

The queen greets her public from an open-topped vehicle as she and her husband, the Duke of Edinburgh, ride down The Mall in London. The royal couple were returning to Buckingham Palace to watch a Golden Jubilee parade after taking part in a banquet at the medieval Guildhall on June 4.

Thousands of people line the streets of central London in front of Buckingham Palace on June 4 as Queen Elizabeth II rides in the Gold State Coach to St. Paul's Cathedral for a thanksgiving service celebrating her 50-year reign.

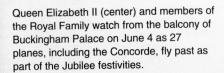

Queen Elizabeth II (center) and members of the Royal Family watch from the balcony of Buckingham Palace on June 4 as 27 planes, including the Concorde, fly past as part of the Jubilee festivities.

Fireworks light the sky above Buckingham Palace on June 3, capping a concert attended by more than 12,000 people. Sir Paul McCartney, Eric Clapton, Tom Jones, Brian Wilson, Tony Bennett, and many others took part, as more than 1 million Londoners watched on television screens set up in parks surrounding the palace.

Queen Elizabeth II pauses to greet ethnic dancers and a mechanical elephant as she tours London's East End as part of her Golden Jubilee tour in May.

ris ordered a reevaluation of 91,000 disputed papers, but the revised results had little effect on actual college admissions.

In her resignation, Morris stated that she felt she was not up to the job of running a large department—an unprecedented admission by a Cabinet member. She was replaced by Labour Party Chairman Charles Clarke. Northern Ireland Secretary John Reid became party chairman, and he in turn was replaced by Paul Murphy.

Conservatives in crisis. Many members of the United Kingdom's opposition Conservative Party became concerned in 2002 about the party's failure to gain substantial popularity with the public under the leadership of Iain Duncan Smith. Duncan Smith had taken over as head of the party after the Conservative defeat in the 2001 election. The new leader, whose personal views tended to be to the right of most of the party, had recognized the need for the Conservatives to reform and move to the center. In particular, the party needed to convince voters it could be trusted to maintain good public services. Duncan Smith insisted that the Conservatives should champion the poor and include more women and ethnic minority candidates.

Duncan Smith fired his rural affairs spokeswoman, Ann Winterton, in May 2002, after she told a racist joke at a rugby club dinner in her constituency. On July 23, he moved party chairman David Davis (a former candidate for the Conservative leadership and an opponent of reform) to the lesser post of spokesman on regional affairs. Davis was replaced by Theresa May, who became the first woman to chair the party. At the Conservative Party conference in October, May told delegates that Conservatives needed to shed their image of being the "nasty party" that was insensitive to the needs of immigrants, homosexuals, and women.

Smith's reforms failed to appeal to the public, however, and by November, political experts speculated that Duncan Smith might be challenged for the party leadership unless the party improved its poll position. The Liberal Democrats, a centrist party led by Charles Kennedy, suggested they might actually replace the Conservatives as the main party of opposition to Labour.

Local elections. The Labour Party's share of the vote declined from 39 percent to 33 percent in local council elections held in May for 5,800 contested seats in England and Wales. The Conservative Party won 34 percent of the vote. Nevertheless, Labour continued to hold the majority of local council seats. The election was notable for the success of the far-right British National Party (BNP) in Burnley, the scene of racial tension and violence in 2001. Three BNP councillors were

elected. The party had fielded candidates for 67 other seats.

Archbishop of Canterbury. In July 2002, Queen Elizabeth II appointed the Archbishop of Wales, Rowan Williams, as the new Archbishop of Canterbury, head of the Church of England (Anglican Church). He succeeded George Carey, who retired. Tony Blair recommended the appointment, based on a list of suggested candidates provided by the Anglican Church. Although Williams was widely admired as an intellectual and a man of deep spirituality, conservatives considered him controversial because he had knowingly ordained a gay man and supported the idea of female priests. Williams also was critical of the U.S.-led war on terrorism.

Train crash. The poor condition of the British railway system, a matter of concern following a train crash at Hatfield in 2000 that killed four people and triggered widespread chaos in the British rail system, returned to public attention in 2002. In May, a train derailed and crashed into Potters Bar station in Hertfordshire, near London, killing seven people and injuring dozens of others. The mainte-

The Cabinet of the United Kingdom*

Tony Blair—prime minister; first lord of the treasury; minister for the civil service

John Prescott—deputy prime minister; first secretary of state

Gordon Brown—chancellor of the exchequer

Robin Cook—president of the Privy Council and leader of the House of Commons

Lord Irvine of Lairg—lord chancellor

Jack Straw—secretary of state for foreign and Commonwealth affairs

David Blunkett—secretary of state for the home department

Margaret Beckett—secretary of state for environment, food and rural affairs

Clare Short—secretary of state for international development

Alistair Darling—secretary of state for transport

Alan Milburn—secretary of state for health

Paul Murphy—secretary of state for Northern Ireland

Peter Hain—secretary of state for Wales

Geoff Hoon—secretary of state for defense

Andrew Smith—secretary of state for work and pensions

Helen Liddell—secretary of state for Scotland

Lord Williams of Mostyn—lord privy seal; leader of the House of Lords

Patricia Hewitt—secretary of state for trade and industry

Charles Clarke—secretary of state for education and skills

Tessa Jowell—secretary of state for culture, media, and sport

Hilary Armstrong—parliamentary secretary to the treasury; chief whip of the House of Commons

John Reid—minister without portfolio; chairman of the Labour Party

Paul Boateng—chief secretary to the treasury

*As of Dec. 2, 2002.

House of Commons

Queen Elizabeth II opened the 2002-2003 session of Parliament on Nov. 13, 2002. As of November 20, the House of Commons was made up of the following:

410	Labour Party
164	Conservative Party
52	Liberal Democrats
6	Ulster Unionists
5	Scottish National Party
4	Plaid Cymru
3	Social Democratic and Labour Party
5	Ulster Democratic Unionist Party
4	Sinn Fein
1	Independent
1	Independent Conservative

In addition, the unaffiliated speaker and 3 deputies attend sessions but do not vote.

nance firm that took care of the rails claimed that the track might have been sabotaged. An investigation in July, however, revealed that the crash was caused by faulty *points*. (Points are mechanisms that divert trains onto different tracks.) A number of nuts were missing from the points, causing the train to jump the tracks.

Firefighters strike. Britain's 50,000 firefighters staged their first national strike in 25 years in November in a dispute over a pay increase. The firefighters initially called for a 40-percent increase and walked off the job twice as government officials continued to refuse their demands. During the strike, some 19,000 army, navy, and air force troops responded to fire emergencies, using outdated equipment. In December, a government panel set up to review pay and work conditions proposed a pay increase of 11 percent over two years if the firefighters agreed to major modernizations in service.

Fox hunting. A group called the Countryside Alliance staged one of the largest demonstrations in British history in London on September 22. The group primarily protested against Labour's plans to ban foxhunting. However, their concerns also included such rural issues as rising housing costs, declines in public health services, and the exploitation of farm prices by supermarkets. Police estimated that 400,000 people protested in central London.

David Shayler, a former member of M15, the British secret service, was found guilty in November of breaking the Official Secrets Act. While at M15, Shayler had provided a newspaper with national secrets. Shayler alleged that M15 had been involved in illegal phone tapping and in a plot to assassinate Libyan leader Muammar al-Qadhafi. Shayler had previously fled to France but returned to clear his name. He was sentenced to prison for six months.

John Major. Britons were amazed in September when former Conservative minister Edwina Currie revealed that she had had an affair with John Major, who had been the Conservative prime minister from 1990 to 1997. The affair had taken place during the 1980's, before Major's rise to power. Major confirmed the allegation and said his wife, Norma, had forgiven him. During his term in office, Major had dismissed several ministers for extra-marital affairs and sexual misconduct.

Royal deaths. Princess Margaret, the younger sister of Queen Elizabeth II, died on Feb. 9, 2002, at the age of 71. Her remains were cremated in a small family ceremony, and her ashes were interred beside her father, King George VI, in St. George's Chapel at Windsor Castle.

Just seven weeks later, Queen Elizabeth, the Queen Mother, died on March 30, at age 101. Her body lay in state in Westminster Hall for three days during which an estimated 200,000 people filed past to pay their respects. At least 1 million people lined a 23-mile (37-kilometer) route between Westminister Abbey in London and St. George's Chapel at Windsor Castle, where the queen mother was interred beside her husband and daughter.

The queen mother had enjoyed great public affection throughout her life. She was particularly admired for the courage she displayed as queen during World War II (1939-1945). During the bombing of London, the queen refused to flee the city to safety and appeared regularly with her husband, King George VI, in bombed-out areas of London, encouraging the residents to persevere.

Jubilee. The public affection for the monarchy displayed after the queen mother's death appeared to have ended a long period of criticism of the royal family that had been especially strong after the death of Princess Diana in 1997. The renewed respect was confirmed during the queen's Jubilee, a celebration in June 2002 to mark the 50th year of her reign. Festivities continued throughout the nation for four days. The Church of England held ceremonies of thanksgiving, including a service at St. Paul's Cathedral attended by the queen. The queen made clear during the Jubilee that she did not intend to abdicate.

Scandal returned to the monarchy in November, following the collapse of the trial of Paul Burrell, butler to the late Princess Diana. The police had accused Burrell of stealing some of Diana's property. The trial ended when the queen recalled that Burrell had mentioned to her shortly after Diana's death that he had taken some objects for safekeeping. Media allegations arose that the royal family had brought the trial to an end to prevent Burrell's revealing royal secrets during cross examination. Tony Blair defended the queen, saying that she had acted properly.   ☐ Rohan McWilliam

See also **Europe; Transportation.**

British Prime Minister Tony Blair, speaking before a special session of the House of Commons in September, voices his support for U.S. President George W. Bush's stand that Iraq must surrender its weapons of mass destruction. Blair's Labour government remained Bush's greatest ally in the U.S.-led war on terrorism despite misgivings by large segments of the British public.

United Kingdom, Prime Minister of.

Tony Blair maintained his standing with the public throughout 2002, after becoming in 2001 the first Labour Party prime minister in British history to win a second full term in office. Nevertheless, Blair faced significant criticism from various segments of the British public and the Labour Party for his stands on such issues as public services and his support of United States President George W. Bush in Bush's threat of action against Iraq.

Blair, during the annual Labour Party conference in October, proposed radical reforms to such long-troubled public services as the medical, education, welfare, and criminal justice systems. He proposed the use of private financing to help fund certain public services. Representatives of trade unions, in particular, opposed Blair's plans.

Blair continued his close relationship with President Bush throughout 2002 and strongly supported the U.S. war on terrorism, begun after terrorist attacks upon the United States on Sept. 11, 2001. Blair also backed Bush's demand that Iraq surrender weapons of mass destruction, by force, if necessary. However, Blair counseled the U.S. president that pressure on Saddam Hussein should come from the United Nations.

☐ Rohan McWilliam

See also **United Kingdom; United Nations.**

United Nations. The United Nations (UN)

General Assembly opened its 57th annual session on Sept. 10, 2002, against the backdrop of the first anniversary of the terrorist attacks on the United States on Sept. 11, 2001, and the ongoing campaign against international terrorism. Jan Kavan, a former foreign minister of the Czech Republic, was elected president of the Assembly, and membership grew to 191 countries with the admission of Switzerland and East Timor.

UN Security Council. On Sept. 27, 2002, the General Assembly elected five countries to replace those countries whose two-year term on the Security Council was to end on December 30. Angola, Chile, Germany, Pakistan, and Spain were elected to join Bulgaria, Cameroon, Guinea, Mexico, and Syria, whose terms were to end Dec. 31, 2003, as well as the five permament members of the council—China, France, Russia, the United Kingdom, and the United States.

Resolution on Iraq. U.S. President George W. Bush appeared before the General Assembly on Sept. 12, 2002, and challenged the UN to make a stand against Iraq, which intelligence sources suggested was stockpiling weapons of mass destruction. He noted that Iraq had already ignored 16 UN resolutions demanding that the country allow inspectors to check for such weapons. Bush warned that if the UN failed to enforce its resolutions, the United States would take the lead in disarming Iraq.

On September 16, Iraqi Foreign Minister Naji Sabri announced that Iraq would allow UN arms inspectors into the country. Iraqi officials and a delegation led by chief UN arms inspector Hans Blix quickly agreed on the practical arrangements for UN inspectors to return to Iraq for the first time since December 1998.

Despite Iraq's apparent concession, Bush continued to press the Security Council for a new resolution that would force Iraq to disarm or face serious consequences. After eight weeks of negotiations that reflected fear among U.S. allies that a strong resolution could trigger a new war with Iraq, the Security Council unanimously approved such a resolution on Nov. 8, 2002. Weapons inspectors were allowed to enter the country on November 25. On December 7, Iraq submitted to the UN a declaration of its weapons programs.

Middle East. The UN, the European Union, the United States, and Russia—known as the Quartet—agreed to the outline of a plan on September 17 for the creation of a Palestinian nation in 2003 with provisional borders based upon a new constitution. The Quartet hoped that negotiations between Israelis and Palestinians would result in a final resolution to the conflict.

International Criminal Court. The first permanent court to try war crimes, crimes against humanity, and genocide was established on July 1, 2002, after more than 60 countries ratified the 1998 Rome Treaty. The court was to begin operating in 2003. The United States opposed the establishment of the court, stating that it feared U.S. troops and diplomats may be targeted in politically motivated indictments. The United States sought to have nations that are party to the treaty sign accords that would exempt U.S. troops and diplomats from the court's jurisdiction. By late 2002, 14 countries had signed such accords.

Millennium Declaration. Kofi Annan in October reminded governments around the world that they had fallen short of pledges they made in 2000 in the Millennium Declaration. The governments had promised to reduce by half the more than 1 billion people in the world living on less than one dollar a day by 2015. Governments had also fallen behind in plans to halt the AIDS epidemic and provide equal primary and secondary school education and health care for all.

Special sessions. In Madrid, Spain, in April 2002, representatives from more than 160 nations and nongovernmental organizations attended the "Second World Assembly on Aging." The purpose of the session was to consider strategies for coping with the growing number of elderly people in the world and their need for health care, housing, transportation, and other services. According to the Assembly, the rapid aging of the global population and the sharp drop in fertility rates is "unprecedented" in human history. Demographers predicted that by 2050, the number of people aged 60 and above would exceed 2 billion, double the number of people under age 20.

The UN General Assembly devoted a special session to children in May 2002. The delegates prepared a new program called "A World Fit for Children," in which governments were called upon to reduce mortality rates for children under 5 years of age by one-third in the next 10 years; reduce by one-third child malnutrition; and expand and improve comprehensive childhood care and education. The program also called for the proportion of infants infected with HIV to be reduced by 20 percent by 2005.

In Johannesburg, South Africa, the World Summit for Sustainable Development met in August 2002 to take action against the rapid deterioration of the global environment. The delegates adopted a nonbinding document, the Plan of Implementation, which spelled out targets and timetables for actions ranging from providing clean water to restoring depleted fisheries and preserving the world's biodiversity.

☐ J. Tuyet Nguyen

See also **AIDS; Iraq; Israel; Middle East.**

United States, Government of the.

The U.S. Congress in November 2002 approved President George W. Bush's plan for a new Cabinet department for domestic defense, setting into motion the most dramatic government restructuring in more than 50 years. The new Department of Homeland Security was created to coordinate government efforts in the war on terrorism.

U.S. troops in Afghanistan continued the war on terrorism in 2002 with mop-up campaigns against scattered Taliban and al-Qa'ida forces. At the same time, the Bush administration prepared for a possible war with Iraq over the suspected development of weapons of mass destruction.

In 2002, the U.S. House of Representatives and the Senate launched an investigation into the failure of the government's counterterrorism measures. The investigation came in response to Federal Bureau of Investigation (FBI) Director Robert S. Mueller III's acknowledgement in May that the agency in 2001 had ignored signs that warned of possible terrorist attacks on the United States.

Governmental reorganization plan. Congress approved legislation in November 2002 creating the new Department of Homeland Security, which was charged with overseeing border security, emergency preparedness, and intelligence analysis. The legislation gave the Bush administration the power to bypass civil service rules in pro-

An agent of the Central Intelligence Agency, concealed behind a screen to protect his identity, testifies in September before a joint Senate-House Select Intelligence Committee about possible intelligence failures related to the terrorist attacks on the United States in 2001. Federal Bureau of Investigation agents also testified about intelligence lapses at the bureau.

moting and firing the new agency's employees, a measure bitterly opposed by Democrats. The Bush administration projected that the department would include 170,000 employees, have a budget of $37 billion, and consolidate 22 existing agencies. The new department would likely become operational sometime in 2003.

War fever. The United States prepared for action against Iraq in 2002. U.S. officials accused Iraqi leaders of stockpiling biological and chemical weapons in violation of a cease-fire treaty signed at the end of the Persian Gulf War (1991). In October 2002, Congress authorized President Bush to use force against Iraqi President Saddam Hussein's regime. President Bush signed the resolution on October 16.

UN weapons inspectors returned to Iraq in November after the Security Council passed a resolution demanding that Iraq surrender weapons of mass destruction. Iraq subsequently issued a 12,000-page document describing its weapons systems. On December 18, President Bush condemned the disclosure as deceptive and full of omis-

sions. U.S. Secretary of State Colin Powell declared on December 19 that Iraq was in "material breach" of the UN resolution's demand that it supply complete details of all weapons programs.

Intelligence failures cited. The Bush administration in September agreed to an independent investigation into the terrorist attacks against the United States on Sept. 11, 2001. The investigation was designed to uncover failures among U.S. intelligence-gathering agencies in regard to the terrorist attacks on the World Trade Center in New York City and the Pentagon Building outside Washington, D.C. Bush named former New Jersey Governor Thomas Kean as committee chairman.

The creation of the independent investigation resulted from the disclosure that officials with the Central Intelligence Agency (CIA) and the FBI were aware as early as 1998 that the al-Qa'ida terrorist network was planning attacks that involved crashing hijacked jets into skyscrapers.

In September 2002, Eleanor Hill, staff director of a joint Senate and House inquiry into the terrorist attacks, testified before a joint intelligence committee that while the heads of the FBI and CIA had not taken the report of such attacks seriously, they did notify senior government officials of the threat. Hill said that the CIA informed "senior government leaders" in July 2001 that al-Qa'ida leader Osama bin Laden had planned a significant terrorist attack against U.S. or Israeli interests. The intelligence agencies did not know the specifics of the planned attacks, which took place on Sept. 11, 2001, but did not bother to adequately investigate al-Qa'ida terrorists known to be in the United States. Hill revealed that U.S. intelligence officials did detect unusual levels of activity among known terrorists and that al-Qa'ida agents had become interested in using airplanes as weapons of terror.

Smallpox preparedness. The Bush administration announced plans in July 2002 to give smallpox vaccinations to approximately 500,000 health care and emergency workers as a precaution against a bioterrorist attack. In December, Bush announced plans to also vaccinate all U.S. military and other strategic personnel.

Scientists *eradicated* (eliminated) smallpox, a potentially fatal disease caused by the virus *Variola major*, from nature in 1980. However, in 2002, U.S. officials feared that some nations, including Iraq, may have developed weapons capable of delivering microbes that could cause deadly epidemics of diseases such as smallpox.

Wiretaps. A special spy review court, the U.S. Foreign Intelligence Surveillance Court of Review, in November overturned a ruling made in May by the Foreign Intelligence Surveillance Act Court that a "wall" must be maintained between spying on foreign agents and investigating citizens suspected of criminal activities. Political experts said that the court's decision granted Attorney General John Ashcroft and the FBI broad new powers to wiretap the telephones of individual U.S. citizens.

Federal budget. President Bush, on Feb. 4, 2002, presented a $2.13-trillion budget to Congress for fiscal year 2003, which began on Oct. 1, 2002. The budget outlined increased military

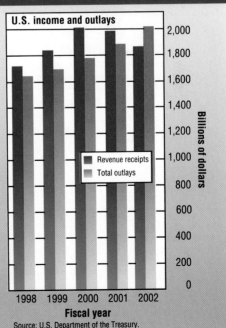

Federal spending
United States budget for fiscal 2002*

Billions of dollars

National defense	347.7
International affairs	22.5
General science, space, technology	21.8
Energy	0.5
Natural resources and environment	27.4
Agriculture	24.3
Commerce and housing credit	–0.6
Transportation	61.2
Community and regional development	13.9
Education, training, employment, and social services	71.1
Health	196.3
Social security	456.4
Medicare	230.9
Income security	311.7
Veterans' benefits and services	51.0
Administration of justice	34.7
General government	17.8
Interest	171.2
Undistributed offsetting receipts	–47.8
Total budget outlays	**2,012.0**

*Oct. 1, 2001, to Sept. 30, 2002.
Source: U.S. Department of the Treasury.

U.S. income and outlays

Revenue receipts
Total outlays

Billions of dollars

Fiscal year
Source: U.S. Department of the Treasury.

Selected agencies and bureaus of the U.S. government*

Executive Office of the President
President, George W. Bush
  Vice President, Richard B. Cheney
  White House Chief of Staff, Andrew H Card, Jr.
  Presidential Press Secretary, L. Ari Fleischer
  Assistant to the President for Domestic Policy,
    Margaret Spellings
  Assistant to the President for Homeland Security, Tom Ridge
  Assistant to the President for National Security Affairs,
    Condoleezza Rice
  Assistant to the President for Science and Technology,
    John H. Marburger III
  Council of Economic Advisers–R. Glenn Hubbard, Chairperson
  Office of Management and Budget—
    Mitchell E. Daniels, Jr., Director
  Office of National Drug Control Policy—
    John P. Walters, Director
  U.S. Trade Representative, Robert B. Zoellick

Department of Agriculture
Secretary of Agriculture, Ann M. Veneman

Department of Commerce
Secretary of Commerce, Donald L. Evans
  Bureau of Economic Analysis—J. Steven Landefeld, Director
  Bureau of the Census—Charles Louis Kincannon, Acting Director

Department of Defense
Secretary of Defense, Donald H. Rumsfeld
  Secretary of the Air Force, James G. Roche
  Secretary of the Army, Thomas E. White
  Secretary of the Navy, Gordon R. England
  Joint Chiefs of Staff—
    General Richard B. Myers, Chairperson
    General John P. Jumper, Chief of Staff, Air Force
    General Eric K. Shinseki, Chief of Staff, Army
    Admiral Vern Clark, Chief of Naval Operations
    General James L. Jones, Commandant, Marine Corps

Department of Education
Secretary of Education, Roderick R. Paige

Department of Energy
Secretary of Energy, Spencer Abraham

Department of Health and Human Services
Secretary of Health and Human Services, Tommy G. Thompson
  Office of Public Health and Science—Eve Slater,
    Assistant Secretary
  Centers for Disease Control and Prevention—
    Julie Louise Gerberding, Director
  Food and Drug Administration—
    Commissioner†
  National Institutes of Health—Elias A. Zerhouni, Director
  Surgeon General of the United States, Richard H. Carmona

Department of Housing and Urban Development
Secretary of Housing and Urban Development,
    Mel Martinez

Department of the Interior
Secretary of the Interior, Gale A. Norton

Department of Justice
Attorney General, John Ashcroft
  Bureau of Prisons—Kathleen Hawk Sawyer, Director
  Drug Enforcement Administration—
    Asa Hutchinson, Administrator
  Federal Bureau of Investigation—
    Robert S. Mueller III, Director
  Immigration and Naturalization Service—
    James W. Ziglar, Commissioner†
  Solicitor General, Theodore B. Olson

Department of Labor
Secretary of Labor, Elaine L. Chao

Department of State
Secretary of State, Colin L. Powell
  U.S. Ambassador to the United Nations, John D. Negroponte

Department of Transportation
Secretary of Transportation, Norman Y. Mineta
  Federal Aviation Administration—
    Marion C. Blakey, Administrator
  U.S. Coast Guard—Admiral Thomas H. Collins, Commandant

Department of the Treasury
Secretary of the Treasury, Paul H. O'Neill**
  Internal Revenue Service—Charles O. Rossotti, Commissioner
  Treasurer of the United States, Rosario Marin
  U.S. Secret Service—Brian L. Stafford, Director
  Office of Thrift Supervision—James E. Gilleran, Director

Department of Veterans Affairs
Secretary of Veterans Affairs, Anthony J. Principi

Supreme Court of the United States
Chief Justice of the United States, William H. Rehnquist
  Associate Justices—
    John Paul Stevens   David H. Souter
    Sandra Day O'Connor   Clarence Thomas
    Antonin Scalia   Ruth Bader Ginsburg
    Anthony M. Kennedy   Stephen G. Breyer

Congressional officials
President of the Senate pro tempore, Robert C. Byrd
  Senate Majority Leader, William H. Frist
  Senate Minority Leader, Tom Daschle
  Speaker of the House, J. Dennis Hastert
  House Majority Leader, Thomas DeLay
  House Minority Leader, Nancy Pelosi
  Congressional Budget Office—Dan L. Crippen, Director
  General Accounting Office—David M. Walker, Comptroller
    General of the United States
  Library of Congress—James H. Billington, Librarian of Congress

Independent agencies
Central Intelligence Agency—George J. Tenet, Director
Commission on Civil Rights—Mary Frances Berry, Chairperson
Commission of Fine Arts—Harry G. Robinson III, Chairperson
Consumer Product Safety Commission—
    Harold D. Stratton, Chairperson
Corporation for National and Community Service—
    Stephen Goldsmith, Chairperson
Environmental Protection Agency—
    Christine Todd Whitman, Administrator
Equal Employment Opportunity Commission—
    Cari M. Dominguez, Chairperson
Federal Communications Commission—Michael K. Powell, Chairperson
Federal Deposit Insurance Corporation—
    Donald E. Powell, Chairperson
Federal Election Commission—David M. Mason, Chairperson
Federal Emergency Management Agency—Joe M. Allbaugh, Director††
Federal Reserve System Board of Governors—
    Alan Greenspan, Chairperson
Federal Trade Commission—Timothy J. Muris, Chairperson
General Services Administration—Stephen A. Perry, Administrator
National Aeronautics and Space Administration—Sean O'Keefe,
    Administrator
National Endowment for the Arts—Chairperson***
National Endowment for the Humanities—Bruce Cole, Chairperson
National Labor Relations Board—Robert J. Battista, Chairperson
National Railroad Passenger Corporation (Amtrak)—
    David Gunn, President & CEO
National Science Foundation—Rita R. Colwell, Director
National Transportation Safety Board—
    Carol Jones Carmody, Acting Chairperson
Nuclear Regulatory Commission—Richard A. Meserve, Chairperson
Peace Corps—Gaddi H. Vasquez, Director
Securities and Exchange Commission—Harvey Lloyd Pitt, Chairperson†††
Selective Service System—Alfred V. Rascon, Director
Small Business Administration—Hector V. Barreto, Jr., Administrator
Smithsonian Institution—Lawrence M. Small, Secretary
Social Security Administration—Jo Anne Barnhart, Commissioner
U.S. Postal Service—John E. Potter, Postmaster General

*As of Dec. 31, 2002.
†Resigned Aug. 17, 2002, to become effective on Dec. 31, 2002.
**Resigned Dec. 6, 2002.
††Announced resignation Dec. 17, 2002, to become effective in 2003.
***Position vacant as of Dec. 31, 2002.
†††Resigned Nov. 5, 2002. Resignation effective upon appointment
    of a successor.

and homeland security spending and called for cuts in labor and environmental programs. Congress failed to pass any of the required 13 spending bills in 2002 prior to the beginning of fiscal year 2003 but approved temporary spending measures to keep the government running without a budget.

Federal deficit. The federal government ran a deficit of $159 billion in fiscal year 2002 (Oct. 1, 2001, to Sept. 30, 2002), the Bush administration announced on October 24. The deficit followed a $127-billion federal surplus in fiscal year 2001. Government officials said the deficit resulted from increased spending on defense and domestic security measures in the wake of the terrorist attacks in 2001. Some economists also cited the slowing U.S. economy. Democratic leaders, however, argued that President Bush's 10-year, $1.35-trillion tax cut enacted in 2001 was a large factor in the deficit, which was the first since fiscal year 1997.

Economic concerns. The Federal Reserve System (the Fed), the central bank of the United States, cut short-term interest rates by one-half of a percentage point on Nov. 6, 2002. The Fed, headed by Alan Greenspan, reduced the federal funds rate—the interest rate on overnight loans between banks—from 1.75 percent to 1.25 percent. The cut was the only reduction in 2002. In 2001, the Fed had cut interest rates 11 times in an effort to stimulate the U.S. economy.

Harvey Pitt resigned as chairman of the Securities and Exchange Commission (SEC) on Nov. 5, 2002. The SEC is a federal agency that enforces laws governing the selling of *securities* (stocks and bonds). Pitt's resignation followed a controversy over his decision in October to appoint William Webster chairman of an accounting-oversight board. Pitt failed to tell SEC commissioners and the Bush administration that Webster was a director and audit committee chairman of a company accused of fraud. Some U.S. senators had called for Pitt's resignation in July after they accused him of being "slow and tepid in addressing accounting abuses" among U.S. corporations.

A report issued on December 19 by the General Accounting Office (GAO), the investigatory arm of the U.S. Congress, described the SEC as "dysfunctional" and "chaotic" and noted that the agency lacked the necessary funding and staff to succeed in its regulatory mission. The GAO also disclosed that appointments to SEC positions had not been adequately examined for possible conflicts of interest or for ethical or legal problems.

Brokerage settlement. At least 10 of the largest U.S. brokerage firms agreed in late December to pay more than $1 billion in fines to end investigations into whether the companies had given customers misleading stock recommendations. The settlement forced the firms to agree to change how stock-research practices are conducted. It also barred brokerages from passing out lucrative stock deals to top executives or directors of public companies in order to curry their favor. Federal regulators and the New York State attorney general had accused the companies of misinforming customers about the true value of stocks in exchange for highly profitable investment banking fees.

Airport security. The federal government began taking over security at U.S. airports in February 2002. The change was mandated by the Aviation and Transportation Security Act, which President Bush signed in 2001. The federal government hired thousands of new employees in 2002 to screen air travelers and check baggage.

INS resignation. James Ziglar, commissioner of the Immigration and Naturalization Service (INS), announced in August 2002 that he would resign at the end of the year. In his resignation, Ziglar wrote that he had made progress in reforming the agency, which had received criticism when the public learned that the INS in 2002 had approved student visas for two of the terrorists who had participated, and died, in the attacks on the United States in 2001. Most of the functions handled by the INS were reassigned to the Department of Homeland Security.

Campaign reform. President Bush signed campaign finance reform legislation in March 2002. The legislation banned *soft money donations* (large contributions made to political parties by corporations, labor unions, and individuals). Political experts said that the legislation was the most sweeping change in the way elections are financed since 1974.

Steel tariffs. In March 2002, President Bush imposed three-year tariffs of up to 30 percent on varieties of steel imported into the United States. The president said the tariffs were necessary in order to allow U.S. steel manufacturers to consolidate their businesses and reduce layoffs. The president later agreed to drop some of the tariffs.

Nuclear arms treaty. President Bush and Russian President Vladimir V. Putin signed a treaty on May 24 in which the governments of both countries pledged to significantly reduce arsenals of nuclear weapons. The treaty obliges each nation to reduce their stockpiles of 6,000 nuclear weapons each by two-thirds by 2012.

☐ Geoffrey A. Campbell

See **Armed forces; Aviation; Cabinet, U.S.; Congress of the United States; Democratic Party; Elections; Immigration; Immigration: A Special Report; Iraq; Manufacturing: A Special Report; People in the news** (Feingold, Russell; Gerberding, Julie L.; McCain, John); **State government; Republican Party; Russia; Transportation; United Nations; United States, President of.**

One System, Two Missions

**The National Park Service struggles to
balance the often conflicting land-use
needs of conservation and recreation.**

By Dianne Hales

Imagine winter in Yellowstone National Park—bubbling
geysers, bald eagles soaring in a clear blue sky, snow drift-
ing from branches, herds of bison crossing frozen fields.
Now add something the creators of the world's first national
park never could have imagined—the roar of snowmobiles, an
estimated 70,000 each winter.

Do snowmobiles belong in America's most prized wilderness lands? The debate over this issue has been raging for more
than 20 years. In 1972, President Richard M. Nixon issued an
executive order prohibiting recreational snowmobile use in sections of the National Park System. President Jimmy Carter issued another order in 1977 banning snowmobiles wherever
they might cause considerable adverse effects on public lands.
However, many parks lacked the money and personnel necessary to create and enforce regulations on snowmobile use, and
the number of snowmobiles skyrocketed, particularly in Yellowstone and Grand Teton national parks in northwest
Wyoming. By the early 2000's, the National Park Service

(NPS) had even issued respirators to Yellowstone gatekeepers complaining of nausea, headaches, and dizziness from toxic fumes at park entrances crowded with idling snowmobiles.

President Bill Clinton, on his last day in office in January 2001, signed a ban on snowmobiling in Yellowstone and Grand Teton national parks, to take effect during the winter of 2003-2004. The International Snowmobile Manufacturers Association challenged the ban with a lawsuit. In November 2002, the administration of President George W. Bush overturned the ban and announced plans that allow for 35 percent increase in snowmobile use in the area.

The heated debate over snowmobiles was the latest in a long series of conflicts about the primary function of national parks. Do the parks exist to preserve natural beauty in a pristine state for future generations? Or do they exist to provide today's citizens with sites for outdoor recreation? "It's a fine line that we walk each and every day," says David Barna, NPS chief of communications. "From the very beginning, the challenge has been to balance preservation of the natural landscape and ecology with public enjoyment of recreational facilities."

The nearly 300 million people who visited the U.S. national parks in 2002 gave the parks high ratings for the quality of sights, staff, and information. In repeated surveys, U.S. citizens consistently gave the National Park Service the highest approval rating of any federal government agency. The vital significance of the national parks to the public remains unchallenged. "Perhaps second only to liberty itself, the national park idea is the finest contribution of the United States to world culture," former NPS director George B. Hartzog, Jr., wrote in his book Battling for the National Parks. However, the parks themselves face a number of ongoing challenges—severe overcrowding, traffic, pollution, and a chronic lack of funds for maintenance and repairs.

Maintaining the national parks is the responsibility of the National Park Service, an executive agency under the U.S. Department of the Interior. The service manages the National Park System— 384 park units covering 84.4 million acres (34.2 million hectares) in 49 states (all except Delaware), the District of Columbia, American Samoa, Guam, Puerto Rico, Saipan, and the Virgin Islands. The system includes 24 national battlefields and military parks; 118 national historical parks and sites; 74 national monuments; 56 national parks; 28 national memorials; and 37 national preserves, reserves and recreation areas.

Preserving the disappearing West

The national parks idea began in 1832 when artist George Catlin visited the Dakota territories (now North Dakota and South Dakota). Catlin, famous for his paintings of Native Americans, worried that the westward expansion of the United States was altering or destroying the places and cultures of the West. He conceived the idea of "a nation's park, containing man and beast, in all the wild and freshness of their nature's beauty." The essence of Catlin's idea became a reality 40 years later.

In 1870, the surveyor general of the Montana Territory led an

The author:
Dianne Hales is a free-
lance writer.

expedition into "Yellowstone country." Impressed by its majestic grandeur, the explorers endorsed a proposal to preserve the area. On March 1, 1872, President Ulysses S. Grant signed legislation designating the Yellowstone area as "a public park or pleasuring-ground for the benefit and enjoyment of the people." The bill placed Yellowstone in the custody of the U.S. Department of the Interior.

In the 1890's, Congress created other national parks—Sequoia, Yosemite, and General Grant (later renamed Kings Canyon) in California; and Mount Rainier in the state of Washington. The legislators' motives were both idealistic and practical. They wanted to preserve the spectacular natural beauty of the West. They also were responding to lobbying by the rail-roads, which saw the parks as tourist des-tinations that would boost their passenger business.

The Antiquities Act of 1906 gave U.S. presidents broad power to place "historic landmarks, historic and prehistoric struc-tures, and other objects of historic or sci-entific interest" in federal custody as na-tional monuments. President Theodore Roosevelt created 18 national monuments, including the Grand Canyon in Arizona and El Morro in New Mexico. Congress later converted many of these monuments into national parks.

U.S. President Theodore Roosevelt and conservationist John Muir, who are of-ten called the fathers of the National Park System, survey Cali-fornia's Yosemite Na-tional Park in 1906. Roosevelt oversaw the creation of five nation-al parks and set aside 18 national monu-ments. Muir cam-paigned for the cre-ation of Sequoia and Yosemite national parks and persuaded Roosevelt to protect 148 million acres (59.9 million hectares) of forests.

An untended legacy

No nationally coordinated agency initially existed to supervise the growing number of national parks. According to many conserva-tionists, the results were disastrous.

In the early 1900's, San Francisco city planners wanted to build a dam to convert the Hetch Hetchy Valley at Yosemite National Park into a reservoir to provide drinking water for the city. De-spite passionate arguments by such famed environmentalists as John Muir, Congress authorized the building of the dam in 1913. Historian John Ise later characterized this decision as "the worst disaster ever to come to any national park."

The Hetch Hetchy controversy led to complaints that national parks were mismanaged. When Stephen T. Mather, a wealthy businessman and outdoorsman from Chicago, voiced his criticism, Secretary of the Interior Franklin K. Lane invited Mather to serve as his assistant for park matters. Mather arrived in Washington, D.C., in 1915 to lead the crusade to create a national parks bu-reau. On August 25, 1916, President Woodrow Wilson approved legislation that created the National Park Service within the De-partment of the Interior to manage the national parks. Mather be-came the park service's first director.

The only national park in the eastern United States in the early

Units of the National Park System

National parks, for example, Yellowstone National Park in northwestern Wyoming, are generally large areas of land that contain a variety of natural features preserved in a natural state.

National preserves, for example, Big Cypress National Preserve in Florida, are large areas which preserve some natural resources but allow activities such as hunting, trapping, and drilling for oil.

National monuments, for example, Devils Tower National Monument in Wyoming, preserve natural landmarks, buildings, and other objects of historic or scientific significance.

National historic sites and historical parks, for example, Valley Forge National Historical Park in Pennsylvania, preserve places or commemorate people, events, or activities important to the nation's history.

National memorials, for example, the Vietnam Veterans Memorial in Washington, D.C., also commemorate historic people or episodes but do not have to occupy sites historically connected with their subjects.

National battlefields, for example, Gettysburg National Military Park in Pennsylvania, preserve the locations of military battles important to the nation's history.

National cemeteries include Gettysburg National Cemetery and Yorktown National Cemetery in Virginia.

National recreation areas, such as the Glen Canyon National Recreation Area in Arizona and Utah, are open spaces that provide for outdoor recreation.

National parkways, such as the Blue Ridge Parkway in North Carolina and Virginia, preserve scenic corridors of park land along roadways.

National trails, such as Ice Age National Scenic Trail in Wisconsin, are long-distance footpaths that wind through areas of national beauty and historic interest.

National seashores and lakeshores, for example, Padre Island National Seashore in Texas, protect shoreline and off-shore areas.

National rivers, such as the Upper Delaware Scenic and Recreational River in New York and Pennsylvania, preserve sections of rivers and the adjacent lands for their natural beauty or historical interest.

Olympic National Park in Washington

years of the NPS was Acadia National Park in Maine. The others lay in the West, where the U.S. government owned vast tracts of land, and new parks were easily acquired. To expand the park system to better represent the entire nation, Congress created three new parks in the Appalachian Mountains in 1926— Shenandoah National Park in Virginia, Great Smoky Mountains National Park in North Carolina and Tennessee, and Mammoth Cave National Park in Kentucky. Eastern sites also grew with the establishment of parks dedicated to the nation's history, such as Morristown National Historical Park in New Jersey, where General George Washington's Continental Army spent two winters during the Revolutionary War in America (1775-1783). In 1933, President Franklin D. Roosevelt transferred 56 parks and monuments from the War Department and the Forest

Acadia National
Park in Maine

Antietam National Cemetery in Maryland

Booker T. Washington National Monument in Virginia

The National Park Service, which is charged with protecting the parks while providing for public enjoyment, protects wilderness resources, such as elk (above), as well as historical sites, such as these ancient cliff dwellings in Colorado (right). Rangers must balance protection efforts while still providing for public enjoyment and recreation (below).

Service to the NPS, along with various monuments, including the White House in Washington, D.C. The park service in the 1930's also began acquiring areas intended for mass recreation, such as the Blue Ridge Parkway between the Shenandoah and Great Smoky Mountains national parks.

During World War II (1939-1945), the NPS faced pressure to yield park resources for national defense. Timber interests sought to cut spruce forests in Olympic National Park in Washington state to be used in the manufacture of wood-framed airplanes. Leaders of scrap metal drives eyed old cannons at various historic battlefields and forts. For the most part, the NPS deflected such proposals. However, the parks did participate in the war effort. Park hotels, such as the Ahwahnee in Yosemite National Park, served as rehabilitation centers for wounded servicemen, and the Armed Forces trained soldiers and tested equipment on such park lands as Mount Rainier, Joshua Tree National Monument in California, and Mount McKinley in Alaska.

The amount of land in the National Park System more than doubled in the 1980's with the addition of more than 47 million acres (19 million hectares) of Alaskan wilderness. One of the new areas, the Wrangell-St. Elias National Park and Preserve, covered an area larger than the states of New Hampshire and Vermont combined and contained the largest number of glaciers and peaks over 16,000 feet (4,877 meters) in North America.

Conflicting mandates

Two missions guided the national park system throughout the long period of expansion. The 1916 legislation that created the agency directed the park service "to conserve the scenery and the natural and historic objects and the wildlife therein and to provide for the enjoyment of the same in such manner and by such means as will leave them unimpaired for the enjoyment of future generations." The park service has struggled to balance these two inherently conflicting missions throughout its history.

The first director, Stephen Mather, and his successor, Horace Albright, believed that in order to flourish, the parks had to attract and accommodate large numbers of visitors. The newly created park service allowed automobiles, which had previously been banned from Yellowstone, throughout the system. The service also licensed private vendors to operate hotels and restaurants on park lands and encouraged the building of museums and other educational facilities. Greater popularity, the first directors of NPS believed, would mean greater public support.

The national parks' popularity far exceeded the wildest expectations of the first directors. The prosperity that followed World War II triggered a travel boom, and visitors flocked to the parks. Attendance soared from 6 million visitors in 1942, to 33 million in 1950, to 72 million in 1960. In 1999, more than 287 million people visited the parks, more than four times as many as attended Major League Baseball games.

The huge crowds not only interfered with individual visitors' enjoyment of the parks, they also threatened the environmental

Air pollution regularly obscures views by up to 80 percent at Great Smoky Mountains National Park in North Carolina (top). Traffic jams such as this one at Yellowstone (above) often clog roads at the nation's most popular parks. Many NPS officials consider pollution, automobiles, and overcrowding to be the most pressing threats to the national parks.

health of the parks. The visitors required food, lodging, and waste disposal facilities, all of which imposed on the pristine wilderness or historic atmosphere of the parks. Visitors leaving designated trail areas to avoid large crowds damaged fragile vegetation and encroached on the habitat of sensitive wildlife. Large crowds also made it difficult for rangers to enforce park regulations and prevent litter and vandalism. In 2001, rangers at Arizona's Petrified Forest National Park estimated that souvenir-hungry tourists made off with an estimated 25,000 pounds (11,340 kilograms) of fossilized wood each year. In many parks, rangers were forced to discourage or destroy animals that had become accustomed to eating human food from handouts.

Trampled wilderness

By the late 1990's, park service employees and many U.S. citizens recognized that the parks' plant and wildlife resources were not infinite, as they may have seemed when the parks were created. According to 2001 NPS estimates, 63 percent of threatened and endangered species within the parks were expected to decline over the next five years. The National Park System Advisory Board, a group of experts that advises the director of the NPS, declared in its 2001 report Rethinking the National Parks for the 21st Century, "It is time to re-examine the 'enjoyment equals support' equation and to encourage public support of resource protection at a higher level of understanding. In giving priority to visitor services, the Park Service has paid less attention to the resources it is obliged to protect for future generations."

Start your engines

While most people agreed that feeding wild animals and pilfering fossils were abuses of the nation's parks, other activities proved more controversial. The heated debate over snowmobiles in Yellowstone was just part of the dispute over off-road vehicles or ORV's. ORV's include a variety of land and water recreational craft, such as four-wheeled motor bikes, swamp and dune buggies, jet-skis, and snowmobiles. Until the late 1900's, few parks established or enforced regulations on the use of such vehicles, allowing ORV users free reign to trample through wilderness areas of the parks, destroying fragile plants and disturbing wild animals. By 2001, unregulated swamp buggy users had blazed some 22,000 miles (35,000 kilometers) of muddy trails across sensitive wetland areas in Florida's Big Cypress National Preserve.

In addition to disturbing wildlife, snowmobiles and most other ORV's used two-stroke engines that produced more noise and air pollution than the four-stroke engines in automobiles. In 2001, the U.S. General Accounting Office, which reviews the operations of federal government agencies, reported that while cars outnumbered snowmobiles at Yellowstone by 16 to 1, snowmobiles generated between 68 and 90 percent of all hydrocarbon emissions within the park and 35 to 69 percent of all carbon monoxide. Two-stroke engines also burned fuel less efficiently. By some estimates, a third of the fuel used by a jet ski ended up in the water. Conservationists and many park rangers proposed restricting or prohibiting ORV's in the national parks. ORV users and industry lobbyists countered that the park service's mandate to provide for public enjoyment protected ORV use.

ORV's were not the only vehicles causing problems for the park system. Inside the parks, "transportation is our number-one

Disrepair due to delayed maintenance of the Sperry Chalet at Glacier National Park in Montana led the National Trust for Historic Preservation to place the historic structure on its annual list of most endangered places in 1996. Lack of funding for maintenance has allowed many historic park buildings and other structures to become dilapidated.

problem" according to NPS communication chief David Barna. On a typical summer day at Grand Canyon National Park in 2001, the drivers of some 6,000 vehicles vied for 2,400 parking spaces. In many popular parks, spaces filled up early, and frustrated drivers often resorted to parking beside the road in wilderness or beach areas. Other parks had different transportation issues. At Glacier Bay National Park in Alaska, environmentalists lobbied for tighter restrictions on cruise ships, arguing that they caused pollution and endangered marine wildlife. Cruise ships in Alaska's waters were cited for illegally dumping garbage and human waste, and the death of at least one endangered humpback whale was attributed to a collision with a cruise ship.

Suffocating the parks

Vehicles contributed to another major problem at many of the nation's parks—air pollution. Great Smoky Mountains National Park drew nearly 10 million visitors annually in the 1990's, more than any other park, and the park had some of the highest levels of air pollution of any monitored site in North America by the early 2000's. Haze generated by automobiles, local industry, and nearby power plants obscured views by up to 80 percent. Smog concentrations rose to hazardous levels on one of every three summer days between 1999 and 2001. Great Smoky Mountains Park was not alone. Park rangers at Shenandoah, Mammoth Cave, Sequoia, and Acadia national parks among others reported high levels of air pollution that obscured scenic views and posed a health risk to people and wildlife. Air pollution in the parks contributed to acid rain (rain, snow, or fog that contains high levels of sulfuric and nitric acid from pollutants). In 2002, environmentalists discovered that clouds near mountaintops at Great Smoky Mountain were as acidic as vinegar according to the National Parks Conservation Association (NPCA), a national park advocacy group. High levels of acid in the park's waters damaged sensitive vegetation and threatened native species of trout.

Like pollution, pressure for new public and private development continued to threaten the national parks. In 2001, the NPS successfully blocked plans to convert an Air Force base in southern Florida into a commercial airport that park system advocates believed would have threatened Biscayne National Park with increased congestion and low-flying planes. In 2002, a proposed project for importing, storing, and pumping water from a natural aquifer threatened the supply of water for vegetation and wildlife at the Mojave National Preserve in California. In 2002, the NPCA placed Georgia's Ocmulgee National Monument on its list of endangered parks because of a proposed highway that would cut directly through a flood plain adjacent to the ancestral home of the Muskogee Creek American Indian tribe.

Starved for funding

Budget shortfalls contributed to many of the problems in the national parks. In 2002, the NPCA estimated that on average, parks were operating with only two-thirds of the funding needed to preserve wildlife and cultural and historical artifacts and to educate and protect visitors. Critical projects to repair infrastructure and preserve resources went unfinished. At the Boston National Historic Park's Old South Meeting House, where Bostonians met in 1770 to discuss ousting British troops following the Boston Massacre, a leaky roof allowed water and mold to severely damage historical documents and artifacts. Lack of funds also left many parks understaffed. In Minute Man National Historical Park in Massachusetts, which commemorates the first battle of the Revolutionary War, only four permanent interpretive rangers served the park's nearly 1 million annual visitors in the late 1990's. In other parks, understaffing made it difficult for park rangers to enforce regulations and manage natural resources. By 2002, not a single national park had the money and staff to produce a detailed survey of all the species of wildlife that existed within its boundaries.

Many of the park service's funding problems stemmed from the rapid expansion of the National Park System. Congress was often enthusiastic about providing money to purchase and construct new parks but less willing to fund maintenance projects to preserve existing parks. Political experts and park advocates have accused some members of Congress of using new parks to please their constituents by increasing tourism revenue in their districts. This has led to some controversial additions to the system. Critics have pointed to the creation of Steamtown National Historic Site, a railroad collection in Scranton, Pennsylvania, as an example of "pork barrel" politics intended mainly to benefit a politician's home district. James Ridenour, NPS director from 1989 to 1993, warned that such acquisitions were "thinning the blood" of the National Park System, diverting needed funds away from the system's "crown jewels," such as Yellowstone and Yosemite.

Paying for the parks

Many park supporters advocated increasing park funding as the first step to fixing the National Park System's problems. In 2001, the administration of President George W. Bush pledged to clear a $5-billion backlog of deferred maintenance repairs by 2006. However, the proposed $2.4 billion operating budget for the NPS for 2003 was only 1.4 percent above 2002 levels. Underfunding of the park system prompted a number of park advocates to push for higher fees to visit and use national parks.

In 1996, Congress began allowing some parks to charge higher user fees under a fee demonstration program. The idea was to generate greater funding for the park and discourage overcrowding. Under the program, as much as 80 percent of the ticket money generated at any individual park was kept inside the park to fund maintenance projects. In 2000, the 100 parks participating in the project raised $133.6 million from user fees. Although the fee demonstration program was scheduled to end in 2004, some members of Congress have proposed making the new rules permanent and extending them to all units of the park system.

Nearly all park advocates agree that the parks need more money, but many people oppose raising user fees, suggesting that fees

Specialized vans called snow coaches (top) provide a cleaner, quieter alternative to snowmobiles for winter visits to Yellowstone National Park. User fees help raise funding for maintenance projects and limit overcrowding at the nation's most popular parks (above).

bar poorer citizens from lands reserved for public use. Others worry that a park service dependent on user fees will promote high-impact uses, such as skiing and ORV use, for which higher fees can be charged. Many park rangers voiced fears that more revenue from visitors will result in less funding from Congress, as politicians expect the parks to become self-sufficient.

Clearing the air

In the 1990's and 2000's, the National Park System tackled its transportation problems with a number of innovative new systems. The directors of Zion National Park worked with the town of Springdale, Utah, to install an environmentally friendly shuttle system. Acadia National Park in Maine used propane-powered shuttles that provided free transportation to hiking trails and beaches. Rangers at Grand Canyon National Park explored the use of a light rail system to shuttle visitors around the park. To meet winter transportation needs, Yellowstone proposed the use of snow coaches—vans fitted with tracks and skis—that would provide a cleaner, more efficient alternative to snowmobiles. To help fund similar projects, a bipartisan group of senators in 2001 introduced the Transit in Parks Act, legislation that would authorize $65 million annually for six years to develop new and expanded mass transit services, pedestrian walkways, and bike paths within and near the national parks. However, Congress had not passed the legislation at the end of 2002.

Also in the 1990's and early 2000's, the park service began responding to the challenge presented by ORV use in the parks.

Rangers at Big Cypress developed plans to establish 400 miles (640 kilometers) of regulated swamp buggy trails and limit permits to use the vehicles. In 2002, personal watercraft, such as jet skis, were banned from most of the national park system. Although ORV enthusiasts and industry groups strongly resisted regulations on ORV use, citing a lack of scientific studies to assess the vehicles' impact on the parks, many park service officials chose to err on the side of caution, prohibiting ORV's in sensitive and wilderness areas until studies could be completed. However, pressure from politicians and industry groups thwarted some efforts to limit ORV use in Yellowstone and other areas.

To improve air quality and showcase clean energy technologies, the National Park Service and the Department of Energy launched a "Green Energy Parks" initiative in 1999, which provided for energy efficient and renewable energy technology in the parks. However, many of the parks' pollution problems could not be solved within their borders. Air pollution was a problem that went well beyond park boundaries, involving emissions from power plants and traffic on nearby highways. Park conservation groups played a strong role in urging the government to enforce tighter restrictions on coal burning power plants and establish higher efficiency standards for motorized vehicles.

Protecting the nation's treasures

While public response to specific measures to protect national parks has been mixed, U.S. citizens generally expressed support for protecting national parks. The debate over snowmobiles in Yellowstone elicited more than 350,000 citizen comments, more than the NPS has ever received on a single issue. They ran more than 4 to 1 against snowmobiles. In a survey conducted by the NPCA, 59 percent of U.S. citizens agreed that it made sense to reduce pollution, noise, and wildlife harassment by ending most snowmobile use in national parks.

In the early 2000's, most experts predicted that the popularity of the national parks would increase regardless of problems, which would continue to challenge the NPS's ability to balance preservation with recreation. "Our growing population will continue to exert pressures on all park preserves—national, state, and local," the National Park System Advisory Board observed in 2001. "These places will become more special, even precious, in the future."

Will the NPS be able to successfully balance its two-fold mission, protecting nature while promoting recreation? The answer will emerge slowly—year by year, budget by budget, administration by administration, even park by park. The payoffs of protecting the national parks go beyond the obvious and immediate. "As a people, our quality of life—our very health and well-being—depends on the protection of nature, the accessibility of open space and recreation opportunities, and the preservation of landmarks that illustrate our historic continuity," the National Park System Advisory Board has stated. "By caring for the parks and conveying the park ethic, we care for ourselves and act on behalf of the future." ■■■

President George W. Bush calls to congratulate a winning candidate following the midterm elections on Nov. 5, 2002. Political experts credited President Bush's popularity with helping the Republican Party regain control of the U.S. Senate and strengthen its hold on the U.S. House of Representatives.

United States, President of the.

The Republican Party, under the leadership of President George W. Bush, gained control of the U.S. Senate and retained control of the U.S. House of Representatives in midterm elections on Nov. 5, 2002. Bush became the first president since Franklin D. Roosevelt in 1934 to see his party gain seats in both the House and the Senate two years into his first term. Many political experts said that the victories gave the president a mandate to pursue his political agenda with Congress.

Iraq. President Bush, in his State of the Union address to the U.S. Congress on Jan. 29, 2002, warned the nation of an "axis of evil"—Iran, Iraq, and North Korea—that threatened world security. The president vowed that the United States would take military action against any regime that sponsored terrorism.

On September 12, in an address before the United Nations (UN) General Assembly in New York City, President Bush offered his rationale for military action against Iraq. The president said that Iraqi President Saddam Hussein had consis-

tently shown contempt for the international organization by refusing to cooperate with UN inspectors. According to the president, Hussein had ignored a series of UN resolutions put in place following the end of the Persian Gulf War (1991) ordering him to destroy all weapons of mass destruction, including stockpiles of chemical and biological weapons.

In October 2002, the House of Representatives and Senate passed a resolution authorizing the president to use U.S. armed forces "as he determines to be necessary and appropriate." The president signed the resolution on October 16.

On November 8, the UN Security Council unanimously endorsed a tough, new resolution to force Iraq to surrender weapons of mass destruction. UN weapons inspectors arrived in Iraq on November 25 to search for evidence of biological, chemical, and nuclear programs.

On December 7, Iraqi officials submitted a 12,000-page document, which they claimed gave complete details of their weapons. President Bush characterized the report as "not credible," and on December 18, U.S. Secretary of State Colin Powell declared that the weapons declaration constituted a "material breach" of various U.N. resolutions.

Homeland security. President Bush proposed a new Cabinet department for domestic defense on June 6. According to the president, the head of the new Homeland Security Department would oversee the domestic war on terrorism. In November, both the House and the Senate approved legislation creating the department, which consolidated 22 existing agencies and 170,000 employees.

Corporate fraud. On July 30, Bush signed corporate reform legislation that increased the penalties for corporate fraud. The legislation also created an independent board within the Securities and Exchange Commission (SEC) to oversee the accounting industry and restricted the amount of consulting work an accounting firm can perform for a company that the firm also audits. The SEC enforces laws governing the selling of securities.

Trade agreements. The president signed legislation in August that gave him broad authority to negotiate trade agreements with other countries through 2007. Congress can approve or reject entire treaties but cannot alter details.

☐ Geoffrey A. Campbell

See also **Armed forces; Congress of the United States; Democratic Party; Elections; International trade; Iraq; Republican Party; Taxation; United Nations; United States, Government of the.**

Uruguay. See **Latin America.**

Utah. See **State government.**

Uzbekistan. More than 90 percent of Uzbekistan's voters turned out in January 2002 to approve a referendum amending the country's constitution. The measures, which were overwhelmingly adopted, called for the creation of a *bicameral* (two house) legislature and an extension of the presidential term from five years to seven years. International observers from Human Rights Watch, a human rights organization based in New York City, called the vote "fatally flawed," citing Uzbekistan's lack of either a free press or opposition parties. Uzbek President Islam Karimov attacked Western critics for expecting Uzbekistan to transform itself into a democracy too rapidly. Karimov, who has served as president since the collapse of the Soviet Union in 1991, claimed that "at a certain stage of historic change you need a strong will ... and you have to use authoritarian measures at times."

In March 2002, Karimov met with United States President George W. Bush in Washington, D.C. Bush praised Karimov's cooperation in the global war against terrorism, in particular Uzbekistan's willingness to serve as a base for air strikes against Afghanistan in 2001. However, Bush also warned Karimov that Uzbekistan must continue to reform its economy and must improve its observance of human rights.   ☐ Steven L. Solnick

See also **Asia.**

Venezuela. The streets of Caracas, the capital, were the scene of several violent clashes between supporters and opponents of President Hugo Chavez Frias in 2002. Chavez's leftist programs, which had benefited people in long-neglected communities, were popular with Venezuela's vast poverty-stricken lower classes. However, Chavez's opponents, comprised mainly of Venezuela's middle and upper classes, denounced his increasingly authoritarian policies in overhauling government institutions, labor unions, courts, and Petroleos de Venezuela—the state-owned oil company.

Failed coup. On April 12, after several weeks of protests and counter-demonstrations, an alliance of Venezuelan military, business, and labor leaders ousted Chavez. The alliance replaced Chavez with Pedro Carmona Estanga, the head of Fedecamaras, Venezuela's largest business association.

The military *coup* (overthrow) stemmed from events of the previous day, when snipers, alleged to be Chavez supporters, opened fire on a crowd of more than 100,000 anti-Chavez demonstrators. Nineteen demonstrators were killed in the gunfire. The bloodshed occurred in the midst of a two-day-old general labor strike, which shut down most commerce in Caracas, and a six-week-old labor slowdown at Petroleos de Venezuela.

Immediately following the coup, tens of thousands of Chavez's supporters, including many soldiers and officers, took to the streets to call for his restoration to power. Developments turned in their favor after Air Force General Raul Baduel demanded the return of Chavez. Carmona Estanga announced his resignation on April 13, and Chavez was reinstated the next day.

Dissent increases. Various conciliatory steps taken by Chavez failed to satisfy his critics. Anti-Chavez demonstrations increased in early October as hundreds of thousands of opponents of the president marched through Caracas. Late in the month, dissident army officers took over a Caracas plaza, which became the main site of public protests. In November, Chavez ordered the military to take over the Caracas police force.

Chavez's opponents organized a nationwide labor strike and large protests in December to try to force the president to agree to a referendum on his rule in early 2003. After three protesters were shot to death in Caracas, the strikers demanded that Chavez resign immediately. When oil workers joined the strike, Chavez ordered the armed forces to seize oil production facilities and force gas stations participating in the strike to open.   ☐ Nathan A. Haverstock

See also **Latin America.**

Vermont. See **State government.**

Vietnam. The Communist Party, the only legal political organization in Vietnam, won 90 percent of the seats in the National Assembly, Vietnam's parliament, in May 2002. The assembly voted in July to reelect Tran Duc Luong to a second term as president, which is primarily a ceremonial position. The assembly also elected Phan Van Khai as prime minister for a second term.

Rumors of widespread corruption plagued Khai and other high-ranking members of the ruling party in 2002. As a result, government officials in July took the unusual step of hiring an independent foreign group to conduct a three-year study of corruption in the party and civil service.

In March, Khai announced that members of the Communist Party could work for private businesses. Prior to this announcement, party members were officially banned from engaging in capitalistic ventures, though this ban was largely ignored. In 2002, privately owned businesses employed 77 percent of Vietnam's workforce and generated nearly 60 percent of the nation's economic output.

In October, a fire in an office building in Ho Chi Minh City resulted in the deaths of 60 people, including 4 foreigners. Officials later urged Vietnamese cities to become better prepared to fight fires. ☐ Henry S. Bradsher

See also **Asia.**

Washington, D.C. Mayor Anthony Williams won a second term on Nov. 5, 2002. His general-election victory came after his name had been struck from the ballot in the Democratic Party primary election on September 10.

The District of Columbia Board of Elections and Ethics had ordered the removal of the mayor's name from the primary ballot after determining that thousands of signatures on his nominating petitions were forgeries. Nevertheless, Williams continued his campaign as a write-in candidate. In the primary election, he received 61,848 votes, compared with 20,689 votes for his main opponent, the Reverend Willie Wilson. The victory of Williams in the Democratic primary ensured that he would win the general election, because registered Democrats outnumbered registered Republicans in the District of Columbia by a ratio of 8 to 1.

Sniper scare. A 21-day killing spree terrorized residents of the Washington, D.C., metropolitan area in October. Between October 2 and October 22, 10 people were killed and three others were wounded in sniper attacks in Washington, surrounding suburbs in Maryland and Virginia, and elsewhere in the area. As the public became more frightened and as police grew increasingly frustrated in their inability to find the elusive killer (or killers), the Department of Defense on October 15 provided the police with military surveillance aircraft to help nab the sniper.

On October 24, a telephone tip from a motorist led police to John Allen Muhammad, a 41-year-old U.S. Army veteran, and John Lee Malvo, a 17-year-old Jamaican immigrant, who were sleeping in a car parked at a Maryland rest stop. Police found a .223-caliber semiautomatic rifle in the car. The trunk, which was open to the passenger compartment, had a gun port cut into it. Following the arrest of Muhammad and Malvo, law enforcement authorities said the men were also suspects in slayings in Louisiana, Alabama, Georgia, and Washington State. In November, U.S. Attorney General John Ashcroft announced that the men would be prosecuted first in Virginia.

Pentagon rebuilt. On September 11—one year after terrorists crashed a jet into the Pentagon Building—the reconstructed wing of the Department of Defense headquarters in Arlington, Virginia, outside Washington, D.C., was reopened. About 3,000 Pentagon employees returned to their offices in the repaired structure.

The reopening of the Pentagon wing was commemorated with a ceremony attended by 13,000 workers, federal officials, foreign dignitaries, and families of the 184 victims of the attack. President George W. Bush delivered a speech in which he reaffirmed his administration's pledge to defeat global terrorism. General Richard Myers, chairman of the Joint Chiefs of Staff, said the Pentagon Building had become a symbol of "American resilience."

Tourism rebounds. Tourists gradually returned to the nation's capital in 2002. A steep drop in tourism after the terrorist attacks had resulted in a loss of $1.25 billion by local businesses in late 2001. Hotel occupancy rose from about 60 percent in October 2001 to 92 percent in April 2002, according to the Washington, D.C., Convention & Tourism Corporation. Returning tourists found that access was restricted to some of the most prominent attractions in the capital. For example, the popular 20-minute, self-guided tours of the White House were no longer available. Only school groups and veterans' organizations were permitted to make reservations to tour the president's house.

World War II memorial. In November, the American Battle Monuments Commission, a federal agency that honors the accomplishments of the armed forces, announced that the National World War II Memorial would be dedicated on May 29, 2004—Memorial Day. Construction began on the memorial, estimated to cost about $170 million, in late 2001. ☐ Howard S. Shapiro

See also **City; Crime.**

Washington. See **State government.**

Water. See **Environmental pollution.**

Weather. Snow blanketed portions of the eastern United States at the start of 2002. A storm deposited snow as far south as Louisiana on January 1 before moving northeast and dumping nearly 5 inches (13 centimeters) in Atlanta, Georgia, and 11 inches (28 centimeters) in Raleigh, North Carolina.

Winter temperature extremes. Sections of the nation enjoyed unprecedented warm temperatures in January. Many cities experienced their highest January temperature on record, including Rapid City, South Dakota (73 °F [23 °C]); Sioux City, Iowa (71 °F [22 °C]); Little Rock, Arkansas (81 °F [27 °C]); and Tampa, Florida (86 ° [30 °C]).

At the end of January, a cold air mass pouring south from Canada triggered a severe ice storm across the Great Plains. More than 2 inches (5 centimeters) of ice toppled trees and power lines from central Oklahoma to eastern Kansas. The storm caused more than 20 deaths and knocked out power for more than 100,000 people. Many counties in Oklahoma and Kansas were declared disaster areas, while power disruptions were the worst on record near Kansas City, Missouri. Heavy snow fell on the storm's northern fringe, with 1 foot (31 centimeters) accumulating in Chicago.

Arctic air that had covered central Canada for much of the winter surged south at the end of February. Tallahassee, Florida, had a record low of 18 °F (–8 °C) on February 28, the latest date that the temperature had ever fallen below 20 °F (–7 °C) in that city.

A snowstorm swept from Texas to Michigan in early March, killing 21 people. A new 24-hour March snowfall record was set in Grand Rapids, Michigan, where 13.6 inches (34.5 centimeters) accumulated. Behind the storm, frigid air enveloped the central states, causing monthly low-temperature records to fall in many cities, including Chanute, Kansas (–3 °F [–19 °C]); Rockford, Illinois (–1 °F [–24 °C]); and Houston, Texas (22 °F [–6 °C]). Despite the late wintry siege, 10 states—including Wisconsin, Michigan, and New York—had their warmest winter on record. Yet, Marquette, Michigan, had its snowiest March on record, with 83 inches (211 centimeters). The city also had its snowiest season on record, with more than 300 inches (762 centimeters) measured between October 2001 and April 2002.

Spring storms and drought. Heavy rain fell from the lower Mississippi Valley to the Ohio Valley on March 19 and March 20. Six to eight inches (15 to 20 centimeters) of rain doused parts of Tennessee. Officials in eastern Kentucky, where 250 houses were destroyed, called the flooding the worst in 25 years.

Much of the nation experienced unseasonably warm temperatures from April 11 to April 18. More than 300 new records were set from the deserts of the Southwest to the cities of the Northeast. In April the temperature in New York City reached 90 °F (32 °C) on three consecutive days for only the second time since 1896.

Killer tornadoes and baseball-sized hail accompanied a powerful storm crossing the East on April 28, 2002. A tornado packing winds near 260 miles (418 kilometers) per hour ripped through La Plata, Maryland, 25 miles (40 kilometers) south of Washington, D.C. The twister killed 3 people and destroyed 80 houses, blowing 6 houses completely off their foundations.

Drought that had covered large parts of the nation during the winter persisted into the spring. State officials declared drought emergencies from Maryland to New Hampshire, and streams along the Middle Atlantic coast were near record low levels. A late season cold spell gripped much of the northern United States, resulting in nearly 500 daily record lows from May 19 to May 25, delaying spring planting by farmers already faced with drought. Bristol, Tennessee; Parkersburg, West Virginia; and Salisbury, Maryland, all had their latest freezes on record.

Record heat and wildfires. A sudden transition to summery heat in late May and June fueled an unusually early wildfire season in the West. The Hayman fire near Denver, which consumed nearly 138,000 acres (60,000 hectares), and the Rodeo-Chediski blaze, which burned 469,000 acres (190,000 hectares) in east-central Arizona, were the largest ever recorded in both states. Meanwhile, fires in the Black Hills were worsened by searing heat that set all-time June temperature records of 109 °F (43 °C) in Rapid City, South Dakota, and 111 °F (44 °C) in Bismarck, North Dakota. Nationally, 2.8 million acres (1.1 million hectares) burned during the first six months of the year, more than twice the 10-year average of 1 million acres (404,700 hectares).

In early July, smoke from at least 85 forest fires that burned across more than 250,000 acres (100,000 hectares) in Quebec, Canada, blew over New York, New Jersey, and Pennsylvania, prompting health officials to advise residents with respiratory conditions to stay indoors.

Conditions in the normally dry Southwest were the extreme opposite. As many as 33 inches (84 centimeters) of rain brought record flooding to parts of south-central Texas. San Antonio received over 16 inches (41 centimeters) of rain from June 30 to July 6. The 9.52 inches (20.2 centimeters) that fell on July 1 surpassed the previous rainfall record for the entire month.

In the West, all-time record highs were tied or set at more than 50 cities from July 10 to July 14, including Reno, Nevada, 108 °F (42 °C); Grand Junction, Colorado, 105 °F (41 °C); Salt Lake City, Utah, 107 °F (42 °C); and Miles City, Montana, 110 °F (43 °C).

A wildfire in the San Juan National Forest threatens a house about 10 miles (16 kilometers) north of Durango, Colorado, in June. More than 7 million acres of forest (2.8 million hectares) burned in the United States in 2002, a near-record that conservationists attributed to severe drought in the West, Great Planes, and along the Eastern Seaboard.

Wildfires continued in the West Coast states in fall 2002. One of the largest fires in Oregon history burned more than 500,000 acres (200,000 hectares) in the southwestern part of the state. By the end of the fire season, more than 7 million acres (2.8 million hectares) in the United States had been charred, just slightly less than during the record year of 2000.

The summer of 2002 ranked as the third-hottest on record for the nation, behind the Dust Bowl years of 1934 and 1936. At the end of August 2002, about 48 percent of the contiguous United States was experiencing moderate to extreme drought.

In central Europe, a series of unusual August storms brought record floods to parts of Germany, Austria, Hungary, Russia, the Czech Republic, and Slovakia. More than 100 people died, and economic losses exceeded an estimated $20 billion.

The hurricane season officially begins on June 1 and ends November 30. Nevertheless, the first tropical storm of 2002—Arthur, which form-ed off the North Carolina coast—did not occur until July 15. The storm moved out to sea without causing damage in the United States, but its remnants brought heavy rain to Scotland later in the week, hampering play in the British Open golf tournament.

The 2002 hurricane season reached a peak in September. Tropical Storm Gustav swept near North Carolina on the 10th. The storm reached hurricane status—winds of at least 74 miles (119 kilometers) per hour—off the East Coast of the United States on September 11, the latest date of the first Atlantic hurricane since modern record-keeping began in the 1940's.

Powerful Hurricane Isidore brought over 2 feet (0.6 meters) of rain to parts of western Cuba and the northern Yucatan Peninsula on September 21 and September 22. After weakening over Mexico, the storm headed north, making landfall in southeastern Louisiana as a strong tropical storm on the 26th. Flooding was extensive around New Orleans, where more than 18 inches (50 centimeters) of rain were reported in some areas. Damage exceeded $18 million in southern Louisiana alone. The storm dropped 2 to 10 inches (5 to 25 centimeters) of rain in the northeast as it raced through later in the week.

At the end of September, Tropical Storm Lili brought flooding and mudslides to Jamaica, where the ground had been saturated by rain from Hurricane Isidore. Lili became a hurricane on September 30 as it sped across the central Gulf of Mexico toward the United States. The hurricane made landfall October 3 near New Iberia in south-central Louisiana. More than 800,000 people, from Texas through Florida, moved inland in advance of high winds, 6 to 10 inches (15 to 25 centimeters) of rain, and flooding.

End-of-the-year storms. A powerful Pacific storm swept into California on November 7, bringing up to 8 inches (20 centimeters) of rain and winds as high as 80 miles (129 kilometers) per hour. Power disruptions in northern California affected more than 1 million customers. The same storm reached the East on November 10 and 11, spawning the deadliest November tornado outbreak since record-keeping began in 1950. Nearly 90 tornadoes were spotted from Arkansas to Ohio, causing 36 deaths.

An early winter storm hit the East on December 4 and 5. Heavy ice accumulation in parts of the Carolinas brought down power lines, causing more than 1.5 million people to lose electricity. New York City had 6 inches (15 centimeters) of snow, its greatest snowfall so early in the season since 1957. □ Fred Gadomski and Todd Miner
See also **Disasters.**

Weightlifting. See **Sports.**

Welfare. State governments increased the amount of money that they spent in 2002 on the current welfare program, known as Temporary Assistance for Needy Families (TANF), announced the Department of Health and Human Services' (HHS) Office of Family Assistance in a report released in April 2002. TANF provides cash assistance and help with child care for low-income workers and the unemployed. State governments spent $24 billion in fiscal year 2000 (Oct. 1, 1999, to Sept. 30, 2000) on the TANF program, an increase from the $22.6 billion spent in fiscal year 1999 (Oct. 1, 1998, to Sept. 30, 1999). Spending in cash assistance fell to $11.5 billion in fiscal year 2000 from $13.4 billion in fiscal year 1999.

Welfare caseloads fell dramatically in the five years since welfare reform began, which the Office of Family Assistance interpreted as a sign that more people in the United States were working instead of receiving benefits. In fiscal year 2001, the average number of TANF recipients totaled 5.4 million people, which was 56 percent lower than the caseload in fiscal year 1996. The fiscal year 2001 total of welfare recipients was the lowest number since 1967 and the lowest percentage of people receiving assistance since 1961, the HHS reported.

According to the 2002 report, the percentage of working recipients had reached an all-time

high. In fiscal 2000, 33 percent of adult TANF recipients were working, compared with 11 percent in fiscal 1996.

TANF funding. President George W. Bush approved temporary funding on Sept. 30, 2002, extending TANF through December 31. The emergency measure was needed because the U.S. Senate failed to approve the required funding before September 30 to extend the welfare program, which was enacted in 1996.

The House of Representatives approved legislation in May 2002 to reauthorize the welfare system. However, the Senate Finance Committee modified the House proposal in June. Political experts expected Senate leaders to reauthorize the welfare program in 2003.

Urban partnership program. HHS Secretary Tommy G. Thompson announced in June 2002 the creation of a new welfare reform initiative. The program, called Urban Partnerships for Welfare Reform, would assist some of the largest U.S. cities in adopting a program to help families make the transition from welfare to self-sufficiency.

Under the program, HHS officials planned on working with 10 cities, typically those with higher numbers of welfare recipients, to develop strategies to support and sustain families that are trying to become economically independent.
□ Geoffrey A. Campbell

West Indies. A 10-percent drop in tourism during the first 10 months of 2002 had a negative economic impact virtually everywhere in the West Indies. The decline in this flagship industry contributed to a worsening of the region's stagnant economies and high unemployment rates. To help revive tourism, the Caribbean Community (Caricom), an association of West Indian nations that fosters economic and political cooperation, kicked off a $16-million advertising campaign in August 2002 focusing on the theme "Life Needs the Caribbean." The campaign, which was financed by Caribbean tourism and hotel associations, aired some 2,000 advertisements on cable television networks in the United States through mid-November. A similar advertising campaign was planned for Europe in early 2003. Caribbean airlines and hotels—with financial support from national governments—offered deeply discounted travel packages in 2002 to lure tourists back.

Jamaican elections. In October, P. J. Patterson of the People's National Party won a third consecutive term as prime minister of Jamaica. A 59-member team of international observers led by former United States President Jimmy Carter monitored the election.

Patterson's party lost 13 seats in Parliament but retained its majority. Patterson pledged to reduce violence and crime and to reinstitute hanging, which was abolished in 1988, as a punishment for murderers. There were approximately 700 murders in Jamaica during the first 10 months of 2002. The majority of the killings were linked to drug traffickers.

Trinidad stalemate. Voters in October in the two-island nation of Trinidad and Tobago handed victory to the People's National Movement (PNM), led by Prime Minister Patrick Manning. PNM candidates, supported mainly by islanders of African descent, won 20 of 36 seats in Parliament. The United National Congress, backed mostly by islanders of East Indian descent and headed by former Prime Minister Basdeo Panday, won 16 seats. The outcome resolved a political stalemate that had existed since December 2001, when elections gave the same number of seats to each party, making it impossible for them to agree on the selection of a parliamentary speaker.

Joaquin Balaguer, who served seven terms as president of the Dominican Republic between 1960 and 1996, died at the age of 95 in July 2002. His rule spanned the country's evolution from dictatorship to democracy.

☐ Nathan A. Haverstock
See also **Latin America.**

West Virginia. See **State government.**
Wisconsin. See **State government.**
Wyoming. See **State government.**

Yugoslavia. Serbian and Montenegrin leaders, under pressure from the European Union (EU), agreed in 2002 to replace Yugoslavia with a more loosely configured joint state to be known as Serbia and Montenegro. Leaders in Serbia and Montenegro pressed in 2002 for closer ties to the EU and to the North Atlantic Treaty Organization (NATO). However, Serbian and Yugoslav cooperation with the International Tribunal for War Crimes in The Hague, the Netherlands, continued to be a precondition for eventual participation in these organizations.

The end of Yugoslavia. In March, Montenegrin, Serbian, and Yugoslav leaders yielded to strong pressure from EU representative Javier Solana to accept an agreement to restructure the Yugoslav nation, which since the mid-1990's consisted of Serbia and Montenegro. Serbia and Montenegro were to have a joint parliament, as well as two individual parliaments. They were to share a United Nations seat but retain separate monetary and banking systems.

The Serbian and Montenegrin parliaments approved the agreement in April, and the federal Yugoslav parliament approved it in May. In August, the Serbian and Montenegrin governments agreed on a proposed Constitution. In late 2002, the change in national status awaited mutual agreement on a few implementation details,

which in turn depended on the resolution of a delayed presidential election in Serbia.

Serbian voters on December 8 failed for a second time to elect a new president. Serbia's Constitution requires a minimum turnout of 50 percent of eligible voters in a presidential election for the results to be valid, but only 45 percent of voters participated in the December polling. The same thing had happened when authorities scheduled the presidential election in October. Yugoslav President Vojislav Kostunica, running for the Serbian presidency, took 58 percent of the vote in the invalid December 8 poll.

War crimes. Serbian and Yugoslav officials came under heavy pressure from the EU and the United States in 2002 to deliver indicted war criminals to the war crimes tribunal at The Hague. In March, the U.S. government froze $40 million in aid to Yugoslavia to force the country to cooperate with the tribunal. The aid freeze was lifted in May.

The war crimes trial of former Serbian leader Slobodan Milosevic, who was extradited to The Hague in 2001, began in February 2002. Milosevic was charged with 66 counts of crimes against humanity in Kosovo, Croatia, and Bosnia. Serbian Prime Minister Zoran Djindjic announced in December that Serbia's outgoing president, Milan Milutinovic, would be turned over to the war crimes tribunal in January 2003.

Kosovo. The Kosovo parliament chose Ibrahim Rugova as Kosovo's first president in February 2002. In May, Kosovo Serbs joined the government. Kosovo, which has an Albanian majority and a Serb minority, has been administered by the United Nations since the 1999 war in which NATO forces drove Yugoslav forces from Kosovo. Kosovo is officially a province of Serbia.

European integration. In April 2002, Yugoslav leaders declared their interest in joining NATO's Partnership for Peace program, a form of association with the alliance that military experts regard as a prelude to full membership. NATO officials said, however, that the presence of war criminals in Yugoslavia's military and the lack of civilian control over its military were serious impediments to prospective partnership status.

In August, the foreign minister of Greece said the EU might sign an association agreement—the first step in the lengthy process of gaining admission to the organization—with Yugoslavia or its successor nation in 2003. Analysts said the statement was significant because Greece was slated to assume the rotating presidency of the EU in January 2003.   ☐ Sharon L. Wolchik
See also **Europe.**

Yukon Territory. See **Canadian territories.**
Zambia. See **Africa.**

Zimbabwe. President Robert Mugabe, head of the ruling Zimbabwe African National Union-Patriotic Front (ZANU-PF), won a new six-year presidential term in an election in March 2002. The election was held amid allegations of widespread vote fraud and intimidation of opposition candidates. Mugabe, in power in Zimbabwe since 1980, received 56.2 percent of the votes cast, compared with Morgan Tsvangirai's 42 percent. Tsvangirai was the leader of the opposition Movement for Democratic Change (MDC).

While presidents Thabo Mbeki of South Africa and Olusegun Obasanjo of Nigeria endorsed the results, most international observers condemned the election as failing to meet criteria for a free and fair poll. They cited a voter registration process that appeared to be designed to frustrate voters; violence directed at MDC supporters; and intimidation of election monitors. More than 20 people—mainly MDC supporters—died during the campaign, according to Western reporters assigned to cover the election.

International response. Mugabe had expelled the head of the European Union's (EU) election observer team in Zimbabwe prior to the election. In protest, the EU withdrew its monitors and imposed so-called "smart sanctions"—sanctions aimed at individuals—that is, Mugabe and 19 of his closest aides. The governments of the United States and other Western nations responded with similar sanctions designed to punish the government, not the people. On March 19, 2002, the Commonwealth of Nations, an association of more than 50 countries, including the United Kingdom and many of its former colonies, suspended Zimbabwe.

Land invasions. Mugabe's regime moved to evict 2,900 white farmers from their land soon after the election. The farmers were ordered off the land by August 8. Critics alleged that many of the vacated farms were awarded to members of Mugabe's family and his associates. Mugabe had begun his campaign against Zimbabwe's white farmers in 2000 by tacitly encouraging so-called "war veterans," guerrillas from the country's civil war (1976-1979), to occupy white-owned farms. Nearly 1,700 such farms had been taken over before the 2002 evictions.

Food shortages. About 6 million Zimbabweans—half the country's population—faced famine in 2002. According to a report from the United Nations World Food Program, the seizure of white-owned farms and subsequent eviction of black farmworkers was a major cause of the crisis. Agricultural experts estimated that food production in Zimbabwe declined by 40 percent during 2002. □ Simon Baynham

See also **Africa; Australia; South Africa.**

Zoos unveiled several spectacular major exhibits in 2002. Such exhibits, the mainstay of zoos, are usually designed to be permanent. However, zoos also turned during the year to splashy, attention-grabbing temporary exhibits to keep visitors coming back.

Permanent exhibits. In May, the Erie Zoo in Erie, Pennsylvania, opened "Wild Asia," an exhibit that re-creates the setting of the ancient Cambodian temple of Angkor Wat. Five hundred tropical trees and other plants, including numerous orchids, complete a jungle habitat that one local newspaper described as "a scene from an Indiana Jones movie." Amid the models of ruins scattered throughout the jungle, visitors can see such Asian creatures as siamang gibbons, tiny barking deer, red pandas, and a pair of Bornean orangutans never before shown at the Erie, Pennsylvania Zoo.

The Woodland Park Zoo in Seattle opened its first exhibit of African wild dogs in June 2002. The dogs roam a flood plain 5,000 square feet (465 square meters) in size. Visitors view the dogs—which are rare both in the wild and in zoos—from the far side of a stream bed or from an overlook. The dogs are also visible through a window that offers views into a heated underground den.

Ohio's Akron Zoological Park unveiled "Wild Prairie" in June. In this replica of a Southwestern grassland live rare black-footed ferrets, prairie dogs, thick-billed parrots, a hog-nosed snake, and a burrowing owl. For children who want to saddle up, there is a pony ring with three ponies.

"Swamp Things" debuted in June at the Mystic Aquarium in Connecticut. Visitors explore the trees, vines, and Spanish moss of a swamp in the American South inhabited by alligators, including a nest with young. There are also snakes, snapping turtles, albino catfish, and gecko lizards.

Catch them while you can. Zoos in 2002 increasingly offered special temporary exhibits, which changed within a relatively short period. The aim was to make people aware that there is always something new at the zoo. The temporary exhibits usually displayed small creatures that were attention grabbers and did not require a large amount of space. These exhibits proved to be enormously popular.

More than 2 million people visited one such exhibit, "Seahorses: Beyond Imagination," at the National Aquarium in Baltimore in its first year. The exhibit, which was scheduled to remain open through 2003, featured 18 species of seahorses.

The Tennessee Aquarium in Chattanooga introduced an exhibit also named "Seahorses: Beyond Imagination" in May 2002. The Chattanooga seahorse gallery offered five separate habitats, including a Tasmanian kelp bed inhabit-

A rhinoceros is evacuated from its flooded habitat at the Prague Zoo in August. The flooding in Prague was the worst the Czech capital had experienced in more than 100 years.

ed by one of the most unusual of all seahorses, the weedy dragon. Covered with fleshy tabs resembling structures on the kelp in which it lives, the sea dragon is a master of camouflage. In another part of the exhibit, children could get right into the swim with a school of pipefish, a seahorse cousin, by standing inside a bubble of plexiglass that bulges into the water.

Jellyfish float in the 10 tanks of "Jellies: Living Art," which opened in April at California's Monterey Bay Aquarium. The exhibit, which was scheduled to run through 2004, featured jellyfish never before exhibited in North America, such as the blue jelly—which ranges in color from light blue to deep purple—and the flower hat, with its multicolored tentacles. A creature of mystery, the flower hat lives in waters off Japan for three months of the year, then disappears into the sea floor. The jellyfish were exhibited among works of art by major international artists.

A scary exhibit called "Danger or Deception? We Dare You" premiered at the Phoenix Zoo in Arizona during November 2002 for a six-month run. The exhibit, housed within a single large structure located along the zoo's Arizona Trail, brings visitors up close and personal with creatures that can be dangerous and others that only seem so. The moray eels lurking within a coral reef can deliver a nasty bite with long, needle-sharp teeth. However, the exhibit's fruit bats,

with faces that resemble a dog's and long, leathery wings, are actually perfectly harmless. And the hairy, bird-eating tarantulas, which grow so large that they can cover a dinner plate, pose no threat to people—even if they do look as if they came from a horror movie.

To leave the exhibit, visitors must walk a gauntlet of creepy critters. Hordes of huge death's head cockroaches crawl around behind clear partitions. Giant scorpions lie in wait above and below, visible through plexiglass. "Danger or Deception?" is the zoo's version of a fright night.

Newcomers. A variety of notable zoo babies were born during 2002. An endangered white-naped crane hatched at the Bronx Zoo in New York City in March. Three white-tailed *trogons* (tropical birds) entered the world at the National Aquarium, also in March. At the Pittsburgh Zoo and Aquarium in Pennsylvania, three rare Amur leopards were born in July. Fewer than 50 such leopards are known to exist in the wild, and only 200 remain in captivity.

The Milwaukee County Zoo in Wisconsin welcomed a Matchie's tree kangaroo in May, when it climbed out of its mother's pouch. And in June, a flamingo chick in a clutch of 12 eggs heading from Florida's Miami Metrozoo to the Fort Worth Zoo in Texas in the care of a zoo staffer hatched in flight aboard an American Airlines jet. The chick was named "Jet." □ Edward R. Ricciuti

New encyclopedia
articles are devoted
to the following topics:

Afghanistan
Circus
Einstein, Albert
Pakistan

2003 SUPPLEMENT

Picasso, Pablo
San Francisco
South Africa
Turkey

AP/Wide World

Kabul, Afghanistan's capital and largest city, has both traditional and modern buildings. Traditional mud-brick dwellings, such as those on the hillside, are found throughout Afghanistan. Some modern buildings rise in downtown Kabul. Parts of the city are being rebuilt after decades of war.

Afghanistan

Afghanistan, a nation in southwestern Asia, has towering mountains, scorching deserts, fertile valleys, and rolling plains. Afghanistan is surrounded by six other countries and so does not have a seacoast. The country is bordered by Turkmenistan, Uzbekistan, and Tajikistan on the north, China on the far northeast, Pakistan on the east and south, and Iran on the west.

Afghanistan is one of the world's least developed countries. Most Afghan workers farm the land, and many use old-fashioned farming tools and methods. Some of the people are nomads, who roam the country with their herds of sheep or goats. Kabul is the capital and largest city of Afghanistan.

Almost all the people of Afghanistan are Muslims. The religion of the Muslims, Islam, is the chief common link among them. The population of Afghanistan consists of about 20 ethnic groups, most of which are divided into several tribes. Most of the ethnic groups have distinct languages and cultures. The variety of ethnic groups has made it difficult for Afghanistan to develop into a unified, modern nation.

Afghanistan has a long and troubled history. In early days, Persians, Greeks, Mongols, and other peoples conquered the region. In modern times, Afghanistan has

continued to suffer foreign interference. The Soviet Union sought to occupy Afghanistan in a war that lasted from 1979 to 1989.

In the 1990's, a conservative Islamic group called the Taliban came to power. The Taliban allowed international terrorist organizations to run training camps in Afghanistan. After terrorist attacks against the United States in 2001, the United States and anti-Taliban forces within Afghanistan drove the Taliban from power. A transitional government was set up to rule the country.

Facts in brief

Capital: Kabul.
Official languages: Pashto (also called Pakhto) and Dari.
Official name: *Da Afghanistan Dowlat* (in Pashto) or *Dowlati Afghanistan* (in Dari), both meaning State of Afghanistan.
Area: 251,773 mi² (652,090 km²). *Greatest distances*—east-west, 820 mi (1,320 km); north-south, 630 mi (1,012 km).
Elevation: *Highest*—Nowshak, 24,557 ft (7,485 m) above sea level. *Lowest*—In Sistan Basin, 1,640 ft (500 m) above sea level.
Population: *Estimated 2002 population*—24,977,000; density, 99 persons per mi² (38 persons per km²); distribution, 80 percent rural, 20 percent urban. *1979 census*—13,051,358.
Chief products: *Agriculture*—barley, corn, cotton, fruits, Karakul skins, mutton, nuts, rice, vegetables, wheat, wool. *Manufacturing*—jewelry, leather goods, rugs. *Mining*—coal, lapis lazuli, natural gas.
Money: *Basic unit*—afghani. One hundred pule equal one afghani.

The contributor of this article, Thomas E. Gouttierre, is Director of the Center for Afghanistan Studies and Dean of International Studies and Programs at the University of Nebraska, Omaha.

A *jirga* (council) is a traditional Afghan community meeting. This jirga near Khowst, in eastern Afghanistan, met in 2002 to choose delegates to send to a national *loya jirga* (grand council) in Kabul.

Noreen S. Ahmed-Ullah © *Chicago Tribune*

Government

In the late 1990's, the Taliban controlled most of Afghanistan, including Kabul. The Taliban imposed their harsh interpretation of Islamic law on the country. However, few nations recognized the Taliban government as the legal government of Afghanistan.

The United States and its Afghan allies drove the Taliban from power in 2001. The United Nations then brought together the leaders of Afghanistan's main ethnic and regional groups, who organized a temporary government. These leaders also developed a plan for creating a permanent, more democratic government. Hamid Karzai, head of the Popalzai, an important clan of the Pashtun ethnic group, became head of the temporary government.

In June 2002, Afghan leaders held a *loya jirga* (grand council) to create a transitional government. Loya jirgas are held at times of crisis or when major political or social changes need consideration. Loya jirgas attempt to include representatives of all of Afghanistan's many regional and ethnic groups. In 1964, Afghan women attended a loya jirga for the first time. Afghan tribes and communities often hold smaller *jirgas* (councils) to decide matters of local importance. Local jirgas include all of a single community's adult men or the leaders from several neighboring communities.

In 2002, the loya jirga created a transitional government to lead the country for up to two years. During that time, it would work to establish a commission to create a new constitution and then hold democratic elections for a permanent government. The loya jirga chose Karzai as president of the transitional government. To gain national support for the government, Karzai selected Afghans from a variety of regions and ethnic groups to serve in his cabinet.

People

Ancestry. Most Afghans are a blend of early peoples who came to the country as invaders or settlers. These groups included Aryans, Persians, Arabs, Turkish-speaking people from central Asia, Mongolians, and people from the Xinjiang region of western China.

Ethnic groups and languages. Afghanistan has about 20 ethnic groups, most of which have their own language and culture. Most ethnic groups consist of several tribes, many of which speak their own dialect of the ethnic language. Many Afghans feel greater loyalty to their ethnic group or tribe than to their country.

The largest ethnic groups are the Pashtuns (or Pakhtuns) and the Tajiks. *Pashtuns* and *Pakhtuns* are also spelled *Pashtoons* and *Pakhtoons.* The Pashtuns and Tajiks make up more than 60 percent of the population. Most Pashtuns live in the southeast, near the Pakistan border. Their language, *Pashto* or *Pakhto,* is one of Afghanistan's two official languages. Most Tajiks live in northeastern Afghanistan and speak *Dari,* the other official language. Dari is also known as Afghan Persian. Most of the country's other ethnic groups speak Dari as either their first or second language.

Way of life. Most of Afghanistan's rural people live in homes made of sun-dried mud bricks. City dwellers live in homes and apartment buildings made of baked brick, concrete, or both. Most of the country's nomadic and seminomadic people live in tents made of goat hair.

Most Afghans wear traditional clothing. In winter, the people wear a heavy coat made of sheepskin, quilted

Symbols of Afghanistan. Afghanistan's flag has black, red, and green vertical stripes and the nation's coat of arms in the center. The coat of arms bears four Arabic inscriptions: at the top, *There Is No God but Allah and Muhammad Is the Prophet of Allah;* near the top, *God Is Great;* near the bottom, the Islamic year *1380* (2001-2002 in the Gregorian calendar); and at the bottom, *Afghanistan.*

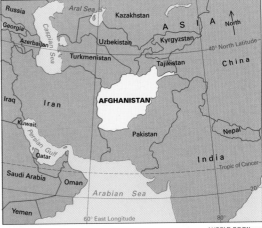

WORLD BOOK map

Afghanistan is a landlocked country in southwestern Asia. It is surrounded by six other countries.

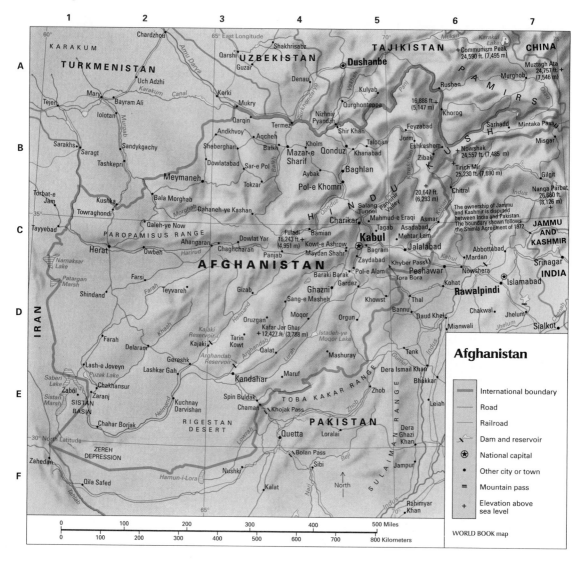

Afghanistan map index

*Does not appear on map; key shows general location.
Source: 1982 official estimates.

Islam greatly influences family and community relationships and almost all other aspects of Afghan life. This beautiful blue *mosque* (Islamic house of worship) is in Mazar-e Sharif.

© John Siceloff

fabric, or felt. Many rural men wear a turban, which may be tied in a certain way to indicate their ethnic group. Most Pashtun women wear a *burqa,* also called a *chadri,* which is a full-length hooded garment that covers the body from head to toe. The Pashtuns believe a woman must not be seen by any men outside of her family. Some rural women in Afghanistan cover their heads with a shawl.

Afghans serve flat loaves of whole-grain, sourdough bread at every meal. They also enjoy vegetables, yogurt, chicken, beef, mutton, and rice. Popular desserts include nuts and fruits. Tea is the favorite drink.

Women have traditionally played a secondary role in Afghan society. Their opportunities for education and careers have been limited, especially in rural areas. Men dominate women in many ways. For example, some Afghan tribes do not allow women to leave their homes without a male relative.

During the 1900's, several Afghan governments at-

tempted to give women more rights. In 1964, for example, a new constitution gave Afghan women equal status with men, and the social and economic position of some women improved. However, most women in rural areas never gained more rights.

In the 1990's and early 2000's, the Taliban greatly limited the freedom of women. For example, the Taliban required all women to cover themselves completely when in public. They also made it illegal for women to work outside their homes. Women who violated Taliban laws were punished severely.

After the Taliban were driven from power in 2001, many Afghan women hoped to reclaim their lost rights. In 2002, several women played significant roles in the national council that created a transitional government and helped decide the country's future.

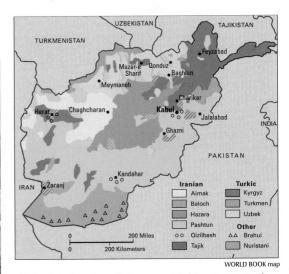

WORLD BOOK map

Afghanistan's major ethnic groups inhabit various parts of the country. The map key arranges the ethnic groups by their language types. For example, the language spoken by the Pashtuns is an Iranian language, but that spoken by Uzbeks is Turkic. Stripes indicate areas shared by more than one ethnic group.

AP/Wide World

The blue *burqa* (or *chadri)* is a full-length hooded garment worn by most Pashtun women in Afghanistan. Some Afghan women drape a shawl over their heads.

© SuperStock

Goat herders lead their herd over an arid mountain path. Afghanistan's economy depends heavily on agriculture. Many of the country's farmers practice sheep and goat herding.

Religion. About 99 percent of all Afghans are Muslims. Their religion strongly influences family and community relationships and most other aspects of life. Almost every Afghan village or nomadic group has a religious leader called a *mullah.* Mullahs lead prayer services and educate the young. They sometimes have great influence in their communities.

Education. Most of Afghanistan's people 15 years of age or older cannot read and write. For the country's literacy rate, see **Literacy** (table: Literacy rates for selected countries). Many children cannot attend school because the country does not have enough schools or teachers. This lack of educational facilities is due largely to the upheaval caused by decades of war. Afghanistan has two universities—Kabul University and Ningrahar University in Jalalabad.

The arts. Because most of the people of Afghanistan cannot read and write, folklore, folk songs, and folk dances play an important part in Afghan life. They enable the people to pass their values and traditions on from one generation to the next. The *attan* (also spelled *atan)* is an energetic folk dance. Pashtuns dance the attan at weddings and other community celebrations.

Recreation. Afghans enjoy sports and games, such as soccer, volleyball, and basketball. Many men in Afghanistan like to hunt, and some of them use the famous Afghan hounds as hunting dogs. Men of the northern plains play a game called *buzkashi.* In the game, dozens of horsemen try to grab a headless calf and carry it across a goal.

The land and climate

Afghanistan is made up of three main land regions. These regions are, from north to south: (1) the Northern Plains, (2) the Central Highlands, and (3) the Southwestern Lowlands.

The Northern Plains stretch across northern Afghanistan and consist of mountain plateaus and rolling hills. The soil is fertile in the Northern Plains but can be cultivated only where water is available. Large irrigation systems have been built along the Harirud, Helmand, Qonduz, and other rivers. Nomadic and seminomadic people raise sheep and goats on the vast grasslands.

Temperatures in the Northern Plains of Afghanistan average about 38 °F (3 °C) in January and approximately 90 °F (32 °C) in July. The average annual precipitation in the region totals about 7 inches (18 centimeters).

The Central Highlands cover about two-thirds of Afghanistan. They consist of the towering Hindu Kush mountain range and its branches. Snow-capped peaks rise about 25,000 feet (7,620 meters) along the Pakistani border in the east. The range gradually descends to a rolling plain in the southwest. Most Afghans live in the high, narrow valleys of the Hindu Kush.

The Central Highlands have an average temperature of about 25 °F (–4 °C) in January and about 75 °F (24 °C) in July. The region receives about 15 inches (38 centimeters) of precipitation yearly.

The Southwestern Lowlands lie in southwestern Afghanistan and consist mainly of desert or semidesert land. The region is crossed by the Helmand River, which flows from the Hindu Kush to the Sistan Basin on the Iranian border. The basin has several slightly salty lakes and marshes. Barley, corn, fruits, and wheat are grown in the Helmand Valley.

Temperatures in the lowlands of Afghanistan average about 35 °F (2 °C) in January and about 85 °F (29 °C) in July. The average annual precipitation ranges from 2 to 9 inches (5 to 23 centimeters).

Economy

Afghanistan's economy once benefited from the country's location along the Silk Road and other ancient trade routes. As these routes died out, the country became isolated. In the mid-1900's, Afghan governments attempted to develop the country's economy and to improve educational opportunities. But decades of war and internal struggles at the end of the 1900's reversed most of these advances. A severe drought in the late 1990's and early 2000's further weakened Afghanistan's economy. However, economic aid flowed into the country following the defeat of the Taliban in 2001.

Agriculture. About 85 percent of all Afghan workers earn their living in agriculture. Wheat is the chief crop of Afghanistan. Other crops include barley, corn, cotton, fruits, nuts, rice, sugar beets, and vegetables. Production is limited by a shortage of modern machinery, fertilizer, and high-quality seeds.

During the late 1900's, Afghanistan became one of the world's leading producers of opium, which is used to make the illegal drug heroin. Many Afghan farmers raised opium poppies because it was more profitable than growing wheat and other food crops. In 2000, the Taliban began enforcing a strict ban on poppy farming, but the practice resumed after the Taliban were driven from power in 2001. The governments that have ruled Afghanistan since then have also tried to stop farmers from growing opium poppies.

Afghanistan's nomadic and seminomadic people raise most of the country's livestock. The chief livestock products are dairy items, mutton, wool, and animal hides. The skins of Karakul sheep, a fat-tailed sheep known for its silky pelt, are especially valuable.

Mining. Afghanistan is rich in minerals, but most of the deposits are largely undeveloped. In the 1960's, large deposits of natural gas were discovered in Afghanistan. Since then, the production of natural gas has become an important part of the nation's economy. Afghanistan also produces some coal, copper, gold, and salt. The country has huge deposits of iron ore, but because of Afghanistan's rugged terrain and frequent conflicts, they remain undeveloped.

Afghanistan has deposits of the world's finest lapis lazuli, a valuable azure-blue stone. Other gemstones mined in the country include amethysts and rubies.

Manufacturing. Afghanistan has little industry. Skilled craftworkers in their homes or small shops make gold and silver jewelry, leather goods, rugs, and other handicraft items. A few mills produce textiles, and small factories turn out such products as cement, matches, and processed foods.

International trade. Afghanistan's leading exports are cotton, fruits and nuts, natural gas, rugs, and Karakul sheep skins. Imports include machinery, motor vehicles, petroleum products, and textiles. Afghanistan conducts its international trade mainly over land, through the neighboring countries of Iran and Pakistan.

Transportation and communication. Afghanistan has about 11,700 miles (18,800 kilometers) of roads. However, decades of war heavily damaged most paved roads, making many of them unusable. The country has no railroads.

Afghanistan's most famous transportation route is the Khyber Pass, which crosses the border between Afghanistan and Pakistan. The pass cuts through the Safid Kuh mountains, which are part of the Hindu Kush range. Conquerors, such as Alexander the Great of Macedonia, crossed the pass to invade South Asia. The Khyber Pass has been an important trade route for centuries. See **Khyber Pass.**

Several newspapers are published in Afghanistan. The country has one national television station and one national radio station. Both stations broadcast from Kabul.

History

Prehistoric hunting people lived in what is now Afghanistan as early as 100,000 years ago. After many thousands of years, the people learned how to farm and to herd animals. Agricultural villages then developed. By about 4000 to 2000 B.C., a number of these villages had grown into small cities.

Early invasions. About 1500 B.C., the Aryans, a central Asian people, invaded the region. They killed many of the area's inhabitants and intermarried with others. In the mid-500's B.C., Persians invaded northern Afghanistan, a region then called Bactria. The Persians ruled Bactria until about 330 B.C., when Greeks and Macedonians led by Alexander the Great conquered the region and much of the rest of Afghanistan.

About 246 B.C., the Bactrians revolted. They eventually conquered Bactria and other parts of Afghanistan. They formed a kingdom that lasted about 150 years, until the Kushans of central Asia seized Afghanistan. Sasanians from Persia invaded in the A.D. 200's, and White Huns from central Asia defeated the Kushans and Sasanians in the 400's.

The coming of Islam. Arab Muslim armies swept into parts of what is now Afghanistan during the late 600's. Three Muslim dynasties—the Tahirid, the Samanid, and the Saffarid—controlled much of the region during the 800's and 900's. Under these dynasties,

© Hulton/Getty Images

The Anglo-Afghan wars of the 1800's resulted largely from the United Kingdom's desire to protect its Indian empire. This photograph shows British troops at a fort in Kabul in 1879.

most local inhabitants became Muslims.

Turkic-speaking peoples from eastern Persia and central Asia ruled Afghanistan from about 900 to 1200. Afghanistan was conquered by Mongols led by Genghis Khan in the 1200's and led by Timur, also called Tamerlane, in the 1300's. Safavids from Persia and Mughals from India struggled for control of Afghanistan from the mid-1500's to the early 1700's.

United Afghanistan. In 1747, Ahmad Khan came to power. He took the title *shah* (king) and adopted the name *Durrani* (Pearl of the Age). Ahmad Shah Durrani united the many Afghan tribes for the first time, marking the beginning of modern Afghanistan. He gained control of territory stretching far beyond the country's current borders.

Ahmad Shah was succeeded by his son Timur Shah. Around 1775, Timur Shah moved the capital from Kandahar to Kabul. Timur Shah and his successors struggled to keep the Afghan tribes united and lost control of most of the territory beyond the current borders of Afghanistan.

In 1819, civil war broke out among rival tribes that wanted to rule the country. The war lasted until 1826, when Dost Muhammad Khan gained control. He took the title of *amir* (prince). Dost Muhammad's descendants ruled the country for the next 150 years.

The Anglo-Afghan wars. During the 1800's, the United Kingdom and Russia competed for control of Afghanistan. Russia wanted an outlet to the Indian Ocean and began to expand toward Afghanistan. The United Kingdom wanted to protect its empire in India, which was threatened by Russia's expansion. In 1839, British troops invaded Afghanistan to reduce Russia's influence in the region. The invasion set off the First Anglo-Afghan War, which lasted until the British withdrew in 1842. Russian influence near Afghanistan increased during the mid-1800's.

In 1878, the United Kingdom invaded the country again, starting the Second Anglo-Afghan War. The British found it difficult to establish control of Afghanistan. In 1880, Abdur Rahman Khan became amir. The British agreed to recognize his authority over the country's internal affairs. In return, Abdur Rahman accepted the United Kingdom's control of Afghanistan's foreign relations. During his reign, Abdur Rahman worked to strengthen the national government and to reduce the power of tribal leaders. After he died in 1901, his policies were continued by his son Habibullah Khan.

Independence. Early in 1919, Habibullah Khan was assassinated. One of his sons, Amanullah Khan, then became amir and attacked British troops in India, beginning the Third Anglo-Afghan War. The United Kingdom had just finished fighting in World War I (1914-1918). It decided to end its involvement in Afghanistan rather than fight another war. In August 1919, Afghanistan became fully independent.

Amanullah began many reforms to modernize Afghanistan, rapidly sweeping away centuries-old traditions and customs. The nation's first constitution was adopted in 1923, and Amanullah changed his title from amir to shah in 1926. But tribal and religious leaders resisted the reform movement and forced Amanullah Shah to give up the throne in 1929.

Late in 1929, Muhammad Nadir Shah became king. In 1931, Afghanistan adopted a new constitution. Under the new Constitution, Nadir Shah began a program of gradual reform. But he was assassinated in 1933, before many of the reforms were begun. Muhammad Zahir Shah, Nadir Shah's son, then became king.

The mid-1900's. By the early 1950's, Afghanistan had developed good relations with the United States and many Western European nations. But the Afghans feared the intentions of the Soviet Union, their country's powerful Communist neighbor. In 1953, Muhammad Daoud Khan, the king's cousin and brother-in-law, took control of the government and made himself prime minister. Under Daoud, Afghanistan took no side in the Cold War, a period of hostility between Communist and non-Communist nations, and it received aid from both the United States and the Soviet Union.

Border disputes with Pakistan and other problems led to pressures that forced Daoud to resign in 1963. In 1964, under the leadership of Zahir Shah and Western-educated scholars and thinkers, Afghanistan adopted a constitution that provided for a democratic government. But many problems arose. Zahir Shah and the legislature could not agree on the role of political parties within the reform program. Parliament often deadlocked on

key issues. In addition, the Afghan people had little experience with, or understanding of, democratic government. As a result, the new democratic system failed to bring about the progress that the framers of the Constitution had hoped for.

In 1973, Daoud led a military revolt that overthrew Zahir Shah. Afghanistan's military, aided by Afghan Communists, took control of the government and established the Republic of Afghanistan with Daoud as president and prime minister.

The Soviet invasion. In 1978, rival left-wing military leaders and civilians in Afghanistan staged another revolt, during which Daoud was killed. This group, which received much financial and military aid from the Soviet Union, took control of the government and established policies that had some features of Communism.

Many in Afghanistan opposed the new government. They believed the government's policies conflicted with teachings of Islam. In addition, they resented Soviet influence on the government. Large numbers of Afghan people joined in a rebellion against the government shortly after it came to power. Widespread fighting broke out between the rebels, who called themselves *mujahideen* (holy warriors), and government forces.

The Soviet Union became concerned that the rebels might defeat the Afghan government forces. In 1979 and 1980, the Soviet Union sent thousands of troops to join the fight against the rebels. The Soviets had far better equipment than their opponents. But the rebels, supplied by countries opposed to the Soviet Union, used guerrilla tactics to overcome the Soviet advantage. The Soviets and Afghan government forces bombed many villages.

In 1988, the Soviet Union began withdrawing its troops from Afghanistan. The withdrawal was completed in February 1989. But the fighting between the mujahideen and government forces continued until 1992, when the rebels overthrew the government.

Afghanistan under the Taliban. After 1992, Afghanistan had several governments made up of various combinations of mujahideen groups. Continued fighting among the groups prevented the establishment of a stable government. In the mid-1990's, a new group,

AP/Wide World

Soviet troops retreated from Afghanistan in 1989. The Soviet Union invaded Afghanistan in 1979 and 1980 to support the Communist government there. Despite their superior military strength, the Soviets failed to defeat the Afghan rebels, known as *mujahideen.*

Hamid Karzai, *left,* led Afghanistan after the fall of the Taliban in 2001. The former king of Afghanistan, Muhammad Zahir Shah, *right,* supported Karzai and helped unify the country.

a conservative Islamic organization known as the Taliban, rose to power.

Pashtun religious students who had fled to Pakistan during the Soviet invasion started the Taliban movement. The Taliban were supported by Pakistan's military and by militant Arab Islamic groups. By the late 1990's, the Taliban gained control of most of Afghanistan. They established a Council of Ministers to rule the country.

The Taliban imposed their strict interpretation of Islam on the nation. For example, they banned television, popular music, and most other modern forms of entertainment, and they established rules for dress and grooming. All women were forced to cover themselves completely when in public, and men were required to grow beards. The Taliban also prohibited girls from attending school and forbade women from working outside the home.

The Taliban destroyed many artifacts of the country's heritage because they claimed they were anti-Islamic. For example, they demolished two ancient statues of Buddha carved into a mountainside near Bamian, Afghanistan. The Taliban also destroyed many works of art in the country's museums.

Through the decades of war in the late 1900's, millions of Afghans fled to neighboring Pakistan and Iran, and thousands more became refugees in their own country. Years of drought in the late 1990's and early 2000's left many Afghans in danger of starvation.

Recent developments. In 2001, members of a terrorist organization called al-Qa`ida attacked the World Trade Center in New York City and the Pentagon Building near Washington, D.C. (see **September 11 terrorist attacks**). The United States accused the Taliban of harboring and assisting al-Qa`ida, which was led by the Saudi-born millionaire Osama bin Laden. The United States demanded that the Taliban arrest bin Laden and the other terrorists and shut down their training camps. The Taliban refused to do so, and the United States and its allies launched a military campaign against the Taliban.

The campaign included air strikes in support of Afghan rebels who opposed the Taliban. This support enabled the rebels to drive the Taliban from power in

late 2001. Meanwhile, the United Nations brought together representatives of Afghanistan's leading groups to discuss the formation of a new and stable national government. The conference agreed on a plan that included the appointment of a temporary government and the eventual creation of a new constitution and a democratically elected government.

An international peacekeeping force arrived in Kabul in late 2001 and early 2002. In the absence of a strong central government, however, warlords and tribal groups continued to compete for territory and power. Also, small groups of Taliban and al-Qa`ida forces continued to battle U.S. and allied troops.

In April 2002, the former king of Afghanistan, Muhammad Zahir Shah, returned to the country. He did not resume his role as king but attended a *loya jirga* (grand council) of Afghan leaders. In June, the loya jirga met in Kabul and chose Hamid Karzai, leader of the Popalzai clan, as the country's transitional president.

Thomas E. Gouttierre

Related articles include:

Asia	Kushan Empire
Bin Laden, Osama	Lapis lazuli
Delhi Sultanate	Muslims
Hindu Kush	Pashtuns
India (History)	Persia, Ancient
Iran (History)	Qa`ida, Al-
Kabul	September 11 terrorist
Kandahar	attacks
Karakul	Taliban
Khan	Turkestan
Khyber Pass	

Outline

I. **Government**
II. **People**
    A. Ancestry   E. Religion
    B. Ethnic groups and   F. Education
        languages   G. The arts
    C. Way of life   H. Recreation
    D. Women
III. **The land and climate**
    A. The Northern Plains
    B. The Central Highlands
    C. The Southwestern Lowlands
IV. **Economy**
    A. Agriculture
    B. Mining
    C. Manufacturing
    D. International trade
    E. Transportation and communication
V. **History**

Questions

What are the largest ethnic groups in Afghanistan?
What is a *loya jirga?*
What valuable stones are found in Afghanistan?
What led to the Anglo-Afghan wars?
What is the Hindu Kush? The Sistan Basin?
How do most Afghan workers earn their living?
What is a *burqa?*
Who first united the Afghan tribes?
What is the chief common link among Afghans?
What country tried to occupy Afghanistan from 1979 to 1989?

Additional resources

Ewans, Sir Martin. *Afghanistan.* HarperCollins, 2002.
Rashid, Ahmed. *Taliban.* Yale, 2000.
Rubin, Barnett R. *The Fragmentation of Afghanistan.* 2nd ed. Yale, 2002.
Vogelsang, Willem. *The Afghans.* Blackwell, 2002.

A circus presents a variety of performers, including acrobats, clowns, dancers, and musicians. A circus traditionally opens with a lavish production number called a *spectacle, shown here.*

Circus

Circus is a live production that features daring and graceful acts by a cast of acrobats, aerial artists, clowns, and other performers. Traditional circuses also feature trained animals. The circus band and dancers in elaborate costumes add to the color and excitement. A ringmaster serves as master of ceremonies, singing and introducing many of the acts.

Audiences enjoy a circus for its pageantry and even more for its thrills and danger. Circus artists risk serious injury or even death by performing in cages with wild animals, flying through the air in a trapeze act, or walking on a high wire many feet or meters aboveground.

The circus is one of the most international of art forms. A large circus will include performers from throughout the world. A show might include acrobats from China, tumblers from Bulgaria, animal acts from Germany, high wire walkers from Spain, trapeze artists from Mexico, and clowns from the United States.

At the circus

Traditional circus performances open and close with a lavish production number called a *spectacle.* As the band plays, the ringmaster sings, and performers in elaborate costumes parade in front of the audience. Such animals as camels, elephants, dogs, horses, llamas, and zebras take part in the parade. The spectacle may end with a trick called a *long mount,* in which the elephants stand in a line with their front legs resting on the backs of the elephants in front of them.

Most of the show consists of circus acts, which take place in round areas called *rings.* A circus may have

LaVahn G. Hoh, the contributor of this article, is Professor of Drama at the University of Virginia and coauthor of Step Right Up! The Adventure of Circus in America.

from one to three rings, though some circuses perform in an open area with no rings. In a three-ring circus, similar acts may appear in all the rings at the same time. These acts are known as a *display.* For example, three groups of acrobats may perform at one time, followed by three animal acts.

Circus acts feature an astonishing variety of talent by people and animals. One circus artist may perform back flips on a high wire. A *flyer* gracefully somersaults through the air into the hands of another aerial artist, who hangs by the knees from a trapeze. Chimpanzees ride around the the ring on bicycles, and dogs jump rope. Tigers leap through hoops of fire. *Liberty horses* (horses without riders) race around a ring and execute intricate maneuvers.

Clowns entertain the audience before and during the performance. In one popular clown gag, about a dozen clowns emerge from a tiny car. Clowns walk on stilts, ride unicycles, juggle, or perform short, silly pantomime plays.

The circus band plays throughout the show. The musicians, directed by a conductor, often make quick adjustments in the music to follow the live action. A typical circus band performs music ranging from traditional circus marches to jazz, blues, and rock music.

Behind the scenes

A number of key people work together to stage an elaborate and complex circus performance. A director supervises the overall performance, assisted by a *choreographer* who creates the many dance routines that are part of the show. Costume designers plan the colorful costumes that have become part of the circus tradition.

Most circuses travel by truck. The performers, staff, and workers travel and live in privately owned motor homes. Animals ride in specially designed stock trailers.

Workers called *roustabouts* unload and set up the equipment for the various acts. The roustabouts must quickly and efficiently erect and take down the equip-

Animal acts provide great excitement for audiences. These lions perform tricks on commands from their trainer. To protect the spectators, the animals perform inside a wire cage.

Ringling Bros. and Barnum & Bailey Combined Shows, Inc.

Ringling Bros. and Barnum & Bailey Combined Shows, Inc.

Clowns in funny costumes and colorful makeup entertain the audience with their playful antics and humorous stunts. They often use comic or unusual objects as props in their acts.

Ringling Bros. and Barnum & Bailey Combined Shows, Inc.

Human cannonballs are circus daredevils who fly through the air after being shot out of a cannon. These performers will land in a safety net on the other side of the arena.

ment during a performance. After the last performance in a city, the workers pack all the equipment so it can be moved to the next location.

A traveling circus is like a small, self-contained community. The circus provides meals for the workers. A circus may also have its own barber, school, veterinarian, and doctor and first-aid unit.

Joining the circus

Before joining a circus, an individual must realize that the circus has its own lifestyle. A performer in a typical circus travels for much of a year, moving from city to city. Some circuses have two or three shows a day for five or six days every week.

For many years, most circus performers grew up in the circus, learning their skills from members of their families. Now a performer can join a circus by training for it. Some noted circus schools are supported by national governments. The Soviet Union had a tradition of training circus artists through state-supported schools, beginning with the Moscow Circus School, established in 1927. But many of these schools closed after the Soviet Union broke apart in 1991. Other countries still have state-supported training schools, including L'Ecole Supériéure des Arts du Cirque (National School of Circus Arts) in France and L'Ecole Nationale de Cirque (National Circus School) in Canada. In the United States, people can learn circus skills at some universities, at training schools sponsored by circuses, and at clubs and YMCA's.

History

Roots of the circus. Many elements of the modern circus have existed for more than 2,000 years. For example, in 2500 B.C., circus-type performers, such as acrobats and balance artists, performed in Egypt. Acrobats jumped over bulls on the island of Crete by the 1500's B.C. Performers spun plates on bamboo poles at a theater school in China in A.D. 714. Many aspects of the modern circus appear in ancient Greek culture. For example, the strong man and the comic mime, a forerunner of the clown, originated in ancient Greece.

Surviving examples of circus activity support the notion that the modern circus had its roots in ancient Rome. Chariot races took place in a round or horseshoe-shaped structure called a *circus*, the Latin word for *circle* or *oval*. These races eventually included circuslike entertainment.

After the collapse of the Roman Empire in western Europe in the A.D. 400's, entertainers called *minstrels, troubadours*, and *jongleurs* traveled throughout Europe, entertaining people with circuslike skills. In the Chinese classical theater, the white-faced clown became one of the four basic types of roles in Chinese drama. In the 1400's, plays in China included people jumping through hoops lined with swords, or turning somersaults on a ladder.

The birth of the circus. The modern circus was developed in England by Philip Astley, a former sergeant major of the British Cavalry. In 1768, Astley opened an *equestrian* (horseback riding) school in London. He taught riding in the morning and performed "feats of horsemanship" in the afternoon. Astley performed in a circular arena later referred to as the *ring*. After two years of demonstrating his "feats of horsemanship," Astley added other entertainment. Between riding acts, he inserted performers who juggled, walked a tightrope, or demonstrated acrobatic skills. He also added a clown. By combining these elements of entertainment, Astley founded the modern circus.

In 1782, two Englishmen, a riding teacher named Charles Hughes and a dramatist and composer named Charles Dibdin, opened an equestrian school that rivaled Astley's. The men called their school the Royal Circus and Equestrian Philharmonic Academy, the first time the word *circus* was used to refer to a combination of equestrian and other acts.

In 1793, Hughes traveled to Russia at the invitation of the Empress Catherine the Great. He introduced the circus at the empress's court in St. Petersburg, and the new form of entertainment quickly spread throughout Russia.

Also in 1793, Hughes's student John Bill Ricketts opened the first American circus in Philadelphia. Ricketts established the first Canadian circus in Montreal in 1797. Philip Lailson, a British equestrian, introduced the circus to Mexico in 1802.

The circus grows. By the early 1800's, the circus had spread throughout Europe and the United States. The first circus performances took place in temporary wooden structures. Soon, however, almost every major city in Europe had at least one permanent building for the circus. Some circuses in the United States also had permanent structures.

While the European circus developed in permanent buildings, the circus in the United States took a different path. Joshuah Purdy Brown wanted to take entertainment and spectacle to America's small towns, so in 1825 he introduced circus performances under a tent. The circus could now travel to more places using this portable structure. By the 1830's, most American circuses performed in tents.

Brown came from the area of Somers, New York, which has been called the "cradle of the American circus." In Somers, a cattle dealer named Hachaliah Bailey bought an African elephant and exhibited it. The popular response to the elephant led Bailey to import more animals from other countries and create a traveling menagerie. Perhaps the most famous menagerie of the early 1800's, called the Zoological Institute, had been formed in the Somers area. The traveling circus and menagerie business had begun.

The American circus started with single acts in one ring and gradually developed into three or more rings.

Astley's Amphitheatre at Lambeth, London, circa 1810. Aquatint by Augustin Pugin and Thomas Rowlandson (Granger Collection)

Astley's Amphitheatre was opened in 1777 in London by Philip Astley, who is credited with developing the modern circus. In the amphitheatre, Astley mixed circus acts with theater. A ring near a stage featured circus tricks with horses.

The Golden Age of the American circus extended from the 1870's through the 1920's. Large circuses, such as the Sells Brothers Circus, traveled throughout the United States, performing in giant canvas tents. This poster from 1895 shows the circus set up next to a railroad station. Patrons could get off a train and walk directly to the circus.

By the end of the 1800's, methods of travel for the circus varied from horse-drawn wagons to riverboats and railroad trains. In 1868 and 1869, a circus and menagerie owned by Dan Castello, a former clown, became the first circus to make a transcontinental tour, much of it by rail.

The Greatest Show on Earth was the name given to his circus by the American promoter and showman P. T. Barnum after he joined with circus owners Castello and William C. Coup to form P. T. Barnum's Grand Traveling Museum, Menagerie, Caravan and Circus in 1871. This show exhibited animal and human oddities, which eventually became a standard part of the American circus known as the *side show.*

Barnum's circus imported the African elephant Jumbo from the London Zoo in 1882. The animal became a sensation. The circus also staged large street parades to promote its shows. Barnum's parades established the practice for other circuses for decades. After a traveling circus arrived in town, a procession of performers, animals, and brightly painted wagons drawn by teams of horses would parade down the main street to attract people to the circus performances.

The circus goes international. During the mid-1800's, the circus expanded to many parts of the world. In 1836, Thomas T. Cooke, an English showman, visited the United States. When he returned to England in 1840, he took with him the idea of the circus tent. An Italian showman named Giuseppe Chiarini managed a touring circus that traveled throughout the world. An Australian

Circus World Museum, Baraboo, Wisconsin

The circus parade was a tradition in the United States for many years. This 1908 scene shows a crowd watching the animals and circus wagons parade through the town. The procession took place after the circus arrived in a town to advertise upcoming performances.

pubkeeper named Robert A. Radford established the first true circus in Australia, Radford's Royal Circus, in 1847. A French equestrian, Louis Soullier, introduced the circus to China in 1854. When he returned to Europe in 1866, he introduced Chinese acts, such as perch-pole balancing, plate spinning, and juggling.

Following the death of P. T. Barnum in 1891, a showman named James A. Bailey, Barnum's partner, acquired the circus and shipped the entire show to Europe for a tour that lasted from 1897 to 1902. During this tour, European circus owners were amazed at how easily Bailey's circus could be loaded, set up, torn down, and moved. Bailey's show traveled on specially designed trains.

The Ringling Brothers. After Bailey returned to the United States in 1902, he discovered that he had serious competition from the five Ringling brothers from Baraboo, Wisconsin. The brothers presented their first show in 1884. They hired an old showman named Yankee Robinson to lend his name and advise them. The show was named Yankee Robinson and Ringling Bros. Great Double Shows, Circus and Caravan, but the Yankee Robinson name was used for only one season.

By 1892, the Ringling Bros. Circus was traveling to 12 states on 31 railroad cars and presenting its show in a tent larger than a football field. After Bailey's death in 1907, the Ringling brothers purchased the Barnum and Bailey circus. They combined it with their show in 1919 to form Ringling Bros. and Barnum & Bailey Combined Shows, The Greatest Show on Earth.

The Golden Age refers to the period in circus history from the 1870's through the 1920's. The circus reached a peak of popularity during this time. Large traveling circuses of the Golden Age included the Cole Bros., Hagenbeck-Wallace, and Sells-Floto circuses in the United States; Lord George Sanger's Circus and Chipperfield's Circus in the United Kingdom; and the Wirth Bros. Circus in Australia. The tent circus expanded from one to three rings. As tents grew longer and wider, they also grew taller to allow for aerial acts. At the same time, because of the great size of the tent, singing and talking clowns began to fade away and clowns turned to mime.

The larger circuses bought out many of the smaller shows. By 1929, for example, virtually every major circus in the United States was owned by the American Circus Corporation, a company based in Peru, Indiana, or by the Ringling Circus led by John Ringling, the last of the five brothers. In 1929, Ringling purchased the American Circus Corporation, making him the undisputed king of the American circus.

The middle and late 1900's. The Great Depression of the 1930's led to a decline in circuses. Many circuses went out of business or combined with other shows during the difficult economic times. The circus also faced competition from new forms of entertainment, first motion pictures and then television.

In 1956, the Ringling Bros. and Barnum & Bailey Circus abandoned the railroad for truck travel, and became an arena rather than a tent show. In 1967, the Ringling Bros. circus was purchased by Irvin Feld, a leader in the entertainment field. In 1969, Feld created a second unit for the circus by buying the Circus Williams of Germany, thus obtaining the services of the famous animal trainer Gunther Gebel-Williams.

Since the early 1800's, approximately 2,000 circuses have come and gone in the United States alone, and hundreds more in other countries. Many of these shows failed to keep up with changes in circus production, the economy, or competition from other forms of entertainment.

The circus today

The circus today survives in two major forms, traditional circuses and an innovative approach sometimes called "new wave" circuses. The Ringling Bros. and Barnum & Bailey Circus is the oldest and best known of the

The Cirque du Soleil is a revolutionary new style of circus that originated in Canada in 1984. The Cirque du Soleil emphasizes modern technology, striking special effects, dramatic lighting, and imaginative costumes. But Cirque du Soleil productions still feature acrobats, aerialists, and other traditional circus acts.

Ringling Bros. and Barnum & Bailey Combined Shows, Inc.

An aerial ballet is a thrilling spectacle. These performers twirl hoops around their arms while they hang suspended by their ankles from ropes high above the floor of the arena.

© Harlee Little

The UniverSoul Circus combines African American acts with entertainers from Africa. This troupe of acrobats from the African nation of Gabon performs in traditional African costumes.

Ringling Bros. and Barnum & Bailey Combined Shows, Inc.

A high-wire team performs on a cable high above the ground. The performer on the bottom uses a pole for balancing. Safety cables attached to the performers protect them in case of a fall.

European Entertainment Corporation

The Chinese State Circus features daring and graceful acrobatic performances. In this act, an acrobat leaps through a hoop and over a row of other performers doing headstands.

traditional American circuses. Traditional circuses in other countries include Billy Smart's Circus and the Blackpool Tower Circus in the United Kingdom, Fossett's Circus in Ireland, and Ashton's Circus and the Lennon Brothers Circus in Australia. Some long-established traditional circuses, such as the Chinese State Circus and the Moscow State Circus of Russia, travel to many countries.

Many new wave circuses are intimate shows, performed in a single ring under a tent. Many omit the spectacle of larger circuses. Some of the best-known new wave circuses include the Big Apple Circus, established in New York City in 1977; Circus Oz, started in Melbourne, Australia, in 1978; Cirque du Soleil (Circus of the Sun), begun in Montreal, Canada, in 1984; Circus

Flora, founded in Camden, South Carolina, in 1985; and the UniverSoul Circus, begun in Atlanta, Georgia, in 1994. The Big Apple Circus is patterned after one-ring European circuses with an emphasis on equestrianism. Circus Oz includes off-beat humor, political jokes, and social satire in its acts. Cirque du Soleil has no animals, only human performers. Live vocalists sing its music in an invented language. Its productions emphasize modern technology, with striking special effects and imaginative, often bizarre costumes. Some of Cirque du Soleil's shows continually tour the world, while other productions reside in permanent theaters in several cities. Circus Flora is a traveling one-ring show that now makes its home in St. Louis, Missouri, under its parent organization, the Circus Arts Foundation of Missouri.

The UniverSoul Circus combines African American acts with acts from Africa.

The new wave shows, with their fresh approach to the circus arts, had a profound effect on the circus industry. Some critics credit these circuses with improving the quality of other circuses in their lighting, music, costumes, pacing, and mix of acts.

Places to visit and annual events

Several important museums and circus collections exist throughout the United States. The Circus World Museum stands in Baraboo, Wisconsin, the original home of the Ringling brothers. Part of the museum is housed in the original headquarters of the Ringling circus. The museum exhibits the largest collection of circus wagons in the world. It also has the largest library and research center in the world devoted exclusively to the circus. Each year, many of the museum's circus wagons travel to Milwaukee for the Great Circus Parade. More than 600 horses pull more than 75 classic circus wagons in the parade.

The Ringling Museum of the Circus in Sarasota, Florida, shows the history of the Ringling circus. It also displays records, wagons, and posters from other circuses.

The Barnum Museum in Bridgeport, Connecticut, offers a unique look at the great showman P. T. Barnum.

The three-story museum displays many objects that led to the creation of "The Greatest Show on Earth."

The Hertzberg Circus Collection and Museum is housed in the San Antonio Public Library in Texas. The museum contains valuable information on the development of the circus in the United States from the 1800's to the mid-1900's.

The International Circus Festival of Monte Carlo in Monaco ranks as perhaps the most important circus festival in the world. The festival presents awards to outstanding circus acts that are considered the Academy Awards of circus performance. The highest award is the Gold Clown.

The Circus City Festival in Peru, Indiana, is held every July. Young people from the age of 7 to 21 present performances over an eight-day period.

The National Circus Festival of Australia is held at various locations in Australia. It provides training in the circus arts, including juggling, trapeze, clowning, and acrobatics. In addition to workshops, the festival presents performances to the public.

The World Festival of the Circus of Tomorrow in Paris is held every year to promote young circus performers. It features performers in two age groups—Circus of the Future (ages 12 to 18) and Circus of Tomorrow (ages 19 to 25).   LaVahn G. Hoh

Related articles include:

Barnum, P. T.
Buffalo Bill
Clown
Hagenbeck, Carl
King, Karl
Lion (Training lions)
Ringling brothers
Rome, Ancient (Recreation)
Stratton, Charles S.
Wisconsin (Places to visit)

Outline

I. **At the circus**
II. **Behind the scenes**
III. **Joining the circus**
IV. **History**
V. **The circus today**
VI. **Places to visit and annual events**

Questions

Who are circus *roustabouts?*
What are considered the Academy Awards of circus performance?
Where and when was Cirque du Soleil founded?
When was the "Golden Age" of the circus?
What was a *side show?*
What was the importance of Philip Astley in circus history?
Where can individuals receive training in circus arts?
Who introduced the tent to the American circus?
Where is the Circus World Museum?
What is a *spectacle?* A *display?*

Additional resources

Burgess, Ron. *Be A Clown!* Williamson, 2001.
Fox, Charles P., and Parkinson, Tom. *The Circus in America.* 1969. Reprint. Hennessey & Ingalls, 2002.
Granfield, Linda. *Circus: An Album.* 1997. Reprint. D K Pub., 1998. Younger readers.
Sugarman, Robert. *Circus for Everyone: Circus Learning Around the World.* Mountainside Pr., 2001.

© Charly Gallo, Centre de Presse

The International Circus Festival of Monte Carlo in Monaco, *shown here,* is perhaps the most important circus festival in the world. Circus acts compete at circus festivals in many countries.

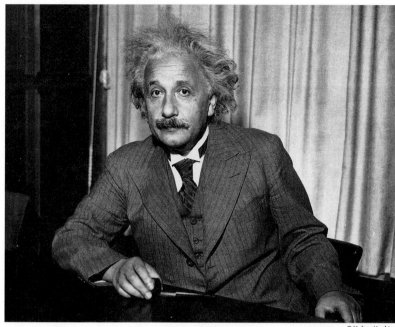

Albert Einstein was one of the greatest scientists of all time.

Einstein, Albert (1879-1955), was the most important physicist of the 1900's, and one of the greatest and most famous scientists of all time. He was a *theoretical physicist,* a scientist who creates and develops theories of matter and energy. Einstein's greatness arose from the fact that his theories solved fundamental problems and presented new ideas. Much of his fame came from the fact that several of those ideas were strange and hard to understand—but proved true.

Some of Einstein's most famous ideas make up parts of his *special theory of relativity* and his *general theory of relativity.* For example, the special theory describes an entity known as *space-time.* This entity is a combination of the dimension of time and the three dimensions of space—length, width, and height. Thus, space-time is four-dimensional. In the general theory, matter and energy *distort* (change the shape of) space-time; the distortion is experienced as gravity.

Einstein also became known for his support of political and social causes. Those included *pacifism,* a general opposition to warfare; *Zionism,* a movement to establish a Jewish homeland in Palestine; and *socialism,* a political system in which the means of production would be owned by society, and production would be planned to match the needs of the community.

Early years

Einstein was born on March 14, 1879, in Ulm, in southern Germany, the son of Hermann Einstein and Pauline Koch Einstein. The next year, Hermann moved the family about 70 miles (110 kilometers) to Munich.

Albert Einstein's younger sister, Maria—whom he called Maja (pronounced *MAH yah)*—recalled that Einstein was slow to learn to speak. But even as a young child, he displayed the powers of concentration for which he became famous.

Einstein recalled seeing the seemingly miraculous behavior of a magnetic compass when he was about 5 years old. The fact that invisible forces acted on the compass needle made a deep impression on the boy.

A booklet on Euclidean geometry made a comparable impression on Einstein when he was about 12 years old. Euclidean geometry is based on a small number of simple, *self-evident* (obviously true) statements about geometric figures. Mathematicians use those statements to *deduce* (develop by reasoning) other statements, many of which are complex and far from self-evident. Einstein was impressed that geometric statements that are not self-evident could be proved clearly and with certainty.

Education. Einstein began to take violin lessons when he was 6 years old. He eventually became an accomplished violinist, and he played the instrument throughout his life.

At the age of 9, Einstein entered the Luitpold Gymnasium, a distinguished secondary school in Munich. He enjoyed some of his classes and performed well, but he disliked the strict discipline. As a result, he dropped out at age 15 to follow his parents to Pavia, Italy, near Milan.

Einstein finished high school in 1896, in Aarau, Switzerland. He then entered a school in Zurich, Switzerland, that ranked as one of Europe's finest institutions of higher learning in science. The school is known as the Swiss Federal Institute of Technology Zurich or the ETH Zurich, from the initials for *Federal Institute of Technology* in German. While at the ETH, Einstein met and fell in love with Mileva Maric. Mileva was a physics student from Novi Sad, in what is now Serbia.

Einstein often skipped class, relying on the notes of others. He spent his free time in the library reading the latest books and physics journals. Einstein's behavior annoyed Heinrich F. Weber, the professor who supervised his course work. Although professors customarily helped their students obtain university positions, when Einstein neared graduation, Weber did not help him get a university post. Instead, a friend helped him find a job as a clerk in the Swiss Federal Patent Office in Bern. He became a Swiss citizen in 1901.

First marriage. Meanwhile, Mileva had become pregnant. Albert and Mileva's child, a daughter they named Lieserl, was born in January 1902 at the home of Mileva's parents. In January 1903, Albert and Mileva married. They had two more children, Hans Albert in 1904 and Eduard in 1910. However, Lieserl never joined them in Bern, and her fate remains a mystery.

Famous theories. Einstein worked at the patent office from 1902 to 1909. Those years were among his most productive. His job reviewing patent applications left him with much time for physics. In 1905, he obtained a Ph.D. degree in physics by submitting a *dissertation* (a long, formal paper) to the University of Zurich. He had already completed the necessary classwork at the ETH.

The year 1905 is known as Einstein's *annus mirabilis*—Latin for *year of marvels.* In that year, the German scientific periodical the *Annalen der Physik (Annals of Physics)* published three of his papers that were among the most revolutionary in the history of science.

The photoelectric effect. The first paper, published in March 1905, deals with the *photoelectric effect.* By means of that effect, a beam of light can cause metal atoms to release subatomic particles called *electrons.* In a photoelectric device, these freed electrons flow as electric current, so the device produces a current when light shines on it.

Einstein explained that the photoelectric effect occurs because light comes in "chunks" of energy called *quanta.*

Albert Einstein Archives from the Hebrew University of Jerusalem, Israel

Einstein and his first wife, Mileva, were photographed with their son Hans Albert Einstein in 1904. Albert and Mileva met in college, where they both studied physics. They divorced in 1919.

Albert Einstein Archives from the Hebrew University of Jerusalem, Israel

Albert Einstein and his younger sister, Maria, were especially close throughout their lives. Albert was 14 years old when this picture was taken with Maria, whom he called Maja.

The singular of *quanta* is *quantum.* A quantum of light is now known as a *photon.* An atom can absorb a photon. If the photon has enough energy, an electron will leave its atom. Einstein received the 1921 Nobel Prize in physics for his paper on the photoelectric effect.

The principle that light comes in quanta is a part of an area of physics known as *quantum mechanics.* Quantum mechanics is one of the "foundation blocks" of modern physics; Einstein's relativity theories are two others.

Brownian motion. The second paper, published in May 1905, explained *Brownian motion,* an irregular movement of microscopic particles suspended in a liquid or a gas. Such motion was named for Scottish botanist Robert Brown, who first observed it in 1827. Einstein's analysis stimulated research on Brownian motion that yielded the first experimental proof that atoms exist.

The special theory of relativity. The third paper, published in June, presented the special theory of relativity. In that paper, titled "On the Electrodynamics of Moving Bodies," Einstein made a remarkable statement about light. He said that constant motion does not affect the *velocity* (speed in a particular direction) of light.

Imagine, for example, that you are on a railroad car traveling on a straight track at a constant speed of one-third the speed of light. You flash a light from the back of the car to the front of the car. You precisely measure the speed of the light. You find that the speed is 186,282 miles (299,792 kilometers) per second—represented by the letter *c* in scientific equations. A friend standing on the ground also measures the speed of the light.

You might expect your friend's result to be $c + \frac{1}{3} c.$ That would be a "common-sense" result consistent with ordinary experience with the velocities of material objects. For example, a ball thrown forward inside a railroad car would have a velocity—as measured by an observer on the ground—equal to the velocity of the car plus the velocity of the ball as measured in the car. But, strangely, in the case of the light beam, your friend's answer turns out to be the same as yours: c.

The strange fact that the velocity of light is constant has even stranger results. For example, a clock can appear to one observer to be running at a given rate, yet seem to another observer to run at a different rate. Two observers can measure the length of the same rod correctly but obtain different results.

Einstein also said that c is a universal "speed limit." No physical process can spread through space at a velocity higher than c. No material body can reach a velocity of c.

Interchangeability of mass and energy. In a fourth paper, published in September 1905, Einstein discussed a result of the special theory of relativity—that energy and *mass* are interchangeable.

Mass is a measure of an object's *inertia,* its resistance to a change in its motion. Due to inertia, an object at rest tends to remain at rest. A moving object tends to maintain its velocity. In addition, an object's weight is proportional to its mass; more massive objects weigh more.

Einstein's paper contains an equation that has become famous: $E = mc^2$. The equation says that a body's energy, E, equals the body's mass, m, times the speed of light, c, *squared* (multiplied by itself). The speed of light is so high that the conversion of a tiny quantity of mass releases a tremendous amount of energy.

The conversion of mass creates energy in the sun and other stars. It also produces the heat energy that is converted to electric energy in nuclear power plants. In addition, mass-to-energy conversion is responsible for the tremendous destructive force of nuclear weapons.

Middle years

Academic appointments. By 1909, Einstein was famous within the physics community. That year, he accepted his first regular academic appointment, as an associate professor of theoretical physics at the University of Zurich. In 1911, he became a professor at the German University in Prague, Austria-Hungary (now Charles University in the Czech Republic). In 1912, he returned to the ETH as a professor.

Einstein moved to Berlin in 1914 to become a member of the Prussian Academy of Sciences, a professor at the University of Berlin, and the director of the Kaiser Wilhelm Institute for Physics, a research center then in the planning stage. He headed the institute until 1933. After World War II (1939-1945), the institute was renamed the Max Planck Institute (MPI) for Physics. Several other MPI's for various branches of physics and for other fields of study were later founded.

Second marriage. Mileva went with Albert to Berlin in March 1914 but returned to Zurich in June. Their marriage had become unhappy; and, in 1919, Albert divorced Mileva and married his cousin Elsa Einstein Löwenthal. Einstein's sons stayed in Zurich with Mileva, and Albert adopted Elsa's daughters, Ilse and Margot.

The general theory of relativity. In 1916, the *Annalen der Physik* published Einstein's paper on the general theory of relativity. This paper soon made Einstein world-famous. He suggested that astronomers could confirm the theory by observing the sun's gravitation

bending light rays. During a solar eclipse in 1919, the British astronomer Arthur S. Eddington detected the bending aside of starlight by the sun's gravitational field. His observation supported Einstein's theory.

In his theory, Einstein also showed that gravity affects time—the presence of a strong gravitational field makes clocks run more slowly than normal. In addition, equations in the general theory are the basis of descriptions of *black holes.* A black hole is a region of space whose gravitational force is so strong that nothing can escape from it. It is invisible because it traps even light.

Attacks on Einstein. Einstein's world fame came at a price. Einstein was of Jewish descent, and *anti-Semitism* (prejudice against Jews) was increasing in Germany. The physicist and his theories became targets of anti-Semitic verbal attacks. Following the 1922 murder of German foreign minister Walther Rathenau, a Jew, Einstein temporarily left Germany. He visited Palestine and a number of other Asian countries, Spain, and South America.

World travel. Threats of danger did not prevent Einstein from using his fame to promote causes dear to his heart. He took his first trip to the United States in 1921. The main purpose of the trip was not to lecture on physics but to raise money for a planned Hebrew University of Jerusalem. In July 1923, he traveled to Sweden to accept the Nobel Prize in physics that had been awarded to him in 1921.

Further scientific work. After creating the general theory of relativity, Einstein worked on a *unified field theory* that was to include all electric, magnetic, and gravitational phenomena. Such a theory would provide a single description of the physical universe, rather than separate descriptions for gravitation and other phenomena. Einstein worked on the theory for the rest of his life but never finished it; to this day, no one has developed a fully successful unified field theory.

Through the mid-1920's, Einstein was a major contributor to the development of quantum mechanics. By the late 1920's, however, he had begun to doubt the theory.

© Hulton/Archive

Einstein played the violin in a trio on board ship in the 1930's on his way to the United States. Einstein took his first violin lesson when he was 6 years old, and he played throughout his life.

© Hulton/Archive

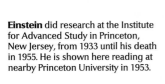

Einstein did research at the Institute for Advanced Study in Princeton, New Jersey, from 1933 until his death in 1955. He is shown here reading at nearby Princeton University in 1953.

One reason for Einstein's doubt was that parts of quantum mechanics did not seem to be *deterministic*. Determinism states that strict laws involving causes and effects govern all events. As an example of apparent nondeterminism in quantum mechanics, consider an atom that absorbs a photon, thus becoming more energetic. At a later moment, the atom reduces its energy level by releasing a photon. But a physicist cannot use quantum mechanics to predict the moment of release.

In 1926, Einstein wrote a famous letter to the German physicist Max Born expressing his doubts about quantum mechanics. Einstein wrote, "The theory produces a good deal but hardly brings us closer to the secret of the Old One [by which Einstein meant God]. I am at all events convinced that *He* does not play dice."

In 1936, Einstein and the German physicists Boris Podolsky and Nathan Rosen published an article, which became known as the "EPR paper," arguing that quantum mechanics is not a complete theory. The EPR paper and a reply from the Danish physicist Neils Bohr became the basis for a scientific debate that continues to this day.

Later years

Einstein in the United States. In December 1930, Einstein traveled to the United States. His trip was the first of what were meant to be annual visits to lecture at the California Institute of Technology. But in January 1933, during Einstein's third trip, the Nazi Party seized power in Germany. The Nazis had an official policy of anti-Semitism, and so Einstein never set foot in Germany again. He returned to Europe in March 1933, staying in Belgium under the protection of that country's royal family. He then went to England.

In September 1933, Einstein sailed to the United States to work at the Institute for Advanced Study, an independent community of scholars and scientists doing advanced research and study. The institute had recently been established in Princeton, New Jersey, and now consists of schools of Historical Studies, Mathematics, Natural Sciences, and Social Science. Princeton would be Einstein's home for the rest of his life. Einstein became a United States citizen in October 1940.

Letter to President Roosevelt. Einstein undertook one of his most important acts in the summer of 1939, shortly before the outbreak of World War II. At the urg-

ing, and with the help, of the Hungarian refugee physicist Leo Szilard, Einstein wrote a letter to President Franklin D. Roosevelt. The letter warned that German scientists might be working on an atomic bomb. The letter led to the establishment of the Manhattan Project, which produced the first atomic bomb in 1945.

Continuing fame. After World War II, Einstein labored tirelessly for international controls on atomic energy. He had a wide circle of professional acquaintances and friends, and he was still a world figure. In 1952, he was offered the presidency of Israel—the modern state of Israel had existed only since 1948—but he declined.

Final days. By the early 1950's, Einstein's immediate family had dwindled. His son Eduard had been confined to a mental institution in Zurich for years, suffering from schizophrenia. Einstein's first and second wives, his stepdaughter Ilse, and his sister Maja, to whom he had been especially close, had died. Einstein's son Hans Albert was a professor of civil engineering at the University of California in Berkeley. Of the people who were emotionally close to Albert Einstein, only his stepdaughter Margot and Helen Dukas, his secretary since 1928, remained with him in Princeton.

Einstein signed his last letter one week before his death. In the letter, to the British philosopher and mathematician Bertrand Russell, Einstein agreed to include his name on a document urging all nations to give up nuclear weapons. Einstein died in Princeton on April 18, 1955.   Don Howard

Related articles include:

E=mc^2
Gravitation (Einstein's theory
    of gravitation)
Manhattan Project
Nuclear weapon
Quantum field theory
Quantum mechanics
Relativity

Additional resources

Bernstein, Jeremy. *Albert Einstein and the Frontiers of Physics.* Oxford, 1996.
Brian, Denis. *Einstein: A Life.* Wiley, 1996.
Clark, Ronald W. *Einstein: The Life and Times.* 1971. Reprint. Avon, 1994.
Fölsing, Albrecht. *Albert Einstein.* Viking Penguin, 1997.

© Piers Benatar, Panos Pictures

Mountains cover much of Pakistan. The Chitral Valley, *shown here,* lies along the border with Afghanistan. Tirich Mir, the highest mountain in the Hindu Kush range, rises in the background.

Pakistan

Pakistan is a Muslim country in southern Asia officially called the Islamic Republic of Pakistan. Its capital is Islamabad, and its largest city is Karachi.

Almost all the people of Pakistan practice Islam, the Muslim religion. Despite their common religion, Pakistanis have strong ties to different cultures. The major cultural groups include Punjabis, Sindhis, Pashtuns (or Pakhtuns), and Baluchi. Each group speaks a different language and inhabits a different part of the country. Urdu is the official language of Pakistan, but less than 10 percent of the people speak it as their primary language. Pakistan has struggled to bring the different cultures together into a unified nation.

Pakistan's natural features are as diverse as its cultural groups—towering mountain ranges, high plateaus, lush green plains, and arid deserts. Most of the people live in the irrigated plains of eastern Pakistan. The most densely populated part is the Punjab, a rich agricultural region in the northeast. The western part of the country is sparsely populated because of its dry climate and its barren, rugged, mountainous terrain.

The majority of Pakistan's people live in rural areas, though Pakistan's cities are growing rapidly. Most of Pakistan's rural inhabitants work in agriculture and follow traditional clan and tribal customs. By contrast, peo-

ple in the urban areas engage in a range of professions, and many have adopted modern ideas and values. Although Pakistan has made rapid strides in industrialization, its economy still relies heavily on agriculture.

Pakistan's history dates back thousands of years. About 2500 B.C., a sophisticated civilization emerged in the Indus Valley, centered around the cities of Mohenjo-Daro and Harappa. Later, over the course of several thousand years, a variety of peoples—Afghans, Arabs, Greeks, Persians, and Turks—came to the region.

In the 1800's, the area that makes up Pakistan and India came under British colonial rule. In 1947, Pakistan was created as a homeland for Muslims, while India was primarily Hindu. The people of Kashmir were Muslim, but the region was ruled by a Hindu prince who tried to join his lands to India. Pakistan and India have struggled over control of the region ever since.

Pakistan initially consisted of two parts called East Pakistan and West Pakistan. More than 1,000 miles (1,600 kilometers) of Indian territory separated the two sections, but the people in both sections were Muslim. West Pakistan tended to dominate East Pakistan, which had a majority of the population. In 1971, East Pakistan won a nine-month civil war and became the independent nation of Bangladesh (see **Bangladesh**).

Government

In 1999, General Pervez Musharraf led a military coup that overthrew Pakistan's democratically elected government. He dissolved the parliament, suspended the Constitution, and declared himself head of a transitional government. Pakistan's Supreme Court ordered that civilian government be restored by October 2002, and

Ayesha Jalal, the contributor of this article, is Professor of History at Tufts University and coauthor of Modern South Asia: History, Culture, Political Economy.

Musharraf agreed. In 2001, Musharraf elevated himself to the presidency, and in 2002, he enacted sweeping changes to the Constitution that cemented his hold on power. Before the coup, Pakistan had a parliamentary system of government.

National government. Before the 1999 coup, an elected prime minister headed the Pakistani government, and the president served as the head of state. The Cabinet and the prime minister were members of a two-chambered parliament. The prime minister was the leader of the party with the most seats. In the upper house, called the Senate, the four provinces of Pakistan had equal representation. Provincial assemblies, elected by the voters, chose the members of the Senate. The people directly elected the members of the lower house, called the National Assembly.

Provincial and local government. Pakistan has four provinces—Baluchistan, North-West Frontier Province, the Punjab, and Sind. Before the military take-over, each province had an elected assembly. Elected and appointed officials govern cities, towns, and villages.

The federal government rules Pakistan's capital, Islamabad, as a separate district called the Capital Territory of Islamabad. Areas called Federally Administered Tribal Territories lie in northwestern Pakistan.

Politics. The Pakistan Muslim League (PML) and the Pakistan People's Party (PPP) are the two largest political parties in Pakistan. The PML's main support base is in the Punjab, while the PPP has a strong following in Sind as well as in parts of the Punjab and the North-West Frontier Province. Other parties include religious parties, such as the Muslim parties Jamaat-i-Islami and the Jamiat-i-Ulama-Islam. Beginning with local elections in 2000, the voting age was reduced from 21 to 18.

Courts. The Supreme Court is Pakistan's highest court. Its decisions are binding on all Pakistani courts, including the Federal Shariat Court, which oversees Islamic aspects of law. Each province has a High Court and other courts with civil and criminal jurisdiction.

Armed forces. An army of more than 500,000 and a smaller navy and air force are the main branches of the armed forces. Military service is voluntary, and the minimum age to volunteer is 17.

People

Ancestry. Pakistan's people are descended from many different cultures. The earliest inhabitants in the region belonged to the same ethnic group as the people in northern India. Over the centuries, Afghans, Arabs, Greeks, Persians, and Turks came with invading armies. Many of the invaders settled in the area and intermarried with the inhabitants. These multiple influences added layers of variety to Pakistani culture.

Cultural groups and languages. Despite the bond of Islam, cultural differences divide the people of Pakistan. Each group has its own language and customs. Some Pakistanis feel greater loyalty to their own cultural group than to the nation.

Language is an important factor that distinguishes cultural groups. Major regional languages include Baluchi, Punjabi, Pashto (also called Pakhto), and Sindhi. Urdu is Pakistan's official language, but less than 10 percent of the people speak it as their primary language.

The Punjabis, the largest cultural group, speak differ-

© Dennis Jackson, Pictor International Ltd.

Karachi is Pakistan's largest city and commercial center. It is also the country's chief port and the capital of Sind Province. Karachi lies in southern Pakistan on the coast of the Arabian Sea.

ent dialects of the Punjabi language. They live mainly in the Punjab but have a presence in other parts of the country, especially Karachi. Members of this group control the government, economy, and armed forces.

Urdu-speaking Muhajirs immigrated to Pakistan from India when the two countries separated in 1947. The Muhajirs became prominent in government after independence, but they have since lost power. Their descendants, most of whom live in Karachi or Hyderabad, blame Punjabi dominance for their declining influence.

Other leading groups include the Sindhis, the Pashtuns (also called Pakhtuns), and the Baluchi. The Sindhis have a slight majority in Sind but are outnumbered by Muhajirs and other non-Sindhi groups in major cities, such as Karachi. Muhajirs and Sindhis have clashed over educational and employment opportunities and political control of Karachi. The Pashtuns, who belong to various tribes and speak Pashto (or Pakhto), inhabit the North-West Frontier Province and the northern part of Baluchistan. Baluchis consist of several nomadic and tribal groups. They speak dialects of Baluchi and live in Baluchistan, the largest but least populated province of Pakistan. Baluchistan is also home to smaller cultural groups, such as the Brahuis, Makranis, and Lassis.

Millions of refugees from Afghanistan form another cultural group in Pakistan. They fled to Pakistan to escape decades of war in Afghanistan. They live mainly in the North-West Frontier Province and Baluchistan but also have a sizable presence in Karachi.

Way of life

Rural life. About two-thirds of Pakistanis live in rural areas. Most of them are farmers, herders, and skilled workers, such as carpenters and bricklayers. Local customs and beliefs play an important part in rural life.

Housing and clothing vary from one region to another, depending on climate, local customs, and economic conditions. Most rural villages consist of clusters of two- or three-room houses made of clay or sun-dried mud.

Pakistan in brief

General information

Capital: Islamabad.
Official name: The Islamic Republic of Pakistan.
Official language: Urdu.
Largest cities (1981 census):

Karachi (5,208,170)
Lahore (2,952,689)

Faisalabad (1,104,209)
Rawalpindi (794,843)

Pakistan's flag has a star and crescent, traditional symbols of Islam. Green stands for the nation's Muslim majority.

A wreath of narcissus, the national flower, encircles a shield on the Pakistani coat of arms.

Land and climate

Land: Pakistan lies in southern Asia, north of the Arabian Sea. It borders Iran, Afghanistan, China, and India. Mountains cover most of northern and western Pakistan. The Thar Desert covers much of southeastern Pakistan, and most of southwestern Pakistan is an arid plateau. A major river system waters the fertile plains of central Pakistan.
Area: 307,374 mi² (796,095 km²). *Greatest distances*—north-south, 935 mi (1,505 km); east-west, 800 mi (1,287 km). *Coastline*—506 mi (814 km).
Elevation: *Highest*—K2 (in Kashmir), 28,250 ft (8,611 m) above sea level. *Lowest*—sea level.
Climate: Most of Pakistan has a dry climate, with hot summers and cool winters. Pakistan averages only about 10 inches (25 centimeters) of rain a year. But the amount of rainfall varies greatly from year to year. Long dry spells may be broken by severe rainstorms that cause rivers to overflow and flood the countryside.

Government

Form of government: Federal republic.
Head of state: President.
Head of government: Prime minister.
Legislature: Parliament of two houses—the National Assembly and the Senate.
Executive: Prime minister and president each have some executive powers.
Judiciary: Highest court is the Supreme Court.
Political subdivisions: Four provinces and the Capital Territory of Islamabad.

People

Population: *Estimated 2002 population*—144,135,000; *1998 census*—130,579,571.
Population density: 469 per mi² (181 per km²).
Distribution: 67 percent rural, 33 percent urban.
Major ethnic groups: Punjabi, Sindhi, Pashtun (or Pakhtun), Baluchi, and Muhajir.
Major religions: 77 percent Sunni Muslim, 20 percent Shiite Muslim, 3 percent other, including Christian and Hindu.

Population trend

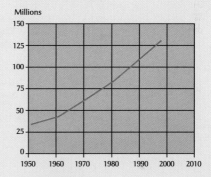

Millions

Year	Population
1951	33,779,500
1961	42,880,000
1972	64,892,000
1981	84,253,000
1998	130,579,571

Economy

Chief products: *Agriculture*—wheat, cotton, rice, sugar cane, milk, chickpeas. *Manufacturing*—cotton textiles and clothing, food products, fertilizer, steel, cement. *Mining*—natural gas, petroleum.
Money: *Basic unit*—Pakistani rupee. One hundred paisas equal one rupee.
Foreign trade: *Major exports*—textiles, including garments, cotton cloth, and yarn; agricultural products; leather goods; and carpets. *Major imports*—petroleum goods, machinery, transportation equipment, and chemicals. *Major trading partners*—United States, United Kingdom, Japan, Germany, Saudi Arabia, United Arab Emirates.

Pakistan map index

Cities and towns

Abbottabad 32,188	C 6	Dera Ghazi		Kamalia 61,107	D 6	Mian Channun* .40,609	D 6	Sangia* 33,771	D 7

*Does not appear on map; key shows general location.
Source: 1981 census.

Most of these homes have little furniture. People sit and eat on earthen floors covered by straw or woven mats. Many homes lack basic plumbing and electric power.

City life. A majority of urban dwellers cannot read or write, or can read and write only a little. Most earn a living as unskilled laborers, factory workers, shopkeepers, or craftworkers. Many live in modest houses in old, crowded neighborhoods or in makeshift homes on empty plots of land. Sanitation is poor in the inner cities.

The middle and upper classes, who make up a small percentage of the population, reside in spacious homes in comfortable urban neighborhoods. Many of these people have been educated in English and know a great deal about Western styles and ideas. They stand in stark contrast to the majority of Pakistanis, who are rooted in their traditional cultures.

Clothing. Pakistanis wear different clothing depending on their region. The most common garment worn by both men and women is the *shalwar-qamiz* (or *salwar-kameez),* which consists of loose trousers and a long, knee-length shirt. Women also wear a *dupatta* (scarf) or a shawl called a *chador* or *chadar* over the shoulders and head. Outside the home, some women cover themselves with a tentlike garment called a *burqa* or *burka.* In parts of the Punjab, some men wear skirtlike garments called *dhotis* or *lungis.* Many Punjabi women prefer the loose, skirtlike *ghagra* instead of the shalwar-qamiz. Turbans and woolen or fur caps are popular head coverings among Pakistani men.

Food and drink. Wheat and other grains are the staple diet of most Pakistanis. They eat flat loaves of bread called *chapattis* or *nans* with cooked lentils, vegetables, and mutton, beef, or chicken curries. *Biryani* and *pilau* are rice dishes mixed with meat, vegetables, raisins, and nuts. Pakistanis like food flavored with spicy seasonings. They do not eat pork, which is forbidden by Islam. Desserts such as *kheer* (a kind of rice pudding) and *halwa* (a confection made with ground seeds or dried fruits or vegetables) are popular. Fresh and dried fruits are also eaten as desserts. Tea with milk and sugar is a favorite drink. In hot weather, Pakistanis enjoy a yogurt beverage called *lassi,* flavored with sugar or salt.

Recreation. Sightseeing, picnics, eating out, fairs, motion pictures, and theater are popular recreational activities in Pakistan. In rural areas, wrestling, horse racing, and *tent pegging* (a horse riding game) are favorite sports. Satellite television and movies on videotape have become popular, especially in urban areas. Interest has grown in organized sports, such as cricket, field hockey, football, tennis, squash, and volleyball.

Religion. More than 97 percent of Pakistan's people practice Islam. The majority of Pakistan's Muslims belong to the Sunni division of Islam. Only about 20 percent belong to the Shiite division. The end of Ramadan, the month of fasting, and the *hajj,* the annual pilgrimage to Mecca, are important religious holidays. People of other religions in Pakistan include Christians, Hindus, Buddhists, and Parsis.

Education. A little over half the men and less than a third of the women above the age of 15 can read and write. School attendance is not compulsory, and less than half of the children of school age attend school. Pakistan suffers from a shortage of schools, qualified teachers, and instructional materials. However, wealthy

Pakistanis have access to high-quality private schools.

Islamic religious schools called *madrasahs* have become popular in both rural and urban areas. These schools teach the Qur'ān and other beliefs of Islam. Some of the schools foster religious extremism, although the government has tried to stop this.

Pakistan has over 20 universities and several private colleges. Some of the largest educational institutions are the universities of Karachi, Peshawar, and the Punjab.

The arts. Each region of Pakistan has its own folk literature, consisting of stories and songs about legendary or historical personalities. Folk theater based on myths and legends is immensely popular in the rural areas. In the cities, motion pictures—either in theaters or on video—are in great demand. Art and architecture in Pakistan show the influence of both Islamic and local cultural traditions. Pakistanis have a passion for folk, classical, and popular music, and several Pakistani musicians have acquired an international following.

Land and climate

Pakistan has five main land regions: (1) the Northern and Western Highlands, (2) the Punjab Plain, (3) the Sind Plain, (4) the Baluchistan Plateau, and (5) the Thar Desert.

Mountains cover much of northern and western Pakistan, known as the Northern and Western Highlands. K2, the second highest peak in the world, towers 28,250 feet (8,611 meters) above sea level in the part of Kashmir controlled by Pakistan. Only Mount Everest is higher. Mountain passes cut through the rugged peaks at several points. The most famous of these passes, the Khyber Pass, links Pakistan and Afghanistan. The mountain regions have the coolest weather. Summer temperatures in the north and northwest average about 75 °F (24 °C), and winter temperatures often fall below freezing.

The Punjab Plain and the Sind Plain occupy most of the eastern part of the country. These regions are *alluvial plains* (land formed of soil deposited by rivers). In the north, the Punjab is watered by the Indus River and four of its tributaries—the Chenab, Jhelum, Ravi, and Sutlej rivers. The combined waters of these four tributaries join the Indus River in east-central Pakistan. South

© Paula Bronstein, Getty Images

Students at an Islamic religious school called a *madrasah* spend most of their time studying the Qur'ān, the sacred book of the Muslims, and other teachings of Islam. Many Pakistani children attend a madrasah instead of a public school.

of this meeting point, the broadened Indus flows to the Arabian Sea through the Sind Plain.

In the Punjab, temperatures average over 90 °F (32 °C) in summer and about 55 °F (13 °C) in winter. The eastern part of the Punjab receives the most rain—more than 20 inches (51 centimeters) a year. Extensive irrigation systems have made the Punjab and Sind plains fertile agricultural regions.

The Baluchistan Plateau lies in southwestern Pakistan. Most of the plateau is dry and rocky and has little plant life. Much of the Baluchistan Plateau receives less than 5 inches (13 centimeters) of rain a year.

The Thar Desert lies in southeastern Pakistan and northwestern India. Much of the desert is a sandy wasteland. However, irrigation projects have made parts of the desert near the Indus River suitable for farming.

Most of Pakistan has a dry climate, with hot summers and cool winters. Pakistan averages only about 10 inches (25 centimeters) of rain a year. But the amount of rainfall varies greatly from year to year. Long dry spells may be broken by severe rainstorms that cause rivers to overflow and flood the countryside. In general, most of the rain falls from July to September, when the summer *monsoon* (seasonal wind) blows across Pakistan.

Economy

Pakistan has a developing economy. About a third of its people live below the poverty line. Agriculture re-

© Robin Laurance, Impact Photos

The Khyber Pass is the easiest land route between Pakistan and Afghanistan. The pass cuts through the Safed Koh mountains, which are part of the Hindu Kush range. This part of the Khyber Pass is near Peshawar, Pakistan.

mains the leading economic activity, but service industries and manufacturing have grown in importance.

Natural resources. Pakistan's rivers are its most valuable natural resource. They supply water to irrigate over 38 million acres (15 million hectares) of farmland and also provide an important source of hydroelectric power. Central Pakistan has extensive natural gas reserves.

Pakistan
terrain map

	International boundary
	Land region boundary
	Desert
	Glacier
	Salt marsh
★	National capital
•	Other city
⤬	Mountain pass
+	Elevation above sea level

Physical features

Arabian Sea	F	1
Baluchistan Plateau	E	2
Chagai Hills	D	2
Chenab (River)	C	5
Dasht (River)	E	1
Hab (River)	F	3
Himalaya (Mts.)	B	6
Hindu Kush (Mts.)	B	4
Hingol (River)	E	2
Indus (River)	E	3
Jhelum (River)	C	5
Karakoram Range	A	5
Khyber Pass	B	4
Kirthar Range	E	3
K2 (Mtn.)	A	6
Makran Coast		
Range	E	2
Mangla Dam	C	5
Mintaka Pass	A	5
Nanga Parbat (Mtn.)	B	5
Nara Canal	E	4
Northern and		
Western Highlands	C	4
Punjab Plain	C	5
Ras Koh Range	D	3
Ravi (River)	C	5
Sind Plain	E	3
Sulaiman Range	D	4
Sutlej (River)	D	5
Tarbela Dam	B	5
Thal Desert	D	4
Thar Desert	E	5
Tirich Mir (Mtn.)	A	4
Toba Kakar Range	C	3
Zhob (River)	C	4

WORLD BOOK map

[Map of Pakistan terrain, with grid columns 1–6 and rows A–F. Locations shown include: Karakum, Mary, Karakum Canal, TURKMENISTAN, Meshed, North, Morghab, Paropamisus Range, Herat, Hariud, Farah, Khash, AFGHANISTAN, Sistan Marsh, Hamun-i-Lora, Hamun-i-Mashkhel, Zahedan, IRAN, Dasht, Makran Coast Range, 5,409 ft. (1,649 m), 25° North Latitude, Arabian Sea, Tropic of Cancer, UZBEKISTAN, Amu Darya, Mazar-e Sharif, Qonduz, Qonduz, Helmand, Kandahar, Rigestan Desert, Quetta, Chagai Hills, Ras Koh Range, 8,133 ft. (2,479 m), BALUCHISTAN PLATEAU, Kirthar Range, Hab, SIND PLAIN, Karachi, TIRICH MIR 25,230 ft. (7,690 m), Hindu Kush, Kabul, Kabul, KHYBER PASS, Peshawar, NANGA PARBAT 26,660 ft. (8,126 m), TARBELA DAM, Rawalpindi, Islamabad, NORTHERN AND WESTERN HIGHLANDS, MANGLA DAM, Toba Kakar Range, 6,363 ft. (1,939 m), Zhob, Sulaiman Range, Multan, Thal Desert, Faisalabad, Chenab, 850 ft. (259 m), Lahore, PUNJAB PLAIN, Sutlej, THAR DESERT, Sukkur, Indus, Nara Canal, Hyderabad, 78 ft. (24 m), Rann of Kutch, MINTAKA PASS, CHINA, K2 28,250 ft. (8,611 m), Karakoram Range, Ladakh Range, Zaskar Range, Himalaya, BEAS DAM, Beas, BHAKRA DAM, Amristar, Ludhiana, Yamuna, Delhi, New Delhi, INDIA, Bikaner, Thar Desert (Indian Desert), Jaipur, Jodhpur, Aravali Range, Ajmer, Chambal, Luni, Banas, Udaipur, Parbati, TAJIKISTAN, Pamirs. Scale: 0–800 Miles, 0–1,200 Kilometers. 60°, 65°, 70°, 75° East Longitude; 35°, 30°, 25°.]

Agriculture employs about 40 percent of Pakistan's labor force and accounts for about 25 percent of its gross domestic product (GDP), the total amount of goods and services produced in the country. In the 1950's and again in the 1970's, Pakistan's government introduced land reforms to distribute land to the poor. It also tried to modernize agriculture by encouraging farmers to use fertilizers, pesticides, and new types of seeds. These efforts met with mixed success.

Wheat is the chief crop in Pakistan. Pakistani farmers also grow cotton, rice, sugar cane, chickpeas, oilseeds, fruits, and vegetables. Although mechanized agriculture has made some inroads, most farmers rely on cattle and water buffaloes to till the land. These animals also provide meat, milk, and hides. Many Pakistani farmers, especially in Baluchistan and the North-West Frontier Province, tend sheep and goats. Some parts of the country have poultry farms. Pakistan exports shrimps, sardines, sharks, and other fish caught in the Arabian Sea.

Service industries employ over 30 percent of Pakistan's work force and contribute about half of its GDP. The service sector has expanded considerably and is especially important in the major cities. Wholesale and retail trade are the largest employers in this sector. Finance, information technology, government, and transportation are other significant service industries.

Manufacturing employs about 18 percent of Pakistan's labor force and contributes about 20 percent of its GDP. Cotton textiles and clothing are the leading manufactured products. Other significant industries include food products, such as flour and sugar; fertilizer and other chemical products; steel; and cement. Craftworkers, operating from home or in small factories, make carpets, embroidered goods, pottery, wooden and leather products, and other handicraft items.

AP/Wide World

Women search for water in the Thar Desert, which lies along Pakistan's southeastern border with India. Much of the Thar is a wasteland, but irrigation has enabled some parts to be farmed.

Energy sources and mining. Fossil fuels, especially coal and petroleum, provide for over two-thirds of Pakistan's energy needs. Hydroelectric power provides the rest. The country imports oil but has rich deposits of natural gas. Salt, coal, chromite, gypsum, iron ore, and limestone are among Pakistan's other mined resources.

International trade. Pakistan's primary exports are textiles, including garments, cotton cloth, and yarn; agricultural products; leather goods; and carpets. Its main imports are petroleum goods, machinery, transportation equipment, and chemicals. Pakistan's chief trading partners are the United States, the United Kingdom, Japan, Germany, Saudi Arabia, and the United Arab Emirates.

Transportation and communication. Railways serve as the principal mode of transportation for passengers and freight in Pakistan. Paved roads link major towns and cities, but motor vehicle travel is limited. In rural areas, camels, cattle, donkeys, and horses provide transportation. Karachi is Pakistan's main seaport. Karachi, Lahore, and Islamabad have international airports.

Pakistan has far more radios than televisions, so radio remains the dominant mode of mass communication. Pakistan has a vibrant newspaper industry. Its publishers produce hundreds of daily newspapers and magazines in Urdu, English, and the regional languages.

History

Early civilizations. Pakistan has a long and complex history, dating back at least 8,000 years to the Mehrgarh civilization in present-day Baluchistan. Later, around 2500 B.C., one of the world's first great civilizations developed in the Indus Valley in what are now Pakistan and northwestern India. Ruins of Harappa and Mohenjo-Daro (also spelled Moenjodaro), the two major cities of the civilization, lie in present-day Pakistan. The ruins show that both cities were large and well-planned. By about 1700 B.C., the Indus Valley civilization had gradually declined. Scholars do not know why it collapsed.

Invasions and conquests. During the next several thousand years, many peoples from southwest and central Asia came into the region that is now Pakistan. About 1500 B.C., a central Asian people called Aryans came through the mountain passes to the Punjab region. In time, they settled across most of India. The Persians conquered the Punjab during the 500's B.C. and made it part of the huge Achaemenid Empire.

In 326 B.C., Alexander the Great of Macedonia took control of most of what is now Pakistan. A few years later, the emperor Chandragupta Maurya made the region part of the Mauryan Empire. The Mauryan Empire began to break up about 230 B.C. Greeks from the independent state of Bactria in central Asia then invaded the Indus Valley. They established a kingdom with capitals near the present-day cities of Peshawar and Rawalpindi.

About 100 B.C., Scythians from Afghanistan came into Baluchistan and Sind. In time, they conquered the Indus region. The Scythians were replaced by the Parthians, who, in turn, were conquered by the Kushans of central Asia. The Kushans ruled what are now Afghanistan, Pakistan, and northwestern India from about A.D. 50 to the mid-200's. They controlled the trade routes from China to India and the Middle East. Peshawar, the Kushan capital, became a commercial center.

During the mid-300's, the Indus Valley became part of

the Gupta Empire, which had expanded westward from northeastern India. Huns from central Asia overran Pakistan during the late 400's.

The Islamic impact. Around A.D. 712, Arab Muslims sailed across the Arabian Sea and invaded Sind, bringing Islam to the region. Beginning about 1000, Muslims invaded northern Pakistan from Iran. Mahmud Ghazni, an Afghan warrior of Turkish descent, established a Muslim kingdom that in time included the entire Indus Valley. Lahore became the capital of the kingdom and developed into a major center of Islamic culture.

In 1206, most of present-day Pakistan came under the control of the Delhi Sultanate, a Muslim empire based in northern India. Under the Delhi Sultanate, a distinctive Indo-Islamic culture developed. The sultanate lasted until 1526, when Babur, a Muslim ruler of Turkish and Mongol descent, invaded India from Afghanistan and founded the Mughal Empire.

The Mughal Empire in time encompassed virtually all of what are now Pakistan, India, and Bangladesh. Under Mughal rule, the Indo-Islamic culture reached its most sophisticated level. It gave rise to a new language, Urdu, which was influenced by both Hindi and Persian. A new religion called Sikhism, which drew upon elements in both Hinduism and Islam, came into being.

In the 1700's, regional rulers acquired greater power at the cost of the central Mughal government. Several groups, including Persians and Afghans, gained control of the region that is now Pakistan. Sikh kingdoms gained strength in the Punjab during the early 1800's, while Sind was ruled by independent Muslim kingdoms.

Colonialism. In the 1500's, European traders began competing for control of the profitable trade between Europe and southern Asia. In the 1600's, after seeking permission from the Mughal emperors, a number of trading companies established settlements along the coastal regions of India. By the mid-1700's, the British East India Company had emerged as the strongest trading power in India. As the Mughal Empire began to break up, the company gradually gained political control over much of India. It fought a series of wars in the Punjab and Sind during the late 1830's and 1840's and added these territories to its holdings.

Resentment of British rule led to many small rebellions and, in 1857, to a widespread uprising. After assisting the British East India Company in crushing the 1857 rebellion, the United Kingdom took control of the company and its territories. Princes controlled the rest of India, and the British made treaty arrangements with these rulers. By 1900, the United Kingdom directly or indirectly controlled all of what is now Pakistan. The territories directly ruled by the United Kingdom were known as British India. See **India** (History [map: British India]).

The British introduced a number of reforms, including a Western system of education. Many Hindus enrolled in the British schools as a way to advance in the colonial system. Some middle- and upper-class Muslims also enrolled, but the majority of Muslims continued to attend their own schools, which stressed religious education. As a result, large numbers of Hindus gained positions in business and government, but the majority of Muslims remained farmers and laborers.

The nationalist movement. The Indian National Congress was formed in 1885 to promote independence for British India. Hindus dominated the organization, and Muslim leaders disagreed on whether or not to cooperate with it. In 1906, some Muslims formed a separate political organization called the All-India Muslim League. The Congress and the Muslim League both sought greater self-government. But differences emerged over how to divide power fairly between Hindus and Muslims. The Muslims feared that Hindus would dominate an independent India.

In 1940, the Muslim League demanded independent Muslim states in northwestern and northeastern India. The president of the Muslim League, Mohammad Ali Jinnah, became the plan's principal supporter. The name *Pakistan,* which means *land of the pure* in Urdu, came to be used for Jinnah's proposed Muslim homelands.

Both the British government and the Indian National Congress rejected the League's demands. To show its strength, the Muslim League declared Aug. 16, 1946, as Direct Action Day. Muslims held nationwide demonstrations calling for the establishment of Pakistan. Violence broke out between Muslims and Hindus. In 1947, hoping to end the violence, the United Kingdom and Hindu leaders agreed to *partition* India—that is, to divide it into separate Hindu and Muslim countries.

Independence. Pakistan became an independent nation on Aug. 14, 1947. The next day, India gained independence. West Pakistan and East Pakistan were carved out of the northwestern and northeastern parts of India, separated by more than 1,000 miles of Indian territory. See **India** (History [map: Independent India]). Jinnah became the first head of state.

Violence between Hindus, Muslims, and Sikhs continued after the partition. Over 10 million people crossed the new borders. Hindus and Sikhs fled to India, and Muslims streamed into Pakistan. Religious riots killed at least half a million people.

Within months of partition, India and Pakistan went to war over Kashmir. A Hindu prince ruled this region, but most of its population was Muslim. When India and Pakistan were partitioned, the prince tried to avoid joining either country. Armed Pakistani tribesmen, backed by government troops, invaded Kashmir to claim it for Pakistan. In response, the prince joined Kashmir to India. Indian and Pakistani troops continued to fight until early 1949, when the United Nations negotiated a cease-fire.

Pakistan became a republic in 1956, but parliamentary elections did not take place as planned. Instead, the military under General Mohammad Ayub Khan assumed control of the state in 1958. Military leaders continued to control the government throughout the 1960's. In 1965, India and Pakistan fought a second war over Kashmir.

Civil war. The people of West and East Pakistan were divided as much by cultural differences as by geography. Only religion united the two groups. West Pakistan controlled the government, economy, and armed forces, which angered East Pakistanis. Bengali-speakers in East Pakistan also resented the government's efforts to impose Urdu as the official language.

In 1970, Pakistan held elections for a National Assembly that would draft a new constitution. East Pakistan had over half of the country's population, so a majority of the Assembly members represented East Pakistan. They hoped to frame a constitution that would give East Pakistan its due share of political and economic power.

In early 1971, Ayub Khan's successor, General Agha Mohammad Yahya Khan, postponed the first meeting of the National Assembly. Infuriated, East Pakistanis took to the streets, prompting a military crackdown. The riots grew into civil war. On March 26, 1971, East Pakistan declared its independence, calling itself Bangladesh. In December 1971, India sent its army to support the rebellion. The war developed into a major conflict with India, and the fighting spread to West Pakistan and Kashmir. On Dec. 16, 1971, Pakistan surrendered. Over a million people died in the fighting.

Yahya Khan resigned, and Zulfikar Ali Bhutto, whose Pakistan People's Party (PPP) held the largest number of seats in West Pakistan, took over as president. He swiftly restored constitutional government and civilian rule.

Struggle for democracy. In 1973, Pakistan adopted its third constitution, which provided for a two-chamber legislature, a president as head of state, and a prime minister as head of government. Bhutto became prime minister and concentrated power in his own hands. In 1977, he called elections in the face of mounting protest against his rule. Bhutto's PPP won the elections, but opponents accused the party of election fraud. Street demonstrations against the government erupted.

In July, General Mohammad Zia-ul-Haq ousted Bhutto from office and declared martial law. Zia assumed the presidency in 1978 while remaining chief martial law administrator. Zia's regime convicted Bhutto of ordering the murder of a political opponent, sentenced him to death, and executed him in 1979.

When the Soviet Union invaded Afghanistan in December 1979, Pakistan's military supported Afghanistan's Islamic resistance fighters. Zia postponed new elections indefinitely and initiated a series of *Islamization* policies, including a system of law enforcement and punishment based on Islamic principles. Many Islamization measures discriminated against women and minorities.

In 1985, Zia allowed new elections to national and provincial assemblies and lifted martial law. However, he also introduced an amendment to the Constitution that gave the president broad powers, including the power to dismiss elected governments and to dissolve parliament.

Zia used these powers in 1988 to dismiss the prime minister and dissolve parliament. In August of that year, Zia died in a plane crash.

After the Soviets withdrew from Afghanistan in 1989, Pakistan's military continued to support Islamic extremist groups in Afghanistan. Chief among these groups were the Taliban, many of whom were educated in religious schools in the North-West Frontier Province. By the late 1990's, the Taliban controlled most of Afghanistan.

From 1988 to 1999, two parties governed Pakistan alternately—the PPP, led by Benazir Bhutto, the daughter of Zulfikar Ali Bhutto; and the Pakistan Muslim League, led by Mohammad Nawaz Sharif. From 1985 to 1996, three presidents used Zia's constitutional amendment to dismiss four elected governments and parliaments. After the Muslim League won elections in 1997 with a two-thirds majority, Pakistan's legislature repealed the amendment. This reduced the powers of the presidency and made the office of prime minister, then held by Sharif, Pakistan's most powerful government post.

Recent developments. In May 1998, India carried out a series of nuclear tests and declared itself capable of producing and using nuclear weapons. Pakistan responded by conducting its own nuclear tests.

In May 1999, conflict broke out again in Kashmir. Militants backed by Pakistani troops crossed the Kashmiri cease-fire line into Indian-held territory. Fighting then broke out between the militants and Indian troops. In July, under pressure from the United States and other countries, Prime Minister Sharif called for the withdrawal of the Pakistani militants.

In 1999, General Pervez Musharraf led a military coup that overthrew Sharif's government. Musharraf dissolved the parliament and suspended the Constitution. He declared himself the head of a transitional government that included a cabinet and a National Security Council, made up of several Cabinet ministers and the chiefs of staff of the army, navy, and air force. Pakistan's Supreme Court ordered that civilian government be restored by October 2002, and Musharraf agreed to follow the order. Sharif was later exiled to Saudi Arabia. In 2001, Musharraf declared himself president.

Following the September 11 terrorist attacks on the United States, Musharraf allowed U.S. forces to use Pakistani military bases and fly over Pakistani territory in a military campaign against terrorists in Afghanistan. Pakistani supporters of Afghanistan's Taliban government protested against the U.S. attacks and against Musharraf for his support of the United States.

In 2001, armed terrorists attacked India's Parliament, killing or injuring over 20 people, though no elected officials were hurt. India blamed Pakistan for the attack, but Pakistan denied that it had supported the terrorists. The incident led both countries to build up military forces along their shared border. In May 2002, militants in the disputed region of Kashmir attacked Indian outposts there. Troops on both sides exchanged artillery fire, and the two countries seemed on the brink of war.

At Musharraf's request, a referendum was held in April 2002 to extend his term as president for five years. In August 2002, Musharraf enacted sweeping constitutional changes that cemented his hold on power. Parliamentary elections were scheduled for October 2002.

Ayesha Jalal

© Hulton Archive/Getty Images

Muslims board trains to Pakistan after the 1947 *partition* (division) of India along religious lines. Millions of Muslims moved to Pakistan, and millions of Hindus and Sikhs moved to India.

Pablo Picasso was the dominant artist of the 1900's. *Family of Saltimbanques* is the masterpiece of Picasso's Rose Period, which began in late 1904. The large painting portrays a group of traveling acrobats. The figure on the left, dressed as the clown Harlequin, is a self portrait of the artist. The rose and pink colors of the painting are typical of Picasso's style during this period.

Picasso, *pih KAH soh,* **Pablo** (1881-1973), was the dominant figure in art of the 1900's. Picasso was primarily a painter, but he also exerted a great influence on printmaking, sculpture, ceramics, drawings, and designs for the theater. All modern artists have been influenced by Picasso's work, either directly or indirectly.

Early life. Pablo Ruiz Picasso was born on Oct. 25, 1881, in Málaga, Spain. In 1895, after living in La Caruña for nearly four years, his family moved to Barcelona. Picasso learned the basic skills of painting from his father, José Ruiz Blanco, an artist and art teacher. In 1897 and 1898, Picasso lived in Madrid, where he spent much time in the Prado museum studying paintings by the great artists who lived before him. He returned to Barcelona in 1899.

The Blue Period. Picasso's artist friends in Barcelona eventually introduced him to the art world in Paris. He made several lengthy visits to Paris before settling there permanently in 1904. From 1901 to 1904, he developed a style known as his Blue Period. During this period, Picasso painted primarily in blue colors, evoking a feeling of sadness and alienation. A classic of the period is *The Old Guitarist* (1903), which appears in the **Color** article. It is typical of Picasso's subjects during this period, which featured the poor of Paris, such as beggars and starving children. The guitarist's stretched-out, distorted body and impossibly long fingers indicate the influence of El Greco, a painter who worked in Spain during the late 1500's and early 1600's.

After Picasso finally settled in Paris, he moved into a tenement in the Montmartre section, nicknamed the *Bateau Lavoir* (Laundry Boat) for the laundry barges that docked on the Seine River there. He lived in the Bateau Lavoir until 1909, with a growing circle of friends, notably painters, poets, actors, and critics.

The Rose Period. In late 1904, Picasso expanded his selection of colors, emphasizing rose and pink. At the same time, he eased the sadness of his subjects. This new style, called the Rose Period, concentrated on acrobats who traveled from town to town. They were called *saltimbanques* and often featured the *harlequin* (masked clown) and other characters who were popular in the traditional Italian theater *commedia dell'arte* and in pantomimes. Picasso often visited the Cirque Médrano near his Montmartre studio, which stimulated his interest in circus subjects. The appearance of circus figures in Picasso's art coincided with his friendship with the French poet Guillaume Apollinaire, whose verse is filled with references to harlequins and saltimbanques as symbols of both friendship and alienation.

The masterpiece of the Rose Period is *Family of Saltimbanques* (1905). At about 7 feet (2.1 meters) high and 7.5 feet (2.3 meters) wide, it was the largest painting of both the Blue and Rose periods. The painting displays almost no activity. The characters hardly notice each other. The stillness of the scene lends it mystery and a sense of melancholy. Picasso portrayed himself as Harlequin, as he did in many paintings. With the self portrait, this painting reflects Picasso's sense of artistic isolation or alienation. *Family of Saltimbanques* includes one figure thought to be from the Cirque Médrano, El Tío Pepe, a fat man in a bright red suit. The identity of the remaining figures remains controversial. Some scholars believe they represent Picasso's friends of the time.

Before Picasso completed *Family of Saltimbanques,* his

work came to the attention of the American writer Gertrude Stein. Stein had lived in Paris since 1903 and was building one of the foremost collections of modern art in Paris. She met Picasso in 1905 and introduced him to the French painter Henri Matisse in 1906.

Early sculptures. In the summer of 1906, Picasso traveled to Gósol, a remote village in the Pyrenees mountains. Before he left for Gósol, he had discovered sculpture of the Iberian peninsula (present-day Spain and Portugal) from the 500's and 400's B.C. Under the influence of ancient Iberian sculpture, Picasso began to experiment with distortion as an expressive element.

At the 1906 annual exhibition in Paris, called the Salon d'Automne, Picasso saw the work of the French artist Paul Gauguin in carved wood along with 10 paintings by the French painter Paul Cézanne. The achievements of these two artists and his response to them preoccupied Picasso over the next year or so and helped define his later work. Gauguin's use of forms found in the Pacific Islands, especially Tahiti, provided Picasso with an important model for using the art of non-Western cultures in his work.

Upon his return to Paris after that summer, Picasso completed a portrait of Gertrude Stein, begun months earlier. He gave the portrait a sculpturelike appearance by painting Stein with a masklike face and massive body of monumental chiseled forms.

Les Demoiselles d'Avignon is a large painting Picasso completed in 1907. Many art historians consider it the most influential painting of the 1900's because it opened the way to modern art. The painting appears in the **Cubism** article. The picture portrays five *demoiselles* (young women), prostitutes from Avignon Street in Barcelona, which Picasso knew well. Picasso reduced the figures to a series of interlocking, angular shapes. He filled the composition with sharp planes, distortions of space, and deliberately disorienting and contradictory points of view. Picasso used this distortion of the female form to express his anxieties about women, love, and sexuality. The painting reveals Picasso's attempt to harness the forms of non-Western carving and the power of magic and ritual in African art.

Oil on oilcloth on canvas edged with rope (1912) Musée Picasso, Paris (Art Resource © 2002 Estate of Pablo Picasso/Artists Rights Society (ARS), New York City)

Still Life with Chair Caning is a *collage*, a technique Picasso invented. He attached a piece of oilcloth printed with a pattern like chair caning and surrounded the painting with hemp rope.

Cubism. Picasso and the French artist Georges Braque became acquainted in 1907, and a remarkable artistic dialogue between the two began in 1908. Together they produced a revolutionary style called Cubism, in which figures and objects are represented by geometrical forms.

In 1909, Picasso and Braque entered a period of great intensity in their work together. Their pictorial vocabularies merged in a phase called Analytic Cubism. Analytic Cubism broke down forms from the natural world and reassembled them into flat planes.

During Picasso's Cubist period, he often painted *still lifes* (pictures of fruit, bowls, bottles, and other everyday objects). He drew his subjects from cafes and artist's studios, settings familiar to him. In 1912, the Cubist search for different styles of representation led Picasso to create *Still Life with Chair Caning,* and with it, to invent a technique called *collage.* Collage is a form of painting or drawing that attaches flat, ready-made materials to the surface (see **Collage**). *Still Life with Chair Caning* shows objects scattered across a cafe table, including part of the newspaper *Le Journal,* a glass, and a lemon. To the painted objects, Picasso applied a real object, a piece of oilcloth printed with a pattern like chair caning. For a frame, Picasso surrounded the oval canvas with a length of thick hemp rope to make the collage look like an old master painting.

Picasso also created illusions in his three-dimensional constructions, beginning in 1912 with a series of sculptures called *Guitar.* One of these works appears in the **Sculpture** article. This *Guitar,* which Picasso completed in 1913, is constructed of sheet metal and wire. He cut away most of the guitar body and expressed its shape as a series of flat, projecting planes. He made the guitar's sound hole a projecting cylinder. In a real instrument, the hole would be an open space. Picasso's use of sheet metal, an industrial material, was highly unusual at that time, but such materials have since become common sculptural mediums. His invention of this radical new sculptural form had a great influence on later developments in sculpture.

By 1912, Picasso discovered that he could give shapes different meanings—real or abstract—simply by rearranging them. He also found that he could use a variety of materials on surfaces. Collage and the *Guitar* construction essentially ended Picassso's Analytic Cubist phase, and he began a second phase, called Synthetic Cubism, which lasted into the early 1920's. Synthetic Cubism generally constructed an image from many components. Instead of dissecting forms, as in Analytic Cubism, the artist added elements to the picture surface, building up the image through each addition, as Picasso did in *Still Life with Chair Caning* (1912).

When France joined World War I shortly after it began in 1914, Braque was called into the French military. Because Spain remained neutral during the war, Picasso continued working on art, but his collaboration with Braque came to an end.

Picasso as designer. A friendship with the French writer Jean Cocteau brought Picasso into the social circle surrounding the Ballets Russes in 1919. The Ballets Russes was a touring Russian dance company that included some of the greatest dancers, composers, and artists of the time. The first ballet Picasso became involved was *Parade.* Cocteau created the story, and Picasso designed the curtain, sets, and costumes. *Parade* premiered in 1917.

Guernica (1937), an oil painting on canvas; the Reina Sofia Museum, Madrid (MAS © Artists Rights Society, New York City)

Guernica is one of Picasso's most powerful paintings. The artist painted this work as a protest against the bombing of the Spanish town of Guernica in 1937. Such images as a gored horse, a woman with a dead child, and a fallen soldier became emotional symbols of the bitter suffering of wartime.

Critics considered the ballet a radical break from traditional ballet, largely due to Picasso's designs. He continued to work on ballets until 1924, while also painting such Synthetic Cubist works as *Three Musicians* (1921).

The 1920's and 1930's. Picasso began to work in a different style in the 1920's, one he practiced alongside Cubism. This style was his version of Neoclassicism inspired by a trip to Italy in 1917. The artist began to use Classical forms and drawing techniques, reflecting the influence of Mediterranean culture. *Three Women at the Spring* (1921) shows its Classical roots in the facial features and clothing of the large, serene figures.

Picasso never became an official member of the Surrealist group during the 1920's, but he had close connections with several Surrealist members. The Surrealists used unexpected arrangements and distortions of images to reflect dreams and the subconscious mind (see **Surrealism**). The Surrealist movement gave Picasso new subjects. It also reinforced his interest in the fragmentation of forms and the expression of suppressed emotions, qualities dating back to *Les Demoiselles d'Avignon.* Picasso's own brand of Surrealism also found a unique expression in poetry. He began to write in the fall of 1935 and continued into 1936. During that time, he concentrated on poetry instead of painting.

In the mid-1930's, Picasso resumed painting with a new political commitment. The outbreak of the Spanish Civil War in 1936 stirred Picasso to produce work supporting the cause of the Spanish Loyalists against the fascists led by Francisco Franco.

The weakened Spanish Loyalist government asked Picasso to paint a mural for the Spanish Pavilion at the Paris world's fair in 1937. The artist struggled to find a subject for the mural until he was inspired by the bombing of the Spanish town of Guernica, ordered by Franco. Dramatic photographs of the destruction of the small town gave Picasso his subject matter.

Picasso painted *Guernica* in about a month in 1937. The canvas stretches more than 25.5 feet (7.8 meters) in length. The imagery of *Guernica*—a gored horse, a woman with a dead child, a fallen soldier—became powerful symbols of bitter suffering. To dramatize the wartime agony of destruction, the artist restricted his colors to stark black, white, and gray.

Later career. After Germany invaded France in 1940, Picasso lived in his Paris studio, though he was banned from showing his work. Skulls began to appear in some of his paintings. They symbolized the tragedies that had touched the artist, including World War II (1939-1945), his mother's death in 1939, and the death of his friend, the Spanish sculptor Julio González in 1942.

After France was liberated in 1944, the Salon d'Automne of 1944 featured Picasso's work of the war years. These somber paintings shocked viewers, as did the announcement that Picasso had joined the French Communist Party. His anti-American painting *Massacre in Korea* (1951) depicts American soldiers as medieval knights slaughtering innocent women and children.

From 1948, Picasso lived and worked in the south of France, at first for part of the year and later permanently. His international reputation had expanded, and his name had become virtually synonymous with modern art.

During the final two decades of his life, Picasso became fascinated with earlier art. He based paintings on works by two masters of the 1600's, the Dutch artist Rembrandt and the Spanish artist Diego Velázquez, and by French artists of the 1800's, including Eugene Delacroix and Edouard Manet. Picasso pitted himself in competition with his chosen masters, breaking their work down, recomposing it, and becoming ever bolder in his methods of painting.

Picasso's style continued to develop through the last decade of his life. At the time of his death on April 8, 1973, Picasso still owned hundreds of his own works in various mediums from all periods of his career. These pieces provided the basis of a gift to the French government by his heirs. In 1985 the Picasso Museum opened in Paris to display the works.   Michael Plante

See also **Chicago** (picture: The Chicago Picasso); **Painting** (Cubism); **Sculpture** (Cubism and Futurism).

Scenic San Francisco is nearly surrounded by water. The San Francisco-Oakland Bay Bridge, *foreground,* which crosses San Francisco Bay, links the city to nearby communities.

San Francisco

San Francisco is one of the largest cities in California and a leading center of culture, finance, and industry in the United States. It is also one of the world's most attractive cities. Its clanging cable cars, fascinating Chinatown, and many hills give the city a special charm. Its scenic beauty and mild climate make it a popular tourist destination.

With more than 775,000 people, San Francisco is one of the largest cities on the Pacific Coast of the United States. It also has one of the largest Asian American populations on the mainland of the United States. About 240,000 people of Chinese, Japanese, Philippine, Korean, Thai, and Vietnamese ancestry live in the city.

San Francisco is built on and around more than 40 hills. Some of the steepest streets in the world lie in San Francisco's downtown area on Nob Hill and Russian Hill. These hills rise as high as 376 feet (115 meters). Cable cars and other vehicles seem almost to stand on end as they climb or descend the slopes.

San Francisco lies on the northern tip of a peninsula. The sparkling blue water that nearly surrounds the city provides a magnificent setting. The Pacific Ocean lies to the west and San Francisco Bay to the east. On the north, a strait 1 mile (1.6 kilometers) wide connects the Pacific Ocean and San Francisco Bay. This strait is named the Golden Gate, and San Francisco is often called the *City by the Golden Gate.* It is also known as the *City by the Bay.*

Indian cultures flourished in the San Francisco region for countless generations before Spanish settlers arrived in 1776. Gold was discovered east of San Francisco in 1848, and the city quickly became a busy mining supply center during the gold rush of 1849. In the late 1800's, the city thrived as the financial and industrial capital of the western United States. Then, in 1906, a terrible earthquake and fire destroyed most of San Francisco. But the

residents soon rebuilt their city. In 1945, the United Nations (UN) was organized in San Francisco.

The city

San Francisco covers 129 square miles (334 square kilometers), including 83 square miles (215 square kilometers) of water, and occupies all of San Francisco County. San Francisco includes several islands in the Pacific Ocean and in San Francisco Bay. Alcatraz, the most famous island, lies in the bay. It was the site of a famous federal prison for dangerous criminals from 1934 to 1963. Today, the prison is a tourist attraction.

Many people consider San Francisco's climate to be ideal. The temperature rarely rises to 80 °F (27 °C) or drops to 30 °F (−1 °C). However, fog often covers the western part of the city. It forms when warm air flows over the cold ocean water.

Downtown San Francisco lies in the northeastern part of the city. Market Street is the main downtown street. It has large department stores and many fashionable shops. Union Square is the main shopping area. The Civic Center stands at Van Ness Avenue and McAllister Street, just north of Market Street. The center includes City Hall, the Asian Art Museum, the War Memorial Opera House, and Davies Symphony Hall.

Nob Hill rises northeast of the Civic Center. Two large luxury hotels, the Fairmont and the Mark Hopkins, have been built on this hill. The business district of Chinatown lies east of Nob Hill. Thousands of people of Asian ancestry live in the crowded Chinatown area. The area includes one of the largest Chinese communities outside Asia. Colorful shops, restaurants, and other buildings with Chinese-style upturned roofs stretch for eight blocks along Chinatown's lively Grant Avenue.

San Francisco's busy financial district is just east of Chinatown and centers on Montgomery Street. Many banks, investment houses, and other financial firms are on this street. It has been nicknamed the *Wall Street of the West,* after New York City's great financial district. The Transamerica Pyramid, perhaps San Francisco's most striking building, stands on Montgomery Street. This sleek, white office building towers 853 feet (260 meters) and looks like a thin pyramid. The impressive 52-story Bank of America building rises nearby. It is the home of one of the world's largest commercial banks.

Farther east, a modern residential and commercial complex called the Golden Gateway Center covers 51 acres (21 hectares) near the shore of San Francisco Bay. The center includes tall, elegant apartment and office buildings, shops, parks, and tiled plazas.

The Port of San Francisco borders the bay, which is one of the largest natural harbors in the world. The bay covers about 450 square miles (1,170 square kilometers). A wide street called the Embarcadero parallels the shore. At the middle of the port, across the Embarcadero from the Golden Gateway Center, stands the Ferry Building with its famous clock tower. The building once was a terminal for ferryboats that carried passengers between San Francisco and the eastern shore of the bay. Today, it houses the World Trade Center, which has offices for firms that deal in international trade.

Russian Hill rises in the northern part of downtown San Francisco. It includes what is called the *Crookedest Street in the World.* This street, a section of Lombard Street, makes eight sharp turns in a single block. The white Coit Tower, a famous San Francisco landmark, stands on top of nearby Telegraph Hill. The 210-foot (64-meter) tower is a memorial to the city's firefighters.

At the northern end of the Embarcadero lies Fisherman's Wharf, once the home of a huge fleet of colorful fishing boats. Today, the wharf is known chiefly for its many seafood restaurants. Nearby are two unusual shopping centers—the Cannery and Ghirardelli Square. The Cannery was once a food-processing factory, and Ghirardelli Square was a chocolate factory. They now house a variety of shops. North of Ghirardelli Square is San Francisco Maritime National Historical Park. The park includes a maritime museum and several restored ships of the 1800's docked at a pier.

Residential districts. North Beach, in northeastern San Francisco, is one of the city's oldest residential neighborhoods. It occupies the western slope of Telegraph Hill. Italian immigrants settled the area in the mid-1800's. Other neighborhoods that developed during this period include Potrero Hill and the Mission District. Potrero Hill lies south of the downtown area, and the Mission District lies southwest of downtown. The historic Mission Dolores stands in the Mission District. The original mission, founded by the Spanish in 1776, was destroyed by fire. It was replaced by another mission, which dates from 1782 and still stands.

The Western Addition, a neighborhood just west of the downtown area, is noted for its nearly 100-year-old houses built in the elaborate Victorian style. Many of these homes have been restored. The Western Addition is also the site of the Japanese Trade and Cultural Center. This huge complex, which includes shops, restaurants, motion-picture theaters, and a hotel, is the center of an area called Japantown.

San Francisco facts in brief

Population: *City*—776,733. *Metropolitan area*—1,731,183. *Consolidated metropolitan area*—7,039,362.
Area: *City*—129 mi² (334 km²), including 83 mi² (215 km²) of water. *Metropolitan area*—1,269 mi² (3,287 km²). *Consolidated metropolitan area*—7,960 mi² (20,616 km²).
Climate: *Average temperature*—January, 50 °F (10 °C); July, 59 °F (15 °C). *Average annual precipitation* (rainfall, melted snow, and other forms of moisture)—22 in (56 cm). For the monthly weather in San Francisco, see **California** (Climate).
Government: Mayor-council (for city and county combined). *Terms*—4 years for the mayor and the 11 members of the council, called the Board of Supervisors.
Founded: 1776. Incorporated as a city in 1850.

Largest communities in the San Francisco area

Name	Population	Name	Population
San Francisco	776,733	San Rafael	56,063
Daly City	103,621	Novato	47,630
San Mateo	92,482	San Bruno	40,165
Redwood City	75,402	Pacifica	38,390
South San Francisco	60,552	Menlo Park	30,785

Source: 2000 census.

Symbols of San Francisco. The city flag was adopted in 1940 and the seal in 1914. Both symbols show the city motto, *Gold in Peace—Iron in War,* in Spanish. Both also have a phoenix, a mythical bird that rose from its own ashes, representing the city's rebirth after the 1906 earthquake and fire.

WORLD BOOK map
San Francisco lies on the Pacific Coast in California.

The Presidio, originally a Spanish army post, covers about 1,500 acres (607 hectares) in northwestern San Francisco. Until 1995, it served as the headquarters of the U.S. Sixth Army. In 1996, President Bill Clinton signed legislation that called for transforming the Presidio into a national park within 15 years. The officers' club, built in 1776, is the city's oldest building.

Almost all the residential areas in western San Francisco began to develop in the early 1900's. Sea Cliff, a community known for its large, well-landscaped homes, lies west of the Presidio along the Golden Gate. Nearby is Lincoln Park. The park includes the California Palace of the Legion of Honor, one of the city's finest museums. Farther south, Golden Gate Park extends from the Pacific Ocean to the center of the city. It covers 1,017 acres (412 hectares) and is one of the nation's largest city parks. The park's attractions include the California Academy of Sciences, Strybing Arboretum and Botanical Gardens, and a Japanese tea garden.

Overlooking the eastern end of Golden Gate Park is Mount Sutro, which rises more than 900 feet (270 meters). Nearby, Mount Davidson and two hills called Twin Peaks reach about the same height. Many expensive homes have been built on the slopes of all these hills.

Most of San Francisco's newest neighborhoods lie in the southwestern part of the city. This area also includes San Francisco State University and Lake Merced, a large freshwater lake.

The metropolitan area of San Francisco covers 1,269 square miles (3,287 square kilometers). It extends over three counties—Marin, San Francisco, and San Mateo. About $1\frac{3}{4}$ million people live in this area. San Francisco forms part of the San Francisco-Oakland-San Jose Consolidated Metropolitan Area. About 7 million people live in this larger metropolitan area.

Two spectacular bridges link San Francisco to other parts of the Bay Area. The $8\frac{1}{4}$-mile (13.3-kilometer) San Francisco-Oakland Bay Bridge crosses the bay. The Golden Gate Bridge connects the city and its northern suburbs. Its main section stretches 4,200 feet (1,280 meters) and is one of the world's longest spans.

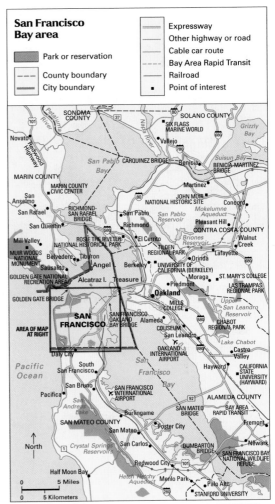

WORLD BOOK map

People

Population. Whites make up 50 percent of San Francisco's population. Asian Americans make up 31 percent. Hispanics, who may be of any race, account for about 14 percent, and African Americans make up about 8 percent.

The largest ethnic groups among whites are people of English, German, Irish, Italian, and Russian ancestry. Chinese make up the largest group of Asian Americans. Many of the first Chinese came to work in the mines during the gold rush of 1849. Thousands of others arrived in the 1860's to help build the Central Pacific Railroad, which formed part of the first transcontinental railroad system in the United States. Other large groups of Asian Americans in San Francisco consist of people who are of Japanese, Philippine, or Vietnamese descent. Mexican Americans make up the city's largest group of Hispanics. San Francisco's black population began to increase during World War II (1939-1945). At that time, thousands of African Americans came from the South to seek jobs in the booming shipyards.

Housing in San Francisco includes many *row houses.* These houses—most of them two-story wood or stucco

buildings—may share at least one wall with the house next door. Single families occupy some row houses, but most such houses have been converted into two or more apartments.

Urban renewal projects south and west of the downtown area have replaced many run-down dwellings with attractive row houses and apartment complexes. However, many other older homes and apartments in these areas remain in poor condition.

Education. The San Francisco Board of Education sets policy for the city's more than 100 public schools. The board consists of seven members who are elected to four-year terms.

San Francisco State University is the city's largest university. The San Francisco campus of the University of California is known for important discoveries in the field of biotechnology. Other institutions of higher learning in the city include City College of San Francisco, Golden Gate University, Hastings College of Law, the San Francisco Art Institute, the San Francisco Conservatory of Music, and the University of San Francisco. Several outstanding universities lie near San Francisco. They include Stanford

© Stone from Getty Images

© The Image Bank from Getty Images

Chinatown, in the northeastern part of San Francisco, has one of the world's largest Chinese communities outside Asia.

The Palace of Fine Arts was built for the 1915 Panama-Pacific International Exposition. It houses a museum, the Exploratorium.

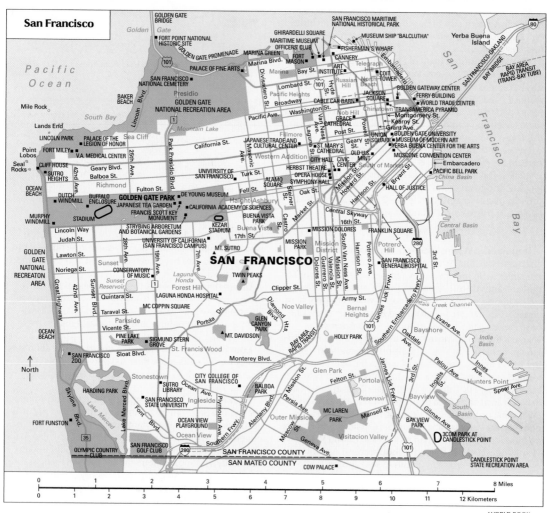

WORLD BOOK map

© Superstock

The Crookedest Street in the World is San Francisco's Lombard Street, which makes eight sharp turns in a single block. It lies on Russian Hill, one of the more than 40 hills in the city.

San Francisco Convention & Visitors Bureau

A cable car carries riders up one of San Francisco's steep hills. The city's cable car system, which includes three lines and covers 10 miles (16 kilometers), is a national historic landmark.

University in Stanford, near Palo Alto, and the University of California in Berkeley.

Social problems. San Francisco, like other large cities in the United States, faces such problems as poverty, homelessness, crime, and drug abuse. Most of the city's poor lack education and necessary job skills.

San Francisco also has had a high rate of people infected with the life-threatening disease AIDS. The disease first appeared in the city in 1981 among young homosexual men and spread rapidly.

Cultural life and recreation

The arts. The San Francisco Performing Arts Center consists of the War Memorial Opera House, Louise M. Davies Symphony Hall, and the Herbst Theatre. The city's opera company and ballet company perform at the opera house. The opera company, founded in 1923, is the oldest major opera company in the western United States. The ballet company, founded in 1933, is the oldest in the nation. The San Francisco Symphony Orchestra performs at the symphony hall. The Herbst Theatre hosts musical, dance, and theatrical performances. The city's American Conservatory Theater is one of the finest professional theater companies in the United States.

Libraries and museums. The Sutro Library, a branch of the California State Library, includes a collection of books printed during the 1400's. The California Academy of Sciences and the California Historical Society also house fine libraries. San Francisco's public library system has about 25 branches.

The California Palace of the Legion of Honor has collections of antique European furniture, paintings, porcelain objects, and sculptures. It is noted for its works by the French sculptor Auguste Rodin and for its French Impressionist paintings. The collection of the Asian Art Museum spans 6,000 years of history and represents the countries and cultures throughout Asia. The San Francisco Museum of Modern Art specializes in art of the 1900's. The California Academy of Sciences includes the Morrison Planetarium and the Steinhart Aquarium.

Recreation. San Francisco has about 160 parks and playgrounds. Golden Gate Park, the city's chief recreational area, includes baseball diamonds, bridle paths, hiking trails, picnic areas, and tennis courts. Many people enjoy boating in San Francisco Bay, as well as fishing and sailing in the Pacific Ocean and Lake Merced. San Francisco's zoo is near Lake Merced.

The Golden Gate National Recreation Area covers parts of San Francisco and Marin counties. Also in Marin County are Point Reyes National Seashore and Muir Woods National Monument, which has the most famous redwood forest in the country.

The city is the home of the San Francisco Giants of baseball's National League. The San Francisco 49ers of the National Football League also play there.

Economy

San Francisco has long been one of the nation's leading financial centers. It is also a major center of commerce, industry, and tourism.

Finance and trade. Loans from San Francisco's banks played a key role in the early development of the mining industry in the western United States. Today, many banks and other financial institutions operate in the city. The Bank of America, one of the largest commercial banks in the world, has its headquarters in San Francisco. The city is also the home of Wells Fargo Bank, which ranks among the largest U.S. banks.

A number of San Francisco's workers have jobs in retail and wholesale trade. Many work for firms that serve the tourist trade. Millions of tourists visit San Francisco yearly and contribute greatly to the city's economy.

San Francisco had the busiest port on the Pacific Coast during the 1800's. But several other ports in the Bay Area developed rapidly in the early 1900's. Today, the Port of San Francisco handles far less cargo than some of these nearby ports.

Industry. The San Francisco Bay area lies at the heart of California's high technology industry. The area from Palo Alto southeast to San Jose has so many computer-related industries that it is called Silicon Valley, for the silicon used to make computer chips. San Francisco itself has large numbers of software firms and Internet companies. Many computer graphics and media firms have offices in the city's South of Market district, an area nicknamed Multimedia Gulch.

Other important industries in the San Francisco area manufacture clothing, process food, and fabricate metal products. The city is a leading printing and publishing center. San Francisco is also a major administrative center for industrial firms. More than 100 large U.S. corporations have headquarters in or near the city.

Transportation and communication. San Francisco International Airport, about 12 miles (19 kilometers) south of the city, serves many commercial airlines. The airport ranks among the busiest in the world. Several passenger and freight rail lines also serve the city.

The publicly owned Bay Area Rapid Transit (BART) operates an electric rail system in the bay region. One BART route passes through the Trans-Bay Tube, a tunnel that runs under San Francisco Bay between San Francisco and Oakland. The Trans-Bay Tube, which is $3\frac{1}{2}$ miles (5.6 kilometers) long, is the longest underwater vehicular tunnel in North America.

San Francisco's cable cars run on rails and are pulled by a moving cable under the street. The cable car system, which is a national historic landmark, has three lines and covers 10 miles (16 kilometers). The system is part of the Municipal Railway, which also operates buses, trolleys, and light rail vehicles.

San Francisco has two major daily newspapers. They are the *Chronicle* and the *Examiner*.

Government

San Francisco was incorporated as a city in 1850. Its government and that of San Francisco County have been combined since 1856. San Francisco has a mayor-council form of government. The voters elect the mayor and the 11 members of the council, called the Board of Supervisors, to four-year terms. The mayor appoints the heads of the chief city government agencies and prepares the city budget. The mayor may also veto bills passed by the Board of Supervisors.

The city government gets most of its revenue from real estate taxes. But taxes do not meet all the government's expenses. As a result, San Francisco depends on grants from the state and federal governments and on the sale of bonds to pay for improvements.

History

Early days. The Costanoan Indians lived in what is now the San Francisco area long before Europeans arrived. Fogs, which often blanket the Pacific Coast for weeks, probably prevented early European navigators from finding the Golden Gate, the entrance to San Francisco Bay. In 1542, the Portuguese explorer Juan Rodríguez Cabrillo saw the Farallon Islands but missed the Golden Gate. In 1579, the English explorer Sir Francis Drake also sailed right by. He may have anchored in what is now known as Drake's Bay, just north of San Francisco. In 1595, the Portuguese explorer Sebastián Rodríguez Cermeño entered Drake's Bay. He named it *Puerto de San Francisco* (Port of Saint Francis) and so established the name *San Francisco* for the region.

Europeans finally reached the site of San Francisco by traveling overland. In 1769, members of a Spanish expedition led by Gaspar de Portolá became the first Europeans to climb the hills and see the bay.

Settlement by Europeans. On Sept. 17, 1776, a Spanish expedition under Captain Juan Bautista de Anza established a *presidio* (military fort) at San Francisco. During that same year, Spanish priests opened a mission nearby. It was named *Misión San Francisco de Asís* in honor of Saint Francis of Assisi. At the mission, Spanish soldiers and priests subjected the Indians to strict discipline and a heavy workload. A number of Indians were exposed to new diseases. Many became ill and died. The Costanoan population declined greatly during this period.

Spanish-speaking families who came with Anza settled near the mission, known as Mission Dolores after nearby Lake Dolores. The settlement was called the *Pueblo de San Francisco* (Town of Saint Francis).

In 1821, Mexico won its independence from Spain and took over California. Mexico encouraged the development of cattle ranches in its new province of California. The ranches in the San Francisco area attracted New England ship captains, who wanted cattle hides for the growing shoe industry in the eastern United States. A lively port developed in the northeastern corner of the peninsula, and a town named *Yerba Buena* (Good Herb) grew up near the port.

The Mexican War. War broke out between Mexico and the United States in May 1846. On July 9, American naval forces under Commander John B. Montgomery captured Yerba Buena. The Americans renamed the town San Francisco in 1847. Mexico lost the war in 1848, and the entire California region became part of the United States.

The gold rush. In 1848, gold was discovered near what is now Sacramento. The discovery led to the gold rush of 1849. Hundreds of ships, jammed with thousands of gold seekers, streamed into San Francisco's harbor. The fortune hunters, who came from all over the world, swept through San Francisco on the way to the gold fields. Gold-hungry crews abandoned many of their ships in the harbor. San Francisco became the main supply center for the miners. Its population jumped from about 800 in 1848 to about 25,000 in 1849. In 1850, the town was incorporated as a city.

Continued prosperity. Adventurers who made fortunes during the gold rush helped San Francisco become rich. Mansions went up on Nob Hill. Theaters opened and flourished. Commerce boomed. But crime also soared. In 1851, a group of citizens formed the San Francisco Vigilance Committee to enforce law and order. They became known as *Vigilantes* and helped rid the city of a number of its worst criminals. But lawlessness still flourished, especially in a district around Pacific Avenue and Kearny Street. In the 1860's, this district was nicknamed the *Barbary Coast,* after a notorious center for sea raiders on the coast of northern Africa.

Following the fabulous California gold strike, mining boom towns sprang up throughout the West. San Francisco became the center of finance and supply for those towns. Manufacturing, especially the production of mining equipment, also thrived in the city.

In 1869, the first railroad from the eastern United States reached the San Francisco Bay area. In 1873, Andrew S. Hallidie, a San Francisco cable manufacturer, invented the cable car. Cable cars provided a safe way to move up and down steep grades and greatly encouraged residential and commercial development on San Francisco's hills. By 1900, the energetic city had a population of about 342,000.

Earthquake and fire. San Francisco suffered one of the worst disasters in United States history when a severe earthquake shook the city at 5:13 a.m. on April 18, 1906. Fires broke out in various sections as stoves and gas lamps overturned, electric wires broke, and gas mains exploded. Firefighters could not battle the flames effectively because the city's water mains had also been damaged. As a result, fires raged unchecked for three days. The firefighters then began to dynamite entire blocks of buildings to stop the spreading flames.

At least 3,000 people died in the disaster, and about 250,000 lost their homes. Most of the city, including more than 28,000 buildings, lay in ruins.

A city reborn. San Franciscans quickly rebuilt their city. In 1915, the new San Francisco held the Panama-Pacific International Exposition to honor the opening in 1914 of the Panama Canal. The canal enabled ships to sail from New York City to San Francisco without having to travel around South America. But Los Angeles and Oakland greatly expanded their port facilities during the early 1900's. As a result, San Francisco lost its position as the leading center of commerce, manufacturing, and shipping in California. The city's population, however, continued to grow steadily. By 1930, it had reached 634,394. The San Francisco-Oakland Bay Bridge opened in 1936 and the Golden Gate Bridge in 1937.

During World War II (1939-1945), San Francisco became one of the world's largest shipbuilding centers. Thousands of new residents, including many African Americans, came to work in the shipyards and other war plants. In addition, thousands of military personnel were stationed in and around the city. San Francisco's population reached a peak of 827,400 in 1945. That same year, delegates from 50 countries met in San Francisco to organize the United Nations (UN).

Building boom. Increasing problems of citywide decay during the 1950's led to large urban renewal projects in the 1960's. Modern row houses and apartment buildings replaced run-down housing in Hunters Point and the Western Addition. Towering new office buildings in downtown San Francisco created an impressive skyline overlooking the bay. The most ambitious project was the huge residential and commercial complex called the Golden Gateway Center.

San Francisco became a center of the counterculture or hippie movement during the middle and late 1960's. Such rock bands as the Grateful Dead and the Jefferson Airplane originated in the city, and thousands of young people flocked there, especially to the Haight-Ashbury district west of downtown.

The downtown building boom continued in the 1970's. The Transamerica Pyramid opened in 1972. That same year, the Bay Area Rapid Transit system began operating. The Trans-Bay Tube opened in 1974. City building codes required that the new structures be built in ways to enable them to withstand earthquakes.

By the 1980's, a debate had reached a peak about the benefits of the city's building boom. Some residents argued that skyscrapers destroyed the city's charm and beauty. Others maintained that the construction was needed to provide jobs and help strengthen San Francis-

California Historical Society

An earthquake and fire in 1906 left most of San Francisco in ruins. The disaster was one of the worst in U.S. history. At least 3,000 people died, and about 250,000 lost their homes. More than 28,000 buildings were destroyed.

co's economy. In 1985, an ordinance called the Downtown Plan was passed. The plan limited the size of future structures, preserved many existing buildings, and called for open spaces to relieve congestion.

Political leaders murdered. Tragedy struck the city on Nov. 27, 1978, when Mayor George Moscone and Supervisor Harvey Milk were shot to death by Dan White, a former member of the Board of Supervisors. In 1979, White was convicted of voluntary manslaughter and sentenced to a prison term of seven years and eight months. Many San Franciscans considered the term too light. White was released from prison early, in 1984. In 1985, he committed suicide.

Another earthquake. On Oct. 17, 1989, a strong earthquake—though not as strong as the 1906 quake—struck San Francisco and the surrounding area. It caused 12 deaths and about $3 billion in property damage in San Francisco County. Some San Francisco neighborhoods, especially older ones, suffered severe damage. The earthquake destroyed about 60 buildings in the Marina District, which was built on landfill in the northern part of the city. Other areas of the city escaped major damage, especially newer areas where buildings had been constructed to withstand earthquakes.

Recent developments. San Francisco's population became increasingly diverse during the 1990's. The city's leaders reflected that diversity. In 1995, San Francisco voters elected the city's first African American mayor, Willie Brown. Brown won reelection in 1999. Asian Americans also held several posts in city government. In addition, San Francisco has one of the nation's largest gay, or homosexual, populations, and gays have experienced growing political power.

In the 1990's and the beginning of the 2000's, San Francisco experienced a cultural renaissance. The Yerba Buena Center for the Arts opened. The San Francisco Museum of Modern Art and the Asian Art Museum moved into new homes. Construction began on new, larger facilities for the Jewish Museum San Francisco and the Mexican Museum.   James J. Rawls

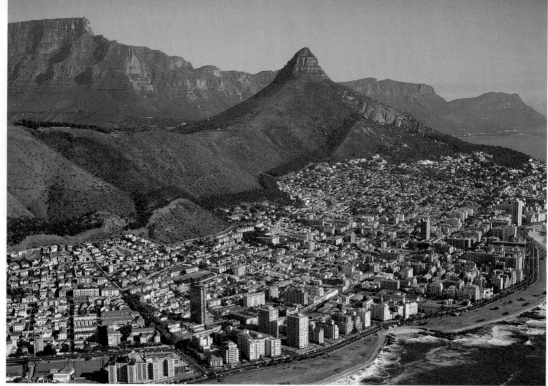

Cape Town, South Africa's legislative capital and oldest city, lies at the foot of the Cape Mountains in a setting of striking natural beauty. The city's location on the country's southwest coast and its excellent harbor make Cape Town an important shipping and trading center.

South Africa

South Africa is a country at the southern tip of the continent of Africa. The country has a wealth of natural resources, especially minerals, and it is the most highly industrialized nation in Africa. South Africa also has great geographical variety and natural beauty.

South Africa was the last nation in Africa ruled by a white minority. From the late 1940's to the early 1990's, the white government enforced a policy of rigid racial segregation called *apartheid* (pronounced *ah PAHRT hayt).* Under apartheid, the government denied voting rights and other rights to the black majority. Many South Africans and people throughout the world opposed apartheid. Protests against it often led to violence.

In 1990 and 1991, South Africa repealed most of the main laws on which apartheid was based. In 1993, the country extended voting rights to all races, and democratic elections were held the next year. After those elections, South Africa's white leaders handed over power to the country's first multiracial government. Nelson Mandela, a civil rights leader who had spent 27 years in prison, became South Africa's first black president.

Government

South Africa has three capitals. Parliament meets in Cape Town, the legislative capital. All executive departments of the government have their headquarters in Pretoria, the administrative capital. The Supreme Court of Appeal meets in Bloemfontein, the judicial capital.

South Africa adopted a temporary constitution in 1993. It provided for a new government that took office in May 1994, following the country's first all-race elec-

tions. In 1996, South Africa adopted a new Constitution. Most of this Constitution, which includes a wide-ranging bill of rights, took effect in 1997.

National government. South Africa's Parliament makes the country's laws, which must be signed by the president to take effect. Parliament consists of two houses: the National Assembly and the National Council of Provinces. The National Assembly has at least 350 members and no more than 400 members, elected for five-year terms. Under certain conditions, the Assembly may be dissolved before the members serve their full terms. The National Council of Provinces represents the interests of South Africa's provinces at the national level. Each of the nine provincial legislatures chooses 10 delegates to send to the National Council. The proportion of seats a political party holds in the provincial legislature determines how many of the 10 delegates to the National Council come from that party.

A president, elected by the National Assembly from among its members, heads South Africa's government. A Cabinet assists the president in running the government. The Cabinet includes the deputy president and the ministers in charge of government departments. The president chooses the members of the Cabinet and assigns them their duties. Cabinet members are chosen mainly from the members of the National Assembly.

South Africa's court system includes the Constitutional Court, the Supreme Court of Appeal, several High Courts, and local courts run by magistrates. In addition, *traditional leaders,* the heads of South Africa's black African ethnic groups, may hear and decide matters of customary law in their own courts.

South Africa's highest court in all constitutional matters is the Constitutional Court, which meets in Johannesburg. The Constitutional Court settles disputes between national, provincial, and local governments that involve the Constitution. It also decides whether constitutional amendments passed by Parliament and laws approved by Parliament and provincial legislatures are legal. In addition, it can determine whether the conduct of the president is constitutional. Members of the Constitutional Court are appointed by the president of South Africa to 12-year terms.

South Africa's Supreme Court of Appeal, in Bloemfontein, hears appeals from the High Courts. It is South Africa's highest court except in constitutional matters.

The government has set up several independent national institutions to strengthen the country's democracy. They include the Human Rights Commission; the Commission for the Promotion and Protection of the Rights of Cultural, Religious and Linguistic Communities; the Commission for Gender Equality; and the Independent Electoral Commission. In addition, a National House of Traditional Leaders advises the government on the role of traditional leaders and on customary law.

Provincial government. Before 1994, South Africa was divided into 4 provinces and 10 areas called *homelands.* The provinces were (1) Cape Province, (2) Natal, (3) Orange Free State, and (4) Transvaal. The homelands were reserved for black Africans. The South African government granted independence to four homelands and allowed the other six a degree of self-government. But none of the homelands had much real power, and black Africans strongly opposed the homeland system.

The 1993 Constitution dissolved the 4 provinces and 10 homelands. In their place, 9 new provinces were created: (1) Eastern Cape, (2) Free State, (3) Gauteng, (4) KwaZulu-Natal, (5) Mpumalanga, (6) Northern Cape, (7) Northern Province, (8) North West, and (9) Western Cape. Each province is governed by a provincial legislature of from 30 to 80 members. The legislature elects the premier of the province.

Local government under apartheid was racially segregated, with separate areas for whites and blacks. In 1999 and 2000, South Africa redrew its local government boundaries to merge previously segregated areas. The local areas, which include districts, municipalities, and metropolitan areas, are each governed by an elected council. Each local government passes laws and provides services for communities within its boundaries.

Political parties. The largest political parties in South Africa are the African National Congress (ANC), the Democratic Party (DP), the Inkatha Freedom Party (IFP), and the New National Party (NNP). The ANC was founded in 1912 to promote the rights of black Africans. Although illegal from 1960 until 1990, it served as the main political voice for blacks, who were not allowed to vote. Its supporters now include people from all ethnic groups. Until 1998, the NNP was called the National Party. It controlled the government from 1948 to 1994. Formerly all white, the party's members now include many *Coloureds* (people of mixed race) and Asians. The DP is supported mainly by white voters. Most members of the IFP belong to the black Zulu ethnic group.

Armed forces. The South African National Defence Force combines the forces of the army, navy, and air force. Men and women of all racial and ethnic groups serve in the National Defence Force. All service is voluntary. Before 1994, most officers in the armed forces were white. The number of black African soldiers and officers increased when armies of the black homelands became part of the National Defence Force. The force also absorbed the military wings of the ANC and another black political group, the Pan-Africanist Congress (PAC).

People

Racial and ethnic groups. From the late 1940's to the early 1990's, the government enforced a policy of racial segregation called *apartheid. Apartheid* means *separateness* in Afrikaans, a language spoken in South Africa. Under apartheid, the government officially categorized the people into four main racial groups: (1) African (black), (2) white, (3) Coloured (mixed-race), and (4) Asian. The government segregated the groups in housing, education, and employment, and in the use of transportation and other public facilities. Even after apartheid ended, the four groups remained generally separated. This separation is slowly diminishing.

Black Africans, often called simply Africans or blacks, make up 77 percent of South Africa's total population. Their ancestors moved into what is now eastern South Africa from the north between about A.D. 200 and 1000. Although black Africans live throughout the country, the largest group, the Zulu, make their homes mainly in KwaZulu-Natal. The second largest group, the Xhosa, live mostly in Eastern Cape. The Sotho are the third largest black group. The southern Sotho live in eastern Free State. The northern Sotho reside in Northern Province. The western Sotho or Tswana, related to the people of Botswana, live near the border of that country.

Whites make up 11 percent of South Africa's people. About 60 percent of the white population call themselves Afrikaners. Their ancestors came chiefly from the Netherlands in the late 1600's, though some came from Germany and France. Until the 1900's, most Afrikaners lived on farms and were known as Boers. *Boer* is a Dutch word that means *farmer.* Today, most Afrikaners live in cities, but they still make up most of the white population in rural areas. English-speaking whites account for about 40 percent of the white population. Their ancestors came chiefly from England, Ireland, and Scotland beginning in the early 1800's.

Coloureds make up 9 percent of South Africa's population. Their ancestors include the Khoikhoi and San peoples of western South Africa; African and Asian slaves brought to the country by whites; white settlers; and passing sailors, soldiers, and travelers. Most Coloured people live in Western Cape and Northern Cape provinces.

Asians—almost all of whom are people of Indian ancestry—make up 3 percent of the country's population. The ancestors of most of them came from India between 1860 and 1911 to work on sugar plantations in Natal (now KwaZulu-Natal). Plantation owners imported them as *indentured laborers,* workers contracted to work for a set time for a particular employer. South Africa also has a few people with Chinese ancestry.

Languages. South Africa has 11 official languages. They are (1) Afrikaans, (2) English, (3) Ndebele (which

South Africa in brief

Capitals: Cape Town (legislative), Pretoria (administrative), Bloemfontein (judicial).

Official languages: South Africa's 11 official languages are (1) Afrikaans, (2) English, (3) Ndebele (isiNdebele), (4) Sepedi, (5) Sesotho, (6) Swazi (siSwati), (7) Tsonga (xiTsonga), (8) Tswana (seTswana), (9) Venda (tshiVenda), (10) Xhosa (isiXhosa), and (11) Zulu (isiZulu).

Official name: Republic of South Africa.

National anthem: Combined version of "Nkosi Sikelel' iAfrika" and "Die Stem van Suid-Afrika/The Call of South Africa."

Largest cities: (1991 census)

Cape Town	854,616	Soweto	596,632
Durban	715,669	Pretoria	525,583
Johannesburg	712,507		

South Africa's flag, adopted in 1994, represents the country's peoples coming together in unity.

Coat of arms was adopted in 2000. The motto, in an ancient South African language, means *diverse people unite.*

Land and climate

Land: South Africa lies at the southern tip of Africa, with a coastline on the Indian and Atlantic oceans. The country borders Namibia, Botswana, Zimbabwe, Mozambique, and Swaziland, and it completely surrounds the country of Lesotho. South Africa's interior is mostly plateau. Coastal lowlands lie in the east. The Cape Mountains are in the far south. The Namib Desert stretches along the west coast. The Kalahari Desert covers much of the northwest interior. South Africa's main rivers include the Orange and its branch, the Vaal.

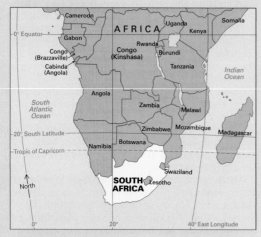

Area: 471,445 mi² (1,221,037 km²). *Greatest distances*—east-west 1,010 mi (1,625 km); north-south, 875 mi (1,408 km). *Coastline*—about 1,836 mi (2,954 km).

Elevation: *Highest*—Champagne Castle, 11,072 ft (3,375 m) above sea level. *Lowest*—sea level.

Climate: South Africa's climate is generally mild and sunny. The Cape Mountains Region has warm, dry summers and cool, wet winters. Much of the Coastal Strip has hot, humid summers and dry, sunny winters. In the Plateau, summer days are hot, but the nights are cool. The winter is cold. The deserts are hot and dry. Only about a fourth of South Africa receives more than 25 inches (64 centimeters) of rain yearly. More rain falls in the east than in the west.

Government

Form of government: Parliamentary republic.

Head of government: President.

Legislature: Parliament of two houses: National Assembly (350 to 400 members); National Council of Provinces (90 members).

Executive: President (elected by the National Assembly) and Cabinet.

Judiciary: Constitutional Court is highest court in constitutional matters; Supreme Court of Appeal is highest court in other matters.

Political subdivisions: Nine provinces.

People

Population: *2002 estimate*—40,952,000. *1996 census*—40,583,573.

Population density: 87 per mi² (34 per km²).

Distribution: 55 percent urban, 45 percent rural.

Major ethnic/national groups: 77 percent black African (mainly Zulu, Xhosa, and Sotho); 11 percent white; 9 percent Coloured (mixed race); 3 percent Asian (mostly Indian).

Major religions: 40 percent Protestant; 25 percent African Independent churches; 8 percent Roman Catholic; less than 2 percent each of Hindu, Muslim, Jewish, and traditional African religions.

Population trend

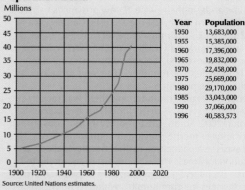

Millions

Year	Population
1950	13,683,000
1955	15,385,000
1960	17,396,000
1965	19,832,000
1970	22,458,000
1975	25,669,000
1980	29,170,000
1985	33,043,000
1990	37,066,000
1996	40,583,573

Source: United Nations estimates.

Economy

Chief products: *Agriculture*—corn, chickens and eggs, beef cattle, wheat, sugar cane, sheep, wool, apples. *Manufacturing*—chemicals, processed foods and beverages, transportation equipment, iron and steel, fabricated metal products, machinery, paper products, textiles. *Mining*—gold, coal, diamonds, copper, iron ore, uranium, manganese, chromite, platinum, vanadium.

Money: *Basic unit*—rand. One hundred cents equal one rand.

International trade: *Major exports*—gold, diamonds, metals and minerals, wool, corn, sugar. *Major imports*—machinery, petroleum and petroleum products, transportation equipment, electrical equipment, computers. *Major trading partners*—Germany, Japan, United Kingdom, United States.

© Porterfield/Chickering from Photo Researchers

Durban is an important city on South Africa's east coast. Many English colonists settled there in the 1800's, and Durban remains the most English of South Africa's cities in language and culture.

© Gisela Damm, eStock Photo

Cattle graze near the Drakensberg mountains in eastern South Africa. About 45 percent of the country's people reside in rural areas. Many earn their living through agriculture.

Africans call isiNdebele), (4) Sepedi, (5) Sesotho, (6) Swazi (siSwati), (7) Tsonga (xiTsonga), (8) Tswana (seTswana), (9) Venda (tshiVenda), (10) Xhosa (isiXhosa), and (11) Zulu (isiZulu). All these languages except Afrikaans and English are black African languages belonging to the Bantu group. Afrikaans developed from Dutch, but it also has words from other European languages and from Asian and African languages. South African English resembles British English with the addition of some words from Afrikaans and Bantu languages.

About 60 percent of South Africa's white people use Afrikaans as their first language, as do about 80 percent of the Coloured population. The other whites and Coloureds speak English as their first language. Many Black Africans speak Bantu languages, and many also speak English or Afrikaans. Most Indians and Chinese speak English, as well as one or more Asian languages.

For many years, English and Afrikaans were South Africa's only two official languages, and the only two used in government. English remains the chief language used in business, industry, and government. However, by law, all government documents must be printed in at least 2 of the country's 11 official languages. Also, the law calls for spoken government transactions to occur in any official language a speaker chooses.

Ways of life

The differing cultural backgrounds of South Africa's people have created contrasting ways of life. In addition, the inequalities created by apartheid and white domination have profoundly affected how people live.

South Africa's racial groups are no longer segregated by law. But black Africans, Coloureds, and Asians still face much unofficial discrimination. Some schools and housing remain segregated by custom. Whites generally enjoy a higher standard of living than other groups do. A growing number of black Africans, Indians, and Coloureds hold executive and professional positions. But most in these groups struggle to earn a living.

Black Africans. The average *per capita* (per person) income of black Africans is about one-tenth that of whites. Large numbers of black Africans are unemployed, and many lack adequate housing. Many still live in areas that were formerly black homelands.

During the apartheid years, strict controls prevented black Africans from leaving the homelands. Agricultural production in the homelands was difficult because of overcrowding, poor soils, and overgrazed pastureland. Many adults, especially men, sought jobs in the cities to support their families. Only black Africans who found jobs with urban employers were permitted to live temporarily in cities. Even then, apartheid laws restricted them to segregated neighborhoods, many of which were far from the center of town.

In the mid-1980's, the government repealed the laws that kept black Africans out of the cities. In 1994, the government ended the homelands system. Today, about 50 percent of black Africans live in urban areas. Many still live in previously segregated black neighborhoods. Others have moved into formerly all-white neighborhoods. Still others have built makeshift shelters on empty land inside the city limits and on land along major roads leading into the cities.

Whites. About 90 percent of white South Africans live in urban areas. Many whites enjoy a relatively high standard of living. Most white families live in single-family homes in suburban areas, and many employ household help who are not white.

Afrikaners and English-speaking whites have traditionally led separate lives. Many still live in different towns and suburbs, go to different schools, and belong to different churches and other organizations. But these distinctions are gradually breaking down. Before 1994, Afrikaners held most government jobs in South Africa. They still control most of the nation's agriculture. English-speaking whites dominate business and industry.

Coloureds. About 85 percent of South Africa's Coloureds live in cities. The Coloured community began

© David & Peter Turnley, Corbis

Association football (soccer) is South Africa's most popular sport. The country's mild climate enables people to spend much of their leisure time participating in outdoor sports.

© Robin Laurance, Impact Photos

A high school in Germiston, a town near Johannesburg, enrolls students of all races. Many schools in South Africa were once segregated but became racially integrated starting in the 1990's.

in what is now Western Cape, and many Coloureds still live there. In cities, many Coloureds have jobs as servants, factory laborers, or craftworkers. In rural areas, many work in agriculture.

Asians. More than 95 percent of South Africa's Asians live in cities. Indians make up almost all the Asian population. Most Indians live in KwaZulu-Natal. Many are poor and work in factories or grow vegetables for city markets. But some are prosperous doctors, industrialists, lawyers, merchants, and government officials.

Food and drink vary among the people of South Africa. Whites eat foods similar to those eaten by Americans and Europeans. They also enjoy traditional specialties, such as *boerewors,* an Afrikaner sausage. *Braaivleis* (barbecues) are particularly popular. Coloureds have a diet similar to that of whites, but less costly. Indians often cook *curries,* dishes of eggs, fish, meat, or vegetables in a spicy sauce. The basic food of most black Africans is *mealies* (corn), eaten as a porridge. Wealthier black Africans eat the same foods as whites and Coloureds. Many poor people suffer from a shortage of protein and vitamins. Popular beverages include coffee, tea, beer, wine, and soft drinks.

Recreation. Many South Africans love sports, and the country's mild climate enables people to spend much of their leisure time outdoors. Association football (soccer) is the country's most popular sport. Cricket and rugby football are traditional sports among white South Africans, although people of other races also participate. Tennis, bowls (lawn bowling), golf, field hockey, boxing, athletics (track and field), and water sports are popular among all racial groups. Many black Africans excel in boxing and in athletic events, such as long-distance running. On weekends and holidays, city dwellers flock to the beaches or tour their country's national parks and game reserves.

For many years, black and white South Africans had to compete in separate sports events and could not attend the same restaurants and theaters. From the 1970's to 1990, the government slowly lifted these restrictions. Some segregation still exists, especially in private sports clubs, even though it is illegal.

Education. Until 1991, most students attended racially separate public schools where far more money per child was spent to educate white children than black children. Since then, many black children have begun to attend previously all-white public schools. In large cities, schools that were formerly all white have become integrated. South Africa's private schools are integrated.

Many areas—especially rural ones—have a shortage of schools. All children from ages 7 through 16 are required to attend school. Until 1981, the law did not require black children to go to school, and many received little education. Today, about 100 percent of whites, 95 percent of Asians, 90 percent of Coloureds, and 75 percent of black Africans can read and write.

South Africa has 20 universities and 15 *technikons* (vocational schools). There is also a large distance-education university in Pretoria. *Distance education* involves the use of satellites, cable television, the Internet, and other technologies to transmit lectures and educational materials to many locations. Most of South Africa's institutions of higher education were originally segregated. Since the mid-1980's, qualified students of any race may attend any university or technikon that will accept them. An increasing number of black Africans, Indians, and Coloureds attend formerly all-white schools.

Religion. About 75 percent of South Africa's people are Christians. Many of the country's churches belong to the South African Council of Churches, which played an important role in the struggle against apartheid.

About 10 million people belong to *African independent churches.* Nearly all of the 10 million are black Africans. African independent churches combine Christian and traditional African beliefs. The largest African Independent church is the Zion Christian Church, with more than 4 million members.

Most Afrikaners, as well as many Coloureds and black Africans, belong to a family of churches called the Dutch Reformed churches. These churches have nearly 4 million members. Other large Christian churches are the Anglican, Roman Catholic, Methodist, Presbyterian, Congregational, and Lutheran churches. These churches have members from all ethnic groups.

South Africa map index

Provinces

Eastern
Cape ......6,436,790 ..E 4
Free State ..2,726,840 ..D 4
Gauteng ....6,869,103 ..C 5
KwaZulu-
Natal ......8,505,338 ..D 6
Mpuma-
langa ......2,921,559 ..B 6
Northern
Cape ....737,306 ..D 2
Northern
Province ..5,201,630 ..A 6
North West ..3,252,991 ..C 4
Western
Cape ......3,633,077 ..F 2

Cities and towns

Alberton* ....76,642 ..C 5
Alexandra* ....124,586 ..C 5
Amanzimtoti‡ ..13,600 ..D 6
Atteridgeville* ..92,008 ..D 5
Beaufort
West ....16,560 ..E 3
Bellville‡ ....78,822 ..F 1
Benoni* .....113,501 ..C 5
Bethlehem‡ ....12,080 ..C 5
Bisho ....E 5
Bloemfontein ..126,867
†300,150 ..D 5

Boksburg* ....119,890 ..C 5
Brakpan* ....53,522 ..C 5
Cape Town ..854,616
†1,869,144 ..F 1
Carletonville* ..118,699 ..C 5
Ceres‡ ....12,260 ..E 2
Cradock‡ ......11,320 ..E 4
Daveyton* ....151,659 ..C 6
De Aar‡ ....14,940 ..D 4
Diep-
meadow* ....241,099 ..C 5
Dobsonville* ...53,091 ..C 5
Dundee‡ ....9,000 ..C 6
Durban 715,669
†1,106,971 ..D 7
East London ..102,325 ..E 5
Elsies River‡ ...82,045 ..F 2
Empangeni‡ ...12,180 ..D 7
Ermelo‡ ....10,860 ..C 6
Estcourt‡ ......10,340 ..D 6
Evaton* ......201,026 ..C 5
Fort
Beaufort‡ ....6,080 ..E 5
Galeshewe* ...72,118 ..D 4
George‡ ....34,940 ..F 3
Germiston .....134,005 ..C 5
Giyani ....A 6
Graaf-Reinet‡ ..14,700 ..E 4
Grahams-
town‡ ....25,120 ..F 5
Grassy Park* ...52,675 ..F 1
Howick‡ ....10,560 ..D 6

Johannesburg .712,507
†1,907,229 ..C 5
Joubertina* ....74,377 ..F 4
Kathlehong* ..201,785 ..C 5
Kempton
Park* ......106,606 ..C 5
Kimberley 80,082
†167,060 ..D 4
King William's
Town* ....14,260 ..E 5
Klerksdorp ....58,923 ..C 5
Knysna‡ ....12,440 ..F 3
Kroonstad‡ ....20,900 ..C 5
Krugersdorp ...81,584 ..C 5
Kuruman‡ ....8,320 ..C 3
Kwa Nobuhle* ..92,381 ..F 4
Ladysmith‡ .....21,880 ..D 6
Lebowakgomo ....B 6
Lekoa* ......217,582 ..C 5
Lichtenburg‡ ..10,700 ..C 5
Madadeni‡ ....60,940 ..C 6
Mafikeng‡ ......6,500 ..B 4
Mahwele-
reng‡ ....14,500 ..B 6
Mamelodi ....154,845 ..B 6
Manguang ....125,545 ..D 5
Mariannhill‡ ...27,940 ..D 6
Mdantsane‡ ..159,360 ..E 5
Middelburg‡ ...18,600 ..B 6
Mmabatho ....B 4
Mossel Bay‡ ...17,600 ..F 3
Motherwell* ...72,999 ..F 4

Namakgale‡ ...20,040 ..B 7
Nelspruit‡ .....14,660 ..B 7
Newcastle‡ ....34,120 ..C 6
Nigel*‡ ....24,520 ..C 6
Nyanga* ....92,896 ..F 2
Orkney‡ ....18,500 ..C 5
Oudtshoorn‡ ..33,480 ..E 3
Paarl‡ ....73,415 ..F 2
Parow ....68,081 ..F 2
Pietermaritz-
burg 156,473
†211,473 ..D 6
Pietersburg‡ ...25,500 ..B 6
Pinetown ......70,001 ..D 6
Port Alfred‡ ....8,920 ..E 5
Port Elizabeth .303,353
†825,799 ..F 4
Potchefstroom‡ .38,920 ..C 5
Pretoria 525,583
†1,025,790 ..B 5
Prieska‡ ....22,280 ..D 3
Queenstown‡ ..15,060 ..E 5
Randburg* .....90,557 ..C 5
Randfontein* ...51,940 ..C 5
Roodepoort‡ ..162,632 ..C 5
Rustenburg‡ ...30,420 ..B 5
Saldanha ....E 1
Sandton* .....101,197 ..C 5
Seshego‡ ......28,880 ..B 6
Sharpville ....C 5
Somerset
West* ....16,500 ..F 2

Soweto ....596,632 ..C 5
Springbok‡ ......8,180 ..D 1
Springs ....72,647 ..C 6
Standerton‡ ...11,960 ..C 6
Stanger‡ ....14,840 ..D 7
Stellenbosch‡ ..37,680 ..F 2
Strand‡ ....25,260 ..F 2
Stutterheim‡ ...11,480 ..E 5
Thabong* ......88,547 ..C 5
Thohoyandou ....A 6
Tongaat‡ ......24,640 ..D 7
Uitenhage ‡ ...67,581 ..E 4
Ulundi ....C 7
Umlazi‡ ......177,100 ..D 6
Upington‡ .....25,880 ..C 3
Vander-
bijlpark* 67,291
†447,526 ..C 5
Vereeniging ...71,255 ..C 5
Verwoerd-
burg* ....80,552 ..B 5
Virginia‡ ......14,080 ..C 5
Vosloorus* .....76,015 ..C 5
Vredenburg‡ ...27,460 ..E 1
Vryburg‡ ....8,980 ..C 4
Vryheid‡ ......11,260 ..C 6
Welkom ....68,111 ..C 5
Wellington‡ ....21,660 ..E 2
Westonaria* ...57,177 ..C 5
Witbank‡ ......38,600 ..C 6
Worcester‡ ....41,880 ..E 2
Zwelitsha‡ .....29,260 ..E 5

*Does not appear on map; key shows general location.
†Population of metropolitan area, including suburbs.

Sources: 1994 official estimates for provinces; 1991 census; 1980 census where indicated by ‡. Data not available for places without figures.

Kruger National Park in eastern South Africa is a world-famous game reserve. Many wild animals, such as impalas, *shown here*, elephants, lions, and zebras, roam in this park.

A small number of black Africans follow traditional African religions, which often involve prayer to the spirits of ancestors. About 66 percent of Indians are Hindus, 20 percent are Muslims, and 12 percent are Christians. A small number of Coloureds known as Cape Malays are Muslims. Fewer than 100,000 South Africans are Jews.

The arts. South Africa has a National Arts Council that distributes public funds to artists, cultural institutions, and private nonprofit groups. There are state-sponsored theaters in Bloemfontein, Cape Town, Durban, and Pretoria. Private companies also perform in many parts of the country.

South Africa has produced outstanding artists in ballet, music, painting, sculpture, and other fields. One of the best-known performing groups is the black vocal group Ladysmith Black Mambazo. The singers perform in a humming style called *mbube,* which is influenced by European and African American harmonies and vocal traditions but retains black African rhythms.

Much of South Africa's literature reflects its political and social tensions. After the Anglo-Boer War of 1899-1902, Afrikaner poets expressed their sorrow over the British conquest of land occupied by the Afrikaners. These poets included Jan F. E. Celliers, C. F. Louis Leipoldt, Eugène Nielsen Marais, and Jacob Daniel du Toit (also known as Totius). Marais also gained critical praise for his writings on nature.

Since the mid-1900's, many South African writers have dealt with racial themes. They include the poet and essayist Breyten Breytenbach and the novelist André Brink, who both wrote in Afrikaans. Major English-language authors include the novelists Peter Abrahams, J. M. Coetzee, Nadine Gordimer, Es'Kia Mphahlele (also known as Ezekiel Mphahlele), Njabulo S. Ndebele, and Alan Paton; the playwright Athol Fugard; the poets Oswald Mtshali, Sipho Sepamla, and Mongane Wally Serote; and the nonfiction author Mark Mathabane. Gordimer won the 1991 Nobel Prize in literature.

Land and climate

South Africa has five main geographic regions: (1) the Plateau, (2) the Coastal Strip, (3) the Cape Mountains Region, (4) the Namib Desert, and (5) the Kalahari Desert. There are slight climatic variations among these regions, but most of the country has a mild, sunny climate.

The Plateau covers most of the interior of South Africa. In much of the Plateau, summer days are hot, but nights are cool. In winter, the days are crisp and clear, and the nights are cold. Winter temperatures throughout most of the Plateau can drop below freezing.

The Great Escarpment, a semicircular series of cliffs and mountains, rims the Plateau and separates it from the coastal regions. The escarpment reaches its greatest heights—more than 11,000 feet (3,350 meters) above sea level—in the Drakensberg mountain range in the east. The highest point, Champagne Castle, is in the Drakensberg. It stands 11,072 feet (3,375 meters) high.

The Plateau slopes gradually downward from the Great Escarpment. It has three chief subregions: (1) the Highveld, (2) the Middleveld, and (3) the Transvaal Basin. The Highveld occupies all the Plateau except for the northwestern and northeastern corners. It lies mostly between 4,000 and 6,000 feet (1,200 and 1,800 meters) above sea level and consists largely of flat, grass-covered land. In places, flat-topped mountains rise above the plain. The area of the Highveld around Johannesburg is called the Witwatersrand. It covers more than 1,000 square miles (2,600 square kilometers) and has rich gold deposits. This area is the nation's chief industrial and business center. Farmers in the Highveld raise cattle, corn, fruits, potatoes, and wheat.

The Middleveld, in the northwestern Plateau, averages less than 4,000 feet (1,200 meters) above sea level. It is a dry, flat area and serves largely as ranch country.

The Transvaal Basin forms the Plateau's northeastern part. It averages less than 4,000 feet above sea level but has mountain ranges more than 6,000 feet (1,800 meters) high. The area is largely a rolling grassland with scattered thorn trees. Farmers raise citrus and other fruits, corn, and tobacco. Elephants, impalas, leopards, lions, rhinoceroses, zebras, and other wild animals roam in Kruger National Park, a world-famous game reserve. The national park is one of South Africa's most popular tourist attractions.

The Coastal Strip extends along the southeast coast from Mozambique to the Cape Mountains Region. Except in the northeast, the region has little low-lying land. In the Durban area, for example, the land rises to 2,000 feet (610 meters) within 20 miles (32 kilometers) of the sea. Much of the Coastal Strip has hot, humid summers and dry, sunny winters. Chief crops include bananas, citrus fruits, sugar cane, and vegetables. Durban is a major industrial center, port, and resort area.

The Cape Mountains Region stretches from the Coastal Strip to the Namib Desert. Mountain ranges in the west and south meet northeast of the great port city of Cape Town. Between the mountains and the Great Escarpment lie two dry plateaus—the Little Karoo and the Great Karoo. There, farmers grow wine grapes and other fruits on irrigated land. They also grow wheat and raise sheep and ostriches. The Cape Mountains Region has warm, dry summers and cool, wet winters.

The Namib and Kalahari deserts. The Namib lies along the Atlantic Ocean north of the Cape Mountains Region and extends into Namibia. The Kalahari lies north of the Middleveld and extends into Botswana. Small bands of hunters and gatherers used to roam the deserts, living on the plants and animals they found.

Rivers. South Africa's longest river is the Orange River. It begins in Lesotho and flows westward about 1,300 miles (2,100 kilometers) into the Atlantic. The Vaal River, the Orange's largest branch, rises in Mpumalanga. It flows about 750 miles (1,210 kilometers) before joining the Orange in Northern Cape. The Limpopo River begins west of Pretoria and winds about 1,000 miles (1,600 kilometers) across northern and northeastern South Africa and Mozambique before emptying into the Indian Ocean. South Africa also has many shorter rivers. Waterfalls, sand bars, and shallow water make even the longest rivers useless for shipping.

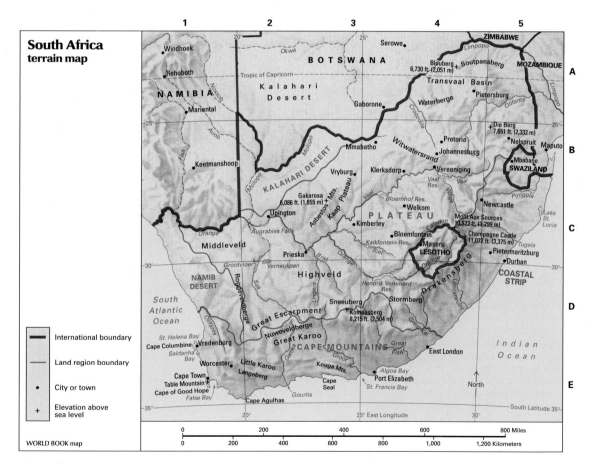

Physical features

Algoa Bay ....E 3	Crocodile River ....A 4	Hendrik Verwoerd	Molopo River ....B 2	St. Francis Bay ....E 3
Asbestos Mountains ....C 3	Die Berg (mountain) .....B 5	Reservoir ....D 3	Mont Aux Sources	St. Helena Bay ....D 1
Augrabies Falls ....C 2	Drakensberg	Highveld (plateau) ......D 3	(mountain) ....C 4	Sneeuberg (range) .....D 3
Bloemhof Reservoir .....C 3	(mountains) ....D 4	Kaap Plateau ....C 3	Namib Desert ....D 1	Table Mountain ....E 1
Blouberg (mountain) ...A 4	False Bay ....E 1	Kalahari Desert ....B 2	Nuweveldberge	Transvaal Basin ....A 4
Caledon River ....C 4	Gakarosa (mountain) ....C 3	Kompasberg	(range) ....D 2	Tugela River ....C 5
Cape Agulhas ....E 2	Great Escarpment ....D 2	(mountain) ....D 3	Olifants River ....A 5	Vaal River ....B 4
Cape Columbine ....E 1	Great Fish River ....E 4	Kouga Mountains ......E 3	Orange River ....C 1	Vaal Reservoir ....B 4
Cape Mountains ....E 3	Great Karoo (plateau) ...D 2	Lake St. Lucia ....C 5	Pongola River ....C 5	Verneukpan (salt flat) ...C 2
Cape of Good Hope .....E 1	Great Kei River ....D 4	Limpopo River ....A 4	Rand, see	Wilge River ....C 4
Champagne Castle	Groot River ....E 3	Little Karoo (plateau) ...E 2	Witwatersrand	Witwatersrand
(mountain) ....C 4	Grootvloer (salt flat) .....D 2	Middleveld (plateau) ....C 1	Saldanha Bay ....E 1	(ridge) ....B 4

Economy

South Africa is the richest, most economically developed country in Africa. It occupies only about 4 percent of the continent's area and has about 5 percent of its people. Yet the value of goods and services that South Africa produces is about 25 percent of the value of goods and services from all African nations combined.

From the 1950's through the 1970's, South Africa experienced spectacular economic growth. Many people from other countries invested in South African businesses. In the 1980's, an economic slowdown and international opposition to apartheid led to the withdrawal of some foreign investments. Some countries reduced or ended trade with South Africa. After the repeal of apartheid in the early 1990's, foreign trade and investment increased. Beginning in the 1990's, however, the AIDS disease spread rapidly and began to hinder growth.

For many years, South Africa's apartheid government owned many businesses and appointed white South Africans to run them. It also passed laws that reserved the best positions in both industry and government for white employees. Today, whites still hold nearly all the executive, professional, and technical jobs. But an increasing number of black Africans, Coloureds, and Indians have moved into these jobs.

Black African workers are generally less educated than whites and receive far lower wages. In 1979, the government for the first time recognized labor unions formed by black African workers. In 1985, many of these unions formed the Congress of South African Trade Unions, which successfully fought for higher wages.

Natural resources. South Africa has long been famous for its vast deposits of gold and diamonds. It also has large supplies of chromite, coal, copper, iron ore, manganese, platinum, silver, and uranium. Although no oil has been discovered in the country, some oil is produced from coal. There are also natural gas deposits near the country's shore.

South Africa is less fortunate in some other natural resources. Only a third of the farmland receives enough rain to grow crops easily. South Africa also has poor forest resources.

Service industries are economic activities that provide services rather than produce goods. Such industries account for more than half of South Africa's *gross domestic product* (GDP), the value of all goods and services produced within the country. They include community, government, and personal services, as well as banking, trade, transportation, and utilities.

Manufacturing. South Africa's chief manufactured products include chemicals, clothing and textiles, iron and steel and other metals, machinery, metal products, motor vehicles, and processed foods. Most factories are in the Cape Town, Durban, Johannesburg, Port Elizabeth, and Pretoria areas.

Mining. Large gold deposits were discovered in South Africa in the 1880's, and gold has been the main force behind the country's growth ever since. Gold mining has attracted huge foreign investments and has led to the development of the transportation and manufacturing facilities in South Africa. Many of the mineworkers come from neighboring countries.

South Africa produces more gold than any other country, supplying about a third of the gold mined in the world each year. South Africa is also a major producer of chromite, coal, copper, diamonds, iron ore, limestone, manganese, phosphate, platinum, uranium, and vanadium.

Agriculture. South Africa's farmers produce almost all the food needed by its people. The leading crops include apples, corn, grapes, oranges, pineapples, potatoes, sugar cane, tobacco, and wheat. South Africa has an extensive sheep industry, and wool is an important agricultural export. Other leading farm products include beef and dairy cattle, chickens, eggs, milk, and wine.

South Africa has two main types of farming—that practiced mainly by whites and that practiced mainly by black Africans. White farmers use modern methods and raise products chiefly for the market. Black farm families produce food mainly for their own needs. Black farms are generally much smaller than white farms. Production on black farms has been extremely low because, for many years, blacks were confined to areas where the

South Africa's gross domestic product

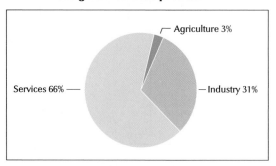

Agriculture 3%

Services 66%

Industry 31%

The gross domestic product (GDP) of South Africa was $131,127,000,000 in 1999. The GDP is the total value of goods and services produced within a country in a year. *Services* include community, government, and personal services; finance, insurance, and real estate; trade, restaurants, and hotels; and transportation and communication. *Industry* includes construction, manufacturing, mining, and utilities. *Agriculture* includes agriculture, forestry, and fishing.

Production and workers by economic activities

Economic activities	Percent of GDP produced	Employed workers	
		Number of people	Percent of total
Community, government, & personal services	23	2,951,000	29
Finance, insurance, real estate & business services	20	931,000	9
Manufacturing	19	1,498,000	14
Trade, restaurants, & hotels	13	2,079,000	20
Transportation & communication	10	539,000	5
Mining	6	476,000	5
Agriculture, forestry, & fishing	3	1,099,000	11
Construction	3	567,000	6
Utilities	3	78,000	1
Total	100	10,218,000	100

Figures are for 1999.
Sources: International Labour Organization; International Monetary Fund.

© Piers Cavendish, Impact Photos

Gold mining has been a major force behind South Africa's economic growth since the 1880's. The country supplies about a third of the gold mined in the world each year.

land was poor. In addition, most black farmers could not afford modern equipment. Since 1994, the government has redistributed some of the country's farmland.

Fishing industry. South Africa's coastal waters yield about 770,000 tons (700,000 metric tons) of fish and shellfish a year. Important catches include anchovies, hake, and herring. Overfishing has reduced the once-plentiful supplies of fish in offshore waters, and so the government has set limits on catching certain types of fish.

Energy sources. Most of South Africa's electric power comes from plants that burn coal. A nuclear power plant near Cape Town produces a small amount of electric power. South Africa imports electric power from Congo (Kinshasa), Mozambique, and Zambia, and cooperates with Lesotho to generate its own hydroelectric power. South Africa exports electric power to other countries in southern Africa.

The country does not produce enough petroleum to support its needs, so it must import oil. South African refineries produce gasoline and other fuels from coal.

International trade. South Africa's chief trade partners—besides other African countries—include Germany, Japan, the United Kingdom, and the United States. Chief exports include gold, diamonds, metals and minerals, wool, corn, sugar, and fruits. Machinery and transportation equipment make up nearly half the value of the country's imports. Other imports include chemicals, manufactured goods, and petroleum.

Transportation. South Africa has the best transportation system in Africa. Paved roads crisscross much of the country. Most roads in the former black homelands remain unpaved. Most white families own at least one automobile. Most blacks rely on buses and trains. The country's freight and long-distance passenger railroads are operated by a government-owned company called Spoornet. South African Airways, British Airways Comair, and other airlines provide domestic and international service. Cape Town, Durban, and Johannesburg have major airports. South Africa has six large, well-equipped seaports—Cape Town, Durban, East London, Port Elizabeth, Richards Bay, and Saldanha.

Communication. The *Sowetan,* published in Johannesburg, is an English-language newspaper for black Africans. It has the largest circulation of any daily paper in the country. Other large English-language dailies are *The Star* and *The Citizen,* also published in Johannesburg, and *Cape Argus,* published in Cape Town. The largest Afrikaans-language dailies are *Beeld* of Johannesburg and *Die Burger* of Cape Town.

A government agency called the Independent Broadcasting Authority (IBA) directs the licensing and regulating of all radio and television stations. The South African Broadcasting Corporation (SABC) provides most of the country's public broadcasting. The country also has privately owned stations. Radio and TV shows are broadcast in English, Afrikaans, and a number of black African languages. The government runs the postal and telegraph systems. In 1997, it partially privatized the national telephone company.

History

Early days. For thousands of years, the San, who were descendants of prehistoric Africans, were the only inhabitants of the region. They moved about in small bands hunting animals and gathering wild plants for food. Around the A.D. 100's, a related group called the Khoikhoi began to move into the area from the north. By about 500, they occupied what is now western South Africa. The Khoikhoi raised cattle and sheep and settled in communities. The other group lived by hunting and gathering. When Europeans arrived in the 1600's, they called the San *Bushmen* and the Khoikhoi *Hottentots.* Both of these European terms are now considered offensive. The two groups have come to be known collectively as the Khoisan.

In the A.D. 200's, peoples who spoke various Bantu languages began to move into the area that is now eastern South Africa. These groups migrated from the north. They raised cattle, grew grain, made tools and weapons out of iron, and traded among themselves.

By the 500's, some Bantu-speaking people had begun to group together and form chiefdoms. Each chiefdom was headed by a wealthy chief who regulated trade, controlled cattle ownership, and settled disputes. Within the chiefdoms, senior men exercised authority over individual homesteads. After the 1200's, some chiefdoms grew to become powerful. Such chiefdoms included those of the Sotho-Tswana and those of the Nguni.

Arrival of Europeans. Portuguese sailors were the first Europeans to see what is now South Africa. They sighted it in 1488, when they rounded the Cape of Good Hope in their search for a sea route east to India.

The first European settlers arrived in 1652. They worked for the Dutch East India Company, a powerful Dutch trading company. The company sent the settlers, headed by Jan van Riebeeck, to set up a base at the present site of Cape Town. The base was to serve as a station where company ships could pick up supplies on the way to and from the East Indies. The company imported slaves—mostly from Southeast Asia—to do manual labor at the base and to work on its nearby farms.

Starting in 1657, the Dutch East India Company allowed some employees to start their own farms. These people became known as *Boers* (farmers). In 1679, the company also began to offer free passage and land to new settlers from Europe. More Dutch farmers, as well as French and German settlers, arrived. By 1700, whites occupied most of the good farmland around Cape Town. Then, they moved into drier areas and became sheep and cattle ranchers. As the white territory expanded, the Khoikhoi and San population declined. White settlers killed some in conflicts and forced many others out of the area. Many Khoikhoi and San also died of diseases, such as smallpox. Most survivors became servants of the whites and intermarried with them.

During this period, the Dutch language spoken in the area began to change. It incorporated words and sounds from the languages of other European settlers, and from Southeast Asian slaves and San and Khoikhoi servants. A new language, called Afrikaans, developed.

About 1770, white settlers spread into the area occupied by the Xhosa, a Bantu-speaking people, in what is now Eastern Cape. The whites called the Xhosa *Kaffirs,* which is now considered an offensive term. Between 1779 and 1879, the settlers and the Xhosa fought several wars in which the settlers took land from the Xhosa.

By the end of the 1700's, the whites had spread about 300 miles (480 kilometers) north and more than 500 miles (800 kilometers) east of Cape Town. The area became a colony known as the Cape Colony. It had a total population of about 60,000. Nearly 20,000 were whites. The rest consisted mostly of Khoikhoi, San, and slaves.

The Zulu and the Mfecane. Between 1818 and 1828, the Zulu kingdom grew to be the most powerful black African kingdom in southern Africa. This kingdom, established by the Zulu leader Shaka, covered most of what is now KwaZulu-Natal. It incorporated a number of Nguni chiefdoms. As the Zulu kingdom grew in size and power, many Nguni peoples fled to other parts of southeastern Africa. The refugees often came into conflict with other peoples during their migrations. This period of forced migrations and battles, known as the *Mfecane* (or *Difaqane),* led to the emergence of new kingdoms, including the Sotho, Swazi, and Ndebele. Other groups, however, were wiped out. The destruction and chaos caused by the Mfecane made it easier for white settlers to eventually expand eastward from the Cape.

British rule. In 1795, after France conquered the Netherlands, British troops occupied the Cape Colony to keep it out of French hands. The British returned the colony to the Dutch in 1803 but reoccupied it in 1806. A treaty between the British and the Dutch in 1814 formally recognized the Cape as a British colony. Thousands of British settlers arrived in 1820. They occupied land that the previous white settlers had taken from the Xhosa.

The Boers soon came to resent British colonial rule. The government made English the colony's only official language in 1828. That same year, the Khoikhoi and Coloured people received the same legal rights as whites. In 1834, the United Kingdom freed all slaves throughout its empire, ruining a number of Boer farmers who depended on slave labor to work their fields.

Many Boers decided to leave the Cape Colony to get away from British rule. Beginning in 1836, several thousand made a historic journey called the Great Trek. They loaded their belongings into ox-drawn covered wagons and headed inland. They traveled into lands occupied by Bantu-speaking peoples, including the Zulu kingdom. The Boers defeated the Zulu and other groups and set-

tled in what became Natal, the Orange Free State, and the Transvaal. The British annexed Natal in 1843 but recognized Boer independence in the Transvaal in 1852 and in the Orange Free State in 1854. In 1858, the Boers in the Transvaal named their government the South African Republic, or SAR.

In Natal and the Boer republics, whites claimed the best land and steadily extended their control over black Africans and Coloureds. In Natal, the British imported Indians to work as indentured laborers on sugar plantations.

Discovery of diamonds and gold. In the late 1860's, diamonds were discovered in South Africa. The richest deposits were found at the site of present-day Kimberley. Miners and fortune seekers from the United Kingdom and elsewhere flocked to the area. Both the British and the Boers claimed the area. In 1871, the United Kingdom annexed it, and it became part of the Cape Colony.

Diamonds began an economic revolution in South Africa and made the region more strategically and commercially important to the United Kingdom. To strengthen its authority over the region, the United Kingdom annexed the Transvaal in 1877.

The British also extended their authority over black African chiefdoms that were still independent. By 1879, the British had conquered the Xhosa, and the Zulu kingdom remained the region's only major African state. The British saw the Zulu as a threat to the eventual confederation of South Africa's colonies, and so they invaded Zulu territory in January 1879. Although the Zulu defeated the British at Isandhlwana later that month, the British army crushed the Zulu in July. By 1898, British rule extended over all independent black African groups.

In 1880, the Transvaal Boers rose in revolt against the British in the Anglo-Boer War of 1880-1881. This struggle is also called the Anglo-Transvaal War. After several victories, the Boers finally defeated the British in a battle on Majuba Hill in 1881. The British agreed to withdraw from the Transvaal. The Boers thus regained independence in the Transvaal and again named it the South African Republic (SAR).

In 1886, the Witwatersrand gold field was discovered north of the Vaal River, where Johannesburg now stands. Fortune seekers rushed to the area. By 1895, these *Uitlanders* (foreigners) made up about half of the SAR's white male population. To maintain control, the Boers restricted the political rights of the Uitlanders, most of whom were British. As a result, tension grew between the United Kingdom and the SAR.

In 1895, Cecil Rhodes, the prime minister of the Cape Colony, plotted to overthrow the government of the SAR. He sent a force led by Leander Jameson, a Scottish-born government administrator, to invade the republic. But the Boers captured the invaders, and the so-called Jameson Raid failed. Relations between the British and the SAR grew more strained. In 1899, the SAR and the Orange Free State declared war on the United Kingdom. During the Anglo-Boer War of 1899-1902 (often called the Boer War or the South African War), the Boers fought bravely against huge odds. They finally surrendered in 1902. The two Boer republics then became British colonies.

The Union of South Africa. The United Kingdom gave colonial self-government to the Transvaal in 1906 and to the Orange Free State in 1907. The Cape Colony and Natal already had self-rule. In 1910, the four colonies formed the Union of South Africa, a self-governing country within the British Empire. The Union's Constitution gave whites almost complete power.

Several black African, Coloured, and Indian groups tried to defend themselves against repression by the white government. A lawyer from India, Mohandas K. Gandhi, worked for greater rights for Indians in South Africa. Gandhi urged the Indians to defy unjust laws, such as a law requiring them to register and be fingerprinted. Gandhi's methods of nonviolent resistance resulted in the Indians' gaining some additional rights. Using the same methods, Gandhi later helped India gain independence from British rule.

Gandhi's example helped inspire black Africans to found the South African Native National Congress (SANNC) in 1912. The SANNC's purpose was to work for black African rights. In 1923, the SANNC shortened its name to the African National Congress (ANC).

In World War I (1914-1918), the British Empire and its allies fought the Central Powers, led by Austria-Hungary and Germany. Two Boer generals, Louis Botha and Jan Christiaan Smuts, led South African forces against Germany. Botha seized German South West Africa (now Namibia) from Germany in 1915, and Smuts drove the Germans from German East Africa (now Tanzania) in 1917. In 1920, the League of Nations, a forerunner of the United Nations, gave South Africa control of South West Africa. Botha and Smuts were the first prime ministers of the Union of South Africa. Botha served from 1910 to 1919. Smuts served from 1919 to 1924, and from 1939 to 1948.

The rise of Afrikaner nationalism. Botha and Smuts had fought the British in the Anglo-Boer War of 1899-1902. But as prime ministers, they tried to unite Afrikaners (as the Boers came to be called) and English-speaking whites. Many Afrikaner authors and religious leaders, however, urged their people to consider themselves a nation. They said Afrikaners had a heroic history, a rich culture, and a God-given mission to rule South Africa. In 1914, James Barry Munnik Hertzog, another Boer general who had fought the British, founded the National Party to promote these ideas.

In 1924, the National Party and the Labour Party joined forces and won control of the government. Hertzog became prime minister. During the next 15 years, he achieved many Afrikaner goals. Afrikaans became an official language along with English. Industries were developed to reduce dependence on British imports. In 1931, South Africa gained full independence as a member of the Commonwealth of Nations, an association of the United Kingdom and some of its former colonies.

In 1934, Hertzog joined with Smuts to form a United Party government. Whites benefited under this coalition government, but black Africans did not. For example, black Africans in Cape Province, who had retained the right to vote after the Union was formed, lost most of their voting rights. The government also passed laws that made it difficult for black Africans to live in cities. In contrast, it made city jobs available for poor Afrikaners, who were leaving their farms in search of work.

Cooperation between Smuts and Hertzog ended at the start of World War II (1939-1945). Hertzog wanted South Africa to be neutral. But Smuts wanted the country to join the United Kingdom and the other Allies against Germany. Smuts won the bitter debate in Parliament and became prime minister again in 1939. During the war, South Africans fought in Ethiopia, northern Africa, and Europe. After the war, South Africa became a founding member of the United Nations (UN).

Apartheid. During World War II, Daniel François Malan, a strong supporter of Afrikaner nationalism, reorganized the National Party. The party came to power, under Malan, in 1948. It began the apartheid program, under which racial groups were legally segregated and given different rights and privileges. Hendrik F. Verwoerd, who served as minister of native affairs from 1950 to 1958 and prime minister from 1958 to 1966, was the main architect of the apartheid state. His government began a program that gave the police and the military extensive powers to enforce apartheid.

Opposition to the Nationalists' racial policies grew. The ANC played the main role in this opposition. In the 1950's, the ANC, along with Coloured and Indian groups and white liberals, demanded reforms through boycotts, rallies, and strikes. The government crushed each campaign. In 1959, some black Africans left the ANC and formed the Pan-Africanist Congress (PAC) because they opposed the ANC's alliances with white groups. They wanted an all-black government instead. PAC first targeted the laws that required black Africans to carry *passes* (identity papers). These laws restricted black Africans from moving freely around the country. PAC leaders told blacks to appear on March 21, 1960, at police stations without their passes—and so invite arrest. In most places, the police broke up the crowd without incident. But at Sharpeville, near Johannesburg, the police

Important dates in South Africa

A.D. 200's Bantu-speaking farmers began to enter eastern South Africa from the north. They were the ancestors of present-day South Africa's black African population.
1652 The first Dutch settlers arrived at the site of Cape Town.
1814 The Cape Colony officially became a British colony.
1818-1828 The Zulu leader Shaka built a powerful kingdom in present-day KwaZulu-Natal.
1836 Boers left Cape Colony on the Great Trek.
1843 Natal became a British colony.
1852 The Transvaal became a Boer republic.
1854 The Orange Free State became a Boer republic.
1867 Diamonds were discovered near what is now Kimberley.
1877 The United Kingdom annexed the Transvaal.
1879 The United Kingdom defeated the Zulu kingdom.
1880-1881 The Transvaal Boers defeated the British in the first Anglo-Boer War (also called the Anglo-Transvaal War).
1886 Gold was discovered near Johannesburg.
1899-1902 The United Kingdom defeated the Boers in the second Anglo-Boer War (also called the Boer War or South African War).
1910 The Union of South Africa was formed.
1912 Black Africans founded the African National Congress.
1948-1994 The National Party governed South Africa.
1961 South Africa became a republic.
1976 Black Africans began widespread protests against the South African government.
1990-1991 The South African government repealed many laws that had formed the legal basis of apartheid.
1994 South Africa held its first all-race elections. Nelson Mandela was elected as the nation's first black president.
1999 Thabo Mbeki succeeded Mandela as the second democratically elected president.

opened fire and killed 69 black Africans. The government then banned both the ANC and PAC.

Opposition to apartheid also came from outside South Africa. Many leaders of the Commonwealth of Nations strongly criticized South Africa's apartheid policies. On May 31, 1961, South Africa became a republic and left the Commonwealth. In 1966, the UN voted to end the country's control over South West Africa. South Africa called the UN action illegal and ignored it.

In the 1960's, South Africa's government introduced its homeland policy. In an attempt to make South Africa a "white" nation, the government set aside separate areas for each racial group. The government granted limited self-rule—and in some cases, full independence—to the black African homelands (also called *bantustans).*

Verwoerd was killed in 1966 by a mentally ill government messenger. Apartheid policies continued under Verwoerd's successor, Balthazar Johannes Vorster. By the 1970's, opposition to white rule was increasing both inside and outside the country. In June 1976, thousands of black African schoolchildren in Soweto marched to protest a policy that required some of their classes to be taught in Afrikaans. Police opened fire on the children, killing one and wounding several of them. Disturbances followed in many parts of the country, and several clashes erupted between black Africans and the police. More than 600 people, almost all of them blacks, were killed.

The dismantling of apartheid. Vorster's successor, Pieter Willem Botha, realized that apartheid was causing South Africa's economy to suffer. In the late 1970's, the Botha government repealed some apartheid laws. It lifted restrictions against multiracial sports. It also abolished most of the *job reservation system,* which had reserved certain jobs for certain races.

In an attempt to gain Coloured and Indian support, Botha proposed a new constitution. White South Africans approved it in 1983, and it went into effect in 1984. The new Constitution restructured Parliament to include representation for whites, Coloureds, and Indians. The Constitution also combined the offices of the prime minister and state president under the office of state president. Botha became state president.

The new Constitution, like the one it replaced, made no provision for black African representation in Parliament or in other parts of the national government. Also, like the old Constitution, it excluded black Africans from voting in national elections. To protest their exclusion from the government, blacks staged numerous labor strikes, demonstrations, and riots. The protesters targeted not only whites but also blacks in the police force and other blacks regarded as government collaborators. Many people, mostly blacks, were killed in these clashes. At the same time, military branches of the ANC and PAC carried out guerrilla attacks on government targets.

In an attempt to maintain control and stop the violence, the South African government declared a national state of emergency in 1986. Under the state of emergency, the government was allowed to arrest and hold people without charging them.

Many countries expressed opposition to apartheid by reducing economic ties with South Africa. In 1986, the European Community, the Commonwealth of Nations, and the United States enacted *sanctions* (bans) on certain kinds of trade with South Africa. Some companies

© Mike Persson, Getty Images

Nelson Mandela, *left,* takes the oath of office for the presidency of South Africa in May 1994. Mandela was elected president in the country's first elections open to all races.

ended or limited their business in South Africa.

In 1986, the South African government repealed more apartheid laws. It permitted black Africans, Coloureds, and Asians to attend white universities. The government also permitted interracial marriages, which apartheid laws had forbidden. It repealed the laws requiring black Africans to carry passes and allowed them to live in cities without special permission. As a result, more than 1 million black Africans moved to the cities. But many apartheid regulations continued. Black Africans were still excluded from participation in government.

In 1988, after several years of talks with major Western powers, South Africa agreed to withdraw from Namibia. In 1990, Namibia gained full independence.

In 1989, F. W. de Klerk became state president. De Klerk realized that white minority rule could not continue in South Africa without great risk of civil war.

In February 1990, de Klerk ended South Africa's state of emergency and lifted the bans on political organizations, including the ANC and PAC. Later that month, de Klerk released Nelson Mandela, the most famous member of the ANC, from prison. Mandela had been arrested in 1962 and sentenced to life imprisonment in 1964 for sabotage and conspiracy against the South African government. While in prison, Mandela had become a symbol of the black struggle for racial justice. In May 1990, the government held its first formal talks with the ANC. Mandela met with de Klerk several times after that to discuss political change in South Africa.

Despite these events, violence continued in South Africa. Some violence resulted from white reactions to de Klerk's reforms, and other fighting broke out between rival black African groups. Much of the violence occurred between supporters of the Xhosa-dominated ANC and the Zulu-dominated Inkatha Freedom Party. Thousands of people were killed in the conflicts.

In 1990 and 1991, the South African government repealed most of the remaining laws that had formed the legal basis of apartheid. In 1991, the government, the ANC, and other groups began holding talks on a new constitution. In 1993, the government adopted an interim constitution that gave South Africa's blacks full voting rights. The country held its first elections open to all races in 1994. The ANC won nearly two-thirds of the seats in the National Assembly, and the Assembly then elected Nelson Mandela president. After the elections, politically motivated violence decreased. In 1994, South Africa resumed full participation in the UN and rejoined the Commonwealth.

Recent developments. In 1995, the government appointed a panel called the Truth and Reconciliation Commission to gather information about human rights violations during the apartheid years. Desmond Tutu, a former Anglican archbishop and winner of the 1984 Nobel Peace Prize, headed the commission. In its final report in 1998, the commission said the apartheid-era government had committed "gross violations of human rights," including kidnapping and murders. The report also criticized opposition groups, including the ANC, holding them responsible for killings and torture.

In 1996, South Africa adopted a new Constitution. It provides for a strong presidency and includes a wide-ranging bill of rights. Among the rights it guarantees are freedom of religion, belief, and opinion; freedom of expression, including freedom of the press; and freedom of political activity. It also establishes the right to adequate housing, food, water, education, and health care.

In 1997, Mandela resigned as head of the ANC. He was replaced in that position by South Africa's deputy president, Thabo Mbeki. In 1999, Mandela retired as president of South Africa. In elections that year, the ANC won a majority in the National Assembly. The Assembly elected Mbeki president.

During the 1990's, AIDS became a major problem in South Africa. More people in South Africa are infected with HIV, the virus that causes AIDS, than in any other country. By 2000, more than 10 percent of the population was infected with HIV.   Christopher Saunders

Related articles include:

Biographies

Barnard, Christiaan Neethling	De Klerk, Frederik Willem
Biko, Steve	Fugard, Athol
Botha, Louis	Gandhi, Mohandas Karamchand
Botha, Pieter Willem	Gordimer, Nadine

Hertzog, James Barry Munnik	Paton, Alan
Kruger, Paulus	Rhodes, Cecil John
Luthuli, Albert John	Shaka
Mandela, Nelson	Smuts, Jan Christiaan
Masekela, Hugh	Tutu, Desmond
Mbeki, Thabo	Vorster, Balthazar

Cities

Bloemfontein	Johannesburg	Port Elizabeth
Cape Town	Kimberley	Pretoria
Durban	Pietermaritzburg	

People

Afrikaners	Khoikhoi	Xhosa
Bantu	San	Zulu

Physical features

Cape of Good Hope	Kalahari Desert	Limpopo River
Drakensberg	Kruger National Park	Orange River
		Walvis Bay

Other related articles

Africa	Drakensberg	Orange Free State
African National Congress	Inkatha Freedom Party	Transvaal
Apartheid	Lesotho	United Nations (Working for self-government)
Boer War	Namibia	
Cape Province	Natal	

Outline

I. Government
A. National government
B. Provincial government
C. Local government
D. Political parties
E. Armed forces

II. People
A. Racial and ethnic groups
B. Languages

III. Ways of life
A. Food and drink
B. Recreation
C. Education
D. Religion
E. The arts

IV. Land and climate
A. The Plateau
B. The Coastal Strip
C. The Cape Mountains Region
D. The Namib and Kalahari deserts
E. Rivers

V. Economy
A. Natural resources
B. Service industries
C. Manufacturing
D. Mining
E. Agriculture
F. Fishing industry
G. Energy sources
H. International trade
I. Transportation
J. Communication

VI. History

Questions

How did South Africa achieve spectacular industrial growth?
What land region covers most of South Africa's interior?
What was apartheid? How did it affect black Africans, Coloureds, and Indians in South Africa?
Who were the Boers?
How does South Africa rank economically in Africa?
How does life differ among South Africa's racial groups?
What was the Great Trek?
What are some black African ethnic groups in South Africa?
When was the African National Congress founded?
Who elects South Africa's president?

Additional resources

Beck, Roger B. *The History of South Africa.* Greenwood, 2000.
Fox, Roddy C., and Rowntree, Kate, eds. T*he Geography of South Africa in a Changing World.* Oxford, 2000.
Nagle, Garrett. *South Africa.* Heinemann Lib., 1999. Younger readers.
Thompson, Leonard M. *A History of South Africa.* 3rd ed. Yale, 2001.

© Giacomo Pirozzi, Panos Pictures

AIDS prevention is a major goal in South Africa, where over 10 percent of the population is infected with the virus that causes the disease. These boys are reading a pamphlet about AIDS.

Turkey has many towering mountains and barren plains. Mount Ararat, *shown here,* is part of the Anatolian Plateau, an area of dry highlands that stretches across central Turkey. The peak is Turkey's highest point, rising 16,849 feet (5,137 meters) above sea level near Turkey's border with Iran.

Turkey

Turkey is a Middle Eastern country that lies both in Europe and in Asia. About 3 percent of Turkey lies in Thrace, at the eastern edge of southern Europe. To the east, the rest of Turkey covers a large, mountainous peninsula called Anatolia or Asia Minor. Istanbul, Turkey's largest city, lies on both sides of the Bosporus (also spelled Bosphorus), a narrow body of water separating Thrace and Anatolia.

Turkey borders Bulgaria and Greece on the northwest; Georgia, Armenia, Azerbaijan, and Iran on the east; and Iraq and Syria on the southeast. The Black Sea lies to the north, the Aegean Sea to the west, and the Mediterranean Sea to the south.

Three bodies of water—the Bosporus, the Sea of Marmara, and the Dardanelles—separate Anatolia from Thrace. The Bosporus and the Dardanelles, often called the Straits, have played a major role in Turkey's history. By its control of the Straits, Turkey could regulate ship movement between the Mediterranean and Black seas.

Turkey has several large cities, including Istanbul and Ankara, Turkey's capital, and areas of rich farmland. But much of the country is rocky, barren, and mountainous.

Caglar Keyder, the contributor of this article, is Professor of Sociology at the State University of New York at Binghamton and Adjunct Professor of Sociology at Bogazici University in Istanbul, Turkey.

About two-thirds of Turkey's people live in cities or towns. Most of the rest live in villages. Nearly all the people are Muslims—that is, followers of Islam. Turkey is a developing country, and nearly half of its workers are farmers. But the economy has become increasingly industrialized since the 1950's. Manufacturing now contributes more to national income than does agriculture.

Various Asian and European peoples have ruled what is now Turkey since ancient times. During the A.D. 1300's, a group of Muslim Turks called the Ottomans be-

Facts in brief

Capital: Ankara.
Official language: Turkish.
Official name: Türkiye Cumhuriyeti (Republic of Turkey).
Area: 299,158 mi² (774,815 km²). *Greatest distances*—east-west, 1,015 mi (1,633 km); north-south, 465 mi (748 km). *Coastline*—2,211 mi (3,558 km).
Elevation: *Highest*—Mount Ararat, 16,849 ft (5,137 m) above sea level. *Lowest*—sea level along the coast.
Population: *Estimated 2002 population*—68,509,000; population density, 229 per mi² (88 per km²); distribution, 66 percent urban, 34 percent rural. *1990 census*—56,473,035.
Chief products: *Agriculture*—barley, corn, cotton, fruits, potatoes, sugar beets, wheat. *Manufacturing*—fertilizers, iron and steel, machinery, motor vehicles, processed foods and beverages, pulp and paper products, textiles and clothing.
National anthem: "Istiklâl Marsi" ("Independence March").
Money: *Basic unit*—lira. One hundred kurus equal one lira.

© Pietro Cenini, Panos Pictures

Istanbul, Turkey's largest city, is divided by a waterway called the Golden Horn, *front,* an inlet of the Bosporus. Two of the city's fine *mosques* (Islamic houses of worship) are the New Mosque, *center,* and the Mosque of Süleyman I, *background.*

gan to build a powerful empire that eventually controlled much of the Middle East, southeastern Europe, and northern Africa. The Ottoman Empire ended in 1922. The next year, Turkey became a republic.

Islamic law had strongly influenced Turkish life for nearly 1,000 years. Beginning in the 1920's, however, Turkey's new republican government introduced sweeping cultural and political changes that discouraged or outlawed many traditional Islamic practices. Most people accepted the changes, but others, especially in rural areas, resisted them. Turkey's people continue to debate the role of Islam in Turkish life.

Government

Turkey is a republic. Its current Constitution was adopted in 1982, following two years of military rule. The Constitution provides for a parliamentary form of government that includes a president, a prime minister and cabinet, and a legislature called the Grand National Assembly. The charter protects state institutions against criticism and attack from citizens. It does not provide for full freedom of speech and other basic rights.

National government. Executive power in Turkey is shared by the president and the prime minister. The president is Turkey's head of state and commander in chief of the armed forces. The Grand National Assembly elects the president to a seven-year term.

The prime minister is Turkey's head of government and directs the day-to-day operation of the government. The president selects the prime minister from among the most influential members of the legislature. General-

ly, the leader of the party with the most legislative seats becomes prime minister. Members of the cabinet, called the Council of Ministers, are nominated by the prime minister and appointed by the president. The ministers supervise the government departments.

The Grand National Assembly makes Turkey's laws, ratifies treaties, and has the power to declare war. The Assembly consists of 550 deputies elected by the voters to five-year terms.

Court system. Courts throughout Turkey handle commercial disputes, family law, criminal trials, and other cases. Appeals courts review the decisions of lower courts. The Constitutional Court determines the legality of laws passed by the legislature.

Local government. Turkey is divided into about 80 provinces. Each province has a governor appointed by the president and a council elected by the province's voters. Provinces are divided into counties, districts, and villages. Settlements with more than 2,000 people are organized as municipalities. The mayor and municipal council are elected by the people of the municipality.

Political parties. Turkey has a number of political parties. Among the largest are the center-right Motherland and True Path parties, the center-left Democratic Left Party, a Turkish nationalist party called the Nationalist Action Party, and a pro-Islamic party.

Armed forces. About 610,000 men serve in Turkey's army, navy, and air force. At some time between the ages of 20 and 32, all men are drafted for service of up to 18 months. The military has high status in Turkey and can, in effect, overrule certain government decisions.

Turkey's flag was adopted in 1936. The crescent and five-pointed star are traditional symbols of the Islamic faith.

WORLD BOOK map

Turkey is a country in the Middle East. It covers the peninsula of Asia Minor, also called Anatolia. In addition, a small part of Turkey occupies a region called Thrace in southeastern Europe.

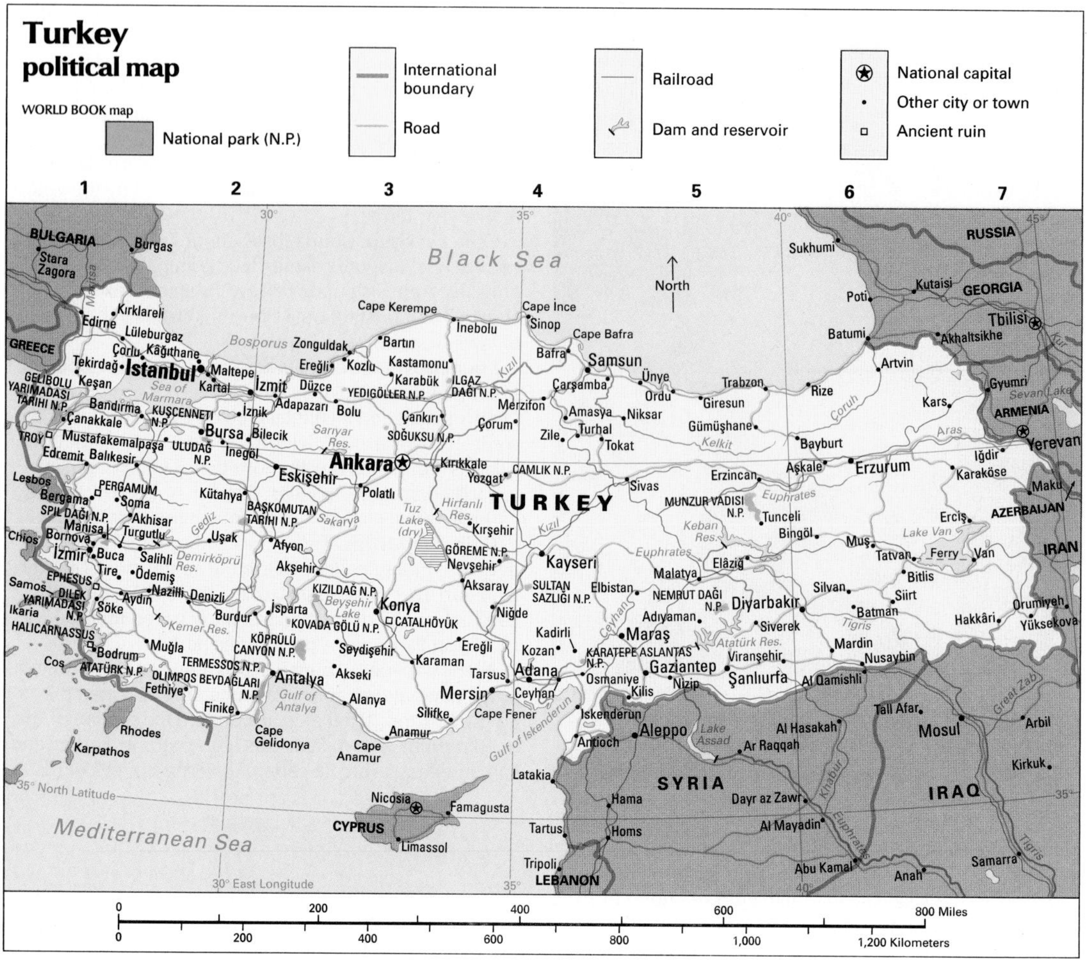

Turkey
political map

WORLD BOOK map

	International boundary		Railroad		National capital
	Road		Dam and reservoir		Other city or town
National park (N.P.)					Ancient ruin

1　　　2　　　3　　　4　　　5　　　6　　　7

0	200	400	600	800 Miles
0	200 400	600	800	1,000 1,200 Kilometers

Turkey map index

Cities and towns

*Does not appear on map; key shows general location.　　Source: 1990 census.

© Adam Woolfitt, Woodfin Camp, Inc.

Ankara became Turkey's capital when the Republic of Turkey was established in 1923. A statue of Kemal Atatürk, the founder of the republic, stands on this Ankara street.

People

Most of Turkey's people live in cities and towns. The number of urban dwellers has increased rapidly since the 1940's. Hundreds of thousands of people have left their farms and villages to seek work in the cities. But the cities do not have enough jobs for all the people. In the 1960's and 1970's, many of Turkey's people went abroad to work. More than 3 million Turkish citizens live in European countries, especially Germany. Other countries where Turkish citizens work include other Middle Eastern countries and Australia.

Ancestry. More than 80 percent of Turkey's people consider themselves descendants of a people called Turks. The Turks began migrating from central Asia to Anatolia during the A.D. 900's. Kurds form Turkey's largest minority group, with about 15 percent of the population. Many Kurds live in mountainous regions in the southeast. Arabs, most of whom are farmers, live near the Syrian border. Caucasians—people whose ancestors came from the Caucasus Mountains region just northeast of Turkey—live in the provinces bordering the Black Sea. Greeks, Armenians, and Jews live mostly in the Istanbul area. During the 1800's and 1900's, many Greeks and Armenians left Turkey, either voluntarily or by force.

Languages. Most people speak Turkish, the country's official language. Many Kurds speak Kurdish. Small groups of people speak Arabic, Armenian, Circassian, Greek, or other minority languages.

The government began to develop the modern Turkish language during the late 1920's. For hundreds of years, the written language was Ottoman Turkish, a complicated language written in Arabic characters and using some Persian and Arabic vocabulary. The Arabic alphabet had no letters to represent many sounds used in spoken Turkish. Ottoman Turkish was so difficult that only scholars and the ruling class learned to read it. In 1928, the government established a new alphabet and eliminated most foreign words from the language.

Way of life

In the 1920's, when the Republic of Turkey was established, the government set out to make Turkey a modern state. Government officials began a program to sweep away the customs and traditions of centuries.

One of the government's major goals has been to change the status of women in Turkish life. Men have dominated Turkish society for hundreds of years. Before the 1920's, women had almost no civil rights. Parents arranged the marriages of their daughters by means of a contract with the groom's family. Women could not vote and had difficulty getting a divorce. During the 1920's, the government outlawed the arrangement of marriages by contract, made it easier for women to get a divorce, and gave women the right to vote. Today, increased educational opportunities are gradually improving the position of Turkish women. Women now make up about 40 percent of all university students in Turkey.

The government also tried to bring the Kurds and other tribal people into the mainstream of Turkish life. Many Kurds lived in tribal groups as nomads or in isolated communities for centuries. During the 1920's, the government began to force these people to abandon their tribal way of life as a means of modernizing Turkish society. The Kurds revolted against these attempts several times in the 1920's and 1930's. Since then, many Kurds have adopted modern Turkish culture. The majority of Kurds now live in large cities. Others are settled in rural villages, where they farm or raise livestock.

City life. The look of most Turkish cities has changed greatly since the mid-1900's. Much new construction has taken place to accommodate the growing population. Most cities are dominated by small factories, retail shops, restaurants, and professional offices. The western part of Turkey has several important industrial cities, such as İzmit and Bursa. Large parts of the cities have many poor people and lack basic services.

© Max Engel, Woodfin Camp, Inc.

Kurds, shown here performing a traditional dance, rank as Turkey's largest minority group. They make up about 15 percent of the population. Many Kurds live in Turkey's mountain areas.

Rural life has changed rapidly since the 1980's. Almost all villages have electric power and telephone connections. Most rural households have a television set and a refrigerator. Villagers in the western regions and on the southern coast are generally well off. Much more poverty exists in the mountainous eastern area and in parts of the northern Black Sea region.

Housing varies throughout Turkey. Peasants who live near the Black Sea build thatch-roofed cottages with timber from nearby forests. Many villagers in central Anatolia live in flat-roofed houses of sun-dried brick. Stone houses are common in southern and western Anatolia. In rural areas of Turkey, many people have replaced their old traditional homes with one-story houses of cinder blocks. New urban construction throughout Turkey is mostly reinforced concrete and brick.

Most wealthy Turks own comfortable private apartments in the city centers, on the outskirts, or in the suburbs. Most middle-class city dwellers live in apartment buildings. The rapid growth of the cities has created neighborhoods of low-quality, makeshift housing. These shantytowns lack good roads and basic services.

Clothing worn in Turkey changed dramatically during the 1920's. The government discouraged or forbade the wearing of certain garments required by Islamic custom. City dwellers and many rural people then adopted Western clothing styles. But some rural people still follow Islamic tradition. A few men wear the traditional loose-fitting cloak and baggy trousers. Some peasant women wear a simple blouse and pantaloons. They cover their head and sometimes the lower part of their face with a scarf as a sign of modesty. A few women, especially in the poorer parts of large cities, wear a long black cloth that covers the head and drapes over their other clothing.

Food and drink. Wheat bread is the chief food of most people in Turkey. Other common foods are rice, vegetables, and lamb. In villages, a meal often consists of *bulgur* (cracked wheat) and yogurt, along with fruit, vegetables, and bread. Turkish cooking is especially famous for *shish kebab,* which consists of pieces of lamb, tomatoes, peppers, and onions cooked together on a skewer. People also enjoy *borek,* a flaky pastry stuffed with meat or cheese. A popular dessert is *baklava,* made of thin layers of pastry, honey, and chopped nuts. Another pastry, *kadayif,* is made with shredded wheat. Favorite beverages in Turkey include tea, thick coffee, and a liquor called *raki,* which is flavored with anise.

Recreation. Many men spend their leisure time in coffee houses playing the ancient dice game of backgammon and various card games. One tradition in the cities is the *meyhane,* a kind of restaurant where cold dishes and drinks, usually beer or raki, are served.

Soccer is extremely popular and a favorite topic of conversation. Everywhere in Turkey, boys and men kick soccer balls around on the street.

Turkish people also enjoy concerts, motion pictures, and stage plays. Large stadium concerts by Turkish and foreign pop music stars draw big crowds.

Religion. More than 98 percent of the Turkish people are Muslims. However, Turkey has no state religion, and the Constitution guarantees religious freedom. Some people are Armenian Apostolic and Eastern Orthodox Christians, Roman and Eastern Catholics, and Jews. The highest spiritual leader of the Eastern Orthodox Churches, known as the patriarch of the Church of Constantinople or the *ecumenical patriarch,* resides in Istanbul.

In the 1920's, the government adopted an official policy of *secularism* (the separation of religion and politics). It declared religion to be a strictly private matter and restricted many traditional religious practices. Many people objected to the restrictions. Today, the dispute continues over what part Islam should play in Turkish life. The army and most citizens prefer a secular state. Some groups, however, dislike the idea of strict separation between government and religion. One dispute concerns regulations that have prohibited women from covering their heads while attending university classes or working in public offices. Many people believe Muslim women should be allowed to cover their heads in public if they wish.

Education. Most of Turkey's people can read and write. For the country's literacy rate, see Literacy (table: Literacy rates for selected countries). The government spends about 10 percent of its budget on public education. But rising costs and teacher shortages prevent the nation from providing enough schools and teachers, especially in rural areas.

Turkish law requires all children to attend an eight-year primary school until they graduate or reach the age of 15. But this law is difficult to enforce. After graduation, students may attend high school for three years, enroll in a vocational school, or enter the work force. Many high school graduates go on to college. They must pass through a highly competitive testing process to determine the universities and fields of study for which they qualify. Turkey has about 60 universities. Istanbul University, the oldest and largest university in Turkey, traces its history back to a religious school that was founded in 1453.

© Dave G. Houser

A Turkish weaver creates an Oriental rug on a traditional hand loom. The country's rug makers have long been famous for their beautiful, elaborately designed Turkish carpets.

The Cappadocia region of east-central Turkey features many unusual volcanic rock formations. Many tourists visit the region each year to see its natural wonders. Tourism has become an important economic activity in Turkey.

© Hans Georg Roth, Corbis

The arts. Turkey's most important contribution to the arts is in the field of architecture. In Istanbul stands the great-domed cathedral Hagia Sophia, a classic example of Byzantine architecture. It was built in the A.D. 500's, when the area was part of the Byzantine Empire. Many of Turkey's finest buildings were built during the 1400's and the 1500's, when the Ottoman Empire was at its height. Many were designed by Turkey's greatest architect, Mimar Sinan. *Mimar* means *the architect.* Sinan's Mosque of Süleyman I in Istanbul is one of the world's most beautiful *mosques* (Islamic houses of worship).

For hundreds of years, Turkish craftworkers have made excellent dishes, bowls, and other ceramic objects. Richly colored ceramic tiles decorate many mosques and palaces in Turkey. Especially famous are elegant tiles with designs featuring a distinctive shade of blue that were made in İznik during the 1500's and 1600's. Turkish weavers have long been famous for their elaborately designed rugs. They made many of the first Oriental rugs used in Europe. Turkish villagers still produce these beautiful rugs on traditional hand looms.

Much Turkish literature before the 1920's was written in the complicated Ottoman Turkish language and deals with religious themes and life during Ottoman rule. Modern Turkish literature centers largely on nationalism, social justice, and history. Two of the most famous modern Turkish writers are the novelists Orhan Pamuk and Yaşar Kemal. Istanbul and Ankara have a lively art scene of young painters and graphic artists.

The land

Turkey lies in the northwestern part of the Middle East. Much of Thrace and the coastal areas of Anatolia consist of lowlands and green, rolling plains. A broad expanse of dry highlands called the Anatolian Plateau stretches across central Anatolia. The plateau is bordered by the Pontic Mountains on the north and the Taurus Mountains on the south.

Turkey has several large saltwater lakes and numerous rivers. But most of the rivers dry up during the hot, dry summers. In the spring, many rivers in Turkey become torrents as waters from the melting snows rush down from the mountains and overflow the riverbanks.

Turkey can be divided into eight land regions. They are (1) the Northern Plains, (2) the Western Valleys, (3) the Southern Plains, (4) the Western Plateau, (5) the Eastern Plateau, (6) the Northern Mountains, (7) the Southern Mountains, and (8) the Mesopotamian Lowlands.

The Northern Plains cover Thrace and extend along the Black Sea coast of Anatolia. Thrace's gently rolling grasslands make it an important farming and grazing region. Along the Black Sea coast, farmers raise corn, fruits, nuts, tea, and tobacco.

The Western Valleys are broad, fertile river valleys along the coast of the Aegean Sea. The region produces barley, cotton, olives, tobacco, and wheat. The value of its crop output is the highest of any region in Turkey.

The Southern Plains are a narrow strip of land along the Mediterranean Sea. A great variety of crops, including cereal grains, citrus fruits, cotton, and *pulses* (peas and beans), grow in the region's rich soil. Farmers must irrigate their fields during the hot, dry summer.

The Western Plateau, a region of highlands and scattered river valleys, extends across central Anatolia. The region receives little rainfall. Farmers raise barley and wheat in the river valleys and wherever irrigation water is available. Goats, sheep, and other livestock graze on uncultivated land.

The Eastern Plateau is an area of towering mountains and barren plains. It extends from the Western Plateau to Turkey's eastern border. The Taurus and Pontic mountains meet in the Eastern Plateau. Mount Ararat, Turkey's highest point, rises 16,849 feet (5,137 meters) above sea level near the Iranian border. Most people in the region have small farms and raise sheep and cattle.

The Northern Mountains, or Pontic Mountains, rise between the Northern Plains and the Anatolian Plateau. Only a few roads and railroads cross the mountains to connect the plateau with the Black Sea.

The Southern Mountains consist of the Taurus Mountains and smaller ranges on the southern edge of the Anatolian Plateau. These mountains almost completely cut off the plateau from the Mediterranean Sea.

The Mesopotamian Lowlands in southeastern Anatolia consist of fertile plains and river valleys. Cereal grains and fruits grow well in the region's rich soil. The

Southeast Anatolian Project, consisting of dams and an irrigation network, is under construction in the region. It will use waters of the Tigris and Euphrates rivers to produce electric power and irrigate fields.

Climate

The climate differs greatly from one region of Turkey to another. The south and west coasts of Anatolia have mild, rainy winters and hot, dry summers. Summer temperatures along the Aegean often rise above 90 °F (32 °C). The Black Sea coast has cooler summers, with an average temperature of about 72 °F (22 °C). Yearly rainfall in coastal areas averages from 20 to 30 inches (51 to 76 centimeters) along the Aegean and Mediterranean to more than 100 inches (254 centimeters) near the Black Sea. Northeastern Turkey has mild summers but bitterly cold winters. Temperatures sometimes fall to −40 °F (−40 °C). Southeastern Turkey and the interior of Anatolia have cold winters with heavy snowstorms. Summers are hot, windy, and extremely dry.

Economy

Turkey has a developing and rapidly changing economy. The western and coastal regions of Turkey are wealthier than the interior and the eastern areas. Also, cities are richer than rural areas.

The government has long been heavily involved in many aspects of Turkey's economy. The government has owned much of the country's transportation and communications industries, and it has controlled other industries as well. However, private companies have become increasingly important. During the late 1980's, the government began a program to reduce its control of

industries and to allow more private ownership.

Agriculture accounts for only about 15 percent of the value of all goods and services produced in Turkey in a year. About 45 percent of the country's people work in agriculture.

Turkey's most productive farmlands are in the coastal regions, which have fertile soil and a mild climate. The desertlike Anatolian Plateau often has long droughts that cause serious losses of crops.

In most years, Turkey's farmers produce enough food for all the people plus a surplus to sell abroad. About 50 percent of the cropland is used for grains. Wheat is the chief grain, followed by barley and corn. Cotton is grown for both fiber and cottonseed oil. Tobacco, a major export, is grown along the Black and Aegean seas. Turkey is a major producer of fruits, nuts, and vegetables, including apples, eggplants, grapes and raisins, hazelnuts, melons, oranges, potatoes, sugar beets, and tomatoes. Many people raise sheep, goats, and other livestock. Wool is the most valuable livestock product.

Manufacturing. When Turkey's republican government came to power in the 1920's, Turkey was almost entirely an agricultural country. Today, Turkey has thousands of factories. Manufacturing employs only about 20 percent of all workers, but the value of industrial production is about twice that of agricultural output.

Turkey's largest manufacturing industries are food and beverage processing and textile production. Other manufactured products include fertilizers, iron and steel, machinery and metal products, motor vehicles, and pulp and paper products. Most factories and mills lie in and around the large cities of the north and west.

Mining. Turkey is rich in mineral resources, but the

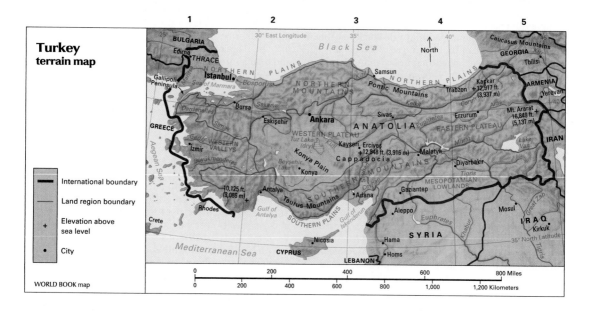

Turkey terrain map

International boundary

Land region boundary

+ Elevation above sea level

• City

WORLD BOOK map

0   200   400   600   800 Miles
0   200   400   600   800   1,000   1,200 Kilometers

Physical features

Aegean Sea	B 1	Bosporus (strait)	A 2	Erciye (mountain)	B 3	Konya Plain	B 2	Sea of Marmara	A 1
Anatolia (region)	B 3	Büyükmenderes		Euphrates River	B 4	Lake Van	B 5	Seyhan River	B 3
Aras River	A 5	River	B 1	Gallipoli Peninsula	A 1	Maritsa River	A 1	Simav River	B 1
Beysehir Lake	B 2	Cappadocia	B 3	Gulf of Antalya	C 2	Mount Ararat	B 5	Taurus Mountains	C 2
Black Sea	A 3	Ceyhan River	B 3	Kaçkar (mountain)	A 4	Murat River	B 4	Thrace (region)	A 1
		Çoruh River	A 4	Kelkit River	A 4	Pontic Mountains	A 3	Tigris River	B 4
		Dardanelles (strait)	A 1	Kizil River	A 3	Sakarya River	A 2	Tuz Lake	B 2

Ephesus, near present-day İzmir on Turkey's west coast, was an ancient Greek city. It was founded in the early 1000's B.C. Archaeologists uncovered the ruins of the city in the late A.D. 1800's.

© M & M Hunn, Photo Researchers

mining industry is largely undeveloped. The country's most abundant mineral is coking coal, which is used in making steel. Turkey is one of the world's largest producers of chromite, the mineral from which chromium is obtained. Turkey is also a major producer of boron. Other minerals produced in Turkey include bauxite, copper, iron ore, and *meerschaum,* a soft, white mineral that is used to make jewelry and tobacco pipes.

Energy. Except for coal and hydroelectric power, almost all of Turkey's energy is imported. Several large refineries process imported oil. Natural gas imports have been growing. Natural gas has been replacing coal in heating urban buildings, helping to reduce air pollution.

International trade. Turkey's chief imports include chemicals, machinery, iron and steel, motor vehicles, and petroleum. The country's major exports include clothing and textiles, iron and steel, and other manufactured goods. Fruits, nuts, and vegetables are also important exports. Turkey's main trading partner is Germany. Other leading partners include France, Italy, Russia, the United Kingdom, and the United States.

Tourism has become a significant activity in Turkey. Millions of tourists visit Turkey every year, most of them from European countries and Russia. The visitors spend beach holidays on the Mediterranean and Aegean coasts. They also visit Turkey's cities; ancient sites, such as Troy and Pergamum in northwestern Turkey, and Ephesus, near present-day İzmir; and the unusual rock formations and other natural wonders of Cappadocia in east-central Turkey and the Eastern Plateau.

Transportation and communication. Turkey's road network varies in quality but reaches almost all the nation's towns. Turkey has about one car for every 15 inhabitants. Most Turks use buses, trains, or taxis. The railroad system links only the largest cities on slow tracks. Cities in Turkey with international airports include Istanbul, Ankara, İzmir, and Antalya. Turkish Airlines serves many cities in Turkey, Europe, and the Middle East. Turkey has many fine natural harbors. Istanbul and İzmir are the primary ports.

Turkey has more than 50 daily newspapers, representing many different political views. Most people, howev-

er, get their information from television. There are more than 20 nationwide TV channels. Most households own a color TV set and have a telephone. Many people own cellular phones. Many members of the middle and upper classes own personal computers.

History

Archaeologists have found evidence of an advanced society in what is now Turkey before 6000 B.C. One of the world's earliest known human settlements is at Çatalhöyük (also spelled Çatalhüyük or Çatal Hüyük). It is near Konya and is still being excavated. The first inhabitants of the area to be recorded in history were called the Hittites. About 2000 B.C., they began migrating to central Anatolia from Europe or central Asia. In the next several hundred years, they conquered much of Anatolia and parts of Mesopotamia and Syria. By 1500 B.C., the Hittites had created a powerful empire that made them the leading rulers of the Middle East. See **Hittites.**

From about 1200 to 500 B.C., large areas of Anatolia fell to the Phrygians, the Lydians, and other peoples. Between about 550 and 513 B.C., the Persian Empire seized control of Anatolia and Thrace. The Persians ruled until Alexander the Great of Macedonia crushed their army in 331 B.C. After Alexander's death in 323 B.C., Anatolia became a battleground in the wars among his successors. Small kingdoms rose and fell until 63 B.C., when the Roman general Pompey conquered the region. Anatolia had peace under Roman rule for about 400 years.

In A.D. 330, the Roman emperor Constantine the Great moved the capital from Rome to the ancient town of Byzantium, on the Bosporus. Byzantium was renamed Constantinople, meaning *city of Constantine.* In 395, the Roman Empire split into the West Roman Empire and the East Roman Empire, also called the Byzantine Empire, which included Anatolia and Thrace. Byzantine emperors ruled all of what is now Turkey until the late 1000's. See **Byzantine Empire.**

The Seljuk Turks became one of the first Turkic peoples to rule in what is now Turkey. The Seljuks were Muslims from central Asia east of the Caspian Sea. During the mid-1000's, they conquered Armenia, Palestine, and most of Iran. Then they invaded Anatolia. In 1071, the Seljuks destroyed most of the Byzantine power in Anatolia by defeating the Byzantine army in the Battle of Manzikert. They set up an empire with Iconium (now Konya) as the capital. From this point onward, the Christian religion and the Greek language of the Byzantine Empire were gradually replaced in Anatolia by Islam and the Turkish language.

In 1095, Christians in Western Europe organized the first of a series of military expeditions called the Crusades to drive the Seljuk Turks from the Holy Land (see **Crusades**). During the First Crusade (1096-1099), Christian troops defeated the Seljuks in western Anatolia. As a result, the Byzantine Empire recovered about a third of Anatolia. But the crusaders then left the peninsula to fight in the Holy Land, also called Palestine. The Seljuk Empire thus endured until 1243, when it was invaded by Asian nomads known as Mongols (see **Mongol Empire**).

The rise of the Ottoman Empire. The Mongol Empire was torn by internal struggles and soon fell apart. As a result, the Turks' influence in Anatolia continued to grow. During the 1300's, a group of Turks who became known as the Ottomans began to build a mighty empire. In 1326, they seized the Anatolian city of Bursa, which became their capital. By the late 1300's, the Ottomans had conquered the western two-thirds of Anatolia; most of Thrace; and much of the Balkan Peninsula, including Greece. All that remained of the Byzantine Empire was the area around Constantinople.

In 1453, Ottoman forces led by Mehmet II captured Constantinople, ending the Byzantine Empire. The Ottomans called the city Istanbul and made it their capital. By 1481, their empire extended from the Danube River in Europe to southern Anatolia.

The Ottoman Empire reached its height in the 1500's. During the reign of Sultan Bayezit II, who ruled from 1481 to 1512, the empire became the leading naval power in the Mediterranean region. Ottoman forces conquered Syria in 1516 and Egypt in 1517. Süleyman I, whom Europeans called the Magnificent, ruled from 1520 to 1566. In 1526, his army conquered much of Hungary in the Battle of Mohács. Süleyman expanded the empire's borders to Yemen on the south, Morocco on the west, and Persia on the east.

The Ottoman decline. After the Battle of Mohács, European powers feared that the Ottomans would overrun Europe. However, European forces successfully defended Vienna, Austria, during an Ottoman attack in 1529. In 1571, European fleets defeated the Ottoman navy in the Battle of Lepanto, near Greece. The Ottomans again failed to capture Vienna in 1683.

During the 1700's, the Ottoman Empire continued to weaken. In 1774, the Ottomans lost a six-year war against Russia and were forced to allow Russian ships to pass through the Straits—the waters linking the Black Sea with the Mediterranean. The Ottoman Empire lost the Crimea, a peninsula in the Black Sea, to Russia in 1783.

The empire lost more territory during the 1800's. In 1821, Greek nationalists revolted against Ottoman rule. France, the United Kingdom, and Russia sided with the Greeks and sent forces to fight the Ottomans (see **Greece** [History]). The Treaty of Adrianople (Edirne) ended the fighting in 1829. This treaty acknowledged the independence of Greece and gave Russia control of the mouth of the Danube River. The Ottomans also lost other Balkan territory in a series of wars with Russia (see **Russo-Turkish wars**). European powers forced Russia to give up much of its gains at the Congress of Berlin in 1878. But the Ottoman Empire continued to decline. The empire had lost Algeria to France in 1830, and France seized Tunisia in 1881. The United Kingdom gained Cyprus in 1878 and began to effectively rule Egypt in 1882, although both areas officially remained part of the Ottoman Empire until 1914.

Ottoman leaders tried to halt the empire's decline through a reform program starting in 1839. They reorganized the military and improved the educational system. In 1876, the empire's first constitution was adopted. It provided for representative government and granted the people various freedoms. But Sultan Abdülhamit II, who came to the throne the same year, set the constitution aside and ruled as a dictator. Government policies became increasingly oppressive, and Abdülhamit ruled by the use of fear. Religious persecution began to spread as members of various religious minorities became revolutionaries. Nationalist feelings were strong among the minorities. Ottoman officials, fearing further collapse of the already declining empire, reacted harshly. Violent attacks took place. Between 1894 and 1918, Christian Armenians in the Ottoman Empire suffered an especially large loss of life (see **Armenia** [History]).

The Young Turks. During the late 1890's, small groups of students and military officers who opposed Abdülhamit's harsh policies banded together secretly. These groups were collectively known as the Young Turks. The most influential group was the Committee of Union and Progress. In 1908, members of this group led a revolt against Abdülhamit and forced him to restore constitutional government. The Young Turks made him give up the throne in 1909. They then ruled the empire through his brother Mehmet V.

The Young Turks wanted to restore the greatness of the Ottoman Empire. However, many people no longer cared about the idea of maintaining an empire. The empire's Christian minorities demanded freedom from Ottoman rule. And so the empire continued to crumble.

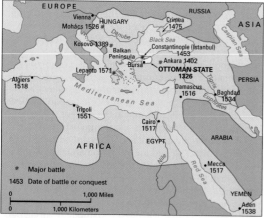

WORLD BOOK map

The Ottoman Empire began during the 1300's as a small state around the city of Bursa. It grew to include much of the Middle East and parts of northern Africa and southeastern Europe.

Important dates in Turkey

1500 B.C.	The Hittites ruled in Anatolia.
63 B.C.	The Roman general Pompey conquered Anatolia.
A.D. 330	Constantine the Great moved the capital of the Roman Empire to Byzantium and renamed the town Constantinople.
1071	The Seljuk Turks conquered most of Anatolia by defeating the Byzantine forces in the Battle of Manzikert.
1326	The Ottoman Turks captured Bursa, which marked the beginning of the Ottoman Empire.
1453	The Ottomans captured Constantinople, ending the Byzantine Empire.
1783-1914	The Ottoman Empire lost much of its territory in a series of military defeats.
1908	The Young Turks revolted against the government.
1914-1918	In World War I, the Ottoman Empire allied with Germany and lost much of its remaining territory.
1923	Mustafa Kemal (Atatürk) set up the Republic of Turkey and began a program to modernize the nation.
1960	Turkish army units overthrew the government and ruled until free elections were held in 1961.
1974	Turkish forces invaded Cyprus.
1980-1983	Army units again controlled the government.
1999	A powerful earthquake struck northwestern Turkey, killing more than 17,000 people.

Soon after the revolution in 1908, Bulgaria declared its independence, and Austria-Hungary annexed Bosnia-Herzegovina. Italy took Libya in 1912. In 1913, the Ottoman Empire surrendered Crete, part of Macedonia, southern Epirus, and many Aegean islands to Greece. By 1914, the empire had lost all its European territory except eastern Thrace.

In 1914, the Ottoman Empire entered World War I on the side of Germany and Austria-Hungary in an attempt to regain lost territory. In 1915, British, French, and other Allied troops tried to gain control of the Straits so that aid could be shipped to Russia. The Ottomans drove back the invaders at the Gallipoli Peninsula west of the Dardanelles, dealing the Allies a crushing defeat. However, the Allies won the war in 1918.

After World War I, the Allies set out to break up the Ottoman Empire. Allied troops occupied Istanbul and the Straits. In May 1919, Greek troops, protected by Allied fleets, landed at the Ottoman port of İzmir and advanced into the country. Turks deeply resented the Ottoman government's inability to defend their homeland.

A Turkish military hero named Mustafa Kemal (later called Kemal Atatürk) quickly organized a nationalist movement. Under his leadership, a series of nationalist congresses met in Anatolian cities and formed a *provisional* (temporary) government. In April 1920, a new Turkish Grand National Assembly met in Ankara and elected Kemal as Assembly president.

In August 1920, the sultan's government signed the harsh Treaty of Sèvres with the Allies (see **Sèvres, Treaty of**). The treaty granted independence to some parts of the empire and gave other parts to various Allied powers. The empire was reduced to Istanbul and a portion of Anatolia. As a result of the treaty, the sultan's popularity among the Turks declined further, while the power of Kemal and the nationalists grew. In September 1922, the nationalist forces finally drove the Greeks from Turkey. The Allies agreed to draw up a new peace treaty with the nationalists. The Treaty of Lausanne, signed in 1923, set Turkey's borders about where they are today.

The Republic of Turkey. The Grand National Assembly proclaimed Turkey to be a republic on Oct. 29, 1923, and elected Kemal as president. Kemal and other nationalist leaders believed that the new nation could not survive without sweeping social changes.

During the 1920's and 1930's, the government did away with such traditions as Muslim schools, the Islamic legal system, and the wearing of the veil by women and the fez by men. It abolished the religious and civil office of the caliph. It also outlawed *polygyny,* the practice of having more than one wife at the same time. Women received the right to vote and to hold public office. All Turks were required to choose a family name. At the same time, the Grand National Assembly gave Kemal his surname—Atatürk, which means *father of the Turks.*

Atatürk held enormous political power. He controlled the Assembly and could appoint and dismiss the prime minister and cabinet without Assembly approval. Some Turks opposed Atatürk's anti-Islamic policies. The Kurds revolted against the policies in 1925, but the government put down the uprising.

Atatürk served as Turkey's president until he died in 1938. Ismet İnönü then became president. Under İnönü's leadership, Turkey avoided entering World War II (1939-1945) until February 1945.

The 1950's and 1960's. The Republican People's Party, established by Atatürk, had governed Turkey since the establishment of the republic. However, in 1950, the Democrat Party won a majority in the Grand National Assembly. Celâl Bayar became president, and Adnan Menderes became prime minister. Unlike the Republicans, the Democrats encouraged foreign investment and wanted less government control of the economy. But by the late 1950's, a rise in the national debt and restrictions on freedom of speech made the Democrat Party government unpopular.

Turkish military forces believed the Democrats had strayed too far from Atatürk's political principles. In 1960, army units seized control of the government and set up a provisional government. The military placed a large number of former government leaders on trial. Prime Minister Menderes was hanged. President Bayar

© Hulton/Archive

Kemal Atatürk founded the Republic of Turkey in 1923 and was its first president. In an attempt to modernize the nation, he introduced major cultural, political, and economic reforms.

was sentenced to life imprisonment but was later released.

In 1961, Turkey adopted a new Constitution. The provisional government then held free national elections.
No party won a majority in the legislature. İnönü, of the
Republican People's Party, was chosen to become prime
minister. In 1965, the Justice Party won a majority, and
party leader Süleyman Demirel became prime minister.

The Cyprus crisis. During the 1960's, Turkey and
Greece nearly went to war over the issue of the
Mediterranean island of Cyprus. In 1964 and 1967, fighting broke out on Cyprus between inhabitants of Turkish
ancestry and inhabitants of Greek ancestry. Turkish
Cypriots make up a minority of the people, and Greek
Cypriots make up the majority. Both Turkey and Greece
threatened to intervene before outside peacemakers
arranged a settlement. But in 1974, Greek military officers overthrew the president of Cyprus. Turkish troops
then invaded the island and captured much territory.
Turkish Cypriots later set up a separate government.
They declared the captured territory an *autonomous*
(self-governing) region in 1975, and an independent republic in 1983. But Greek Cypriots protested strongly
against these measures. See **Cyprus** (History).

Political changes. In the late 1960's, radical groups of
Turks began staging bombings, kidnappings, and murders in an attempt to overthrow the government. In the
1970's, deep divisions developed between secular and
religious groups. No political party could form a stable
government. During this period, Demirel headed several coalition governments. In 1980, the military seized
control of the government and ruled until Turkey returned to civilian rule in 1983.

The Motherland Party, led by Turgut Özal, controlled
the government from 1983 until the True Path party won
the most legislative seats in 1991 elections. Süleyman
Demirel, who had become leader of the True Path, again
became prime minister. The legislature elected Demirel
president in 1993. Tansu Çiller of the True Path then became Turkey's first woman prime minister.

In elections in 1995, the Welfare Party, a strongly pro-
Islamic party, won the most seats in the legislature. In
1996, the Welfare and True Path parties formed a coalition government. Necmettin Erbakan, the Welfare Party
leader, served as prime minister until the coalition lost
its parliamentary majority in 1997. He was the first person from an Islamic party to head the government since
Turkey became a republic.

In 1998, the Constitutional Court banned the Welfare
Party, ruling that its goal of creating an Islamic state was
unconstitutional. Some Welfare Party members joined
the more moderate pro-Islamic Virtue Party. Following
elections in 1999, former Prime Minister Bülent Ecevit,
the leader of the Democratic Left Party, became head of
a coalition government. The Constitutional Court
banned the Virtue Party in 2001. Moderate Islamists then
formed the Justice and Development Party.

Recent developments. A Kurdish nationalist movement developed in southeastern Turkey in the 1980's.
The Turkish government has battled Kurdish guerrillas
since the mid-1980's. About 30,000 people have died in
the fighting. In 1999, Turkish intelligence agents arrested
the Kurdish guerrilla leader Abdullah Öcalan. A Turkish
court convicted Öcalan of treason and separatism and

sentenced him to death. Since Öcalan's capture, the
fighting has decreased.

In August 1999, a powerful earthquake struck northwestern Turkey. More than 17,000 people were killed.

In 1999, the European Union (EU) accepted Turkey as a
candidate for membership. Turkey must make several
political and economic reforms before the EU will set a
timetable for membership.   Caglar Keyder

Related articles in include:

Biographies

Atatürk, Kemal	Mehmet II	Osman I
Barbarossa	Muhammad Ali	Süleyman I

Cities and towns

Ankara	Edirne	İzmir
Antioch	Istanbul	Tarsus

History

Armenia	Greece (History)	Seljuks
Balkans	Janissaries	Sèvres, Treaty of
Berlin, Congress	Kurds	Sultan
of	Ottoman Empire	Thrace
Byzantine Empire	Russo-Turkish	Turks
Crimean War	wars	World War I
Cyprus		

Physical features

Ararat	Dardanelles	Marmara, Sea of
Bosporus	Euphrates River	Mount Ararat

Other related articles

Asia Minor
Census (Censuses around the world)
Middle East

Outline

I. **Government**
   A National government   D. Political parties
   B Court system   E. Armed forces
   C. Local government
II. **People**
   A. Ancestry   B. Languages
III. **Way of life**
   A. City life   F. Recreation
   B. Rural life   G. Religion
   C. Housing   H. Education
   D. Clothing   I. The arts
   E. Food and drink
IV. **The land**
   A. The Northern Plains   E. The Eastern Plateau
   B. The Western Valleys   F. The Northern Mountains
   C. The Southern Plains   G. The Southern Mountains
   D. The Western Plateau   H. The Mesopotamian Low-
                                lands
V. **Climate**
VI. **Economy**
   A. Agriculture   E. International trade
   B. Manufacturing   F. Tourism
   C. Mining   G. Transportation and com-
   D. Energy   munication
VII. **History**

Questions

What are Turkey's chief economic activities?
Why was a new Turkish language developed?
What are the Straits?
How has the role of Turkish women changed since 1900?
Who are the Kurds?
Who was Kemal Atatürk?
How did Atatürk's modernization program affect Turkish life?
Who were the Young Turks?
What are the chief foods of most Turks?
What was the Ottoman Empire?

Index

How to use the index

Each index entry gives the page number or page numbers—for example, **Semiconductors, 175.** This means that information on this topic may be found on page 175.

When there are many references to a topic, they are grouped alphabetically by clue words under the main topic. For example, the clue words under **September 11 terrorist attacks** group the references to that topic under numerous subtopics.

The indications (il.) or (ils.) mean that the reference on this page is to an illustration or illustrations only, as in **Shanghai.**

When a topic such as **SIERRA LEONE** appears in all capital letters, this means that there is an Update article entitled Sierra Leone. References to the topic in other articles may appear after the topic name.

When only the first letter of a topic, such as **Silk,** is capitalized, this means that there is no article entitled Silk but that information on this topic may be found on the pages listed.

The "see" and "see also" cross-references—for example, **Skating,** refer the reader to other entries in the index or to Update articles.

An entry followed by "reprint" refers to a new or revised encyclopedia article in the supplement section, as in **SOUTH AFRICA.** This means that an article begins on page 472.

Acknowledgments

The publishers acknowledge the following sources for illustrations. Credits read from top to bottom, left to right, on their respective pages. An asterisk (*) denotes illustrations and photographs created exclusively for this edition. All maps, charts, and diagrams were prepared by the staff unless otherwise noted.

6 Dale DeBolt*; U.S. Geological Survey; National Park Service; Dale DeBolt*
7 National Park Service
8 AP/Wide World
9 © Spencer Platt, Getty Images
10 AP/Wide World
11 Goddard Space Flight Center from NOAA/ Goes-8 DATA/Hal Pierce/Fritz Hasler/NASA
12 © Getty Images
15 AP/Wide World
17 © Scott Nelson, Getty Images
18-21 AP/Wide World
22 © Reuters/Getty Images
24 AP/Wide World
27 © Ralf Hirschberger, Agence France-Presse
28 © Spencer Platt, Getty Images
30 © Reuters/Getty Images
32-35 AP/Wide World
36 Rendering of planets by Sylvain Korzennik, Harvard University; photograph by Till Credner, Max Planck Institute for Aeronomy
38 AP/Wide World
41 © Reuters/Getty Images
44 © Agence France-Presse
47-49 AP/Wide World
50 Maurico Anton © National Geographic Society
51 © Nature M.P.F.T. from Getty Images; Alfred J. Smuskiewicz*
52 Kenneth Garrett © National Geographic Society; John R. Anderson Jr. © National Geographic Society
54 © Matt Campbell, Agence France-Presse
55 © Agence France-Presse
57 © Warren Zinn, Getty Images
59 The Champion Single Sculls (Max Schmitt in a Single Skull) (1871) oil on canvas by Thomas Eakins: Metropolitan Museum of Art; Purchase, The Alfred N. Punnett Endowment Fund and George D. Pratt Gift 1934 (photograph © The Metropolitan Museum of Art)
61 AP/Wide World
65-66 NASA/Space Telescope Science Institute
69 AP/Wide World
74 BMW.AG; AP/Wide World
75 GM Media Archives
76-89 AP/Wide World
92 The Falkirk Wheel
97-110 AP/Wide World
112 © Reuters/Getty Images
117 © Jack Vartoogian
119 Dale DeBolt*
120 Dale DeBolt*; The Craftsman Farms Foundation, Parsippany, NJ
121-127 Dale DeBolt*
128 © Gail Mooney, Corbis; Dale DeBolt*
129 © Eyewire/Getty Images
130 Dale DeBolt*
131-138 AP/Wide World
140 © Terry Harris, The Chicago Tribune
143 AP/Wide World
145 © Reuters/Getty Images
147 © Andrea Tamoni, Teatro alla Scala

149 AP/Wide World; © Corbis/Bettmann; AP/Wide World
150 © Hulton/Getty Images
151 © Wally McNamee, Corbis; AP/Wide World; AP/Wide World
152 AP/Wide World
153 © Hulton/Getty Images; AP/Wide World; © Hulton/Getty Images
154 AP/Wide World
155 AP/Wide World; Collection, The Supreme Court Historical Society; © Hulton/Getty Images
156 AP/Wide World
157 © Corbis/Bettmann
160-164 AP/Wide World
167 Allergan, Inc.
168 © Agence France-Presse
170 AP/Wide World
173 © Reuters/Getty Images
177 NASA/National Snow and Ice Data Center
180-189 AP/Wide World
192 © Reuters/Getty Images
193 Garfield Park Conservatory
195 U.S. Geological Survey
196 AP/Wide World
197 © Agence France-Presse
198-201 AP/Wide World
203 © Agence France-Presse
206 © Gary M. Prior, Getty Images
208 AP/Wide World
211 U.S. Dept. of Justice, Immigration and Naturalization Service
212 Library of Congress (National Photo Company Collection)
213 Library of Congress (Ansel Adams photographer)
214-215 AP/Wide World
216 U.S. Dept. of Justice, Immigration and Naturalization Service
218-219 AP/Wide World
220 © Reuters/Getty Images
222-224 AP/Wide World
227 © Agence France-Presse
228 © Reuters/Getty Images
230 © Agence France-Presse
231 © Reuters/Getty Images
232-234 © Agence France-Presse
236 AP/Wide World
238-242 © Reuters/Getty Images
246 © Agence France-Presse
253 AP/Wide World
255 © National Geographic Society
256 © Reuters/Getty Images
258 © Alamy Images
260 Jay E. Bensen, Bensen & Associates*
261 © Robert A. Davis
262 © Hulton/Getty Images
263 Calumet Regional Archives/Indiana University Northwest
265 © Gao Feng, Imaginechina
266 AP/Wide World
271 © Agence France-Presse
273 © David Silverman, Getty Images
278 © Timothy Street Porter, Rockwell Group; © Universal/Dreamworks from Shooting Star
279 AP/Wide World
281-282 © Reuters/Getty Images
284 AP/Wide World

285 Hawaii Undersea Research Laboratory; © Sotheby's /Getty Images
286-287 AP/Wide World
288-290 © Pete Souza, The Chicago Tribune
291-292 AP/Wide World
293 © Scott Peterson, Getty Images; AP/Wide World
294-295 AP/Wide World
296 © Robert Nickelsberg, Getty Images
298 © Agence France-Presse
302 AP/Wide World
303 © Donald Miralle, Getty Images
304 AP/Wide World
305 © Getty Images
306-307 AP/Wide World
308 © Doug Pensinger, Getty Images
309-314 AP/Wide World
315 Judith River Dinosaur
317 AP/Wide World
318 U.S Senate
319 Centers for Disease Control and Prevention; AP/Wide World
320 AP/Wide World
321 U.S. Senate; AP/Wide World
322-326 AP/Wide World
330 © Mario Tama, Getty Images
335 © Dan Currier, The News Star
338 © Reuters/Getty Images
339 AP/Wide World
341 © Reuters/Getty Images
342-345 AP/Wide World
349 © Reuters/Getty Images
350-351 AP/Wide World
354-355 NASA
356 © Agence France-Presse
358-362 AP/Wide World
364 © Mike Luckevich, Creators Syndicate
369 © Reuters/Getty Images.
372 © Mike Siegel, Seattle Times
375 Paul Perreault*
376 Paul Perreault*; © Hulton/Getty Images
377 © Hulton/Getty Images
378 © Hulton/Getty Images; Intelsat
379 © PhotoDisc, Inc.
380 © Forms.com; © CNN/Getty Images
381 Motorola Corporation
382-383 Everett Collection
385-386 AP/Wide World
389 © Erin Patrice O'Brian
391 Heeling Sports Limited
394 © David McNew, Getty Images
396 © Getty Images
398-406 AP/Wide World
410 © David W. Hamilton, Getty Images
411 AP/Wide World
413 National Park Service Historic Photography Collection
414-415 National Park Service
416 U.S. Fish and Wildlife Service; National Park Service; National Park Service
418 © Larry Neubauer, Corbis; National Park Service
419 AP/Wide World
422 National Park Service
424-432 AP/Wide World
443 San Francisco Convention & Visitors Bureau